Marginal Europe

Marginal Europe

The Contribution of Marginal Lands since the Middle Ages

SIDNEY POLLARD

CLARENDON PRESS · OXFORD

1997

Oxford University Press, Gt. Clarendon Street, Oxford OX2 6DP
Oxford New York
Athens Auckland Bangkok Bogota Bombay
Buenos Aires Calcutta Cape Town Dar es Salaam
Delhi Florence Hong Kong Istanbul Karachi
Kuala Lumpur Madras Madrid Melbourne
Mexico City Nairobi Paris Singapore
Taipei Tokyo Toronto
and associated companies in
Berlin Ibadan

Oxford is a trade mark of Oxford University Press

Published in the United States
by Oxford University Press Inc., New York

British Library Cataloguing in Publication Data
Data available

Library of Congress Cataloging in Publication Data
Data applied for

ISBN 0–19–820638–0

1 3 5 7 9 10 8 6 4 2

Typeset by Jayvee, Trivandrum, India
Printed in Great Britain
on acid-free paper by
Biddles Ltd., Guildford & King's Lynn

ACKNOWLEDGEMENTS

Many obligations are incurred in the writing of a book of this kind. I am particularly grateful to the University of Bielefeld for granting me a research semester free of teaching duties, and to the Leverhulme Trust for an 'Emeritus Fellowship' research grant which enabled me to visit archives and libraries in Britain and on the Continent.

Librarians and archivists and their staffs have been invariably helpful. I have benefited from the facilities of the Bavarian State Archive (*Hauptstaatsarchiv*), the Zurich Cantonal Archive, and the County Record Offices of Calderdale (West Yorkshire), Cheshire, Derbyshire, Northumberland, North Yorkshire, Shropshire, and the Borders Regional Records Office; and the libraries of the Universities of Bielefeld, Cambridge, Delaware, Sheffield, and Zurich, the libraries of the Institute of Historical Research, of the German Historical Institute (London), the Bavarian National Library, and the public libraries of Calderdale Central, Carlisle, Chester, Derbyshire Local Studies, Harrogate, Newcastle upon Tyne, North Yorkshire County, Scarborough, Sheffield, and Shrewsbury. I have also had the benefit of friendly criticism and the contribution of positive ideas from audiences to whom some of the matters contained in this book have been presented, in the Universities of Bielefeld, California (Davis and San Diego Campuses), Cambridge, Chicago, Delaware, Exeter, Leicester, Oxford, Sheffield, and York, as well as of two anonymous referees. Rudolf Braun, Ulrich Pfister, Hansjörg Siegenthaler, and Mathias Weishaupt allowed me to draw on their extensive knowledge of Swiss economic and social history. None of them is responsible for any remaining errors. The Department of History at Sheffield University has generously made its facilities available to me after my retirement.

My main thanks goes to my wife Helen, for her companionship, her skilled secretarial help, and her unfailing encouragement and inspiration, which has made it all worth while.

S.P.

Sheffield
October 1995

CONTENTS

1

Introduction

This study is the outcome of reflections on a puzzle familiar to many British economic historians: the curious geographical distribution of the leading regions in the British Industrial Revolution. Instead of developing out of the background of the richest and in many ways most advanced regions such as London and the Home Counties, Bristol or East Anglia—just as we tend to explain Britain's pioneer role by her wealth and technical lead—the great spurt in technological, economic, and social change which we term the Industrial Revolution and which was destined to change the course of world history had its origins, rather surprisingly, in the main in parts of the country which may be termed 'marginal', defined, for the moment, as relatively poor, relatively backward, and located far from the centres of power and wealth. Lancashire and Yorkshire, the West Midlands, and the Durham–Northumberland coalfield, together with south-west Scotland, took the lead in technical and commercial innovations, and, having once taken it, succeeded in keeping it for well over a century.

Does this paradox, if paradox it is, represent a simple aberration of the path of world history? Some see it as a unique occurrence with its own particular causes; but the argument in favour of this view is much weakened by the fact that in other parts of Europe also, industrialization originated and was driven forward from regions which looked, at first blush, anything but destined for such a role. The Ruhr area, for example, which was to contain the most powerful industrial concentration of Germany and of continental Europe as a whole by the end of the nineteenth century, had been described at its beginning as nothing more than 'an impoverished region of backward agriculture bordering on the proto-industrial areas of the Siegerland, Sauerland and the Wupper Valley'.[1] In other parts of Europe north of the Alps, too, it was surprisingly often the marginal lands and the uplands which proved to be the most fertile grounds for the process of industrialization.[2]

By contrast, capitals and other large cities, with all their accumulated advantages, very seldom turned out to be the venues of the new industrialism. Britain, as Paul Bairoch has remarked,[3] was one of the least urbanized of European countries at the beginning of the eighteenth century; the most urbanized ones, including Italy, the Netherlands (a special case), Spain, and Portugal, were all among the late industrializers. London was certainly not lacking in entrepreneurship in the

[1] Hohenberg and Lees (1985), 187. [2] Jones (1981), 138–9.
[3] Bairoch (1981), 64.

eighteenth century, yet it supplied little direct drive, though no doubt much indirect encouragement, towards industrialization, and neither did Amsterdam, Paris, Venice, Genoa, Antwerp, or Naples.[4]

Have we then tended to misjudge the character, the role, and the potential of marginal regions? Have innovatory movements arisen elsewhere and at other times, too, from the less favoured areas of the globe? Even if there were no other fundamental transformation whose origin can be pinpointed in quite the same way as the Industrial Revolution, other major innovations of a technical or economic nature did occur, and it might be worth while to investigate the role of marginal areas in them over a wider field.

These thoughts were the starting-point of this book. They give it its perhaps unusual character, of being essentially in the nature of a confrontation of a widespread, almost dominant view with some contradictory historical reality. This involves two linked tasks: first, to set out a general framework of the history and the role of marginal areas, after these are suitably defined and delimited, and secondly, to investigate how these came to take a leading role in the industrialization process and possibly in other significant innovational movements, while being generally considered to be backward, poor, and without initiative. If marginal areas are indeed the poor relations in a society, dependent and lagging behind the others, one would surely not expect them to generate innovation and progress: or does a mechanism exist whereby their very qualities of poverty and hardship encourage a pioneer role? What is it that distinguishes marginal areas from other regions of a country? The original enquiry related to the Industrial Revolution in Britain, but the focus has shifted to the history and role of marginal areas in general.

Such an approach immediately brings us up against the problem of the role of geography in history, and the relationship of man, or rather of society, to the natural environment, using the 'natural world in historical explanation'.[5] To the charge of geographical determinism one could urge that the social sciences, and Economics and Sociology in particular, all too often ignore location and geographical configuration altogether, and there might thus be some value in attempting to redress the balance. This attempt is made here, and the intention therefore is to combine an economic and historical approach with geographical realities.[6]

Clearly, by taking marginal areas as our point of departure we start with units of study, and with categories, which are essentially geographical: they are areas delimited on the map. We are likely to look for spatial causes and spatial results. Even if we take other factors into account from time to time, including those with strong spatial associations, such as class relations, inheritance traditions, military organization, or political influence, our approach will inevitably appear geographically deterministic, stressing above all the impact of the environment and the location factor on societies and their history.[7]

[4] Sella (1979), 136; there may be some doubt about London: Lee (1986), 126 ff.

[5] Beinart and Coates (1995), 2.

[6] Nutley (1980), 112 ff., citing K. H. Stone; also Ruffieux (1980), 346.

[7] Viazzo (1989), 3.

There was a time when such extreme views would find widespread support. More recently, however, even geographers interested in marginal lands have felt such a one-sided approach to be inadequate. The environment is a constant in only a very restricted sense. Human action has profoundly altered the impact of geography in the course of history, and the very concept of marginality, as we shall see, is always in part a socially determined, rather than a purely spatial one. Former deserts may be made into rich cities when oil is discovered and delivered, bleak hillsides may sprout coal-mines and steelworks, and forest land can be turned into arable fields—and vice versa.[8] It is in fact the interplay of spatial juxtaposition and the history of society which forms the main theme of this book, rather than the area on the map as such.

While there exists an extensive literature on theories dealing with these relationships, it is not the intention to contribute directly to it. This approach is empirical. By tracing the economic fate and impact upon others of one kind of region, seen as a type, we may well add to our understanding of the dynamics of historical geography in general; but the intention is merely to illuminate a specific and time-bound series of relationships. This book is to be judged by its success in establishing that such relationships existed, rather than by any success in erecting theoretical constructs.

Even if it is granted that a regional approach is justified, it may still be questioned whether a region's marginality is, indeed, a useful category of classification. In due course we shall attempt to define marginality more closely; but right from the start we have to justify the assumption that the fact that a region may be considered 'marginal' in some sense explains much of its history or makes it useful to search for common characteristics shared with other marginal regions, as against regions which are more centrally located and classifiable as such. Moreover, there are various kinds of marginality. Is what is common to, say, areas in difficult mountainous country and areas in marshy coastlands more important than what separates them? Even if we limit ourselves, as we mainly do in this study, to the relatively narrow range of qualities which propelled a region into a leading or innovating role in Europe at certain times, it still has to be established whether, and in what way, its marginality is an element in an explanatory chain of argument. Thus Lancashire and the West Riding of Yorkshire pulled ahead of other, more 'central' areas from the late eighteenth century onward: so did the Alpine uplands, according to a widespread consensus, between the tenth and the sixteenth centuries, when they turned to specialization in animal husbandry.[9] Is what these regions had in common more significant for their leadership role than what separated them? Can any useful generalization be deduced from these facts?

The question may be put in a slightly different form. Much of the substantial literature on the economics of location attempts to define an economic region either

[8] Perrot (1983), 91–2; Toynbee (1959–64), xii. 147–8; Kruker (1979), 103; Massey (1984), 13, 101–2.

[9] Bergier (1988), 32–3 and (1980), 166, 223 ff.; also Guichonnet (1980*d*), 222–3 and p. 115 below.

by a certain degree of homogeneity within it, or by its differentiation from areas around it; alternatively, enquirers like Lösch have looked for a definable structure or *Gestalt* of such a region.[10] Having established such a congeries of regions, is there much to be gained by grouping together the 'marginal' ones among them? Once again, the choice must be justified by our empirical results, rather than be decided on theoretical grounds beforehand.

There is yet another preliminary problem. There is no a priori guidance available to help us define a margin in terms of its relative extent. It may be thought of as a frontier, a thin line, or it may be thought of as a broad belt, a region among others. Those who divide the world into 'core' and 'periphery' sometimes define the latter—if it is permitted to equate it with our notion of marginality—as extending over half or even more than half of the inhabited globe. For our purposes we consider the margin to be a good deal less than that, as the margin of a page is expected to extend to less than the printed core. At the same time, since we are interested in societies living in marginal lands, we opt for a broad belt, a territory with a history of its own, rather than as a thin line beyond which there is a territory of a different kind.

Finally, we have to set limits to the range of this study in terms of time and place. In order to keep it within manageable proportions and preserve some kind of homogeneity, our investigation will be limited to Europe excluding the Mediterranean regions, and to the period from the Middle Ages onward, with but occasional glances at other areas and times, where the context demands it.

The plan of the volume is as follows. The first part, consisting of Chapters 1 to 5, will attempt to explore some general issues relating to marginality in our chosen area and its role in economic development. Chapter 1 will deal with definitions and a preliminary classification. Chapter 2 will examine, in a general way, one particular type of marginality, the dynamic or moving margin derived from the process by which a society fills out its territory in the course of growth and expansion. It will also serve as an introduction to some factors affecting the whole of the economic history of Europe north of the Alps from the Middle Ages onward. Chapters 3 to 5 are intended as reviews of the existing literature on marginal societies: Chapter 3 will discuss the view that these are by their nature poor and backward; the next chapter will cite examples of the opposite view; and Chapter 5 will follow the line of thought that margins are neither necessarily inferior nor superior, but are different and often fulfil a complementary role to the regions located in the 'core'. These three chapters, therefore, concern themselves with the existing literature, including contemporaneous knowledge, ignorance, special pleading, and prejudice which it reflects, rather than representing this author's own views.

Chapters 6 to 10, forming the second part of this study, consist of case studies of marginal regions of different periods and in various parts of Europe. They have been chosen with the deliberate intention of showing at least the potential, and in

[10] Lösch (1954), esp. Stolper, Introd., p. x.

some cases the actual achievement, of marginal regions for playing a more than negligible role in European economic and social development. Chapter 6 will focus on the German colonization of the European east in the Middle Ages and its various ramifications. The following chapter will consider the role of the monasteries in the Middle Ages as agencies of technical and commercial innovation. Chapter 8 has as its subject the mining areas of central Europe in the boom period of the fifteenth and sixteenth centuries, particularly those engaged in silver and copper mining and metallurgy. Several other examples of advanced activity in marginal areas are dealt with, in rather less detail, in Chapter 9. They include mountain areas as well as forests and regions of marshes and fens. Finally, Chapter 10 will return to the original example, the British Industrial Revolution and the contribution made to it by some of the 'marginal' areas of England, Scotland, and Wales, against a setting of other European 'proto-industrial' regions and their experience.

A concluding chapter will attempt to summarize the results of this study, and point to some remaining open questions.

PART I

The Problem in Outline

1

The Concept of the Margin

What makes a marginal region? The concept, particularly when applied to an economic margin, lacks precision in at least two senses: in the sense of what constitutes marginality, and in drawing the boundary of such an area, even if the meaning itself could be clearly defined. Such lack of clarity makes a poor beginning for our study. Our justification must be that the phrase is in common use, and is found scattered far and wide in the literature, both as a topic of enquiry, and as an aside which need not be defined, since everyone may be expected to know its meaning. Innumerable authors, and presumably their readers, assume or imply the existence of marginal regions in Europe: thus even if their reality is doubted, there is no question of their proliferation on the printed page. To this extent, this book is about the literature as much as about real historical developments.

The concept of marginality need not in principle imply a locational dimension. It is possible to think of marginal men as people on the periphery of society such as the old, the non-unionized, the immigrants, the unskilled, even the peasantry: marginality, it has been said, has been 'increasingly used in sociological parlance as a synonym of weakness, poverty and ignorance to indicate—in a meaning taken over from economics—a position of deprivation (alienation) with respect to power, wealth and culture'. Alternatively, Ian Inkster's 'marginal men' were those not necessarily underprivileged, but those who had found no place in the existing classes or strata of society, as for example medical men and scientists at the time of the English Industrial Revolution.[1] Much might be said about this interesting and significant topic; it will not, however, be considered further in this study, except to note that the use of the word in this context may have helped to establish it as denoting a poor and underprivileged condition.

Marginality has also been defined in terms which, though they do contain a spatial element, are essentially political or social. Thus the core or centre of a country may be thought of as that part of it which imposes its values on the men living on the margin: 'the values and beliefs of the centre gradually extend over the peripheral societies as an agreed basis of government'. Again, the 'central value system is the central zone of society . . . The power of the ruling class derives from its incumbency of certain key positions in the central institutional system . . . The mass of the population in most premodern and non-Western societies have in a sense been *outside*

[1] Inkster (1975); Linge (1988*b*), 18–19; Strassoldo (1980), 50. Also Gottmann (1980*b*), 17 and literature quoted by Hoffman (1980), 112–13.

society.'[2] In this view the margin is an area which passively receives, but does not create, cultural values, if indeed it possesses any.

History is full of examples to support this view. The classical world thought of itself as 'a central area of refined civilization [from Babylonia to Italy and Sicily] . . . surrounded by a larger outer zone [from the Ganges to the Atlantic] of assimilated barbaric kingdoms in which there were islands of *polis* economy or Roman municipal settlements'.[3] In the Middle Ages, Anglo-Normans and Germans saw the men in marginal areas known to them, like the Welsh, the Scots, the Irish, the Scandinavians, or the Hungarians, not only as poor in an economic sense but also as barbarous and lacking the civilizing influence of effective government. At the same time, from the viewpoint of Europe as a whole, England and Wales were marginal in turn. On a somewhat larger scale, Christian Europe, including the Germanic and Romance language speakers, was the core, and the pagan Slavs formed the margin. It is arguable that in some sense Europe has had a centre which has maintained a continuous existence lasting from the days of the 'prosperous core' of medieval Italy, Flanders, the Rhineland, and south Germany to the 'golden triangle' of north-western Europe of our own day.[4]

In all this, clearly the political-cultural elements predominate, though there is also an economic content visible in the relationship of centre to periphery. Once again, the mental picture evoked by this approach tends to confirm the marginal areas as backward, poor, and uncivilized.

Arising out of this notion of the overriding significance of the centre, some observers began by assuming that the evolution of the European landscape into a grid of well-defined (nation) states took place by the outward growth from dominant cores: typically, according to this view, the centre brings into subjection, opens up, and colonizes the fringe. Thus England evolved from the Thames basin, Scotland from the Lowland core, France from the Île de France, Switzerland from the valleys bordering the 'lake of the four forest countries', and Hungary from the Buda hill; the capital then tends to be in the core—or at an exposed frontier.[5] Conversely, the areas last to be incorporated, such as the two north-western counties of England—Cumberland and Westmorland—would remain the least integrated into the country's culture and society.[6]

This view has not, however, found universal acceptance. 'Unlike the Chinese and Roman State-builders of earlier times', according to Charles Tilly, 'the Europeans of 1500 and later did not ordinarily expand from a highly organised centre into a weakly

[2] Turnock (1982), 7; Shils (1975), 4, 12, 13; Hansen (1978), 247–62; Rokkan (1973*b*), 74; Bintliff (1977), 107.

[3] Heichelheim (1956), 168; Folz (1980), 4.

[4] Glennie (1990), 199; Wolf (1990), 123; Colley (1984), 53; Bartlett (1982), 158–9, 162–3, 166; Wallace (1990), 67; Keeble *et al.* (1982), 61; Juillard and Nonn (1976), 18; Lösch (1954), 258; Wijkman (1990), 89–105; Denecke (1992), 307; Unwin (1990), 123; Rokkan (1980), 168 ff.; Friedmann (1966), 10; Hechter and Brustein (1980).

[5] Toch (1989), 65; Whittlesey (1939), 2–4; Turnock (1982), 15; Hechter (1975), 4; Hechter and Brustein (1980), 1062; Russell (1972*a*), 19; Hoffman (1980), 112, 116; Rokkan (1980), 173.

[6] Winchester (1987), 13; Wilson (1901), 296.

organised periphery.' Rather, numbers of scattered islands of population coalesced and grew into states over the centuries according to local conditions. Some writers would even give precedence to the margins: the 'decisive thrust towards the formation of nation states', noted Rokkan, 'came at the edges of the Old Empire . . . the only efforts of aggressive state building took place on the fringes of economic Europe', while France, Germany, and Italy started later and less decisively. Toynbee, indeed, saw the key developments taking place not in the cores but on the marches. Frontier regions, according to some, may even 'come occasionally to dominate the whole system of which they were a crucial periphery'.[7] This is most likely to happen in the case of those marginal areas of a more backward country which adjoin the territory of a more advanced neighbour. Finland has been termed a case of 'relative over-development' in relation to the Russian Empire, and the same has been said about Poland.[8]

The alleged political and cultural weakness of marginal areas is often put down to their remoteness, which could derive from their sheer distance from the centre, but may also be due to physical barriers. It is this remoteness which may combine political/cultural and economic marginality. In one view, 'the periphery is defined by its economic marginality to the political and economic powers dominating states and empires'.[9]

Provinces distant from the capital often complained of the economic consequences of their neglect. Thus Tyrol, in 1798, felt discriminated against not only because it missed out on the subsidies available to regions nearer to the capital, but still more because its goods were charged tariff duties when entering the rest of the Habsburg dominions. The Lower Engadine has been held to have been 'marginal' in the later seventeenth and the eighteenth centuries in no fewer than four different senses: its distance from the main centres of economic activity; its location between two very different states—hierarchical and centralized Austria and the communally governed Grisons; its location on the edge between Protestantism and Roman Catholicism; and its location at a language margin—Romansh.[10]

In modern terms, a substantial literature asserts that regions far from the political centre also lack markets and infrastructure, and tend to be fobbed off with branch activities, whereas the central areas house company headquarters, research and marketing, knowledge, and access to resources, and above all they possess the decision-making power and possess the capital to back it; it has even been possible to construct a 'peripherality index' based on some of these criteria.[11] This has given rise to the notion that

[7] Tilly (1975*c*), 24; Rokkan (1980), 576–7; Jones (1981), 106 ff.; Toynbee (1959–64), xii. 112 ff.; Gottmann (1980*b*), 16; also Linge (1988*b*), 4 ff.; Merritt (1974), 190; Mellor (1989), 22–3, 63–5; Medick (1993), 205–6.

[8] Alapuro (1982), 117–18; Topolski (1991), 207–8.

[9] Brush (1982), 160; also Williams (1991), 108; Smout (1979), 11–12.

[10] Zwanowetz (1977), 431; Mathieu (1987), 12.

[11] MacMillen (1991); also Keeble *et al.* (1982), 61 ff.; Juillard and Nonn (1976), 4–6; Conti (1988), 42–3; Asheim (1988), 66; Barta and Dingsdale (1988), 167; Gripaios *et al.* (1989); Harrison and Hart (1990), 386; Tödtling (1984); Keeble (1976), 3, 51 ff., 67.

> National economic development is, to a large extent, identical with the development of core regions . . . core regions perform a critical role in the process of industrialization and are major centres of trade, finance and government activities.
>
> In each individual country and internationally, capital presses outward from the centre—in other words, its historic birthplaces, towards the periphery . . . In certain circumstances productive capacity is attracted to the periphery by its resources and cheap labour. But control remains in the core or metropolis.[12]

Statements of this kind, referring both to remote frontier regions within countries and to countries marginal to the world economy as a whole in the modern period, could be multiplied almost indefinitely in current writing.

Economic marginality, however, the centre of our interest, turns less on location as such than on the natural features of a region. It is broadly agreed that there were essentially three types of characteristics which have made regions marginal in recorded history: mountains, forests, and fens and marshland. These are the features that have given regions a bad press in the past, and it is with these that the rest of this book will mainly be concerned.

This emphasis on mountains, forests, and marshland makes it clear that, not unnaturally, in ages when food production formed the main occupation of the people, any region deficient in that respect were the most likely to be deemed marginal. With the rise of manufacturing industries as a major source of incomes, regional classifications were bound to become much more complex.

There were important distinctions between these three types of region. Mountains were seen as immovable, though methods of tackling the problems of surviving on them changed over time. Forests, however, were affected very directly by human action, usually by encroachments so that their extent was diminished, but occasionally they were affected also by replanting or neglect, which expanded the area covered by woodland. Marshes and fens could also be drained and their marginality removed by deliberate social action.

Yet they are often considered to have much in common. Jennet called them 'deserts': 'The obvious deserts are moors and mountain tops; there are other desert areas, of a different kind, by the sea or on the mouths of rivers—saltings, sand dunes and beds of oozy ground.' Among the English 'deserts' he listed the Lake District, the Forest of Bowland, the Yorkshire Dales, the High Peak, Dartmoor, Exmoor, and the Long Mynd in Shropshire. Similar language was used by Le Goff: 'In the Middle Ages the fundamental opposition was between the town and the desert . . . the desert was the uncultivated and the wild; most characteristically it was the forest'.[13]

Little needs to be said about mountains, though there is always room for debate as to what constitutes a 'mountain'. It is obvious that they are more difficult of access than locations on plains, and that tillage there is harder if not impossible because of the slope of the land and, usually, also because of the harsher climate. It was there-

[12] Friedmann (1966), 67; Smith (1981), 229, 230.

[13] Newell (1925), 9; Le Goff (1972), 72; also Pfister (1994), 22; Macaulay (1913), 300–2.

fore an easy, even if not scientifically based assumption that primitive man shunned the higher mountains, and settled on them only if driven from the plains by enemies or by population pressure, making them truly marginal areas.[14]

The marginality of mountains can, however, differ, as can the height at which they become marginal. Thus, in the Middle Ages, while the Lake District may have been fairly unknown in England, it appeared to be well known in Scotland, and Scottish travellers moved around the Highlands without much difficulty. The Alps were crossed by the Romans along major roads—Hannibal's feat being thus perhaps less astonishing than is usually assumed—and a number of alternative routes over the Alpine passes were available in the Middle Ages, when goods traffic of considerable extent was carried across them.[15] It seems that traffic on two or four legs was less hampered by the height of the land than wheeled traffic. Forested mountains were generally more difficult to cross or inhabit, and it is widely held that forests and deserts were more effective barriers to human settlement and communication than most mountains.

Forests are thought to have presented themselves to primitive man as barriers: 'the forest appeared to neolithic man as an enemy'.[16] It had to be cut down to make settlement possible: civilization was where woodlands were not, and vice versa. The forest formed the edge, or boundary of civilization: 'The forest was the great obstacle in the necessary extension of the economic space of a permanent settlement.'[17] Up to the High Middle Ages cutting down the forest in order to convert it to arable and settlement was considered an action beneficial to society and to progress all over Europe. Woodlands were considered either inexhaustible or useless in themselves, or of such little value that access and usage were free: they belonged to no one; anyone, at least any dwellers nearby, might come and help themselves to wood for timber or fuel.[18] In some cases, forests were cut down for political reasons, as having given shelter to bandits, outlaws, and enemies of the state.[19]

The point in time at which forests ceased to be an obstacle to progress, and came to be valued and thus to be preserved and husbanded, differed greatly in different regions. Some protection of woodlands was enacted even under the Carolingians, and it became widespread in many parts of Europe in the twelfth century when population growth led to steady encroachments on all marginal lands, including the forests. Forest protection laws were enacted in Berne in 1304, in Schwyz in 1344,

[14] Fox (1932), 53 ff., 64; Niederer (1980*a*), 5; and Ch 3 below.

[15] Cole and Wolf (1974), 28; Hassinger (1969), 137 ff.; Mutschlechner (1969); Müller (1905), 363–4; Barrow (1973), 369–72. Also cf. p. 124 below.

[16] Renouard (1958), 10; Devèze (1961), ii. 334; Deffontaines (1933), 19 (S. P. translation), 20; Helmolt (1896), 244; Loyn (1970), 151; Frödin (1940), 39; Kötzschke and Kretzschmar (1965), 25; but see Timm (1960), 77, for a contrary view.

[17] Messerli (1989), 11; Jegorov (1930), ii. 365; Zon (1920), 140; TeBrake (1985), 36; Fox (1932), 52; Hammersley (1957), 136.

[18] Russell (1967), 42; Sombart (1922), ii. 1143; Helmolt (1896), 237, 240; Timmermann (?1959), 216; Berthold (1964), 12; Blache (1933), 172; Devèze (1961), ii. 21; Rollinson (1978), 42; Hedley (1950), 97.

[19] O'Dell and Walton (1962), 56; Latouche (1967), 274 ff.; James (1981), 130.

and from 1500 onward there were repeated bans on glass-making in the Swiss cantons because of its vast consumption of timber. In England several areas had to cease iron production in the early fourteenth century because of a shortage of charcoal fuel.[20] The decline of population from the fourteenth century onward relieved the pressure on the forests temporarily, and the area covered by trees may even have expanded in places, but in the sixteenth century widespread anxiety began to grow about the continued survival of forests, and about the problems of timber and fuel shortage, which has, with some exceptions, continued until the present day.[21] Careful coppicing could preserve woodland for long periods for the use of ironworks: in 1754 the Empress Maria Theresa ordered a full register of all the forests in Upper Styria with detailed orders for replanting. There was always also the possibility of importing timber, especially from the Baltic.[22] Difficulties of supply and rising prices, leading to the replacement of forest resources by coal and iron, respectively, are among the standard explanatory features of the British Industrial Revolution of the eighteenth century.[23] Nevertheless, even at a time when their value was recognized, forests were frequently considered to be marginal lands, and those who dwelt in them were thought of as people who led a marginal existence.

Europe also had some extensive marshlands which were marginal in a similar sense. Much new land was gained by drainage and embankment, with occasional relapses, in Flanders and the northern Netherlands from the tenth century onward. The English fens saw some drainage works performed under the Romans, although many parts of the Fenlands were still relatively empty at the time of Domesday. There was much localized reclamation throughout the later Middle Ages, and large-scale drainage began in the seventeenth century.[24] Other difficult areas were Romney Marsh, the Isle of Axholme, the Somerset marshes, the meers of Cheshire, and the Thames and Humber estuaries. Defoe described Chat Moss in Lancashire, a stretch of 5–6 miles, as 'entirely waste except for the poor cottagers' fuel'.[25] Much of the wet lowlands of the north German and Polish plain had to wait until the seventeenth century to be made habitable: in the Duchy of Oldenburg even until the late nineteenth century. In the Pripet Marshes, 'primitive people lived for centuries

[20] Hornstein (1951), 21; Berthet (1951), 145–9; Piuz (1967), 78; Wrightson (1982), 121–2; Wessely (1853), i. 475 ff.; Ziekursch (1978), 146; Hildebrand (1992), 87; Haushofer (1986), 91–4; Glacken (1956), 74; Witney (1990); Gradmann (1901), 442; Koebner (1971), 80–1; Rubner (1967), 28–35; Bloch (1966), 17–18; Devèze (1961), i. 64; Timm (1960), 18–19, 92–3; Slicher van Bath (1963), 74; Quirin (1954), 94, 96; Hauser (1972), 39–41; Grossmann (1934), 19; Schubert (1957), 112–14; Pounds (1973), 385; Rowley (1972), 165.

[21] There is a large literature. Good summaries in James (1981); Radkau (1983), 525 ff.; also Constantinescu (1982), 3; Curtis (1956), 723.

[22] McDonnell (1992), 119 ff.; Parry (1967), 177–8.

[23] Darby (1951), 80; Albion (1926); Thomas (1986), 129 ff.; Wrigley (1988); also see p. 121 below. For a contrary view cf. Hammersley (1957), 57; Flinn (1958–9); Rackham (1990); Riden (1991), 64; Schremmer (1970), 99; for Ireland cf. McCracken (1958–9).

[24] Andreae (1952); Hodges (1982), 139; Duby (1974), 10; Lambert (1971); van Houtte (1977), 4–6; Beresford (1967), 77–8; also p. 34 below.

[25] Darby (1968), 15–16 and (1977), 160; Hallam (1958), 356; Cantor (1982*b*), 18; Heichelheim (1956), 168; Weber (1976), 3, 488; Finn (1967*b*), 185–6; King (1973), 84; Denholm-Young (1934), 402; Fox (1932), 73; Lennard (1959), 18; Rowley (1972), 162–3, 166 and (1986), 3; Plymley (1813), 223.

beyond the ken of the outside world', while the Mazurian and Lithuanian Lakelands 'form belts of sparsely inhabited terrain which interrupt free movement and inhibit settlement'. The drainage and reclamation of parts of the Hungarian Alföld as late as the nineteenth century 'can be regarded as a phase in the colonization history of a frontier area'. The estuary of the Danube remained marshy until the same period, and in France, also, extensive marshlands along the Atlantic coast and in the Camargue remained to be drained and cleared as late as in the nineteenth century. As late as 1826 the Landes were called 'our African Sahara', a 'trackless desert', where, so the saying went, 'birds crossing the moors had to carry their own food'.[26] There were impassable wet stretches also on uplands, such as the mosses of Wales and the Pennines, and the Irish bogs. In Camden's time, the Tindale hills were 'so swampy as to be inaccessible to cavalry'.[27]

Deserts affected some of the Mediterranean countries, but were hardly a problem north of the Alps. In some mountainous areas, lack of water dictated the location of settlement boundaries. In Russia, the well-watered lands of the Black Soil region gradually turned to steppe towards the south-east and beyond a certain point these areas might be considered marginal also. In the north, the forest gave way to tundra, but this does not strictly come within the orbit of European economic development and is thus not considered further in this study.

In the nature of things, none of these areas can have any clear boundaries, such as we expect to see in political units. Nor is there an a priori size range which would qualify a region as marginal. It is possible to think of units of very different orders of magnitude. Villages could have marginal lands on their edges, which in certain circumstances could have considerable economic and historical significance. Most English villages, for example, had some land technically termed 'waste', though this was normally by no means worthless, but on the contrary performed valuable functions, including the carrying of game, the provision of scavenging for pigs or, if wooded, a supply of fuel and timber. If these lands, usually not in any individual's ownership, did not exist, other resources would have had to be used to furnish equivalent supplies.

A further significance of these village marginal lands was that they offered the possibility of expansion. As long as much of Europe was still only thinly populated, villages could spread outwards, into surrounding forests perhaps, as their population grew—until they came up against the edges of expanding neighbouring villages.[28] Even when western Europe had become pretty well settled, which was the case by the thirteenth century, and this kind of internal colonization then had to come to an end in its core regions, it continued in marginal areas. Thus, on the edges of uplands, villages under population pressure might move their tillage uphill,

[26] Hollander (1960–1), 165; Davies (1981), 30, 35; Smith (1978), 184; Kahk (1989), 168; Berthold (1964), 21; Brockstedt (1989), 90–1; Clout (1983), 47–54; Hay (1966), 14; Nicholas (1991), 30.

[27] Camden (1974), 847; O'Grada (1994), 321; Kenworthy (thesis, 1949), 14; Sylvester (1969), 53.

[28] Duby (1968), 14; Moore (1965), 23; Berthet (1951), 147; Lennard (1959), 3; Latouche (1967), 63; Miller (1964), 23.

where formerly only animals had grazed, and drive their herds one stage higher into former no man's land.[29] So the infilling may be seen to resolve itself in large measure into numerous small-scale advances and the use of marginal land at village levels.

We may also look at the other extreme in terms of size of territory. For Britain as a whole, for example, it has been held that all the northern half was 'marginal' from the early Middle Ages onward, the line between the Humber and the Severn dividing the south-eastern core from the thinly settled, relatively unimportant north. Macaulay suggested the Trent as the dividing line. An alternative view was that the northern counties themselves could be divided into a perimeter of the four border counties, and an inner core of Yorkshire and part of Lancashire: 'the outer perimeter was poor and sparsely populated: the core was comparatively rich and eventually became a great reservoir of military manpower and resources'.[30]

As a final step there is the even wider concept of marginality on a world scale. This is a very recent construct, and usually defines Europe and North America together with some other advanced areas as the 'core', while what has come to be known as the 'Third World' forms the periphery. It is favoured by Marxists and by politicians from the poorer countries, and it has been given a very firm structure in the works of Immanuel Wallerstein and his supporters.[31]. In Wallerstein's world picture the 'periphery' is much larger, and much more populous, than the core, while being disadvantaged both economically and politically, in part because of the deliberate actions of the core countries.

The nature of our interest demands that we mainly consider regions within these extremes, being large enough to have a clear economic character and complex inner life of their own, yet small enough to have a recognizable homogeneity as against neighbouring territories. It will also be evident that, being interested in *societies* living in marginal lands, we exclude areas which are so inhospitable that no human life is possible in them, as for example the tops of the Alpine peaks. These may be termed extra-marginal, and will not be considered further.

There is a final point to be made. While our definition of the margin has been spatial and locational, it is not necessarily immobile. On the contrary, it is one of the main themes of this study that not only might the boundary of any given marginal area change, but its degree of marginality itself is mutable, rendering a previous periphery into a central area, or vice versa. These changes in character may be associated with developments originating in the marginal areas themselves, or they may arise from changes in other areas affecting the marginal position of the area under observation.

[29] Williams (1982), 86; Smith (1978), 168; Duby (1974), 201–3; Grigg (1980), 32; Owen (1976), 71; Harvey (1976), 199; Hansen (1976), 56; Darby (1973*b*), 28; Timmermann (1959), 203 ff.; Nef (1987), 719; Vinogradoff (1905), 168.

[30] Musgrove (1990), 175; Darby (1977), 92–3, 228; Jewell (1991); Kapelle (1979), 3, 197–200; Barta and Dingsdale (1988), 168; Macaulay (1913), 274—but he seemed to think that there were only border counties north of the Trent.

[31] Linge (1988*b*), pp. xi, 2–3; Raumolin (1982*b*), 4–6; Rauch (1984), 209 ff.; Wallerstein (1989).

It was frequently rising population pressure which pushed out a border of cultivation into previously marginal or unoccupied land and, in extreme cases, might push the periphery back 'to sites which are totally unusable for agriculture, such as cliffs, rocky ground, barren sands, ravines and swamps'. But it might also be technical improvement which allows a previously unworkable territory to be fruitfully occupied. Among the causes of a contrary move towards contraction was the erosion of marginal lands by intensive usage so that the limit of cultivation had to recede.[32]

Further, backward regions might catch up and even overtake lead areas, thus changing their place in the hierarchy, as well as changing their status of marginality: in Europe, 'lead and laggard areas were constantly being remapped'.[33] Economists have studied this as a regular development, speaking, in Myrdal's phrase, of a 'spread effect', where such catching up takes place, but expecting normally a 'backwash effect' in which the backward region falls further and further behind.[34]

However, while economists are largely concerned to convert observed developments of this kind to relationships which may be generalized, our historical examples cannot be explained merely from the logic of their existing position and network of relationships within their economies, linked perhaps to their resource base and the available technology: they also have to be related to their position in the preceding phase. The distribution and character of marginal areas in Europe at any one time will thus be quite different from what they might have been, had they started from a *tabula rasa* in the preceding period and been formed according to some ideal theoretical construct taking into account merely location as well as natural resources, property relation, and the like.[35] Marginal areas were an element as well as a product of European economic *history*. The next chapter will explore some aspects of this dynamic dimension.

[32] Curtis (1956), 725; Turnock (1982), 78; Higham (1986), 336–7.
[33] Dodgshon (1987), 356; also Verlinden (1983).
[34] Myrdal (1957), 31; Linge (1988*b*), 38–9.
[35] Weber (1969), 213.

2

Filling out the Land

Having in the last chapter attempted to define, in a preliminary way, the concept of marginality used in this study, we proceed in this chapter to follow through one particular type of marginal area, that associated with an expanding territory and a moving frontier of occupation. There are clearly some differences between societies occupying economic frontier areas of this kind and those in which the marginal status has greater permanence, but more significant are the basic similarities. In particular, like the permanent marginal lands, the frontier lands were far from the centre—they were areas of hardship, of limited communication and uncertain prosperity, but they were also often areas of vigour and of promise which provided favourable conditions for enterprise and innovation.

Although it illustrates one special type only of the broader group which is the topic of our interest, this chapter has its rightful place at the beginning of our study, because, in describing the long-term moving frontier of European occupation, it highlights a major factor in European economic history which is too often neglected. Expansion has been a feature of life in Europe in the past millennium; and the people at the cutting edge of this expansion were people of the margin.

The drive for territorial expansion was provided above all by the growth of population. Ever since the dawn of recorded history, the long-term trend of Europe's population has been upward. There have been occasional reversals, when population declined temporarily, but numbers in each phase of renewed expansion easily exceeded those of the previous peak.

There were three main ways of feeding a population growing for centuries at an exponential rate. One was improved technology, permitting more food to be drawn from a given acreage. A second method, which has become available only in the two past centuries, was to import food from outside Europe and pay for it by products of European industry and by services. There was also a third way: this was to expand the land used for food production in one's own region. It is the one most appropriate where agriculture is the main occupation and opportunities for technical change are limited, and it is that which forms the topic of this chapter.

When a population extends its area of agrarian occupation, its edge of settlement becomes a moving margin. It is marginal at least in the sense of having been occupied last, while the previously marginal area becomes sub-marginal as soon as more land is occupied, possibly to be incorporated into the core in due course. This phenomenon of the moving margin had an important influence on Europe, as Turner thought it did on America, until region after region became fully settled, and no

room was left for further spatial extension. What is notable is that as long as the process continued, some of the key changes and developments of the age took place at the margin, where new land was being won, and the contemporary population was well aware of this fact.

The newly acquired land may, however, be considered to be marginal in a second, different sense. If we assume that a population will occupy the best land first, and take over inferior land only when it is forced to do so because the best land has been used up, then the marginal land thus defined is also inferior land, and it becomes increasingly inferior, the longer the process of outward expansion continues. That some such process is at work, in other words, that every society will choose to settle on the best land first, occupying the inferior 'margin' only when the superior land is no longer available, seems entirely logical to a priori reasoning. It has, in fact, been the assumption of most historians describing the process of European internal colonization and expansion.

Even neolithic man is said to have settled on the best land available to him, as did the Roman and Saxon settlers in England.[1] This continued to be the case in later centuries wherever in Europe the density of population had reached a certain level. From the twelfth century onward, as the good land became occupied 'settlements were established even where the elevation, the density of the forest, or the risk of flood had hitherto been insuperable obstacles'. 'Any increase in population . . . led to clearing of woodland and waste for extra arable land; much of this would be marginal land, giving lower yield and liable to soil erosion.' 'Continued population growth eventually forced the people of the manor to take up land of inferior quality, having in the past already cleared the best virgin land available.' New colonizers had to take 'unpopulated land which had been unattractive to earlier settlers, or perhaps had been avoided due to their proximity to the border'.[2]

For England, the process has been described in some detail for the first sustained period of population increase for which adequate records exist, which lasted from the eleventh to the fourteenth century. What has come to be known as the 'Postan thesis' refers to English conditions, but it may be taken that similar processes were at work elsewhere in western and central Europe, wherever the population had reached the limits of profitable cultivation at existing and available technology.

As population began to increase in what proved to be an extended boom period and began to press on the means of subsistence, additional land had to be taken under the plough. This extension may be viewed as a process occurring both on a small scale in individual estates and villages, and on a macro-scale for the country as a whole. In as far as the land had been previously left fallow or under rough grazing on the margins of settlement, the theory assumed that it must have been inferior,

[1] Grenier (1930), 28–9; Dyer (1980), 20, also 84, 96; Moore (1965), 21, also 37–9.

[2] Quotations from Koebner (1971), 3; Grigg (1980), 27, also 65, 105; Janeczek (1994), 24; North and Thomas (1973), 35. For other examples, see Jegorov (1930), 362; Kötzschke and Kretzschmar (1965), 149; Higounet (1986), 22, 25; Rösener (1992), 33, 4; Ladurie (1977), 12 and (1974), 16, 75; Cole and Wolf (1974), 73; Born (1957), 136; Smith (1978), 136.

yielding less output in terms of input so that the spatial extension meant invariably a reduction in overall productivity. At the same time, there was also a second process at work as a result of the internal colonization. This was to turn grazing land on which animals had been kept, whether within or without the village or estate boundaries, into arable. By replacing animal husbandry with grain production, more people could be fed per acre, but the amount of manure available was simultaneously reduced, and this reduced productivity still further. The rising numbers of people thus led directly to diminishing returns on the land, and these in turn were responsible for the falling standards of living of the age, for the rising death rate and, according to some, even for lack of resistance to the epidemics, culminating in the Black Death, which from the early fourteenth century onward reduced population levels once more in a clearly marked Malthusian cycle.[3] 'There is no doubt', it has been asserted, 'that by the end of the thirteenth century the boundary of productive land in Western Europe had been pushed to its limit': if population growth was met by putting new land under the plough, 'much of the land taken in was marginal, and the moment its productivity declined men went hungry'. 'It is clear that continued expansion led gradually but inexorably to the settlement of uncongenial lands, "the journey to the margin".'[4] Declining marginal returns could thus be linked to the most significant aspects of the social history of the age.

The Postan thesis did not remain uncontradicted. Instances were shown to exist where the better land was taken under cultivation later than land which was clearly inferior, and it has also been held that the connection of falling agrarian productivity with the wave of epidemics remains unproven.[5] But the central notion—that the expansion into new marginal territory was bound to mean the taking under cultivation of inferior land—found proof in many parts of Europe. These were areas which had been left until dire need forced resort to them, and they must have been less desirable, and worth less, than the land in the open plains that had been settled first. Marginal clearly meant inferior.

In due course, population recovered from the disasters of the fourteenth century, but it is widely believed that a second Malthusian cycle, with its crisis in the seventeenth century, followed the recovery from the first. This would make the remarkable population increase which was observed all over Europe in the eighteenth century part of a third cycle. In Britain, the pressure of a growing population on food supplies was aggravated during the French wars: resources were withdrawn for the war; sea communications, bringing in food from overseas, became difficult; and the country was also hit by a series of bad harvests. High food prices again led

[3] Postan (1972), 59 ff. and (1971), 552 ff. and (1973), 14 ff.; Titow (1972), 20, 32 and (1969), 35, 51–2; Farmer (1977), 56; Harvey (1966), 23, 32; Williams (1982), 87; Saltmarsh (1941), 28; Outhwaite (1986), 14–17; Miller (1988), 257–8; Hallam (1988*d*), 348–52; Dyer (1988*b*), 382–3; Jack (1988*b*), 443–4; Hatcher (1977), 33–4; Mate (1991), 79; Kershaw (1973*b*), 36–43.

[4] Hay (1966), 31; Hatcher (1988*a*), 242; Miller and Hatcher (1978), 55, 56; Jones (1960–3), 117; also Campbell (1991*b*), 176.

[5] Hallam (1988*b*), 287–9 and (1972); Clark (1992); Harvey (1966) and (1991); Dyer (1989).

to an expansion into marginal, inferior land which would not have been worth cultivating in normal years.[6] These circumstances gave rise to what was probably the most influential economic theory based on that phenomenon, the Ricardian theory of rent.

The ideas underlying Ricardo's theory were not new—the connection between the later occupation of agrarian land and its inferior quality had even then a long pedigree. Steuart (1767) and Ortes (1774) had clearly described the effect of the extensive, poorer margin as population increased and less fertile soil had to be taken under cultivation, while Turgot (1776) saw that increased application of capital to land brought decreasing returns.[7] James Anderson, publishing in Dublin in 1777, had in mind much the same fully market-oriented agriculture which also formed the framework of Ricardo's theory:

> In every country there are various soils, which are endowed with different degrees of fertility; and hence it must happen, that the farmer who cultivates the most fertile of these can afford to bring his corn to market at a much lower price than others who cultivate poorer fields. But if the corn that grows on these fertile spots is not sufficient fully to supply the market alone, the price will naturally be raised in that market to such a height, as to indemnify others for the expence of cultivating poorer soils.[8]

In a new colony, added Adam Smith, 'when the most fertile and the best situated lands have all been occupied, less profit can be made by the cultivation of what is inferior both in soil and situation'.[9]

Ricardo, similarly, thought in terms both of location and of natural fertility, which included the climate, as determining whether a particular plot was marginal or not. Additionally he took into account, as did most of his contemporaries, that while the produce of land could be raised by successive applications of capital, these themselves would also be subject to diminishing returns.

> After all the fertile land in the immediate neighbourhood of the first settlers were cultivated [he wrote] if capital and population increased, more food would be required, and it could only be procured from land not so advantageously situated.
>
> If, in the progress of population and wealth, the produce of more land were required . . . it might be necessary to employ, either on account of distance, or of the worse quality of land [more capital but] instead of employing capital at a distance on new land, an additional capital . . . could be employed on the land first cultivated.
>
> In the progress of society when no importation takes place, we are obliged constantly to have recourse to worse soils to feed an augmenting population.[10]

The concept embodied in these quotations, which was repeated in various forms in Ricardo's writings, was used by him as an integral part of his famous theory of rent. Strictly speaking, however, it was not a necessary ingredient. The Ricardian

[6] See p. 45 below. [7] Schumpeter (1972), 259–61.
[8] Cited in Hollander (1979), 42.
[9] Smith (1863), book I, ch. ix, 42. A contemporary of Ricardo holding similar views was Edward West, Schumpeter (1972), 476 and Sraffa, Introd. to Ricardo (1951*b*), 6; Ramana (1985), 78.
[10] Ricardo (1951*b*), iv. 13, 14, also 212. Also see Bailey (1989*b*), 4.

theory of rent, which was based on the differential between different pieces of land, did not require a moving frontier, but only a situation, no matter how arrived at, in which some land produced more with the same non-land inputs than some other land. A variable structure of land fixed for ever would have done equally well to explain both the existence of rent on all lands except the least favourable, and the direct relationship between the productivity, in monetary terms, of any given piece of land and the rent it yielded. That Ricardo chose to emphasize the moving frontier and the expanding population may have been due to the fact that he hit upon the theory in the attempt to explain his own observation of British conditions under the pressure of a rising population in the French wars. It may, however, also derive from his belief that the assumption of a relative land shortage as population increased was common ground among his readers, and would appear to them to be a plausible precondition. But it did mean that the marginality of a piece of land was a temporary attribute, arising in the course of expansion, and would be lost again in the further process of expansion, when areas that were still more marginal were opened up.

To Ricardo, an intensely logical thinker, it seemed reasonable to postulate that every society would choose the 'best', i.e. the most fertile or most accessible land, first since any alternative would have been irrational. There would also, presumably, have to be a trial and error mechanism to ensure that those who had chosen wrongly could return to the better land and this, in turn, implied a degree of mobility of the population to allow it to make these choices and changes. No doubt, in abstract terms, these were valid assumptions. They did not, however, necessarily apply to real historical situations which were not as simple and schematic as Ricardian societies, and in which other simultaneous dynamic changes might affect choices and priorities. Among those changes which Ricardo failed to take into account were the power derived from the association of larger numbers of people, as well as improvements in technology in the broadest sense, *pari passu* with the process in which population increased and filled up more and more of its land.

One economist who has used these and other related elements to propose, with equal dogmatism, a theory directly opposite to that of Ricardo is the American, H. C. Carey. Well aware of Ricardo's doctrine, he attempted to show, not that Ricardo was wrong sometimes, but that he was bound to be wrong always.

Like Ricardo, he began with new settlers on empty land. Thus the first English settlers on the barren soils of Massachussetts had, 'like other colonists, to take what, with their means, they could obtain . . . leaving the clearing of timber and the draining of swamps to their more wealthy successors'. Indeed, in North America generally, what were settled first were 'high and dry lands requiring little clearing and no drainage: those which can yield but a small return to labour: and as invariably travelling down the hills and clearing and draining the lower and richer lands, as population and wealth increased'. Drawing on examples from South and Central America, from England and Scotland, France, Germany, Italy, Greece, Egypt, Asia, and Australia, among others, he found that everywhere,

When population is small, and land consequently abundant, the work of cultivation is, and always must be, commenced upon the poorer soils; that with the growth of population and wealth, other soils yielding a larger return to labour, are always brought into activity, with a constantly increasing return to the labour expended upon them.

Carey was consistent enough to claim the converse development, too; thus when a rich and well-settled land loses much of its population and wealth, as did Mexico after the conquest, the population returns to the poorer uplands from which its former wealth and power had allowed it to descend to the more fertile lowlands in better times.

With an expanding population, however, the move is always from the worse to the better land: 'We know of no exception to the rule, and we feel assured that none exists, or can exist. That it would be so, would be contrary to the laws of nature.'[11] Turner expressed this generalization more elegantly by arguing that as more labour and capital were applied to land, land would become the scarce factor, and this would justify the movement from the poorer lands to the richer.[12]

It would not be difficult to find examples of such reverse Ricardian developments. Apart from Carey's own numerous historical descriptions, it has more recently also been confirmed in other contexts, such as North America and South Africa, where 'hinterlands once considered worthless were reappraised in the light of technological advances such as steel ploughs and windmills'. Even Postan conceded that as the medieval Winchester estates, his best-researched source, expanded their territory, the yields in the newly won acres were higher than those of the 'core' of the estates, though this may have been due to the unspoilt natural fertility of unused land. Conversely, the declining yields caused by over-use did not always occur on the marginal lands.[13]

The relevance of the Carey thesis to the topic of our discussion is that it predicts that, at least during the process of growth, the marginal land would be the better land. It would be 'better', in part, because it would react more favourably to the increased powers of production derived from larger numbers and the division of labour and large-scale operations made possible by them, as well as to purely technological progress. Modern historians would tend to lay more stress on the latter as enabling a society to proceed from the worse to the potentially better land in the course of time. A commonly quoted example is the heavy plough, with which heavy soils, which ultimately turned out to be more fertile, could be cultivated, and which helped to sustain the expansionary boom from the eleventh century onward in Europe by making good land available for cultivation which had up to then been beyond the reach of agriculturists. Fox gave the conquest of heavy soils an even higher positional value:

Porous soils are more easily worked, but claylands are more fertile. Hence the progress from subjection to, to control of, environment, which is that from barbarism to civilization, is

[11] Carey (1967), quotations from 24, 25, 37, 34.

[12] Turner (1985), 58–62; also see Fox (1932), 79; Outhwaite (1986), 8.

[13] Curtis (1956), 727–8; Postan (1967), 576; Titow (1972), 26; Campbell (1990), 94; Harvey (1966), 32–5; Zon (1920), 154; Beinart and Coates (1995), 6.

expressed physiographically by the utilization of the damp oakwood forests and their gradual replacement by arable fields.[14]

Among other technical innovations which turned formerly inaccessible, but potentially very fertile land into successful agrarian regions were drainage and transport improvements, better manuring, and the three-course rotation. 'Our forefathers', according to the agricultural reporter on Argyllshire in 1798, 'ignorant of the art or advantage of draining, pitched not upon the best, but upon the driest fields . . . Hence a great deal of our best soil still remains in a state of nature.'[15] The view of those economists who were brought up in the classical tradition—that Ricardo was wholly right and the outsider Carey was wholly wrong—is thus untenable. Both were wrong in being dogmatic, claiming truths valid for all places and all times—a not uncommon failing among economists. Neither had discovered a 'law' of development, strictly speaking, beyond the rather banal statement that any group of men will choose that method, and that location, which seems best to them *at the time*. The difference between them would lie in the time-scale. Ricardo's view was static, assuming an unchanging range of possibilities; Carey's was historic, or dynamic, based on the quite different assumption that changes were occurring over time.[16] It was Carey who sensed that the margin could at times be the area where new and better methods were first successfully applied.

The dispute between them is, however, also a dispute of principle, and it is one which in some sense lies at the heart of this study. For while the vast majority of historians adhere to the Ricardian doctrine that societies on marginal lands were underprivileged, our quest, induced by the observation of the Industrial Revolution, is to search for examples and causes of Careyan developments, in which marginal lands provide the background for innovation and economic leadership.

Interestingly enough, the study of the very earliest settlement of man on the European continent north of the Alps, including Britain, has been rent by a major debate which almost exactly duplicates that between Ricardo and Carey. While this is not the place to review the relevant literature in detail, still less to judge between the opposing views, it may be worth observing that the debate has ranged over different periods, from the mesolithic and neolithic to the Bronze Age, the Iron Age, and into the medieval Dark Ages, that it has also covered different parts of Europe for these different periods, and that some, at least, of the contestants were aware that their differences might arise because their views were based on observations in different times or places. In recent decades, the debate has also been

[14] Titow (1969), 37; Fox (1932), 79; Darby *et al.* (1979), 190; Hoskins (1955), 29; Slicher van Bath (1946), 116; Duby (1974), 200; Diener (1974), 36; Russell (1967), 169; Mann (1986), 79; Postan (1972), 45; White (1972), 147–8.

[15] Smith (1798), 171; Offer (1985), 156–8; Åström (1978), 60–1; Ladurie (1974), 81; Hallam (1972), 219–20; McDonnell (1992), 116–17; Eyre (thesis, 1954), 9; Watts (1967*a*); Gülich (1844), 7; Campbell and Overton (1993), 97–8; Messerli (1989), 11; Holroyde (1988), 18; Franklin (1952), 33; also Hoskins (1943), 91; Postan (1972), 19; Perrot (1983), 91.

[16] Schumpeter (1972), 517–18; Turner (1985), 62; Jenks (1885), 97 ff.; also East (1938), 66; Schwarz (1959), 171 ff.; Timmermann (1959), 198.

affected by newly available evidence, particularly by the results of pollen counts, and by changing views as to the sequence of the climatic ages. However, in the end, data relating to prehistoric times have to be interpreted through a veil of anterior theories and preconceptions, and it is precisely these controversial preconceptions of the process by which an expanding population progressively fills a given area which are of relevance to our enquiry.

In principle, there have been two types of theory current about the process and sequence of early settlement in Europe, each of them being presented in several variants. They may be termed the Ricardian and the Careyan. Probably the leading representative of the Careyan view was Robert Gradmann, whose writings were most influential in the early years of this century. Gradmann started with the commonly held view that much of Germany must have been covered with forest in prehistoric times. Primitive man, when moving into the area, was incapable of cutting it down in order to clear for his own use the fertile soils in which the dense forest flourished, and was forced instead to settle in natural clearings, on the steppe or on moors, even though the soil there was relatively less fertile. Valley bottoms which were wet and overgrown were also shunned.[17] This *Steppenheide* theory, which was actually later somewhat modified by Gradmann himself, may be interpreted as asserting that the earliest, primitive settlers had to take to the poorer lands, because they were the only ones they were capable of working. Only later, when population expanded and was able to use better methods, could the potentially more fertile forest soils be cleared and taken under cultivation. The outer 'marginal' areas in that process of expansion were thus the better endowed ones, once more advanced technology was available.

Similar Careyan assumptions may be found in numerous other accounts of the sequence of territorial occupation by prehistoric man. Among British historians, a long line of observers, from Fox to Hoskins, assumed that Bronze and Iron Age man settled on moors and sandy uplands, from which the descent to the richer forest lands was made only much later; others placed the early settlements in gravelly river valleys, but the sequence was much the same.[18] On the continent of Europe, the Germanic tribes were said to have started with land on the plains that was easily worked; only later did they expand into the forests or the hills. An interesting example is provided by a painstaking study of the Bavarian settlement on the Erdinger Moor which showed how its prehistoric settlers and the later Baiovarii invaders stuck to the inferior gravelly ground of the moor, ignoring the much better tertiary hill landscape nearby, because they could use that land at once. Moreover, being near the edge of the river they could send their animals to graze on the wet moor, while tilling the drier lands, using manure to develop a form of mixed farming.[19]

[17] Gradmann (1901). Good summaries in Schlüter (1952–3), i. 36 ff.; Firbas (1949), 354–6; Dudley and Webster (1962), 2.

[18] Fox (1932), 82; Hoskins (1955), 22; Hallam (1988*d*), 178; also Hatcher (1988*a*); Ford (1976), 288–9; Zon (1920), 139.

[19] Diener (1974).

Settlements which fit a similar pattern may easily be found in other parts of Europe, including the Brecklands of East Anglia.[20] 'The clearing of land was a slow business', according to Latouche, but he added, rather ambiguously, 'and the soils most easily broken up and most fertile were naturally the first to be attacked' in various parts of France.[21]

More recently, the contrary view has tended to prevail, not least because it seems to accord more nearly with the results of the pollen counts which have become possible since Gradmann first formulated his thesis. According to this view, possibly most clearly expressed by Nietsch, primitive man was quite capable of clearing the forest, with axe or fire or a combination of both, and did so to get at the richer soil which was generally to be found where the forest had also flourished. The method of cultivation that was applied is usually thought to have been extremely wasteful, but forested lands were plentiful. Tillage is also thought to have been linked with animal husbandry, some domestic animals, like the pigs, actually subsisting on what they found in the forest, others feeding on the newly cleared grasslands. The soil that neolithic and later man was looking for was loess, or loamy soil, above all, and to make it available he was prepared to undertake a great deal of laborious work. If this thesis is correct, the forest was by no means an enemy, and the Ricardian principle provides a valid model for the European experience.[22]

It is not necessary to visualize the actual development in one or other of these extreme forms; each can be modified in detail. Upland choices might have been dictated for protection, or in the Mediterranean area in order to avoid malaria; other locations may have been chosen to be close to water, or to avoid flooded or swampy land, or to be near the hunting grounds. There was also a tendency, widely remarked on, for newcomers to occupy areas cleared already, rather than choose to make clearings of their own, unless driven by local over-population.[23] Even those who think only in terms of the settlement of empty territories might admit that early man might have entered thinly grown forest land, while those holding the opposite view, who saw him attacking the forest from the start, would accept that he preferred to do it in easily cleared rather than thickly wooded growth, so that there could be a certain *rapprochement* of views. It can also be held that even if neolithic man was quite capable of cutting down trees, at least up to a certain size, he would prefer easier or safer ground if it could be had. All schools of thought would assume that early man looked for the best soil in the circumstances and that that system would

[20] e.g. Kuhn (1973), 187–8; Duby (1968), 15; Smith (1978), 134; Bailey (1989*a*), 108; Schwarz (1959), 120; Koebner (1971), 13, quoting Tacitus.

[21] Latouche (1967), 62.

[22] Grenier (1930), 28; Nietsch (1939); Clark (1945); Schlüter (1952–3), i. 39 ff.; Firbas (1949); Evans (1989), 217–18; Garnett (1945); East (1938), 65–6; Raistrick (1970), 23; Stewart (1956), 121; Narr (1956); Darby *et al.* (1979), 188 ff. There was the further interesting thought that the land gained so laboriously would not lightly be returned to wilderness after only a few years' extensive cultivation, but was more likely to be incorporated in a tight system of crop rotation: Loyn (1970), 148–9.

[23] Braudel (1976), i. 52; Schumer (1984), 11; Butlin (1973), 96; Advusin (1989), 135; Russell (1967), 25; Smith (1978), 49; Lambert (1971), 53; Sitwell (1986), 29.

prevail which proved itself by some method of trial and error or the survival of those who had chosen wisely.

If we now make the jump forward to recorded history, it appears that at the time of the Roman Empire, most of the forests around the Mediterranean had been cleared, in some regions disastrously so. Towns tended to create ever-widening circles of deforestation around them, also eating their way up the mountainsides and as a result frequently having to import their timber from distant coasts.[24]

In northern Europe, the situation was less clear-cut. Southern Gaul, where an urban network had arisen to serve a fairly densely settled population on the ground, may have borne some similarity to Italy itself, but the landscape looked very different in northern Gaul, Germany, and Britain, let alone Scandinavia and eastern Europe. Even within the limits of the Empire, the Romans had advanced very little into the forests. There were some towns along the defensive edge of the Empire, along the Danube and the Rhine, for example, many of them associated with fortifications or the headquarters of legions and cohorts. In England, too, some military headquarters had become surrounded by urban developments. There were towns also along the Rhône and along the coastline of Roman Gaul. The major towns, in turn, were connected by good roads, and the larger villas and more advanced estate developments seem by preference to have chosen sites along the major routes. Beyond these narrow cultivated belts, however, Roman influence seems to have petered out rapidly, again with the exception of the settlements along the frontiers which had a defensive purpose. It was probably the native population which cleared much of the forest in England and even drained some of the fens,[25] while Germany was described as consisting largely of marshes and impenetrable forests.[26] It may be taken for granted that the regions to the east and north of it were no more developed.

In consequence of this tenuous hold of urban life over rural and nomadic communities, much of what civic network there was declined when Roman rule collapsed. Some towns remained centres of trade and distribution, serving the original Celtic or newly arrived Germanic populations; some became the seats of bishops or of monasteries; but most of them shrunk in size and population. The rural population also declined in the Dark Ages which set in, and the forests once more reconquered some of their former territory. One estimate suggests that in the sixth century only perhaps 5 per cent of the land in temperate Europe was cultivated.[27]

Some accounts seem to contradict that gloomy view. Saxons in England and Franks in Gaul were said to have pushed back the forests in new settlements even

[24] Semple (1932), 265–6; Bekker-Nielsen (1989), 111–14; Meiggs (1982); McNeill (1992).

[25] Map in Michaud (1959), 13, 27; Russell (1972*a*), 77; Smailes (1960), 83–4; Smith (1978), 70–1, 87, 93; Devèze (1961), i. 39 ff.; Koebner (1971), 43; East (1938), 107; Birley (1981), 78–9; Randsborg (1992), 21; Febvre (1973), 211–12.

[26] Gradmann (1901), 368; Latouche (1967), 36; Hodges (1982), 49.

[27] TeBrake (1985), 38; Rokkan (1980), 171; Myres (1989), 206 ff.; Higham (1986), 244; Duby (1968), 5; Schumer (1984), 5; Russell (1967), 145.

before the tenth century, when by common consent a new expansion began. There appear also to have been some towns in existence for the Vikings to sack.[28] Yet the overall picture is scarcely altered thereby: movement and insecurity in 'outer' Europe, decay and decline in inner Europe. By *c.* AD 800, 'no cities survived in Western Christendom comparable to Constantinople . . . Baghdad . . . or Cordoba'.[29] Yet it was out of this unpropitious setting that the rebirth of Europe began, much of it taking the form of an outward expansion from townships of Roman origin. Like cells in a nourishing tissue, they turned marginal land into fully settled land, conquering ever new margins in the process.

The territorial expansion of human settlement in Europe, which began in the tenth or eleventh century and went on unabated until the early fourteenth century, had as its main cause the increase in population, though other causes, such as the rising costs of feudal control, may also have played a part. Little is known about the causes of that remarkable population increase: it may just be that various blocks, which had inhibited it in the past, were at least temporarily cleared out of the way, but it may also be, conversely, that it was the opportunity of moving into newly available land in widening margins that either encouraged an increase in the birth-rate, or helped to keep alive those who might otherwise have perished. No exact figure for the population increase can be given, but it seems likely that the numbers living in England and in the territories which later became France as well as in central Europe increased by a factor of three, a remarkable rate of growth by any standard. We cannot even be sure that the growth had not started much earlier on. Certainly, in some regions the expansion of the cultivated area at the expense of marginal land seems to have started as early as the sixth or seventh century.[30]

Territorial expansion took two forms which might be characterized as outward and inner colonization. The outward push included the drive of German settlers and conquerors eastward into Slav lands, the Scandinavian drive into western Europe and Russia, and the southward drive of the Christian population into the Iberian peninsula.[31] Here we shall be mainly concerned with the inner colonization, the filling up of empty spaces between existing settlements, as forests were cleared, swamps and marshes drained, and settlements pushed up difficult sides of mountains.

> The expanding frontier [for England] lay not in the wide open spaces but in the heart of long settled shires, in the Weald and among the forests and swamps of the heavy Midland clay soil.
>
> Around the year 1050 [it was said of France] . . . a new era dawned, which was to last until the late thirteenth century. This was the period of large-scale land clearances, and to all appearance it saw the most considerable addition to the total area of land under cultivation in this country since prehistoric times.[32]

[28] Duby (1974), 78; Hohenberg and Lees (1985), 60; Bloch (1966), 3; Latouche (1967), 217; Loyn (1970), 6–7, 161.

[29] Wolf (1990), 103.

[30] Abel (1966), 30–2; Williams (1982), 88–9; Herrmann (1989), 227; Koebner (1971), 43; Darby *et al.* (1979), 192–3; Nitz (1983), 107; Wolf (1990), 108–9.

[31] e.g. map in *Times Atlas of World History* (1988 edn.), 120.

[32] Loyn (1970), 332; Bloch (1966), 5; also Gerhard (1959), 220.

Although there was to be some shrinkage of the cultivated area thereafter, symbolized by the 'lost villages' of England and the *Wüstungen* of central Europe, of which more below, this internal expansion, the eating up of the free margin between the settlements, could happen only once, and it was largely completed in the boom phase of the High Middle Ages. The extension to create new land out of the wilderness was, according to Duby, 'without question the great economic venture of the twelfth century'. 'During the three centuries which began the second millennium AD', added North and Thomas, 'this extension of the boundaries of settlement was destined to convert Western Europe from a vast wilderness into a well-colonized region.'[33]

In a relatively old populated country like France, the drive to add to the settled and tilled or grazing land had many sources, corresponding to the complex structure of rural society. Some encroachment on marginal lands was carried through by peasants, individually or within their village communities, gaining thereby not only land but also frequently improved conditions of tenure or other reliefs and privileges from their lords. Elsewhere it was the temporal lords or the monasteries which provided the impetus for opening up empty lands, by assarting and drainage on the edges, or by founding new settlements in the middle of the wilderness.[34] In Artois settlement proceeded along two lines, along the sea by draining the water-logged plains, and in the upland by clearing the forest. Forests were cleared in the southern Alps, in Auvergne, in Brittany and Normandy. In Dauphiné peasants started to encroach on the upland forests where hitherto only hermit monks had settled. The Poitou heathland was cultivated, and Maine became repopulated in the eleventh and twelfth centuries.[35]

In some cases, settlements were the product of deliberate policy by the ruler. Some of the *bastides* of south-western France fell into that category. While a few were suburbs of existing towns, most were founded on new land cleared for cultivation. Saint-Blanquat counted around 400–500 such *bastides* founded in the region mostly between 1230 and 1350. Apart from marking out and securing the boundaries of the area under the ruler's control, they also served to repopulate areas denuded of population by migration southward into Spain and by the losses of the crusades, and this was underlined by the attempt to attract settlers from areas outside the ruler's own lands. They were also meant to increase the ruler's income, and to form administrative centres, while the settlers, for their part, were given a number of privileges by their communal *pariage* contracts, including the rights of market towns. Some, however, merely regrouped existing villages to give the optical illusion of new settlement in previously empty territory.[36]

33 Duby (1974), 200; North and Thomas (1973), 33. Also Lewis (1958), 476–80; Abel (1966), 34; Jegorov (1930), 364; Grigg (1980), 32–3.

34 Dodgshon (1987), 258; Berthet (1951), 147.

35 Pesez and Ladurie (1965), 148, 167 ff.; Latouche (1948), 44 and (1967), 280–5; Bloch (1966), 8; Pounds (1973), 243–4.

36 Saint-Blanquat (1949); Higounet (1950), 69 and (1975); Lyon (1957–8), 48; Deffontaines (1933), 23; Berthe (1990); Beresford (1967), 58–9, 351–2.

Elsewhere the foundation of new townships (*villeneuves*) began earlier, from the early twelfth century onward: in the Paris basin alone, around 500 have been counted. In Maine, similar developments of new towns with market and other privileges, granted by the monasteries in order to settle population on their land, were known as *bourgs*.[37] Thus, driven by these relatively large-scale, as well as local small-scale assarts, the 'unremitting work of clearance' of forests together with the drainage of marshes went on,[38] transforming the population increase into a spatial expansion, and turning marginal land into settled territory.

In Flanders, the filling-up process consisting largely of the draining of marshland was probably completed by the end of the ninth century. Further north, in Holland, dykes to keep the sea out of low-lying land were begun by the beginning of the eleventh century, and there was much reclamation of the wetlands, on a large comprehensive scale: 'much of fourteenth-century Holland was, in effect, a new country', though the most rapid expansion occurred only from the fifteenth century onward. There was drainage also of river valleys. The reclaimed lands in Flanders and Holland were quickly settled.[39]

In the regions which later became Germany, it was mainly the deep forests and the hills and mountains of middling height that were being cleared for cultivation and settled. The valley of the Moselle was among the first to be cleared, from the west. In Bavaria, forests and low hills were being cleared from the tenth to the twelfth century, which was also the period when the population advanced into the hilly regions of the Taunus and the Swabian and Frankish Alps, the Black Forest, the Harz, and the Weserbergland. The marshy regions south of the Harz were also being settled, as were the forests of the north German plain as far to the east as today's Hanover. Further north, early population was found on the Geest, i.e. the raised dry land, rather than the marshy plains bordering the North Sea and the Baltic. Pathways and bridges began to appear in the forests around Magdeburg, an area of departure for the conquest of the east. Somewhat later took place the clearances of Saxony and Thuringia, of the Silesian Oder, of Little Poland and Bohemia and Moravia and the Lower Carpathians, accompanied by signs of over-population in various parts of Germany. Altogether, the German peasant 'had to wrest from virgin forest, from moorland and sometimes from bog, the land on which he settled, and the task of bringing Central Europe into cultivation was a slow and unremitting process of land clearance which went on until late into the Middle Ages'. 'Land clearance in Germany was a long, slow process and was achieved almost everywhere at the expense of the forest.'[40]

[37] Lyon (1957–8), 48, 54; Koebner (1971), 78; Duby (1968), 76; Pesez and Ladurie (1965), 141; Higounet (1965), 253; Latouche (1948).

[38] Latouche (1967), 278; Devèze (1961), i. 61–2; Pesez and Ladurie (1965), 181. Also cf. p. 122 below.

[39] De Vries (1974), 27; van Houtte (1977), 7; Schlüter (1952–3), i. 12 ff.; Grigg (1980), 71–2, 150–1; Bloch (1966), 8; Duby (1968), 15 and (1974), 205; Latouche (1967), 273; Cipolla (1949–50), 182; Pounds (1973), 280.

[40] Latouche (1967), 256; Higounet (1986), 42 ff.; Quirin (1954), 23; Herrmann (1989), 227; Koebner (1971), 73; Abel (1966), 35; Nitz (1983), 109; Helleiner (1967), 24–5; Schmidthenner (1923), 121–4; Madurowicz-Urbanska (1986), 301–2.

In the highlands themselves, settlers began to occupy land which up to then had been temporary summer pastures only, and these, in turn, were taken further up the Alpine slopes. Styria and Carinthia saw 'intensive' colonization between 1000 and 1300, mainly by driving uphill from the valleys.[41] In the Swiss Alps and Jura mountains also, a remarkable expansion of the population from the tenth century onward led to settlements further up the valleys, into the side valleys and even on to slopes facing north, clearing forests in the process. The 'free' Walsers, being last, were forced up to heights of 1,400–1,900 m. above sea-level.[42]

For the developments in England at about the same time, the Domesday census of 1086 provides a source for which there was simply no parallel on the other side of the Channel. Though not fully comprehensive, it yet greatly exceeded in its range and reliability anything that can be matched elsewhere. It provided, moreover, a solid base for one given date with which information of later provenance may be compared to give some indication of change; indeed, there is much internal information in Domesday Book itself to allow some idea of the direction of change between 1066 and 1086, such as the cutting down of much wood in East Anglia in those two decades.[43]

Yet Domesday Book is not without its difficulties, and its interpretation has undergone modifications in the course of time. This applies above all to marginal lands, like forests and 'wastes'. Forests, in particular, were often ignored in Domesday, because they were the king's, and thus paid no tax, or else because there was no income from them for other reasons, or yet again, because their income was allocated to and appeared under the heading of outside parishes to which the rights in the forest belonged, as in the Weald.[44]

By the time of Domesday, areas still outside the boundaries of settlement had been reduced essentially to three types: forests, notably the king's forests; fens, marshes, and other wetlands, termed the 'technological margin' by Postan; and areas difficult of access because of their mountainous nature, or lying along insecure borders.[45] Forests constituted a much smaller proportion of the available land than in prehistoric times, or, to put it differently, a great deal of clearance had gone on before Domesday. According to one calculation, Domesday England devoted 35 per cent of its land to arable cultivation, 25 per cent to pasture, 15 per cent to woodland, and the remaining 25 per cent to settlements, moorlands, heaths, and wastes made by the wars.[46]

[41] Latouche (1967), 256; Gradmann (1901), 440; Diener (1974), 64; Viazzo (1989); Hornstein (1951), 18; Jäger (1954), 169 and (1958), 36, 49; Riedmann (1988), 44; Jones (1971), 355; Schlüter (1952–3), ii. 26–36; Toch (1989), 66; Darby *et al.* (1979), 195; Timmermann (1959), 300–1; Helleiner (1967), 27; Pickl (1986*b*), 43–4; Stolz (1955), 231; Messerli (1989), 12.

[42] Meyer-Marthaler (1944), 15; Joos (1946), 294; Mathieu (1987), 7; Bucher (1974), 141–3; also p. 83 below.

[43] Darby (1977), 188–90 and (1971), 236–7.

[44] Moore (1965), 23–4; Sawyer (1976*a*), 1 ff.; Darby (1967*b*), 378 and (1954*b*), 443; Wightman (1975), 57–71.

[45] Postan (1972), 20–2; Hoskins (1955), 61.

[46] Cantor (1982*b*), 17–18; Rackham (1990), 74–6; Darby (1951), 71 and (1950–1); Lennard (1959), 4; Hoskins (1971), 75; Winchester (1987), 37; Schumer (1984), 5; Higham (1986), 184; Everitt (1977).

Without taking this to be a precise statement, it yet gives a fair indication of the extent of the clearances in the centuries before the Conquest.

The king's forests represented a legal rather than a vegetative category, introduced by the Normans. Only parts of the areas thus designated were wooded—according to some estimates, these might account for well under half the total. Forest law implied that the right of the chase, as well as rights of collecting wood, allowing animals to graze and other possible uses were reserved for the king, though in the following centuries encroachments on rights of this kind were increasingly permitted to outsiders for suitable payment, while some of the restrictions also fell into disuse. In all, some 86 royal forests existed. They covered a broad belt from Hampshire to Berkshire, with another running from the Thames to Rockingham Forest; they included the counties of Essex and Huntingdon, also Cannock, Dean, and Sherwood, and much upland territory including the Peak, Exmoor, the Mendips, Allerdale, and Inglewood, among others. There were also private 'chases', of which 56 have been counted. Altogether, there were at least 143 forests in England just before Magna Carta.[47]

The largest extent of wetlands in England was to be found along the fens. There were also undrained and largely uninhabited marshes in the south-east (Romney, Thames estuary, Pevensey), Sedgemoor in Somerset, the Isle of Axholme, and the Humber estuary on the Yorkshire bank.

Thirdly, there were the upland moors and the borderlands. The tops of the Mendips and much of Dartmoor, the Cornish uplands, the Pennines, and much of the Lake District were not cultivable with contemporary technology. On the Welsh marches, villages in Herefordshire and in Shropshire had been devastated by raiders, and much of the upland there was also still largely empty.[48] The northernmost counties of England, constituting the other border area, were not covered by Domesday.

Particularly interesting are the areas laid waste by William's soldiers in the 'harrying of the North' in 1069–70. Both the extent and the consequences of that campaign are in some dispute. The areas most affected were the uplands of Staffordshire and Derbyshire, and much of Yorkshire, as well as Cheshire in a separate campaign. There is no doubt that the Yorkshire Pennines were almost wholly devoid of settlements at the time of Domesday, but it is not clear whether this was because they had never been fully settled, because the soldiers had destroyed what there was, or, to adopt what has come to be known as the Bishop thesis, because William devastated the more accessible lowlands, which induced the hill dwellers to leave their marginal lands and settle on the now available more desirable land in the valleys. Could a relatively small army, moving on foot or on horseback, create so much havoc in so short a time by devastating the whole of the 'North'? Or did they

[47] A good map will be found in Bazeley (1901); also see Baring (1901); Cantor (1982*b*); Hoskins (1955), 73. Also details in the Domesday volumes by Darby (1971), Darby and Finn (1967), Darby and Terrett (1954); Darby (1950–1), 40–2; Rackham (1990), 131 and (1980), 177–80; Tubbs (1986), 48, 68.

[48] Darby and Terrett (1954), 85, 143–4; Darby (1977), 257.

cut a swathe across the hostile territory, which gave those living on the edge their chance? There is evidence that in some areas, at least, the soldiers actually did attack upland settlements—not least because that was where some of the most rebellious people dwelt. In any case, it may be held that it would be 'the poorest soils, that is the marginal lands, which would be likely to carry longest the impact of devastation, and also be the first to revert to waste during lean years'. There is, however, also the view held on the basis of more recent research that the destruction wrought by William's men has been exaggerated, that 'waste' in Domesday does not necessarily mean that the lands were empty, and that the population living in marginal areas was greater than is often assumed.[49]

Without attempting to resolve this dispute we may note that the relative emptiness of the area was an inducement to both Norman rulers and local lords to pursue a particularly vigorous policy of colonization and the founding of towns. In part, this policy was based on the perceived need to fortify the frontier against the Scots. Some of the devastation found on the Pennine uplands and valleys in 1086 had, in fact, been caused by Scots raiders rather than the Norman soldiery. Thus the marginal nature of the territory is seen to have a double origin: remoteness and rebelliousness on the one hand, enemy incursions on the other.

Whatever the cause, there followed the creation not only of castles and settlements associated with them in the valleys of the northern marches but also the foundation of planned towns or villages. No fewer than 30 towns were planted in Northumberland, Durham, and Yorkshire, constituting a 'genuine development area in twelfth-century England', while a remarkable number of new monastic foundations also settled there at the time. On the Welsh border, the lords settled 'hospites' out of a similarly mixed motivation.[50]

Quite apart from the settlements established on the margins for military reasons, there was also the more peaceful process of assarting from upland forests and taking in moorlands on high ground, for the same reasons as were found on the Continent. The Derbyshire Peak District and the Scottish and English border hills furnish good examples.[51]

As the population increased in the following centuries to perhaps 4–5 million people—some estimates go even higher—some of the pressure was relieved by improvements in agrarian techniques in the settled villages.[52] However, much of the innovative drive of the age was also directed to occupying and making habitable the marginal areas still unoccupied at the time of Domesday. Perhaps nowhere else is the push into marginal land in the boom of the Middle Ages as well documented as it is in England.

[49] Terrett (1962*a*), 266 and (1962*b*), 365 ff.; Holly (1962), 315–17; Darby (1962), 453; Maxwell (1962*a*), 68 and (1962*b*), 145–50 and (1962*c*), 217, 230; Kapelle (1979), 162 ff.; Bishop (1935) and (1948); Whealey (1954), 172.

[50] Musgrove (1990), 101; Millward (1974), 205–6; Loyn (1962), 453; Sheppard (1973), 183; Wightman (1975), 56; O'Dell and Walton (1962), 90; Winchester (1987), 5–6, 37–8; Darby (1977), 80–1.

[51] Dixon (thesis, 1984), 140; Parry (1978), 114–18; Wrathmell (thesis, 1975), 138–40; Harrison (1990); Austin (1990); Fox (1991*a*), 152; Miller (1991*b*), 34–5, 43; Winchester (thesis, 1978), 302; Eyre (1954), 7.

[52] Thirsk (1964), 8–9.

Much effort was devoted to draining the fens and other waterlogged territory to create new acreage for pasturage and tillage. Between *c.*1140 and the mid-thirteenth century, colonization there proceeded on a truly heroic scale. Highly skilled drainage engineers carried out the work in Lincolnshire, and the existence of a dyke-reeve, whose job it was to organize and supervise the maintenance of the vulnerable structures by which land was won from the marsh and the sea, is attested by 1160 at the latest. In the townships south-east of Spalding alone, 50 square miles of new arable and pasture land were added in the eighty years to 1241, and 18 square miles were added later. Other areas showed similar achievements, though fewer details can now be reconstructed. The work was basically planned and organized by local villagers, who showed themselves capable of an 'impressive exercise in co-operative action and mutual aid'. Further, the agriculture practised in the lands thus gained was among the most progressive and productive of the day, while retaining flexibility to meet the sometimes difficult conditions. The draining of the marshland has been described with some justification as an 'astonishing example(s) of the engineering skill of the early middle ages' and the most 'spectacular' reclamation of the age. The clearing of the Somerset marshes was, unlike that of the fens, planned and directed from above and Romney Marsh was cleared partly by Canterbury Priory, and in part under instruction by a public 'Commission of sewers'.[53]

The clearance of forest land may have been less spectacular than the drainage schemes, but the acreage added to cultivation thereby was probably a good deal larger. Methods varied much in detail, but the drive was everywhere ultimately traceable to the increase in population and the consequent local shortage of land. In some places it was the monasteries which provided the initiatives: thus in Rockingham Forest and in Northampton it was Peterborough Abbey which was responsible for much of the assarting, though individual freeholders were active, too. In the Forest of Arden, it was the peasantry, among whom there were many freeholders, who cleared the forest lands. The most vigorous period of colonization occurred there in the period from 1180 to the mid-thirteenth century under charters granted by the Earl of Warwick. Thereafter only small grants for the occupation of the wasteland remained to be awarded. In the Weald, the main period of encroachment from the twelfth to the fourteenth centuries was marked by settlement of cloth-makers, ironworkers, and woodturners as well as agriculturalists.[54] In due course the settlers proceeded also into the most barren of the woodlands, such as Sherwood, the higher reaches of the Weald, and the Pennine uplands, though of course the further up they advanced, 'the less rewarding many of their gains were apt to be and the more restricted the uses to which they could be put'. The proportion of woodland may have shrunk from 15 per cent in 1086 to around 10 per cent

[53] Hallam (1965), 219–20 and (1954), 15 ff. and (1958), 361 and (1988*a*); Williams (1982), 94–107; King (1973), 84–5; Darby *et al.* (1979), 250–2; Rackham (1990), 384–7; Smith (1943), 166 ff.; pp. 14 and 90 above and below.

[54] King (1973), 72–84; Skipp (1970), 84–5; Roberts (1968) and (1973); Brandon (1988*a*), 176; Raftis (1974); Baker (1973*b*), 423–4; Schumer (1984), 50–6.

of the land of England in 1350, a share similar to that of today. There was forest clearing also in Scotland.[55]

The occupation of the margin in those centuries implies a certain degree of mobility, at least where moves farther than the edge of a village or an estate were concerned. But such mobility as there was, was insufficient to even out the effects of the increasing population as between different districts. These effects depended in part on conditions at the outset. An interesting local study of two hundreds in Warwickshire—Kineton and Stoneleigh—will furnish an illustration.[56] Kineton was much the more densely settled and the more prosperous of the two in 1086; it had more villeins and serfs and may thus be said to have had a more traditional structure. Stoneleigh, on the edge of the Forest of Arden, was less prosperous, and much more thinly occupied at the outset. By 1279, after a period of vigorous growth, Stoneleigh's population had grown much faster, so that in terms of the density per square mile it had caught up with its neighbour. But in the process of absorbing, or attracting, a large addition to the population, Stoneleigh had also seen a period of 'vigorous colonization', into good fertile soil gained from the forest; it had become, by comparison, a society full of enterprise and emancipation, richer now than Kineton, although it disposed over a much smaller proportion of arable.

It cannot, of course, be argued from this single example that the communities on marginal land were everywhere more enterprising and more successful or, indeed, that they tended to attract the more vigorous settlers. Yet neither can the notion that the clearance of forests, like the drainage of fens and marshes, brought forth the more active spirits and the more advanced technology of the age be rejected out of hand. The margin offered, at the time, a greater challenge than the older settled lands. It is not entirely surprising that it should also, on occasion, bring forth a more vigorous response.

When we now turn from western Europe, which we have considered so far, to eastern and northern Europe in the same period of the Middle Ages, we find a different situation, and the differences become more pronounced the farther we move away from the European 'core'. There, the margin of cultivation had not been reached in the sense that it had in the West. Villages were not generally limited in their expansion by abutting on neighbouring villages. When new land was occupied by settlers away from their own villages or hamlets, it did not have to be 'marginal' land, but was frequently of the same type and quality of soil as that which earlier settlers had cleared.[57] There was no sign yet of over-population in the western sense, though there might be some clearly defined local problems here and there. On the contrary, then and for many centuries to come, local rulers, like western rulers at the onset of the medieval population expansion, would set out to attract immigrants by offers of land and privileges, to increase their revenue and help to secure their territories against potential invaders.

[55] Miller (1988), 257; Raftis (1988), 194 ff.; Brandon (1988*a*), 184–5 and (1988*b*), 312; Smailes (1960), 97; Dyer (1980), 57, 90–2; Rackham (1990), 88 and (1980), 133–7; Liddell (1966); Lythe and Butt (1975), 20.

[56] Harley (1958); also Hilton (1950).

[57] Brunner (1968), 200, 210.

As had been the case on a small scale in every village, on the large European scale the existence, side by side, of densely settled lands in the west in which the population was dangerously pressing on the means of subsistence, and relatively empty lands in the east, in some cases actively seeking settlers, could not but set up an active relationship between the two. Seen from the west, the whole of eastern Europe might appear to be 'marginal' land, beckoning with its opportunities or, at the least, offering a chance of some complementarity. We shall find similar but more active links of mutual interdependence in the upswings of the later two European population cycles, in the fifteenth and sixteenth centuries, and the eighteenth century, respectively. In the Middle Ages, however, means of communication were primitive, and in their light the distances appeared enormous. It would have been hard to exchange products in large quantities, especially over land: people could move more easily. Thus the main connection between the broad bands of eastern and western Europe, leaving out the extreme north and the extreme south for the moment, was the move to colonize adjacent areas of the east, the first recorded German *Drang* or *Zug nach Osten.*

This move forms the subject-matter of Chapter 6 and will therefore be noted only briefly here. The main thrust came in the twelfth and thirteenth centuries, and much of what the settlers occupied consisted of forest and marsh; the latter they generally gave a wide berth, though there were exceptions. Some territories such as Upper Saxony and the Vogtland had been virtually empty. Elsewhere there was a thinly settled, scattered Slav population, which was itself expanding. The Slav rulers on the whole welcomed the German settlers, who they hoped would increase their own power and incomes.

The Scandinavian lands, and especially the three northern ones, Norway, Sweden, and Finland, must also be reckoned among the thinly populated outer margin of Europe at that time. However, the massive Viking raids from the late eighth century onward and the drive of the Scandinavians into Russia pose a puzzle in this regard, if we assume that the raiders were driven by land hunger and over-population. Historians are, however, by no means agreed that the Viking raids and overseas settlements are to be explained wholly or even partially by the push of population pressure. There was, indeed, a rapid rise in the population which hostile observers attributed to the large numbers of children caused by the practice of polygamy, especially among the chieftains: the Mälar valley in Sweden, for example, had 1,000 farmsteads in AD 800 which had increased to 4,000 by 1100.[58] But Nordic society was described as a rich society before AD 800; possibly because of its production of bog iron, it was engaged in active trade with the Mediterranean and other areas, and there were hints of rising prosperity rather than poverty, including some evidence that the stature of men was increasing, a sign commonly of good nourishment, in the period leading up to AD 800.

[58] Ambrosiani (1985), 103.

Two other explanations for the expansionist drive of the Scandinavians have been put forward. One would place the cause of emigration on the dynastic squabbles which drove the losers to seek their fortune elsewhere, and on the encroachment of newly gained royal power over a proud and independent people. Certainly, what is known of the history of these countries at the time includes a great deal of violence and internecine strife. A second possible cause was greed for the riches of other countries and the ease with which these could be obtained in view of the weak defences put up by the inhabitants of many coasts compared with the military and naval skill of the Viking raiders: 'They wanted land to farm, wealth to make life splendid, or bearable, and some of them wanted dignity and fame. Trade, colon-ization, piracy and war would get them these things.'[59]

By the European standards of the time, the Nordic countries were clearly thinly populated. By the end of the thirteenth century Sweden is estimated to have had a population of 600,000, Norway of 400,000, and Denmark of perhaps one million. Much of the forest land of north Scandinavia was empty; forests were still often treated as no man's land in Norway and farmsteads might remain unoccupied for a long time after the death of the occupier. In Sweden and Denmark, the margins of villages were often neglected and, if it came under pressure, a village might found a completely separate daughter settlement in the empty territory beyond.[60] Given their long coastline and good water communication, some of these countries' timber surplus was exported to western Europe even between the eleventh and thirteenth centuries—an early harbinger of a type of relationship between periphery and core which was to take on quite different dimensions in later centuries.[61]

Yet land shortage and over-population are relative terms, especially where the climate is severe and much of the land consists of steep mountainsides and bleak mountaintops, as in Norway. Even today only 3 per cent of the land surface is cultivated in that country. There was in fact much clearance of forests before 1350, and it has even been possible to speak of over-population, and the increase of burdens imposed by landlords on farmers in consequence of it, until the population decline after 1350 realigned markets there as elsewhere in Europe. The odal system of tenure inhibited the alienation of land, so that holdings had to be split into ever smaller portions on the death of the owner, or some sons were left without land.[62] It may well be that a key factor here was a low rate of mobility, for legal or technical reasons, which tied people to their overcrowded settlements even though there were immeasurable acres of empty forest elsewhere in the kingdom. From their point of view, the margin was inaccessible, and, when the population came under pressure, the open sea seemed to offer a better prospect.

[59] Jones (1973 *a*), 196; also Wilson (1970); Logan (1983), 25–6; Arbman (1961), 49.

[60] Smith (1978), 170, 235; Bjorkvik (1965), 583; Hansen (1976), 56; Åström (1983), 435–6; Blache (1933), 105–6; Bolin (1971), 633–9; Gissel *et al.* (1981), 108.

[61] Clow (1956), 87; Clarke (1985), 116; Rackham (1990), 88.

[62] Bjorkvik (1965), 601; Gissel *et al.* (1981), 110, 216–18; Derry (1957), 10; Kendrick (1968), 21; Jones (1973*a*), 196.

In Russia the population had made less impact on the environment at the time than anywhere else in Europe, with a tendency for the settlement to thin out as one proceeded from west to east, though even parts of Poland were still largely empty. Much of the land, particularly in the north, was marshy or inaccessible and, in any case, climatically unsuitable for the European type of agriculture. Elsewhere, the forest dominated the scene. It was cut back vigorously, timber being almost a free good, and towns like Novgorod and Moscow were built almost entirely of timber. The ores of the Urals would ultimately become economically exportable as smelted metal because of the quantity of wood fuel available, and meanwhile furs, wax, and other forest products, as well as timber, could be produced for export. Settlers, attracted to Novgorod from the second half of the twelfth century onward, 'fulfilled the function of opening up, cultivating, and managing newly acquired farmlands'.[63]

In these lands it was clear to existing communities that there was always plenty of forest land freely available elsewhere of a quality equally as good as their own. The Ricardian margin, in other words, had not yet been reached. Partly for that reason, land was used extremely wastefully, being tilled for perhaps one to three years after a slash and burn operation, before communities moved on. Though authority attempted to fill up land by settling people between existing villages—it was labour which was in short supply—the freely available land elsewhere provided a classical framework for marginal existence with some of its traditional consequences: the ability to escape authority, and the lack of incentive to engage in technical progress: 'The very abundance of new land which might be brought under cultivation provided little incentive to intensify production beyond a certain level, and afforded means of escape to those who wished to avoid demands they considered too exacting.'[64]

Part of the pressure which drove western Europe into the search for better methods and enlarged freedom was thus absent. Russia would have had to continue the process of inner colonization for a very long time before her population hit the limits of subsistence in the western sense. Meanwhile her promising urban development[65] was, like so much else, cut short by the Mongol invasions.

It was a sign of the abundance of land, especially when under forest, that no great efforts were made to draw clear boundary lines in early medieval Europe. Occupied territory would peter out into no man's land. Thus in Anglo-Saxon England, typically 'frontiers tended to coincide with areas of "negative" land, where communication was difficult and settlement largely lacking'. At the time of Domesday, Yorkshire had no clear boundary towards the north and west, nor had Cheshire a firm frontier towards the Welsh lands. Part of the reason why the frontier between England and Scotland, first established in 1237, was in dispute well into the sixteenth century, some of it even after the amicable settlement of 1552, was that some open

[63] Birnbaum (1987), 31; Kuhn (1973), 188; Hohenberg and Lees (1985), map on p. 52; Zon (1920), 157; Wyrobisz (1978), 67; Rutkowski (1971), 487.

[64] Smith (1971*b*), 518, also 508 ff.; Rubner (1967), 25; Schwarz (1959), 111; Stökl (1975), 762.

[65] Hohenberg and Lees (1985), 55; Birnbaum (1987).

land had been grazed over by subjects of both kingdoms from time immemorial.[66] In forested lands, the frontier forest, or *Grenzwald*, was a common device to demarcate the Germanic *Gaue*; but countries might define their frontiers in such terms as 'as far as the middle of the forest'. Thus 'In the early Middle Ages, the frontier mountain ranges and their foothills in Bohemia were covered by inaccessible forests and swamps, with the imaginary border line of the Czech state running vaguely through the middle.'[67] We find forest ribbons to be the frontiers separating Poland and Hungary from their neighbours, Denmark from the German lands, Livland from Prussia, Lithuania, and Russia, Norway from Sweden, and even parts of the Frankish kingdom or empire from each other. It need hardly be stressed that the European-Russian frontier to the Asiatic East was even less clearly marked than the internal European frontiers.[68]

Clearly determined borders with their inevitable quarrels and occasional warfare had to await the clearance of the forest. It may be significant that the territory of the Teutonic Knights, being perhaps the earliest 'modern' political construct, did set up something like real frontiers. By contrast, the boundary between France and Spain in a remote Pyrenean valley was settled only in 1866–8, and then largely to stop smuggling.[69]

In many ways forests, which separated one group of settlements from others, were preferred as frontiers to mountains and rivers, which could unite as well as divide, though lakes and marshes were also found useful as demarcation lines.[70] At the same time, in many cases, as in 'Red Ruthenia' with its Polish and Ukranian population, frontiers were not barriers, but areas where two peoples mixed.[71]

The defensive system of medieval Silesia was the *Grenzverhau* (*Preseka* in Polish) in which trees were cut and intermeshed to become an impenetrable protective barrier with just a few paths left open through it. Similar systems were in use also by Mecklenburg, Pomerania, Prussia, and Lithuania, as well as by Hungary. After German colonization and the clearing of the forests such barriers were replaced by castles as the basis for frontier protection.[72]

Whatever growing population pressure there was, was reversed from the middle of the fourteenth century onward, when a catastrophic decline of population set in all over Europe. It is usually associated with the Black Death, though that was only the most spectacular assault on human survival in a long phase of disease and undernourishment. Exact figures are hard to come by, but

66 East (1938), 101; Winchester (thesis, 1978), 31; Atkin (1954), 57; Maxwell (1962*a*), 1; Darby (1962), 421 and (1977), 321; Kapelle (1979), 147–8; Tough (1928), 23; but see Barrow (1973), 141–2. For a parallel in the Maghreb, see Rokkan (1973*a*), 29–30.

67 Jelecek and Bohac (1989), 150, 160.

68 Kuhn (1957), 362; Deffontaines (1933), 20; Zon (1920), 144–5; Schlüter (1952–3), i. 20; Higounet (1986), 215; Zajchowska (1976), 121; Smith (1971*b*), 418; also Semple (1911), 215.

69 Kötzschke and Kretzschmas (1965), 89; Jegorov (1930), 434–5; Peyer (1979); Kasiske (1941), 291; Sahlins (1989), pp. xv, 239–43.

70 Jegorov (1930), 365; Helmolt (1896), 239 ff.; Semple (1911), 357; Mellor (1989), 76.

71 Janeczek (1994), 19–20.

72 Kuhn (1971), 32 ff.

the widespread assumption that populations were reduced by between a quarter and one-third seems reasonable.[73]

After an interval, population began to grow again in all parts of Europe, and with it, there was renewed pressure on the margins. It is sometimes referred to as a Second Malthusian crisis. Many of the reactions of the Middle Ages were repeated, but there was now far less free land available to be occupied by marginal encroachment. For those reasons, we shall treat this period more briefly.

In England there were widespread expressions of apprehension that the country was becoming dangerously overcrowded, there was talk of land hunger, and temporary food shortages made their appearance there as elsewhere.[74] Signs of encroachment on the uplands, moors, forests, and marshlands had appeared even in the later fifteenth century, but the movement became stronger in the sixteenth century. The enclosures of common land of that period, generally assumed to have taken place for gaining land for sheep rearing, but which was also for purposes of cattle rearing (as distinct from enclosures for converting arable to pasture), took place to a considerable extent on these marginal lands. There are some indications that it was precisely in these areas along the moors and the fens, as well as in those which still possessed extensive commons at the outset of this period, that population grew fastest, and the forests were also being invaded by waves of settlers. It appears that it was in these marginal areas, particularly in pastoral regions, that domestic, part-time industries appeared to expand most strongly.[75]

In southern England expansion into marginal land occurred notably in the Weald and in Devon and Cornwall. There, population pressure led both to the nibbling at the edges of wastes and moorland, and to larger enclosures of what had been commons and of woodland. In the Cotswolds, some industrial employment eased pressure, and there were complaints of the overstocking of the commons. There was also massive drainage of the fens engineered by Vermuyden, of which more below, though it is not clear how far the drive for this derived from population pressure, and how far it was the result of the search for profits, allied to temporary powers to override ancient rights and privileges on the part of the proprietors, though this in turn may have been helped along by the background of rising rents and land values associated with over-population. We hear of encroachments on the wastes, as well as improvements in husbandry in Staffordshire and also in Wales, while in the Forest of Arden there was not only encroachment on the woodland waste, but changes in tillage, including some conversion from pasture to arable. The spread of employment in both woodland crafts and textile trades provided income and food for greatly enlarged numbers.[76]

[73] Ziegler (1982), 239; Helleiner (1967), 5–9; Bean (1963), 423 ff.; Born (1957).

[74] Helleiner (1967), 30–1; Fisher (1957), 6, 16; Wallerstein (1974), i. 110, 251.

[75] Manning (1975), 138; Baker (1973*a*), 211–14; Wrightson (1982), 121–7; Clay (1984), 72–3, 93 ff.; Swain (1986), 91–2; Campbell (1960), 72, 96.

[76] Moore (1965), 36; Hoskins (1943), 80–8; Clay (1984), 107; Lindley (1982), 1–4; Rackham (1990), 390; Carus-Wilson (1962); Frost (1981), 32; Skipp (1978), 41 ff.; Jones (1973*a*), 459; Rowse (1969), 36; Pierce (1972), 211; Griffiths (1988), 71–2.

It was the north of England which had the largest stretches of unused land, in the Pennines, in the border hills, and in the Lake District. In Cumberland and Westmorland, a commission in 1619 reported 757 encroachments in Inglewood, including 602 for houses. In Lancashire, both the occupation of wasteland and the rise of part-time industrial occupations were very marked. The Forest of Bowland, which was still sparsely populated in the early sixteenth century, was shown to have been almost entirely cleared of trees by 1650, and—apart from the high ground—enclosed and used as grassland. Between 1550 and 1630 there was almost as much land enclosed in south-eastern Bowland as in the whole of the previous seven centuries. In the Yorkshire dales also, cultivation was creeping up the sides of the valleys, and industrial employment was increasing.[77]

There were similar developments on the Continent. In region after region, wasteland was being taken under the plough, forests cleared, marshes drained, higher slopes reoccupied or newly settled.[78] As the peak of the population cycle was approached, reaching the limits of subsistence, it was accompanied by social disasters and economic depression. Among the Malthusian positive checks were wars and civil wars, of which the worst, the Thirty Years War, reduced population in parts of Germany by as much as 40 per cent. There were also epidemics, bad harvests, and temporary famines.[79]

Yet it has to be stressed that the disasters of the sixteenth and seventeenth centuries did not compare in severity with those which had hit Europe two centuries earlier. Overall, the population decline was very modest; in some countries, indeed, it was represented only by population stability or even by slowed-down growth rather than by an absolute decline. Among the causes for this more successful weathering of the storm was a higher level of technology, particularly in agricultural practice and in transport.[80] The former allowed a larger number of people to subsist on the same number of acres, as well as enabling productive cultivation to extend also to the margins on marshes and moorlands. The ability to feed the growing proportion of the population which was employed outside agriculture, in various forms of part-time or full-time industry, was another consequence of that improvement. Better transport facilities permitted a certain amount of regional specialization in cultivation to be introduced. More significantly, it allowed the European 'core' to use its external margins more effectively. This was done, in part, by the outward migration from overcrowded European countries. Thus the eastward colonization from German territories was resumed, Iberians poured into South and Central America, and the Dutch into their eastern colonies, while Switzerland exported a

[77] Winchester (1987), 52 ff.; Wadsworth and Mann (1965), 26–7; Elliott (1959), 85–7 and (1973), 46; Appleby (1978), 34; Porter (1977), 20 and (1974); Rackham (1990), 318; Tupling (1927), 28–9.

[78] e.g. Podraza (1986), 286; Morard (1971), 276; Fel (1962), 104; Bloch (1966), 19.

[79] Helleiner (1967), 40 ff.; Chambers (1972), 18, 135–6; Coleman (1977), 27; de Vries (1980), 5–24.

[80] For improvements in Britain, see Pollard and Crossley (1968), 85, 95, 113; Coleman (1977), 113–17; Holderness (1976), 62–9.

large proportion of its male population as soldiers. However, emigration from England to overseas colonies, though frequently mentioned in the literature, was still modest.

Improved transport also permitted the western European population to make better use of the acreage of Europe's marginal land in the east and the north of the Continent. Sweden, indeed, actively encouraged colonization in her northern territories. Some exports of food and raw materials from the Baltic to western Europe had taken place even in the Middle Ages. This traffic was now much enlarged to the point where it played a not insignificant role both in the core countries, and in the margins of Europe. It even helped the Dutch economy to enter upon its 'Golden Age' at a time when much of Europe was gripped by what has been termed the 'crisis of the seventeenth century'. Two commodities above all were involved: timber together with associated products, such as tar and ashes, and grain.

It was the Dutch who were mainly dependent on Baltic timber. Much of what was constructed in the United Provinces in their golden age was made of timber: this included their ships and bridges, their windmills and much of their houses, and countless timber piles were used to line canals and to carry the weight of the buildings of Amsterdam on marshy ground. Yet it has been said, with only slight exaggeration, that 'the Dutch never had any supply of natural timber worth mentioning';[81] at any rate, much of the woodland which they had once had, had by then been used up and cleared for agriculture. Timber was a costly product to carry over long distances, and was basically dependent on water transport. In consequence, most of the Dutch timber imports came from the Baltic. At first the Dutch wholly dominated that trade, but in due course the British also became significant importers from the same area, except for an interval in the first half of the nineteenth century, when the North American colonies were given preference.[82]

Originally the major part of Baltic supplies came from Norway but later Sweden, north Germany, and Poland became more important, and later still they were joined by Finland. Russia, which first developed an extensive timber market in the sixteenth century for inland distribution, also began to export forest products in the nineteenth century.[83] The case of Finland is perhaps the most interesting. Originally exporting furs and later tar, in the eighteenth century, when the region acquired political stability, the Dutch began to supply the capital and the technology for new types of saws to develop the huge timber resources of the country that were easily accessible by water. 'Finland as initially a peripheral area', it has been said, found it possible eventually to become 'a "post-colonial" type of economy to utilize in a more sophisticated way the principal natural resource, the forest'.[84] The case of Finland, striking though it is, is not unusual: it would probably be true to say

81 Parry (1967), 177–8; Zeeuw (1978), 5; Wilson (1966), 7; Barbour (1930), 119–24; Öberg (1990), 146.

82 Åttman (1981), 197–8; Sombart (1922), ii. 1149; Wallerstein (1974), i. 212; Davis (1962).

83 Schlenger (1965), 79–80; Bruland (1989), 27; Knoppers and Nicholls (1981), 75–81; Wyrobisz (1978), 66–72.

84 Åström (1978), 60–1, also (1975) 14, (1981), and (1983).

that it is the export of timber to the advanced world which has more often helped peripheral, marginal, or 'colonial' countries to make the transition to modernity than the export of any other raw material.[85]

The grain trade, however, had the opposite effect on some of the supplying countries on the southern shore of the Baltic, and in particular on Poland. Here, also, it was in the sixteenth century that exports, in the first place to the Netherlands, began to take on significant proportions. Stimulated by this foreign demand, empty lands began to be brought into cultivation, the shipments of grain being largely paid for by manufactured products from the advanced countries. But instead of helping to develop east Elbia, as timber exports had done in Scandinavia and North America, the specialization of these countries on grain exports led to the introduction of a 'second serfdom' and the decline of what native urban and industrial development there had been up to that time. Why a rising demand for peasant labour, and the disproportion between available land and a labour shortage, should lead to aggravated unfreedom in the east when, after the Black Death, the same circumstances had helped to complete the emancipation of the serfs in the west has been the subject of a large and inconclusive debate. More recent research has pointed out, however, that only a small proportion of Polish grain production, never exceeding 2.5 per cent, was ever exported, and only from the largest estates, most easily accessible from the Baltic ports. The effect of the western grain trade on the reintroduction of serfdom in the east may thus have been exaggerated in the literature. There is no doubt, however, that a similar development in the Balkans, where grain exports to the west at about the same time seem to have had a larger impact than in the Baltic lands, caused a marked loss of rights and a deterioration in the position of the peasants. In Russia, the availability of open land, and therefore the need to tie the peasant to his village and his lord, also went hand in hand with the reimposition of even more severe serfdom than in Poland or Turkey, without substantial sales to western markets.[86]

Thus, compared with the similar crisis of the later Middle Ages, when the core countries of Europe had reached the ceiling of their food production because their margins were used up and there was no additional land available at the current state of technology, it proved possible to ease the population pressure of the sixteenth and seventeenth centuries by improved agrarian techniques, and by the fact that Europe had become more integrated. Considerable quantities of bulky goods such as timber and grain could now be transported over long distances by water, helped by an elaborate mercantile network together with adequate credit facilities. Typically, the vast storehouses for grain in Amsterdam as well as in such export ports as Danzig were available not only for their regular customers, but also to help out in temporary famines in any part of Europe accessible by water transport.[87]

85 Radkau (1983), 527–8.

86 There is a large literature: e.g. Malowist (1959); Zytkowicz (1983); Wallerstein (1974), i. 85, 96, 301 ff.; Kula (1976); Topolski (1982); Bogucka (1982); Mironov (1992); Davies (1981), 279 ff.; for the Balkans, cf. McGowan (1981), 3–5, 16, 46, 56–9; Lampe and Jackson (1982), 29 ff.

87 Helleiner (1967), 77.

Thus, as the marginal land in the west was being used up, a new type of marginal land came to the rescue. The European margins in the north and the east now took on a new significance. That was where a great deal of the expansion of output was now concentrated, aiding, as well as being aided by, the creation of new trading and credit links among the European states, and permitting the growth of the population of Europe to continue. Much of this new land was in no way inferior in fertility to the land previously cultivated, though it was less favourably located in relation to the population concentrations in the west.

A further, third population cycle could now begin in Europe. It can be treated here even more cursorily than that of the sixteenth and seventeenth centuries. Population growth was resumed and became widespread, almost universal in the eighteenth century, though the actual rates of increase, as well as the causes of the long period of uninterrupted expansion which followed, differed between countries. In Germany, population expanded into the empty spaces left by the losses of the Thirty Years War, but in addition, new clearances were particularly widespread in east Elbia, including Silesia. In many respects, these areas with their uncleared territories of marshland and forest resembled the regions still further east where, 'in the frontier regions of Europe growth was and had been rapid because there was space to be filled'.[88] There was a deliberate population settlement policy in Prussia, for her newly won territories of Silesia after 1740 and in Poland after the partition of 1772, and in Tsarist Russia in the eighteenth century, and this was not entirely unconnected with the land shortage and regional over-population in the west.[89]

In Russia the population increase was absorbed more by extensive rather than intensive land use, even into the late nineteenth and twentieth centuries, by clearing forests in the north, ploughing up steppe land in the south and occupying new territory in the Siberian east. In the Scandinavian countries also, margins continued to be occupied as people moved 'farther into forest and peat-bog areas'. The Norwegians advanced higher up into their valleys; in northern Sweden, 'one of the last major frontiers of colonization in Western Europe' was crossed; and even in Denmark, the Jutland heath could be settled thanks to new agricultural techniques, to help absorb the population increase.[90]

The west, with very little uncultivated land left, had to depend mainly on other solutions when population exceeded local resources. One was emigration overseas, and the stream of emigrants leaving Europe, particularly in the century to 1914, was larger than any voluntary migration had been before or since. Another solution was to turn to better technology. Ultimately, the problem of feeding the inhabitants of western Europe was solved in part by industrialization and by the importing of food from other parts of the world in exchange for industrial goods

88 Habakkuk (1971), 49 and (1953), 123–4; Kuhn (1955), 34–5 and (1957), 200 ff.; Ziekursch (1978); Berthold (1964), 20; Harnisch (1984), 148; Wrigley (1969), 153.

89 Smith (1978), 184; Kuhn (1973), 229; Lund (1974), 3–4; Schwarz (1959), 140–1.

90 Merl (1989), 178; Rubner (1967), 175–6; Schmidthenner (1923), 117; Darby *et al.* (1979), 208; Blanchard (1989), 258, 265, 271–2; Smith (1978), 215–16; Lund (1974), 2; Derry (1957), 16; Dovring (1966), 618.

and for services; but in part it was also solved by improvements in the techniques of food production itself.

In Britain, this process was well under way in the eighteenth century, when the country for a time even became a net exporter of grain. The improvements involved—new crops and crop rotations, the seed drill and the mechanical hoe, improved selective breeding of farm animals, marling and manuring, fencing and drainage, among others—are well known.[91] Many of these required changes in the patterns of landholding; above all, they depended on successful enclosures. On marginal land, of which there was now little left, what was frequently involved was the enclosure of the common land on moors and uplands, as changing relationships between costs, techniques, and prices made it worth while to devote more resources to those lands than had been the case up to then.

In some areas, the cultivation of marginal land was driven forward by families engaged in domestic industry but prepared to devote some time to their smallholdings. In Lancashire many thousands of acres were enclosed for that purpose, 'bringing into use . . . common pasture and large tracts of moorland, moss, marsh and sandhills'. Under the pressure of the rising rural industrial population, 'oats and potatoes were cultivated over what now appear to be impossibly barren hill tops'. In the West Riding, similarly, weavers settled on 'intakes' from moors, which provided pasture for their horses and perhaps for other domestic animals. The remaining moorland carried sheep, besides quarrying and mining. In Durham, 25,000 acres of common land were 'reclaimed' between 1809 and 1856.[92] In France, 'population growth and land hunger in the eighteenth century led many to turn to less and less productive parts of mountain, moor or forest, and even to encroach on rural woods'.[93]

Among the belligerents, it was the Napoleonic wars which made enclosure temporarily profitable and 'drove the plough to bleak moorlands and steep hillsides where it had not been since the late 13th century'.[94]

> Farmers had relentlessly pushed back the edge of cultivation across heaths and up hills. Thousands of new homesteads clung precariously to footholds beyond the present limits of settlement. In 1801 many places in England and Wales had more people than they were to have in the twentieth century; they were situated in mountains and moorlands, in the Lake District and fells of the North country, in remote Pennine dales, in central Wales, in the south-west peninsula.

On the Weald, there were large intakes between 1813 and 1818. In the south-west there was reclamation not only of the Somerset 'levels', but also of the common grazing grounds of Cornwall, Exmoor, and the Mendip hills. In Wales also, most of

91 e.g. Chambers and Mingay (1966); Chambers (1972), 23; Beckett (1990).

92 Wadsworth and Mann (1965), 313, 321, 322; Raistrick (1970), 113–16; Smailes (1960), 71; Gilchrist (1907), 360.

93 Weber (1976), 119.

94 Prince (1973), 392; Mingay (1990), 6; Holderness (1976), 46; Wells (1988); Outhwaite (1986); Williams (1970), 56–7.

the marginal land had been brought into cultivation by the intake of 'waste' by the end of the French wars. Farms also crept up the Shetland hillsides.[95]

This was the period which provided the object-lesson out of which Ricardo constructed his theory of rent.[96] The land occupied last was really the least fertile, or least favourably placed in relation to the market. When, after this, the tide receded, much truly marginal land once more fell into disuse. Farming could not be pursued beyond the limit set by the prices of foodstuffs imported from abroad, which kept falling in the long run with the repeal of the Corn Laws, the opening up of new lands overseas, the railway and the steamship, until the subsidy policies of the twentieth century changed the rules of the game once more. The issue has been raised particularly in the debate on the 'deserted villages' and the *Wüstungen* which made their appearance in the centuries following the Black Death. The theme is worth pursuing: was it indeed the marginal lands in the sense of being the least fertile and the least desirable, those on the edges of cultivation occupied last of all which were 'deserted' most frequently?

Many thought that it would be so in principle. 'It is probable', Saltmarsh judged, 'that on marginal lands, colonized during the period of expanding demand and high prices in the Middle Ages, whole villages were being abandoned' when the pressure was off. Mingay speaks similarly of the 'retreat of cultivation. Farms in marginal areas, where soils, altitude and climate were not well suited to grain production, went out of arable and might be converted to pasture for sheep or cattle, or perhaps abandoned altogether'. In England as in Germany, 'it was often the marginal land whose cultivation was given up, often soils that had been won for the plough only in fairly recent times'. In Wales also, 'soils of marginal productivity, which had been brought into cultivation as a consequence of the population explosion of the thirteenth century, were now abandoned and agrarian activity was increasingly concentrated on the richer and more productive lands'. Darby and Terrett thought similarly that the 'agriculturally marginal lands', the last to be occupied, would be the first to be abandoned.[97] Beresford, having these areas under consideration in the following period, when the gaps left by the population decline were being filled up again, expressed similar views: 'In the marginal lands no one came to occupy all the empty spaces'; 'at the end of the queue . . . were villages to which no one wanted to come'. These consisted of 'particularly unattractive fields . . . described as stony and uncultivable' even before the Black Death.[98]

Postan's view was somewhat more complex. According to him, the receding land was to be found in 'the marginal acres in most villages or the entire villages on the outer periphery of settlement and cultivation', especially in such areas as the upper

[95] Moore (1965), 36; Williams (1976), 105–8 and (1971), 65–72; John (1950), 170; Rowe (1953), 211, 225–7; Dodd (1954–6), 28; Richards (1982–5), i. 78; Knox (1985), 115.

[96] See p. 21 above.

[97] Saltmarsh (1941), 24; Mingay (1990), 2; Helleiner (1967); Owen (1991*a*), 104; Whealey (1954), 202; also Duby (1968), 306–7; Darby and Terrett (1954); Hoskins (1955), 92; Tuck (1991*a*), 38.

[98] Beresford (1965), 199, 202, 209.

reaches of the Yorkshire dales, the South Downs, or the heath and sands of north-west Suffolk. This movement is confirmed by many other studies relating to England and Scotland. But Postan also thought that at the time when this kind of 'decolonization' occurred, there was simultaneously also some expansion by intakes from the king's forests, from marshes, or from other marginal soils. Possibly some of the land recently reclaimed had better yields than the old lands.[99]

Clearly, a Ricardian reaction did take place in some areas: there the last acres occupied were also the worst, they had been occupied only reluctantly, and were let go at the first opportunity. But it is evident that not all cutbacks in cultivation, and possibly not even the majority of them, can be explained in this way. Beresford, in his pioneer study of the 'deserted villages', found that most desertions had taken place in a broad Midland belt of counties, and there the most vulnerable settlements proved to be the smaller ones which had few freeholders but strong and greedy lords of the manor, rather than those on marginal land. By contrast, villages in the typically marginal higher, pastoral areas were little affected; though, to be sure, Beresford's study concerned itself less with the abandonment of land as such than with the conversion from arable to pasture by enclosure which involved removing the population and pulling down their houses to make room for perhaps a solitary shepherd. He also listed examples of the conversion of cultivated village land and the destruction of dwellings to make a park for the manor house.[100]

His evidence is confirmed from other sources. According to Baker, while there were deserted villages where there was 'retreat from marginal soils as the pressure of population upon land was relaxed', there were also abandoned villages as a result of reverting from arable to pasture in marginal areas. There were no more desertions from the poor soil of the Brecklands than from the rest of East Anglia. The core as well as the periphery was found to have lost population, and there were wholesale losses even among market towns and those assigned market status after the Black Death. Thus Norfolk saw the number of such towns go down from 130 to 31, Gloucestershire from at least 53 to 34, and Lancashire, which had charters for 85 markets and fairs plus 50 by prescription, was down to only 50 by 1640. Many of these had been 'founded on a wave of enthusiasm . . . and were left high and dry when it subsided'.[101]

In Germany, also, where according to some estimates up to 50–60 per cent of settlements disappeared between the early fourteenth and the mid-fifteenth centuries, only some of the *Wüstungen* were laid at the door of the poor returns from marginal land taken in hand last during the period of population increase. As in England, there were wide variations in their incidence. They were strongly marked in the central mountainous region including Hesse and Thuringia, as well as in Lower Saxony and the province of Saxony, but less so in southern Germany. The most

99 Postan (1971), 591 ff., and (1972), 25, 64; Parry (1978), 118, 166; Wrathmell (thesis, 1975), 10, 160.

100 Beresford (1965), also (1971).

101 Baker (1973*a*), 193, 207–9 and (1966), 519–20; Everitt (1967), 469; Campbell (1990), 102; Dyer (1980), 257–60; Holderness (1976), 53–4; Bailey (1989*a*), 315.

recently settled land east of the Elbe was much affected, and so was the Vienna basin, but there were hardly any cases found in the north-western and the west-central parts of Germany. Many desertions took place from good quality land. This might be where villages were pulled together in larger settlements, or to operate a new three-field system, which might be considered an aspect of progress. In other cases, the causes of the desertion were migration into the towns, and the destruction wrought in wars. At the same time, some town fields were also deserted. There was also a climatic explanation, to the effect that cultivation on dry, sandy soils was abandoned in the warm phase of 1360–1430, and on wet, impervious ground in the wet phase after 1430. In mining areas, settlements were abandoned when the ore gave out.[102]

The French experience was similar: in many areas it was 'the marginal, infertile lands, which were awkwardly situated on the rocky slopes of mountains and hills, which were quite simply abandoned', but elsewhere villages might be deserted because the population moved, more or less voluntarily, into *bastide* towns founded by their lord. Here, also, climatic change was said to have led to some abandonments, and the silting up and salting of coastal areas created other examples.[103]

The desertion of land in the Scandinavian countries has been the subject of a major collaborative study. It has been shown that while there were few abandoned settlements in Finland, they were widespread in the other four countries (i.e. including Iceland). Norway and Iceland having been populated mostly by isolated farmsteads in their 'marginal areas' of woodlands and heaths and Sweden and Denmark mostly by villages and hamlets. All these countries tended to have a rather higher proportion of freeholders than was common in the rest of Europe. Moreover, it should be stressed that all of them had available much unoccupied land to which dissatisfied peasants might migrate. Of the desertions listed, many took place on marginal land, in the sense either of possessing poor soil, or of being located near a frontier. Other causes named were climatic changes and the ravages of warfare in particular cases. Conversely, the best soil saw the least desertions, though there were some examples of abandonment also on good soil, such as the Horns Hundred. Norway was the worst affected country, and farm holdings there were calculated to have decreased from 36,000 in 1300 to 16,000 by 1520, a loss of 56 per cent. Norway also had the least amount of alternative usable land to escape to, and there were in fact few new clearances at that time, except in some 'peripheral areas'.[104]

It might be held that the many examples of the abandonment of villages and townships in other than marginal areas for the reasons cited here can tell us little about the history of marginal areas themselves. The evidence certainly points to an exceptionally heavy loss of population and settlement in the margins of the

[102] Pohlendt (1950), 16–21; Abel (1966), 81 ff. and (1943), 5–13; Krenzlin (1959), 153–5; Kötzschke and Kretzschmar (1965), 149; Jäger (1958), esp. 36 ff., 73 ff., 84; Simms (1976); Darby *et al.* (1979), 198; Kuhn (1955), 60–71; Singer (1971), 8–13.

[103] Ladurie (1977), 40; Marsh (1974), 131, 156, 207; Pesez and Ladurie (1965), 181–2; Abel (1966), 84–5.

[104] Gissel *et al.* (1981), esp. 83, 94, 110 ff.; Bjorkvik (1965), 583–91; Abel (1966), 89; Parry (1978), 129.

occupied area of Europe, which were deserted by their populations because their soil or location was unfavourable, making them undesirable precisely because they were marginal. Yet the fact was that other kinds of areas were abandoned also. Moreover, not all marginal lands were unloved by their occupiers, some of whom were driven from the land only by force to which they offered strong resistance. The tenacity with which many dwellers in marginal lands held to them had, in turn, many causes. Some of them are to be sought in the countryman's particular relationship to his land, the land which he worked and, possibly more than anything else, the land which he or his ancestors had wrested from nature.

The theme of this chapter, to sum up, has been the expansion of the occupied territory of Europe north of the Alps and of the Pyrenees, a process which has gone on, with some interruptions and subject to great regional differences, since the collapse of the Roman Empire and the arrival of the Germanic tribes. The process has to some extent imposed its own logic on the experience of Europeans or, to put it differently, much of Europe's history becomes explicable only in the light of this process of internal and external colonization, until the eighteenth century if not later. It provided a dynamic which played its part, together with other dynamic effects, such as technical change or the emergence of the nation state, in helping to shape the evolution of European society as we know it.

In the context of this study, the significance of this expansionary dynamic lies in the effects which it had on the margins of settlement and cultivation. Frequently, the margin was marginal not merely because it lay on the rim of a village, a region, or a state. It was also marginal because it was newly settled.

Two opposing doctrines have attempted to generalize from this process of expansion into territories located beyond the edge of the currently occupied, to establish a regularity or 'law' of the way in which empty spaces have been filled up. In spite of much compromise, and much interpenetration of ideas, they do represent quite different sets of assumptions and conclusions. One doctrine, termed here the Ricardian, assumes that the best land (however defined) will have been occupied first, and the later stages of expansion will therefore be forced to absorb worse, and indeed ever worsening territories. The other theory, termed Careyan, argues the opposite, namely that the first settlers are forced to take over poor land, because it is easy to work, and that only with the growth of the power of expanding communities and the improvement in technology can the better, but more difficult, lands be occupied at a later stage. One sees the dynamically marginal lands as being by their nature inferior, the other holds them with equal certainty to be superior.

History knows no such all-or-nothing laws. Examples of Ricardian expansion can be found without difficulty, and their prominence has led to a widespread acceptance of the Ricardian sequence as the normal one: the expansion of the population base forces men to move onto ever less desirable lands, located on hills, in marshes and fens, and in forests. By the same token, should the population pressure be reduced and the population shrink, for whatever reasons, the process would be reversed and these undesirable margins would be abandoned first. Yet a

'Careyan' sequence of an opposite nature was by no means rare. There were many reasons why a society should choose one initial location rather than another, including access, security, water supplies, or similarity with the known, as well as fertility and convenience. Above all, as conditions changed, as new technologies became available or as larger numbers operating in concert had it in their power to do what smaller ones could not, what was once the 'best' territory may have ceased to be so later, and what had once been inferior or marginal land may overtake it in desirability. Moreover, the lands left unoccupied at first may have riches unsuspected by the early settlers, which are discovered only as men move into them.

It follows, then, that marginal lands are not always the poorest, as is frequently believed, still less does it necessarily follow that their populations are more backward than those of the 'core' areas. On the contrary, it would not be unreasonable to suppose that the newly settled lands, precisely because they are new, and attract the more enterprising in the population who are then forced to adapt to new situations, will call forth an unusual degree of initiative, and become the location of pioneering achievements. We are not, to repeat, setting out a doctrine that marginal societies are always among the technical or organizational leaders, still less that no progress is ever originated from the cities or the core areas. Our objective is to establish whether the marginal location of the pioneers of the Industrial Revolution was wholly exceptional or whether, on the contrary, it fitted into a pattern and was therefore not unexpected in the light of the properties of such locations. Some examples of this are cited later. We must begin, however, in the next chapter with an account of what has traditionally been the predominant view, to the effect that marginal areas are poor, backward, and undesirable, and that their populations are the poor relations of society.

3

The Negative View

> Without exception all scholars present cores as advantaged and peripheries as disadvantaged . . . without exception [in their view] peripheries are poorly developed, primary economies, with low technology and high labour intensive activities . . .
>
> For other authors peripheries are also distinguished by distinctive culture, usually defined as marginal, without distinctive institutions, fragmented and parochial as non-producers of culture. Cores, on the other hand, are the locus of culture as well as political powers and decisions and possess military superiority.[1]

'Periphery', in this quotation, is not exactly identical with marginal lands in our definition, and the author is thinking of contemporary rather than historical relationships, yet the overall impression of a consensus of negative judgement in the literature might well be applied to our definition of marginality also. While not all authors believe marginal lands to be inferior, there is no doubt that the large majority of those who have considered the question would concur in the judgement that they were culturally and politically dependent and incapable of originality.

A similar near-consensus exists with regard to the history of societies on the *economic* margin. In perusing the present chapter which is devoted to a cross-section of views of this kind the reader should be aware that if this volume were to reflect accurately the balance of the literature, virtually every chapter would have to express what is here called the 'negative view', though much of the traditional writing would be found to be of a rather superficial nature. The single chapter devoted to it here is intended to reflect the range, not the weight, of received opinion. The widespread agreement on inferiority encompasses a number of variations. There are those who think that it is the natural conditions of margins which are inferior—their infertile soil, harsh climate, distance from the centre of things; there are those who believe the population living in marginal areas to be in some way inferior to those living in core areas; and there are those who hold that one was the cause of the other, that is to say, that it was the unfavourable environment which made the dwellers in it poor, backward, or uncultured.[2] These views are by no means the same thing. Quite the contrary: those who hold that it is the conditions that are to blame might even have a certain admiration for the peculiar qualities required to overcome an adverse environment. However, whether their view is wholly or only partly negative, the observers all do assume that there is a significant influence of recognizable importance of the marginal location on the nature of men and

[1] Wellhofer (1989), 342. [2] Weber (1969), 21.

societies dwelling in them, though it is modified by history, by technology, by political events, and by many other factors.

Mountainous country is frequently picked out as the type of landscape in which natural conditions made for poverty and harsh living conditions. Above a certain height, depending on latitude north and on other circumstances, no settlement whatever was possible. But below it there would then be a belt of country permitting some sort of occupation, possibly seasonal only, possibly shifting with changing technology, with increasing population pressure, or varying market demand, on which a precarious living could be had. This was truly marginal land.

Our earliest reasonably reliable overview, the Domesday census, showed the Pennine uplands to be practically void of population or plough-teams.[3] The border hills were even by the sixteenth century a 'miserable, distressed and wasted country', a 'remote, mountainous and infertile region'. 'Westmorland', reports another observer, 'is nothing else but a Western moorish country . . . which cannot easily, by the painful labour of the husbandman, be brought to fruitfulness'. These were the poorest counties of England: even their gentry and middle classes were impoverished compared with the rest of the country. Much of the High Peak, according to Defoe, was as late as the eighteenth century a 'waste and houling wilderness', 'perhaps the most desolate, wild and abandoned country in all England'. Pilkington, the local historian, agreed: 'civilization does not take place so early in a mountainous as in a champaign [*sic*] country. This may, in some degree, account for the rude manners of those who live in the Peak District of Derbyshire.' Wales did not come off much better: parts of it were 'barbarous and he surmised that the Devil dwelt there'. The Scottish Highlands and Islands outside some of the large estates were described as 'seats of oppression, poverty, famine, anguish and wild despair'. The Pennines, the north Yorkshire moors, and Wales were other areas described as bleak and therefore poor.[4] Devon and Cornwall were stated to have had similar 'barren and empty moorland and mountainside'. 'The significance of the highland line in the pre-industrial setting', it has been said starkly, 'can be simply stated as the demarcation of good land from bad.'[5]

Reports from the Continent tell a similar tale. In the Massif Central and other highland regions of France, poor soil and climate led to forced emigration. The lowest tax returns, per head or per acre, were registered in the nineteenth century in the Massif Central, the Alps, the Pyrenees, and the Landes. The Alps were seen as obstacles to civilization, a land in which no one could hope to make a fortune: 'La pauvreté a régné de tout temps dans les Alpes'; and, from Switzerland, 'Gebirge sind Regionen, die für die dort beheimatete Bevölkerung erschwerende Lebens-

[3] Maxwell (1962*a*), 47–8, 79–80 and (1962*b*), 99–100; Holly (1962), 286–7; Darby (1962), 430–1.

[4] Pease (1913), 22; Bean (1958), 14–5; Fleming (1882), 1; Fraser (1968), pp. xvii ff.; Duxbury (1985), 227; Thirsk (1984), 10–11; Somerville (1977), 16; Dodgshon (1981), 319; Evans (1987), 414; Pilkington (1789), ii. 57; Swain (1994), 70–1; Marshall (1788), ii. 221, 245, 275 and (1794), 21; Youngson (1973), 18 and (1974), 179; Richards (1982), 48; Jewell (1994), 58, 136.

[5] Newton (1974), 7; Winchester (1987), 2; Williams (1960–3), 2; O'Dell and Walton (1962), 131; Hechter (1975), 52; Price (1969), 124, 125; Butlin (1976), 145.

bedingungen bedeuten. Dies ist allgemein bekannt.' In the north of Europe, Norway consisted to a large extent of a 'large, mountainous, inhospitable land mass', and in general, 'in the mountains, society, civilization and economy all bear the mark of backwardness and poverty'. The Serbian census of 1863 shows average lowland incomes to have been 153 dinar, foothills 98 dinar, and uplands 64 dinar per capita.[6] It is intriguing to note that those areas designated as 'less favoured' by the European Community, being engaged in mountain or hill farming or suffering 'specific handicaps' such as remoteness, insularity, or liability to flooding, correspond closely to the areas designated as 'marginal' in the past.[7]

Forests were more rarely viewed as wholly waste and inhospitable; as we shall see below, there were good reasons for this. Nevertheless, Maitland noted, in Germany, as in England, forest acres were larger than common acres, and forest rods were longer than normal ones, the implication being that it took more land to provide the same return. The County Agricultural Reports, written around 1800, also grouped 'waste, common, fen, bog, salt-marsh, moor, forest, heath or warren' as wasted lands. A map structured by counties showed the counties with the highest proportion of such 'waste' to be Northumberland, Yorkshire, Cumberland, and Westmorland in the north, and in the rest of the country Derbyshire, Bedfordshire, Rutland, Cambridge and the Isle of Ely, central Wales, and Cornwall.[8] These were almost all counties possessing either much high ground or fens and marshes.

In the late Middle Ages, as Postan put it, 'most of these lands were marginal "because they were, to use a humdrum adjective, poor", though some were poor only because the technology then available could not cope with the conditions, because of legal or administrative impediments, or because they were situated on the "geographical periphery of medieval England" '.[9] Modern writers have added some other considerations. The periphery, in their view, is

> poor because it is outlying and handicapped by greater costs of transport to the centre, by which it is forsaken. It is marginal, weak, alienated, provincial and backward. Innovations come late and investments tend to have a purely exploitative and colonial character, with no spin off effects because of lack of locational advantages other than natural resources.[10]

One wonders how much of this might also apply, *mutatis mutandis*, to earlier periods of history.

It was a small step from this position to argue that life in marginal areas also tended to affect directly the people and the societies dwelling there, from which a further step might follow, to the effect that the changed character of the marginal

[6] Nadal and Giralt (1960), 106 ff.; Lindgren (1987*a*), 7; Bruland (1989), 26; Braudel (1976), i. 30–3; Niederer (1980*a*), 75; Guichonnet (1980*d*), 194; Poitrineau (1986), 103–4; Moch (1983), 43; Weber (1976), 181; Bielmann (1972), 194–6; Bucher (1974), 92–5; Kruker (1979), 122; Zurfluh (1986), 232; Palairet (1986), 410 and (1995), map p. 81.

[7] Map in Kerr (1986), 86.

[8] Terrett (1962*a*), 275; Maitland (1960), 437; Williams (1970), 57–8.

[9] Postan (1972), 19.

[10] Quoted from Strassoldo (1980), 52; also Rauch (1988), 23; Conti (1988), 42; Keeble *et al.* (1982), 61; Lösch (1954), 205; Perrot (1983), 91; Wallerstein (1974), i. 301–2; Juillard and Nonn (1976), 18, 24–5.

population itself contributed to the marginality of their region. North-west Wales, for example, was said to have been 'marginal' in the nineteenth century not only because the land was mountainous and far from the core, but because the mountains had made for a culturally divided population. Camden thought Northumberland to be 'infinitely remote, rough and uncultured, afflicted alike by a harsh climate and by harsh and violent men'. The founder of Queen's College, Oxford, laid it down that preference should be given in it to the inhabitants of Cumberland and Westmorland, 'on account of the waste, desolate and illiterate condition' of those counties: 'isolation, a difficult physical environment, absentee landownerships and peculiar tenures combined to retard improvement in both animal husbandry and field management in Cumberland in 1700–1850', according to another judgement. A campaign in the later eighteenth century in favour of enclosing the upland pastures and commons blamed the conservatism of the Cumbrian 'Statesmen' for their misfortunes and pictured them as oppressed, hard-working, yet poverty-stricken—in contrast to the traditional favourable view of an upright, independent peasantry.[11] Cornish agriculture was similarly described in the Middle Ages as primitive, backward, and poor, and even in the eighteenth century it was said to 'present a wild and strange appearance. There are few signs of any fertility or cultivation.'[12]

In relation to Europe as a whole, there were areas of 'difficulty', defined as those unsuitable for grain growing, 'conserving old layers of culture and resisting change': they were the 'cloudy pastoral corners of Europe', which included the Basque country, the Romansh-speaking valleys of Switzerland, as well as the Celtic fringes in Brittany, Wales, western Scotland, and western Ireland. 'A pastoral economy surviving on the [French] upper slopes would be reflected in the clinging to old ways that were rapidly disintegrating below.' The Hungarian plain, in its poverty and backwardness, had also become a 'permanent frontier' and in France, 'the high parts of the Massif Central, much of the Alpine area and the Landes were . . . all areas of sparse and scattered population with relatively little activity of any kind'.[13]

In Switzerland, the accusation of laziness against the inhabitants of mountainous areas was common: the people of the canton Uri, in the heart of the Alps, were said to be as dirty and dishonest as Italians, doing only what was strictly necessary. The appearance of idleness might only have been a reflection of the seasonal character of upland stock breeding, which created long periods of underemployment, but contemporaries also commented on the neglected roads and meadows, and on the unwillingness to learn a proper trade: too many of the craftsmen were foreigners. In the uplands generally, 'as with most mountain people, all is organised for comfort',

[11] An article in the *Gentlemen's Magazine* appearing in 1766 was widely quoted in this context. Searle (thesis, 1983), 53 ff.; Hutchinson (1794), 39; Bailey and Culley (1813), 283; Jones (1980), 199; Watts (1975), 37; Jewell (1991), 22; Musgrove (1990), 2; Dilley (thesis, 1991), p. vii; Richards (1982), 126–8.

[12] Hatcher (1970), 8; Jenkin (1972), 145.

[13] Evans (1956), 220; Hollander (1960–1), 166; Weber (1976), 261; Smith (1978), 570; also Duby (1974), 29.

said one report of 1804, 'what does not have to be done is left alone'. They were 'happy with their modest income, and do not wish to exert themselves to get more, and laugh about those who do'.[14]

Almost exactly the same was said about the Scottish Highlander. James Loch, who did more than any other agent to introduce sheep into the Highlands and drive out the Highlanders, thought that 'Contented with the poorest and most simple fare and, like all mountaineers, accustomed to a roaming, unfettered life . . . they deemed no new comfort worth the possessing which was to be acquired at the price of industry'. The Highlander's poverty, according to others, was to be explained at least in part, by his 'laziness'. He does what is necessary, in the harvest and in peat cutting, but otherwise is totally idle, for which his excuses are 'dictated by nothing but what must be considered constitutive sloth'. According to James Ray in 1747, they 'have been reckoned an indolent people; although . . . it may appear that they are ingenious and industrious'. In the eighteenth century 'Lowland Scots traditionally regarded their Highland countrymen as members of a different and inferior race, violent, treacherous, poverty-stricken and backward. They called them savages or aborigines.' In the century following they were still regarded as 'feckless, guilty of overbreeding', 'notoriously indolent', characterized by 'sluggishness and ignorance' in need of being 'civilized'. Galloway people also were said to be 'very lazy and mismanaged the land . . . [their] shiftlessness in workaday life, indifference to comfort and neatness, might well go, as it did in the Highlands, with a martial spirit, a readiness for adventure, all the more so because in the conditions of the Scottish countryside labour was likely to be so unrewarding'.[15] Much the same has been said about other similar regions:

> The mountain dweller is apt to be the laughing stock of the superior inhabitants of the towns and plains. He is suspected, feared and mocked . . . [In the Ardèohe] the lowland peasant had nothing but sarcasm for the rude fellow from the highlands, and marriages between their families were rare.[16]

More generally,

> Mountain regions discourage the budding genius because they are areas of isolation, confinement, remote from the great currents of men and ideas that move along the river valleys. They are regions of much labour and little leisure, of poverty today and anxiety for the morrow, of toil-cramped hands and toil-dulled brains. In the fertile alluvial plains are wealth, leisure, contact with many minds, large urban centres where commodities and ideas are exchanged.
>
> The important characteristic of plains is their power to facilitate every phase of historical movement; that of mountains is their power to retard, arrest and deflect it.[17]

[14] Bielmann (1972), 14; Bircher (1938), 11, 127, 159, 164.

[15] Colley (1984), 15; Prebble (1963), 64; Tough (1928), 14; Nutley (1980), 112; Dubuis (1986), 5; Russell (1967), 169; Kiernan (1988), 75; Ray quoted in Womack (1989), 21; Devine (1988), 127–30, 138; Williamson (1996), 60–1.

[16] Braudel (1976), i. 46; for a similar Swiss view, see Bergier (1980), 247 and for France, Rosenberg (1988), 1.

[17] Semple (1911), 20, 521; Hufton (1983), 308.

The records of the French army showed much under-nourishment among the men from the Massif Central, the Alps, the Pyrenees, and Dauphiné.

The inhabitants of the fens were held in similarly low esteem. 'Fen-men were depicted impressionistically as a race apart, fiercely independent, ague-ridden, web-footed, who lived precariously on birds and fish.' Camden, reflecting the prejudices of his age, thought them to be 'a kind of people according to the nature of the place where they dwell, rude, uncivil and envious of all others'. W. Dugdale added in 1662 that they were a 'rude, and almost barbarous, sort of lazy and beggarly people', and Celia Fiennes, in 1695, thought them to be 'a slothful people'. They were 'a population sub-human in its lawlessness, poverty and squalor'. But at the same time it was also said that the Fenland was a country 'overflowing with food, and as a consequence the people degenerated into a thriftless race, whose only strong passion was a love of freedom'. But this in no way endeared them to Macaulay, who thought them 'half-savage'. The similar amphibious life of the Dutch was believed by some to have been responsible for their 'coolness of blood [which] bred phlegm and sluggishness'; their 'celebrated addiction to alcohol [was] needed to kindle the passions of love and war'. Others maintained that 'the scourge of the country was the humidity of its atmosphere, resulting in continuous mists . . . Saumaise and Descartes both complained that the softness of the air was prejudicial to intellectual activity.'[18]

It is interesting to note that while some critics despised mountain dwellers and the inhabitants of the fens because of their overwork, others held them in low esteem because of their idleness. Forests, as we noted above, were less harshly judged, and there was, in general, less prejudice against those dwelling in them. But even they were often thought of as isolated, backward, and ignorant.[19] Miners living in remote mountainous districts aroused what was perhaps the most devastating prejudice of all. 'The common people here', a traveller reported from Cornwall as late as 1776, 'are a very strange kind of beings, half savages at the best. Many thousands of them live entirely underground, where they burrow and breed like rabbits. They are rough as Bears, selfish as Swine, obstinate as Mules and hard as the Native iron.'[20]

Even such extreme examples of ill-informed and prejudiced reporting, however, seem nevertheless to rest on the unspoken assumption that it was their environment which made people what they were. The inhabitants of the Cornish uplands, we are subtly led to believe, act as they do because they were born into and reared by their particular society. Had they been born in London, they would have behaved like Londoners, and vice versa, and part of the attraction of travellers' (tall) tales lay precisely in the thrill of putting oneself in the position of the savages, or half-savages, out of the smugness of one's own civilized superiority.

Yet there existed an even more extreme and hostile critique to the effect that it was less the environment than the character of the people themselves which had made them marginal, backward, and poor. The Scottish Highlander, for example,

[18] Rackham (1990), 374; Tawney, Introd. to Thirsk (1953), 4; Darby (1968), 23, 112 and (1940), 119; Schama (1988), 265; Zumthor (1994), 26.

[19] Zon (1920), 148.

[20] Quoted in Jenkin (1972), 146.

may have found himself in an unfavourable environment, but he was also the victim of his own 'native indolence, low animal spirits, backward-sloping supply curve of labour and . . . peasant psyche'. Moreover, while the inhabitant of the mainland is 'barbarous for the most part yet mixed with some sort of civility, the other that dwelleth in the Isles . . . are bitterly barbarous', according to King James VI and I. The view was expressed most crudely by John Pinkerton in 1790. The Highlanders, he held, were savages and will 'infallibly remain so till the race be lost by mixture'.

It has similarly been held that wherever two ethnic groups meet on the lower boundaries of mountain slopes, in the piedmonts which often divide populations racially as well as geographically, 'superior peoples from the lowlands are found expanding at the cost of retarded mountain folk'.[21] More generally, some believe, national characteristics are important: 'timidity and daring, discretion or rashness, a liking for tradition or for innovation, a conservative or a flexible mind, thorough or superficial training, stability or frivolity.' The shape of the economy is important too. August Lösch, the well-known pioneer of the economics of location and author of those lines, went on to say: 'The Swabian economy cannot be entirely grasped without an understanding of Swabian philosophy which has probably formulated [its] national character in a most apt way.'[22]

The marginality of a region, in the negative sense, may thus be derived not only from its natural location and resources, but also from the way these have influenced their populations, and even, in the extreme view, from the culture and the historical experience of the societies living in them.

Such extreme views are rare, to be sure. Even the more prejudiced contemporaries, who professed to see the causes of the weaknesses of marginal societies in the inborn moral or intellectual failings of their populations, yet generally provide unspoken hints (evidenced clearly in some of the statements cited here) that these failings themselves were, in the long run and possibly over generations, derived from their adverse environment. There was, however, also the more rational view: the inferiority of the inhabitants of marginal areas was explained, not so much by the inferiority of the men born there, but by the fact that, as was said about the 'debatable lands' along the Scottish border, they became the 'sink and receptacle of proscribed wretches'[23]—about which more below.

Barring these exceptional cases, most observers thought the environment was to blame. The examples given here of adverse judgements on marginal areas contain a number of hints as to what was thought to have caused their poverty and backwardness. We must now proceed to examine these more closely.

Traditionally, the 'natural' inferiority which would make an area marginal has been found to be its infertility and lack of natural resources on the one hand, and its

21 Richards (1988), 195; Semple (1911), 524; Fiennes (1988), 168; Youngson (1973), 192 and (1974), 142, 153; Smout (1969), 104; Handley (1953), 94; Pilkington quoted in Womack (1989), 21.

22 Lösch (1954), 193, 194, 196. The meaning is clear despite the awful translation.

23 Graham (1911), 36.

remote location on the other. These were the two qualities which Ricardo, for example, thought relevant for his theory of rent and they are still echoed today: the 'peripheral or marginal status [of an area] can be defined in terms of physical distance or environmental quality'.[24] Although, as we have seen, both depend to some extent on the social framework, including the distribution of settlements in the rest of the country and the available technology, especially in the fields of agriculture and transport, yet they form a good starting-point as major causes of marginality, particularly in ages before the Industrial Revolution and the extended power of man to change his environment.

In Europe north of the Alps, most ascriptions of natural infertility relate to mountainous districts. It is the uplands which failed to yield returns to effort, comparable with the bulk of a society's territory, in part because of their poor or thin soil, and in part also because the ground was too steep. As for the soil, on English northern hills the tops carried heather and furze at best, or were covered by peat bogs. In Switzerland today it is calculated that while in the valley bottoms 75 per cent of the soil is cultivable and on the lower hills somewhat under 40 per cent, on higher hills this drops to 15 per cent and in the mountain zone to 4 per cent. On the High Alps grazing peters out into sheer rocks. The steepness prevented ploughing and, on higher Alpine grounds, it limited grazing to sheep and goats. Wheeled transport was impossible.[25]

Added to this was the harsh climate, and especially the severe winters. Thus in the Urseren valley, with villages at 1,400–1,500 m. above sea-level, there were only 153 growing days in the year, six months being winter. Spring in Entlebuch, at 520–860 m. up, started 4–6 weeks later than in the nearby Lucerne valley; and in Wallis, it needed two summers for the corn to ripen. In many areas avalanches threatened, and these and similar problems have remained to the present day. Beyond a certain height, snow would lie permanently on the ground.[26] Mountains, therefore, were marginal because not merely one but in fact a number of adverse factors came together to make them less fertile, and therefore less attractive to settlers, and less productive of comfort and riches, than most of the land on the plains.

There were, however, important differences between different mountainous areas in the way in which soil, configuration, and location affected settlement and its marginality, without negating the general rule that the higher up, the colder.[27] One such concerned the latitude north of the Equator; the farther south, the higher up could settlement proceed, other things being equal. Whereas at latitude 64° N settlement based on agriculture ceased at 300 m. above sea-level, it reached 1,000 m. at 54° N, and 2,000 m. and over at latitude 40° N, which covered the southern tip of

[24] Dodgshon (1987), 274.

[25] Hodgson (1827–58), Part III, ii. 113; Ramm *et al.* (1970), 2; Elliott (1959), 89–90; Kiefner (1983), 18; Pfister (1986), 365; Mathieu (1992), 133, 143.

[26] Zurfluh (1982), 294; Bucher (1974), 3; Mathieu (1992); Bielmann (1972); Veyret (1978), 76–7; Arnold (thesis, 1989), 12; Siebter Bericht (1992).

[27] The experience on the northern slopes of the Alps being that the temperature fell by 2 °C for every 400 m. of height, Cépède and Abensour (1961), 26.

Italy and bisected Anatolia. In the Alps, the average temperature dropped by 1 °C for every 150 km. move northward. The south and west permitted growth to greater heights than the north and east in the Alpine lands. There were significant differences also between southern slopes in comparison with slopes facing north and rarely touched by direct sunlight.[28]

In the Engadine, protected by high mountains, forests reach up to 2,200 m. above sea-level, and orchards and corn fields up to 1,760 m.; in Wallis there were forests up to 2,250 m. In the Swiss Jura beeches were said to have grown up to a height of 800 m. above sea-level, above which there were conifers. At about 1,300 m. those gave out too, though it was not clear how far this was a natural dividing-line, and how far caused by the human and animal action of encroaching on the forest from above, for above it were the summer grazings. Below the trees were the permanent pastures for the mountain villagers. In the Swiss Alps there were similar bands of trees, those of the beeches being about 300–500 m. wide, and those of the conifers above them, about 700 m. There was a mixed band of conifers and pasturage above it, of a width of perhaps 150–200 m., before the upper, summer pasture land began. This would start at a height of around 2,000–2,200 m. above sea-level, to be followed by true 'Alpine' land of brush, moorland, and rough grazing at 2,500–3,000 m. In the eastern Alps the upper forest line was to be found at 1,700–2,300 m., and somewhat higher in inner, drier areas. Again, there was 'Alpine' vegetation above it. In all cases, some grazing would also be found in clearings in the forests and pasture land would make up between one-fifth and two-fifths of Alpine territory.[29]

Settlement thinned out with ascending height, but there might be great differences of the actual population density at any given absolute height, depending on the lie of the land, on local fertility, and other factors. Thus it was found in the early years of this century that at a height of 400–500 m. above sea-level, the density of population was 39 persons per square kilometre in the Flysh zone of the Alps, 120 in the Grauwacken zone, 50 in the Hacker Mühlviertel, and 118 at Tangl in Carinthia. At 800–1,000 m. there was no one in the first-named, 10 in the Grauwacken, 31 in the Mühlviertel, and 32 in Tangl. In Tangl, there was an average of 20 to the square kilometre even at 1,100–1,200 m. This is well above the top of Snowdon (1,085 m.). In the German Tyrol in 1910, 50 per cent of the population lived at 700 m. or below, 23 per cent at 700–1,000 m., 16 per cent at 1,000–1,300 m., and 11 per cent above 1,300 m. In the canton Uri in 1799, while 59 per cent of the population lived at 400–800 m., 20 per cent lived above the 1,200 m. line. It should be noted, however, that the climatic changes of the last millennium made substantial differences to the levels to which cultivation could proceed.[30] On the Alps, for example, there is evidence of much higher levels of arable fields in the late Middle Ages than today.

[28] Schwarz (1959), 3–4; Bätzing (1991), 20; Bowes (1990), 4; Schwarzenbach (1931), 335; Weiss (1941), 53; Niederer (1993), 159; Cépède and Abensour (1961), 7; Bielmann (1972), 69; Leibundgut (1986), 15.

[29] Frödin (1940), 81 ff., 198–209, 221 ff., 281. Also Blache (1933), 43; Kuhn (1957), 260; Morsel (1972), 558 ff.

[30] Günther (1930), 172; Stolz (1955), 205; Ulmer (1935), 65; Zurfluh (1986), 243; Barber (1974), 86; Parry (1978), 65 ff.

The mountainous regions of Britain differed in two major respects from the Alpine lands. One was the lower heights at which all vegetation ceased; the other was the prevalence of moors and heather, coupled with the inability to carry any other vegetation, on high plateau or flat-topped mountains. Only in Scandinavia were mountain conditions similar to Britain's. Upland marginality had therefore frequently a different connotation in Britain and on the Continent outside Scandinavia.

British uplands, including those of Devon and Cornwall, Wales, the Pennines, the Border country, and the Scottish Highlands and Islands, were universally considered to be infertile 'wastes', covered as they were with moss, heather, furze, or very poor grass. The latter would allow some grazing of animals, at least in the summer, and in some other areas furze, and peat where it existed, might be used as fuel. But otherwise these were thought of as inhospitable, their bleakness made worse by severe weather conditions, including heavy rains, flooding, and snow. The lands bordering on these upper slopes were, in turn, truly marginal lands in the context of British history.[31]

'The greater part of the country', it was reported in a review of the estate of the Earl of Northumberland in 1570, 'consists of waste and mountains . . . the country consists most in waste ground and is very cold, hard and barren in the winter'. It was, according to another view, a 'remote, mountainous and infertile region'. On the other side of the border, in the eighteenth century, the Lammermuir hills were said to be all moor and mosses, which it would not pay to cultivate. Other Scots border uplands had 'thin, dry, heathy and poor' soil. On the north Yorkshire moors with their 'extremely bleak' climate it was necessary to cut the crops before they were ripe, or run the risk of seeing them covered with snow. In the Lake District, the sheep picked 'their meagre tufts of grass under the sheltered side of craggs [*sic*] and stones, earn[ing], like their owners, a hard subsistence', while the late ripening crops were 'often a prey to autumnal rain'. According to Aikin, the north Staffordshire 'moorlands is a region which is generally high, sterile, and open'. The eastern 'horn' of Cheshire ran up to the 'wild country bordering on Yorkshire and the Peak of Derbyshire', the Peak consisting of 'bleak, barren heights'.[32]

Again, the upland soil of Cornwall was said to be capable of sustaining only heath, furze, and poor grasses. In Wales the useful land in the valleys was found to be severely limited: the uplands could be used for grazing, at best. In the 'bleak moorlands' of Montgomeryshire, 'this forlorn part of creation', 'much of the land [was] marginal'. It was 'poor quality land, which it was uneconomic to improve'. Breconshire and Radnorshire, 'including some of the wildest and grimmest uplands in Mid-Wales', were tough on 'those who were forced to win a thin living from [the] steep slopes and barren, windswept heights'.[33]

[31] Eyre (1954), 27, 126; Dilley (1967), 126–7.

[32] Winchester (1987), 81, 1 also 3; Low (1819), 2, 150; Sinclair (1979), 1, 17; Marshall (1788), ii. 275; Tuke (1800), 4; Gilpin (1792), i. 173, 206; Farey (1811–17), i. 96; Virtue (1976), 25; Aikin (1795), 66, 98, 450; Dilley (1991), 9, 14, 92, 337.

[33] Williams (1964), 2; Rowe (1953), 210; Hatcher (1970), 9; Darby and Terrett (1954), 52, 119, 154, 172; Jones (1960); Tough (1928), 25; Hey (1972), 16; Parry (1978), 122; Bailey and Culley (1813), 202; Jenkins (1990), 82; Powell (1967–8*a*), 67, 72: Sylvester (1969), 411, 501; Carr (1992), 46.

Yet the Border country and the Derbyshire Peak District seldom rise above 2,000 ft. (700 m.), the Staffordshire Pennines over 1,500 ft. (500 m.), and Cornwall and mid-Wales rarely reach even such heights. Above the tree line of 1,000–1,500 ft. (300–500 m.), according to Fox, there were only peat, grass and sedge, and heath in drier areas: 'Man cannot support himself on such peaty soils'.[34]

In the Highlands and Islands of Scotland 'where nature has been so niggardly [that] man has a constant struggle . . . to garner a subsistence', only a population of low density could survive, while cattle were small and stunted because of the shortage of fodder. By the seventeenth and eighteenth centuries, they could not feed their population. Much land was so steep and stony that ploughs could not be used and spade cultivation was the only way of tilling it. Even in Argyllshire there was twelve times as much acreage of heath, hill, and pasture than there was arable. Woodlands also 'tend to have survived on soils that were of little use for anything else, on areas of poor soil according to medieval or earlier ideas of land capability'.[35]

The Massif Central accorded more with British and Scandinavian rather than Alpine conditions. The upland, much of which had 100 days or more of frost per year, consisted mostly of rough grazing. Robert Louis Stevenson was struck by its similarity to Scotland. The road from Cheylard to Luc, he reported, went through 'one of the most beggarly countries in the world. It was like the worst of the Scottish Highlands, only worse; cold, naked, and ignoble.' Some of the Pyrenean uplands, too, had a severe climate, either too much rain or a drought, and a 'fragile' economy.[36]

With all the differences, however, a similar general pattern emerges for the whole of Europe. The population prefers the lower-lying valleys, and thins out on the higher slopes because of poor soil, poor climatic conditions, and the steepness of the land. Heavy crops are limited to the lower reaches: the upper slopes and plateaux beyond the possibility of cultivation are used for grazing, the highest areas being limited to summer grazing only: the higher the pasture, the thinner the grass.[37] It is the inferior 'fertility' of the land, in its wider sense, which explains the marginal existence of the upland dwellers, according to this view.

Turning from Ricardo's 'natural fertility' to remoteness, the second criterion of his definition of undesirability, more or less the same areas will be found to have the same stigma of being handicapped and marginalized. Moreover, while we can distinguish three forms of 'remoteness'—namely distance, poor quality of transport and communications linkage with the outside world, and poor communications within the area[38]—the marginal areas will once again seem to be defective in all three.

34 Fox (1932), 45.

35 Tough (1928), 45; Shaw (1980), 108–9, 129; O'Dell and Walton (1962), 130, 143; Barrow (1973), 366; Rackham (1980), 33; Dodgshon (1981), 294, 299 and (1993); Handley (1953), 91; Grant (1930), 526; Smith (1798), 3; Youngson (1973), 15 and (1974), 100–2, 184–5; Devine (1988), 14.

36 Fel (1962), 31, 45, 70–2; Stevenson (1911), 179; Rosset (1984), 138, 141–2.

37 Wessely (1853), i. 397–8; also Pounds (1973), 383; Grainger (1908), 126; Caputa (1984), 153. For the Carpathians, see Podraza (1986), 285.

38 Barrow (1969), 25.

Any map of the means of transport, whether by road, by water, or by rail, and of any period since the Middle Ages, will show the areas here considered marginal to be poorly provided for compared with the rest of the country.[39] Some areas, such as the western shore of the Scottish Highlands, or the Atlantic coastline of Norway, were practically inaccessible from the landward side before modern roads and railways were built, and could be reached only from the sea, difficult though that might itself be. The abbot of Holme Cultram, owning lands all over northern Cumberland, depended on food supplied by sea from Ireland, since regional roads were too rough for transport. Inhabitants of Furness and the Border counties were declared to be too far from London to attend the courts, or to send soldiers to the royal army.[40] In consequence, most of the mountain areas and forests here termed marginal appeared 'remote' or 'inaccessible' to outsiders. This was also true of marshy areas. 'In English history, much of the significance of the marsh, like that of the mountain, lay in its inaccessible character.' Similarly, 'geography, in the seventeenth century, had isolated the Netherlands from the rest of Europe. On one side was the sea, on the other sandy moors and marshland; the country seemed to be surrounded by deserts.' In eastern Europe 'the enormous marsh of the River Pripet in Western Russia was an obstacle to the economic and political exploitation of the no-man's-land between Poland and Russia'.[41]

From the economic point of view, what mattered above all were the outward transport facilities of an area's potential export goods, though the facilities for imports were also of significance. From most mountain areas the export of bulky agricultural products was normally unthinkable; at best, products in concentrated form, such as butter or cheese, could be sent down to market. Even the transport of products of high value, such as textiles woven on the Pennines, or the minerals found in the mountains surrounding Bohemia in their golden age of the early modern period, proved exceedingly difficult and costly. The transport of lead from Caldstanes (Nidderdale) to Boroughbridge, a distance of some 20 leagues (probably around 20 miles) took 24 days by ox-wagon drawn by 10 oxen in 1365. Camden reported that the exploitation of the mineral riches of 'Richmondshire' was held back 'perhaps because of the difficulty of carriage', while in the borderlands of Scotland as late as the 1790s it could be stated that 'the principal obstacle to improvement is distance from fuel, manure and markets'. The uplands of southern Poland, rich in timber, were virtually cut off from their markets by distance: timber, altogether, could bear only short distance transport by land before it became prohibitive in cost; from the Alps timber could often be transported downhill more easily in the snow of the winter months. It need hardly be stressed that minerals from the Ural mountains had a particularly high level of transport costs to bear, using river

[39] e.g. O'Dell and Walton (1962), 129, 206; Unwin (1990), 145.

[40] O'Dell and Walton (1962), 241–2; Bryden and Scott (1990), 90; Grainger (1908), 120–1; Farrer (1911), 208; Hinds (1896–1922), iv/2, 137.

[41] Darby (1940), 142; Zumthor (1994), 24; Hay (1966), 14; also Higham (1986), 317; Postan (1972), 22; Turnock (1982), 8; Barrow (1969), 25; Kreiner (1919), 113; Slawinger (1966), 228; Marshall (1958), 82.

transport in spring, when the water level was high, or sledge transport in winter.[42] Animals, easiest to transport because they could move themselves, and frequently the product for which mountains, fens, and marshes enjoyed comparative cost advantages, were among the main exports of marginal areas.[43]

In many respects, inward traffic faced even greater difficulties in the mountains than the export of local products because it meant dragging the load uphill. Cornwall, for example, without coal of its own, was gravely handicapped by the costs of transporting it there. In France it can be shown that even in the nineteenth century, prices in the uplands—including the Massif Central, the Alps, and the Pyrenees—were consistently higher than in the lowlands. Even the successful central European mining districts in the Erzgebirge, in Slovakia and elsewhere had problems getting their food and other supplies sent in. In the Alps, imports were moved in winter, when snow made transport easier.[44]

Nor were internal communications much better in many of these marginal lands. In the Scottish Highlands, roads were so bad that there was no wheeled traffic until well into the eighteenth century. The same applied to upland Cornwall, to the Massif Central of France, to upland Switzerland, and to the Pyrenees. According to Adolphe Blanqui in 1851, 'in the high Alps and parts of Var and Isère, a simple wheelbarrow would be as extraordinary a sight as a locomotive'. Loads were carried on the uplands of the Lozère and in the Pyrenees on the backs of people or mules until late into the nineteenth century. In parts of the Alps, the whole of the harvest and the manure for fields and vineyards had to be carried in baskets on peasants' heads. Even in the twentieth century, many loads were still carried on the backs of men, or pulled on sledges: at Visperterminen the wheel was allegedly unknown as late as 1901. The Lake District lacked roads and even navigable rivers, and communications were equally primitive in upland Wales until the late eighteenth century.[45]

One almost universal impression gained from the numerous descriptions of what we have called marginal areas is their self-sufficiency and their independence even from the next valley or glen. Arthur Young found that in the Yorkshire uplands even in the late eighteenth century cash was very little used, as there was so little commercial intercourse, and in some Alpine valleys a kind of autarky persisted well into the twentieth century. The French mountain areas kept their population isolated 'far from the mainstream of men, their products and their ideas'. In 1846 the population of the French Alps was reported to be 'further from the French influence

42 Wyrobisz (1978), 72; Radkau (1983); Braun (1960), 57; Raistrick and Jennings (1965), 27; Probszt (1966), 253–6; Yatsunsky (1974), 83–8; Camden (1974), 758; Douglas (1798), 337.

43 Jones (1971), 385–9; O'Dell and Walton (1962), 112.

44 Jenkin (1972), 71–2; Price (1983), 53; Zytkowicz (1983), 269 ff.; Wessely (1853), i. 441.

45 Shaw (1980), 110; O'Dell and Walton (1962), 99, 124–6; Watts (1975), 37–8; Weber (1976), 9, 200–1, also 42–2; Bouch and Jones (1961), 117; John (1950), 20; Pettit (1968), 5; Hallas (1990), 214; Rowe (1953), 229, 233; Netting (1981), 11–12; Gravier (1964), 290; Moch (1983), 50, 52; Derruau-Boniol and Fel (1970), 21; Marshall (1794), 15; Dilley (1991), 135; Jeffrey (1857–64), iv. 249; Goodman (thesis, 1978), 1; Hopkinson (thesis, 1958), 19; Bouch (1948), 353; Kiefner (1983), 18; Pfister (1986), 365; Mathieu (1992), 133, 143.

than those of the Marquis Islands'. It does not surprise, therefore, that there were few markets, and even fewer market towns in those areas. Celia Fiennes made the heartfelt comment about a place near Windermere: 'they are 8 miles from a market town and their miles are tedious to go both for illness of way and length of miles.'[46] Goethe's reaction to Schiller's praise of Swiss freedom is worth recording: 'Free, those poor devils on their crags and cliffs? Yes, they freed themselves from a tyrant . . . but . . . up in the mountains, where they . . . affect to speak of freedom, but are trapped like marmots by six months of snow.'[47]

The inaccessibility of markets affected adversely the incentive to increase output or improve productivity. It was the peasants and farmers near the urban markets who led in improvements in agrarian technology, in northern Italy, in the Netherlands, in Germany as in the present-day United States and elsewhere.[48] Those far from potential purchasers had less cause to follow suit, and, indeed, numerous examples may be found of backward agrarian technology and an unwillingness to adopt innovation in marginal areas—though in others the periodic threat of over-population and famine might have been thought to have provided incentive enough. The quality of the wool from sheep reared in Cornwall, the Scottish Highlands, and the Lake District, for example, was known to be much inferior to that of more central areas even in the boom years of the sixteenth century, and the yield ratios for grain cultivation were also much lower in the northern uplands. New crops were eyed with suspicion in the more remote corners: there was much resistance in the Scottish Islands to the introduction of wheat, and prejudice in the Highlands to the introduction of the potato. When harvesting grain, the practice of pulling up the whole plant, rather than cutting it with a sickle, then separating the grains by burning off the husks and the straw, meant that the infield would lack the stubble, and thus the manure of the animals grazing on it, and the farm would be short of straw. Even in the early eighteenth century the Highlander scorned green vegetables: 'you might as well ask for bananas as a cabbage, a leek or an onion'.[49]

It is precisely the distance from the market which features very largely also in present-day discussions about the economic disadvantages of marginal or peripheral areas. The periphery, it has been held, 'is poor because it is outlying and handicapped by greater costs of transport to the centre' and greater cost of access to services, in part because of the longer distances, but in part also because it had failed

[46] Braudel (1976), i. 33; Frödin (1940), 267; Weber (1976), 96; O'Dell and Walton (1962), 90, 102; Sandgruber (1989), 88–9; Heaton (1965), 401; Cole and Wolf (1974), 87, 120; Williams (1980), 21; Donkin (1973), 122–4; Campbell (1990), 83; Smailes (1960), 269; Poitrineau (1986), 103; Fiennes (1988), 168; Marshall (1794), 35.

[47] Quoted by Barber (1974), 9–10.

[48] Slicher van Bath (1963), 14–5; Hausmann (1975), 14; Chisholm (1979); Russell (1967), 183; Smith (1978), 548–50; Ziekursch (1978), 42 ff.; Jones (1975), 333; Nicholls (1961); von Thünen (1966), esp. pp. 8, xxix.

[49] Salaman (1987), 348, also 357–8; Bouch and Jones (1961), 27; Shaw (1980), 94–5; Rowe (1953), 222; Appleby (1978), 65; Hallam (1988*e*), 497; Smailes (1960), 298; Lund (1974), 8; Prebble (1963), 29; Dodgshon (1981), 306; Richards (1982), 48–9, 84–5; Naujoks (1982), 170; Bergier (1980), 247; Niederer (1980*a*), 6.

in the past to get adequate means of transport built to connect it to the rest of the world. It is isolated from other peripheral areas, with which it can communicate only via the centre, and it lacks the 'agglomeration economies' from which firms in central locations benefit. The cost of distance, it has been said, is hostility to innovation.[50]

Thus the poverty and backwardness of marginal areas may be explained, to a considerable extent, by physical, or non-social factors. But there are also man-made, or historical causes which can be held responsible for the alleged disadvantages of existence on the margins. These fall logically into several groups. Some are the consequences of having to deal with the natural disadvantages of the region. Some are said to arise out of the way in which existence in marginal lands affected the character of individuals and of society. A few even appear as random weaknesses, unconnected with the marginality of the region as such. In the literature, these are often confused, and they are not altogether easy to keep apart.

One group of explanations starts with the assumption that knowledge and science, as well as art and even religion, have their origins, and are located, near the centre of societies from which marginal regions are by definition cut off. Thus in the Middle Ages, it has been observed, much of what there was in the field of culture was to be found in the towns. It was in the towns where churches and monastic houses, especially of Dominicans and Franciscans, were said to have been built—though many monasteries, as we shall see, were also to be found on marginal land. It was the urban centres which held the hospitals, the schools, the academies and universities, the booksellers and writers, the knowledge of what passed for science and of the world outside the immediate region. The towns also had the clocks, the information on technical innovation, the festivals and the works of art. To have its share of culture and civilization, a region had to have towns—yet towns of any size were not to be found in marginal areas in the thirteenth and fourteenth centuries, in mountains or in the midst of forests, or in the 'areas of limited urbanisation on the European periphery', such as Scandinavia, Poland, Russia, Ireland, and Scotland. The whole of the Alpine territory outside the French Alps had no towns of any size until very much later, and there were only two universities there in the past, Grenoble and Innsbruck, the former of which was soon moved to the more congenial location of Valence.[51]

The churches were built in the towns as well as in villages in the flatlands: hilly regions were usually allocated to parishes of the plains, and were given chapels and part-time clergy at most. In consequence, the provision of schooling was also poor even after the Reformation: in the Scottish Highlands and Islands, where every parish nominally had to provide a school, it was the poverty of the district which prevented the practical execution of this rule. Matters were not helped by the fact

[50] Strassoldo (1980), 52; Nutley (1980); Wellhofer (1989), 343; Keeble (1976), 54 ff.; Collins (1978), 82; Messerli and Brugger (1984*b*), 610; Virtue (1976), 46; Mitchell (1968), 41–3; Merlin (1971), 126 ff.

[51] Hohenberg and Lees (1985), 53, also 38–40; de Vries (1983), 156; Guichonnet (1980*e*), 250; Bergier (1980), 214, 245–6.

that the richer parents sent their children out of the countryside into the towns where there was schooling, thus reducing whatever incentive there might have been to make the effort locally. Nor were matters helped by the clash between the Gaelic of the vernacular and the English (let alone the Latin) used in the main centres of learning. The language of the Celtic fringe was, in any case, deemed inferior and not worthy of preservation, as were the languages of other fringes, such as the Basque country, Brittany, Slovakia, and Macedonia, but even the English spoken in marginal areas, such as the upland northern England where some remote dales preserved elements of a Celtic language, was considered to be incomprehensible and provincial, and its speakers suffered from their 'cultural remoteness' from the centre of things.[52]

The relatively poorer provision of schooling in the marginal areas has remained largely unchanged through the centuries. Thus in the sixteenth century the illiteracy in Languedoc was much higher than that of north-eastern France and a similar difference still existed in 1830–3 between the French north-east on the one hand, and such areas as Brittany and the Massif Central, the latter with its 'non-literate, intensely Catholic-culture', on the other.[53] Macaulay's claim that 'within the memory of some whom this generation has seen' there lived, around the sources of the Tyne, 'a race scarcely less savage than the Indians of California' may be largely the result of prejudice, evident in other comments about the north of the country, but clearly reflected some kind of reality.[54]

As the cultural needs of marginal lands, like so many of their other needs, were neglected by those in power at the centre,[55] these lands were necessarily left in a position of inferiority. 'Location on a frontier involves remoteness from the centre of national, cultural and political activities; these reach their greatest intensity in the core of the nation.' The Paris salon awards of 1896, it has been alleged, showed a 'lack of artistic instinct' in the highlands of Savoy, the Alps, the east Pyrenees, the Auvergne plateau, and the 'barren peninsula of Brittany', while talent flourished in the river valleys. 'French men of letters, by the distribution of their birthplaces, are essentially products of alluvial valleys and plains, rarely of upland and mountains.' In England, also, the frontier regions were considered to be 'unremarkable for intellectual excellence or any inclination to abstract thought.' 'The mountain dweller is essentially conservative. There is little in his environment to stimulate him to change, and little reaches him from the outside world.' Wordsworth, surveying the Coniston area, spoke of 'a constitutional indisposition towards novel enterprise—a common failure among people who live in solitude'. At the same time, those who were more sympathetic to societies living on the margins in general and in the mountains in particular, recognized that, being close to the

[52] Winchester (1987), 2, 23; Shaw (1980), 139, 144–6; Watts (1975), 86; Tough (1928), 32; Jewell (1991), 21; Mercer (1991), 131; Hechter (1975), 63 ff.; Bouch and Jones (1961), 22; Lucas (*c.*1880), 11, 35–40; Jewell (1994), 175; and p. 76 below.

[53] Ladurie (1977), 234, 342; Viazzo (1989), 138; Moch (1983), 60.

[54] Macaulay (1913), 276.

[55] Musgrove (1990), 10–11; Devèze (1961), ii. 222–3; Hilton (1980), 58.

subsistence level, they would have been unwise to risk untried innovations, and often unable to bear their costs.[56]

So much for culture in general. In the matter of the more limited field of the source of entrepreneurial initiative and innovation, marginal areas were also considered to be lacking and inferior. Even in the past, it was the cities, and not the countryside, which were said to have aided innovation, including those which were to benefit agriculture: 'remoteness is partly a question of distance from centres where new ideas and impulses are generated'.[57] Thus Cumbria did not adopt the agricultural improvements of the seventeenth century until the eighteenth, and the inner Swiss cantons failed to change to a specialist market economy in the fifteenth and sixteenth centuries, when the more accessible valleys did so. Both areas were said to need pressure from the lowlands to make any changes. There is similar evidence from other regions, such as the Upper Palatinate, the Pyrenean valleys, and the Balkan mountains.[58] Men of the French Massif Central, who lacked neither intelligence, nor tenacity, nor ingeniousness, yet chose traditional, 'atavistic' jobs; the mountain regions of Catalonia were said to have been dominated by a 'backward-looking populism'; and the Alps have even been described as 'ethnological museums, keeping primitive tools and methods long after they had been discarded elsewhere'.[59] Goethe, when shown the first steam engine in Tarnowitz, marvelled that this should happen 'fern von gebildeten Menschen, am Ende des Reiches'. Another visitor remarked in the following year that the 'iron trade had brought civilization [*Kultur*] to Upper Silesia, hitherto an area of ill repute'.[60]

Modern economic literature is inclined to conflate the effects of distance from the centre, location near frontiers, political dependence, and the kind of marginal location traced in these pages in a single concept of 'periphery'. As the 'periphery' is contrasted with the core, it is the core where entrepreneurial and other initiatives are said to have their origin, sending their impulses outward, so that they reach the marginal areas late, in a weakened form or not at all: 'Major centres of innovative change', according to one definition, 'will be called "core regions"; all others within a given spacial system will be defined as *peripheral*... peripheral regions can be identified by their relations of dependency to the core area.' 'Development will tend to have its origins in a relatively small number of *centres of change* located at the points of highest potential interaction . . . Innovation will tend to spread downward and outward from these centres . . . Peripheral regions . . . [are] territorially organized sub-systems of society whose development path is determined chiefly by core

[56] Semple (1911), 19, 230, 600; Musgrove (1990), 15; Wordsworth (1974), 311; Viazzo (1989), 12; Bergier (1988), 30; Fox (1932), 31; Smith (1978), 50; Poitrineau (1986), 105; Kruker (1979), 119–20; McNeill (1992), 5–6.

[57] Barrow (1969), 25; Bairoch (1981), 68–9.

[58] Mathieu (1992), 113; Hogg (1972), 2; Arnold (thesis, 1989), 144–9; Veyret (1978), 59; Bainbridge (1947), 56; Götschmann (1985), 225; Hughes (1965), 12–15; Palairet (1986), 392; Young (1770), iii. 114, 169; Marshall (1794), 38, 42; Sahlins (1989), 134.

[59] Gravier (1964), 291; Vilar (1988), 332; Niederer (1993), 149 and (1979), 235.

[60] Pierenkemper (1992*b*), 77; Plaum and Witthöft (1993), 358; Fuchs (1992), 145–6; p. 201 below.

region institutions with respect to which they stand in a relation of substantial dependency.'[61]

The logic behind this notion of a kind of a dual economy is not only that it is in the core that entrepreneurial and technical talent—as well as capital—are to be found; there will also be found the larger and more sophisticated markets, the shorter distances and lower transport costs, and the marketing information. Moreover, successful entrepreneurs need a favourable 'local culture', a 'dynamic region' to be had above all in the core.[62] Marginal areas will therefore drop behind in terms of both enterprise and the level of technology. Thus arises what in modern terms has been called the 'colonial' character of their economies, their lower standard of living, their poorer facilities, and their inability ever to catch up.

The periphery is also far from the centre of political power and influence. This generally means not mere distance, but also subordination, and the difficulty in getting its needs considered and its wishes met. However, this may well also mean that the power of the central authority is weakened at the margin which is to some extent out of its reach: and there often arise demands from the periphery for autonomy or even for independence.[63]

Border areas, if they are exposed to a raiding enemy, tend to be impoverished for that reason. The English-Scottish Border country, additionally, was marginal by its natural configuration: mainly consisting of bleak uplands, its soil was poor and its wet and cold climate adverse for arable cultivation with the exception of narrow coastal strips and some inland valleys. The Scots valleys were rather more fertile. To this the insecure border added a further cause of marginality and impoverishment, though there were at least some observers who saw the chain of causation running the other way, the very poverty of the ground and its overpopulation forcing the men of the border to eke out a living by raiding the lands on the other side, or, for that matter, some lowlands on their own.[64] Though freed from some military duties to the Crown, the local inhabitants were obliged to serve for their own border defence and were subject to the jurisdiction of the Wardens of the Marches, as well as to some tough legislation, including summary execution for aiding the Scots. Moreover, all the additional costs incurred in fortifying their dwellings, building peel towers and bastles,[65] moving their cattle in convoy and under protection only, did not preserve the border folk from repeated losses by the destructive raids and robberies of reivers from the other side, inadequately compensated by the proceeds of raids from their own. The carefully compiled lists of

[61] Quoted in Linge (1988*b*), 14; Gore (1984), 124; Conti (1988), 40–1; also Asheim (1988), 59.

[62] Sweeney (1987), 14; MacMillen (1991), 97; Keeble (1976), 51 ff.; Keeble *et al.* (1982), 62 ff.; Perloff and Wingo (1975), 329; Tödtling (1984), 402.

[63] Gottmann (1980*b*), 16; Linge (1988*b*), 14; Semple (1911), 230; Hechter (1975), 4–11; also Wellhofer (1989), 340; Kapelle (1979), 232; Smailes (1960), 4–5. The advantages of distance from the centre are dealt with in pp. 96–103 below.

[64] Appleby (1978), 52; Tough (1928), 48–9, 73; Watts (1971), 68.

[65] McDowall and Mercer (1970); Hogg (1972), 6; Tuck (1991*b*), 181–2; Wright (1986), 56–8; Rowley (1986), 179.

losses due to Scots depredations sent from time to time to ministers in London show a rather pathetic picture of poverty preying on poverty, of a 'people . . . poor and rude . . . [who] could never keep their goods in safety, nor scarcely their own lives'.[66] Even after pacification the area continued to be a centre of unrest, as in the case of the Kaber Rigg plot of 1663, 'set within the craggy dales and damp moors of Westmorland'.[67]

In England the devastation caused by Scots raids as well as other invasions reached beyond what were normally considered border regions, into Yorkshire and Lancashire. Geoffrey of Monmouth described the whole of the land north of the Humber in around 1135 as

> a frightful land to live in, more or less uninhabited, and it offered a safe lurking place to foreigners. Indeed, by its very geographical position it is open to the Picts, the Scots, the Danes, the Norwegians and anyone else who came ashore to ravage the island.[68]

The Welsh border was also subjected to Marcher Lords whose tough and often arbitrary rule added to the burdens on the population settled there. Despite the range of castles built by the Normans, occasional raids from beyond the defensive line caused much damage to the husbandmen in the Middle Ages.[69] Here, too, the causes were to be sought in political as well as in economic marginality.

There were similar burdens to be borne by the people living in marginal frontier areas on the Continent where borders were sometimes even less clearly defined than the frontier between England and Scotland. This included the south-west of France, Languedoc, most German states, and the frontiers of Poland and Lithuania. The *voivod* of the Hungarian border had powers not dissimilar from those of the Marcher Lord. Almost invariably, frontier existence also involved military duties, as well as being subject to raids from the other side, on top of being impoverished by the natural configuration of the land, while road building was sometimes kept to a minimum in order not to give the other side easy access.[70]

There were, too, other uncertainties of life in pre-modern ages which frequently affected the dwellers on marginal land more than others. To quote one example, the Scottish Highlander was liable to suffer periodic famines not only because his land was poor and its climate harsh—and in years of a bad local harvest he was

[66] Bain (1894–6); Hodgson (1827–58), Part III, ii; Elliott (1959), 89; Rae (1966), 4.

[67] There is a large literature. See, in addition to works cited in nn. 45 and 46, Winchester (1987), 3; Mercer (1991), 132; Smailes (1960), 103–7; Wilson (1901), 295–6, 323–6; Bouch and Jones (1961), 16, 22, 32–3; Newton (1974), 2–9, 19; Millward (1974), 203–4; Kapelle (1979), 124, 144 ff.; Barrow (1973), 139–49; Harbottle and Newman (1973), 142; Clarke (1988), 162. For some accounts of the Scottish side, cf. Borland (1898); Parry (1978), 112–13.

[68] Jewell (1991), 9; also Miller (1988), 258–9; Bishop (1948); Wightman (1975); Kapelle (1979), 86 ff., 118; Kershaw (1973*a*), 3, 41; Darby (1977), 248 ff.

[69] Darby and Terrett (1954), 85, 143–4, 157; Darby (1977), 326–7; Graham (1976); Denholm-Young (1964), 3; Williams (1960–3), 20, 23; Sylvester (1969), 112–15; Rowley (thesis, 1967), 24.

[70] e.g. Ladurie (1977), 251–2; Saint-Blanquat (1949), 282 ff.; Kuhn (1971), 16, 35; Jelecek and Bohac (1989), 153, 161–2; Rosenberg (1988), 96; Davies (1981), 81; Ritschel (1983), 43; Arnold (thesis, 1989), 22–4; Sahlins (1989), 23 ff.; McNeill (1964), 16.

virtually cut off from aid by neighbouring glens by the mountains—but also because of the archaic social form under which land was held and its lack of incentives.[71] The upland miner, another typical dweller on the margin, was subject to the vagaries of the weather and water in his turn, as well as the uncertainty of the extent and richness of the metal lodes. This helps to account for the almost proverbial poverty of the Cornish miner and the Derbyshire lead-miner until well into the modern era.[72]

From the point of view of the lowlander and city dweller—and it was they who composed most of the literature which has come down to us and which is cited here—a major source of the insecurity of marginal areas did, however, derive less from their unfortunate location on poor land near a frontier than from the behaviour of their inhabitants themselves. To men living in the 'core', the marginal lands were areas of lawlessness, brutality, and barbarity—a view in which some elements of truth were typically overlaid by ignorance and the consequent fear of the unknown.

One factor which strengthened this view of lawlessness in marginal lands was the inability of those who administered the law to make their power felt effectively there. These regions in consequence became the refuge of criminals, as well as of those persecuted for their religious beliefs, their political opposition, or for other causes. What might they not get up to in the mountains and forests, unsupervised by authority? 'It is a commonplace that brigands flourish in remote and inaccessible areas such as mountains, trackless plains, fenland, forests or estuaries with their labyrinth of creeks and waterways.' Thus Sir Hugh Oldcastle sought refuge in the forests of the Welsh marches after the failure of the Lollard rebellion of 1413–14. Redesdale and north and south Tynedale attempted to maintain their status outside the king's writ, dating from before the Conquest, into the sixteenth century, and at different times, the western and eastern Pennine slopes, and the Border country, were known to have become havens for those who were for one reason or another outside the law. The Borders bred 'wild and misdemeaned people', forming a '*terra incognita*, as a waste of evil repute, the haunt of thieves and border reivers, where the King's messenger . . . dare not show himself'.[73]

In the 1530s King James V of Scotland attempted to end the lawlessness, the brutal vendettas, and the robberies among the barons on the Scottish side of the border, but to no avail: he had no central force to overcome the regional power of the Marcher Lords. Nor did King James VI do much better before the unity of the Crowns in 1603.[74] On the English side, the Pilgrimage of Grace of 1536 is

[71] O'Dell and Walton (1962), 102; Dodgshon (1988), 28; Salaman (1987), 356–7; also Hoffmann (1975), 31; Wrightson (1982), 145.

[72] Jenkin (1972), 49–50; Hatcher (1973), 82–3; Barton (1967), 87.

[73] Hobsbawm (1969), 16; Higham (1986), 173; Kapelle (1979), 128; Watts (1975), 24; Mingay (1990), 24; Musgrove (1990), 69; Tough (1928), 37; Hodgson (1827–58), Part III, ii. 228; Summerson (1982), 113; Jones (1969), 151; Charlton (1859), 147; Rowley (1986), 153; Fraser (1972), 27; Phillips (1977), 91–3; Beresford (1967), 83.

[74] Jeffrey (1857–64), iv. 249; Chambers (1864), 92 ff.; Graham (1905), 17–18; Grant (1930), 535.

sometimes, rather more controversially, linked to similar conditions: 'dearth was a common phenomenon in the region, and a factor likely to stimulate lawlessness'. Richard Aske, one of its leaders, believed 'that if the King took the wealth of the North Country abbeys out of the province, the inhabitants would, of very poverty, be forced either to ally themselves with the Scots or make commotions and rebellions'. This was because of 'the sheer poverty of the North and the fact that it was, essentially, a border province'. Forests and the less accessible marshes and fens had a similar reputation, and robberies and depredations were indeed frequently committed from there. English forests in the Middle Ages, 'unpoliced and remote, were also the haunts of criminals and outlaws, who might live for years in the vastness of the forest with little fear of disturbance'. Irish forests were worse.[75]

More generally, it was alleged that 'marauding propensities are marked among all retarded mountain people of modern times': thus the Highlander raided the Lowlander and the Caucasus tribes raided the plains Russians.[76] The Scots Highlanders had altogether a very bad press in Britain. Out of reach of the king's power in their remote and 'rugged terrain', it was in part their 'cultural values' which were said to have inspired their autonomous and anarchic behaviour, including their clan vendettas. Cattle stealing was considered an honoured tradition, and punishment for it was deemed unjust. The best that could be said for them was that because the Highlands were so poor, their people 'have more of the predatory instinct of the hunter than the peaceful emotions of the cultivator of the soil'. Following the fighting in Scotland especially in the years between 1640 and 1655, much banditry and lawlessness remained. Mounted 'moss troopers', rather like those appearing in the Border country, ravaged the countryside, the clans had to arm against them and then, in turn, raided the Lowlands. Gaelic in speech and catholic or episcopalian in religion, 'bands of highlanders continued to sweep into lowland farms to plunder cattle and other livestock', well after 1680. After Culloden, the Highlands were at last placed under the direction of what has been described as a committee of Edinburgh lawyers. These worked under the assumption that 'Highland peasants were ignorant, idle and culturally savages, and they therefore strove all they could to eliminate the mores of the clan'. They were supported in their notion by Defoe, according to whom the West Highlanders were 'some of the worst, most barbarous, and ill governed of all the Highlands of Scotland; they are desperate to fight, cruel in victory, fierce even in conversation, apt to quarrel, mischievous, and even murderers in their passion'.[77]

As for the marches of Scotland and Wales, they were 'sanctuaries for roving bands of thieves and other brigands who would subject the relatively wealthier

[75] Brooks (1954), 3; Harrison (thesis, 1975), 9, 172; Smith (1970), 198; Clark (thesis, 1990), 344; also Beinart and Coates (1995), 6.

[76] Semple (1911), 586–7; Novosel'tsev (1986).

[77] Turnock (1982), 192–4; MacInnes (1988), 58–61; Dodgshon (1988), 33; Barrow (1973), 363; Hechter (1975), 112–14; Shaw (1980), 120; Defoe (1992), 239; Pease (1913), 34–6; Grant (1930), 525; Youngson (1974), 23, 203; Handley (1953), 91; Anderson (1968), 12–13; Smout (1969), 39; Richards (1982), 44; Johnson (1984), 615; O'Brien (1919), 43; Butlin (1976), 142–3.

border counties to plunder with alarming regularity'. These were 'outlying parts where government was less normal and regular'. While the border hills were the 'upland haunt of the wolf and the outlaw', the fault was generally thought to be that of the people rather than of the location as such. One visitor in 1598 who was not entirely unsympathetic found them to be 'barbarous more of speech than manner, active of person and speech, stout and subtle, inclined to theft and strife, factious and seditious, full of malice and revenge . . . they lived worse than infidels'.[78] This rather acute observation, combining the horror of the good citizen when faced with lawless violence with a sneaking admiration for the power and freedom of that kind of life, summarizes the most common reaction of the pre-modern age to those living on the margin.

The Cornishmen of Elizabethan times had an equally poor image. The tinners were described as 'ten or twelve thousand of the roughest and most mutinous men in England . . . lawlessness was a feature of stannary life throughout our period [i.e. before 1550]'. 'The Cornish tinners, from Elizabethan times onward, seem to have been regarded as a rough, hardy, and lawless crew, dwelling more or less without the pale of civilization, in the confines of "West Barbary".'[79]

Many mountainous areas on the Continent enjoyed a similar reputation for lawlessness. The Pyrenees and sub-Pyrenees were said to be the home of brigandage, as were the Balkan uplands, where 'raiding and cattle rustling were a part of the economy', while the regions of the Massif Central in France were 'perpetual zones of fiscal rebellion'. 'The traveller in Italy, in Spain, in France, whose path crossed stretches of moor or high hill went in fear of the wild, independent and lawless folk who were not averse to augmenting their slender income with money extorted by terror or worse', according to Hay. The people of the Cévennes, strong-minded men of mountains and forests, were responsible for repeated insurrections, most effectively in 1702–4. The Caucasus was alleged to give shelter to tribes dedicated to fighting and slave-trading into the nineteenth century, and had to be 'pacified' and 'civilized' by the Russian state. The mountain Vlachs raided lowland villages and held up travellers.[80]

Woodlands were similarly difficult to control, and similarly feared. 'The forests became a by-word for lawlessness and roguery' in the early modern period in England: Robin Hood and his men were naturally placed there. In the real Middle Ages, trenches were made along the major highways where they passed through woods, and wood and woodbank had to be destroyed for a width of 200 ft. along each side, to reduce the risk of highway robbery by people lurking behind trees. In Wales, monasteries were urged to clear woodlands where rebels had been hiding.

[78] Quotations from Hechter (1975), 57; Winchester (1987), 2; Rowse (1978), 287; Tough (1928), 32, 33; also Jewell (1991), 19–20; Appleby (1978), 50; Smailes (1960), 105–6; Williams (1964), 14.

[79] Hatcher (1973), 86; Jenkin (1972), 48.

[80] Nadal and Giralt (1960), 102 ff.; Hay (1966), 29; Tilly (1975*c*), 47; Novosel'tsev (1986), 20–1; Wace and Thompson (1972), 157–8, 192, 198, 258; Vilar (1988), 322–4, 329; Palairet (1986), 413; McNeill (1992), 117–18, 267; Garnsey (1986), 9; Weishaupt (1992*a*), 37, 136; Ligou (1967), 133; Jelavich (1984), 247; Venturi (1991), ii. 679–80.

Strata Florida, for example, was set the task in 1278 of clearing certain woods 'where robberies, homicides and other enormities against the king's peace have been wont to be committed'. The woodlands west of Lough Erne in Ireland were so wild in 1700 that they were 'scarce inhabited by any human creatures but the O's and the Macs', 'who pillaged all who came their way'. Anything irretrievably lost was said to be 'gone beyond the Arney'.[81] On the Continent, too, forests were thought of as retreats for criminals—or for religious groups seeking solitude; forest tribes were considered inferior, isolated, and ignorant.[82] Nor did fens and marshes escape a similar reputation: they were also held to be rebellious and free and anarchic: 'So wild a country nurses up a race of people as wild as the fen', according to Arthur Young in 1799.[83]

Marginal areas were also regarded with suspicion as breeding grounds for witch crazes and heterodox religious beliefs. LeRoy Ladurie has traced this tendency in a sensitive study in relation to Languedoc and the Cévennes: 'The natives of the mountains of the Cévennes (a harsh, inhospitable country if ever there was one in France, and that would seem the least capable of receiving the Gospel on account of the rudeness of the spirit of the inhabitants)' took to belief in witchcraft in the 1490s, and in 1550–1600.

> The coarse, ungodly mountain folk were ignorant of the Bible, and because they lived in isolated farmsteads or hamlets far from any church, they did not go to Mass and were easy prey to every sort of demonic obsession. Not far away, in the country of Saint-Pons, a den of astrologers and hotbed of superstition, the Devil was equally at home.

In view of the large extent to which witchcraft and associated phenomena were a fabrication of the Catholic Church and its methods of obtaining 'confessions', and the fact that the area of the Cévennes was a stronghold of the Huguenots in the sixteenth century, how are these regional predilections to be explained? Part of the explanation, according to Ladurie, lies in the simple neglect by the Church of the mountain people and their increasing poverty caused by their increased numbers, so that they were forced to seek solace by unorthodox means. But it may also be that they were brutalized by the spectre of misery and death created by the war after 1560, and further that they were roused to opposition to urban ideologies, and the hope for a reversal of fortune: 'the first shall be last', expressed in the role inversion of All Fools' Day, in revolts, and possibly also in witchcraft frenzies. In the late seventeenth century the region was once again a centre of unorthodox religion, brought to it by the 'Camisards' with their 'prophesying, and their fanaticised messianic preaching'.[84]

Witchcraft also haunted other isolated mountain areas. One of them was located in the Jura mountains, between Vaud and Fribourg on the Swiss side, and Franche-Comté on the French side, where the 'obsession' with witchcraft started around 1420.

[81] Thirsk (1987), 50–1; Rackham (1980), 155; Williams (1969), 49; McCracken (1958–9), 276.

[82] Zon (1920), 146–8; Probszt (1966), 14; Braudel (1986), 128–30; Weber (1976), 55.

[83] Quoted in Darby (1968), 154; also his (1940), 42, 119–20; Beresford (1967), 84; and p. 56 above.

[84] Ladurie (1974), quotations from 165, 205–6, also 276 ff.; also Jones (1975), 340; Moch (1983), 40.

A detailed study of the region found that from the French point of view, witches were early on associated with heresy, and indeed the eastern Jura was said to be the first region in which the terms for witch and heretic were conflated, and one of the very few in which there were more male witches condemned than female ones. This appears also to have been the reason why the authorities in Geneva, who were themselves somewhat sceptical about the existence of witchcraft, were prepared to pronounce convictions for it. On the German-speaking side, however, witchcraft was associated more with sorcery than with unorthodox Christian belief.

More generally, according to Lord Dacre (H. R. Trevor-Roper),

> The Alps and the Pyrenees, the original cradle of the witch craze, would long remain its base . . . as a continuing social phenomenon, involving not merely individuals, but whole societies, the witch craze would always be associated particularly with the highlands. The great European witch-hunts would centre upon the Alps and their foothills, the Jura and the Vosges, and upon the Pyrenees and their extensions into France and Spain. Switzerland, Franche-Comté, Savoy, Alsace, Lorraine, the Valteline, the Tyrol, Bavaria, and the North Italian Bishoprics of Milan, Brescia and Bergamo: Béarn, Navarre and Catalonia: these would be the primary centres.[85]

In the Lake District also, the belief in witches lingered on until the end of the eighteenth century, if not later.[86]

Among the explanations for the association of witch crazes particularly with highland zones was the experience of such exaggerated natural phenomena as avalanches, electric storms, the cracking of mountain ice, and the hallucinations generated by the thin air on the tops. Being exposed to incalculable catastrophes, people turned to superstition, the belief in miracles and 'unnatural' causes. 'The physical strenuousness of alpine existence may have made men sturdy and independent . . . but it also made them bitter, solid, cold, superstitious, irrational and violent.' The modern Derbyshire well-dressing practised in upland villages, a revival of the eighteenth century, has been held to be a return to a pagan practice as well as a reflection of local irregular water supplies.[87] Another explanation for witch crazes was the survival in the mountains of different races—such as the Basques—with differing social organization. The persecutions were in part explained by the hatred and unease of those in authority in the plains at the defiance of mountain people of their feudal order and religious orthodoxies.

These areas were also centres of religious heterodoxy, for much the same reasons. The official Church, whether Catholic or Protestant, was apt to neglect the population in distant valleys and hillsides. Thus the first Gaelic New Testament had to wait until 1767, and even then few Highlanders could read. Mountains 'are the home not only of sorcery and witchcraft, but also of primitive religious forms and resistance to new orthodoxies.' The Waldenses, for example, after a brief early

[85] Cole and Wolf (1974), 110; Monter (1976); Weber (1976), 23 ff.; Trevor-Roper (1969), 105, 106.

[86] Rowley (1986), 25, 86 ff., 141; Burgess (thesis, 1984), 545; Jewell (1994), 177–8.

[87] Bucher (1974), 252; Bielmann (1972), 16; Veyret (1978), 69; Trocmé (thesis, 1977), 39; McCall (thesis, 1976), 102; Henderson (1879), 2; Weiss (1941), 356; Braudel (1976), i. 37; Barber (1974), 103.

efflorescence in the late twelfth century, survived in strength in the valleys of the Cottian Alps on the border between France and Italy, mainly in Dauphiné and the valleys leading into the Piedmont plain. There they lived in 'high, compact communities', and were strengthened in part by the degree of autonomy and self-government which all Alpine regions had achieved for themselves. Though concerned with the purity of their religion in contrast to what they saw as the offensive corruption of the Catholic Church, the cohesiveness of the Waldenses derived also from their common experience as upland peasants and country people, just as the interests of those who waged a crusade against them were to rob them of their property, 'to enrich the few at the expense of a marginal group'.[88] Tyrol became one of the main strongholds of the Anabaptists. The Albigenses or Cathars, who had their greatest successes in Languedoc, were also strongly supported by mountain people, as were their spiritual ancestors, the Bogumil sect in the Balkans. Their movement, however, had a much wider, partly urban and even cosmopolitan basis. The mountain area was also the breeding-ground of the Fratricelli zealots and the Béguines. In Transylvania, the millenarian belief spread by Franz David that the world would come to an end in 1570 found a widespread echo, especially among the Szekler people.[89]

The Reformation on the Continent is often stated to have been largely an urban phenomenon, strongest where towns depended on distant trade. Yet it was remarkably successful also in marginal areas. Luther found early support in Tyrol, among the miners, though the interest there was quickly transferred to the Anabaptists, before they in turn were swallowed up by the Counter-Reformation.[90] In the eastern Alps, too, miners turned to Protestantism, as did a significant number of people living under the clerical dictatorship of Salzburg. The upland peasants of Styria and Carinthia were said to have kept to their 'secret protestantism' for 180 years after the Counter-Reformation by virtue of their 'inner strength and proud self-assurance' (innere Kraft und stolze(s) Selbstbewusstsein). In Switzerland and in the French Alps, too, Protestantism reached out early on, beyond its centres in Geneva and Zurich, into the surrounding mountains.[91] Holland became a centre not only of Calvinism but of a remarkably widespread adherence to Anabaptism.[92]

In England, 'at the time of the Reformation, the Border was most probably the most ignorant and barbarous district in England, amongst whom is neither faith, virtue, knowledge of God, nor regard for any religion'. Yet it quickly adopted

[88] Howell (1963), 136; Bain (1896), 80, 87; Burgess (thesis, 1979), 3; Newell (1925), 39–40; Smout (1969), 432–3; Jennings (1983), 394; Trevor-Roper (1969), 107, also 116, 135 ff., 183–6; Cohn (1975), 38; Cameron (1984), 46; Rosenberg (1988), 49; Guichonnet (1980*c*), 274; Bergier (1980), 248; and p. 66 above.

[89] Wakefield (1974); Rocquebert (1982), 265–6, 288–9; Douie (1932), 82, 248 ff.; Wandruszka (1980), 376.

[90] Egg *et al.* (1986), 151–3; Riedmann (1988), 97–107; Niederer (1979), 252; Wolfstrigl-Wolfskron (1903), 206, 219; Laube (1976), 203, 235. Also Ch. 8 below.

[91] Ludwig and Gruber (1987), 215, 303; Stolz (1955), 267; Niederer (1993), 221, 256; Pickl (1986), 88; Kiefner (1983), 5; Mathieu (1987), 10–12.

[92] Tracy (1990), 160 ff.

Protestantism, if not for ideological reasons, at least because it promised a lighter yoke. As is well known, the Quakers gained an early foothold in the Lake District, the 'Galilee of Quakerism', where the Plymouth Brethren, the Inghamites, and the Sandemanians also found support. However, the population there retained 'more than a hint of paganism into modern times'. 'In those remote northern areas, religious conformity was notoriously difficult to enforce, hence dissent flourished with only intermittent interference.' In Swaledale, Methodism appealed to the 'rugged hard-living miners', as did Quakerism, and much the same was said of the miners and others in the Derbyshire Peak District. Wales and Cornwall were other marginal areas strong in Nonconformity.[93] In general, dissent also flourished in the larger parishes in fen and forest areas, where control was weak.[94]

Yet at the same time marginal areas were also said to cling to the old religion because of their conservatism. In England the survival of the Catholic rituals was generally limited to regions 'which modern historians term the "highland zone" and which in sixteenth-century terms would crudely be characterised as "conservative" in religion'. The same applied to the Scottish Highlands. In France, too, 'the plains went Left and the mountains remained obstinately Right and Catholic'.[95]

The reputation of marginal lands of being wayward and anarchic, which was clearly connected with the inability of central authority, such as it was, to establish itself and maintain its own kind of 'peace', began to decline as soon as better means of policing, aided by the shrinking of the 'free' territories such as forests and marshes by encroachment and settlement, allowed them to be controlled effectively. There was a curious echo of this in the way in which contemporaries looked at the railway navvy in the middle of the nineteenth century:

> Rough alike in morals and manners, collected from the wild hills of Yorkshire and Lancashire, coming in troops from the fens of Lincolnshire, and afterwards pouring in masses from every country of the empire; displaying an unbending vigour and an independent bearing . . . impetuous, impulsive and brute-like, regarded as the pariahs of private life . . .[96]

Nowadays it tends to be the centres of the largest cities which are thought of as the hiding places for criminals and the location where most crimes are committed, and it is therefore not easy for us to place the fierce murderer and robber in the peaceful countryside and the healthy mountain air. Until the beginning of the modern age, however, isolation, poverty, backwardness, and crime were associated together in the minds of many: they were thought of as features of the marginal lands.

Because so many marginal lands were unknown, they were also mysterious in a supernatural sense. Possibly the normal laws did not apply: possibly there were

[93] Clarke (1988), 162; Raistrick (1975), i. 112; Austin (1973), 75, 82; Burgess (1980), 103 and (thesis, 1984); Hinds (1896–1922), iv. 104; Tough (1928), 187; Anonymous (1874), 82; Graham (1911), 54; Williams (1980), 41; Davie and Hearl (1991), 215; Bouch and Jones (1961), 179; Jenkins (1990), 76; Phillips (1977), 115, 120; Dickens (1966), 8–11; Smail (thesis, 1988), 188; Musgrove (1990), 223; Marshall (1958), 143; Cornholme (1986), 46.

[94] Everitt (1970), 188–97; Clark (thesis, 1990), 189, 194; Holroyde (1988), 19.

[95] Hutton (1995), 113; Weber (1976), 261.

[96] Quoted in Bagwell (1988), 91.

strange animals and spirits to be found there, and for many nations, forests and mountains were the seats of their gods. Many found these places awesome and even horrifying; others were prepared to be intrigued, perhaps even amused by the suspension of humdrum reality and the appearance of the unexpected on unfamiliar ground.

When travellers like Defoe found the mountains terrifying, this was inspired partly by their lurking menace but also by their barrenness, and the danger of being lost without resource in them. 'These hills', he wrote of northern Lancashire, 'were not high and formidable only, but they had a kind of unhospitable terror in them . . . all barren and wild, or no use of advantage either to man or beast.' From there he entered Westmorland, 'a county eminent only for being the wildest, most barren and frightful of any I have passed over in England or even in Wales itself'. Worse still were the Scottish Highlands, 'a frightful country full of hideous desert mountains and unpassable'.[97]

If travellers crossed mountains in fear and trembling, as they often did, it was in part because of the feeling of powerlessness, and because of the tales of others having perished in them. The dangers of snow and ice, of torrents, gorges and avalanches, of getting lost in eerie mist and falling into crevasses or down a rock face were real enough, and so were, in some areas, the dangers from wild animals or criminal bands. The Alps were seen as 'horrible mountains, full of dangers and threats, of bears, wolves and other wild beasts' while the Lake District with its avalanches, wild winds, and rock falls was seen as a 'scene of terror'. But beyond these there was also a more primitive, irrational fear. The northern uplands of England 'seemed to all who visited them the very birthplace of hauntings and mysterious powers'. Not only gods, but terrible sorcerers and demons dwelt in mountains. But there were also sagas and tales of benign rulers and inaccessible terrains, of treasures and secrets of happiness, of the *Alpenkönig* and Shangri-La.[98] In the Middle Ages the miners in their distant uplands, bringing forth rare metals from the earth, and the glass-blowers with their uncanny skills were also viewed with some awe and superstition as having supernatural powers.[99]

It is interesting to note that in spite of the differences between the bleak moors, rarely covered in snow or ice, which characterized British mountains, and the tree- and snow-clad higher mountain ranges of the Continent, the sentiments of travellers and lowlanders towards them showed such similarity, though there were rather fewer supernatural beings, such as trolls, and fewer mysterious treasures, in the English and Scots imagination. It is possibly a primeval fear of the unknown, rather than the experience of the known, which coloured these reactions.

Forests, also, gave rein to fear, awe, and superstition. In Europe it was possibly the Germanic tribes whose culture was most closely identified with forest lore.

[97] Defoe (1992), 195, 238.

[98] Lindgren (1987), Introd. 7; Gilpin (1792), 137–9; Brown (1971), 36; Bouch (1948), 353; Günther (1930), 23–4; Blache (1933), 98–9; Wandruszka (1980), 389; Guichonnet (1980*d*), 176–9; van Berchem (1980), 206, 219; Laube (1976), 203, 235.

[99] Nef (1987), 731; Schreiber (1965), 201.

While the Romans looked upon the forests north of their lines with some dread—Caesar's *regio sylvis horrida* of the north—the Celts and the Germans peopled them with their gods.[100] In the Middle Ages, when wolves and bears, as well as robbers and outlaws, still roamed the European forests, imagination also peopled them with demons, witches, and the Wild Huntsman. At the time of the French Revolution, when 'there were no longer any chance encounters with the devil, fairies or Merlin the Enchanter [in the forests], there were plenty of wolves and evil-looking men'. In the Alps, it was believed, one might still encounter wild men known as *Fanggen* or *Fänggen*, who had knowledge of weather and herbs, were hairy all over, with a wreath of leafage, and often carried a fir-tree with its roots. They might be a danger, but could also be protective. Their women were dressed in furs, were friendly and helpful, but had goats' feet. The Riesengebirge was the haunt of *Rübezahl*. Even the relatively open Teutoburg Forest had something dreadful and ominous about it, as is clear from Droste-Hülshoff's famous tale, 'Die Judenbuche'.[101]

Elsewhere, also, imagination peopled the forests with elfins, fauns, and naiads, with opportunity as well as danger. Weber's *Der Freischütz* and Schiller's *Die Räuber* have not without reason been held to be near the heart of German culture, as were those of Grimm's fairy tales which had forests as their setting. Poetry and art turned frequently to the forest, and not only in Germany, as a place of solitude and unspoilt nature, but also a place of hardship, of danger and having to rely on one's own resources.[102] In the case of the forests, it seems that it was ignorance rather than some inkling of real danger which determined an attitude that was essentially irrational.

Outsiders' prejudices, and travellers' tall tales, no matter how numerous, consistent, and plausible, may not by themselves be proof of the hardships, the poverty, and the disadvantages of living in marginal lands. They may merely reflect ignorance or irrational fear. But there was one aspect of the behaviour of their inhabitants themselves which lent credence and strength to that belief: it was the tendency for these areas to give rise to large-scale emigration and to become population reservoirs for other, more favoured territories. There was, of course, emigration also from other regions; but marginal lands seemed to be particularly liable to exhibit this proof of their undesirableness.

Some aspects of this have been discussed in Chapter 2 above, in connection with the 'desertions' and *Wüstungen* which followed the population decline of the Middle Ages, and which were often exceptionally heavy precisely in marginal areas. But these 'desertions' left the affected areas empty of people, and their dwellings often in ruins, merging with the ground and visible only to archaeology some centuries

[100] Koebner (1971), 21; Nietsch (1939), 219; Russell (1972*b*), 39; Helmolt (1896), 235; Sitwell (1986), 15.

[101] Lefebvre (1973), 22; Hauser (1972), 81; McDonnell (1992), 110; Wilsdorf and Quellmalz (1971), 288; Leiser (1983), 43–4.

[102] For a sensitive review, see Grill (1987), also Schlender (1987); Zon (1920), 151–2; TeBrake (1985), 48; Schlüter (1952), 19; Helmolt (1896), 235; Devèze (1961), i. 35.

later. The emigration which we are concerned with here, by contrast, had its source in populated areas which remained populated, perhaps even over-populated, after the migrants had left. What is of interest in this context, therefore, is not that barren land was left behind, but that there was a population which continued to dwell in territories which others, possibly the most energetic and able, had found too inhospitable and had felt obliged to leave.

The incentives to migration are commonly divided into push and pull factors. No doubt pulls played a part here, as elsewhere, from time to time, but what we are concerned with is the push, that is to say, the negative factors expelling people from their regions. The changes which provided the push can be classified into three groups: (1) an increase of population which exceeded the capacity of the land to carry it; (2) the decline of a local resource, such as mineral ores, or its replacement by cheaper supplies from elsewhere, or by a newly available alternative; and (3) deliberate human action, such as clearances or expulsions. In the marginal areas considered here, especially the mountain areas, the first of these was much the most important. Its variations provided an indication of the range of disabilities suffered by people living in these lands.

Possibly the best-known emigration stream from marginal lands is the exodus of young Swiss men to serve as soldiers elsewhere. The earliest of these to take mercenary service outside their country were reported from the thirteenth and fourteenth centuries, 'an indication of the early over-population of the Alpine valleys'. The first formal treaties with a foreign potentate to supply troops were made in 1373 with the Viscontis of Milan, and more formally in 1474 between Louis XI of France and eight Swiss towns, while Swiss still fought for their own country as well as for others. After the battle of Marignano (1515) in which 40,000 of them were said to have taken part, 12,000 of them being killed, the Swiss gave up any political ambitions of their own, confirming the right of the French Crown to enlist mercenaries. Henceforth Swiss mercenaries were to hire themselves out to foreign rulers.

The total loss of Swiss population by death or settlement abroad has been estimated at 50,000–100,000 men in the fifteenth century, 250,000–300,000 both in the sixteenth and seventeenth centuries, and 300,000–350,000 in the course of the eighteenth century. In the first half of the nineteenth century there were 100,000 emigrants from Switzerland, of whom perhaps one-half went into mercenary service; of the rest, many went to the United States seeking better opportunities in civilian life. The total number of those who served abroad between 1373 and 1848–59 is estimated to have been around one million, of whom 700,000 were in French service, and they were involved in forty-three battles and wars. In the seventeenth and early eighteenth centuries, the Swiss regularly had 50,000–70,000 men abroad; later a good deal fewer. According to another calculation, of the natural population increase of the country of *c.*2.00–2.23 million between 1400 and 1800, about one-half, or 0.95–1.15 million, were lost by 'migration', mostly by being killed in foreign service. The poverty of their homeland is often said to have

been one factor of that movement, and it was commonly the most able-bodied who tended to be lost in that way.[103]

Other relatively barren uplands also sent young men into foreign armies, including numerous Germans and the Scots Highlanders who served the French king in the fifteenth and Gustavus Adolphus in the seventeenth century, and who took part in many later British campaigns. In the Napoleonic wars, over 10 per cent of the *whole population* is said to have enlisted.[104] The Scottish Highlands have, however, become infamous for a different type of emigration, that induced by deliberate clearances undertaken by all-powerful landlords against legally helpless tenants. This was done first in the late eighteenth and early nineteenth centuries, in order to replace cattle by sheep, which needed few men to mind them, and later still in order to replace the sheep, in turn, by deer which promised even higher returns to the landowners and provided even fewer local jobs. Some evictions were carried through with a cruelty and indifference to the fate of the original inhabitants which shocked even contemporaries, but it has become clear since then that there was in any case no chance of the survival of the traditional Highland economy under modern conditions. From around 1650, 'put in simple terms, the Highlands and Islands had too many people dependent on too little arable land' and there were many signs of a 'population rapidly outstripping its resources'. Most of the 'problems of the Highlands pre-dated the clearances . . . the clearances were imposed upon a society already under strain and dislocation derived from both population and landlord pressure'. There had been some emigration even before the clearances, in part to the Lowlands, but also to North America, often in groups led by the local tacksmen. The evictions and clearances, mainly from the first decade of the nineteenth century onwards, continued a process in which the 'push' factor clearly predominated. Nevertheless, the natural increase of the Highland population, possibly aided by the potato, was such that it increased in absolute terms despite emigration until the 1840s, declining only thereafter.[105] The Orkneys which benefited from varied proto-industrial enterprises, yet lost population by emigration in the eighteenth and nineteenth centuries.[106]

Emigration was also a feature of other British uplands. Whereas upland Scotland had a population index of 130 in 1880 (1801 = 100) against the whole of Scotland standing at 232, Cumberland and Westmorland's 199 compared with England

[103] Bergier (1983), 52, made it a million for 1474–1792; Mayer (1952), 192, also 114–17, 196; Bührer (1977); Ruckstuhl (thesis, 1990), 85, 91 ff.; Kistler (1962), 53 ff.; Schelbert (1976), 158; Netting (1981), 54, 97; Günther (1930), 229; Bergier (1980), 255–6, 284; Ruffieux (1980), 317, 330; Niederer (1980*a*), 86–7 and (1993), 220; Bickel (1947), 89–91; Meyer-Marthaler (1944), 7; Braun (1960), 30; pp. 138–9 below.

[104] Semple (1911), 581; Richards (1982), 147 ff.; Symon (1959), 272–3; Douglas (1899), 341; Smout *et al.* (1994), 76–7; Potter (1996).

[105] O'Dell and Walton (1962), 131–2, 140–2; Gray (1957), 63; Dodgshon (1981), 277, 298; Richards (1982–5), ii. 141 and i. and (1988), 193–4; Turnock (1982), 95; Lythe and Butt (1975), 98; Handley (1953), 245; Franklin (1952), 168; Devine (1983), 137 ff.; Gailey (1962), 157; Smith (1798), 25; Youngson (1973), 161–3; Prebble (1963); Hamilton (1963), 131; Devine (1988), 69 ff., 197.

[106] Schrank (1992), 372, 387.

at 295, and upland Wales at 183 compared with the Welsh average of 252:[107] for these results emigration was largely responsible. In the eighteenth and nineteenth centuries Furness and the Border country furnished labour for the expanding industrial districts further south, the Northumbrian border and Cumberland supplying mainly the coalfield areas of the north-east, and Westmorland and Furness sending their surplus population into Lancashire.[108] Within Northumberland itself, a rough calculation of the change in the number of houses or families between 1665–6 or 1734–6 and 1821 reveals that among the ten fastest growing parishes, five were in the lowlands and two in the uplands (the remainder being in the foothills); among the ten declining parishes, the proportions were reversed, six being in the mountains and only one in the plain. A similar crude division, based on the Census of Population, shows the lowland parishes to have increased their populations by 108.5 per cent between 1801 and 1851, those in the foothills by 48.1 per cent, and those in the uplands by 29.4 per cent. Yet the available parish records, such as those for Haltwistle and Whitfield (Blanchland is misleading because of the immigration of lead-miners), show a consistent healthy surplus of baptisms over burials, pointing to the likelihood that it was emigration which slowed their growth. The Yorkshire dales, Lincolnshire, central Wales, and Cornwall were among other marginal areas noted for their high emigration figures.[109]

France is not known for any significant emigration in modern times, yet its marginal areas were as active as any in sending their surplus population into the plains and cities when additional numbers exceeded the local resources. The Alps, and Savoy in particular, were a significant source of emigration, and this also applied to the marginal areas of Languedoc.[110] Large numbers also left the Massif Central and the French Pyrenees, 'what is today "poor France" ', and while some of them went to Bordeaux, many crossed the Pyrenees into Catalonia. That movement between 1553 and 1717 has been the subject of a major study.[111] It found the causes for the emigration from the Pyrenees and their foothills to lie mainly in over-population, in religious intolerance, and in brigandage. Migrants left Languedoc and the Garonne basin because of the effects of religious wars and because, having large families, they could not provide all their children with a holding, a form of local over-population. They came from the Massif and the highlands because the poor soil and climate put

[107] Collins (1978), 14.

[108] Howell (1963), 148; Marshall (1969, 1970), 284–5; Marshall and Walton (1981), 19, 67 ff.; Appleby (1978), 27; Searle (thesis, 1983), 123; Rees (1951), 14; Sylvester (1969), 415.

[109] Marshall (1958), 110; Watts (1975), 41; Hallam (1958), 358; Hallas (1991); Dixon (thesis, 1984), 243–4; Northumberland Parish Registers; Hartley and Ingilby (1988), 33 and (1979), 139–40; Hastings (1981), 28, 137; Pickles (1981), 73; Rees (1951), 14; Knowles (thesis, 1990), 29–31; Lucas (*c.*1880), 66.

[110] Monter (1976), 44; Blache (1933); Ladurie (1974), 237–45 and (1977), 11; Moch (1983), 37–8, 200; Hufton (1974), 72; Rosenberg (1988), 134; Juillard (1976), 80–2; Braudel (1976), i. 47; Merlin (1971), 8–11, 34 ff.

[111] Nadal and Giralt (1960); also Hohenberg and Lees (1985), 141; Poussou (1970); Braudel (1986), 57; Gravier (1964), 291–2; Marsh (1974), 206–7; White (1989), 23; Hanagan (1989), 78 ff.; Ogden (1989), 121–2; Pinkney (1953), 3; Lucassen (1987), 108–19; Derruau-Boniol and Fel (1970), 6, 69; Fel (1962), 159, 168 ff.

limits to the numbers which the land could carry, and again, because their inheritance system gave the holding to a single heir, leaving other children without land. At the same time, empty holdings in Catalonia because of wars and epidemics may have added a 'pull' element to that migration. It is noteworthy that most of those who moved were poor agriculturalists and shepherds, and they went to inland rural districts rather than to Barcelona or other coastal cities, in their search for forms of employment with which they were familiar. It is possible that not all who left the Massif Central region did so because of the push of poverty in the later nineteenth century. According to Robert Louis Stevenson, some rather felt the pull: 'the lads go forth pricked with the spirit of adventure and the desire to rise in life'.[112]

German emigration was also mainly regional in modern times, upland and forest areas once more being the source of most of it, though the agrarian plains of east Elbian Prussia proved to be equally active in driving their inhabitants into exile. The mountainous areas of Baden and Württemberg furnished the largest contingents after 1815 and particularly from the famine years of the 1840s onwards (see Table 1 below). In their case, it is said that it was the system of partible inheritance, which created ever smaller dwarf holdings for a sizeable part of the population, which was responsible for the high level of emigration. Some, in the earlier period, went in groups to eastern Europe and even to Transcaucasian Russia; later it was North America which proved to be the main attraction. Alsace and parts of Bavaria, particularly the Böhmerwald in the east, were also considered over-populated and lost large numbers by emigration, an aspect of the *Höhenflucht* more typical of the High Alps. Frankfurt am Main, the Palatinate, and Wuppertal were among the growth centres which drew some of their population increase from the surrounding mountains and hills.[113]

The emigration from the Alpine uplands was particularly strongly marked. While earlier emigration was partly triggered by religious persecution, or by the attractive offers of German and eastern European rulers intent on a policy of *peuplation*, the emigration of the nineteenth and twentieth centuries came largely from the higher reaches of the valleys and appears to have been caused by the poverty and lack of opportunity for the growing population. Between 1887 and 1938, the proportion of emigrants was highest in the Swiss upland cantons (apart from the large cities): Tessin led with 29.3 per cent, followed by Obwalden (27.8 per cent), Schwyz (20.6 per cent), Glarus (18.3 per cent), and Uri (16.5 per cent). Altogether, between 1850 and 1970, the Swiss Alpine population declined from 14.2 per cent to 10.3 per cent of the national total. Yet its birth-rate remained high, which points to a substantial emigration.[114] The story of the so-called 'Walser' movement is of par-

112 Stevenson (1905), 181.

113 Walker (1964); Erickson (1976), 41–4; Günther (1930), 170, 211–12; Kreiner (1919), 42–3; Schremmer (1979*c*), 1–2; Reulecke (1980), 56; Müller (1938), 204–5; Fehn (1979), 694 ff.; Guth (1989), 112–13, 131.

114 Schelbert (1976), 191; Cépède and Abensour (1961), 161; Löhr (1971), 19–20; Bergier (1983), 33, 54; Hauser (1972), 335; Pfister (1986), 362, 371–2; Head (1979), 186–91; Hagmann and Menthonnex (1979); Bickel (1947), 98; Nabholz (1924), 19; Bätzing (1991), 105; Schuler (1984), 244; Meyer (1979), 258.

ticular interest in this context. Moving out from the Upper Wallis in the thirteenth century, having apparently arrived there from the Bernese Oberland some two centuries earlier, they travelled over the southern Alpine slopes and settled eventually in the Upper Grisons and other uplands, finding everywhere the best lower slopes already occupied. Bringing with them their particular freedoms and privileges, they were widely referred to as the 'free Walsers'.[115]

In Tyrol, the migration movement was well under way by 1835, settlements at over 1,000 m. above sea-level being affected first, others from the 1870s onward, at a time when the rest of the country showed an increase of population. Settlements lying above 1,300 m. lost 7.5 per cent of their population between 1869 and 1910 while those between 200 m. and 1,000 m. gained 46 per cent. Moreover, the top zones had markedly fewer women—a disproportion which increased over the period 1869–1910. Similar examples of the *Höhenflucht* may be found in other Alpine parts of Austria, including Styria and Lower Austria, as well as in the upland parts of Bavaria.[116]

Table 1 shows emigration rates from some European regions and countries in the nineteenth century, in each case taking the emigration rate for Europe as a whole measured in emigrants per 100,000 population as unity. *Only periods in which the rate exceeded the European rate by more than 2.5 times are entered.*

TABLE 1. *Rates of Emigration from some Selected European Areas and Countries, 1841–1900 (annual averages, by decades)**

	1841–50	1851–60	1861–70	1871–80	1881–90	1891–1900
Ireland	21.4	16.7	11.4	13.8	9.3	9.0
Sweden	—	—	2.8	3.3	4.4	3.1
Norway	—	—	3.9	4.2	5.8	—
Scotland	—	6.2	2.8	2.8	3.4	—
Württemberg	4.0	6.9	3.0	3.7	4.2	3.8
Baden	5.1	6.1	—	3.9	—	—
Alsace-Lorraine	3.8	4.8	4.6	7.9	2.6	—
Italy	—	—	—	—	—	3.9

*For detailed explanation, see text.
Source: based on Erickson (1976), 29.

Sweden and Norway, it will be seen, also belonged to the major emigrant areas in some decades. In Norway, the emigrants rather curiously did not come from the harsh northern regions in the main, but from the south-west, the most fertile part of the country, where primogeniture, leaving the younger children without land, together with other accompanying social changes, was said to have driven them out. Sweden, however, bore all the signs of Malthusian crisis from the 1860s

[115] Joos (1946), 289–90; Meyer-Marthaler (1944), 4; Weiss (1941), 171–2; Bätzing (1991), 43; p. 101 below.
[116] Stolz (1955), 277; Ulmer (1935); Haushofer (1986), 72–3; Fehn (1979), 696.

onward. Italy began to have heavy emigration only towards the end of the century, the real growth occurring only after 1900, but as most of the emigrants came from southern Italy, their problems lie outside the framework of this study. From at least one Alpine valley, fully 40 per cent of those born after 1800 and surviving into adulthood left their village for good.

In Austria-Hungary there was substantial internal migration around 1900, from the marginal areas of Goritz and Gradisca, Carniola, Galicia, and Dalmatia, into Lower Austria (Vienna), Salzburg, and Trieste. There was heavy emigration also to North America from the province of Galicia, as well as from the Balkans, particularly 'from the villages of the densely populated but infertile limestone uplands in the Western half' of Croatia-Slavonia and from the Greek mountains. Many mountain dwellers in the Balkans, including some notorious cattle thieves, left their upland hideouts and moved into the plains in the eighteenth and nineteenth centuries when it became safe to do so, as did the Romanians in Transylvania.[117]

Summing it up, some observers formed the opinion that 'depopulation, abandonment of settlement and intensification of land use are among the features common to most of the high mountain regions of Europe'. In the past, it has also been said, 'mountains and rugged hills furnished many emigrants, while major cities were favoured destinations . . . mobility was often the consequence of misery or despair and was forced rather than voluntary'.[118]

In this extreme form, such views, though widely held, are hardly borne out by the facts. If emigration 'is an almost universal phenomenon in higher regions', this is normally not because these areas are being left denuded of population, but because they are unable to provide for a population increase, living literally on a narrow margin, and it is only the equivalent of the additional population, in numbers, which is forced to leave. The legal forms of inheritance which many historians have stressed as having significance in this process are found to have been of little, if any, importance, since in some areas it is partible inheritance, and in others it is its precise opposite, primogeniture, which is held responsible. Neither would by itself tend to drive out any resident population if total numbers remained stable. But with rising numbers, each generation cohort being larger than the preceding one, both systems would lead to enforced emigration if no new land is available at home.

To this effect of sheer numbers pressing on constant resources a new element has been added in more recent times. This is the effect of the rapidly improving standards of living in all European countries in the twentieth century, which marginal lands sometimes cannot match, either because their incomes stagnate, or because they lack certain facilities, such as good TV reception or convenient petrol stations. Moreover, while in the period preceding full industrialization many industrial employments, being domestic and part-time, were well suited for the dwellers in the

[117] Erickson (1976), 57–9, 83, 90–3; Cole and Wolf (1974), 160; Palairet (1979), 44, 424; Semmingsen (1960); also Baines (1991), 32; de Rosa (1988), 477–8; Davico (1972), 476–9; Broers (1990), 82; Blache (1933), 77; Dovring (1966), 615–16, 619; Lampe and Jackson (1982), 195–7; Hoffman (1977), 477.

[118] Lichtenberger (1978), 181; Hohenberg and Lees (1985), 93, 94; O'Grada (1994), 79.

uplands, given that their work was generally seasonal and their severe winters kept them indoors, modern industry tends to require large units and level, accessible sites, which draw the more enterprising mountain dwellers down into the valleys and plains.[119] It is largely in the modern period, when a 'pull' factor has been added to the traditional 'push' of relative over-population, that marginal populations have actually declined in absolute terms, endangering in some cases the whole ecology of their settlement when the men and women remaining behind are no longer able to maintain the terraces, the irrigation channels, or the drainage on which the settlement depends.[120]

If the normal tendency has been for upland populations to stabilize at a level which their country could bear, balancing over longer periods in some way the opportunities which the lowlands could offer, there have in the past been occasions when lowland people have pushed into the mountains. In some cases, as shown in a remarkable study for the Zurich Oberland, where the lowland towns and villages had enacted strict rules to prevent the settlement of newcomers, it was the uplands which were in a position to welcome the additional population.[121]

Nevertheless, the overwhelming one-way direction of migration out of, rather than into, the marginal lands forms perhaps the most powerful argument for the view that these are undesirable, ill-favoured, and generally poor and backward areas, the regional step-children of society. Large-scale emigration over many ages, from many types of marginal region, under various conditions, seems to point to a common factor of inferiority, at least in the eyes of contemporaries and of those who were obliged to live there. It helps to complete the negative picture of marginal areas which is without a doubt the dominant one in the historical literature.

The evidence assembled in this chapter, to repeat, is meant to provide a sample of a voluminous and dominant 'negative' literature, without necessarily endorsing it. In order to make sure that it is represented fairly and comprehensively, it has been loaded with direct quotations and has ranged widely over many centuries and many countries. Despite the numerous variations in detail, it shows a consensus to the effect that marginal regions are poor and backward, in many ways outside the comforting circle of civilization, to be feared or pitied, but not to be treated as equals of the core areas.

Taking the picture thus created as a whole, it would make these regions most unlikely locations for progressive or innovatory action. On the contrary, they are represented as likely to resist, or being incapable of absorbing, such progressive influences as may reach them from outside: they would certainly never lead the 'core'.

Yet, reading between the lines, a second, perhaps more positive consensus may also be discerned: marginal societies, it appears, are inferior not because of their own human failings, but because they face adverse circumstances. True, there has

[119] Semple (1911), 579; Hunt (1986), 955–7; Viazzo (1989), 60–3, 144, 295; Verlinden (1983), 256; also Braudel (1976), i. 43

[120] McNeill (1992), 6.

[121] Braun (1960), 37 ff.; Dubuis (1986), 7; Viazzo (1989), 133–5.

been much prejudice, condescension, and contempt regarding them. But with few exceptions, most descriptions of marginal populations as ignorant, lawless, uncouth, technically backward, and conservative in outlook also seemed to imply that their environment had made them such. Only rarely was there also the suggestion that these marginal areas were a kind of sump in which less desirable elements, above all those of criminal intent or those escaping from the law, had sought refuge, and that there was therefore a negative selection process in being which accounted for the deplorable character of these regions.

Beyond this, there was even frequently a sneaking admiration for the ability of their denizens to survive amidst harsh conditions, bereft as they were of many of the benefits of civilization, far from the fleshpots of the cities and far from the centres of power. On the whole, this approach would still leave the marginal populations handicapped and subsisting in a lower form of social life. Yet it makes it possible to take a different view altogether. It makes it possible to emphasize the power of adverse conditions to bring out hidden human qualities left dormant in a life of ease, qualities which allowed these populations not only to survive, but even, at times, to excel. To this, more positive literature, we must now turn.

4

The Positive View

The last chapter showed a widespread consensus to the effect that the areas defined here as marginal, namely mountains, forests, and marshes, were inferior and undesirable as places of settlement. People today, fleeing overcrowded, noisy, and polluted cities, and equipped with technical means to make life comfortable even when away from the centres of population, might well prefer these regions, and settle there by choice, if profession or retirement permits. In past times, however, such preferences would be likely to be rare. Nevertheless, life there was not always considered relatively undesirable and, more importantly, the populations living there were not always rated as inferior. In the same way as in the 'negative' literature surveyed in the last chapter, this chapter will trace two aspects of the 'positive' view: the belief in a desirable environment, and the esteem in which the population on marginal land was held.

It is no doubt difficult to reconstruct people's preferences from their actions: we cannot now be sure what was voluntary choice as opposed to enforced movement. Yet in some cases deliberate preferences were unmistakable. Thus it has been said, not unreasonably, that in the early modern period 'the inhabitants [of the forests] valued the variety of their resources and their freedom to use their ingenuity. The poor were better equipped for survival than in the arable country.' The Alpine highlands, similarly, had their obvious attractions in difficult times such as the fourteenth century: the Black Death, it seems, was less ferocious in the high valleys. Moreover, the mountain dwellers were spared much of the warfare of the time, and, relying as much on stock breeding as on the products of the fields, they stood up to the famine years caused by crop failures such as that of 1315–17 much better than the plainsmen who lived mostly on grain-based food. There is evidence that at the time the Alpine dwellers were altogether richer than the population living on the plains.[1] For the eighteenth century there are similar scattered references to the desirability of living in the (French) Alps: 'Some government officials openly admired the area's peasants.' A report of 1708 commented that 'there is hardly a region whose lands produce more than these mountains', and military observers agreed that the inhabitants lived in comfort and had plenty of land to graze their sheep: their well-known migratory habits should not be construed as a sign of poverty.[2]

In part, the advantages of the uplands, in the Alps and elsewhere, lay in the fact that they *were* marginal, that, in particular, there was still much free and unoccupied

[1] Thirsk (1987), 51; Bergier (1980), 222–3; and p. 3 above.

[2] Rosenberg (1988), 3, 7.

land to be had.[3] It was commonly the open spaces of the marginal lands which attracted migrants seeking to better their circumstances, and much of the colonization movement in Europe, referred to in Chapter 2 above, had this as its driving force, at least as far as the colonists themselves were concerned.

It is doubtful whether the modern tendency to leave the cities for the more attractive countryside can be discerned in quite the same form in earlier centuries, though of course the rulers of the sub-tropical plains of India, or for that matter the rich merchants of Renaissance Florence, would escape to their favourite mountain retreats in the hot summers. There is, however, some evidence for a tendency for people who had migrated in search of jobs to return at the end of their working days to the periphery whence they had originally started out.[4]

These scattered examples of a preference for marginal lands quoted here, drawn from many countries and various times, could easily be multiplied; yet the impression remains that they were isolated cases. If positive views about their populations were expressed, these arose not so much from the attractive features of the environment, but on the contrary from the harsh or at least unpromising environmental conditions. Tough conditions, it was held, breed hardy and active people.

Probably the best-known advocate of the positive effects of a challenging environment on the populations living in them was Arnold Toynbee. His syndrome of challenge and response has wider applications than the effects of marginal regions traced here, but is certainly intended to apply to them also. Thus, according to him, the origin of the British Industrial Revolution in the north rather than the south of the country is to be explained by 'the stronger stimulus of a more difficult environment prevailing over the weaker stimulus of an environment in which the difficulty is less'. The people of northern England, Scotland, and Wales had to 'exercise their ingenuity' to make the best of the 'badlands beyond the Severn–Humber line', and it was their drive which ultimately resulted in the breakthrough to the Industrial Revolution. More generally, the areas providing the most effective stimulus to 'peoples, states or cities which are exposed to . . . pressure fall, for the most part, within the general category of marches'. A faint echo of this very broad characterization may be found in the equally well-known 'Turner thesis' relating to the North American frontier. Men of the frontier, then at the margin of the country's occupation, showed, according to this thesis, 'coarseness and strength . . . combined with acuteness and inquisitiveness'. They are alleged to have been known for their 'practical, inventive turn of mind, quick to find expedients . . . (their) restless, nervous energy . . . dominant individualism . . . and that buoyancy and exuberance which comes with freedom'.[5]

Attributions of qualities of this kind to men on marginal lands were common. The community in one of the areas most affected by Anglo-Scottish border violence

[3] Price (1981), 46.

[4] 'We, the Auvergnians, we are different, we will end our days peacefully in the shade of the old tree which embowered our infancy', Lucassen (1987), 197; Conti (1988), 44–5.

[5] Toynbee (1959–64), ii. 62–3, 112; Taylor (1965), 17.

was described as 'of a very rude fashion and yet, of their sort, right expert and wise men'. According to Camden (1586), 'the [border] country is mostly rough and barren, and seems to have hardened the very carcasses of the inhabitants: whom the neighbouring Scots have rendered yet more hardy'. The Scots, needless to stress, were equally tough: the physical hardihood of the (West Highland) crofter was 'remarkable' even in the nineteenth century. Upland Northumbrians, it was asserted in the sixteenth century, 'have but little tillage, by reason whereof they live hardly and at ease, which makes them tall of personage and able to endure hardness when necessity requires'. In the Lancashire Pennines, men had the 'freedom of the frontiersmen', and their 'self-reliance'. The men of Halifax, in the later sixteenth century, were said to 'excel the rest in policy and industry, and . . . surpass the rest in wisdom and wealth'. The Derbyshire Peak District 'bred hard, forthright men, intelligent, tenacious, always practical'. Mountain people in general were characterized by 'initiative, self-reliant thrift, scorn of dependence upon . . . charity, combined with mutual help in times of need'. Significantly, the Poor Law Assistant Commissioner, observing the people of the Derbyshire Peak District in 1834, 'feared lest easier communication with other districts should cause them to lose their self-reliance'.[6]

Around 1800, the French administration of Piedmont noted that in contrast to the 'inhabitants of the low valleys [who were] less active, less hard-working and less sober, the inhabitants of the hills are . . . energetic, intelligent, lively and courageous', although, alas, 'as most of the hill country provides a large quantity of wine, the inhabitants tend to consume too much and this renders them quarrelsome'. Further north in the High Alps, families were said to be more individualistic and self-reliant, and in the Jura mountains, similar phrases were used to describe the population engaged in the domestic industry of watchmaking. There was a spirit of emulation about and an aptitude for the mechanical arts. 'Indeed, one frequently finds in these mountains people who exercise certain trades without ever having been apprenticed.' As for the Pyrenees, the local saying was that 'the Catalan pulls his bread out of the rocks'. Similarly, there was no doubt that the mountains of 'Teutsch-Böhmen voller nahrhafter, grundarbeitsamer Leute stecken'. The Avergnat was noted for the hardness of his life, his sobriety—and also the devotion of his family.[7] More generally, there has been speculation that the dull plains inhibit development, while the more varied highlands stimulate it. One highlander stereotype makes him 'vigorous, honourable, healthy, patriarchal, frugal, industrious and provident'.[8]

Similar judgements were not lacking for other marginal areas. The impressive reclamation of the Lincolnshire Fenland 'would never have taken place without the

[6] Musgrove (1990), 4, 51; Winchester (1987), 1; Farnie (1979), 47; Heaton (1965), 77; Kirkham (1968), 10; Newell (1925), 80; Lander (1970), 334; Robson (1989), 240–1; Pease (1913), 22–4; Houseman (1800), 69; Marshall (1794), 18; Wordsworth (1974), 311; Cregeen (1979), 115.

[7] Broers (1990), 80; Günther (1930), 368; Landes (1983), 306; Niederer (1993), 350; Vilar (1988), 321; Kuhn (1955), 266; Hufton (1972), 104.

[8] Müller (1938), 203–4; Netting (1981), 57.

abundant energies of a numerous and growing population of peasants. The immense dykes which they built . . . are astonishing examples of . . . the powers of co-operation which their peculiar institutions gave them'. Those who maintained the dykes of the Netherlands 'must be accustomed to hard work from childhood; men who have greased leather boots on their feet and who can stand a rough and harsh climate. In times of storm, wind and hail they must be able to persevere.' Again, in Languedoc, the areas with poor soil had a much more active population than the fertile higher-lying territories. There is also a widespread consensus that the European Far North, the Viking country, was where 'the dynamic forces of Europe were to be found' in the ninth century. 'The Viking civilization of the North, vibrant, untamed and raw, had a strong and unmistakable impact on much of the rest of Europe.'[9] We shall return later to the alleged link between the vigour and hardihood of people living on the margin, and the dynamics of economic growth and expansion.

It should be noted that those who characterized the populations living in difficult territories as alert, enterprising, and hardy did not generally specify the mechanism by which such adaptation to the environment might have been achieved, any more than did those who characterized them as lazy and backward. Several different mechanisms are conceivable in theory. It might be that from childhood onward, men and women in those areas were taught, by precept and example, frugality, industry, and adaptability, or that by practical experience they became inured to hardship and forced into being alert and finding expedients when faced with the unexpected. In such districts, 'an exceptional spirit of self-help and self-defence would grow up, merely tolerated at first but gradually consecrated by custom'.[10] This would be a process of individual adaptation. On the other hand, a process of selection might have been at work, letting only the hardiest and most adaptable survive in the tough conditions of marginal lands, eliminating the weaker individuals, and thus changing the genetic make-up by the survival of the fittest over generations. It might also have been the case that these areas had attracted the hardy and the enterprising among migrants in the first place.

A further possibility springs to mind: it might also be that the observers were mistaken, that they saw what they expected to see, imparting their positive prejudices in the same way that those who pronounced their negative judgements might have done. Therefore, while we contented ourselves merely to reproduce opinions in the last chapter, because their near-universality seemed sufficient support, in what follows we shall attempt to subject unsupported judgements, wherever possible, to the test of such concrete data as may be available.

One piece of evidence relating to the alleged economical and spartan tendency of marginal living may be made available at once: there is no doubt that, typically, wages were lower there than in cities and central locations, and that in more recent

[9] Hallam (1958), 361; Schama (1988), 43–4; Thomson (1983), 64; Logan (1983), 16; and p. 34 above.

[10] Coulton (1933), 127.

times workers were less likely to organize and make militant demands.[11] Examples of the movement of work to the periphery in recent times may be likened to the well-known phenomenon of the 'product cycle', in which novel products or processes are tried out and perfected in central, high-wage regions first, to be transferred, when their mass production becomes possible, to the periphery or to low-wage countries to capture the benefits of cheap labour. However, it may well be that these lower wages in the margins sometimes merely reflected lower skills, so that labour costs there would be no lower and might even be higher than elsewhere. The independence enjoyed by farmers and others on marginal lands might also mean that at times they demanded higher wages than the norm.[12]

The hardihood and toughness of men living in marginal lands were frequently associated with martial skill, courage, and military prowess. There are here at least three different notions which are frequently confused and conflated in the literature: that these societies are by nature warlike, quarrelsome, or aggressive; that, irrespective of who started the fighting, their men make good soldiers; and that, thirdly, in warlike actions they are favoured by their terrain.

According to Toynbee, the 'vitality' of people in what he called the 'marches' would vary with the pressure on them; but most accounts assumed that it would be the marchers themselves who would initiate the violence, or at least be willingly involved in warlike actions. Thus the Scots Highlanders needed no outside pressure to engage in their raids and clan vendettas, in view of their 'wild independence, for which they were not less indebted to their poverty than to their valour', just as the Northumbrians, according to Camden, 'made fierce by their Scots neighbours', had 'addicted themselves, as it were, wholly to Mars and Armes'.[13]

The lawlessness of marginal regions has been touched on in Chapter 3 above, but here we might note the more favourable, even admiring accounts of the martial skills and prowess of their menfolk. The Swiss Alpine herdsmen have come in for the most fulsome romanticizing, in a literature which reached an apex in the eighteenth century but has continued in different forms until the present day. One strand of it, which has become part of the Swiss national myth, asserts that it was the courage and fighting ability of simple country lads which gained the cantons of the 'Inner' (High) Alps their early and much-envied freedom. In another, they are compared to the knights of old, men above all of honour, 'in remarkable affinity with the nobler form of life, albeit that is marked by the horse rather than cattle'. Some accounts went even further, claiming that 'these stockbreeders are the founders of many states'. Count Friedrich von Stolberg's panegyric—'I visit the battlefield where a handful destroyed whole armies, in fertile valleys I hear the sound of bells of cattle that provide food for the best and the happiest people, who are free as the

[11] Marshall and Walton (1981), 63; Gripaios *et al.* (1989); Plaum and Witthöft (1993), 359–60; Storper (1981), 29; Smith (1981), 230.

[12] Keeble (1976), 64,71; Erickson (1981), 141 ff.; Sweeney (1987), 200–1; Bailey and Culley (1813), 259.

[13] Toynbee (1959–64), ii. 171, 275; Armstrong (1883), 69; Richards (1982), 41; Tough (1928), 10; Camden (1971).

eagles of God and simple as doves'[14]—may be taken as a typical example of the extensive romanticizing literature. It was the independence and self-reliance needed by cattlemen on the mountains that was, according to some cultural anthropologists, responsible for the bundle of qualities which characterized mountain herdsmen alike in Inner Asia, in the Balkans with their 'Dinaric myth', and in the Scottish Highlands, as well as among plains herdsmen like Huns and Mongols. They included a patriarchal kinship culture, ancestor worship and blood feuds, traditionalism, self-assurance, and an honoured place for women in society. But above all, they included courage and a fighting spirit.

Thus, while the negative view saw the widespread recruitment of mountain people to have been the result of their poverty, as noted in Chapter 3 above, the positive view put it down to their military qualities: the Swiss were favoured among the rulers who hired mercenaries because of their reckless courage and the impetus of their attacks in battle. Other mountain people were similarly valued as hired soldiers. The Scottish Highlanders with their 'independent temper', 'martial spirit [and] readiness for adventure' were widely said to 'make excellent soldiers'. 'Mountaineers are warlike', according to Dr Johnson, 'Among a warlike people, the quality of highest esteem is personal courage.' 'All accounts agree', according to Salaman, 'that the Highlanders of the seventeenth and eighteenth centuries were an outstandingly sturdy folk; the endurance of their fighting men on long marches over trackless hill and dale, constantly excited the admiration and envy of the officers and men of regular English troops.' In similar vein, the Cumbrians were described as 'a hardy set of men; bear the greatest fatigue with patience'. Medieval Wales, too, bred 'men of an animal type, naturally swift-footed, accustomed to war'.[15]

In similar belief the French under Napoleon were eager to recruit Piedmontese from the Alpine valleys, while the Tyrolese impressed contemporaries by their vigour and their accurate shooting, as well as, apparently, by the love of their country. Venice, Genoa, Naples, and Spain recruited actively among mountain-dwelling Balkan Christians from the fifteenth century onwards. Later, soldiers from these regions also fought for France, Britain, and Russia. The Montenegrins were said to be capable of putting 20,000 fighting men into the field out of a population of 120,000. In turn, Muslim Albanians were recruited by the Sultan and earned themselves the nickname of 'Swiss of the Near East'. Among the Netherlanders, 'the men of Gelderland were known to be unparalleled as warriors'.[16]

[14] Much the best account is in Weishaupt (1992*a*), citation here on p.136, and his (1992*b*); also Braun (1984), 82; Niederer (1993), 261; Wandruszka (1980) 389. For the equivalent romanticized phase for the Scottish Highlands in *c.*1746–1811, see Womack (1989), 2, 77 ff.

[15] Kiernan (1988), 55, 62, 75; Defoe (1992), 238; Womack (1989), 35; Salaman (1987), 356; Jollie (1974), 35; Burgess (thesis, 1979), 3; Davies (1991), 34; Giraldus (1919), 16; Douglas (1899), 308; Phillips (1977), 84–5.

[16] Stolz (1955), 393; Daisenberger (1859–61), 135–8; Pappas (1981); Zumthor (1994), 27; Roglić (1970), 231; McNeill (1964), 76; Jelavich (1984), 84.

In some areas of the world, the martial reputation of mountain folk is still alive today. A soldier of the Karabakh Armenians, 'most [of whom] were and many remain mountain shepherds, accustomed to hardship', had this to say in the war of 1993–4:

> You can't blame the Azerbaijans for fighting so badly. They are peasants from the plains, and mountain people make better soldiers. Look what sort of people we are. There are only 150,000 of us and seven million of them but we have beaten them again and again.[17]

Something similar is frequently remarked of the nomad of the steppes who 'is economically a herdsman, politically a conqueror, and chronically a fighter': 'the nomad's whole existence', added Semple, 'breeds courage'. The 'constant cycle' in North African states, 'running from the conquest of the centre by a peripheral tribe, through the establishment of this tribe in the capital and its progressive disintegration under urban conditions, to the conquest of the centre by the next peripheral tribe', was found in Europe, too. Thus the Turks emerged in the fourteenth century out of their 'freeebooters' frontier principality' to conquer a large part of Europe and threaten the rest, before succumbing to soft urban living.[18]

By contrast, the mountains, and to a lesser extent forests and marshes, favour the defenders and make it difficult for an outside conqueror to subdue and hold down their denizens. The geographic configuration hampers the deployment of large numbers of regular troops in the form to which they are accustomed; it neutralizes the power of heavy artillery, which frequently could not be taken into the upper fastnesses or the swamps at all; and it reduces the value of the cavalry. The defenders, knowing the country, enjoy the power to inflict losses on the enemy from ambushes and by guerrilla tactics generally. Wales was said to be 'defended by high mountains, deep valleys, extensive woods, rivers, and marshes': Edward I in his conquest of the country 'had relay after relay of workmen to cut through the natural barrier of forest, and made a road . . . The axe was his weapon as much as the lance and the bow.' There were similar good military reasons for the English to cut back the woods of Ireland in the seventeenth century. The Turks were unable to use their cavalry and bowmen in the Transylvanian forests, the Baltic pagans could defeat the heavily armed Teutonic Knights by luring them into forests and swamps, and it was a similar use of terrain which enabled the Camisards to defy the French royal army for two years in 1702–4. Deep forest, 'where the enemy could not chase them without great company and great time to do it', and the deepest fens, like Crowland, inaccessible from all sides, 'except the North and East, and that only by narrow causays', defied the technology of the day until modern times. That is where the legend of Hereward the Wake was located. The barren Karst mountains became 'a frontier, a refuge and fortress in time of war'. It is also important to note that herdsmen's property and supplies were more mobile than those of the plainsmen, and therefore less easily ravaged and destroyed by an invading army. Conversely,

17 *The Times*, 13 July 1993.
18 Semple (1911), 486–93; Rokkan (1973*a*), 35; Wolf (1990), 35; Sugar (1977), 64.

conventional armies would be difficult to keep supplied in their areas.[19] Though large imperial armies might normally be in a position ultimately to crush rebellions and resistance in the forests or mountains, the costs would often be felt to be too high, particularly in view of the poverty and poor prospects of these areas, so that their low taxable or exploitable capacity became another deterrent aspect.

Thus it is not altogether surprising that 'the high mountains always were regions of retreats for people anxious to retain their cultural identity and political independence', while forests, also, became hiding places for refugees. Interestingly enough, Weber suggested that in the nineteenth century 'in the forests of the Pyrenees and notably the Ariège, people took up arms against police and administrators who were "newcomers to the region and ignorant of our rights, our needs, and the local situation" '. Nor will it be wondered at that when Napoleon undertook his (most unpopular) recruiting campaigns, evasions, 'as one would expect . . . were most numerous in areas where the physical terrain facilitated [them], in mountains, heavily forested or frontier areas'. Britain, recruiting Civil Defence volunteers at about the same time (1798), found that 'counties such as Brecknockshire, Carmarthenshire and Radnorshire which were isolated and mountainous, sparsely populated and heavily dependent on agriculture, responded poorly . . . On the eastern borders of Craven, in the isolated and sparsely populated Upper Wharfedale there was scarcely any enthusiasm.' Men living in mountainous country were also more able, and more likely, to kindle rebellions and anti-tax campaigns, while people living around high passes enjoyed considerable strategic power, either to levy tolls on, or to rob, travellers crossing their territory.[20]

All these are essentially strategic considerations. But there was also a second group of causes generally listed for the remarkable relative freedom from political domination and oppression on the one hand, and from economic and feudal exploitation on the other, enjoyed by marginal areas in the past. This was the frequent need of rulers and owners to attract settlers to these areas, requiring in many cases the offer of special privileges and immunities to compensate them for the costs of moving and the strangeness as well as the harshness and dangers of their new surroundings.

Marginal areas, as a matter of fact, frequently got away with lighter taxation burdens than 'core' areas, which 'invariably . . . become the most heavily taxed areas', including the Province of Holland in the Dutch Republic, Castile in Spain, the *pays d'election* in France, the Kingdom in Denmark, and southern English counties in Great Britain. In the France of the *ancien régime*, Parisians were taxed at ten times the rate levied on Bretons. The provinces of the Midi and the frontier were the most

[19] Giraldus (1919), 155; Morris (1901), 105; Urban (1975), 270; Ligou (1967), 129 ff.; Stevenson (1911), 214–17; Richter (1976), 66; Camden (1971), 410; Rowse (1978), 78; Barber (1974), 96; Boehm (1982), 27 ff.; O'Brien (1919), 106; Butlin (1976), 154; Johnson (1984), 613; Lampe and Jackson (1982), 74; McNeill (1964), 47; Sugar (1977), 219; Hoffmann (1977), 464.

[20] Lichtenberger (1978), 184; Colley (1984), 296–7; Weber (1976), 487, also 59, 106–7; Blache (1933), 169; Woolf (1991), 161; Ladurie (1974), 198, 269; Semple (1911), 552–3; Armstrong (1960), 53.

lightly taxed. The Isle of Skye, Dr Johnson noted, 'pay no customs, for there is no officer to demand them'.[21] The case has even been made, though not widely accepted, that it was the European states which arose in the periphery which turned out to be strongest and most durable, while those of the heartlands, Italy and Germany, remained fragmented far longer.[22]

All these are aspects of political freedom. Of at least equal significance was the relative freedom from personal exploitation and control, and in particular, from feudal domination and exactions. This has caused surprise in some quarters. In the case of England, where feudal services were commuted much earlier into cash payments in the marginal areas than in the more 'advanced' core areas, it has indeed been asked: 'how are we to explain the greater speed of commutation in the most economically backward part of England and the survival of a natural economy, in the shape of labour services, in areas of most active money turnover'—'a case of the periphery seemingly being more progressive than the core'. The Scottish case, where commutation occurred first in the 'peripheral areas' of the Hebrides and the Northern Isles, and only later in the 'more fertile areas', posed a similar question.[23] This was indeed a puzzle to those who took it for granted that marginal areas were both poor and backward.

In fact, the weakness of feudalism in the marginal lands was the rule rather than the exception. ' "Feudal" civilization was a civilization of the plains. In poor mountain areas, pastoral and individualistic, this "feudalism" had never fully established itself.' The view that it was the pastoral nature of the upland societies which helped to hold off the grasping hands of potential feudal lords was widespread. In addition, the open and originally plentiful spaces of the upland pastures made overall control and organization of village life less necessary. 'The pastoral regions . . . were largely free from manorial control.' In the marshy lands of Friesland, the cattle economy is similarly said to have inhibited exploitation by landlords. Forest areas also were frequently less tightly feudalized.[24]

Apart from their geographic configuration, it may also have been their more recent colonization which spared the marginal regions the feudal control suffered by the core areas. As population moved into 'marginal woodland and pastoral areas [the] limited regulation of their right to reside and to practice unlicensed trades was a factor in their attractiveness'. The great land reclamations of the eleventh and twelfth centuries in Europe 'contributed to the emancipation of the common man', which was thus owed to the 'hardy pioneers who cleared the forests, drained the marshes, and won land from the sea'. As another account put it succinctly: 'colonization bred freedom'. The fact that in the Alps feudalism hardly took root at all or, if it did, disappeared again rapidly, was said to have been due

21 Johnson (1984), 623; t'Hart (1993), 100; Jones (1955), 203–6; Crouzet (1993), 85; Vergil (1950), 39; Lebon (1935), 278.

22 Urwin (1982), 55.

23 Dodgshon (1987), quoting Kosminsky 271, 270 and (1981), 98.

24 Trevor-Roper (1969), 107; Pickl (1986*b*), 62–6; Hechter (1975), 58; TeBrake (1985), 130–1; Baltzarek (1979), 339; Morris (1995), 216.

partly to the extensive royal domains, where the pressure would normally be less, but also because of the privileges granted to those carrying out the necessary clearances. 'C'est donc une paysannerie libre qui vit et qui travaille dans les Alpes.' The widespread belief that marginal areas generally secured more freedom and earlier independence than others, and that it was, indeed, from there that the impulses went out which rolled back feudalism in the rest of Europe, provides possibly the most potent source of the admiration found for these areas in the literature.[25]

The terms 'freeedom' and 'independence', to repeat, thus conceal at least two different meanings: they may refer to the early shaking off of distant control by kings or emperors on the part of marginal areas; or they may refer to the privileges gained by peasants and others regarding their feudal service obligations and personal dependence, or, in more modern times, their tax burdens. There may also be, moreover, significant gains in some regions from escaping the restrictions imposed by urban guilds or other local authorities. Lastly, there are the peculiar privileges and freedoms enjoyed by miners, glass-workers, and others over the centuries. Many of these skilled workers were important in the life of marginal areas. We shall look at these in turn.

The freedoms granted to marginal populations took various forms in different parts of Europe. Regional variations were based on different traditions, on political contexts and legal provisions, as well as on the natural differences of the terrain, among other factors. It is therefore all the more remarkable that the lightening of the burden on marginal folk turned out to be so similar in principle in all the regions examined.

The northern English border counties, and in some respects their Scottish counterparts, qualified as marginal regions on at least two counts: they were hilly, bleak, and difficult of access, and they were far from the centre and close to the frontier. As one consequence of this, the border peasantry of Cumberland and Westmorland enjoyed an uncommon privileged form of tenancy, known as 'customary tenure' or 'tenant right'. It involved the obligation to undertake military service, which included an active campaign of up to eight days in Scotland, when called upon, as well as to pay rent, to be subject to fines and heriots, and possibly also to work boon days, to use the lord's mill, and meet other similar obligations; but, in return, the tenants had full rights of inheritance over their land and were free to dispose of it at will, while rents and usually also fines were fixed and low, and service dues were minimal. Additionally, they had the right to cut wood and bracken on paying a rent. Altogether, it has been held that this bundle of rights was 'tantamount to freehold'. Similar tenancies applied to Northumberland, as well as to border holdings in Scotland.[26] The Crown intervened periodically to protect these rights against encroachments by local magnates in order to maintain a ready and cheap defence force along the border.

[25] Smith (1990), 173; Clarkson (1971), 96; Dodgshon (1987), 254, 279–80; Bergier (1980), 215; Lyon (1957–8), 47–50; Barber (1974), 132, 141.

[26] Bouch and Jones (1961), 67; Bailey and Culley (1813), 205; Appleby (1978), 68–9; Tough (1928), 57; Winchester (1987), 62; Smith (1970), 204; Beckett (thesis, 1975), 140; Bean (1958), 57; Tuck (1991*c*), 590. For the negative aspects of life on the Anglo-Scottish border, see pp. 68–9 above.

As always, however, there was the danger that an armed border population could turn against its own ruler, and the northern marches were no exception. The Tudors faced rebellions in the north in 1489, 1513, and 1523, during the Pilgrimage of Grace in 1536–7, which was 'virtually the entire northern community in action: aristocrats, gentry, abbots and yeomen', and in the Northern Rebellion of 1569, the last expression of such independence. Until the Reformation, 'Cumberland had been a law unto itself'.[27] It was in part to curb the traditional, but dangerous indiscipline of the northern Marcher Lords that Henry VIII transferred much of the power of command of the levies to centrally appointed Marcher Wardens. By then, however, Scottish raids, as well as the custom of partible inheritance, which diminished the size of holdings, had greatly reduced the fighting powers, and especially the supply of horses, in the northern parishes—the latter a subject of almost unceasing complaint in the last decades of Tudor rule.[28]

The value of tenant right to the peasants is shown by the tenacity with which they tried to maintain it, as well as by the vigour with which the lords sought to abolish it, as soon as the justification of military border service had fallen away with the unification of the English and Scottish Crowns in 1603. In the event, the county of Northumberland fared differently from the two western English border counties. In the former, a region of powerful lords and large estates facing small tenant holdings, the lords were quickly able to turn the holdings into leases which allowed them to raise rents and, if need be, repossess the holdings: a law case won by the Percy estate in 1613 set the precedent, and others followed quickly. The Percys increased their revenues no less than fourfold between 1590/1 and 1632/3.[29]

In Cumberland and Westmorland, however, the lords were weaker and the tenants had greater resources. They repeatedly and successfully challenged in the courts the attempts to raise rents arbitrarily or deprive them of their rights over the land, finally winning their case in the Star Chamber. As a result, two-thirds of the land in the two counties were still held by 'customary tenure' in the 1790s,[30] and there survived into the modern era, in the two north-western counties, the phenomenon of a peasantry with rights to its land, practically unique in England. Known as 'statesmen' or, more romantically, as 'yeomen', their best time was in the seventeenth and much of the eighteenth centuries. It was only towards the end of this period that they had begun to suffer a relative decline owing to their inability to apply many of the new agricultural methods. In the nineteenth century the larger holders among them were eager to accept the landlords' offer of turning their holdings into freeholds, in return for allowing the restrictions on the pasture land to lapse. By the end of the nineteenth century, only about one-third of

27 Musgrove (1990), 198 ff.; Jewell (1991), 16; James (1966), 47 ff.; Clark (thesis, 1990), 381; Harrison (thesis, 1975).

28 Musgrove (1990), 20 ff.; Dixon (thesis, 1984), 31; Bain (1894–6).

29 Dixon (thesis, 1984), 188 ff.; Wrathmell (thesis, 1975), 164 ff.

30 Searle (thesis, 1983), 27–45 and (1986), 115; Watts (1971), 71 ff.; Ford (1908).

Lakeland farmers could still be termed 'yeomen', men of some independence, though now also fully integrated into a market economy.[31]

The liberties of the northern counties went back to the Middle Ages. From the twelfth to the fourteenth century, central Government largely left the north to fend for itself, to make its own treaties and buy off the Scots on its own. Many Saxon institutions survived there. Among them was the 'Cornage' tenure which obliged the holder to limited military service, but made him a subject of the sovereign rather than of his immediate lord. The 'drengage' vills, which had to do service in forest or hunting, also probably antedated the Conquest. The Anglo-Saxon term 'thane' similarly survived in the north, and the absence of hundreds as county divisions reflects the freedom from subsidies before the pacification under James I which made border service unnecessary and permitted the privileges associated with it to be abolished.[32] It remains to be added that the Welsh Marcher Lords were similarly 'ready to band together to preserve their cherished independence and to check the centralizing policy of the King' in the Middle Ages, while the upland Welsh kept largely 'free from more oppressive features of the manorial system'.[33]

On the Yorkshire uplands, and even in the Vale of York, the burden of the feudal manor also rested more lightly than in the southern counties, probably because of their late colonization. A form of tenancy similar to that of the yeoman or 'statesman' survived in the less accessible Yorkshire dales, and the lack of 'deference' shown by the dwellers on both sides of the Pennines is a recurring theme into the modern era. In general, the English moorlands had more 'generous' common rights, and the forests 'gave refuge to a great many people whose living depended on their common rights rather than a secure tenancy of land'. The fens, for their part, were not much 'disturbed by gentlemen, who did not choose to live in such an uncongenial climate. But . . . the fenlands attracted many landless poor in search of refuge. There was a connection between assarting and relative freedom of the peasant.'[34]

An older, non-feudal landholding system based on the Norse odal tenancy also survived in the Orkneys and Shetlands: the tenants there were freeholders, paying only a scat, the old land tax, and other public taxes but no feus or duties. Conversion to a more oppressive system, forced in part by the introduction of heavy taxes and fines, began only in the sixteenth century.[35]

[31] Beckett (1982) and (thesis, 1975), 139 ff.; Jones (1962); Searle (thesis, 1983), 133, 193 and (1993), 147; Walton (1986); Marshall (1972), 250; Hutchinson (1794), 39, 41; Smailes (1960), 298; Humphries (thesis, 1993), 342–5; Wordsworth (1974), 321; Dilley (thesis, 1991), 96 ff.

[32] Musgrove (1990), *passim*; Hinde (1857), 44–5; Hodgson (1827–58), Part III, ii. 251, 258; Smailes (1960), 93; Vinogradoff (1908), 61–4; Wilson (1901), 315–20; Fleming (1882), 4 and (1889); Kapelle (1979), 11, 132, 158; Joliffe (1926), 1–2; Sawyer (1979), 8; Reid (1920); Graham (1925); Harrison (thesis, 1975), 116.

[33] Hechter (1975), 57; Evans (1949–50), 24; Owen (1991*c*), 649.

[34] Quotations from Thirsk (1987), 51, 49, 55; also Moore (1965), 28; Hudson (1989*c*), 74; Mingay (1990), 24; Smith (1990), 173; Dyer (1989), 52; Pettit (1968), 152, 162; Dodgshon (1975), 332; Beresford (1954), 231; Bohstedt (1983), 177; Newell (1925), 77; Spencer (1991), 56; Lucas (*c*.1880), 60; Ashcroft (1984); Hartley and Ingilby (1979), 61.

[35] Shaw (1980), 34 ff.

One type of peasant found in the Domesday Book who enjoyed relative freedom, the Sokeman, does not, however, appear to have been associated with marginal land, except perhaps in the fens. The origin of the Sokemen's status, which clearly antedates the Conquest, is in dispute; but since the greatest concentrations of them were enumerated in Lincolnshire and East Anglia, the most common explanations are that their freedom was either linked to the Danish occupation of the area, or derived from the extensions and liberties associated with the marshlands of those counties.[36]

The impressive schemes of drainage and extension in the Fenlands in the Middle Ages, noted in Chapter 2 above,[37] of necessity required the kind of co-operation among the villagers which gave them self-confidence and a taste for self-government; they also obliged the landlords—mostly religious houses—to offer concessions, including at times freedom from tithes, to attract colonists, and to allow some tangible return on the investment in land reclamation which would otherwise not be made at all. Both these factors tended to give the fen population privileges beyond those of the neighbouring dry lands and evolved the tradition of having 'always been distinguished for their sturdy independence'.[38]

While it has been pointed out that the fens became a 'refuge for successive rebellions', and that 'in English history much of the significance of the marsh, like that of the mountain, lay in its inaccessible character', the rebelliousness there tended to look inward rather than taking the outward form found among mountain folk, and to be military rather than social. The cycles of revolts around 'Hereward' in the eleventh century, in Stephen's reign (1139 and 1142), of the barons (1216), and in 1265 (in the reign of Henry III) were said to be of this type.[39]

The history of the marshlands on the opposite shore of the North Sea, in the Netherlands, shows some remarkable parallels. Here also, not only the 'peripheral location and the late colonisation of the peat bog', but above all the impressive drainage schemes and polder works were said to have led to a relatively early freedom from feudal obligations and oppression, not least because of the terms on which the authorities, the Count of Flanders and the Bishop of Utrecht, encouraged marshland colonization, but also because of the effective co-operative nature of village dyke and polder work. The task of maintaining the dykes and associated works required specialist knowledge on the part of the dyke-reeve, of local boards (*Waterschappen*) and their wider regional associations, rather than feudal exploitation. Moreover, it provided a 'determination not to yield to foreign tyrants what had been laboriously wrested from the sea'. Stockbreeding, as ever, also made for independence. By the early thirteenth century, the lands of the Count of Flanders

[36] King (1973), 55–8; Hallam (1965), pp. vii–viii, 201 and (1954), 8; Bailey (1989), 46; Vinogradoff (1908), 431; Darby (1971), 50, 168; Kapelle (1979), 64–5; Lyon (1957–8), 58.

[37] See p. 34 above.

[38] Darby (1940), 119; Williams (1982), 87–8; Hallam (1965), 218 and (1954), 40; Spufford (1974), 302, 306; North and Thomas (1973), 143.

[39] Darby (1940), 106 ff., 143–4.

were free of imperial authority; in 1323 the Estates pushed out the clerical lords of Utrecht and in 1430 the 'Federation of Freedom' determined to abolish all arbitrary power over drainage and embankments.[40] The manorial system may have entered the Netherlands from the south in the tenth century, but bloody battles halted its progress three centuries later. 'Serfdom . . . was rare and short-lived, leaving few traces past the twelfth century.' The northern provinces of the Netherlands were hardly touched by feudalism at all, possibly because of their poverty, as well as because of the difficulty of access to them. 'The uncommonly weak position of the nobility in the northern Netherlands stands out clearly in a Europe' of *c.*1500.[41] Thus the Dutch freed themselves early on from both imperial and feudal governance.

Possibly the most remarkable achievement was that of the people of Dithmarschen, a boggy land lying between the lower Elbe and north Frisia. On the basis of the success of its collectively undertaken drainage work, their 'clan' organization was given increasing autonomy by the Archbishop of Bremen and Hamburg, and in 1447 their sworn communities received a constitution that gave them virtual independence. They defeated a superior Danish army sent to put them down in 1500 and were subdued only in 1559. The Stedingerland on the lower Weser, being smaller, fared less well, though its people were able to defeat feudal armies sent against them in 1229 and 1231. A massive crusade supported by the pope finally overcame their resistance in a bloody battle in 1234.[42]

Whether, as has been stated, it was the early liberation from feudal rule which made England, in common with other marginal areas,[43] into one of the earliest bastions of liberty which spread outwards from there into Europe may well be debatable. There is less doubt in the case of the Netherlands that it was the fight against the natural hardships of their marginal location which prepared their people for their similarly successful early adoption of the free bourgeois spirit, which blossomed out in due course in the form of Dutch sea power and hydraulic engineering in the battles for independence from Spain. But it is perhaps in the Swiss Alps, above all, that the marginal character of the landscape has been held responsible for the development of free institutions. There, the freedoms first won in the high valleys of the 'Inner Alps' are almost universally believed to have radiated outwards to neighbouring cantons to create the most remarkable bastion of liberty in the midst of feudal, and later absolutist, Europe.

The beginnings are shrouded in mist and in much myth-making: much of what passes for Swiss history in the critical thirteenth and fourteenth centuries is surmise tinged by ideology, rather than historical knowledge. In particular, it is not clear

[40] Van Zanden (1993), 19; de Vries (1974), 25–6, 34 and (1983), 156–7; Schama (1988), 35, 39–40; Andreae (1952), 162–4; Slicher van Bath (1982), 25 and (1946), 122; TeBrake (1985), 122; van Houtte (1977), 7; Rösener (1992), 156; Tracy (1990), 9–10.

[41] Thompson (1918–19), 161–2; de Vries (1973), 194 and (1974), 41; Lambert (1971), 181; Slicher van Bath (1946), 119.

[42] Rösener (1992), 233–47.

[43] See p. 96 above.

that in 1291, the foundation date of the oath-bound confederation, peasants were concerned at all: it may well have been the squires who wanted freedom, as later it was to be the patricians of the towns who led the fight for it: 'Berceau des libertés médiévales, les Alpes adoptèrent tacitement le principe oligarchique qui devait fournir la base de l'Ancient Régime en Suisse et à l'étranger.'[44] Some early relief from feudal burdens was achieved by purchase in the case of Uri (1230) and Schwyz (1241), but there is no doubt that freedom from the Habsburgs had ultimately to be won in tough battles.

Beyond the strategic advantages provided by the terrain, there were several other factors which favoured the cantons that joined together in the Confederation, as it was also to favour the later comers. Among them was the poverty, and the difficulties of collecting feudal dues, especially from the higher slopes of the Alps; the privileges granted to peasants who cleared land; the necessity for the peasants to develop village or parish communal organization which stood them in good stead in battling against authority; the urban liberties in northern Italy which were taken as models by Alpine villages; and possibly also the population losses in the fourteenth century, after which it became impossible to maintain any form of serfdom in the uplands.[45]

It will be noted that these factors favoured both types of freedom—from foreign domination and from feudal exactions and servile status. These freedoms were also achieved later in other parts of Switzerland. Thus the Engadine uplands put up an early resistance to their bishop's rule, while in the isolated valleys of the Grisons, the 'land of the three confederations', there were no fewer than fifty tiny village democracies. The Lower Engadine, too, developed a full democracy in which each (male) villager took part. Appenzell gained its freedom in the fifteenth century by military action, though it took another 150 years to get rid of its landlord burdens. Finally, in Zurich, to take a canton of the foothills dominated by its city, it was the town patriciate against which the peasants rebelled in their 1525 rising, demanding an end to the payments of rent for land which they held by *Erbrecht*, the kind of fully secure and heritable tenancy familiar also to other marginal regions.[46] As noted above, the 'Walsers', who apparently had not fully shaken off their servile status before they set off on their migration, achieved a free status and special privileges when they settled on the upper mountain valleys of the Grisons and neighbouring territories from the thirteenth century onward.[47]

The people of Fribourg achieved their liberty in the sixteenth century, but other Romance-speaking Alpine dwellers generally lagged behind in their move to freedom.[48] An important, and in its way striking exception to this was formed by the

[44] Ruffieux (1980), 321; Mayer (1937), 230–1, 282 and (1965*b*), 12–13; Hauser (1972), 27; Nabholz (1924), 16; Gilomen (1991), 470; Veyret (1978), 67; Odermatt (1981), 49 ff.; and pp. 91–2 above.

[45] Bätzing (1991), 82; Mathieu (1992), 63, 83; Niederer (1993), 261; Mathieu and Stauffacher (1986), 320–2; Bergier (1983), 78, 83 and (1980), 181–5; Clavadetscher (1976), 5–6; and, in general, Coulton (1933), 125.

[46] Schwarzenbach (1931), 58–64; Mathieu (1987), 6; Schläpfer (1984), 3; Nabholz (1938), 491–2.

[47] See p. 83 above.

[48] Bätzing (1991), 37, 49; Bergier (1983), 95; Morard (1971), 275.

League of Briançon, an area in Dauphiné on the Alpine watershed between France and Italy. The origins of this 'peasant republic', organized into five *escartons*, were to be found in the early freedom purchased by the city of Briançon—according to some, the highest city in Europe—itself; in part in the need of the Dauphin for immediate cash, but not least also in the strong democratic and communal tradition of the Alpine peasantry. By a contract concluded in 1343, and in return for an immediate payment of 12,000 gold ducats down, and 4,000 gold ducats a year thereafter, the region was granted a remarkable degree of self-government. In addition to being freed from all taxes and other exactions, it had charge of all its woods, roads, and markets, as well as its own lower jurisdiction; it had rights of unobstructed trade across the Alps, which it was able to turn to lucrative account; and its citizens became free men, *libre, franc et bourgeois*, and had the freedom to dispose of their property at will. The Dauphin remained formal ruler and military commander and retained the right of superior jurisdiction, but each new ruler had to confirm the liberties on his accession. In contrast to the Swiss cantons, however, the *Grand Escarton*, which represented the whole of that area, was too weak to stand by itself in its external relations, and when the area of three of the *escartons* was awarded to Piedmont by the Treaty of Utrecht in 1713, the soldiers of both Piedmont and France soon moved in to clear the forest and erect their frontier barriers.[49]

Tyrol was another area in which the peasant population was granted some early privileges. Among the causes are thought to have been the need to attract settlers, the difficulty of enforcing feudal obligations in the mountainous terrain, the influence of the freedom of the north Italian cities with which active trading links were established from the early Middle Ages, possibly also some remnants of a primitive democratic tradition among the Germanic settlers and, not least, the peculiar position of the rulers, the Counts of Tyrol, who 'had no interest to keep the peasants in unfree servitude', but on the contrary, sought to win them as allies in their fight to reduce the power of the nobles.[50]

In terms of property holding, the *Erbleihe* or *Erblehen* gave the peasant full rights of disposal over the land, provided he paid his rent and dues, and kept the land in good order; only in the case of alienation did the lord have first right of refusal. The legal breakthrough came when the jurisdiction over this tenant right was removed from the manorial to the territorial (ruler's) court. Moreover, the commune had long had rights over police and fire regulation, tax collection, poor relief, and conscription. More important still in the view of many observers was the right of the peasantry to send delegates to the Land Assembly by 1400 at the latest, which was of particular significance since the Margrave Louis of Brandenburg had promised in 1342 not to raise taxes or enact new laws without the consent of that assembly; at a census in 1427 all inhabitants, free and unfree, were listed together, in a near-modern notion of citizenship. Serfdom, abolished earlier on the estates of the ruler, was abolished

[49] Rosenberg (1988), 7, 39 ff.; Nabholz (1931); Cameron (1984), 13–4; Bätzing (1991), 80–1; Bergier (1980), 241–2.

[50] Mayer (1965), 13.

everywhere by the sixteenth century as incompatible with the *Landrecht.* In consequence, the decrees of the Emperor Joseph II towards the end of the eighteenth century which freed the serfs in Austria had no need to mention Tyrol, which had long since passed that stage.[51] The similarities with Switzerland are striking, but so are the differences: in particular, there was no political independence for Tyrol which remained within the Habsburg Empire.

There were some early signs of privileges and freedoms for the peasants in other Alpine lands also. They were awarded usually for similar reasons, the need to attract and hold settlers in harsh conditions on the one hand, and the difficulty of enforcing feudal obligations on the other, but nowhere did they reach the extent found in Switzerland and in Tyrol. Thus Salzburg's early liberties were lost in the Counter-Reformation of the sixteenth century. Upland peasants in Styria and Carinthia, though not those in the plains, had by the mid-eighteenth century achieved *Freizügigkeit* (freedom to move), control over the commons, and the right to their own jurisdiction, and they could count, moreover, on being supported by the ruler against their lords. Vorarlberg, like Tyrol, benefited by the early emancipation decreed on the ruler's estates. Some peasants in Upper Bavaria also obtained hereditary tenancies, and in Upper Austria there were special rights granted on the assart of new lands.[52]

Examples of early emancipation from feudal obligations can be found also in other German mountain areas, such as Swabia, the Siegerland, and the Black Forest. On the marginal lands of Scandinavia, also, farmers were free of most feudal constraints. The pioneers who cleared forests and wastes in Russia in the fourteenth and fifteenth centuries were similarly rewarded with privileges in an environment of general labour shortage.[53] The Basques of the Pyrenees, to cite another example, were not only freed from taxation and military conscription but were in 1526 even given a kind of collective status of nobility. These privileges were modified only in 1876.[54]

The advantages, especially for economic development, of freedom from the burdens of feudalism, however defined, are numerous, as is frequently stressed in the national histories of the Netherlands or Britain. Two of them stand out: one is the encouragement, or at least the removal of barriers, for able individuals from the lower orders to strike out into economic enterprises of their own; the other is the opportunity for economic surplus to be invested in a productive way instead of being wasted in conspicuous consumption or aggressive warfare.

It is worth asking why the people of the Balkans failed to gain the kind of privileges and self-government achieved by a large part of the Alpine population. Conditions

[51] Günther (1930), 99–100; Mayer (1959*a*), 231 ff. and (1959) and (1965), 13 and (1937), 245 ff.; Wopfner (1903), 6 ff., 62 ff. and (n.d.), 18; Cole and Wolf (1974), 31–5, 70–2, 108; Stolz (1955), 396; Blickle (1973), 395–6.

[52] Blickle (1973), 60, 396 ff.; Toch (1989), 69; Daisenberger (1859–61), 71 ff.; Mayer (1937), 271; Pickl (1986*b*), 72–4, 86; Rösener (1992), 155.

[53] Plaum and Witthöft (1993), 325; Mayer (1937), 232; Gissel *et al.* (1981), 21–7; Koebner (1971), 82; Smith (1971*b*), 542–3; Rösener (1992), 39; Birnbaum (1987), 31.

[54] Barahona (1983), 273.

were not dissimilar: high mountains, inaccessible valleys, and the attempted rule by an alien empire, in this case the Turks rather than the Habsburgs. According to Braudel, the reason was because the Balkans lacked the resources, the collective discipline, the quality of the human population, and the good roads of the Alps.[55]

Those who know Balkan history more intimately, however, favour a quite different explanation: until the mid-eighteenth century, at least, the Balkan people did very much better under Turkish rule than they had under their 'own' rulers; they had been freed from their servile status and their overlords, and they enjoyed security of tenure, subject only to eminent domain. Moreover, their taxes were lower, they were left a large degree of cultural and political autonomy, and they enjoyed more religious freedom than under the previous dominion of the Catholic Church. In 1519 the Ottomans granted to the Christian subject population a form of self-government, a local administration of justice, the right to bear arms, and exemption from some taxation. There was also the fact of internal disunity among the several groups, with their tribal loyalties and their different Greek, Bulgar, Serb, Croat, and Vlach languages and traditions. As was made clear in the case of Briançon, a certain minimum critical mass was necessary to give a community the power to resist domination from outside and keep a necessary minimum foothold in the valleys. However, Albanians and Montenegrins were never really under Turkish control. By the nineteenth century, when conditions had deteriorated, the 'mountain villages became centres of resistance against foreign domination' and vigorous and ultimately successful drives for independence were set in train.[56]

The fate of the Carpathians was slightly different. Some of the Magyar plains people fled to those mountains for security, and the Turks made little effort to follow them there, probably because of their dense forests and general difficulties of access. However, while the peasants of the Sub-Carpathians had become relatively free by the sixteenth century, thereafter local freedoms were more likely to have been granted because of mining activity there.[57]

Farther east, privileges and freedoms were generally limited either to colonists to encourage them to settle on marginal lands, or to those who had to guard a dangerous frontier. Possibly the most extensive settlement movement which used the promise of enhanced freedom and privileges to attract colonists was the medieval German colonization drive to the east. This will be treated in greater detail in Chapter 6 below. It was preceded by the hill settlements of central Germany, which may well have been the model for the methods used in the drive eastwards. The motto was 'Rodung macht frei'.[58]

[55] Braudel (1976), i. 33, ii. 664.

[56] Hösch (1972), 104–6; Hoffman (1980), 114; Dujcev *et al.* (1977), 249, 262–4; Pappas (1981), 37; Boehm (1982), 30–2; Stoianovich (1989), 259; Wace and Thompson (1972), 254; Hoffman (1977), 439, 473; Jelavich (1984), 30, 35, 83, 157; Sugar (1977), 96, 220, 231; McGowan (1981), pp. x, 54–5; Lampe and Jackson (1982), 6.

[57] Hollander (1960–1), 82; Probszt (1966), 170–5; Stefanescu (1989), 93–6; also Ch. 8 below.

[58] Timm (1960), 95; Mayer (1937), 231–2; Rösener (1992), 26, 227.

Following the devastation of the Thirty Years War, which was particularly widely felt in Germany, a number of rulers there set out to repopulate their lands by offering special terms to immigrants, some of whom were skilled and possibly even propertied men driven out by religious persecution. Other examples of the promises of privileges could also be found in the eighteenth century, and in lands of eastern Europe.[59]

As for fortified frontiers, the English-Scottish border was by no means the only one which required a defensive line of settlements in which military readiness was traded for privileged forms of tenancy and of self-government. On the continent of Europe, the Austrian Military Frontier was the most prominent such arrangement. It was established originally as a defensive line in 1522, when the advancing Turks, having captured Belgrade in the preceding year, succeeded in penetrating in temporary raids as far as Carniola and Styria. It was manned originally by Christian refugees driven northwards by the Turks, and financed by the Austrian provinces closest to the border. The first recorded charter granted to the *Uscoce* (refugee) settlers was dated 1535 and awarded them, in return for hereditary military service, land allotments as hereditary fiefs and freedom from all taxes and robots for twenty years, thereafter payment to the Archduke Ferdinand of a quitrent only. Interestingly enough, a similar 'military frontier' was built up on the Turkish side of the border.

The Austrian privileges granted to the borderers were confirmed by a statute of the Emperor in 1630, which incorporated the family organization of the Zadruga into the military framework and allowed the leaders to be elected, subject to the veto of the Austrian Colonel Commandant. A law of 1667 reduced the judicial self-government of the frontier people, and by the eighteenth century, as the Turkish threat receded, the administration of the region became both slack and confused. Reforms over the period 1735–48 brought the region directly under the control of Vienna, tightened military discipline, and permitted the *Grenzer* troops to be used outside their area. From then on they were increasingly aligned with the regular army and used mainly to suppress rebellion at home, but they also acquitted themselves well in the Napoleonic wars, and as a reward had the right to their land made perpetual once more in 1807, as long as the family provided military service. The Military Border District was abolished in 1881.[60]

The other major group in Europe to enjoy privileges on the basis of frontier military service was formed by the Cossacks. Recruited first in informal arrangements in the fifteenth century to protect Muscovy from roving Tartars on the southern frontier, their ethnic and social origins are obscure and controversial. In the course of the following centuries, the Cossacks helped to settle, as well as defend, the empty frontier lands and, as their counterparts in Austria, were used increasingly to secure

[59] Hauser (1972), 335–44; Fehn (1979), 686; Weiss (1979), 458; Layer (1979), 886; Rösener (1992), 39; Denecke (1992), 312; Davies (1981), 282; Franz (1939).

[60] Rothenburg (1960); Amstadt (1969); Kampus (1981); Valentinitsch (1981); Sugar (1977), 104 ff.; Jelavich (1984), 145 ff.; Lampe and Jackson (1982), 62.

the Tsar's rule internally as well as forming part of the imperial army in campaigns outside their territory. The grant of a wide measure of self-government in the beginning, together with freedom from taxation, rights to their land, and freedom from personal serfdom were secure only as long as there was some balance between Russia, Poland/Lithuania, and the Tartars or Turks, respectively. With the growing supremacy of the Tsar's government in the eighteenth century, the Cossacks' freedom of manœuvre was much reduced, though they were never repressed to the level of the rest of the peasantry.[61] Freedom from some dues and services in return for military service at the frontier or the 'marches' was also not unknown in other parts of Europe, such as Banat, Bohemia, or Transylvania.[62]

Some responsibility for driving those seeking freedom into the margins of Europe was also shared by the numerous town guilds which prohibited technical innovations and prevented the settlement of newcomers. Expanding and new trades were thus forced to settle outside the jurisdiction of the towns, and in some cases this drove them into marginal territories, which in that way became areas of freedom as well as of innovation. The related case of the Zürcher Oberland, where the cotton industry took root because the lowlanders refused to allow new settlements, is well documented, as is the move of settlers into the Black Forest to escape the restrictions of guild towns, and the replacement of the guild-dominated textile centres of York and Beverley by the free settlements on the West Riding slopes.[63] Even in England, it was not unknown for jealous villagers to drive fullers or farmers into marginal areas. Not least among the causes of the spread of the textile industry into the Lancashire and Yorkshire uplands in the sixteenth and seventeenth centuries was the fact that these areas were exempt from the restrictive Weavers' Acts.[64]

Lastly, miners, whose skills were eagerly sought after by medieval and early modern rulers, were granted special privileges and freedoms in all parts of Europe. Possibly these went back to Roman practices, but in the twelfth and thirteenth centuries, 'it was almost as if an invisible lawgiver inspired miners, landlords, and territorial rulers from one end of Europe to the other with a single conception of right or wrong, which could be translated into custom or positive law. For a brief spell . . . the Western Europeans almost managed to universalise among the miners freedom and self-government.'

The earliest known charters of the miners date from the twelfth century, but these, in turn, were often based on existing practice. Thus the Bishop of Trient granted privileges in 1175 to the local silver-miners, who by the early thirteenth

[61] Goehrke (1980); Stökl (1953) and (1975), 775; Davies (1981), 144; Longworth (1970); Gerhard (1959), 225–8; McNeill (1964), 49, 111–13, 193.

[62] Wilson (1901), 326–7; Morawitzky (1856–7); Mellor (1989), 76; Graus (1975), 60; Schreiber (1965), 172; McNeill (1964), 10–11; Lampe and Jackson (1982), 64.

[63] Mauersberg (1960), 330 ff.; Pfister (1989), 637; Braun (1960); Kellenbenz (1965), 409; Gothein (1970), 58; Smail (thesis, 1988), 41; Jennings (1992), 42; François (1966), 259; Kisch (1964); Dodgshon (1987), 261–2.

[64] Daniels (1920), pp. xxviii–xxix, 3–6; Outhwaite (1986), 12; Kerridge (1985), 12; Kellenbenz (1965), 382–3; Ch. 10 below.

century had their own court, were freed from taxes, and had other rights, including fishing rights and the right to catch birds.[65] The first extant Cornwall charter, dated from 1201, confirmed ancient freedoms and privileges of miners. Though partially revoked on pressure from the Barons in 1215, it was soon renewed, and a new charter was granted in 1305. The Cornish miners had the right not merely to search for tin, but also to divert streams and use turves for fuel. The Alston silver and lead mines were taken under the special protection of King Henry III in 1234, confirming all the liberties and customs which they had enjoyed from times past. These included the right to search for timber for smelting, and to have their own judge and bailiff. It was in 1288 that an enquiry in Derbyshire set out the mining laws and practices which were then thought to exist there.[66] Privileges in the Harz mines were confirmed in 1219, and in the Erzgebirge the old Iglau code of 1365 was modernized by the Annaberg code of 1509. Upper Franconia worked under the law of 1323. The Balkan mining code dates from 1412, while the famous Schwaz mine in Tyrol enacted its own rule book in 1427. The silver-miners in particular had privileges, including the 'right of faggot and water, exemption from ordinary taxes and tolls, from military service, from the obligations of a service tenure, and from disability and forfeiture', nor could they have their tools seized for debt, and they usually had their own jurisdiction.[67]

It is noticeable that while the original regulations favoured the miner as both principal and active producer, later legislation was obliged to recognize the rising power of capital and the growing divergence of interest between the shareholders on the one hand who inherited the privileges granted earlier, and the actual miners. Thus in the Gastein/Rauris gold and silver mines in Salzburg, an order of 1477 included safety rules for the protection of the workers and decreed a 44-hour week; similarly, in south Tyrol, an 8-hour day and a free labour contract became the rule in the sixteenth century. The extensive bureaucracy which evolved in the mining industry in the German lands had as its task not merely to control the operations in a technical sense, but to regulate wages, conditions, and social welfare provisions for the mining communities.[68]

Some mines were located in forests, as in the Forest of Dean, and it was in woodlands that glass-makers, another free and privileged class of men, were to be found. Some details for these groups will be discussed later in this book.

It was thus a widespread feature of marginal lands that the settlers on them had extensive rights over their holdings, amounting in many cases to the equivalence of

[65] Quotation from Nef (1952), 456; also Palme (1984*b*); Forbes (1956), 66; also pp. 160 and 189 below.

[66] Lewis (1907), 34–7, 69–70; Salzman (1950); Hatcher (1973), 48; Hodgson (1827–58), Part II, iii. 46–8; Ford and Rieuwerts (1968), 4–10; Lander (1970), 323, 331; Farey (1811–17), i. 356–65; Rees (1968), ii. 45 ff.; Agricola (1950), 77 (note), 84–5; Kirkham (1968), 100; Raistrick and Jennings (1965), 92 ff.

[67] Lewis (1907), 73; Poller (1970), 319–20; Ritschel (1983), 39; Egg *et al.* (1986), 102; Wilsdorf and Quellmalz (1971), 532; Cirković (1987), 167.

[68] Ludwig and Gruber (1987), 13; Palme (1984*a*), 114. Also in general, Raistrick and Jennings (1965), 47, 92–5; Salzman (1950), 88; Jenkins (1972), 33 ff.

freehold. They provided, in other words, early examples of private real property among the mass of a region's population.[69] This remained true even if some land, such as mountain pasture, was not individually managed, but communally held and administered: this should in no way be taken to mean that it did not constitute a form of private property.

It was always good agricultural logic to hold pastures and wastes of the village in common, and to operate common pasturing (including the separate summer pasture) further up the valleys. This clearly saved resources and reduced the number of people necessary to guard a flock or herd of a given size. At the same time, animal husbandry was always a vital part of the village economy, and a village's pasture was a highly prized and controlled possession.

The ability of mountain folk to organize, allocate, and husband their vital grassland resources has, like their freedoms, excited the admiration of contemporaries and historians alike. The exact form of administering the pastureland varied with local circumstance and with historical development. It would be usual in the early stages of settlement, when the population was thin on the ground, not to trouble too much about the use of the upland or summer pasture. As population and the number of animals increased and adjacent villages began to dispute what had now become valuable territory, boundaries were drawn and grazing stinted in some form. In some cases, though by no means everywhere, a later stage still might be the division of the common pasture into separate holdings.[70]

Thus what appeared as common pasture on the top of the Mendip hills was in fact carefully stinted land, watched and guarded. When, in the period 1771–97, it looked as though enclosing such land would pay dividends, each village enclosed 'its' part of the hilltop.[71] Such developments were typical also for the north of England where, in some cases, a rent or cornage was paid for the village upland pasture. In the Swiss High Alps, the mountain summer pasture became what was possibly the key element of the economy, determining the character of village and public life and frequently controlling the timetable of its agricultural activities. The form of ownership in the higher valleys was generally either communal or corporative.[72] One peculiar system found in many upland areas was the *Markgenossenschaft*. This form of organization, which had ancient roots, might combine the people of several villages sharing upland commons and forests. Allocation of use would often depend on the size of an individual's valley holding, but a main purpose of the organization was to prevent outsiders from sharing in the benefits. In the canton Uri, a poor mountain community, the increase in the price of sharing in the commons developed a startling momentum in the sixteenth century, as soon as its value became

[69] Léon *et al.* (1976), 646; Veyret (1978), 77; de Vries (1974), 50, 55.

[70] Searle (thesis, 1983), 100–4, 150; Marshall (1958), 11–13; Zimmermann (1989), 105–6; Sandberger (1979), 737; Günther (1930) 368.

[71] Neale (1976), 93; Williams (1971), 66–8; Joliffe (1926), 10–13.

[72] Kistler (1962), 127; Weiss (1941), 163, 174; Mathieu (1992), 79, 182; Odermatt (1981), 78 ff.; Nabholz (1924), 9; Schwarzenbach (1931), 131–2; Bergier (1980), 213; Niederer (1980*a*), 20; Viazzo (1989), 111.

apparent: the charge for purchasing membership rose from fl. 4 at the beginning of the century to fl. 300 at its end. In 1621 a ten-year stop was decreed, and by the end of the eighteenth century, the fee had risen to fl. 1,000: the money raised in this way was used to boost the poor-law funds. For the whole period 1800–50 only ten persons gained new citizenship. Somewhat unusually, the grazing rights in Uri were tied to individuals rather than to valley property, though they were modified by the size of the holding.[73]

Similarly, the intercommoning on drained land gained from marsh and sea in the Fens should not be taken to mean that it was considered of little value. It was considered a valuable property, it was stinted, its usage was regulated, and grazing from outside the village was paid for.[74]

Many observers concur in the view that it was precisely their marginal existence in difficult terrain which forced the communities on mountains, in forests, and in marshlands to maintain an unusually close cohesion and to collaborate generally more effectively in order to survive than was necessary for people living on the plains. They were, in Braudel's words, battling with nature, and they were therefore much more conscious of existing in a precarious eco-system, though, as always, the actual methods used depended on traditions and historical experience.[75]

Possibly the most obvious need for co-operation as a condition of survival obtained on lands gained by embankment from the sea. The exact methods for allocating rights and duties varied, but the obligation to keep dykes in repair and drainage channels cleared was common to all these lands and had to be regulated in detail in a manner which ensured that it remained effective over the centuries. In the mountains, the threat represented by avalanches and by torrents as the snows began to melt was only a degree less urgent, and there, too, only common action could avert disaster. Mountain communes were also normally responsible for maintaining paths, bridges, and the like, and sometimes other tasks were added, such as keeping the Alp huts in repair.[76]

The high degree of initiative shown in this respect in past centuries was forced on people living in marginal areas not merely by the exigencies of their natural environment but also by their isolation. The outside world was rarely willing to help, often ignorant of their needs, and sometimes hostile. The self-help imposed on them strengthened the inner cohesion of the marginal communities.[77]

We may summarize the evidence presented so far by stating that the favourable, even romantic notions current about life on the margin thus concentrated largely on the alleged sturdiness, the heroism, the freedom, and the

[73] Arnold (1989), 61 ff.; Schwarzenbach (1931), 58 ff.; Hauser (1972), 27 and (1964), 5; Bielmann (1972), 97–8.

[74] Darby (1940), 18, 67; Vinogradoff (1908), 289; Semple (1911), 575.

[75] Braudel (1976), i. 57–8; Viazzo (1989), 24–8; Braun (1984), 63; McNeill (1992), 7.

[76] Bergier (1988), 30; Semple (1911), 323; Hoskins (1955), 78; Hallam (1965), 38–9, 166, 222 and (1954), 24; Darby (1940), 155; Messerli and Brugger (1984*a*), 58; Kienholz (1984), 395; Weiss (1941), 249–50; Niederer (1993), 350.

[77] Novosel'tsev (1986), 15–16; Braudel (1976), i. 30; Cole and Wolf (1974), 120 ff.

necessary social organization to be found there. But beyond it, the healthier living, the family relationships, and the intellectual development in marginal areas also received much attention.

The better health attested to mountain people was to some extent a consequence of natural conditions rather than social action. The relatively low density of population, and the rarity, in many valleys, of contact with outsiders most likely accounts for the lesser impact of contagious diseases, including the Black Death.[78] The absence of malaria was notable, as was the low incidence of tuberculosis. The thin, clean air of the Alpine uplands had commended itself as early as the eighteenth century as a form of therapy for consumptives: the first sanatorium was opened in Switzerland in 1841. But at the same time, the high incidence of goitre in Alpine lands, as in upland Derbyshire—because of the lack of iodine—was also commented on.[79]

More commonly, human agency, including a healthy and adequate diet, clean living, and care in the upbringing of children, was held responsible for the superior health of the mountain folk. Contrary to much prejudice, by the eighteenth and nineteenth centuries, certainly, the rural population tended everywhere to be taller than the stunted workers of the towns; and the widespread impression that the upland districts in many parts of Europe were inhabited by 'tall men and hard of nature', 'vigorous, honourable, healthy', 'strong, robust and well-built', with 'children [who] are healthy and strong, and look quite fresh and jolly'[80] was too definite to be merely the result of prejudice. Statistics of death-rates and of age at death, where available, confirm the advantages, from the health point of view, of living on marginal uplands.[81]

Mountain villages and hamlets were also believed to be morally unpolluted. The idealization of people living in marginal lands was particularly prevalent in the later eighteenth and early nineteenth centuries. Thus the sheep farmers of upland Cumberland were, according to Jollie in 1811, 'modest, unassuming and civil to strangers. [A] happy people, among whom luxury has scarcely set foot, and Discord is held in contempt.' While Wordsworth enthused over the 'perfect Republic of shepherds and agriculturists' there, Thomas Gray, a generation earlier, had found all to be 'peace, rusticity and happy poverty, in its neatest and most becoming attire', and Gilpin saw 'the sons and daughters of simplicity enjoy health, peace and contentment'. In the West Riding, in 1814, 'simplicity and industry characterise the manners and occupations of the various humble inhabitants of Wensleydale'; in Upper Swaledale 'every man holds himself to the simple tenets of conduct, fearing God'; and Aikin, in 1795, found 'the whole face of the [manufacturing]

78 Bergier (1980), 222; Swiss Economy (1991), 25; Marshall (1958), 114–15.

79 Guichonnet (1980*b*), 33 and (1980*e*), 278; Ladurie (1977), 40 and (1974), 17; Pfister (1986), 370; Palairet (1986), 407–8.

80 Quotations from Winchester (1987), 1; Netting (1981), 57; Broers (1990), 80; also Nicholas and Steckel (1992).

81 Mathieu (1992), 19; Niederer (1980*a*), 81; Hallas (1991), 146; Viazzo (1989), 216–17; Blache (1933), 77; Zurfluh (1986), 240; Rosenberg (1988), 29; but see Cépède and Abensour (1961), 41.

country highly favourable to their morals and happiness . . . [they] are for the most part blessed with the comforts, without the superfluities of life.' The Wicklow mountains provided 'ever-lasting happiness and roast meat', and the Scottish 'Highland family lived . . . in comparative ease, contentment, prosperity and enjoyment, free and independent, leading a life conducive to health, vigour and longevity, to morality, manliness and high religious principles'. 'The Highlander', it was said, had a 'superior degree of fancy and feeling . . . when not fighting or hunting, the herdsman's time was taken up with music, poetry and lounging in the sun'. 'Untainted by the vices that too often accompany affluence', the nobility of Caithness boasted at the time of the American War of Independence, 'our people have been inured to industry, sobriety'. If they raided and robbed, stealing (or retrieving) cattle was not considered an offence; breaking one's word was. Like the upland borderer and the Welshman, the Highlander was also noted for his hospitality to strangers.[82]

All this could certainly be matched by the mountain folk of the Alps, as seen by their admirers: they were men of a free nature, 'pure and true', the 'noble savage' in the heart of Europe.[83] The peak of that literature, as noted above, was reached in the eighteenth century, with works such as Rousseau's *Nouvelle Héloïse* (1761), or Albert de Haller's poem, *Die Alpen* (1736), which had gone through 30 editions by 1777. Dwellers in forests were also romanticized.[84] But none could match the enthusiasm of the Archduke Ferdinand of Austria, who found the people of the Austrian Alps 'free and upright, but also simple and faithful'. They were, in the Archduke's words, a 'splendid, unspoilt people, firm and true like their rocks', which he would protect from all outside poison. And again (1822):

> I found in the mountains strength, faithfulness, sympathy, an unspoilt people . . . as God has set the mountains as a protective wall against time, their poverty and fight against natural forces has its reward, in keeping their inhabitants strong in body and spirit . . . It is my aim to preserve the mountains, to keep them in their faith, their loyalty, righteousness and simplicity, and while all else is frantically [*krampfhaft*] on the move, to stand firm as a model of how things should be everywhere.[85]

Whatever we may think of such extravagant claims, there must have been some core of truth and, perhaps, envy in observations of this kind. The longing for the simplicity of the bucolic life, found so frequently among sophisticated city dwellers, was not, of course, limited to marginal lands, and might light on peasant or village life and even uninhabited wilderness anywhere. Yet there appeared to be something special in the isolation which was the fate of the mountain dweller, as it was of the denizens of marshes and forests. It preserved them from the vices of the city, or

[82] Jollie (1974), 36; Wordsworth (1974), 206; Gilpin (1792), i. 205; Hartley and Ingilby (1988), 40; Bogg (1908), 358; Aikin (1795), 574; Cullen (1981), 102; Colley (1984), 141; Richards (1982), 82–3; Gaffney, (1959), 20; Humphries (thesis, 1993), 27–8; Giraldus (1919), 168–9; Watson (1877), 11; Armstrong (1960), 45; Douglas (1899), 308; Smith (1798), 33; Youngson (1974), 121, 202–3.

[83] Houseman (1800), 70; Weishaupt (1992*b*) 30 and (1992*a*) 18, 64; also Bircher (1938), 137, 142–4.

[84] Guichonnet (1980*d*), 199 ff.; also Landes (1983), 272–3; Ubersfeld (1967); p. 92 above.

[85] Pickl (1986*b*), 89 (S. P. translation).

of any large concentration of people, as it withheld from them the superfluous wealth which was the feeding ground of these vices.

In a small, inward-looking community transgressions are less easily hidden than in an impersonal city society, and often more cruelly punished. The tight family control, necessary, among other reasons, because of the precarious existence on land at the margin, also helped to preserve the society's traditional mores. All accounts agree on the peculiarly influential role of the family in marginal areas. Possibly it was because the extended family alone could keep the agrarian production unit going.[86] More commonly, a pronounced tendency to endogamy was observable: by keeping the search for marriage partners within the village or its immediate vicinity, the economic management remained in the hands of those who understood its local needs. Thus a study of the parishes of Matrei in Tyrol over the period 1580–1900 shows that 61 per cent of marriage partners came from the parishes themselves and a further 20 per cent from the surrounding *Gerichtsbezirke*; only 3 per cent came from outside Tyrol. In Uri, in the period 1765–85, 96.2 per cent of marriages were of both partners from within the village area, 3.4 per cent had one partner from outside, and only in 0.4 per cent of cases were both partners immigrants.[87] Upland valleys in the Border country of the north of England and of Scotland were noted for the fact that the same family name recurred repeatedly in villages, neighbourhoods, or shielings. Some speak, with some justification, of 'clans' in those hills, not entirely unlike those of the Scottish Highlands—though the blood-related kinship of the Highland clans is now known to be largely mythical.[88]

It was therefore not unnatural that the traditional lore, by which people locate their own place in the unfolding of history, should in marginal lands highlight the family. Songs tell of the deeds of forefathers, and bards relate the past of the clan.[89] The outside world does not loom nearly as large as it does in areas easier of access.

Even if a priori reasoning might suggest that the kind of life led in these relatively isolated, inward-looking communities might well have created a stable, possibly even a virtuous society, yet it would also be one which remained backward and intellectually sluggish. Such indeed was the common view of those who looked down on the marginal population, that is to say, of the large majority of observers, as noted in Chapter 3 above. Yet the reality was often different. Intellectually no less than morally, the marginal population was by no means always behindhand.

One striking aspect of this was the incidence of schooling and of formal education at a time when these had not yet become universal. Possibly because of the long winter leisure hours in which little agricultural work could be performed, or possibly also because they were conscious of having to work harder to get as far as those born

[86] Ladurie (1977), 86; Asheim (1988), 69; Fel (1962), 114; Beckett (thesis, 1975), 157.

[87] Stolz (1955), 266; Zurfluh (1986), 238; Bielmann (1972), 40; Ruesch (1979), 169; O'Dell and Walton (1962), 104; Bucher (1974), 49; Giraldus (1919), 195; Rees (1951), 31, 79; Knowles (thesis, 1990), 15.

[88] Dixon (1972), 251; Graham (1907), 58–61; McDonnell (1990), 31; Jones (1969), 139; Watts (1975), 25; Carter (1980), 359–62; Richards (1982), 50–6; Jeffrey (1857–64), iii. 230; Kermack (1967), 49; Rae (1958), 6 and (1966), 5; Grant (1930), 483; Smout (1969), 41,313.

[89] Tough (1928), 36; Shaw (1980), 149; Johnson (1984), 616–17.

into easier circumstances, the people in marginal areas were not infrequently found in the forefront of the drive for education.

The Briançonnais region in the French Alps, for example, whose exceptionally independent status was noted above, was unusual also in its cultural role in the France of the eighteenth and nineteenth centuries. There, 'peasants hired locally trained schoolteachers to instruct their children in French, Latin and arithmetic during the long Alpine winters': the teachers were paid by the community, so that schooling was free to the children. In the course of time, the district became a significant training ground for the teaching profession in France. In 1807 the Prefect of Hautes-Alpes, the *département* concerned, noted that of 4,319 emigrants from his region, no fewer than 705 were schoolmasters. Parents in Chantal and Puy-de-Dôme made extreme efforts to impart literacy to their children, and military recruits from the region showed above-average literacy.[90] In the Swiss mountains, also, education enjoyed a high priority, though most of the schools were kept open in winter only. Some upper valleys in Valais were also known for supplying an exceptional number of teachers. Others were known for their collections of books, and their interest in studying foreign languages, the arts and sciences.[91]

A parallel could be found in England, where the northern hills were centres of a high degree of literacy. Bible reading fostered the 'puritan, questioning spirit' among the statesmen of Cumberland and Westmorland, and the region had a favourable ratio of teachers to population and exceptionally large numbers of booksellers and printers, publishers and newspaper distributors. It is possible that the large number of schools founded after the Reformation in Cumbria and the Pennine uplands was linked to the perceived need to induce godliness and civic obedience there, but the result was that in Westmorland, for example, 'a rash of early 17th century foundations was to transform the county into one of the most literate'. By 1814, a school existed 'in every parish and almost in every village in Westmorland; and education to learned professions . . . continued the favourite method of the Westmorland yeomanry of bringing up their younger sons'. The proportion of people able to sign their marriage certificates in the period 1839–45 was much above the average in both Lake counties, as it also was in Northumberland and the East Riding of Yorkshire, beside the better-known example of Scotland. Farther north, in the Wenlockhead lead mines, 'the miners . . . soon gained a reputation for literacy and intelligence that astounded visitors coming unawares on the isolated communities' in the eighteenth century.[92] Miners as well as the builders of dykes and drainage schemes would almost inevitably gain some scientific understanding of natural phenomena.[93]

90 Rosenberg (1988), 1, 29; Niederer (1980*a*), 82; Viazzo (1989), 140; Weber (1976), 288.

91 Friedl (1982), 39; Bielmann (1972), 9; Niederer (1993) 102; Bircher (1938), 130.

92 Marshall (1969), 295–301; Marshall and Walton (1981), 15, 141–2; Hodgson (1827–58), Part II, i. 86; Smout (1962), 155; Clark (thesis, 1990), 361,363; Jones (1955), 198; Beckett (thesis, 1975), 47; Wordsworth (1974), 44; Bouch (1948), 344; Nicolson and Burn (1976), i. 9; Dickens (1966), 5.

93 Semple (1911), 327.

Some of the industries which settled in marginal areas demanded a high degree of craftsmanship, of which more below. In particular, 'the difficulties of life in . . . forests often developed the ingenuity of the inhabitants and led to the flourishing of artisan life'. On the whole, however, these regions were known rather for the facility with which people turned their hands to anything that was required, in the absence of local craftsmen, than for their particular skill in any one craft.[94] More significant was the ingenuity with which the people of those areas, individually and collectively, solved the peculiar problems posed by their environment. We are here, indeed, somewhere near the heart of the question which this study has set out to explore. Did the difficulties with which nature confronted the people lead to resignation, backwardness, and poverty, or did they spur them on to exceptional effort, to forethought and ingeniousness? What were the circumstances most likely to incite the latter reaction?

The second part of this study will deal with some particular examples in their historical setting. Here we merely enumerate some random cases to illustrate not merely that solutions were often found, but that it was the very scarce resources and the nature of life close to the margin of existence which led to innovations, sometimes well ahead of the stage reached by the plainsfolk. It is worth noting that very few of these indeed are linked to the name of an individual inventor or innovator. Instead, nameless and numberless dwellers on the margin must have contributed to evolve solutions which not only kept their own heads above water, but frequently also represented a step upward on the ladder of human progress. Indeed, even some modern observers reflect that 'peripheral regions appear to record a proportionally higher occurrence of process innovations'.[95]

Thus in the Swiss Alps we find ingenious crop and grass rotations, within the valleys and the Alpine pastures, respectively, and between them. We find irrigation systems, sometimes by channels many miles long, to bring badly needed water to meadows and arable, as early as the year 1270. There were turnable butter churns reported from around 1700, the scythe was in use from around 1500, and there are early records of methods to protect the harvest from rain or rotting. Beginning with the eleventh century, and becoming widespread by the thirteenth, the uplands dropped uneconomic attempts to maintain a mixed agriculture and switched to stockbreeding instead, for which their terrain was much better suited, and which led them to develop an exchange economy with the lowlands to acquire the kinds of food they no longer produced themselves. Thus, according to Jean-François Bergier, by the thirteenth century the 'mountains had an advantage, I would even say were advanced in development [over the lowlands]'. In like manner, by the later eighteenth century 'the mountain and Alpine husbandry was far superior to the arable [lowland] sector in its capacity to absorb change and its commercialised, market-oriented readiness to react to it'.[96] By then, the uplands cattle breed had

[94] Deffontaines (1933), 91; Niederer (1993), 218; Bircher (1938), 121; Stolz (1955), 395.

[95] Harrison and Hart (1990), 386.

[96] Braun (1984), 61; pp. 3 and 87 above.

become famous and much sought-after, some breeding control having been introduced from the sixteenth century onward. By watching their cattle, it was said, the herdsmen developed a workable method of weather forecasting. Possibly most interesting was the agreement among the cantons Uri, Schwyz, Unterwalden, Zug, and Lucerne in 1587 to allow only cattle with a health certificate to pass through on their way to Italy, their major export market. In 1646 a 'sanitary authority' for cattle was created, and in 1702 a compulsory cattle examination for Uri, Schwyz, Unterwalden, and Lucerne was introduced.[97] All this was well in advance of the lowlands areas.

Similar ingenious adaptations could be found in the Austrian and Bavarian Alps. Among other typical examples of mountain innovation is the Laiten plough for use on the steep hillsides in Tyrol. As far as the French Alps were concerned, the early irrigation works, and the active steps taken to fight the plague threat of 1720–3 might be mentioned. In the Scottish Highlands and Islands, hampered as they were by their general poverty, it was the rotational systems which were, to some observers, 'impressive in their variety': for both the two main types, the infield–outfield system, and the arable–grass sequence, there was in the eighteenth century no mere standard pattern, but careful local adaptation. Livestock was managed to provide the maximum of the desperately needed manure while their numbers were strictly stinted; other fertilizers, including seaweed, peat soil, and shell sand, had to be carted up laboriously to the fields. As in Tyrol, a special light plough was developed to deal with the uneven soil conditions. Appropriate methods to deal with difficult agrarian conditions were found also elsewhere in marginal lands; the manner in which the people living on the north Yorkshire moors overcame the problem of the loss of water in the porous ground by an ingenious system of impervious channels deserves special mention.[98]

In many of these cases, as observers were at pains to state, the successful search for solutions was made possible, or helped along, by the freedom from outside control and restrictions enjoyed by the typical marginal area. A similar observation has been made of the East Anglian Breckland 'marginal economy'. There a system effectively of infield–outfield management was in use, probably since the Middle Ages, joined to particular regulations for the grazing of sheep to obtain their manure. These cropping and pasturing arrangements were 'sophisticated and flexible', forming 'an advanced and complex variation' of the infield–outfield model, as they had to be, precisely in order to overcome the poor soil and the 'constraints of their environment and location'. The changes towards specialization

[97] Bergier (1983), 92, also 88–9 and in discussion after Smout (1983), 350; Bucher (1974), 162; Niederer (1980*a*) 70 and (1993), 179–82; Mathieu (1992), 201–26 and (1987), 56 ff.; Netting (1981), 43–5; Weishaupt (1992*a*), 39; Kistler (1962), 29; Weiss (1941), 351; Marty (1951) 22, 38; Bätzing (1991), 56; Wopfner (1931).

[98] Wopfner (n. d.), 5; Haushofer (1986), 207–8; Rosenberg (1988), 7, 34–5; Dodgshon (1993), 685–6, 694; Rösener (1992), 134 ff.; Hamilton (1963), 45; Symon (1959), 280; Humphries (thesis, 1993), 316, 468; McDonnell (1963), 211–15; Hellen (1972).

and integration into a market economy dated there from the population increase of the thirteenth century.[99]

About the same time the Frisians, on their marshes, were similarly forced to trade, exchanging their animals, butter, cheese, their fish and sailing services for the produce of more fertile regions. Their 'marshes were famous for their cattle'. Windmills were found in the Netherlands from the thirteenth century onward, possibly brought back from the crusades. The drainage and enclosure of the English fens also involved the use of a precocious technology.[100]

This random list of innovative technology developed in marginal areas is not intended to suggest that all the innovations of the age had been made there. Its object rather is to indicate that marginality has been no obstacle to originality and initiative at various times and places in the past.

At the same time, it is scarcely necessary to stress that not all the technical advances made in marginal areas turned on the poverty of their resources. On the contrary, many of them depended on being able to exploit gifts of nature and locational advantages. We may now turn to some of the favourable locational aspects of these areas. One obvious advantage associated with the lesser density of population was the larger number of acres per head. Though, almost by definition, these were inferior acres for agricultural purposes, they provided space and alternative possibilities of settlement; and with technological improvements, they could sometimes be turned into productive lands. Apart from the land itself, it was mineral ores which played a leading part.

The remarkable way in which minerals were found, from the Middle Ages if not earlier, mainly in marginal areas, and particularly on mountains, was not entirely accidental. For one thing, mineral ores reveal themselves more easily where the earth tilts, as the covering soil slips away or streams carry traces of the metal to alert the miners: Nef has suggested that the extension of cultivation into upland areas exposed more outcrops. For another, they are more easily brought out on slopes, where the nature of the ground allows accumulating water to flow off naturally, than on level ground which beyond a certain depth requires costly pumping arrangements.[101] As for the smelting stage, large forest resources and much water-power were required, most plentifully available on mountains or where there was no large resident population.[102]

Of perhaps equal significance was the relative ease with which it was possible to prospect for minerals on mountains and in deep forests, because, at least until the minerals were found, the land was considered to be of little or no value and no one had much interest in claiming ownership and control. Thus 'a large part of the ores

99 Bailey (1989*a*), 57–8, 86–7, 145.

100 Van Houtte (1977), 17; Lambert (1971), 106–12, 197; Hallam (1965); Rösener (1992), 134; pp. 99–100 above.

101 Semple (1911), 477–8; Purrington (1982), 9; Bailey (1989), 12; Braudel (1976), i. 43; Kuhn (1955), 180; Nef (1952), 437.

102 Devèze (1961), ii. 43; Lopez (1976), 143; Beinart and Coates (1995), 59.

dug up in Central Europe during the thirteenth century were in mountainous country, and so in waste land, in no-man's land. Territorial princes claimed such land as part of their demesne', and so were enabled to award the special rights and privileges which it became the rule to extend to miners. As late as the seventeenth century, Welsh landlords remembered their rights on the bleak hills only when iron ore and coal were discovered there.[103] Conversely, population tended to move into inhospitable uplands—or, for that matter, into the Siberian wilds—only because ores had been discovered and were being mined. Typically, these settlements were located in areas which were in other respects so inhospitable that they could not feed themselves but had to rely on food imports.[104]

In the Alps, salt and iron have been mined since prehistoric times, certainly in Roman days, and uninterruptedly into the modern period. There was also plentiful mining of copper from the Bronze Age onward, silver in Styria from the fourteenth century and in Tyrol in the fifteenth and sixteenth centuries, and even gold in the Hohe Tauern in the sixteenth century.[105] In other parts of Germany, there had been iron mining by the Romans in the Eifel, and there was documentary evidence for iron mining there from 1240; in the Frankish Alb evidence dates from before AD 1000; in the Thüringerwald from the fourteenth century; in the Fichtelgebirge from the thirteenth; in the Upper Palatinate, the 'Ruhr of the Middle Ages', from the fourteenth century or earlier, and in the Siegerland from the thirteenth century, to list merely the more prominent ones. For other minerals, above all silver, the Harz mountains, where the first reference dates from AD 968, and the Saxon uplands, extending into Bohemia, were in their day among the leading producers in Europe.[106]

If we look briefly at the rest of Europe, in France there were minerals in the Massif Central, and in the forested area between the Sambre and Meuse, among others, worked early on. In the Swedish bogs and forests iron ore was produced from the twelfth century if not earlier, copper from the mid-thirteenth century, silver from the fourteenth. Cracow and Transylvania furnished the largest supply of rock salt in Europe in the sixteenth and seventeenth centuries. The mineral wealth of the Ural mountains began to be exploited from the eighteenth century onwards.[107]

In the British Isles, the production of tin in Cornwall and of lead in Derbyshire, Wales, and Yorkshire in Roman times is well attested. All these areas were productive again in the Middle Ages. Further north in the Pennines, in the Alston region,

[103] Citation from Nef (1987), 709; Dilley (1967), 136; Osborne (1978).

[104] Darby (1977), 36, 40; Mitterauer (1974*b*), 234; Hatcher (1970), 29; Blanchard (1989), 364; Hoffmann (1975), 31.

[105] Nef (1987), 696; Sandgruber (1974); Bergier (1980), 237 and (1982); Ress (1954); Schwarzenbach (1931), 172–4; Guichonnet (1972), 549; Wiessner (1950), 23. Also see Ch. 8 below.

[106] Müller (1938), 5, 21, 131, 152; Götschmann (1986); Schmidtill (1963); Schremmer (1979*b*), 1371 ff.; Kellenbenz (1965), 404; Schulte (1959); Kiesewetter (1988), 424; Jakob (1984), 81; Fehn (1979), 670; and Ch. 8 below.

[107] Kellenbenz (1965), 394; Heckscher (1963), 41–4; Molenda (1976*b*), 151; Seebass (1928), 55; Yatsunsky (1974).

there was a (royal) silver mine in existence by 1133. Jervaulx Abbey nearby was granted the right to dig for lead and iron in 1145 and by *c.*1179–1223 was associated with Alston Moor mines. Substantial lead production in the area, including Swaledale, Wensleydale, and Wharfedale, has continued into the modern period. As late as the end of the eighteenth century their surroundings were still 'barren and mountainous, inhabited by miners and shepherds; the scene on every hand is dark and deplorable, the mines only inducing inhabitants to this desolate spot'. And in mid-Wales, 'most of the mines . . . were situated in the heart of the uplands, in rugged country often over 1,000 ft. [330 m.], and in which communications were very poor'. Even today these areas are bleak and empty.[108]

The Lake District was rich in minerals, including copper, lead, gold, silver, wolfram, and shale, as well as a rich type of iron ore and coal. Copper was mined from the early thirteenth century, but its high peak of activity occurred in the Elizabethan period, when a German company of mine adventurers took over the workings. The first reference to slate quarrying is dated to 1283, in Sadgill. Iron was found in the Weald, the Forest of Dean, and the Cleveland hills, among other areas. Lead was mined in the Wenlockhead region of Scotland, and jointly with silver in Wales.[109] Some coal was also found in upland areas, such as Staffordshire in the thirteenth century,[110] north Wales, and Cumberland, as well as the Forest of Dean, but its significant expansion had to wait until the eighteenth century, and then much of it occurred in more easily accessible regions.

Next to mines, it was forests which provided communities on marginal lands with a natural resource on which a social life could be built. In the literature, forests appear in two guises with an uncertain dividing line between them. We find them, on the one hand, as wooded areas surrounding towns and farming villages, furnishing fuel, building material, and possibly pannage for the inhabitants, being encroached on as more land was required, perhaps for a growing population, and thus being part of the 'core' areas of settlement with which we are not concerned here. Our concern is with the second type, composed of large stretches of forested land in which settlements, if any, are dominated by the trees and their growth, which are usually difficult of access, and are often the source of mystery, fear, or contempt for the rest of the population. These were locations of truly marginal settlement, playing their own particular part in the unfolding of economic history.

Like the mineral ores, the forests could be a rich source of income and sustenance for those dependent on them. In the margins of Europe, in Scandinavia and Russia in the Middle Ages, they yielded furs. The trees provided timber as building material

108 Donald (1961); Hodgson (1827–58), Part II, iii. 40 ff.; Bowes (1990), 41; Raistrick (1975), i. 18 ff.; Raistrick and Jennings (1965), ch. 1 and 46–7; Louis (1907), 348 ff.; Hinds (1896–1922), iii. 101; Powell (1967–8*b*), 118; Goodman (thesis, 1978), 50; Plymley (1813), 50; Rowley (1972), 211; Hardy (?1988), 15; Kirkham (1968), 96.

109 Millward and Robinson (1970); Marshall and Davies-Shiel (1969), 154–5; Bean (1958), 15, 28; Donkin (1973), 109; Baker (1973*a*), 228; Fowler (1976), 67; Athill (1976), 146–7; Smout (1962).

110 Frost (1981), 29; Hatcher (1993), ch. 5; Nef (1966), i. 56 ff.

or raw material for industrial products, including barrels, carpentry work, musical instruments, toys, clogs, and brushes; they provided the best fuel available until replaced by coal from the Industrial Revolution onward. They also provided tar, tree bark used in tanning, potash used in glass-making, honey from bees, fruit from fruit trees, oil from beechmast, and food for animals. To the outsider, the forests of the Middle Ages and of the early modern period might appear empty and forbidding. In fact, they were often teeming with population and with economic activity, though within a framework of a different kind of living: 'The forest had its own population [in the Middle Ages] often highly suspect in the eyes of the more sedentary folk, who roamed about the woods as they lived in shacks they built themselves: huntsmen, charcoal burners, blacksmiths, gatherers of wax and wild honey . . . dealers in wood ash, which was important in the manufacture of glass and soap, and bark strippers, whose wares were used for tanning hides or could be plaited to make cords'.[111]

Since timber, but especially fuel, was often the heaviest input, it was rational to locate a certain type of industry in the forest, not unlike the locational concentrations on the coal districts in a later age. In Britain, indices such as the Poll Tax of 1660 and the Hearth Tax of 1664 tend to suggest that there was relative prosperity in forest districts. Though it would be going too far, even for France, to state that 'a map of industries in the 18th century shows a close correspondence with the map of forests',[112] there is some truth in the observation.

The users who were said to be the most closely dependent on the forests were the glass-makers, for they needed wood not only for fuel, but far more wastefully, for the ashes required in their process of production. Although other materials, such as quartz, sand, and limestone, were also required, these were widely available, and it was forest supplies that tended to determine the location of the glass-works: to produce 100 kg. of potash, 189 cu.m. of wood had to be burnt, plus 5–6 cu.m. for boiling and calcining. In terms of weight, before the nineteenth century between nine and twelve times as much wood was needed as the quantity of glass produced. A comparison of the ratio of final output to wood input shows potash to lead with 1 : 2,000, while silver rated at 1 : 300, forge iron at 1 : 30, and the boiling of brine at 1 : 15 in the sixteenth and seventeenth centuries, and 1 : 7 in the eighteenth century; according to another calculation in English terms, 1,920 cu.ft. of hardwood were required for a hundredweight (or 112 lbs.) of potash. In the eighteenth century, the larger glass-houses used up to 4,000–8,000 cords of wood a year; St Gobain, the largest, used 12,000–16,000 cords.

In consequence, the glass industry tended to denude whole forest areas, and was not infrequently forced, either by the devastation it had caused, or by fiat of the

[111] Wolf (1990), 158–9; Bloch (1966), 6; also Birrell (1962); Rey (1967), 79 ff.; Butlin (1976), 164–5; Braudel (1986), 127; Radkau (1983), 529; Timm (1960), 68–72; Berthet (1951), 150; Duval (1953), 482; Devèze (1961), i. 37, 129 ff.

[112] Deffontaines (1933), 89; also Raumolin (1982*b*), 9; Weber (1976), 213; McDonnell (1992), 111; Mate (1991), 89; Porter (1974), 40–1; Clow (1956), 90; Witney (1990), 23–5; Pettit (1968), 158–60; Winchester (1987), 100–4; Parker (1908), 30 ff.; Hammersley (1957), 144; Thirsk (1961), 70; Swain (1986), 93.

authorities, into less accessible areas, such as the uplands of Lorraine, the Alpine foothills, the Bavarian forest, the Carpathians and the Jura mountains. In Bavaria in 1784 the extension of potash working was banned, and the local works were obliged to import their potash from Bohemia and Hungary, where the forests were less under threat. Against this, some rulers, like the Dukes of Lorraine, who had extensive forests which brought no income otherwise, actually invited glass-makers to them.[113] Though usually away from the more densely settled areas, the hamlets of glass-makers deep in the forests were often surrounded by the cottages of charcoal burners, pitch makers, coopers, carvers, timber merchants, and others.[114]

Apart from the charcoal burners, who might be considered to be subsidiary to the others, it was ironworkers and salt-workers who were the other main users of forest produce. Both were dependent on the location of the mineral as well as of the fuel, so that ironworks, in particular, were found in populated as well as marginal areas, if ores were found there. To meet their needs, they might be given privileged first call on the timber resources, as in the Upper Palatinate and in Bohemia, or be enabled to draw them from nearby mountains, as in the county of Mark; alternatively, where there was a choice of ores, the furnaces and forges moved to the areas in which there was no competition from other fuel users. In some cases, as in Sweden, in Upper Silesia, or in the Styrian mountains, ironworkers found themselves in isolated territories to begin with, with only woodcutters, charcoal burners, and huntsmen for company. Though not as rapacious in its fuel consumption as a glass-works, a charcoal iron furnace, according to Mushet in 1824, would use 30,000 sacks of charcoal a year, equal to 120 acres; at a coppicing replacement rate of twenty years, it would therefore need the sole use of 2,400 acres (*c.*970 ha.) of woodland. The iron furnace at Charcotte on the Welsh border had to draw its wood supply from as far away as 12 miles in 1720–50 and up to 15 miles in 1750–80.[115]

Salt-works were possibly even more tied to their mineral source than ironworks, because of their consumption of fuel in boiling the brine. Thus Reichenhall used 59,000 cu. m. in 1770–82 and nearby Traunstein 41,000 cu. m.; their consumption in 1786–98 was 53,500 cu. m. and 31,500 cu. m. respectively. Thus salt-works had to husband their timber resources carefully; some even had to move the brine-boiling plant to another part of the forest after they had denuded their own area. Cheshire was the first important production area to be driven by wood shortage to use coal in the seventeenth century, though the evaporation of sea water by coal had been practised much earlier in Scotland and on Tyneside.[116] In the Scandinavian countries

[113] Grossmann (1934), 20–1; Slawinger (1966), 229; Schremmer (1970), 99; Rubner (1975), 99; Gleitsmann (1981), 54 and (1984), 30; Rose-Villequey (1971), 80, 95; Wilsdorf and Quellmalz (1971), 434–5; Knoppers and Nicholls (1981), 61; Scoville (1968), 57; Kenyon (1967), 48.

[114] Pischel (1928), 37.

[115] Götschmann (1986), 59; Seebass (1928), 158; Eversmann (1804), 5–7, 128, 341; Haushofer (1986), 71; Husa (1965), 475; Lange (1976), 70; Ziekursch (1978), 147–8; Wessely (1853), i. 475; Schulte (1959), 21; Mazoyer (1932), 350–2; Gleitsmann (1982); Evans (1982), 39; Rowley (thesis, 1967), 151.

[116] Schremmer (1970), 268–70; Piuz (1967), 73; Wagner (1931), 40 ff.; Riedmann (1988), 54; Phillips and Smith (1994), 51–2, 99.

with their substantial timber exports, it was woodcutters and sawmill workers who formed settlements in the forests.[117]

As noted above,[118] the relentless advance of settlements and their forest clearances threatened timber supplies everywhere. By the early modern period, Britain probably had fewer areas of extensive forest left than the Continent north of the Alps, and there was a heavier demand for timber for shipbuilding and metal smelting, so that fears for timber and fuel supply were expressed very early, particularly on a local basis. For a brief period, iron furnaces had to be moved to the Scottish Highlands in search of fuel.

It is true that Acts were passed, or conditions imposed on companies, to replenish the woodlands they had exploited. The problem was to some extent eased also by the practice of coppicing which can certainly be found from the period of Domesday Book onward: 'Industries undoubtedly had a protective effect on woodland . . . it is farmers who grub out the stools, and cattle that eat the spring.' Moreover, since much of the country was accessible by water, imports of timber, and particularly of wood ashes, became possible from an early period.[119] Nevertheless, there can be no doubt that the search for coal, and for methods of using coal for metal smelting, glass-making, brewing, and other industrial purposes, a field in which Britain took the technical lead in Europe, was not unconnected with the perceived shortage and the price rise of local wood fuel supplies.[120]

Until the development of the coal economy, the main industrial source of energy, next to wood fuel and, in some districts peat[121], was water-power. Supplied by rivers and streams, water-power was available in populated plains also, but there were signs in different parts of Europe even as early as the fourteenth century that the demand for it might be greater than the supply. By the early years of the Industrial Revolution there was an acute shortage of it in such British industrial towns as Stockport, Oldham, Bolton, Bradford, and Nottingham.[122] The quest for water-power was one of the main reasons why the British textile industry moved out of the towns and into 'remote valleys and townships where both transport and labour could be a problem',[123] until steam-power brought the mills back into the centres of population.

Water-power, it has long been accepted,[124] is most freely available in uplands, where streams move faster and location on river banks is cheap. It has helped to locate industries in such German mountain areas as Saxony, the duchy of Berg and

117 Aström (1983) and (1978); Heckscher (1963), 22; Søderberg (1982), 389.

118 See pp. 13–14 and 31–2 above.

119 Rackham (1980), 153; Donald (1955), 120; O'Dell and Walton (1962), 56; Rowley (thesis, 1967), 111; Kent (1955–6), 62; Godfrey (1975), 141; Knoppers and Nicholls (1981), 63; Curtis (1956), 723; Marshall and Davies-Shiel (1969), 165.

120 There is a large literature. See esp. Clow (1956), 58 ff. and p. 14 above.

121 Chandler (1991), 65–8; Hartley and Ingilby (1968), 63–4; Davies (1991), 32; O'Grada (1994), 321.

122 Lohrmann (1979), 297, 303–5; Unwin *et al.* (1924), 123–8; Hills (1970), 91–4; Phillips and Smith (1994), 70, 97; Jenkins (1973), 263; White (1972), 156.

123 Phillips and Smith (1994), 169.

124 Semple (1911), 527; Purrington (1982), 9.

county of Mark, the Böhmerwald, the Upper Palatinate, the uplands of Württemberg and the Bavarian Alps, as well as on the Alpine slopes of northern Italy, the Swiss Alps, the French mountain areas, the Ardennes, the Bohemian ring of mountains and the Urals.[125]

In the British Isles, important early industrial users of water-power were to be found in Cornwall and Devon, and in the woollen districts of the West Country. By the later eighteenth century, upland water-power had become significant also in south and north Wales, along the edges of the hilly country flanking the Scottish Lowlands, in the Lake District, and, above all, along the Pennines, for cotton mills in Lancashire and Cheshire, woollen mills in Yorkshire, and the cutlery industry in the Sheffield region. No detailed statistics exist, but it appears from the factory inspectors' reports that in 1838 the textile industry used close on 28,000 hp derived from 2,230 waterwheels; for the Lake District alone, some 30,000 b.h.p. derived from water has been estimated for the mid-nineteenth century. It should be stressed, however, that hills were not the only environment to generate water-power. Domesday Book shows the densest concentration of mills to have been in Norfolk, though no doubt many of them were very small. By the eighteenth century, much ingenuity was employed to make larger quantities of water-power available also in more central and flatter areas, such as the Thames valley and the West Midlands, and even in Lincolnshire.[126]

For people dwelling in marshlands the natural resources available not only included fish and various waterfowl, but in fact had a much wider range. The English Fens had rich meadowland which benefited from being flooded in winter, or being improved by drainage, and which provided nourishment for numerous cattle and sheep. Reeds, rushes, and sedge, carefully husbanded and stinted, were the basis of thatch and basket work, or could be sold as raw material. Flax and hemp were available for weaving. Rich turbaries yielded fuel, wanted in part for the salt pans which again provided a saleable product. A cheap and ready means of transport was furnished by a network of waterways. Lastly, there was also a considerable extent of arable, and early examples of crop rotation and other advanced agricultural techniques are known to have been introduced there.[127]

It is therefore not entirely surprising that the English Fens registered a quite exceptionally rapid increase in population between Domesday and the mid-fourteenth century and again in the seventeenth century,[128] and enjoyed wealth and

[125] Forberger (1958), 137; Kiesewetter (1988), 424; Eversmann (1804), 195; Lange (1976), 45, 69; Schulte (1959), 29; Kreiner (1919), 3–5; Götschmann (1985), 9; Megerle (1982),122, 166–7; Ladurie (1974), 66–70; Dewerpe (1984), 897–9; Günther (1930), 419; Yatsunsky (1974), 82; Tunzelmann (1978), 280; Guichonnet (1972), 548.

[126] Ponting (1971); Ramsay (1965), 2; Millward and Robinson (1970), 249–51; Hills (1970), 95; Musson (1976), 417; Tunzelmann (1978), 139; Farnie (1979), 51; Marshall and Davies-Shiel (1969), 57; Hodgen (1939); Tann (1973); Tupling (1927), 195, 205.

[127] The best account is in Darby (1940), also his (1971) and (1968), 26, 153; also Hallam (1965), esp. 195, 220; Thirsk (1987), 49–54 and (1953), 24 and (1961), 84–5; Williams (1982), 95; Camden (1971), 409.

[128] Donkin (1973), 71; Hallam (1958), 340–1 and (1965), 200; Wrightson (1982), 126–7.

income well above the average for English counties. It has been held that 'the Fenland communities formed the most successful culture in medieval England'. In the fourteenth century they boasted 'much the greatest concentration of agricultural prosperity in England': according to the lay subsidy of 1334, 31 of the 106 richest places in all England were located there.[129]

None of this was achieved without a great deal of effort. There are indications that some drainage schemes go back to Roman times, but it was the fenmen's own efforts in the twelfth–fourteenth centuries which made the greatest contribution both to drainage and to extending the usable land by erecting defences against the sea, in what was a remarkable technical and organizational achievement at the time. Their bitter if unavailing opposition to the great drainage schemes arranged by the Earl of Bedford and other courtiers in the seventeenth century was not directed at change as such, but was caused by the realization that they would have to bear much of the costs, but would get few of the benefits.[130]

Other marshland, such as the Humber estuary, Romney Marsh, and the Somerset levels also boasted rich meadowland or extensive fisheries. Drainage permitted an extensive sheep and wool economy to develop there, paralleled by the worsted industry in the region of the Norfolk Broads from the early fourteenth century onward, if not earlier. As for the Essex marshes, they 'were unhealthy but rich. The Dengie people made a lot of money . . . selling salt, butter, cheese, corn, fish and timber to London merchants. With no great houses and no powerful county families, the marshes lay happily outside the usual class arrangements of rural England . . . The people of Dengie were left largely to their own smelly and profitable devices.'[131]

The Cumbrian lakes also provided fishing, sufficiently valuable to be allocated to different proprietors by imaginary lines drawn across the water. Fishing was also a valuable source of income for the men of the Shetlands as well as of the Western Highlands and Islands, from the early eighteenth century onward. For a brief period, *c.*1735–1815, these latter areas also benefited by the collection and processing of kelp as a source of potash. Some fortunes were made with kelp during the Napoleonic wars, but the industry was wiped out when Spanish barilla became freely available.[132]

In Norway, fishing and sea transport helped to eke out a living on poor soil. Elsewhere fishing communities could be quite well-to-do. In the coastal zone of the Netherlands—the most important marsh zone in Europe—where the human effort to create drainage schemes and polders eclipsed even the achievements of the fenmen, rich and 'valuable' meadows were created, there were copses for fuel and to

[129] Hallam (1965), 222; Rackham (1990), 387; Glasscock (1973), 179–81; Thirsk (1953), 42; Darby (1940), 130.

[130] Rackham (1990), 374–84; Hallam (1965); Lindley (1982); Manning (1975), 143–8; Cunningham (1892), 187–8. For opposition to drainage in Shropshire, see Rowley (1972), 162–3.

[131] Quoted in Neeson (1993), 4; also Darby (1977), 159–60; Maxwell (1962*c*), 210–11; Kerridge (1985), 2, 8.

[132] Gilpin (1792), i. 160–1; Youngson (1973), 101–4, 134; Hamilton (1963), 110–28, 357–62; Lythe and Butt (1975), 38 ff.; Gray (1951–2); Carter (1980), 370–2; Franklin (1952), 167; Knox (1985), 15.

feed pigs, and sods of heath for fertilizing the rest. Gathering peat became a widespread occupation for the population in that marginal land, as well as fishing, fowling, and sea transport. Their products were exchanged for Baltic grain and timber from the fourteenth century onward, and by the seventeenth century that landscape was destined to carry the richest province of the richest country in Europe.[133]

Finally, the widespread view[134] that mountains presented obstacles to transport, and that their difficulties of access were an important cause of the poverty of their populations, must be examined.

> Mountain ranges, [it has been observed] are commonly thought of as barriers to interchange, but in many cases their barrier quality may be more than compensated for by the differentiation or complementarity which they produce. The climate, in many instances, differs on two sides of a mountain range . . . More directly, mountains may be so different as to generate interaction, as in the case of transhumance.

Experience in many areas shows indeed that mountains need not be barriers between peoples, even though they inhibit military movements. On the contrary, they could be links or filters, and passes and gaps in upland ranges often became the location of cities and of vigorous economic enterprise. In the Middle Ages, the kingdoms of Navarre and Aragon and the county of Savoy straddled some of the highest mountain ranges of the Alps and Pyrenees.[135]

Thus the Alps, the highest and most extensive range in Europe, were never an absolute barrier in historical times. The main through route in the eastern Alps crossed Tyrol and the Brenner Pass into Italy. It contributed to the prosperity of the Tyroleans and earned the region, in parallel to the equivalent Swiss regions, the title of a 'pass country'. The route provided tolls, cartage income, and easy access to foreign goods such as Italian wines, though it tended to suffer in wartime from marauding troops and the obligation to quarter them and their officers.[136]

Active trade via the Brenner Pass, from Venice to Germany, is documented from the thirteenth century onward; before it was made, monasteries were known to have aided pilgrims and other transalpine travellers. Later on, towns on the route were given staple and other rights, and roads were improved. Peasants along the way were obliged, as part of their tenancy, to provide transport for the lord, and that duty was then extended to all comers. Persons engaged in transport were organized in *Rod* companies or guilds, operating a carefully regulated system of stages within which they provided horses and carts. Estimates for the traffic across the Brenner in *c.*1300 vary between 3,000 and 4,000 tons a year. By 1500 this had reached 5,000 tons and by 1800, some 19,000 tons, amounting to around three-quarters of the

133 Semple (1911), 230–1; Lambert (1971), 59; Slicher van Bath (1946), 122; Hallam (1988*e*), 504; Nicholas (1991), 25–6; Harris (1957), 300–1; Petri (1975), 696–700; de Vries (1974), 56, 71; van Houtte (1977), 5, 66–7, 91, 152; van Zanden (1993), 31–2; Sandvik (1979), 37; Tracy (1990), 21.

134 Bergier in Lindgren (1987), 119; Guichonnet (1980*e*), 253–4.

135 Ullmann (1956), 872; Bergier (1988), 29 and (1989*b*), 1–2; Blache (1933), 171; Lösch (1954), 206; Heller (1993), 181; Russell (1972*a*), 232; Renouard (1958), 10; Guichonnet (1980*b*), 12–13.

136 Stolz (1955), 252, 389; Mayer (1965), 11; Klein (1965), 275; Bosl (1979), 15; also p. 13 above.

Tyrolean transalpine traffic. Just before the railway was built, in 1867, some 25,000 vehicles a year crossed the Brenner Pass. Curiously enough, traffic was often heavier in winter, possibly because the peasants did not need their animals then in the fields, or because sledges were easier to pull than wheeled vehicles and carried more than pack animals.[137] The northern extension of the Tyrolean route through the Bavarian foothills was similarly organized, the guild of carters known as *Rottfuhrmänner* receiving their right of staple in 1332. Salzburg also derived much gain from its through traffic.[138]

There were several passes across the central and western Alps in Switzerland. The route exerting the strongest influence on the local communities through which it passed was probably the one running south from Lucerne over the St Gotthard pass, after it was opened in the thirteenth century by the bridge over the Schöllenschlucht. Though much less important before 1500 than the Brenner, carrying only an average of 852 *Saum*, or perhaps 170 tons in 1493–1503, it was considered the shortest route across the Alps, and its traffic increased thereafter, including cattle driven south on the hoof. Here, also, organization and staple rights provided an income for the valleys, considered 'vital for the survival' for the Uri population,[139] which involved them in the costs of keeping the roads in repair; these ensured a safe, if slow and costly journey. By the end of the seventeenth century, two posts a day (on foot) crossed the St Gotthard, and in the eighteenth century, about 20,000 animals a year used the route. In 1790 one estimate calculated that 30–5 pack horses a day crossed in both directions. The other main routes were over the Splügen and Bernina passes. Travellers and goods crossing by the Grisons had to meet high charges, but were assured of 'scheduled delivery, and security from bandits and other Alpine hazards' in return.[140]

It clearly paid the dwellers along main routes to keep them open, even at considerable expense, in order to derive an income from the tolls and freight charges. Thus Halifax gained as a 'border town' by being accessible for traffic on both sides of the Pennines. Where there were no roads, or inadequate ones, successful businesses had to build their own—like Thurzo's road across the Carpathians in the late fifteenth century—or force a lane across the country, as did the cattle drovers in the undeveloped Scottish Highlands. Elsewhere, routes across difficult terrain were made hazardous not merely by the obstacles of nature, but also by robbers and highwaymen who might lurk there. In Sweden it was thought that the advantages of snow and ice in the winter lay not merely in the reduced costs of using sledges, but also in avoiding blockages by tolls and robber barons.[141]

137 Müller (1905), 382 ff.; Srbik (1947); Hassinger (1969); Cole and Wolf (1974), 35, 75, 100; Löhr (1971), 38; Gramulla (1977), 151; Kramer (1977), 241; Wessely (1853), i. 406 ff.; Kellenbenz (1988), 15–16.

138 Daisenberger (1859–61), 83; Mayer (1965), 14; Klein (1965), 278; Riedmann (1988), 78.

139 Bielmann (1972), 155.

140 Barber (1974), 149; Mayer (1959), 234–5; Schnyder (1973), i. 1, 14, 23–4; Gilomen (1991), 481; Gilliard (1929), 178; Arnold (thesis, 1989), 34–47; Glauser (1979); Caroni (1979); Bielmann (1972), 86, 124 ff.; Mathieu (1992), 65, 145, 159; Bircher (1938), 42. Marty (1951), 63 has a much larger estimate.

141 Heckscher (1963), 38; Molenda (1976*b*), 166; Richards (1982), 85; Hamilton (1963), 228–32; Crump (1941), 21; Bonser (1970), 148; Laube (1976), 45.

People living along frontiers could add to their income by smuggling. In some Pyrenean valleys, 'contraband trade was not just an activity, it was a morality, a way of life'. For some coastal dwellers, such as the men of Cornwall or the Western Highlands, there were similar opportunities.[142] Marginal islands might derive their own advantages from lying across trade routes. The Orkneys, for example, were situated in what was considered for the Middle Ages a 'linchpin' position in a political, cultural, and trade network. It was a society always in touch with the outside world, and though remote, was not really poor.[143]

Summing up the evidence presented in this chapter, we may begin by recalling that it had set out to convey the views of those observers and historians who were opposed to the predominant vision of marginal areas as containing a segment of the European population that was, because of its location, disadvantaged, backward, and poor. Many of these authors seemed surprised that the populations studied by them were doing relatively well. They did not expect to find, for example, that wages in the Lake District were above average, that the Scottish Highlands were 'full of pasturage grass for cattle and comely with verdure in the glens along the water courses' and that their inhabitants had a 'wealth of cattle, sheep and horses', or that Breckland and Fenland people were prosperous, or that Cornish agriculture had high yields.[144] On the Continent, similarly, there was astonishment that the estates in upland Silesia or in Bohemia were highly profitable, that the watchmakers in the Jura mountains were happy and extremely prosperous, or that Tyrol had been made 'fertile, plentiful, attractive and prosperous', and many mountain people were vigorous and well fed.[145]

There were two aspects to the more positive judgement on these marginal lands. One starting-point was to view them as actually favoured by nature: thus the people dwelling in them were thought to live in healthier surroundings, to be better protected from feudal or guild oppression, from foreign occupation or warlike action on their territories, and to be able to avoid the temptations and evils of city life. They were also blessed with rich natural resources, including timber, minerals, the fauna and flora of marshlands, abundant water-power and, frequently, much unoccupied land.

More commonly, however, observers recognized that marginal lands presented difficult conditions, but judged that it was precisely these conditions which would develop and bring into play a number of admirable qualities among the people living in these lands. The logic behind this has been most clearly expressed in Toynbee's 'challenge and response' syndrome, and is akin to what is sometimes known as

142 Sahlins (1989), 129; Youngson (1973), 117–18.

143 Schrank (1992), 369–71.

144 Hatcher (1970), 35; Hey (1972), 5, 22; Marshall (1969), 286 and (1989), 143; Bailey (1989*a*), 117 ff., 128–35, 192–3 and (1989*b*); Collins (1978), 15; Thirsk (1953), 9, 42; Evans (1985), 113–14; Haldane (1953), 7; Grant (1930), 473; Jones (1955), 202.

145 Ziekursch (1978), 135–6; Landes (1983), 272–3, 307; Stolz (1955), 388; Klima (1989), 511; Ladurie (1974), 48; Braudel (1976), i. 31.

the Boserup thesis, which holds that it is basically the adverse effect of population pressure which has induced agricultural progress in world history.[146]

Even without necessarily developing an overarching thesis, however, the common explanation favoured by numerous authors was that these marginal populations had been made industrious, flexible, self-reliant, hardy, active, even martial, by the conditions facing them. They had been forced into forms of village co-operation and to devise effective and generally egalitarian social institutions and appropriate sanctions in order to survive. Above all, they had to be observant, inventive, and ingenious in order to overcome their handicaps and eke out a living in tough surroundings. The necessary understanding of natural phenomena had helped to make them aware of scientific laws, while the peculiar climate, with its long winter months, together with the consciousness that they were destined to face more obstacles than most, had tended to make them aware of the benefits of a formal education.

Handicaps, difficulties, lack of political clout and of access to the seats of power remained and could not always be avoided; yet we have seen how often these could be overcome by the inner resources combined with the positive locational advantages of marginal folk. The 'positive' literature provides some clues why it is not altogether miraculous that they should, from time to time, be found among the technical and cultural leaders of their societies. It may help to explain how it came about that the Industrial Revolution found such fertile soil in some of what seemed outwardly the least favoured regions of Britain.

[146] Boserup (1965); Clark (1977), 133–7; p. 88 above.

5

The Complementarity Thesis

Both the points of view sketched so far, that which considers marginal areas to be inferior, and that which considers their population to have enjoyed certain advantages in the past, are anchored to the assumption that these areas are clearly separate from their surrounding territories. It is, however, also possible to view them, not so much as regions going their own separate way but rather as regions integrated into the national economy which, because of their distinctiveness, developed mutually beneficial relations with their neighbouring territories on the basis of some form of division of labour. This view, which emphasizes both the symbiosis[1] and the innate differences, may be referred to as the complementarity thesis. Complementarity implies a degree of mutual dependence rather than inferiority or superiority,[2] and it is therefore compatible with both the negative and positive theses, though in particular cases it may well be that one region was at times more dependent on the relationship than the other.

One of the oldest and most common ways in which a marginal area can establish such mutually beneficial economic relations between itself and a 'core' area, appropriate particularly to mountainous grounds, is the practice of transhumance, the movement of domesticated animals for pasturing between different regions in certain seasons of the year. In this system, both parts, the upland with its wide expanse of grazing in the summer but inhospitable climate and possible snow cover in the winter, and the lowlands, sheltered in the winter but with limited acreage, are combined to carry a population of herds or flocks which neither of them could have fed on its own. It has been found to have existed in one form or another in the past in practically all parts of upland Europe.[3]

Transhumance was widely practised in classical times in the Mediterranean basin, and is believed to have played a part in affecting adversely and transforming drastically the vegetation of many of the areas concerned. Its most spectacular but destructive example which has survived almost into the modern period is the Spanish Mesta.[4] Its origins go back to before Moorish times, but it was formalized in 1273 by King Alfonso of Castile, and because of its importance for the

[1] Dubuis (1986), 6–7.

[2] Mann (1986), 81–2; Linge (1988*b*), 5; Conti (1988); Brugger *et al.* (1984*b*), 11; Messerli and Brugger (1984*a*), 59.

[3] Slicher van Bath (1963), 167; Pounds (1973), 383–4; Frödin (1940), p. xii; Semple (1911), 573–7.

[4] Klein (1920); Slicher van Bath (1963), 167–8; Garnsey (1986), 10–11; Russell (1967), 165–6; Smith (1971*a*), 439.

national economy does at least deserve a mention, though it falls outside our self-imposed geographical limits.

There are generally held to be three forms of seasonal animal migration: nomadism, the Alpine economy, and transhumance proper.[5] Nomadism is found on the Mongolian steppes and was possibly a feature also on the Hungarian plain, but is otherwise rare in Europe. Its distinguishing mark is that there is no recognized route which is followed in an identical manner year by year, as is the case with the other two types. The Alpine economy is characteristically a carefully regulated system linking the upland summer pastures with the inhabited valley below. On the tops are buildings providing rough accommodation for the 'Senne' workers together with butter and cheese-making facilities. The extent of the upland pasturing rights belonging to a household is then typically determined by its ability to produce the winter feed and by its possession of land in the valley below. In this system, the cattle or sheep are moved between them according to guidelines laid down by the village. Sometimes an intermediate stage, called *Maiensäss* in the Grisons, and perhaps yet another, called *Vorwinterung*, allow a further specialization of crops and pasturing half-way up in spring and autumn. This form, which is found in the High Alps in Switzerland and in parts of Austria but was known also in Wales and the Scottish Highlands and Islands, effectively operates wholly *within* the marginal area and therefore does not quite qualify for our definition of mutual dependence.[6] But it is the third form of migration, or transhumance proper, in which a similar movement takes place between upland and lowland, which exemplifies the complementarity existing between the two types of region.

One of the most significant European movements of this kind, continuing at least from the Middle Ages to our own century, was centred on Provence. At its climax, in the mid-nineteenth century, 400,000 sheep, in flocks of up to 20,000, were driven annually down from the French Alps as well as the Massif Central into the warmer lowlands to overwinter, and because of the very extent of the movement and its duration—it might take ten days or more before the destination was reached—it had to be accompanied by carefully defined regulations over routes, grazing rights, and the like. In Auvergne, the flocks might have to travel up to 120 km. to graze on high land. From Navarre, sheep travelled to Aquitaine in the winter, and from the Montagne Noire to the Toulouse region. The Vosges form another area in France in which this form of transhumance occurred. Both there and in Dauphiné may be found what some have termed 'reverse transhumance', the owners bringing the animals down for the winter, rather than taking them up to the mountain pastures in the summer.[7]

[5] Niederer (1993), 149, 157, 162–7; Evans (1940); Jones (1971), 380; Braudel (1976), i. 86.

[6] Cole and Wolf (1974), 124; Netting (1981), 12; Weiss (1941), 26–7, 199, 269; Bätzing (1991), 41–2; Arnold (thesis, 1989), 136; Stolz (1955), 294; Kruker (1979), 111; Frödin (1940), 273 ff.; Sayce (1955–6), 141.

[7] Bloch (1966), 203; Cleary (1988); Frödin (1940), 36, 351 ff.; Blache (1933), 45; Smith (1978), 246–7; Rosenberg (1988), 15–16; Niederer (1980*a*), 8 ff. and (1993), 150; Fel (1962), 103; Rosset (1984), 135; Châtelain (1976), i. 337 ff.

In other parts of the Alpine chain also, where the uplands bordered on lowland areas, true forms of transhumance were the rule, generally involving cattle rather than sheep. In the uplands facing the Italian valleys, there might even be a seasonal migration between mountain meadows and wine-growing valleys, while Italian shepherds would bring their flocks into the Grisons in the summer.[8] In the Mediterranean area, it should be remembered, transhumance could be as much a method of escaping the dry valleys in summer, as an avoidance of the harsh mountains in winter. Similar movements took place in the Bavarian foothills, as well as in the Jura mountains.[9]

Transhumance was practised also in the mountains of eastern and south-eastern Europe. This includes the Carpathians, Transylvania, and the Balkans. In parts of the Balkans, peasants would stay on the upland grazings with their sheep and goats over the summer and make cheese; as population growth drove peasants ever higher up the mountains, some of these sites became foundations for permanent settlements.[10] There were also cases of transhumance without any great differences in height between the areas concerned, usually for particular reasons. Thus it was the practice among the Magyars to let their sheep graze in the hills surrounding the Alföld plain in summer, bringing them down to their camp, fixed near a river or a swamp, in winter. In northern Germany, in more modern times, farmers reared their lean cattle on the Geest, after which they drove them into the nearby marshland to be fattened. A similar practice can be discerned in Cornwall and in some Border country hills.[11]

In the British Isles, transhumance was widely practised in the hilly region north and south of the Border, the northern Pennines, and the Lake District. Where the upland pastures were a good distance away from the valley settlement, herdsmen lived in rude shelters called 'shielings', known in the Cumbrian dialect also by the Norse name of saeter (or Gaelic *erg* or *airigh*). In terms of acreage, the upland possessions would be much larger than the valley holdings, and might be shared by several settlements. As population increased, division and more careful allocation became necessary; at the same time some shielings would develop into permanent settlements. The study of place-names suggests a 'broad evolutionary sequence in which shielings were pushed further into the mountains and to higher altitudes as margins of permanent settlement advanced'. This was possibly helped by the fact that, unlike the Alps, where only a small number of specialists spent the summer on the 'Alp' or 'Alm', in the Border areá the whole family might migrate temporarily, leaving the lowland settlement deserted. Where, on the other hand, the villagers had more pasture land than they could use themselves, they might let it out to others in a form of agistment. Normally, however, the upland pastures were stinted.

8 Schwabe (1984), 128–9; Mathieu (1987), 75.

9 Fehn (1968), 36 ff.; Sandberger (1979), 737; Haushofer (1986), 207–8; Morard (1971), 273.

10 Blache (1933), 20, 24; Kuhn (1957), 364; Wace and Thompson (1972), 258; Hocevar (1987), 566; Podraza (1986), 295; Roglic´(1970), 232–5; Lampe and Jackson (1982), 4–5, 44–5.

11 Hollander (1960–1), 77; Schwarz (1959), 212; Rowe (1953), 23; Collins (1978), 13.

As a lease of 1734 stipulated, rather like those in the Alps, each tenant could graze the number of cattle 'he might reasonably keep or feed in winter and no more'.[12]

In the Scottish Highlands, the outlying grazing areas might be up to 20 miles away, but not necessarily much higher up. In their case, as in the Alpine system, both termini of the transhumance route would be within the marginal area, rather than linking it with plains settlements. On Skye, butter and cheese would be made on the tops. In some places, summer grazing could be on a different or separate island altogether. There are signs of the decline of the practice in the eighteenth century.[13]

In the Midlands and in southern England, varieties of transhumance, mainly for sheep, were found on the Mendips, in Cornwall, and in the Cotswolds, whereas in the Middle Ages journeys by the flocks of up to 40 miles, from manor to manor in search of pasture, were recorded. There was also a form of transhumance into the forests, in the West Midlands, in Kent, and elsewhere.[14] Wales possessed a similar and widely practised form of transhumance, called 'Hafod'. Here also, population increase gradually led to the stinting of the upland pasture as 'cultivation . . . crept slowly up the mountainside as squatters carved new holdings out of the waste', and upland sites turned into permanent settlements.[15]

Transhumance is an intelligent method of making the most of the different natural conditions obtaining in the marginal area as against the settled plains. The uplands, and to some extent the forests, offered richer pastures in the warmer seasons; in the winters, cattle and sheep survived better on lower land or indoors. Marginal lands were in this way wholly and vitally integrated with the lowland economy. In this system, there is no change in the ownership of herds and flocks: they remain in the same hands—though there were cases known of the same flock of sheep being sold to mountain people in the summer, and resold by them to the plains people in the winter.[16] However, the traffic of property remaining in the same ownership is exceptional. The more common relationship between marginal area and core consists in buying and selling, in the trade in goods and services.

We may begin with cattle and sheep which, having been reared on marginal territories, would be driven for sale to towns and lowlands. The Scottish drovers took their cattle to England for centuries, the numbers rising from 20,000 head a year at the end of the seventeenth century, when a law of 1671 attempted to regulate the

[12] Searle (1993), 130; Whyte (1973), 108; Smailes (1960), 95; Winchester (1987), 3, 81–4, 159, 228 ff.; Bowes (1990), 31–8; Watts (1975), 42; Higham (1986), 333; Wrathmel (thesis, 1975), 250 ff.; Brassley (1984), 34; Ramm *et al.* (1970), 1–3; Butlin (1964), 116; Barrow (1973), 261; Dixon (thesis, 1984), 86; Gaffney (1959), 22; Dilley (thesis, 1991), 263 ff.; pp. 108–9 above.

[13] Dodgshon (1993), 694–5; McDonnell (1988), 16; Whittington (1973), 567–9; Shaw (1980), 91; O'Dell and Walton (1962), 108; MacSween (1959), 81–2; Youngson (1974), 21, 100–1; Marshall (1794), 45; Gaffney (1959), 30–4; Haldane (1953).

[14] Hooke (1982), 230; Neale (1976), 98; Dyer (1980), 136; Rowse (1941), 32; Thirsk (1987), 50.

[15] Dodd (1951), 5; Williams (1969), 66; Cowell (1984), 70–1; Jones (1973), 444–5; Winchester (1973), 89; Jones (1960–3), 124; Sayce (1955–6), 117 ff.; Pierce (1972), 329 ff.; Griffiths (1988), 71–2.

[16] Frödin (1940), 379.

trade, to 60,000 a century later; by the mid-eighteenth century about 80,000 head a year fed on Cumbrian grassland on the way south, and by 1800 the numbers driven south over the border reached 100,000 a year, in addition to those driven to the industrializing and urbanizing Scottish Lowlands. For the breeders, it has been stated, probably somewhat optimistically, that the cattle trade 'lifted the economy from mere subsistence farming to farming for profit'. As for the economy as a whole, Adam Smith thought it the main advantage accruing to Scotland from the Union with England. It required, and created, an elaborate credit system, the cash flow permitted tenants to pay their rent, and the profits derived from it were said to have made a significant contribution to the rebuilding of classical Edinburgh. After the Highland Clearances, it was sheep, first introduced in the Highlands in 1762, that were sent down to the markets in increasing numbers. Cattle droving was of considerable importance also for the Welsh economy.[17]

The Swiss upland herdsmen exported their cattle, including calves, as well as horses, to the cities of northern Italy, and also to the lowland towns of northern Switzerland. It is estimated that in the eighteenth century the traffic amounted to 6,000–10,000 head a year, and in the nineteenth, 7,000 head from the canton Schwyz alone. This trade had been carried on at least since the twelfth century; before that, it appears, it was mainly wool that was sent south.[18] Elsewhere, from the Middle Ages onward when communications became easier, 'in the marginal areas tillage was reduced, stock raising expanded. These marginal areas included the German marshes on the North Sea and the Netherlands, large areas of Eastern Europe and the northern rim of the Alps'. 'High mountains', it has been said even more comprehensively, 'always were and still are among those regions of Europe characterized by producing a surplus of either cattle or sheep. Therefore a strong market relationship with the neighbouring lowlands has existed at all times.' In Norway, poor soil forced farmers to engage in fishing, cattle rearing, mining, and forestry in 'regional economies . . . each with certain foreign connections'.[19]

The market-oriented economy which was found to have developed early in mountainous marginal areas, as noted in Chapter 4 above, derives both from the inability of the population dwelling there to supply all their needs out of their upland fastnesses themselves, and from their comparative advantages in supplying certain products to the people in the cities. They are two sides of the same coin: marginality and exchange usually, even if not always, go together. In Switzerland, the upland product which above all others captured outside markets and boosted the development of the 'Inner Alps' as well as of other upland areas was cheese. It

[17] Quotation from Hamilton (1963), 89, also *passim*; Searle (1993), 134; McDonnell (1988), 15; O'Dell and Walton (1962), 112–14; Gregson (1989), 31; Gray (1957), 36, 86 ff.; Smout (1983), 330–3; Lythe and Butt (1975), 113–16; Turnock (1970), 17 ff.; Bonser (1970), 21, 37 ff., 90; Grant (1930), 544–6; Richards (1982), 49, 80; Carter (1980), 362, 370–1; Franklin (1952), 130–1.

[18] Bielmann (1972), 11; Marty (1951), 32; Arnold (thesis, 1989), 145; Bergier (1987), 121; Kistler (1962), 36.

[19] Bätzing (1991), 45; Lichtenberger (1978), 182; Sandvik (1979), 39.

became an exportable commodity as soon as the Swiss learned how to produce the hard types of cheese which would stand the long journey down to the outside world.

One study has crystallized out four stages of this development in the mountain 'herdsmen's country', the original 'inner' cantons. In the first stage, the top grazings could not be fully used, as there was not enough feed for the winter in the valleys; mostly goats and sheep were kept, while cattle, if any, had to be slaughtered in the autumn. Tithes were paid in goats' cheese. In the second stage, calves were grazed on top, and sold as such in the autumn: this was profitable and allowed many communes to buy out their tithes. In the third stage, when markets became more easily accessible, tillage in the valley bottoms was restricted and ultimately ended, thus increasing the capacity to overwinter cattle and make fuller use of the summer pastures, buying in grain and other food with the proceeds of the dairy industry, much of which originated in butter exports. The development of hard 'fat rennet cheese' around 1550, which was more popular and kept better than traditional products, introduced the fourth phase. To operate this cheese-making economically, a herd of at least 24–30 well-kept Alpine milch cows became necessary. This benefited the richer peasants and disadvantaged the mass of poorer ones, so greatly widening class differences in the Alpine villages.[20]

Some cheeses, including those of Greyerz and Emmental, acquired a high reputation from the beginning and had no difficulty in finding wide markets abroad. They were formed into standard sizes so that in many places rents or payments were reckoned in cheeses. Their weight was such that they could be manhandled and carried downhill on the backs of men. It is recorded that some mountain peasants delivered their cheese dues to the monastery of Visachbachau over a distance of 110 km. as early as the twelfth century. Though butter could also be exported, it was cheese which became the lifeblood for the more distant mountain communities from the sixteenth century onwards when the new technology was introduced. Thus Entlebuch, a virtually closed valley, sold 400–450 tons a year by the end of the seventeenth century, rising to 501 tons by 1889, when the whole canton produced 3,840 tons of fat cheese; by then, however, much of the production had been transferred to the valleys and Entlebuch was mainly selling cattle. By the nineteenth century, something like an effective regional specialization had taken place, some valleys specializing in rearing cattle and others in marketing dairy products.[21]

With marketing linkages to the lowland towns established, the mountain population exported other products, including wool, skins, and leather. Similar produce, as also meat, cattle, and fish, was exported from other marginal areas, such as the English marshes and the Breckland. The Scottish Highlands did a profitable trade in exporting (partly illicitly distilled) whisky. Alpine forests delivered timber to the outside world, and forests everywhere were linked to outside buyers by their sale of

[20] Bircher (1938), 23 ff.; also Pfister (1986), 364, 381; Bergier (1988), 32; Kistler (1962), 18; Weiss (1941), 338–40.

[21] Glauser (1971), 2 ff., 36; Toch (1986), 35; Arnold (thesis, 1989), 145; Weiss (1941), 240; Bucher (1974), 209; Bergier (1982), 181, Viazzo and Albera (1986), 194; Mathieu and Stauffacher (1986), 337.

forest products, including iron and glass, barrels and furniture, charcoal and wooden utensils and many others. In modern terms, they were also part of the leisure industry: in some areas, considerable costs were incurred to preserve them as hunting grounds for the privileged, or, in our century, make them accessible for tourism.[22]

Today it is commonly the mountains and other marginal regions, such as the Norwegian fjords, together with the beaches, which attract mass tourism. Although travelling in search of remote wildernesses by the select few began in the second half of the eighteenth century, and Alpine climbing became fashionable in the middle of the nineteenth, mass tourism as a phenomenon came too late to be included in this study in any detail. Two comments may, however, be in order. One is that the provision of services may be as much a complementary activity of a marginal region as the provision of goods. The other is to point out that, once the opportunity presented itself, the population living on the margins showed just as much initiative in the building of hotels, the marking of paths, or the participation in cable-car companies as it had shown in other enterprises at any time in the past.

The picture which thus emerges is one of early and increasing specialization of marginal areas as soon as transport and commercial conditions allowed: in difficult terrain, as on the Massif Central in France, or in the Derbyshire Peak District, economic specialization in fact had to wait for the transport technology of the later nineteenth century.[23] In that sense, their otherness did not exclude them from economic life but, on the contrary, made for a certain dynamic in developing market relations, by the exchange of commodities and services which they were particularly fitted to supply for those which they conspicuously lacked. It is noteworthy how often in the description of upland life we find the statement that the main relations of the dwellers of a valley were not with those of neighbouring valleys, but with lowland communities.[24] By the same token, marginal regions also provided a market for producers in the core areas for commodities which it was out of their power to produce, or the production of which had been allowed to wither away in the interests of developing their own specialization. The most important of these were foodstuffs, especially corn and fruit.

The population of the higher Swiss mountains was supplied with food not only from nearby lower-lying cantons, but ultimately also from the rich agricultural lands of Swabia, situated north of Lake Constance, and the Rhine valley, as well as from the Po valley. This became even more marked when industrial employment began to spread to the Swiss uplands from the seventeenth century onward. Upland Tyrol was similarly dependent on the import of grain and animals for slaughtering.

[22] Hamilton (1963), 105–10; Bergier (1980), 234; Blache (1933), 84; Bailey (1989*a*), 111; Hooke (1982), 240; Niederer (1993), 187; Cantor (1982*c*); Winchester (1973), 93; Sella (1979), 107; Turnock (1970), 56 ff.; O'Dell and Walton (1962), 329–36.

[23] Pilkington (1789), 301; Derruau-Boniol and Fel (1970), 87–8; Fel (1962), 185; Hanagan (1989), 89. Also Ch. 9 below.

[24] e.g. Smailes (1960), 283; Price (1983), 58; Gray (1957), 9.

It has been said that 5,000–6,000 Hungarian oxen yearly were delivered to the mining towns there in the sixteenth century. Oxen as well as other foodstuffs are also particularly mentioned in the imports needed in the Swedish mining community of Bergslagen.[25] In the same way, the Scottish Highlands had to import grain from the Lowlands, and the Cotswold woollen areas imported their food from the Avon valley and from Somerset.

As for the Pennine uplands, according to Defoe, in the 1720s Halifax together with other textile towns imported corn from Lincolnshire, Nottinghamshire, and the East Riding, black cattle and horses from the North Riding and Lancashire, sheep and mutton from adjacent counties, butter from the East and North Ridings, and cheese from Cheshire and Warwickshire. By the end of the century, Aikin believed that Rochdale had to import nineteen-twentieths of its grain needs, while 'the whole country from Leeds westward into Lancashire, does not provide grain or feed for cattle sufficient to supply one-fifth of the inhabitants'. The Lake District and other northern uplands, as well as mid-Wales, sold wool and cattle in return for the produce of plains agriculture.[26]

The bleak mountains of the Erzgebirge, in which silver-and copper-mining towns shot up in the boom period of the fifteenth and sixteenth centuries, had to be supplied with grain and wine, cattle and meat from below. Those of the Slovakian/Hungarian mining area also depended on cloth, salt, and lead for the separation process from the outside. The position was revealed in a particularly striking form in the kingdom of Saxony, which found itself deprived, by the Peace settlement of 1815, of the agricultural provinces which had hitherto fed its industrial uplands. In consequence, special tariff agreements had to be made with Prussia, to which the agrarian territories now belonged, to ensure that the industrial and upland population continued to receive their grain supplies.[27]

The area of the county of Mark and the duchy of Berg, in western Germany, offers another interesting example of territorial and economic symbiosis. The area north of the river Ruhr was mainly agricultural, at least before the middle of the nineteenth century, and capable of feeding the mountainous regions further south, all of which lacked agricultural land but were rich in other resources. The Süderland south of the river had timber, which could be combined with the iron found in the Siegerland further south still, an upland and food import area. Some iron-finishing industries, including cutlery and wire-making, settled in the Süderland where there was water-power and charcoal. The Siegerland, in turn, was becoming short of timber by the eighteenth century and lacked coal altogether, which was

25 Strätz (1976), 118; Wolfstrigl-Wolfskron (1903), 183; Schläpfer (1984), 13; Pfister (1991), 155; Giger-Eschke (thesis, 1985); Göttmann (1991), 1; Stolz (1955), 280; Pfister (1994), 2; Søderberg (1984), 6.

26 Gray (1957), 112–13; Ramsay (1965), 3; Raistrick (1970), 79–80; Hamilton (1963), 357–62; and, in general, Petran (1965); Jones (1977), 501 and (1975), 341; Owen (1991*b*), 240–1; Miller (1991*c*), 188–92; Williams (1960–3), 32; Dilley (thesis, 1991), 131–6, 295 and (1991), 134 ff.; Hey (1979), 126; Rosset (1984), 134–6; Defoe (1927), ii. 606; Aikin (1795), 574; Hastings (1981), 13, 16; Fletcher (1971), 7; Searle (thesis, 1983), 57; Sylvester (1969), 135; Nicolson and Burn (1976), i. 11; Thirsk (1961), 73.

27 Kiesewetter (1988), 41–9; Unger (1983), 77; Probszt (1966), 257; Agricola (1950), 14.

part of the reason why the semi-finished iron and steel was sent north. Finally, without the industrial and mining uplands south of it, the northern parts of the county of Mark would have had no market for their agricultural produce, being surrounded to the west, north, and east by similarly endowed areas.[28]

It may well be argued that the existence of marginal agricultural deficit areas was an important factor, at certain times and in certain regions, of stimulating agricultural productivity and technical improvements in core areas. At a time of population growth, in particular, the developing regional division of labour would play a significant part in absorbing the additional consumers without lowering their standard of living, while at the same time laying the foundations for future advance.

In addition to trade, the economic interdependence of marginal areas with their neighbours also took the form of sharing part of the labour force by means of the widespread practice of the seasonal migration of labour. This is not entirely unconnected with the emigration movement sketched in Chapter 3 above, since regular seasonal absence might in time turn to permanent settlement; but there remains a fundamental difference. For in emigration, the link between marginal land and city is severed; in seasonal migration, it is the link which is important.

From the upland areas in particular, it was common for workers who would otherwise have been seasonally underemployed to fill temporary gaps in the lowland economies. Broadly, two types of movement may be discerned. There was the temporary absence of mountain people in the summer, including the harvest period: here the pull factor, the need for their labour in the lowlands, usually exerted the greater power. But there were also cases of absence in the winter: for this the push factor of enforced idleness and harsh conditions in the uplands may have provided the greater impetus, though the pull was by no means absent.

In eighteenth-century France these movements presented themselves in part as a problem of poverty, as many of the vagabonds, pedlars, and beggars to be found in the towns and on the road came from the mountain areas—the Massif Central, the Alps, and the Pyrenees. In drought years, in particular, 'armies of beggars descended into the plains' from Ariège. But migrant workers also performed useful functions as tinkers, repairers, suppliers of goods to outlying villagers, and road workers.[29] Many of the migrants, then and later, were skilled, and even those who went as harvest hands, labourers, or domestics contributed in significant ways to the economy of the areas to which they moved. At the same time, even those regarded as unskilled who took the lowest-paid jobs available mostly still lived frugally enough to send, or take, some cash home to help out in the mountain villages. In this manner, they made a vital contribution to the economy also of the marginal territory.

The Massif Central was a major source of such migrant labour. In 1808–13 it supplied 54,400 of the 120,000 migrant workers counted in France, and in 1852

[28] Eversmann (1804); Schulte (1959), 9 ff.

[29] Weber (1976), 17, also 63–4; Hufton (1983), 307–8 and (1972), 100–4 and (1974), 73 ff.; Lucassen (1993); Woolf (1986), 7.

this had risen to 115,000 out of 363,000. From its northern settlements, there was a regular stream of building workers to Paris, forming a significant part of the labour force which rebuilt the city in the nineteenth century. They lived closely together in certain parts of the city, preserving their own traditions and their own language. In some upland places up to 90 per cent of the male labour force was said to be engaged in building work away from home in the late eighteenth century. In the Creuse, the wandering building workers (*maçons*) were said to have increased from 6,000 in 1789 to 13,000 in 1814 and 34,000 in 1848. From the southern slopes of the Massif, temporary migrant workers covered both the cities and the countryside of Provence. In towns like Nîmes, as well as in Lyons, the men would work as chimney sweeps, bootblacks, knife grinders, tinkers, cobblers, and pedlars, and the women as textile workers or domestics: 'Within certain limits, mountain girls had always sought the plain . . . for much the same reason as their brothers did, because the prospect it held of a less lean life.' Cantal in particular was the home of the pedlars. Much of this would be winter labour.

In the countryside, apart from salt gathering, migrants would help to bring in the harvest, then return home for the later mountain harvest season, then back south again for the grape picking, to return home finally for lifting potatoes and bringing in the chestnut harvest.[30] 'In the Dordogne the ancient symbiosis between the poor, birch-covered highlands and the more prosperous chestnut country below endured until 1900, with tribes of hill people coming down to work for the valley farmers, gathering chestnuts on a 50–50 basis.'[31]

The French Alps similarly lost much of their labour force in the winter to the towns, while in the summer many of their people moved to the lowlands for the harvest. By the end of the eighteenth century it has been estimated that 100,000 people left every winter for the Po valley, the Rhône valley, and other areas. From the Middle Ages onward, the building activity in several Italian cities came to depend on the migrant workers from the Piedmont mountains and from Ticino, who also furnished tin and coppersmiths, coopers and weavers, beside agricultural workers. Men from one upper valley in the Alpes-Maritimes 'were known over the whole of Europe as puppeteers', while those from the slopes of the Lure were herbalists, distilling their product from the native flowers.[32] Temporary workers from the Pyrenees came down mainly for harvest work, but the region also furnished winter migrants. These were among the poorest. In general, skilled workers came from less poverty-stricken backgrounds. In some of the valleys, villagers spent one winter

[30] Weber (1976), 174, 282; Chevalier (1973), 228; Gravier (1964), 291; Moch (1983); Poitrineau (1986), 115–17; Bickel (1947), 101; Châtelain (1976), i. 44–6, 177; ii. 776; Fel (1962), 145–56; Derruau-Boniol and Fel (1970), 71–2; Hanagan (1989), 78. Curiously enough, masons (together with bakers and tailors) were similarly prominent among temporary migrants out of the Balkan mountains, Todorov (1983), 383.

[31] Weber (1976), 118.

[32] Merlin (1971), 32–3; Blache (1933), 83, 88–90; Frödin (1940), 271; Woolf (1986), 57; Niederer (1993), 217; Cépède (1961), 172; Viazzo (1989), 102–3, 130–1, 145–50.

knitting and weaving woollen goods, which the men would then peddle in the following winter in France, Germany, or Switzerland, returning with manufactures which they then peddled in Spain.[33]

From the Swiss cantons a stream of confectioners and café proprietors went out every year to many parts of Europe: many of these, as indeed other skilled migrant workers, ultimately settled in lowland towns. But there were also the more common harvesters including grape pickers, water carriers, pedlars, butchers, tinkers, cobblers, and skilled and unskilled building workers. Typically, they would concentrate on trades not protected by guilds.[34] Tyrol also furnished harvesters in the summer months—some 20,000 a year according to an estimate of 1789—and pedlars and labourers in the winter. Like some Swiss, many of them, especially youngsters known as *Schwabenkinder*, worked in the Swabian fields which supplied food to the mountain people, thus tying the two areas together with a double link. Other German regions also obtained their seasonal harvesters mostly from the poorer, mountain districts.[35] Similar groups of seasonal workers emerged from Balkan mountains and Welsh hills, from Lakeland and Pennine villages and Highland glens, from Ireland, and from forests in Scandinavia and the Alpine slopes.[36]

The Swiss military mercenary trade, mentioned in Chapter 3 above, formed a particular type of migrant labour, justifying to some extent the statement that 'for balancing the economy of mountain communities war, it has been said, was an essential industry'.[37]

By the seventeenth century the system had become highly organized. At one level, there were treaties between the cantonal authorities and foreign rulers to allow recruitment on conditions laid down, which included pension payments to the canton and, for a time, valuable tariff concessions for imports into the foreign country, above all into France. At the other level, the trade was managed by 'captains' who made contracts with foreign rulers to supply troops for payment, with the intention of emerging with a profit at the end. After returning from service, the senior officers tended to receive high civic honours in their home towns; they occupied leading political posts and in due course their families frequently also came to own and manage large industrial enterprises.[38]

The effects of the mercenary system on the Swiss economy has been much debated. About half of those who went abroad never came back, either because of

[33] Caron (1978), 456–7; Poussou (1970), 64–5; Grigg (1980), 39; Sahlins (1989), 142.

[34] Niederer (1993), 102; Mathieu (1987), 228–9 and (1992), 106; Weiss (1941), 300; Schwarzenbach (1931), 34; Veyret (1978), 82; Mayer (1952), 200; Pfister (1994), 2–6, 14–15.

[35] Zwanowetz (1977), 427; Cole and Wolf (1974), 82–3; Kocka (1990), 208.

[36] Gray (1957), 53; Marshall (1970), 286; Schwarz (1959), 238; Wessely (1853), i. 429 ff.; Palairet (1986), 424; John (1950), 66; Hamilton (1963), 11; Lythe and Butt (1975), 92; O'Grada (1994), 79; Hastings (1981), 147; Devine (1988), 146 ff.

[37] Jones (1971), 420; p. 80 above.

[38] Bührer (1977), 41–5, 55 ff., 79, 89, 124 ff.; Ruckstuhl (thesis, 1990), 56–60, 85, 91 ff.; Kälin (thesis, 1985); Niederer (1993), 200; Schelbert (1976), 161; Suter (1971), 37–8, 126; Bucher (1974), 123–4.

death or because of permanent emigration. This represented a considerable loss of manpower, mostly of young, healthy men; but if, as has been frequently stated, recruitment occurred because of over-population, it was a preferable cure compared with permanent emigration or starvation. Among other significant gains were the favourable tariff treatment by France, and the annual pensions from abroad, which greatly helped the Swiss balance of payments. Further, the system called into being a class of rich, active entrepreneurs who knew their way around other countries. The returning ordinary soldiers were also sometimes said to be marked out as active, enterprising men in their villages.

Against this, and in addition to the grievous human loss, former soldiers were said by others to have returned as drunkards and idlers. The loss of their production was incalculable, and among other disadvantages, a surplus of women emerged in many communities.[39] Perhaps the best that can be said is that, as long as the country could not feed its growing numbers at the current state of technology, the mercenary system was one method of transferring labour to the food supplies available elsewhere.

Mercenaries in considerable numbers were also recruited from the Scottish Highlands, from Corsica, Albania, the Caucasus,[40] and other upland areas. However, nowhere else did they involve their countries in such close and long-lasting significant economic relationships with the outside world as was the case with the young Swiss men, who for centuries left their native mountains to fight in wars for foreign rulers for money.

Finally, we have to examine the role of capital as a linkage between the marginal areas and the rest. In past centuries, capital may have been of less economic significance than it is today, but it nevertheless played an important role at times.

Modern observers, viewing regional interconnections from the point of view of core–periphery relationships, in which, moreover, the 'periphery' is often thought of as colonial or occupied territory, tend to argue that the core will attract capital from the periphery, sucking it dry, hampering its progress, and thus widening the gap between them as time passes. This would be consistent with Myrdal's 'backwash effect', referred to in Chapter 1 above, and Hirschman's polarization effect.[41] Even where the rich centre invests in the margin, so runs the argument, it will be merely for the purpose of exploiting its resources: the 'surplus value' is still transferred to the core, without benefiting the periphery.[42] In a less extreme form it may be argued that the periphery tends to depend on the outside world for funds, while governments are less likely to provide for its infrastructure than for that of the core areas, unless particular factors apply.[43] There is, however, also a contrary view,

[39] Bickel (1947), 93; Bircher (1938), 48; Schelbert (1976), 155–7; Mayer (1952), 192; Netting (1981), 54, 97; Günther (1930), 229.

[40] Braudel (1976), i. 48; Kiernan (1988), 55; Novosel'tsev (1986), 19; Lythe and Butt (1975), 12; p. 80 above.

[41] Williamson (1975), 161; p. 17 above.

[42] Wellhofer (1989), 345.

[43] Clark (1981), 101; Williams (1991), 111.

especially if the periphery is within the same country, summarized by Myrdal's thesis of the 'spread effect'. According to this, as the resources of the core become exhausted, as traffic and environmental problems arise, and high wage demands and social insecurity begin to make the existing centres less attractive, investment moves outward and even governments favour the marginal areas: thus, typically, regional divergence is followed by convergence.[44]

Past European history furnishes examples of all these possible relationships, though seldom in such a clear-cut form. Examples of capital being drawn, in any quantity, away *from* the marginal areas are, however, rare. Bergier has argued ingeniously that as the Swiss developed a flourishing export trade in the High and Late Middle Ages, selling animals and their products, including cheese, butter, and hides to the lowlands as far away as Lombardy, Burgundy, Bavaria, Swabia, Alsace, and the Swiss lowland itself, they were able to accumulate substantial capital sums. With those they extended their herds, improved the infrastructure, including the route over the Gotthard, and were able to dominate their markets. They had thus turned the tables: they were now the centre, and their markets had become periphery. However, as is the case with all marginal areas which take the lead, their economic hegemony did not last long. After 1500 the uplands lost their relative advantage, and became impoverished once more. In spite of this, Swiss cities such as Basle and Geneva continued to be sources of capital for outside areas,[45] leading directly into the modern era of huge capital transactions centred on Switzerland.

The movement in the opposite direction, of capital flowing *into* the marginal areas, was, however, much more common. There were, essentially, two types of driving force in this process, though they were not unconnected. Capital was sent into the margins, mainly by governments, to develop the infrastructure, by building roads, harbours, and the like. This might be for the purpose of subduing a rebellious population, as in the case of the military roads built in the Scottish Highlands in the 1720s, or it might be to open the region up for development of a kind favoured by the government of the day: English attempts to 'civilize' the Celtic fringe have been said to have been of such a nature.[46] This might also be undertaken by private capital with strong political backing, as in the case of the large-scale drainage schemes for the English Fens in the seventeenth century.

The second type of investment was targeted at the exploitation of specific natural resources. Typical for this was the Dutch and later British capital which developed the forest resources of Norway, Sweden, and Finland. But probably the most impressive examples of this type of investment were the large-scale mining enterprises of the fifteenth and sixteenth centuries, in the mountains of Bohemia–Saxony, Slovakia–Hungary, and Tyrol. There, ownership, as well as management, passed into the hands of the capitalists of Augsburg, Nuremberg, Cologne, Frankfurt,

[44] Williamson (1975), 164, 178 ff.

[45] Bergier in discussion following Smout (1983), 351; Lösch (1954), 448–50; Morsel (1972), 564; Introduction, n. 9; pp. 87 and 115 above.

[46] Hechter (1975), 114–15.

Antwerp, and other cities as soon as the enlarged capital needs exceeded the resources of the miners and the territorial rulers. This will be discussed in greater detail in Chapter 8 below.[47] We shall refer to the other major form of lowland and city investment in marginal areas, namely the provision of work by proto-industrial putters-out or *Verleger*, in Chapter 10 below.

Where no outside capital could be attracted, marginal regions might have difficulty in raising their own. Conditions varied greatly, but quite frequently the general poverty of the area meant that miners, farmers, or herdsmen fell heavily into debt. The typical peasant villager, in the uplands as well as in the plains, would be either mortgaged or in the clutches of a usurer.[48]

Thus the links between marginal areas and the rest could be many and varied. Frequently they were substantial. The marginal area itself was clearly affected by its economic relationships with its neighbours, but those neighbours, also, derived not inconsiderable benefits from the proximity of regions possessing assets and resources different from their own. Far from being isolated, as they were frequently described, most marginal areas of Europe have been shown to have made up a part, and a not unimportant part, of the complex and intricately patterned network of the European economy at every stage from the High Middle Ages onward. Moreover, far from being always the weaker and more backward partner helped along by the advanced inhabitants of the plains and the cities, they were not infrequently the source of activity and initiative, and sometimes even of capital.

[47] Also Kellenbenz (1965), 407; Wolfstrigl-Wolfskron (1903), 121; Strieder (1929), 6–7; Paulinyi (1971), 565; Vlachovic (1971), 603–4; Stromer (1984), 51; Günther (1930), 423,

[48] Cole and Wolf (1974), 166–7.

PART II

Case Studies

6

The German Colonization of the East

We now turn, in this second part of the book, to some examples of marginal areas which were among the most advanced economically in the Europe of their time, or were, at least, at the cutting edge of technological innovation. Other examples could have been found, but our selection is intended to indicate, in its variety, the kind of contribution which marginal areas were able to make, and were peculiarly fitted to make.

As noted in Chapter 2 above, Europe experienced a substantial increase in population in the eleventh–thirteenth centuries, and possibly into the early fourteenth century. Given the limited advances in technology of an agricultural sector operating only slightly above subsistence level, the increased food supply needed to feed the additional population had to be produced mainly by extensive rather than intensive expansion: more people meant more land under cultivation. The inner colonization in Bloch's 'period of large-scale land clearances'[1] has been described above. But there was also an outward push by west Europeans, into northern Scandinavia, into the Iberian peninsula,[2] and into eastern Europe. It is with this last that the present chapter is concerned.

Eastern Europe was by no means empty territory. It was occupied at the time by Slavic, Baltic, Magyar, and other populations who had some agriculture, as well as a fishing and gathering economy, and the beginnings of statehood. The status of the peasant is obscure, but there was a church which collected tithes, a modest nobility, and an incipient differentiation of property.[3] Nevertheless, with one important exception, the colonization movement appears to have encountered remarkably little resistance from the settled populations as it penetrated into their territory. The causes for this are, or at any rate were, a hotly debated issue among nationalist historians. German historians are wont to stress the superior organization and technology which the migrants brought with them, and which explained the welcoming invitations by native rulers; against this, Polish, Czech, and Baltic authors tend to deny the technical superiority of the Germans or at least to minimize it and emphasize rather their aggressive behaviour.[4] Because of the influence of nationalist pride,

[1] Bloch (1966), 5; Smith (1978), 163 ff.; Rösener (1992), 22; Duby (1974), 201 ff.

[2] Lopez (1984), 153.

[3] Aubin (1971), 449–52. There is an enormous literature on the German eastern colonization. The English-speaking world is much indebted to Aubin's magisterial account for an overview of it, as the German is to the work of Kuhn (1955) and of Higounet (1986), on which much of this chapter is based.

[4] For typical examples see Kasiske (1941) and Kahk (1989), 169–174, respectively. Cf. also Kluge (1969); Schlesinger (1975*b*); Graus (1975), 32 ff.; Menzel (1975), 136–7; Trawkowski (1975), 350; Wenskus (1975), 417; Piskorski (1991).

but also because of the patchy nature of the source material, there has been much myth-making in the past regarding the colonization drive as a whole.

The eastward movement proceeded slowly over some centuries. It may be thought of as advancing along several parallel routes. The southernmost thrust followed the Danube valley and the eastern Alps. Here much of the best land on valley bottoms was already settled, and the immigrants had to be satisfied with the upper reaches, but there were enormous forests still left, and their clearance was fostered by the foundation of numerous monasteries in the region, while the settlers were protected by strategically sited castles. Thus Styria, Carinthia, and Slovenia were occupied, and by the twelfth century also the Marchfeld and Burgenland. With the immigrants came the miners: there was mining in Styria, near Leoben and Hüttenberg, from the twelfth century if not earlier, reaching Eisenerz in the thirteenth century. Some townships were founded, though the uplands remained sparsely settled, being used for summer grazing, at most.

In the Danube valley itself, the Weinviertel was occupied by 1040, protected by two marches: the approximate frontiers established then turned out to be the permanent limits of cohesive German settlement. The settlers of the Waldviertel meanwhile pushed up against the Bohemians and a frontier was fixed between them in 1179. By that time, the first towns as well as mining enterprises had been founded in Tyrol.[5] Later movement advanced further east. In the Carpathians the Germans found valuable minerals and they ultimately reached Transylvania, turning it into a German enclave among Hungarians and Romanians.

A second thrust proceeded along the mountainous arc of the Böhmerwald, the Erzgebirge, the Riesengebirge, and the Sudeten. Although the lower grounds, with their fertile loess soil, had been settled early, there was still much empty space, and the mountains were still thickly forested. It was there that rich mineral ores were found, which in turn led to the early foundation of towns. There were some signs of Germans in Komorn in the twelfth century: Duke Boleslav, who had called in some monks earlier, permitted peasant settlement in 1175. By 1202 colonists are mentioned in Silesia, miners in 1217, and after the Magyars were driven out, there was a further extension of mining settlements, including a 'Saxon' mine at Neusohl (Banská Bistrica) in 1255, and the gold-mining area of Kremnitz, which was given its charter early in the fourteenth century. In the second half of the thirteenth century, there were signs of overpopulation and settlers moved further into Upper Silesia and higher up the mountains, while others settled on the Bohemian side of the mountain ranges.[6]

A third line of advance occupied the plains north of this mountain range. Much of this was boggy and marshy land, the best of which was already occupied; nevertheless, there were still empty spaces and uncleared forest land to be found. Advance did not proceed without resistance on the part of the Slavs, but the line of the Elbe was reached around the year 1000, and the Oder about 1150.

[5] Klein (1980); Pickl (1986*b*), 38 ff.; Tremel (1981), 89; Kötzschke and Ebert (1937), 10–12; Darby (1956), 197; Vilfan (1975); Kubinyi (1975), 546.

[6] Kuhn (1971), 9–22; Probszt (1966), 27–9; Sieber (1954), 7.

The northernmost thrust occupied the coastal strips along the Baltic and the lands south of it. This can be considered as having consisted of two separate movements: the foundation of trading ports, colonized from Lübeck, which was established in 1143 by Henry the Lion, and ultimately reaching as far as Riga on the one hand; and a land advance on the other. This second movement, in which the Teutonic Knights played a prominent role, is the one which most resembles a series of warlike campaigns and which appears most often in the history books. Here also there were bogs and marshes as well as sands and lakes, but some fertile soil was also found, and while, again, there was some pre-existing settlement, there were empty spaces as well. In all this, something like a chronological sequence can be discerned, running from south to north: the Austrian drive, having been thrown back in the eighth–tenth centuries, was in full swing by the eleventh century, while this would apply to Brandenburg only around 1230.[7]

It should be emphasized that the movement as a whole was by no means the outcome of any unified plan or co-ordinated advance. Decisions were made locally, by princes, prelates, and entrepreneurs as opportunity seemed to offer, though the experience and apparent success in a neighbouring territory would obviously affect the plans regarding one's own. Nevertheless, there seemed to be a forward movement on a broad front, almost like a military thrust with a recognizable, though much broken front line. Thus by 1200, some 80–100 km. had been 'gained', and the line of the three northern fronts extended roughly from western Bohemia and the Lusatias, to the middle mark of Brandenburg, and on to central Mecklenburg. Among the towns founded were Chemnitz (market rights in 1143), Leipzig and Brandenburg (both before 1170), Lübeck (1143–57), the Hamburg bishopric (mentioned in 1158), and Schwerin (1160). By 1150, as noted above, the Oder was reached, after 1200 the Vistula: Danzig was given full town rights in 1224. The Teutonic Knights founded Reval in 1219 and Dorpat in 1225, and Memel (1252) and Königsberg followed. In the ore mountains were Karpfen (1238) and Schemnitz (1244). Prussia was effectively settled between 1300 and 1350, and more southerly German colonization had reached the Dunajec before 1300 and had crossed the San by about 1350.[8] The total number of settlers between the Elbe and the Saale was estimated at 200,000 in the twelfth century, with a similar number in the thirteenth. By the fourteenth the movement had come to a halt, even going into reverse. In one way it could be seen as a levelling out of population densities, which under Slav occupation was not likely to have exceeded 1–2 persons per sq. km., but by the end of the medieval drive had settled down around 10–20 persons per sq. km.[9] It was to start up again after an interval of about one hundred years.

[7] Zernack (1975), 785.

[8] Aubin (1971), 455; Kuhn (1955), 41–7; map in *Times Atlas of World History* (1988 edn.), 119; and in Smith (1978), 173.

[9] Kuhn (1973), 199, 209, 228; Blum (1957), 816–18; Higounet (1986), 32, 86; Krenzlin (1952), 14–19; Pounds (1973), 335.

There was some tendency for the pioneers who formed the advance guard of this movement to be drawn, not from the long settled areas further behind, but from areas only recently covered by colonization, rather as in the case of the North American westward movement in modern times. Some settlers, however, were attracted over long distances and there were colonists from all parts of the German-speaking world, with a tendency of the northern lowlanders, including Rhinelanders and Westphalians, to stick to the plains, the southerners to move to the mountainous territories in the south, Flemings and Hollanders to move to the marshy lands, and miners to the metalliferous and the salt-bearing ranges. In most areas, a fairly representative cross-section of western society was re-created in the new lands, containing monks and knights, burghers and craftsmen, but above all peasants. In the eastern Baltic lands conquered by the Teutonic Knights, however, there were relatively fewer German peasant immigrants. Similarly in the regions which have remained non-German to the present day, including Poland, Bohemia and Moravia, and Hungary, Germans were more strongly represented in the towns rather than the country, above all by merchants and churchmen.

The conquests by the Teutonic Knights advancing eastward and northward along the Baltic littoral stand out as being of a different character from the rest. They are to be seen as a parallel to the more famous crusades into the Holy Land—a mixture of religious mission and personal greed. In their case, the populations encountered by the Knights were mostly pagan, they had little political cohesion, and encroachments on their territories had been made at different times by Swedes, Danes and, later, Russians, while the Poles had made efforts to convert the Pomeranians and the Prussians to Christianity. The original order licensed by the pope to undertake the conquest was that of the Knights of the Sword of Livonia, founded in 1202. They were not very numerous and fell to squabbling with the bishops and the Cistercians; after they suffered a devastating defeat in 1236, the pope transferred in 1237 the remaining members of the sword order, and the task of spreading Christianity, to the Order of the Teutonic Knights. These had been formed as a nursing brotherhood at the siege of Acre in 1190 and transmuted into a knightly order in 1198. The original scheme was to divide the conquered territories between the bishops and the order in the ratio of two-thirds to one-third.

The Knights had been called upon earlier to fight heathen neighbours on behalf of King Andrew of Hungary in 1211 and by the Duke of Masovia in 1230, while other knightly orders were to be similarly engaged by Duke Boleslav the Bashful of Cracow in 1256 and by a later Hungarian king, Bela IV, in 1247. None of these had any lasting success apart from the Teutonic Knights in the north. In a series of bitterly fought wars the latter conquered, first Prussia, after their victory of 1249, and later large territories further along the Baltic coast, right up to Estonia, annexed from Denmark in 1346, the Newmark being purchased in 1402.

The treatment which the Teutonic Knights meted out to the non-German population has been the subject of much controversy. Recent research suggests that it differed substantially according to the ethnic composition of the people they

encountered—Prussians, Poles, Pomeranians, Cours, or Lithuanians—and according to the degree of resistance they offered. According to one account, following a series of raids and rebellions, 'the mild attitude towards the natives was abandoned, and a policy of extermination was the German answer to the atrocities of the Prussian rebels'. Sambia, for example, 'was reduced to such a desert that forests grew where once a numerous people had dwelt'. By 1263 the Sambians were 'practically exterminated'.[10] It was also not long before the religious impulse of this 'sanctified aggression' fell wholly into oblivion. Many Prussians, for example, were killed rather than converted, though the numbers killed have often been exaggerated in the literature: in 1308 the Archbishop of Riga was forced to beg the pope to stop the Knights' persecution of Christians. Instead, the conquests were used to settle the Knights on large and lucrative estates. When worked by German peasants, these enjoyed, as elsewhere in the east, more freedoms than they had had in the west, and while they worked in part for the army, the Knights also offered them protection from raids originating outside their borders. Where natives were used to work their estates, as in Livonia and Estonia, they were made serfs. The Knights also had exclusive trading rights granted by the pope, which they used to become members of the Hanse, within which they obtained certain privileges on the basis of their military might. Their trading profits, together with the healthy surplus from tax and toll incomes in their heyday, were used in turn to pay their mercenary soldiers.[11]

The maximum extent of the order's territory was reached around 1400, when there were some 3,000 knights, priests, and serving brothers. In all, some 1,400 villages and 76 towns were founded. The order maintained itself by efficient military organization and by development of its estates and trade links, but it could not stand up to the onslaught of Poles and Lithuanians, once these had been united. After the disastrous battle of Tannenberg (1410), the order declined and there was little new settlement.

In contrast to that drive, whose object was conquest coupled with conversion, the main objective for much of the rest of the European east was extension of settlement, although at least on the part of the authorities, here too motives were mixed: for example, the attraction of 'abundant open space and the principle of expanding Christendom, its culture, power and economic development towards the periphery . . . The ideology of the core and periphery, linked to the perceived advantages of the periphery, helped to mobilize colonists from the core areas.' It was sometimes, like other crusades, cloaked in a garb of righteousness, 'to suppress superstition, barbarism and anarchical tribal warfare'. At the same time, 'the crusade was in great measure a trading adventure'.[12] Typical of these mixed motives were the large

[10] Boswell (1932), 257; also Wenskus (1975); Urban (1973) and (1975), 156–9; Kuhn (1975*a*), 232; Schreiber (1965), 74–5.

[11] Anderson *et al.* (1992), 358 ff.; Halecki (1952), 69–73; Seward (1972), 110 ff.; Lönnroth (1971), 375–91; Krollmann (1928).

[12] Denecke (1992), 309, 310; Urban (1975), pp. xii, 269.

grants awarded to monastic houses. The monks were expected both to spread Christianity and to clear and open up territory to cultivation and occupation, applying the same skill which they had shown in the process of the internal colonization in the west. None expressed this better than the Bishop of Magdeburg when calling for a crusade against the pagans to the east in 1108:

> The pagans are evil, but their land is good in meat, honey, flour . . . and poultry, and when it is tilled, full of rich harvests beyond compare. Thus say those who know it. Therefore, oh you Saxons, Franks, Lorraineans and Flemings, you famous men and conquerors of the world, here you can save your souls and if it so please you, gain the best land for your dwelling.[13]

It is worth remembering in this context that several of the areas into which the settlers moved were Christianized already, leaving an economic motive as the single most pervasive driving force of the eastward expansion.

Settlement was in principle always organized. Leaving to one side the bloody conquest of the Knights, there were two main sources of initiative: on the one hand, the attempt by German rulers, lords, and ecclesiastics to extend their territory thereby or gain new lands; and on the other, the invitation from native rulers among the Slavs and Hungarians who invited settlers into their realms. In both cases, the colonists came in groups rather than as individuals.

Where Germans had taken the initiative, they generally appointed middlemen known as *locatores* who organized the colonization in detail. Typically the peasants came from crowded areas, 'lured by the prospect of larger holdings and greater personal freedom, lower dues and an end to labour services'. According to the traditional account, these colonizers moved into 'empty' lands, mostly forests or moors which they had to clear themselves for their own settlement. Where the terrain permitted, the cleared area would be laid out in the planned form of a 'street village', the houses being lined up along each side of the main street, with their land allocations running in strips at a right angle away from the road. That pattern was apparently first worked out by the Ascanic margrave, for an area which had Frankfurt an der Oder, founded in 1253, as its centre.[14] On hilly ground, as along the foothills of the Alps, for example, villages would take on more complex shapes, and holdings had less regular sizes. But, in essence, they would reproduce a German village structure, with the important difference that the settlers were granted a more generous land allocation.

While it was German princes, lords, and bishops who encouraged colonization of the lands still empty *within* their realms, the settlements which pushed outward were often undertaken with the connivance and possibly even on the initiative of Slavic lords. In those cases the immigrants tended to find themselves under Slavic jurisdiction and surrounded by a large pre-existing Slavic population, while the 'foundation' of towns, too, frequently consisted of enlarging and immigrating into existing Slavic towns, rather than founding completely new ones. Much of the process is, however, still obscure.[15]

[13] Cited in Higounet (1986), 88.

[14] Rösener (1992), 41; Krenzlin (1952), 78.

[15] Jegorov (1930).

Finally, where there was a properly formed non-German political unit or 'state', as in Poland, Bohemia, or Hungary, it is generally agreed that it was the territorial rulers, or lords or ecclesiastics authorized by them, who took the initiative in inviting and regulating settlement. There were thus three types of framework of colonization, in three rough bands moving from west to east: there were 'German' lands being colonized by filling out empty spaces; there were, next, lands without firm internal control, sometimes known as 'Germania Slavica'; and there were, lastly, properly governed kingdoms and dukedoms whose rulers actively encouraged settlement.

The drive eastwards tailed off in the fourteenth century, most probably because of the catastrophic decline of population associated with the Black Death as a result of which German rulers and landlords, far from wishing to encourage emigration, were in many areas desperately trying to attract migrants into their manors or territories, while preventing their own people from leaving. Where they were strong enough to do so, the lords in fact managed to tie the peasant to the soil by legal rules, which turned into a main ingredient of the 'second serfdom' that was to become a prominent feature east of the Elbe. Meanwhile, by the late fourteenth century among the areas abandoned were also some of the newly settled lands, which were either reoccupied by Slavs, or turned into *Wüstungen*—deserted villages.[16]

Thus brought to a halt, the eastward movement was never resumed in quite the same form, though a new wave of migration began in the sixteenth century and continued well into the seventeenth. The nearest approach to a similar extension of colonization eastward occurred into the forests of Posen, west Prussia, central Poland, and Volhynia, referred to by some as a 'second eastern colonization'. Slobody, a suburb of Moscow established by Tsar Alexey Mikhailovich in 1652, was largely settled by German craftsmen and traders.[17] Taking both waves together, at least one million German settlers had by then moved to the east.[18] There were also Dutch settlers who drained some of the remaining marshes, and from the seventeenth century onward, there were religious refugees from the west who moved east, as well as specific groups invited by Russian rulers as late as the nineteenth century.[19] In all these cases, circumstances differed in material respects from the medieval drive that was part of the territorial expansion of the west.

For as long as these colonized areas were in the process of settlement, they formed the true margin of Europe. This was so not merely because they consisted largely of forest, marsh, or mountain, the typical marginal landscapes, but also because they were at the edge of 'expanding Christendom, its culture, power and economic development towards the periphery'. The settlers were the frontiersmen of their age—a likeness which had not escaped the observation of the originator of

[16] Higounet (1986), 329; Rösener (1992), 267–70; Kötzschke and Kretzschmar (1965), 149.
[17] Berthold (1964), 10–11; Kuhn (1955), 110; Aubin (1939), 21; Birnbaum (1987), 32.
[18] Kuhn (1973), 210.
[19] Zajchowska (1976); Druzhinina (1991), 220–1; Kuhn (1973), 213–16; p. 82 above.

the American 'frontier' thesis, Frederick Jackson Turner.[20] It is indeed possible to discern a number of similarities in the two frontier societies.

As hinted above, settlers could not have been attracted without the offer of more generous conditions than they had enjoyed at home. These would necessarily have differed, but apart from runaways, the migrating peasants would have had to be among the minority of 'free' peasants in order to be permitted to move at all. The inducements to leave home were essentially of two kinds: more land, and greater freedom combined with various legal privileges.

Land was cheap for whoever claimed rights as a landlord, and peasants were generally given very much more of it than they had occupied at home. Their new tenancies were often described as 'full land' holdings. The size of these could vary with the quality of the soil, local custom, and the varying size of the standard measure, the *Hufe*, best translated as 'hide'. In Brandenburg and east Prussia an allocation of two *Hufen* per settler was likely to have been the rule; elsewhere it might be one *Hufe* or even less. On marshland, after it was drained and improved by Flemish settlers, the holdings might consist of 2 Flemish hides, or about 33 ha.; in the Erzgebirge, where the holdings were based on the Frankish hide, the allocation tended to be some 24 ha.[21]

Among the privileges granted to the settlers in the East was a greatly enlarged scope for personal freedom, an exchange, in Darby's phrase, of the 'old western feudal Germany' for the 'new eastern colonial Germany'—though it must be remembered that 'freedom' is a somewhat elastic term in view of the numerous ways in which it could be circumscribed. In practice, the colonists could count on strict limitation of personal services owed to the lord. Privileges were granted on exceptionally generous terms in the marshy areas, where the Netherlanders and Flemings expected their own favourable *Hollerrecht* traditions to apply, and in certain wooded areas, where the *Hagen* rights were applied. Others achieved a great deal of independence because of the 'natural difficulties of the boggy terrain'. It is 'beyond doubt', a recent study asserted with only slight exaggeration, that the east Elbians 'enjoyed what was the greatest degree of personal freedom anywhere in the Middle Ages'.[22]

Perhaps most significant for the peasant, his land became heritable and disposable at will, being burdened with a relatively limited and fixed quit-rent only, together with possibly other low dues. The tithe also was fixed, but since it was normally paid in kind, its relative burden was to increase over time as the value of money, in which most rents were expressed, declined. Additionally, taxes to the territorial ruler were payable, though there were usually some years of tax freedom on settlement. The few scattered references that have survived do not allow us to venture any estimate of how much peasants generally paid for their land allocation. It

[20] Faber (1979), 15–16; Gerhard (1959), 206–7.

[21] Aubin (1971), 466; Rösener (1992), 41; Nitz (1983), 105–6; Kuhn (1973), 203–6.

[22] Rösener (1992), 231; Darby (1956), 195; Urban (1975), 11.

can be taken for granted that all dues and burdens were lighter on land which had to be laboriously cleared, as compared with settlement on formerly cultivated land newly laid out on German lines.[23] Terms were also more favourable in exposed distant or frontier areas. Thus settlers in the newly conquered eastern lands of Little Poland, roughly corresponding to the later Galicia, were offered twenty years' tax freedom and reduced tithes, and those on the even more exposed areas in the north-east of the country, around Lublin, were given thirty years' exemption from tithes.[24]

In addition to the privileges granted to individuals, the settlements were awarded collective benefits. These included their own lower jurisdiction, and a rather larger degree of juridical independence from the state in non-German territories. So-called German law, sometimes referred to as 'Magdeburg law', was applied, being considered superior to the protection afforded by Slavic codes, as indeed it was superior to anything known in the German west. In due course Slav peasants who were able to pay full taxes also gained the privilege of being made subject to German law, so that after a time it was difficult to distinguish those descended from settler families from those of native descent.

Where the settlement had taken place on the invitation of a foreign ruler, the privileges tended to be even more extensive. As an example, Henryk the Bearded, Prince of Silesia may be quoted, who launched a campaign in 1205 to attract 10,000 peasant families into 400 new villages. Each family was to get a generous arable holding, together with pasture and forest land to be held in common; all were to be freed from all services and dues for an agreed period, after which they were to be liable to military service only; and they were to enjoy the benefits of German law. Similarly favourable offers are recorded of King Koloman of Hungary (1096–1114), Duke Sobieslaus of Bohemia (*c.*1175) and King Andrew of Hungary (1205–35) in his code of 1224.[25] There are indications that some of these plans were stillborn, and that there were never enough potential immigrants to meet the wishes of the eastern sovereigns.[26]

The *locatores* noted above were the entrepreneurs who directly organized the transfer of population and settled the families on the land. In exchange for what for many must have been a considerable investment, they could count on an allocation of land which exceeded that of the peasants, and would be free of rent and often free of tithe; they might also receive part of the rents paid by the peasants. Additionally, they would be granted the right to build mills or inns, to keep bakers' and butchers' stalls, to enjoy a monopoly of brewing, and many other rights of a like kind. As *Schulze* or village magistrate, the former *locator* would also claim part of the revenue of justice. Some *Schulzen* acquired a hereditary right over the magistracy which, together with the larger land allotment and the other rights, would lift them

[23] Carsten (1941), 73–6; Halecki (1952), 73; Rösener (1992), 26; Rutkowski (1971), 499–506.

[24] Kuhn (1975*b*), 397, 409.

[25] A good list will be found in Kuhn (1975*a*), 255–6; also Davies (1981), 77; Quirin (1954); Kasiske (1941), 294; Sugar (1977), 146. But see Aubin (1971), 483.

[26] Trawkowski (1975), 353, 361.

well above the level of the ordinary peasant socially and economically, though still only as members of the lower orders. It was clear that the occupiers of that office formed a village entrepreneurial class in the making, though in the circumstances of east Elbian development, this would be within a rural rather than an urban or industrial context. Equivalents of these *locatores* were found also in France, Tyrol, and Russia.[27]

The kings and dukes of the region who fostered German and other western immigration were motivated by three main considerations. The first was strategic: to secure the frontiers. Numerous allocations of land were made in frontier areas, not without, at times, obliging the ruler on the other side of the border to match the initiative by a similar colonization of his own. The second was the wish to settle empty lands and wastes with a population of productive cultivators. Finally, it can be shown that some invitations to westerners were intended to bridge the technical and cultural gap with the west, to catch up.[28] These last two motives may be termed economic.

In this competitive bidding by eastern European rulers, there were often particular efforts made to get the Germans to establish towns in addition to agrarian settlements. The term 'town' must not be taken too literally in this context, but no matter how low we pitch the definition, the east was at a very rudimentary stage of urbanization only when the migration phase began. The foundation of towns then proceeded apace. Thus in Mecklenburg, the earliest town, Rostock, was first noted in 1211, but by 1276 there were records of 26 towns. Again, in the principality of Rügen, Richterberg was noted in 1231, followed by Stralsund in 1234: by 1278 there were 6 more towns. Western Pomerania, where Bahn and Prenzlau (1234) led the field, counted 44 towns by 1278. Goldberg is the first documented town in the dukedom of Breslau, dated 1211; by the end of the century, details of 88 towns are known. Lastly, it is estimated that in Oppeln there were 46 foundations between 1217 and 1300. There were strong German burgher communities even in the Hungarian capital city, Ofen, and in Prague in Bohemia.[29] All in all, we can take it that towns with trading links arose as part of the colonization drive, even if with some delay, in the east as they had in the west.

Thus the scene was set. On the margins of Europe there now came to be settled a peasant population, who by a process of self-selection consisted of some of the most energetic and enterprising of the age, and they were led by a class of entrepreneurs who might almost be called capitalist. They were given sufficient freedom and independence, together with a favourable tenancy structure on adequate holdings, to leave them with most of the gains of any improvement they introduced. Before long, some of the more prosperous peasants even hired outside labour for their plots, drawn generally from the labourers or the virtually landless so-called 'gardeners' who were required on the demesne lands. There was no question but

[27] Stökl (1975), 771–3; Zernack (1975), 797; Jones (1971), 357; Gerhard (1959), 223–4.
[28] Kuhn (1975*a*), 233–6, 259, and (1975*b*), 377–83; Zientara (1975), 337; Helbig (1975), 519–20.
[29] Kuhn (1975*a*), 238 ff.; Fügedi (1975), 488; Kubinyi (1975), 545 ff.

that they understood, and largely worked within a money economy. Thus almost from the first they required and demanded markets, to sell their surplus produce and buy manufactured goods and produce from outside. The experience of Brandenburg, Silesia, Greater Poland, Bohemia, and Moravia, among others[30] showed that this necessity for urban markets was accepted also by the rulers, who, as we have seen, were most active in founding towns.

Conditions were now ripe in the new settlements on the eastern margins of 'Europe' for increases in production and productivity by means of technical and organizational improvement. Did the men on the new lands grasp their opportunity to take the lead in the advance of European agriculture? Did they become pioneers of progress?

Given the extremely limited possibilities of the age for agrarian technical innovation and the scattered nature of the settlements as they were pushed forward in a thin line over a wide front, one would not expect the kind of striking and concentrated breakthroughs that marked later leading industrial regions. At most, one would expect a stream of the kind of small, imperceptible improvements which are significant in total yet will escape the eye of the historian. If we find nevertheless the literature to be of the unanimous opinion that the colonization of the East was associated with substantial innovations of a progressive agriculture, as we do, it must be because of better organization, and wider application of known technologies, rather than because of inventions in the narrow sense. After all, even in modern agricultural practice, years, decades, possibly even centuries pass before an innovation, after it has proved itself, is sufficiently widely adopted to make an economic impact: it is its wide adoption, rather than the initial spark, which provides the significant date. It is indeed the effective diffusion of innovations which appears to have taken place on Europe's eastern margin.

About the broad facts there is no dispute. Possibly the greatest achievement of the colonists was the introduction of grain growing into an area which had known little, if any, of it before, successfully enough to allow them to provide a substantial exportable surplus of bread grains for sale outside their region. The shipping of corn from Brandenburg to Flanders and England may be demonstrated from about 1250, after which it became a regular trade of increasing importance for the whole area. Among other consequences, it led to the development of transport routes, especially along the lakes and rivers, and the building up of ports on the Baltic.[31] The methods and implements of husbandry and the forms of agrarian organization which the German settlers introduced into their areas to achieve these results were greatly superior to those in use among the Slavic and Baltic peoples, though there may well have been one or other progressive unit among the latter before. Moreover, even if the colonists merely transferred to the east methods which were developed and known in the west, they used them more consistently and modernized on a broad front, while in the old Europe, advanced units were at best islands of modernity in a sea of backwardness.

[30] Aubin (1971), 473.

[31] Aubin (1971), 485; Smith (1978), 180–1.

Among these new methods was the introduction of the German three-field system of rotation. The advantages of this—including the reduction of fallow, the improved management of manure economy, and the opportunity of introducing new crops—are well known and need not be stressed. But while this rotation system was developed in the west essentially within a village open-field economy in which any change from time-worn methods, from traditional timing or types of crops had to be approved by the village as a whole and was therefore very hard to introduce or improve, the eastern settlements provided solid blocks of land which each peasant controlled for himself from the start. Elsewhere that advantage could be gained only at great cost and much later by a long drawn-out process of enclosure. The enterprising individual on the German frontier of cultivation, on the other hand, could from the start experiment and adapt more freely, to be followed rapidly by the rest, if he proved successful. Additionally, the immigrants also succeeded in introducing new crops, including the vine, hops, woad, vegetables, and fruit trees. The rearing of cattle and sheep was also greatly extended, and there are indications that the *Schulze*, as entrepreneur, opened up new possibilities for such local produce as timber.[32]

Among implements, it is the heavy iron plough, with coulter and mould-board, which is mentioned most often. It may well be that it was known on individual Slav farms, and it may also be that the older hook plough, which did little more than scratch the surface, was useful on newly cleared land where tree stumps obstructed progress. But overall, it was the colonists who introduced the heavy plough, and with it, they were able not merely to cultivate all types of soil, including sand and heavy clays which had defeated the natives, but to cultivate it more effectively by cutting and turning a deeper furrow. Moreover, by using horses rather than oxen, with an improved harness, the colonists were able to develop a much greater pulling power, though a more expensive one. They also had larger carts and better working tools of all kinds, including the scythe. Further, the waterwheel and windmill should be mentioned. 'The consequence was an extraordinary economic, cultural and political strengthening of these countries.'[33]

The drainage of the marshes along the sea coast and the river valleys deserves special mention. The technical skills to achieve this were beyond the powers of the German settlers, and expert Flemings, Hollanders, Zeelanders, and Frisians who had acquired their skill in their home countries were brought in to do the work. Almost invariably they came because they were formally invited by a ruler for work on a specific territory. Their main task was drainage and dyke building, but in the dry Geest they created irrigation channels, and there are indications that they also introduced some of their own forms of animal husbandry.

The first formal contract of which details are known was issued by the Archbishop of Bremen and Hamburg in 1113 (an older reading made it 1106) to a number of

[32] Fügedi (1975), 503.

[33] Kuhn (1975*a*), 256 and (1971), 100; Higounet (1986), 270; Seward (1972), 105; Slicher van Bath (1963), 155; Carsten (1941), 62; Rösener (1992), 24, 50–2, 109–16, 125; Kahk (1989), 174; Kuhn (1971), 100; Trawkowski (1975), 366; Jope (1957), 88, 91; Mokyr (1990), 32–7; Piskorski (1991), 64; Koebner (1932), 342.

Dutch peasants from the Utrecht region who were to clear some of the Weser marshes. They were to pay a fixed rent, plus in tithes one-eleventh of their crops and one-tenth of other produce. They were to have their own jurisdiction and were granted large holdings in return for developing land that had hitherto been barren. In this and subsequent contracts, the favourable Dutch or Flemish law was to apply, which gave the settlers secure hereditary tenure. They thus had 'favourable property rights, low rents and far reaching autonomy'.[34] Typically, the Flemings built villages on German lands that reproduced the kind of structure they had known at home.

Broadly speaking, the drainage work proceeded from west to east. The lower Elbe, including the 'Altes Land' south of the river delta, was drained first, together with the lower Weser. Then came the marshes of the Alte Mark (*c.*1160), the Oder, Saale, and Warthe followed, and by the end of the thirteenth century the Vistula and Nogat were reached: the town of Prussian Holland on the Vistula was founded in 1297.[35] Of particular interest in this context is the region of Dithmarschen, mentioned briefly in Chapter 4 above. There, on land nominally belonging to the Archbishop of Bremen and Hamburg, the settlers who had reclaimed their land from the sea by dykes and embankments were given a great deal of autonomy, which they exercised first at local village level and later extended to claims of virtual independence in an increasingly unified province, until overrun by superior feudal forces in the sixteenth century.[36]

The Vistula delta and lower Vistula had, however, not been firmly secured by dykes and dams, and when the population receded, the maintenance work was neglected and the land flooded again, forcing the remaining settlers to leave; only the fishermen stayed. In 1527 Duke Albrecht of Prussia brought in a group of Dutchmen to refortify the work once more. Their *Freibrief* included the right to found six villages, to be free of labour duties, and to enjoy 'Colmar rights', including having their own *Schulze* and parish priest, free fishing and bird hunting, and paying a fixed rent only, after three years free of all payments.[37] The particular contribution of the Dutch everywhere was an organized system of straight channels in place of the rather ragged scheme of construction typical for earlier works. While Dutch experts also undertook other drainage schemes on the German northern plain from the sixteenth century onwards, as well as in Italy, in England, and elsewhere, as far as the High Middle Ages were concerned they had made their main mark (outside their own country) along the German North Sea and Baltic coastal plains and estuaries, as part of the great German colonization drive eastwards.

[34] Rösener (1992), 38–9; also Higounet (1986), 90; Darby (1956), 196; Hauser (1972), 335–6; Menzel (1975), 138–9; Petri (1975), 728; de Vries (1974), 27; van Houtte (1977), 8.

[35] Hallam (1988*e*), 504; Aubin (1971), 484; Krenzlin (1952), 23; van Houtte (1977), 8; Petri (1975); Schlesinger (1975*c*); Thompson (1918–9).

[36] Rösener (1992), 235–6; p. 100 above.

[37] Franz (1939), 38–9; Kuhn (1957), 57–61, and (1975*b*), 411. For a detailed map showing the work of Dutch engineers from the Middle Ages to the end of the 17th century, see Goudie (1986), 153; also Slicher van Bath (1977), 68.

In the years from around 1050 to at least 1350, much of Europe's energy, enterprise, and technical innovative spirit was thus concentrated along the moving frontier to the east. What elsewhere took place at best in small and privileged enclaves of progressive agriculture was practised there on a broad front, by a population which was better prepared than most others to meet and overcome difficulties of terrain and climate. The pioneers engaged on this programme were given, or had gained for themselves, a greater degree of freedom and independence than most others, within a framework which rewarded innovation and enterprise. It was therefore no accident, but almost inevitable, that new and better methods should be applied by them rather than by the oppressed and exploited peasantry in the older settled areas. In many respects, the men on this moving frontier were at the cutting edge of European expansion in a cultural and technical as well as territorial sense, playing, as a community of frontiersmen, a role of economic leadership which pointed to the future. Many details are lacking for the period and some historians are sceptical of the claims made for it; but at the least, the claim that conditions were favourable for progress, and that techniques and organization on these marginal lands were up to the state of the art, cannot be denied.

This role of the eastern *limes* of Europe needs emphasis because it is not often recognized, possibly because it is not tied to a particular political unit of the kind which historians normally take as their subject. There is one exception to this: that is the State of the Teutonic Knights, which has been described as the 'first modern state', possessing 'unified laws and administration, [a] co-ordinated foreign policy, trade and industry'. At the least, according to a second opinion, 'the State of the Teutonic Order . . . was the best organized and best endowed power in the region'; and, according to a third, the Knights kept in touch with the most advanced seats of learning in Vienna, Prague, and Cracow, and made in Riga, Reval, and Dorpat 'real cultural advances . . . to a level of refinement comparable with that of any contemporary German centres'. 'By the fourteenth century', in the view of yet another source, 'Prussia had the most contented peasant freeholders in Europe'. More than that, in the lands of the Teutonic Order, a fifth informs us, 'art and learning flourished, particularly in the construction of magnificent castles and cathedrals and in the account of human events recorded by the accurate rhymed chronicles and the fine history of such an annalist as Henry the Lett. Generally speaking, the history of the Teutonic Order is one of the most glorious achievements of the Middle Ages, and, in a narrower sense, it is the greatest triumph of German medieval civilization.'

If this kind of eulogy seems somewhat exorbitant, it should be stressed that most of it comes not from nationalist German sources but from non-Germans who were, on the whole, rather critical of the methods of conquest used by the Knights.[38] Not everyone will accept their judgements in full; but few would deny them a certain validity.

[38] Citations from Anderson *et al.* (1992), 359; Lönnroth (1971), 374; Schreiber (1965), 104; Seward (1972), 105; Boswell (1932), 268.

Yet there is still one more—possibly the most significant—contribution of the importance of the moving margin to European economic progress to be mentioned: that is the work of the pioneers who went east to open up the mineral riches of the region and who developed an appropriate technology to do so.

As noted above,[39] little of the extensive and sophisticated mining activity of classical times had survived the collapse of the Roman Empire and the centuries of the Dark Ages. Some iron mining and working, and salt mining in the eastern Alps, and surface or shallow mine-ore working elsewhere, including the Rhineland, Saxony, and Spain appear to have had a continuous existence, though details are lacking. There are signs of an increase of the iron output in Styria from the ninth century onwards, and mining in Schemnitz (Hungary) is said to have been taken up by AD 745. The expansion in metal mining and working which began thereafter is closely associated with the German drive to the east.

The first major discovery was made on the Rammelsberg behind Goslar in 968, and by 970 there is evidence of active mining there. In addition to silver, other metals—including copper, zinc, and lead—were found, and Goslar became the main centre for the Harz mineral industry. A second major centre developed in Freiberg, where rich silver ores were discovered about 1170. In 1215 mining in the Mansfeld area began. Further east, Iglau and Kuttenberg (Kutná Hora) in the Sudeten, and silver mining at Rodna (1242), the mining towns of Neusohl (Banská Bistrica) in 1255, Pukkanz, Königsberg (Nova Bana), as well as the gold-mines of Kremnitz (1328) in Hungary became important. In Silesia gold was found in Goldberg (before 1211) and Löwenberg (1217).

Meanwhile, the expansion of iron mining in Styria, spreading from Leoben and Hüttenberg in the twelfth century to Eisenerz in the thirteenth and to Carinthia and Carniola in the fourteenth should not be forgotten, nor the expansion of salt-mining in the Alps. In the Balkan mountains, mines of gold, silver, copper, and tin, 'in many cases . . . in places difficult of access and a long way from the main communication arteries', some of which had been worked by the Romans, were opened up in the thirteenth and fourteenth centuries, allegedly with the help of 'Saxon' miners.[40]

A good deal of the mining activity outside the German orbit, such as tin mining in Cornwall and lead mining in the Peak District and the northern Pennines, was also performed by Germans, so that the term German or Saxon became almost synonymous with the term for miner. Moreover, since nearly all the mining took place in the mountains, it is no accident that the German word for miner also means 'mountaineer', a mine is a 'mountain works' (*Bergwerk*) and the overman even today is known as the *Steiger* or climber.

[39] See pp. 117–8 above.

[40] Nef (1952); Kuhn (1975*a*), 247; Forbes (1956), 62 ff.; Fügedi (1975), 503; Higounet (1986), 158, 182, 193; Bromehead (1956), 11; Probszt (1966), 27–9; Lopez (1984), 144; Jelecek and Bohac (1989), 162; Herrmann (1989), 233; Aubin (1928), 177; Schulz (1931), 16 ff.; Carter (1977*b*), 157; Sugar (1977), 172; Hoffman (1977), 470–1; also p. 146 above.

Many of the German mining towns mentioned were given privileged borough status, including self-government and taxing powers, parallel to the privileges and special codes developed for the mine enterprises themselves. 'Mining made a positive contribution of its own to the new freedom', according to Nef, and, because of its high status, it 'added to the prestige attaching in a small degree to many kinds of manual labour, and especially to the artistic work in building and decorating churches and monasteries'. 'Like the gothic arch and the great cathedral spires,' Nef continued, 'the community of free miners was a creation of western civilisation.' However, it should be stressed that '[t]he most striking progress in mining of all kinds, particularly of silver-bearing ores, took place on the margin of western civilisation, away from the chief centres of cultural and economic life'.[41]

It is evident that there were innovations both in prospecting for minerals, and in their mining and smelting in this period of vigorous expansion, though we have no reliable details. All we can be certain of is that the men of the eleventh–thirteenth centuries knew more than their predecessors. At the same time, they proved ultimately incapable of solving the problems of pumping out the water at any depth, and their mines drowned where they did not give out altogether. In consequence, mining output, especially of precious metals, declined in central Europe in the later fourteenth century, awaiting a technical renaissance which only came a hundred years later.

Meanwhile, the new finds of gold, silver, and copper had not merely made rulers and some miners rich; they also provided the monetary base for the economic expansion of the age. The sequence of cause and effect is necessarily obscure. But there is no doubt that the remarkable expansion of mining activity was in one sense a consequence of the eastward drive out of the western, mainly German, lands, and the enterprising and innovative society in the mining towns, experimenting with new social organizations as well as in the field of mineral technology, was a part of that drive. At the same time, the metal extracted from the earth by these miners, was a significant and possibly an indispensable element of the medieval leap forward in the European economy. In that sense, too, a key aspect of the advance of the European economy was to be found in its margins.

[41] Nef (1952), quotations from pp. 436, 454, 455, 456. Also pp. 106–7 above.

7

The Medieval Monasteries

There was a second source of economic advancement on marginal lands in the Middle Ages, not entirely unconnected with the drive to the east discussed in the last chapter. It was to be found in the economic actions, and particularly the agrarian initiatives, of the monastic foundations in western and northern, and ultimately also in eastern Europe. Monasteries are not, by themselves, 'regions' in the sense in which this word is used in the rest of this study; but they exemplify the not uncommon tendency for advanced techniques to be found in marginal lands.

The religious impulses which led in the eleventh century of our era to a reawakening of the drive to carry the Christianity of the Western persuasion outward from its European centre lie outside the scope of this study. But given that drive, and given the well-established tradition of monasticism at the time, it was to be expected that one element in it would be the foundation of monasteries in new locations. Monasteries and convents, it is evident, required men and women willing to lead dedicated communal lives within the discipline of one or other monastic order. But the enlargement of their number also required donors willing to provide resources, which essentially meant land, for the religious houses to live on. Among those who possessed large enough tracts of land to make the appropriate gifts available were rulers and the more powerful lords. It was one of the pre-conditions of the enormous expansion in the number of religious houses which was to take place in the eleventh–thirteenth centuries that sufficient of these owners would be willing to provide the land, and where necessary, appurtenances and privileges to go with it.

There were, in principle, two types of land which could be made over to the religious foundations. They could be given settled and cultivated land, with villeins and other peasants upon it to furnish labour services, pay rents, and be liable for the payment of tithes; or they could be granted tracts of still uncleared land, including forest land or marshes, which the monks would be called upon to clear and make cultivable. Both types occurred, but within the framework of the theme of this study it is the foundations which were settled on empty, but possibly potentially fertile land which are of particular interest.

Assarting, drainage works, and the conversion of grasslands or moors into arable were also proceeding concurrently on the initiative of peasants or landlords. However, a number of advantages could accrue to a donor from making the kind of grant which would permit a monastery or convent to be set up for the purpose. For one thing, the larger co-operative resources which a religious house could muster made it possible to tackle some kinds of comprehensive schemes, such as the draining and

embankment of a larger area, which separate individual actions could not easily accomplish. While, as we have seen, group collaboration, especially under the leadership of a *locator*, was quite capable of undertaking work of that kind in certain conditions, a monastery provided an alternative mechanism, with some additional advantages, such as the internal discipline maintained by the organization. It could also be sent further into hitherto intractable forest. Once settled, it could, as we shall see, run an estate-type rather than small-scale peasant agriculture.

Secondly, monasteries settled in no man's land, near borders or on the edge of a territory, could help to protect the frontier and strengthen the claim of the owner over the intervening empty territory. Some religious houses even had clear military duties.[1] In certain favourable circumstances, such a monastic foundation might be held inviolable by invading foreign troops who would think nothing of razing lay property to the ground, though at other times the wealth accumulated by some monasteries acted as an additional lure for the invader.

A third, and unique, advantage of having the clearing of lands performed by monasteries lay in the hope of laying up credit in heaven by making gifts to religious organizations on earth, sometimes referred to as a 'spiritual insurance policy'.[2] It was frequently the lords and rulers noted for their piety, as for example King David I of Scotland, or rulers and their consorts who had just converted to Christianity, who were particularly likely to endow religious foundations, including monasteries. The Church itself might also contribute from its enormous holdings: in England at the time of Domesday it held more than one-quarter of the land.[3] The common disputes between bishops and abbots, and indeed between one monastery and another, over the ownership or control of land as well as other possessions derive from that fact.

The founding of monasteries thus became part of the internal, and in due course also the external colonization drive of the age. It was fortunate that it was matched by complementary simultaneous developments within monasticism. The reawakening of interest among a growing number of people in the monastic life was accompanied by changes in attitude which encouraged the settlement in remote areas requiring land clearance and development, for which monastic communities were often considered to be particularly suitable. There were therefore two kinds of motivation for this kind of colonizing activity: the desire to spread Christianity among the heathen or fortify the faith among recent converts; and the drive to open up the land. The latter could also be set in a religious connotation, for while it was a pious deed to improve land use and ensure agricultural progress, it was also considered that to engage in physical work would be good for the monks' souls.[4]

The ideal of a life devoted to religious observance far from the vanities of the world, of simplicity of lifestyle, perhaps even poverty and hard work, has been the

[1] e.g. Musgrove (1990), 22; Hill (1968), 59–61; Raftis (1960–1), 460; Wordsworth (1974), 197; Haigh (1969), 58.

[2] Williams (1969), 35.

[3] Lennard (1959), 25–6.

[4] Latouche (1967), 86; Mokyr (1990), 203–4.

basis of much of the monastic movement throughout the ages. Its closest expression was found in the Benedictine trinity of duties of obedience, poverty, and chastity, but not dissimilar rules were enjoined also upon Augustinians and on the Premonstratensians who derived from them. It was for these reasons, as well as for solitude and avoidance of entanglements in this world, among others, that many of the monasteries founded in earlier centuries had been located in remote and empty areas. This was particularly so in the case of those derived from the Celtic inspiration, but it was not at all uncommon also among the Latin houses. Thus, typically, the Abbey of Kremsmünster, founded in 777, was told to go into the forest and clear as much land for arable as it wished. Freising, established in 769, was similarly granted ever larger territories in the following centuries, to cultivate the land and Christianize and Germanize the Slav populations to be found on it.[5]

However, in the course of time these rules had been relaxed in practice, and towards the end of the first millennium of the Christian era monasteries had become centres of luxury and idleness. As in other periods of religious reawakening, this moral decline came to be challenged by reformers who wished to re-establish the original high ideals.

The new monastic order which proved most insistent in stressing the need to return to the original discipline as well as in placing the taming of the wilderness and life in solitude among its leading concerns was that of the Cistercians. Established in 1098 by the Abbot Robert of Molesme as a monastic community at Cîteaux near Dijon, they determined to return to the Benedictine rules in their original purity. The intention was, further, for 'the white monks to live by the labour of their hands'. This was partly so as not to have to live on the tithes or feudal contributions from others, and partly it was thought that it would be for their own spiritual good. At the same time, it would also help to drive back the wilderness according to the words of the Bible.[6] Aiming 'to achieve complete self-sufficiency, to be independent of the world outside', they would almost of necessity have to have 'unencumbered lands on the margins of existing settlement', to settle 'in a remote or at least an unencumbered site', in 'remote and uninhabited districts', 'in places practically unknown to the world before their arrival', so as to be able to 'evolve order and plenty out of a wilderness'.[7]

Following the foundation of the original house, the Cistercian form of monasticism spread across Europe with remarkable speed, given the restrictive rule which laid down that new communities had to be set up by brothers from established ones at least for an initial period. Clearly, their work struck a chord among contemporaries, and it might well be worth while to speculate how far their appeal was purely religious or moral, one designed to overcome the betrayal of their professed

[5] Quirin (1954), 49; Zahnbrecher (1907), 3–4. Also cf. Latouche (1967), 55–6; Nitz (1983), 106; Darby (1940), 10; Hornstein (1951), 209; Décarraux (1964), 356–8; Gallagher (1976), 106–8.

[6] Bloch (1966), 12; Duby (1968), 70; Gottschalk (1966), 68–9; Schnath (1963), 79–80, 91; Micklethwaite (1899).

[7] Quotations from Cruden (1960), 33; Platt (1969), 11; Knowles (1940), 215 and (1955), 64; Franklin (1952), 51; Bishop (1936), 210; also Le Goff (1972), 72.

ideals on the part of the existing orders, or how far it was an unconscious reflection of the growing pressure of population on agrarian resources, which made it harder for younger sons to inherit adequate property, and for which the cultivation of waste land would be an obvious solution.

By 1124 the number of Cisterican houses had risen to 26, by 1151, 307 new ones had been founded, and in the following 100 years, there were 313 more. Thereafter expansion slowed down, and by 1500 only another 90 new foundations were recorded, making altogether some 750 Cistercian monasteries in Europe by the end of the fifteenth century. The first English house was established at Waverley in Surrey in 1128, followed by Tintern in Wales in 1131, and Rievaulx and Fountains (both 1132) in Yorkshire, and by 1153 there were 40 of their foundations in England and Wales, plus another 11 by the end of the century and a further 12 later. Wales alone had 14 monastic foundations between 1136 and 1273, and in Scotland, 10 Cistercian houses were established between 1136 and 1229. The Savigny houses deserve particular mention: originated in the woods of Mortain in 1093 by some hermits who set up a community in Savigny *c.*1112–15, there were 13 houses in England between 1124 and 1153. In 1147 they joined the Cistercian order.[8]

In a large number of cases—the exact proportion would depend on definitions—these Cistercian monasteries were located on marginal land, on wastes, marshland, moors or deep inside forests, as indeed were the foundations of some other orders. It is possible that some were placed deliberately on sites ravaged by the 'harrying of the North'. In general, however, in England, some of the largest grants were made on the bleak upland 'wastes of Yorkshire' (including Rievaulx, Byland, Fountains, and Jervaulx) and in Cumberland, in the case of Holme Cultram even right on the Scottish border; in Scotland, several were sited on the Border ranges, and some of the Welsh ones were in isolated mountainous spots; Blanchland in Northumberland was founded on a trackless moor, 1,300 ft. (*c.*425 m.) up. The first location assigned to the group of monks who had left St Mary's Abbey in York in 1132 and were later to become the founders of Fountains was 'a place remote from all the world, uninhabited, set with thorns, and among the hollows of mountains and prominent rocks on every side, fit more, as it seemed, for the dens of wild beasts than the uses of mankind', at Skelldale: in their case, they had to be rescued from these extreme conditions, to be relocated after two years.[9] Others were settled in fens and marshes, including Romney Marsh,[10] or in forests such as Selwood or the New Forest.[11] Among monasteries of other

[8] Musgrove (1990), 101; Donkin (1963), 181 and (1960), 141 and (1978), 21; Fossier (1983), 55; Donnelly (1954), 399; Coulton (1933), 38; Knowles and Hadcock (1953), 22; Hill (1968), 84 ff.; Darby *et al.* (1979), 194; Williams (1969), 15; Cantor (1982*d*), 146.

[9] Hope (1899), 272; Mingay (1990), 4; Hodgson (1827–58), Part II, iii. 2, 312; Smailes (1960), 98; Miller and Hatcher (1978), 33; Bishop (1935), 21; Waites (1959–62*a* and *b*); Cowan and Easson (1976), 4–6; Morton (1832); Cameron (1954), 36; Franklin (1952), 10, 31; Rowley (1986), 132–3; Waites (1967), 5.

[10] Darby (1940), 44; Hallam (1954), 39; King (1973), 6, 71; Donkin (1978), 116 and (1973), 104; Smith (1943), 166 ff.

[11] Neale (1976), 87; Tubbs (1986), 72.

orders placed in marginal lands, the Augustinian Bolton Abbey could be named, set in a 'remote region of England', in a 'highland zone economy', or Kelso in the Scottish border uplands, granted to the Benedictines in 1128.[12]

Given that at the beginning of the population explosion around 1050 much of the British Isles was thinly settled, and densely populated areas were few and far between, it does not surprise that the large grants of land which were necessary if a monastery was to be equipped properly were so frequently made in zones remote from these populated areas. It should astonish rather how many were placed in settled areas, or on the margins of them, in defiance of the injunction to move into the wilderness.[13] It is a point to which we shall return.

These developments in the British Isles reflected and were part of a general European movement. Chapter 6 noted that the foundation of religious houses on marginal lands or beyond was used, among other means, to open up empty territory or secure frontiers in eastern Germany. Many of these houses were of the Cistercian order. It has been argued that this was in a relatively unpopulated, 'economically underdeveloped territory', 'a colonial area, a frontier, and as such it should have presented the monks with a relatively large degree of freedom to develop along the lines they desired to follow'.[14] New monasteries were set up also elsewhere in marginal regions of Germany, such as Bayerisch-Zell and Vischbachau in the Alpine foothills, Herrenalb in the Black Forest, and Tennenbach in the Breisgau, while the Cistercian monastery at Walkenried in the Harz mountains took up mining.[15] Similar foundation policies were pursued also in other countries, such as France, Switzerland, or the Netherlands: on the Frisian coastline monastic foundations, starting with Mariengaarde in 1163, shared in the task of organizing the sea defences.[16] For Russia we even have an estimate of the proportion of monasteries that were founded in the wilderness: in the fourteenth century, it was 42 out of 84 new foundations, in the fifteenth century it was 57 out of 84, and in the sixteenth century it was 51 out of 86, an average of 59 per cent.[17]

It can therefore not be doubted that the founding of monasteries in this phase of expansion was an activity which went on to a large extent in the marginal areas of Europe: in uncleared forests, on hillsides, and among marshes. Did these foundations in some respects represent a progressive part of the economy? Were the monasteries, especially though not uniquely those of the Cistercian order, agrarian

[12] Kershaw (1973*a*), 3; Jack (1988*a*), 260 ff.; Jeffrey (1857–64), iii. 40.

[13] Donkin (1978), 103, 116.

[14] Roehl (1972), 95–6; Kuhn (1971), 9–10 and (1975*a*), 229–32 and (1975*b*), 375; Slicher van Bath (1963), 153–4; Koebner (1971), 75; Schich (1979), 133–4; Gottschalk (1966), 77 ff.

[15] Toch (1986), 31; Zahnd (1990), 59–60; Henschke (1974), 21; Riedmann (1988), 44; Daisenberger (1859–61), 70.

[16] Higounet (1975), 663 ff. and (1950); Petri (1975), 717; Bergier (1980) 194–5; Devèze (1961), i. 63 ff.; Barrière (1983); Pounds (1973), 278; Lambert (1971), 86–8; Slicher van Bath (1963), 153; Ladurie (1974), 11; Nabholz (1931), 19; Fel (1962), 109; de Vries (1974), 41.

[17] Stökl (1975), 769; Darby (1956), 207.

or organizational innovators, so that we can, once again, identify some marginal regions as being on the cutting edge of progress?

Virtually the whole of the appropriate literature is inclined to take an extremely favourable view of the role of the monasteries, and especially the Cistercian houses, in the economic and social life of their age. To quote one typical account:

> The inmates of these houses carried not only the gospel into the wilds and waste places of the land, but peace and civilization followed in their footsteps; they stood between the oppressed poor, the serf, and slave, and the feudal tyrant and military spoilers . . . the abbeys were the sole repositories of learning and the arts through many centuries of ignorance. . . . They were the greatest farmers of the early times, and the first agriculturists who brought intellect and science to bear on the cultivation of the soil. Wherever they carried the cross, the plough also appeared.[18]

Fulsome praise of this kind, which could be matched many times over in the literature, derived in part from the piety of the authors and in part from the fact that much of what we know of those times is based on the writings of the monks themselves, who were not inclined to underrate their own contribution. One consequence of this is that the first mention of an innovation may well appear in a monastic document, and thus be credited to the monks, when in fact it might have arisen outside the ecclesiastical sphere altogether; in similar manner, the monks' own contribution to clearances or drainage schemes may well have been more restricted than their documents lead us to believe.[19]

Present-day historians view the surviving medieval documentation more critically. Statements like the one quoted above scarcely stand up to the evidence available today. Only the reference to the monks' agrarian skill accords to some extent with our present state of knowledge and may contain more than a modicum of truth.

It need not be doubted that the monks who settled in empty territories turned them into productive arable or pastureland. Like others engaged in expanding from settled landscapes, they cut down trees, drained marshes, and ploughed up former wastes, and thereby pushed European civilization outward in a geographical sense. But as in the case of the German settlement in the east, there are here two distinct questions. What we are concerned with, and what is frequently in the minds of historians of the monastic movement, are cases of actual innovation, making the monasteries the pioneers and leaders in European advancement in the economic field. The evidence commonly presented, however, concerns the introduction, not of new practices, but of established methods into hitherto waste or underdeveloped territories. There is merit in that activity, too, but in our terms it represents a catching-up by the marginal areas, rather than their leadership. In the light of the patchy nature of the sources, it will not be possible to avoid entirely a certain confusion of these two developments, which are, in truth, not wholly unrelated to each other.

There are those who even today would affirm that both these developments occurred. The monks, say some, were well known as 'converters of wastes and

[18] Jeffrey (1857–64), iii. 45, 46.

[19] Pounds (1973), 277; Sylvester (1969), 123, 396.

barren lands into fertile soil capable of producing abundance of food . . . They were great flockmasters, horse and stock breeders, gardeners, foresters, millers, brewers of beer and bee-keepers.' The Cistercian 'brothers' advanced techniques' benefited others, they 'played their part in the promotion of economic development', and their work, it has been said, amounted to 'nothing less than an agricultural revolution': 'no estate owner obtained more from the soil.' And again, 'all the historians agree on the importance of the role [the Cistercians] played in improving methods of cultivation and cattle breeding.' This was in part because the 'monasteries were among the first to introduce new methods' and 'were among the first . . . to organize the labour service into something approaching a scientific system'; using this 'scientific system', they 'became the repositories of the economic wisdom of the age'. They copied innovations made in other countries to ensure 'faster economic development', and as far as the Alps were concerned, 'la plupart des [unspecified] innovations dans l'exploitation du sol ont êté le fruit de leur initiative'.[20] In the case of the English monasteries, at least, it has become fashionable to speak of a period of 'High Farming', 'that was', in the view of some, 'in itself a peak and a turning point in medieval society, the genesis, through its accompanying urban and commercial expansion, of the world we are familiar with today'.[21]

Common though these judgements are, they are very rarely backed by any evidence, even in well-informed literature.[22] It is no doubt difficult to prove that any specific innovation or improvement originated among the monks in Cistercian or other religious houses,[23] yet one cannot help feeling critical of the standards of a literature which considers apodictic statements to that effect sufficient in themselves. It is therefore particularly important to go beyond the easy generalization and examine such direct evidence as has survived.

One of the achievements frequently attributed to English, Scottish, and Welsh monasteries, as well as to many of those settled on marginal areas on the Continent, was their specialization in stockbreeding on a large scale. This was made possible by the generous grants of land they received, including moors or other upland waste and potential pasture. While it had been a long-standing practice among other farmers in marginal areas, too, to graze their animals on uplands which could not be turned into arable, either close by or some distance away by a system of transhumance, it was the monasteries which were able to develop animal husbandry on a large commercial basis with a view to deliveries to outside markets. In the case of Switzerland, it has even been suggested that it was the monasteries which pioneered the use of the uplands in this way—leading to the prosperity of the Alpine cattle

[20] Quotations from Franklin (1952), 21; Smailes (1960), 98; Lekai (1977), 313; Platt (1969), 12; Knowles (1940), 441, 443; Schreiber (1965), 219; Gille (1980*a*), 559; Raftis (1960–1), 455; Cantor (1982*d*), 144; Bergier (1980), 195.

[21] Platt (1969), 13; also Smith (1947), 104, 106 and (1943), 143; King (1973), 126; Knowles (1948), 32, 36 and (1955), 310; Kershaw (1973*b*), 35; Brandon (1972), 407–8; Dyer (1980), 50.

[22] See also Gottschalk (1966), 71 ff.; Higounet (1986), 245–6; Titow (1969), 46; Postan (1967), 576.

[23] Cameron (1954), 35; Donkin (1978), 65; Schnath (1963), 89.

country in the Middle Ages; they also introduced horse breeding.[24] In the case of the British Isles, it was rather in the breeding of sheep that the scale and the skills developed were said to be innovatory.

Some of the monasteries, mostly of the Cistercian order, which had settled in hilly districts, including the Pennines, the Cotswolds, Devon, and the Scottish border, but also Lincolnshire and Romney Marsh, did indeed become the owners of very large flocks of sheep, as did some of the older foundations. At the time of Domesday, Ely had 13,400 sheep. In the period around the year 1300, for which more information is available, Melrose in Scotland had around 12,000 sheep, Canterbury, with its possessions in Romney Marsh, had 13,760 (in 1322), Peterborough and Crowland in the Fens had 16,300 between them, Holme Cultram, Fountains, Rievaulx, and Newminster had about 10,000 each, Kelso perhaps 7,500, and even Kirkstall disposed over 4,000. For Wales there is an estimate of 21,000 sheep owned between all the religious houses in 1291.[25] The popular picture of the medieval abbey as a place of quiet contemplation, surrounded by peacefully grazing sheep, is thus not entirely fanciful.

Much of the information on English and Scottish sheep rearing and wool sales comes from Florentine merchants. They were the main agents who exported the wool to the Continent, and at times even advanced money to breeders before the fleece became available, though for some monasteries their flocks represented a significant form of capital investment.[26] Their information on the approximate size of flocks at a certain point in time tallies with that available from elsewhere and thus carries some credibility. It shows that the monks furnished only a small fraction of the wool exports from the British Isles, some 3–4 per cent in quantity according to one estimate, 2,700 sacks out of a total of 33,000 sacks, or about 8 per cent, in 1273 according to another. Even then, some of the wool sold by them was grown on neighbouring pastures and merely passed on by them.[27]

Was there anything in their practice to distinguish them from other suppliers, other than sheer quantity, and were they responsible for any innovations? Some observers think that they did lead the market, that the monasteries were 'the producers of the finest fleeces', that they gained by cleaning, grading and packing their wool, and that the wool sold by the Cistercians fetched 15–20 marks per sack, compared with an average market price of 10 marks only. There is also some evidence that their sheep were sought after for breeding purposes. Against this, however, there are no signs that improvements in breeding were attempted, and it is known that the wool produced on upland pastures of such monasteries as Furness was of

[24] Bergier (1983), 89 and (1980), 186, 212.

[25] Cameron (1954), 40, 42; Jack (1988*b*), 479–80; Smith (1943), 152–3; Lythe and Butt (1975), 17; Hatcher (1988*b*), 398; Donkin (1963), 190; Lekai (1977), 320; Franklin (1952), 80; Kermack (1967); Knowles (1948), 40; Rowley (1986), 133; Waites (1967), 29 ff.; Wroot (1930); McDonnell (1963), 115.

[26] Kershaw (1973*a*), 129; Prestwich (1979), 93; Rutkowski (1971), 502; Lloyd (1977), 39–40, 288–90.

[27] Lekai (1977), 313; Franklin (1952), 80; Denholm-Young (1964), 53–5.

very poor quality and fetched the lowest prices in England.[28] Thus no firm conclusion is possible on the quality of wool supplied by the monasteries as a whole, quite apart from the fact that it depended not merely on the skill and knowledge of the monks, but also on soil and climate, among other factors.

While sheep appear to have formed the mainstay of the monks' animal husbandry in England and Scotland, most also had cattle and pigs, and some, like Jervaulx or Holme Cultram, bred horses. Fountains, by the fifteenth century, had installed the intelligent system of grazing the sheep on the limestone fells, the cattle on the rich damp grasslands of Nidderdale, and turning the lowlands around the abbey to arable farming. It is no clearer in their case either, however, that any of this was in advance of the prevailing practice of peasants and lay estates. Some of the continental mountain monasteries which did well in the breeding of cattle, as noted above, also bred sheep.[29]

There are some hints in the literature, but again not conclusive ones, regarding the monks' agricultural practices in their arable fields and orchards. Some historians profess to see a distinctly progressive, and possibly even innovatory attitude to arable farming among religious communities. The Benedictine houses of Battle Abbey and Canterbury Cathedral Priory, for example, were said to be 'employing advanced and efficient agricultural techiques,—sowing at a high rate of seed, using legumes as a partial alternative to fallow, and improving the soil with the addition of marl—they received substantial grain yields from their Sussex and Kent manors'.[30] Regrettably, these were not marginal areas. There are indications that some of these methods were also applied in outlying regions, such as the Scottish monasteries, and in various parts of continental Europe. Another point made in favour of the Cistercians is that they used their international contacts to introduce fruit and vegetables, including vines, into new regions.[31]

Much of this evidence is vague and not entirely convincing, nor could it be expected to be otherwise, given the available sources, and the need to compare with current practice outside the monasteries, of which even less is known. Some information on grain yields is rather more tangible. Yet that information too is scattered and sparse, and mostly not strictly comparable because of the differences of soil and climate. In Scotland, some yields were said to have doubled between 1190 and 1285, but it is not clear whether these returns refer to the same areas and conditions. Kelso's oat yield in 1285 at $5\frac{1}{4}$ times the seedcorn is rather better than Walter of Henley's standard of a fourfold yield, which was all that was achieved in Tavistock. Tavistock's wheat yields, however, were generally better than Walter of

[28] Knowles (1955), 65; Lekai (1977), 313; Prestwich (1979), 93; Collingwood (1928), 115; Donkin (1963), 195; Lloyd (1977), 295–6.

[29] Niederer (1993), 155; Higounet (1975), 666; Jennings (1983), 100–1; Speight (1892), 295–301.

[30] Mate (1991), 80, also (1985); and Smith (1943), 136.

[31] Franklin (1952), 71, 156; Coulton (1933), 122–3 and (1925), 217; Fossier (1983), 68–9; Lekai (1977), 316–17; Schreiber (1965), 218.

Henley's fivefold return, and its expected rye yield of 12 times the seedcorn very much better.[32] Other information is even less precise, nor do we know what the usual yields were on plains or on the uplands, on old tillage or newly cleared land. Two additional thoughts might be borne in mind in this context: yields could not very well be much lower than those recorded for the monasteries, given the need to provide for next year's sowing even in bad years; also, they were pathetically low, even at their best, compared with modern returns, and these low yields allowed little room for experimentation.[33]

The Cistercians are known to have made sure always to be located near to flowing water, which they used to provide power as well as for other purposes. They are alleged to have 'played a major part in the development of machinery and in particular in the various applications of the water mill'. Thus at Clairvaux the river was first led to the corn mill, including a winnowing machine; then one after another it fed the boiler for the brewing of beer, drove the fulling stocks, raised the hammers, and supplied the tannery, before being divided into branches to serve cooking, washing, and grinding activities in the monastery. There were piped water systems in operation also at Obazine (Corrèze), Le Châtellier (Deux-Sèvres), Noirlac (Cher), Bonport (Eure), and Vaux-de-Cernay (Seine-et-Oise) among others. In Fountains, the river was led underground, to supply the brewery, a corn mill, and various workshops. The abbey at Foigny had 14 corn mills, a fulling mill, 2 rope-making shops, 3 furnaces, 3 forges, a brewery, 3 wine presses, and a glass-works in the Middle Ages. The first fulling mill actually recorded in Britain, in 1185, belonged to the Templars, though that is not to say that this was indeed the first one in operation: there is some evidence of fulling mills in Italy about the year 1000. Numerous references to fulling mills in religious houses follow soon after, most of them, not surprisingly, from hilly districts. They are, however, found in lay estates also. It has been held, interestingly enough, that the need for water-power for the fulling stage in the production of woollen cloth was instrumental in shifting the location of the industry from town to country, and from the eastern lowlands of England to the uplands of the West Riding, the Lake District, Cornwall, Devon, Somerset, and Wiltshire, as well as the Kennet valley, with the introduction of the water-driven fulling mill.

As another example of monastic innovation, the connection of its lake with one at a higher elevation by the Soro Abbey has been hailed as 'one of thirteenth-century Denmark's greatest engineering achievements'. Bertrand Gille, somewhat exuberantly, even credited the medieval Cistercians with having 'invented the factory'.[34]

A wide range of other industrial and craft activities were to be found in at least the larger monasteries who had their own skilled blacksmiths, leather workers,

[32] Franklin (1952), 73; Cameron (1954), 39; Smith (1943), 133–8; Fox (1991*b*), 308; Oschinsky (1971), 417 ff.; Mate (1985), 26.

[33] Wiswe (1953), 131–2.

[34] Zahnd (1990), 62; Schich (1979), 151; Gille (1956), 650 and (1980*a*), 559–60; Donkin (1973), 114; Carus-Wilson (1954), 45–51; Lekai (1977), 311–12; White (1963), 279, 290.

carpenters, coopers, weavers, and others, beside the fishermen, bakers, butchers, and brewers among the monks. The monks at Beaulieu Abbey in the New Forest specialized in forestry, while some monks were active as medical men, and others ran schools. In 1245 the Cistercians founded a college in Paris adjacent to the university. None of this was necessarily innovatory, though there is some evidence that glass-making was introduced into the Alpine lands by the monasteries, as at St Gallen in the ninth century, and at Tegernsee around 1000.[35] Possibly more significant was the monastic activity in mining, metallurgy, and in salt works. Welsh monasteries worked lead and iron, as did Newbattle in Scotland, and the Yorkshire houses of Fountains, Byland, and Bolton Priory operated lead mines and smelt works. The Cumberland monasteries worked sea salt, and Furness Abbey was calculated to have derived one-sixth of its temporalities in 1292 from ironworks.[36] On the Continent, it has been estimated that at least 35 monasteries were engaged in the iron trade by the early fourteenth century, particularly in Lorraine and Champagne, as well as in Dauphiné. Monastic salt works were also widespread in the Alpine area and on the north German plain.[37]

It may well be that some of these were pioneering activities on the part of the monks. The chances for this are highest in glass-making, mining, and metal working, though we cannot hope to gain reliable evidence even for these. We can be certain only that the monks brought several of these activities newly into their marginal areas, and we know that in addition to draining marshes and clearing forests they were often obliged to build roads and bridges to allow their agricultural and commercial activities to be carried on. Rievaulx built a canal half a mile in length to convey its building stone; it later drew its stone from 6 miles distance. It has been estimated that 200 men must have been employed in the building, some of whom must have come from afar. At Fountains Abbey an enormous building programme, much of which was completed within six years, must also have used a labour force well above local resources.[38]

In the absence of much reliable direct information, it may be permissible to look for circumstantial evidence. There are some a priori reasons for expecting the monks, particularly in marginal areas, to have been innovators. One of these is the notion of return for effort. The peasants of the day would have had no interest in exerting themselves when working for the lord, and could not be sure that even on their own plots, any additional produce would not be taken away from them, or that

[35] Douglas (1899), 64; Donnelly (1954), 414; Burgess (1988), 24; Rackham (1980), 140, 158; Grossmann (1934), 16; Schremmer (1970), 100; Le Goff (1972), 85; Thrupp (1972), 230; Décarreaux (1964), 357; Hefner (1839), 20 ff.

[36] Williams (1969), 78; Coulton (1933), 209; Lekai (1977), 323; Raistrick and Jennings (1965), 57; McIntire (1942), 3–5; Collingwood (1928), 121; Raistrick (1975), ii. 18; Jennings (1983), 59 ff.; Vellacott (1912), 342.

[37] Volk (1984), 9–15; Schich (1979), 155; Chauvin (1983), 30; Bergier (1980), 237; Lekai (1977), 323; Gille (1980*a*), 560.

[38] e.g. Jeffrey (1859–64), iii. 47, 57; Coulton (1933), 208; White (1972), 170; Clark (thesis, 1990), 101; Wright (1986), 46–8; McDonnell (1963), 114.

any permanent improvement they made to their holdings would accrue to their own benefit. In contrast to this, the monks' perspective could be a long-term one. The land was theirs for ever by mortmain, and the monastery could be presumed to have a perpetual existence, even if the individual monk was mortal: 'It was doubtless this continuity of administration which gave, first to the Cistercians and later to the black monks, a leading place among the pioneers of commercial sheep and dairy-farming, as well as among the first promoters of the corn trade of England', in the view of Knowles. It should also be stressed that the monasteries were not tied to manorial rules and decisions on crop rotation or other matters, so that their 'fields [were] virtually free of any collective restraints, thus permitting long periods of innovation and experiment'.[39]

Secondly, we do know that the monks were fertile in organizational innovation, which was likely to have both improved the management of existing technologies, and encouraged the experimentation with new ones. Among the most promising of these was the organization of granges.

Granges were found most commonly in the larger Cistercian houses, though they were known also among other monastic orders such as the Benedictines. They were designed to deal with problems of agricultural management arising from the nature of their possessions. Typically, monastic estates consisted of scattered holdings as donors had gifted them, sometimes with differing pre-existing rights, and frequently including outlying territories that were too far from the central building complex to be comfortably worked directly from it. A grange was a portion of the estate that was in effect managed separately, though under the ultimate control of an officer of the monastery—the 'cellarer' or storekeeper and accountant—who maintained close contacts by frequent visits to the different granges.[40]

A grange would have its own farm buildings and equipment, including, if necessary, housing for the staff and perhaps some of the serfs. Frequently it proved possible to use the scatter of granges of any monastery with their different types of soil or configurations to specialize in the type of product each was most suited for, such as grain production or stockbreeding, or in France, Germany, or Hungary, in wine growing or cheese making. In some cases a grange might specialize in salt panning or metal mining; in others, the upland shieling would form a grange. In Wales, with much mountain pastureland still unoccupied, the Cistercians were able to choose their own pastoral grange. Where, on the other hand, the Cistercians moved into land that was already occupied and they thus had to drive out the existing inhabitants, 'the grange was the spearhead of the monastic blitzkrieg'.[41] Generally, granges lay close enough to the main buildings to have their produce, or animals,

[39] Knowles (1948), 33; Brandon (1972), 406; Franklin (1952), 24; Cameron (1954), 38; Coulton (1933), 122; Denholm-Young (1964), 1.

[40] Williams (1969), 14; Platt (1969), 12–13.

[41] Waites (1959–62*b*), 653, also 627, and, in general, (1967), 21; Franklin (1952), 53, 68; Barrière (1990), 150; Owen (1991*a*), 94; Millward and Robinson (1970), 161; Knowles (1948), 65; Williams (1969), 15; Lekai (1977), 295; Jennings (1983), 95.

conveyed there for consumption or sale, though in some cases, where the monastery had been granted gifts of land that were far apart, this caused some difficulty. There were also granges which, far from fitting into a specialist division of labour, were intended to be self-sufficient; others were expected to send food up to the main house in rotation.[42]

Granges could be of different sizes: in upland grazing areas they might be quite large. Aberconway had a grange on the slopes of Snowdon extending over 10,000 acres (*c.* 4,000 ha.), and Strata Florida one of around 5,000 (*c.* 2,000 ha.) acres. The number of granges maintained by any given monastery would necessarily vary with circumstances. In Wales, at the high point of the system, some 70 are known for the 12 Cistercian houses. England had around 350, of which two-thirds were north of the Severn–Wash line. Fountains Abbey, at 26, had the most; Meaux, engaged in the reclamation of the Humber marshes, had 22, Rievaulx and Byland 13 each. In Burgundy, the average lay around 10–12 each, though Obalin had 25, Villers, in Belgium, had 20 and Poblet, in Spain, 27. Clairvaux had 12, plus two wine-growing ones.[43]

Normally, a grange had a resident manager who might be a specialist of some kind, and he supervised the serfs or villeins who performed the actual farm work. He would in most cases be a lay brother, rather than a monk. This was one of the many useful functions performed by the lay brothers, or *conversi*, which allowed the monks to occupy more central key posts, to devote themselves to religious duties, or simply to live in comfortable idleness. It is clear that with a dozen or more granges to supervise in the case of the larger houses, efficient working required a complex supervisory and administrative structure. This, according to the indications we possess, many of the monastic houses were indeed able to create.

Monastic government was strictly hierarchical. The abbot was all-powerful, and might even be considered to have more authority than a baron, since he had, within limits, considerable judicial power within his house and disposed of a wide range of patronage. Typically, after the initial years of genuine enthusiasm in the period of the monastic revival, when piety might count for more than descent, he was likely to be a member of a noble family; in Scotland he might well be one of the king's illegitimate sons. The monks, particularly those holding offices within the house, such as cellarer, flockmaster, or land officer, also tended to come from families of high social status, and this tendency would increase in the later years of decline of monasticism, when many of the offices had, in practice, become hereditary, part of a privileged family's possessions. Below them were the lay brothers, used by the Cistercians and Benedictines 'to carry out their farming [which] left their ordinary monks for religion'.[44] These lay brothers might well also be motivated by religious

[42] Donnelly (1954), 414; Knowles (1948), 35.

[43] Williams (1982), 118; Butler (1988), 948; Donnelly (1954), 406–7; Chauvin (1983), 23; Barrière (1983), 89; Lekai (1977), 296.

[44] Franklin (1952), 22, also 25–7, 56–8; Donnelly (1954), 455; Platt (1969), 12; Knowles and Hadcock (1953), 20; Wordsworth (1974), 7; Coulton (1933), 47–51; Smout (1969), 50.

inspiration, but were commonly illiterate and not of the same social class. In numbers they would match or exceed the monks: thus Rievaulx in its heyday in 1167 had 140 monks and 500–600 *conversi*, and Meaux in 1249 had 60 and 90 respectively. After the Black Death and the decline of the system the numbers shrank drastically. Below them, as noted above, were villeins and, later, tenants.

Under this centralized system it was possible, to quote Knowles's words, 'to secure a greater efficiency, economy and uniformity of policy and management than was possible under the obedientary system'. It made, we are assured by Lekai, 'consistent planning and efficient administration' possible. 'The Cistercians were bound to succeed and out-distance all their competitors, not through a determined pursuit of wealth unbecoming to monks, but through hard labour, intelligent planning and efficient organization.' The hard labour, presumably, was that of the serfs who actually dug the ditches and worked the land, but the words 'management', 'planning', and 'efficiency' occur so often in the literature[45] that we may be sure that the written records left by the foundations do indeed exude that spirit. 'We can speak with some assurance', a textbook on Scottish history informs us, 'of positive management on monastic estates down almost to the eve of the Reformation.' Bolton Abbey, already vigorously managed, showed 'increased interest in estate administration' by the end of the thirteenth century. Several historians speak of a 'managerial revolution'.[46] For some houses, the acquisition of granges was not merely the result of haphazard benefactions, but was pursued methodically and deliberately, including even using the method of purchase or the swapping of parcels of land. Estates came to be managed by experts rather than lay brothers, by 'able and literate estate managers', as the management became simultaneously systematized by rules.[47]

One important aspect of this was the introduction of rational accounting methods, including departmentalized bookkeeping. There were also signs of rudimentary budgeting, and the auditing of accounts.[48] It might well be argued that several centuries were to elapse before the methods of management control evolved by the monks were improved on.

It is quite probable that similar practices were also being introduced into the administration of some of the larger lay estates: the textbook on estate management by Walter of Henley, essentially designed for the large landlord, is proof of a widespread interest in the subject. Curiously enough, although 'monastic estates might be expected to have taken up and copied any advice on estate management available, specially when associated with Robert Grosseteste', they showed little interest

45 Knowles (1955), 310 and (1948), 66; Lekai (1977), 282, 301; Fox (1991*b*), 309.

46 Lythe and Butt (1975), 25; Kershaw (1973*a*), 13–14, 36; Dyer (1980), 50; King (1973), 127; Thornton (1991), 202.

47 Bishop (1936), 201; Smith (1947), 109, 115; Neale (1976), 90; Postan (1972), 101; Knowles (1944), 45–8; Drew (1947); Roehl (1972), 87–90.

48 Lekai (1977), 315; Kershaw (1973*a*), 2, 34; Raftis (1960–1), 462–4; Wiswe (1953), 132; Harvey (1994).

in that collection of writings. Instead, they seem to have compiled their own text-books or rules on accounting, and no doubt learnt from each other's practices.[49]

To some extent, these developments may be seen as one aspect of the commercialization of monastic life which proceeded in stages. In the first phase of enthusiasm, men (and women) felt the call for life in an exclusively religious community, ready to go out and conquer their own human weaknesses by undertaking to make wild and desolate land habitable and fruitful, rather like the kibbutz pioneers of our own century. That generation, and their unstinted idealism, soon passed, and for a century or more, monks and nuns found satisfaction in turning their enterprises into efficient going concerns, with ever less emphasis on the ascetic, dedicated, physically strenuous life that had inspired the pioneers, and correspondingly growing stress on the fruits of economic success. In due course the foundation of new religious houses came to a halt, the number of recruits fell off, and the disaster of the Black Death further weakened the communities; but meanwhile they had discovered that they might do better by leasing their land rather than working it directly in the demesne modified by the grange system which had evolved. With the 'immer mehr steigende Erwerbslust der Klöster'[50] they came to live on rents and tithes, and ceased to do any work themselves, even that of mere supervision; it was precisely what the founders had vowed not to do.

Growing efficiency in wool sales and related marketing was one early sign of commercialization: Tintern Abbey became a member of the Bristol staple. Scottish monasteries were given town properties in the twelfth and thirteenth centuries partly to organize their buying and selling from there. They benefited from and did not scruple to exploit their freedom from tolls and tithes, and their monopoly rights. On the Continent, where the brethren had evolved banking methods and bills of exchange, unified weights and measures, and minted their own coins, they become members of the Hanse. British houses also went in for moneylending, taking land in pawn and forfeit. 'The Abbey of Crowland', we are told, 'was a great capitalist establishment which geared its product to the market.' Further, 'the monasteries were almost alone as agricultural capitalists', according to Knowles. 'The white monks and canons were henceforth capitalist employers of labour', and the switch to leases, and to maximize the income from leases, certainly exhibited a capitalistic, 'rational' and 'cost-oriented', rather than a monastic spirit.[51] Expensive lawsuits between monasteries over property point in the same direction, as do the examples of sharp practice, coming close to criminality, which have come down to us.[52] It may surely be reasonably inferred that institutions engaged in

[49] Oschinsky (1971), 5 ff.; also Blanchard (1973); Roehl (1972).

[50] Hoffmann (1910), 706.

[51] Owen (1991*b*), 245; Seward (1972), 105; Knowles (1940), 443 and (1948), 32, 66; Coulton (1933), 136, 206–9; Donkin (1963), 191; Kershaw (1973*a*), 113; Stevenson (1981), 99; Williams (1969), 69; Wiswe (1953), 133; Lekai (1977), 307, 392; Hallam (1988*c*), 311; Knowles and Hadcock (1953), 48; also Dyer (1980), 51; King (1973), 154; Whitwell (1904), 8, 16.

[52] Burgess (1988), 27; also Zahnd (1990), 61, 65; Wiswe (1953), *passim*; Lloyd (1977), 291–3; Wroot (1930), 16–17; Mol (1992), 88–9.

rational, surplus-maximizing management innovations of this kind would also welcome, and possibly pioneer, improvements and innovations in agrarian and mechanical technology.

Centuries later, at the time of the Reformation, many members of monasteries, though by no means all, had completely turned away from their intended purpose and had allowed themselves to fall into sloth, luxury, and self-indulgence, scandalously misusing the resources of their establishments contrary to their original avowal. The modern mind may puzzle over why men and women should trouble to submit to solemn vows of chastity, poverty, and obedience when they proceeded immediately to break them, unless it were merely to provide themselves with undeserved honour and pelf. The monastic foundations had simply become one of the methods by which members of the higher orders of society managed to live on the labour of the lower ones, without contributing to society in any way whatever.

These are developments with which we are not directly concerned. However, modern research has also subjected to critical scrutiny other aspects of the monasteries' records for which many of the accounts of the chroniclers have been found to have been informed by piety rather than honesty. We have noted already that by no means all, and possibly not even the majority of the Cistercian foundations, still less those of the other orders, were actually set in the wilderness of marsh, mountain, or forest, as has been pretended. In France, the Cistercians showed great reluctance to enter deep forests; in the Alpine areas, they took good care not to move onto the high ground, but stayed in the valley bottoms, as they did also in the Lake District of England.[53] Even when moving into wasteland, they would often start out, and did not move too far, from existing villages.[54] If they were given poor land, they soon saw to it that they would obtain something better. The brothers who were to found Jervaulx, for instance, first settled on a site near Aysgarth in 1144, but when the 'half-wild suspicious moormen dwelling round about' demolished their rude shelters, the Abbot of Savigny, their erstwhile superior, showed little sympathy, and censured them for their 'headstrong folly in venturing into such a remote district as the head of [Wensley]dale then was'. Thus, 'owing to the bleakness of the position and the poorness [*sic*] of the land', they soon, in 1156, moved to the easier Jervaulx site.[55] There has been much myth-making on this score, particularly on the role of the Church in the opening up of Eastern Europe. It is now known, for example, that neither Loccum (1163), nor Doberan (1171), nor Dargun (1172), nor Kolbatz (1173) was founded on wasteland, as had been alleged,

[53] There is overwhelming evidence: e.g. Dodgshon (1981), 121; Waites (1959–62*b*), 632; Cowan and Easson (1976), p. xiv; Millward and Robinson (1970), 155; Schich (1979), 150; Schnath (1963), 82; Donkin (1978), 103; Duby (1968), 70; Deffontaines (1933), 22; White (1973), 97; Zahnd (1990), 64; Chauvin (1983), 21.

[54] Donkin (1963), 188.

[55] Hill (1968), 48; Bogg (1908), 551–3; Page (1914), 280–1; cf. also the origins of Fountains, p. 164 above.

but on the contrary, settled on populated, well-prepared ground, and this probably applied to the whole of Lower Saxony and much of Thuringia.[56]

Moreover, having had gifts made of cultivated land, many monastic communities, perhaps most, then proceeded to expel the working population that was settled there, at times with considerable brutality, or to turn them into serfs, though at other times they were resettled nearby and employed to work the religious brothers' or sisters' farms.[57] It was therefore not entirely surprising that in some areas the Cistercians acquired a reputation of being depopulators of villages.[58] Their greed also turned on other Church property. 'Though they be good men', Archbishop Peckham complained in 1284, 'still they are the hardest neighbours that prelates and parsons could have. For wherever they plant their foot, they destroy villages, take away tithes, and curtail by their privileges all the power of prelacy.' A community like that of Rievaulx, which soon rose to 640 members, set in an infertile territory which could not possibly feed them, must have placed a substantial burden on the sparse local population. In Scotland, in particular, the monastic houses impoverished the already poorly provided parishes, to enrich themselves.[59]

Where they found serfdom, they left it in place, and in Eastern Europe they were hard taskmasters of Slav unfree labour. In Britain they may possibly have given their villeins an easier life than did other feudal lords, but there were exceptions: there were desperate rebellions on the lands of the Abbey of Bec by oppressed peasants throughout the fourteenth century.[60] In all those cases, far from furthering civilization, they brought misery and poverty, and far from labouring themselves to subdue raw nature, they immediately proceeded to live on the labour of others.

Finally, and of major importance for our enquiry, reservations have also been expressed about the claim that the agrarian technology or efficiency of the monasteries was superior to that of lay estates or of the peasantry of their day. 'There is no evidence that the monks farmed better than the layfolk' according to Coulton; he is echoed by Donkin: 'there is comparatively little direct evidence of improvements in arable farming by Cisterican houses.' Still less, argue some, can any innovation be clearly attributed to them.[61] Negatives are notoriously difficult to prove, but these widespread impressions must be taken seriously.

It appears that the history of the monasteries in their heyday to the end of the thirteenth-century has thus gone into a remarkable reversal. The earlier, nineteenth-century description of the monks, and the Cistercians in particular, was that of

[56] Jegorov (1930), ii, p. xiii; Epperlein (1967).

[57] Platt (1969), 92–3; Slicher van Bath (1963), 154; Lekai (1977), 299; Knowles (1948), 64; Fossier (1983), 65; Higounet (1983), 167; Coulton (1925), 224; Gottschalk (1966), 75; Postan (1971), 578; Cruden (1960), 33; Beresford (1965), 152; Harrison (thesis, 1975), 48; Schreiber (1965), 215; Roehl (1972), 103–4.

[58] Donnelly (1954), 412; Donkin (1978), 39 and (1960), 152–7.

[59] Williams (1969), 41; Franklin (1952), 84; Coulton (1925), 223–4; Cameron (1954), 44; Smout (1969), 52; McDonnell (1963), 112.

[60] Franklin (1952), 20; Lekai (1977), 342; Coulton (1933), 142; Smith (1970), 117.

[61] Coulton (1925), 214; Donkin (1978), 65; Gottschalk (1966), 76; Brandon (1972), 419; Epperlein (1967), 329.

dedicated, ascetic pioneers who opened up empty and difficult terrain on the margins, to cultivate by their own labour, spreading at the same time the best available agricultural, industrial, and organizational methods throughout many parts of Europe. Present-day scholarship, by contrast, tends to deny almost the whole of that idealized picture: with few exceptions, the monks did *not* seek out the marginal terrain, they did *not* labour themselves, and they did *not* innovate in the fields of either technology or accounting, though they were as eager for profit as other members of contemporary society.

Neither extreme judgement seems to square fully with the evidence, nor do we, for our purposes, need to judge with any exactitude between them. Given the large number of foundations, examples of all kinds of location and types of management are bound to have occurred, and given the patchy nature of our sources, there is bound to be room for differing interpretations. We may, indeed, do an injustice to manorial and even peasant farms which were perhaps just as progressive as the monastic granges but for which no records survive. Yet in view of their opportunities, their priorities, and the unique concentration of literate members they possessed, it must surely be granted as a minimum that it is highly likely that monasteries would practise and spread widely the best available technology even if we cannot be sure how far they went on to improve on it. Similarly, there can be no doubt that at least *some* of the monastic foundations were settled on marginal land.

By the conjunction of these circumstances—which may not be entirely accidental—it appears that for a significant period in the expansion of medieval Europe some of the leading economic units were to be found on the slopes of the Pennines, the Alps, and other upland regions, in the deepest forests, and on difficult bogs and marshlands of Britain and the Continent. It would therefore not have been entirely unexpected if some of the innovations of the age also had first made their appearance there.

8

The Central European Mining Regions in the Early Modern Period

As we saw at the end of Chapter 6, the impetus of the drive eastwards in Europe had petered out by the early fourteenth century. From the mid-century onward, the tide even began to recede. As population declined, outposts were deserted, and some marginal lands again became wastes. The metal mines opened up in the expansion phase went into decline, too. In part, the causes for this have to be sought in the economic field, but there were also technical reasons, such as the working out of easy seams and the inability to deal with the flooding of the deeper mines. Additionally, there were political problems: in Bohemia, the Hussite wars (1420–36) destroyed some of the leading mining towns, such as Kuttenberg (Kutná Hora)—which was said to have employed 4,000–4,500 miners—Eyle, and Deutsch-Brod.[1]

Mining revived in central Europe in the mid-fifteenth century. The causes for the revival lay in both supply and demand conditions. As far as supply is concerned, two factors in particular favoured expansion: new finds of metal ores, and technological innovations. Whether these favourable developments were purely accidental, or whether they were the result of an intensified search for solutions to problems of supply because a revived market beckoned, will probably remain unknown—just as we still cannot be sure if it was pure coincidence that the great gold discoveries in the nineteenth century occurred in the 1840s and 1890s, just when prices were at their lowest and thus the value of gold at its highest.

Whatever the cause, it is clear that skilled miners began to swarm over the well-known slopes of the Harz, the Erzgebirge, the Carpathians, the eastern Alps, the Balkans, and other ore-bearing regions, as well as territories previously unexplored, to search for metallic ores, and their efforts were rewarded. At the same time, a whole range of new techniques improved the methods available for pumping water out of mines and for conveying ores, while methods of smelting were also improved: the key problem of separating the silver from the copper with which it usually occurred was greatly eased by the discovery of the Saiger process, based on the use of lead. Thus not only could new sinkings be taken in hand, but formerly abandoned mines could be reopened.

The rise in demand also had several facets. For one thing, an increased population, together with technical innovations in various fields and rising urbanization, increased the industrial demand for metals, above all iron, copper, tin, and lead.

[1] Nef (1952), 458; Unger (1983), 92–3; Wilsdorf and Quellmalz (1971), 226; p. 160 above.

These metals were also key elements in warfare, though, once more, we cannot be sure if the needs of war, especially in the German lands, should be accounted part of the demand pressure, or if it was the broadening stream of supplies which enabled the princes to equip their armies.

Possibly even more urgent was the search for gold and silver for monetary purposes, and there is no doubt that this was actively encouraged by some rulers at least, who issued new codes and employed various means to attract metallurgists to their lands.[2] The question of metallic money is complex, for a sophisticated economy can, in theory, bypass a shortage of precious metals by the suitable creation of paper money in various forms. Whether fifteenth-century European states were in a position to do so, if forced by circumstances, must remain forever uncertain.[3] The fact is, however, that coinage problems were destabilizing a number of economies before the new ore finds, and that when gold and silver were delivered in larger quantities and came to be minted, they not only enriched the fortunate rulers who held the regalia, or the merchants to whom they had pawned their lucrative coinage rights, but also helped to shift the centre of European economic life away from the Mediterranean to Germany, where the metal was found, and to the north-west of Europe, where it was traded. It need hardly be stressed that the discovery of even larger sources of the precious metals in the Americas—equally, possibly, the result both of accident and deliberate search—had an even greater impact on the economic fortunes of different parts of Europe.

Some discoveries of silver ores had been made in Grummbach, near Annaberg, in 1411, but the upper reaches of the mountains had still been unexplored. The phase of mining on a larger scale was inaugurated in 1445 with the opening up of Altenberg in the east, followed in 1452 with discoveries around Geisingberg and in 1453 at Schneeberg, which became one of the main centres of silver mining in the Saxon Erzgebirge: 'a rush for the Zwickau silver set in, such as Europe had never seen before'.[4] Soon 1,200 miners were at work in 150 pits in Schneeberg, and the yield there between 1476 and 1485 was 3.5 million gulden. Another important ore discovery was made around 1492 in Schreckenberg, the town of Annaberg was founded, and among a whole series of new discoveries and mining enterprises on both the Saxon and Bohemian slopes of the mountain range, the rich silver veins of Joachimsthal (Jáchimov), discovered in 1516—origin of the thaler and the dollar—and Marienberg (1521) stand out. Joachimsthal had 800 active pits within 14 years of its start, allegedly employing 13,000 miners, while Marienberg was credited with 559 working pits, and Annaberg with over 900 in 1514. In the 1520s the older sites at Rammelsberg (Harz), Freiberg, and Kuttenberg (Kutná Hora) became active again, and Tarnowskie Gory in Poland was also reopened, using new drawing and

[2] Sieber (1954), 25; Kraschewski (1984), 134; Nef (1952), 480–6; Ludwig and Gruber (1987), 56; Braunstein (1983), 573–4.

[3] For an excellent introduction to the problem, see Braudel and Spooner (1967); also Spooner (1972), 14; Vilar (1976); Sombart (1987), I, chs. 31–2.

[4] Schreiber (1965), 194; Wilsdorf and Quellmalz (1971), 22 ff.,135; cf. also p. 159 above.

pumping techniques. This last was said to have had 867 pits (*Zechen*) working in 1536 and 2,528 in 1559, but this may be a mistranslation, referring to working places. It is likely that the period 1526–35 saw the peak of silver output from European mines.[5]

Further east also, in what is sometimes referred to as Slovakia, at other times as Hungary, since it was ruled by that country over much of historical time, silver as well as gold mining received a boost in this period. The most productive area was to be found in the Gran valley and its tributaries in the western part of the territory. Schemnitz (Banská Stiavnica) had been worked there from the twelfth century, if not earlier (there had been mining at nearby Dilln from the seventh century onwards), and Kremnitz from 1328, while the Königsberg (Nova Bana) discovery dates from 1345. Wars—including the Hungarian civil war and the Hussite wars—invasions, and destruction then held up developments. Recovery followed in mid-century. An early pump was installed in 1445 in Kremnitz, which by 1480 was minting 12,000 ducats per annum, and other technical innovations were made towards the end of the century, in part by Johann Thurzo (Jan Turzo), a partner of the Fuggers. The Fuggers' capital financed other improvements, including road construction, but in the sixteenth century the mines had a disturbed time. A report of 1535 speaks of desolation and decline, and the Turkish occupation of Ofen in 1541 further destabilized the region. Though the Turks never attacked the mining towns directly, the repeated raids on the settlements lower down affected them also. Neusohl (Banská Bistrica), however, first documented in 1255, did well until the 1560s, when it employed 1,900–2,000 men, selling its copper and silver to the Low Countries. Output between 1494 and 1546 totalled 74,281 tons of copper and 119 tons of silver. Its crisis came only as a result of the collapse of the Antwerp market in 1568.[6]

The second major concentration of silver and copper mining was found in the eastern Alps, with Schwaz in Tyrol as its main centre. There are signs of copper working in the region going back to at least 1500 BC, but the first documentary evidence dates from the second half of the twelfth century, and it refers to southern Tyrol. There, the silver mines on Kalisberg, north-east of Trient, appear to have been worked in the eleventh–thirteenth centuries. In Schwaz itself, the first known finds were made in 1408, the Falkenstein mine was opened in 1420, and the richest vein, the *Erbstollen*, was discovered in 1448.[7] The dramatic expansion phase which followed thus coincided in time with that of the Saxon-Bohemian-Carpathian field.

Older statements tended to exaggerate numbers engaged in Tyrol, but even those derived from a recent study of the archives are impressive enough. In 1492, when it was still growing, it is estimated that the Schwaz field employed 4,000 miners. A more detailed summary for 1554–6 put the number of miners at the Falkenstein mining

[5] Sieber (1954), 24 ff.; Kuhn (1955), 180ff.; Nef (1941*b*); Spooner (1972), 16–17; Wyrobisz (1976), 759–60; Kötzschke and Kretzschmar (1965), 151; Henschke (1974), 24; Laube (1976), 115; Molenda (1976*b*), 152; Wilsdorf and Quellmalz (1971), 315–16.

[6] Probszt (1966) offers a detailed account. Also see Paulinyi (1971), 525 ff.; Vozár (1971), 568; Vlachovic (1971), 604–27; Strieder (1929), 5; Schreiber (1965), 199; Wilsdorf and Quellmalz (1971), 255 ff.

[7] Egg (1964), 3, 9; Egg *et al.* (1986), 42; Wolfstrigl-Wolfskron (1903); Jäger (1875), 339.

complex at 6,900, while Ringenwechsel employed around 1,850 and Alte Zeche, together with some others, some 2,250. Adding some 500 employed as carters, smelters, and coalmen, this would amount to 11,500 employed in or about the mines. With their dependants, and the miners employed elsewhere in Tyrol, they represented about one-fourth of the whole of the county's population. Decline set in soon after, Falkenstein, for example, being down to 1,600 miners—still a considerable concentration—in 1606.[8]

The most important metals produced in the Schwaz district were silver and copper. At the time of its greatest prosperity, in the first half of the sixteenth century, the district produced over 10 tons of silver and 250 tons of copper a year. The peak output was achieved in 1523, when possibly 18 tons of silver were produced. A careful calculation for the whole period 1420–1827 came to a total of 2,571 tons of silver and 190,999 tons of copper; of this, Falkenstein (and Erbstollen) had yielded some two-thirds, Ringenwechsel and Alte Zeche sharing the remainder.[9]

In the mountains nearby other mines were also active at the time. They include Sterzing-Grossensass, as well as the Zillertal centres of Rattenberg (1447–1661) and Kitzbühel (1481–1664), where Röhrerbüchel had its maximum output in 1550; Prettau (copper, maximum 1525), Brixen, Taufers and Persen, situated in other parts of Tyrol. Röhrerbüchel employed 1,547 men in 1583, and Rattenberg 1,001 in 1589.[10]

It does not surprise that Tyrol, with its rich yield particularly of silver at a critical time, became a main source of the financial strength of the Habsburgs and of the Fugger empire, a 'political centre of energy'. Its mining code of 1427, amended in 1447 and 1449, became a model for other areas, and its silver supply became the basis of a new coinage, after the mint had been moved from south Tyrol to Hall, nearer to the Schwaz mines, in 1477.[11]

Of other precious-metal mines in the eastern Alps, those of Gastein-Rauris were probably the most important. Situated at heights of up to 2,800 m., they were discovered by 1340 at the latest, since the Archbishop's mining code (*Bergordnung*) dates from 1342, a new one for Salzburg being introduced in 1477, amended further in 1521. The peak of output was reached in the mid-sixteenth century, the yield for 1557 being 830 kg. of gold and 2,723 kg. of silver. Employing in 1541 a total of 625 miners, 202 woodworkers and charcoal burners, and 181 in the furnaces and elsewhere, or 1,008 persons out of a population of around 5,000, it was clearly of great regional economic importance. There were signs of decline soon after, and in due course (as in the case of the Schwaz mines) the workings had to be taken over by the state in 1616.[12] Among smaller mining enterprises of the time, the Bosnian/Serbian

[8] Egg (1964), 9; Egg *et al.* (1986), 129; Strätz (1976), 89; Wessely (1853), i. 460; Viazzo (1989), 158 ff.; Mitterauer (1974*b*), 237, 306; Klein (1980), 93; Riedmann (1988), 126.

[9] Egg *et al.* (1986), 73–4; Jäger (1875), 345; Riedmann (1988), 79, 125.

[10] Nef (1941*b*), 583–5; Strieder (1929), 4; Wolfstrigl-Wolfskron (1903), 154 ff., 172 ff.; Riedmann (1988), 127 ff.; Mitterauer (1974*b*), 237.

[11] Niederer (1979), 236; Egg *et al.* (1986), 100, 109 ff.; Kellenbenz (1988), 36; Mutschlechner (1969), 294; Pölnitz (1960).

[12] Ludwig and Gruber (1987); Viazzo (1989), 158; Egg *et al.* (1986), 156.

silver mines financed from Ragusa, and the lead, zinc, and silver deposits at Davos in the Grisons might be mentioned. Some Turkish mines were worked by Spanish Jews or German experts, respectively, at this time. The main French silver mines were located at Saint-Nicholas de la Croix-aux-Mines in the Vosges, in Pampailly in the Lyonnais mountains, and at Rosemont in Alsace.[13]

In the most important English copper-mining district, in Keswick, the leap into modernity was directed by German experts. The Höchstetters had learnt their trade in the Tyrol–Salzburg area, and had later been bankrupted in an unequal struggle with the Fuggers. Unlike the competing mining associations typical of the German ore fields, the English enterprise was financed and run by a single large privileged company, constituted, after some years of working, as the chartered Society of the Mines Royal in 1568. There had been some copper mined in the district in the thirteenth century, and a group of Germans, one of whom bore the somewhat transparent name of Hans Ducheman, searched for metals there in the 1470s at the time of the dramatic finds in Saxony. Renewed searches were instituted in 1526–31, and real large-scale operations began in the 1560s.

Enormous sums were sunk in the workings, which were designed to yield silver as well as copper. Much the best method of separating them was the recently developed Saiger process, for which the lead was planned to be brought in from the Alston mines, and possibly also from Brandley south of Derwentwater. By 1568, £18,612 had been spent, and by 1581 the total had risen to £50,000 and further investment continued thereafter. The latest technology was brought into play, some of it hitherto unknown in the British Isles, and around 150 skilled Tyrolese and South Germans, together with unskilled local labour, put up some two dozen buildings and sank ten mines. They brought to that remote and backward district a brief period of prosperity and employment, as well as a glimpse of the modern world, but although much copper was delivered and some graphite worked, the enterprise could not be made to pay, mainly because there was practically no silver found, while Sweden could produce cheaper copper with lower-paid labour. The works were closed in practice in 1633 and abandoned in 1636.[14] Sweden's enormous copper resources at Stora Kopparberg, developed from the fourteenth century with the help of German specialists and extended in the sixteenth century partly on the initiative of Dutch entrepreneurs, had fewer dramatic fluctuations. This was in part because it was less directly associated with the production of silver.[15]

The age also saw an expansion of the mining and smelting of other metals, much of it, once again, in mountain regions[16] which were otherwise remote, thinly populated, and difficult of access. This distribution was, of course, directly due to the

[13] Kovacevic (1960); Hügi (1984), 201; Braunstein (1983), 579, 584; Jeannin (1974); Wilsdorf and Quellmalz (1971), 279 ff.; Spooner (1972), 296–7; Cirković (1987), 160–71; Hoffman (1977), 470–1.

[14] The best brief account is in Hammersley (1991), also his (1973*b*) and (1988); Collingwood (1928), 128; Rollinson (1978), 55; Donald (1955) and (1961); Millward and Robinson (1970), 225 ff.; Bean (1958), 49–50; Bouch and Jones (1961), 119–27; Rees (1968), 370 ff., 409; Raistrick and Jennings (1965), 86–91.

[15] Nef (1952), 439 and (1950), 13; Forbes (1956), 65; Heckscher (1963), 44, 71.

[16] Kuhn (1955), 180; Blache (1933), 105; Kellenbenz (1965), 398.

location of the ore finds; but there is scarcely a single regional mining history which does not also mention the significance of the availability of forests for the charcoal fuel, and of streams to drive waterwheels and perhaps also bellows, which reinforced the locational advantages of these areas.

Among the important iron-working districts in central Europe were those of Styria, where *c.*1550 some 92 large iron forges and around 180 smaller ones were in operation; in Innerberg alone, with about half the region's capacity, some 19 furnaces used half a million barrels of charcoal, equivalent to about 18,400 tons a year around 1600. There were 150 miners employed there in 1605, and applying the ratios obtaining later in the seventeenth century, there would have been 500–600 smelters, hammermen, charcoal burners, and other workers in addition. Other concentrations of ironmaking were to be found in the Upper Palatinate (Fichtelgebirge), sometimes dubbed the 'Ruhr region of the Middle Ages', and the Erzgebirge itself, where furnaces of a new type (*Wolfsofen*) reached heights of 5–6 metres by 1500. Among other important areas, the Siegerland, the areas around Liège, the 'regions regarded as virtually uninhabited' of Bergslagen, mid-Wales, north Derbyshire, and south Yorkshire, and the Weald might be mentioned.[17]

Central Europe was also rich in other metals. The Erzgebirge worked tin deposits, for which the 'golden age' was the fifteenth and sixteenth centuries, as did the Fichtelgebirge and the Kaiserwald; lead was found in the Harz, in inner Bohemia and Upper Silesia, zinc in Tyrol, Carinthia, and Upper Silesia, and mercury in Carnolia (Idria), while bismuth and cobalt were other ores worked in the Erzgebirge at the time. There were brass works at Stainenberg (Tyrol) from about 1509 and at Gailitz near Arnoldstein from the late fifteenth century. The period 1550–1650 also saw the opening, or reopening, of numerous salt mines. Non-ferrous mineral mines were also worked in other parts of Europe, usually in mountainous areas, as tin in Cornwall, zinc in the Mendips, or lead in the Pennines, in the Peak District, in Wales, and at Wanlockhead. Coal-mining was developed in Britain above all.[18]

The surviving archival material relating to the mining centres of the fifteenth and sixteenth centuries is incomparably richer and more reliable than that on which the preceding two chapters have been based, and it is therefore possible to concentrate on more restricted areas and occupations. In the remainder of this chapter we shall focus our attention on the gold, silver and copper mining and smelting activities in the leading areas of central Europe, with but occasional glances at the iron industry and at other districts. That is in no way to be taken as an indication that some of the other areas did not also contain seeds of technical or economic progress.

[17] Pickl (1986*a* and *b*); Götschmann (1985); Sieber (1967), 4; Singer (1971), 13 ff.; Nef (1987), 737; Schremmer (1979*a*); Paulinyi (1974); Mitterauer (1974*b*), 238; Kellenbenz (1976), 108–11; Coleman (1977), 83; Goodman (thesis, 1978), 90, 192–3; Hopkinson (thesis, 1958), 180; Søderberg (1984), 6.

[18] Bilz (1975), 5; Kuhn (1955), 181, 247; Blanchard (1971) and (1989), 45; Sieber (1954), 7–10, 20–2, 34–5; Nef (1934), 16 ff., and (1987), 727; Petran (1965), 219; Bergier (1982), 87; Blendinger (1977); Rainer (1977); Wolfstrigl-Wolfskron (1903), 379; Riedmann (1988), 128; Rees (1968), 134; Hatcher (1993); Rowse (1978), 126 ff.; Raistrick and Jennings (1965), 46 ff.; Crossley and Kiernan (1992); Vellacott (1912), 351.

The developments described here were part of the European Renaissance. Against that background, the favours extended by territorial rulers to mining and smelting enterprises were coloured by changing social attitudes which rewarded successful enterprisers by high social status, possibly even by titles of nobility, as well as by monetary returns; at the same time it is highly likely that that more favourable attitude to business was itself called forth by the economic successes of some of the new mining and metallurgical enterprises. These successes, based on the achievements of the new technology, might also help to account for the more open-minded attitude towards science and its generalizations, which in turn made further technical advances possible. The European Renaissance had numerous other dimensions, and had its mainspring in the cities of Italy, in Paris, and in other core areas. Yet the ore mountains also made significant contributions not merely by providing the necessary monetary base and supplying other important metals, but by actually taking the lead in a broad range of key technologies and pioneering some of the sciences that went with them. While Leonardo worked on paper, they worked in metal, timber, and stone.

In many respects, conditions in metal mining and the reduction and refinement of ores were favourable at this time for innovation to have taken place. Incentives are normally taken as most potent when higher rewards are out of reach, but only just, and the technical preconditions exist for bridging the gap. Thus, in the metal mines, valuable ores were known to be there but were inaccessible because they were waterlogged. A small improvement in pumping or drainage would open up their riches; once this step was taken, the next level became visible, once again encouraging the search for a still better pump. The same favourable set of incentives, of prospective success beckoning as a result of a relatively minor step forward, applied to organizational innovation, such as the formation of companies and the provision of capital for them, the mobilization of resources for area drainage, or the construction of an infrastructure in the wider sense. The whole has to be seen as set in a framework—of a technology which had reached a certain level, of sufficient social savings to provide capital, of a favourable social attitude to money-making, and of sufficient and secure commercial links, among others.

The technical innovations which were made by the miners of the day have often been described. Many arose from the fact that shafts had to be dug ever deeper as the shallower deposits were worked out. In the Middle Ages, Kuttenberg probably had the deepest shafts, reaching 500–600 m., but that was exceptional. It was in the Renaissance period that depths were much increased. The iron mines in the Upper Palatinate were sunk to 50 *Klafter* or fathoms (perhaps 100 m.) in 1600; a similar depth, 50 fathoms, was reached in Cornwall and elsewhere by 1585–1600. But where necessary, miners were able to penetrate the earth's crust much deeper in their search for ore deposits. Thus in the Röhrerbüchel mine in Tyrol, the two deepest shafts, *Gesellenbau* and *Geisterzech*, reached 377 and 363½ *Klafter*, respectively, or depths of *c.*754 m. and 727 m., in 1567. By 1618 the *Heiligengeistschacht* and the *St Daniel-Schacht* in the same mine had been sunk to depths of 886 m. and 885 m.

respectively. The former was at its deepest point actually 144 m. below sea-level, and worked 17 levels or floors; the latter touched 108 m. below sea-level, with 14 floors. There were then in that mine complex four other shafts which descended deeper than 600 m. At Schneeberg, in the Erzgebirge, depths of 200 fathom were reached, and both at Kuttenberg and St Andreasberg in the Harz, the maximum was said to have been 500 fathoms, or about 1,000 m.[19]

Once the workings approached depths of that kind, and often well before that, the most persistent problem was posed by accumulations of water. Two types of solution were possible: drainage, which would let the water flow downstream; or pumping, which forced it upward. In hilly locations, underground tunnels called adits or soughs—which let the water flow to an exit on a slope below the workings—were widely known and had been put in place over short distances. Where the workings reached a depth lower than any nearby valley bottom, extended soughs would become necessary in order to make use of outfalls further away. These would not only be technically difficult to drive, but were likely also to overstrain the financial resources of a single company. The solution was for several companies to act together, and perhaps to set up a separate specialist company to drain a group of pits, which would be financed directly or indirectly by the mining partnerships that stood to benefit from it. On the Erzgebirge a network of adits financed in this manner was started in the early sixteenth century and ultimately expanded to a length of 44 km.; in the Upper Silesia–Cracow area there were 18 adits totalling 50 km. underground. They had cost an average of 7,000–8,000 zloty per km., the equivalent at that time of building a ship in Gdansk.[20] In an interesting variant of this idea, the Hallstatt salt works began to build a pipeline in 1595 to allow it to transport the brine to Ebensee where there were much larger timber resources to fuel the boiling plants.[21]

It was the alternative solution, of pumping out the water, which led to what many observers have judged to have been the most impressive technical innovations of the age. Even today, we can only marvel at the ingenuity of the engineers who constructed the pumps for the Saxon-Bohemian-Hungarian fields. The best account of them, beautifully illustrated by easily understood drawings, is in *De re metallica* by Georg Bauer ('Agricola'), which was first published in 1556 but had been written over the twenty-five preceding years.

In earlier times, buckets of water were hauled up by windlass; increased flow of water led, in due course, to chains of buckets or dippers, followed by rag and chain pumps, of which six different types were shown by Agricola, and pumps using the suction of pistons moving in cylinders. Some were powered by horses; the more elaborate ones required waterwheels. The largest waterwheel then in use, which

19 Kellenbenz (1981), 366–7; Pickl (1981), 414; Wolfstrigl-Wolfskron (1903), 197, 199, 206; Jenkin (1972), 85; Wilsdorf and Quellmalz (1971), 226, 340; Molenda (1976*b*), 153.

20 Götschmann (1986), 77; Sieber (1954), 28; Henschke (1974), 204; Molenda (1981), 404–6; Raistrick (1975), ii. 25.

21 Koller (1987), 774–8, 803; also Hägermann and Ludwig (1984) and p. 204 below.

had a diameter of 36 ft., was constructed so that its direction could be reversed by controlling the water-flow over it. It was equipped with ingenious safety devices, and built so that parts could easily be replaced. Probably the most inventive of the local engineers was the Pole Jan Turzo (Johann Thurzo, 1437–1508), who entered into partnership with the Fuggers in 1494. He designed a reversible waterwheel *c.*1475, the first probably at Kremnitz (Kremnica) and another for Neusohl. One of his most spectacular constructions was the pumping machinery at the gold mine of Nagybany: the wheel, of 10 m. diameter, was placed 65 m. underground, to deal with a network of galleries going down 280 m. A water head of 110 m. was built up, fed by a system of dams which began at a distance of some 15 km. from the mine. Where water had to be raised to a height that exceeded the suction power of the pumps, a set or battery of pumps was built, one above the other, driven by a set of waterwheels, similarly placed one above the other. Wherever possible, the water was lifted only to the nearest adit whence it could flow out by gravity. Zellerthal had 24 waterwheels, mostly underground. The extensive and ingenious use of gearing is also noteworthy.[22]

The advanced nature of the technology described in Agricola's work is underlined by the fact that it remained in use as a textbook for 180 years, being replaced by a more up-to-date work only in 1738. Yet there is no doubt that it was describing actual practice, and not theoretical constructs such as can be found in other examples of Renaissance literature. As regards pumping, the Saxon-Bohemian-Hungarian district was well ahead even of the famous Schwaz mine in Tyrol. The method used there was to drain the water from several levels into a single sump which by 1533 had reached a depth of 125 (Tyrolean) *Klafter* or 237 m. By that time, 600 men were engaged in raising the water from the sump by passing leather buckets to each other, working six/4-hourly shifts per day.

It is not clear why such an out-of-date method was still in use in the 1530s, as there seems to have been no lack of capital or ingenuity. At any rate, threatened by high costs and technical problems, that primitive system was replaced in 1537 by a machine of which no details have survived. When this failed, it was followed by a set of pumps worked by 250 men, and in 1554 by a machine which became one of the wonders of the age. Driven by two waterwheels of 8 m. or 10 m. diameter (reports differ), whose movement could be reversed by applying different water channels, it was connected to a double-conical capstan with ropes in opposite directions so that as one was wound up, the other was let down. The axle was in three parts, for lifting water, ores, and men: used as a pump, it could lift 300,000 litres of water per day. However, the relief was temporary only, for as the mine was extended, the limit of the pump's capacity was reached in 1580 and parts of the mine had to be shut down in order to be able to keep the rest drained. In 1615 the whole mine had to be abandoned. A new shaft was sunk in 1660, ultimately to a depth of 265 m., with a waterwheel of 12 m. diameter which provided power to cams that operated on a set of

[22] Agricola (1950), book VI; Wilsdorf and Quellmalz (1971), 262–4; Braunstein (1983), 585–6; also Nef (1941*a*), 211; Bromehead (1956), 13–22; Aitchison (1960), 375–7; Bartels (1992), 33–42, 103.

pump rods, each lifting water from one level to the next, with a capacity of 640,000 litres per day. Later a second wheel and an even larger third wheel of 16 m. diameter were added which increased the lifting capacity to 1.2 million litres per day.[23]

Similar innovative ingenuity was shown in the building of winding mechanisms and ventilation machines, and in lining shafts and underground passages. The wooden rails laid down for the *hund*, a carriage fitted with a central peg to stop it running off the rails, which greatly reduced the energy needed in horizontal transport in and out of the mine, are first documented in 1427 for Grossensass in Tyrol, but were widely used in the other central European mining areas later in the fifteenth century[24]. Quite remarkable also was the progress made in mensuration, including the surveying of dead ground and of underground layouts by triangulation. Extensive instructions on the assaying of the ores will be found not only in Agricola's work, which is unique in many respects, but significantly also in a number of other books which appeared at the time as textbooks and guides to miners and metallurgists, including those of Lazarus Ercker (1574), Ciriacus Schreittmann (1578), and Samuel Zimmermann (1573).[25] Rocks were still split by using fire; the first use of gunpowder in mining was recorded in the same region, in Schemnitz (Hungary) in 1627, though there had been some early trials in *c.*1470.[26]

There were innovations of great significance also in the preparation, refining, and smelting of the ores. Agricola devoted no fewer than five of the twelve 'books' or chapters of his work to smelting and separation, including the preparation of the ores. Possibly the most important new technique was the Saiger process, noted above, of separating silver from copper by means of lead: it required large plants including furnaces, bellows, hammers, and stamping machines, all driven by water-power, as well as other equipment. Licensed by the Duke of Saxony in 1451, the process, according to Nef, 'more than any other invention . . . accounts for the great prosperity in mining and metallurgy during the century which followed'.[27] Higher temperatures reached in smelting also allowed other improvements, and it is significant that the slagheaps of former gold mines were worked over several times in 1530–40 in areas like the Fichtelgebirge to extract more of the metal which earlier methods had failed to refine. The cupellation process for silver was another important step forward.[28] The water-driven stamps, bellows, and hammers noted above were widely introduced also into other smeltworks. Towards the end of the fifteenth century Annaberg had 37 stamp works, 4 ore washeries, 7 *Flutwerke* (meaning unclear), and 12 private smeltworks in addition to the two owned by the ruler.

[23] Details will be found in Egg *et al.* (1986), 53–5, 166; Henschke (1974), 113, 201–2, 217; Götschmann (1986), 79; also cf. Braunstein (1983), 583.

[24] Lewis (1970), 10; also Gille (1980*b*), 64–7.

[25] Agricola, books v and vii; Kellenbenz (1981), 365; Nef (1952), 462; Smith and Forbes (1957); Henschke (1974), 106–7; Long (1991), 320 ff.

[26] Editors' note in Agricola (1950), 119; Probszt (1966), 136; Braunstein (1983), 586.

[27] Nef (1941*b*), 576, also (1952), 479; Stromer (1984), 51 and (1986), 89; Braunstein (1983), 587–8; Vlachovic (1971), 604.

[28] Ritschel (1983), 43; Aitchison (1960), 387.

Tin-plate works and wire-drawing mills, though they were based on innovations which had originated elsewhere, were also established in this period in the same busy central European mountain regions. A new method for rolling silver plate in preparation for coinage was introduced in Hall in Tyrol in 1575.[29]

It is evident that the copper- and silver-mining regions of central Europe formed a lively, stimulating, and competitive environment for technicians and entrepreneurs. As a society which was eager to adopt the latest technical know-how and the innovations introduced elsewhere, it also nurtured men who were constantly pushing out into the unknown themselves.

All the signs are that the technical leaders of the various mining communities were in touch with each other, where they were not indeed actually working for the same firm, as in the case of the Fugger combine with branches all over Europe. But the spread of the new technology was also furthered by deliberate initiatives. One of these was the publication of textbooks and guides already mentioned. A second method, though it was one which did not have the spread of technology as its primary objective, was the introduction of mining codes by the territorial rulers. These codes, as they developed in this period, covered several aspects of the mining community's life. They were concerned, for example, with providing encouragement for prospectors and for miners, reducing quarrels between the different companies, regulating labour relations, and providing for safety measures and insurance. But they also laid down technical details for mining practices, some of which obliged operators to introduce up-to-date methods, and the authorities set up under them were even known to take the initiative themselves in introducing such innovations as pumping equipment and drainage soughs, especially where the collaboration of several mining companies would have been required.[30]

Thirdly, and probably most importantly, the transfer of technology was accomplished by the movement of people. Students, who were often proprietors' sons, would naturally be sent to other works for technical training. But skilled miners and metallurgists would also migrate. This was clearly so within the leading districts themselves. One example concerns the process of wet-stamping of ores. This was brought to Joachimsthal in 1519 by one Paul Grommestetter, a native of Schwaz; a little before that he had introduced the same improvement at Schneeberg. One Hans Pörtner brought the process to Schlackenwalde in 1525, and it was installed at Wildenmann (in the Harz) by Peter Philip, the assay master, about 1524.[31]

Beyond their own districts, the German (or 'Saxon') miners and metallurgists also carried their know-how to all corners of Europe. In some cases, as in central Italy (1479), Spain (1553), Ireland (1561), Scotland (1593), France, and England they were specifically invited by rulers, or leading companies, to develop the local mineral

[29] Sieber (1954), 31; Usher (1957), 341–2; Kellenbenz (1981), 367–74; Götschmann (1986), 120; Henschke (1974), 114 ff., 262; Mitterauer (1974*b*), 306; Kuhn (1955), 212 ff.; Mokyr (1990), 48.

[30] Henschke (1974), 103 ff., 111–12; Niederer (1979), 243; Poller (1970), 319; Agricola, book IV. For the relevance of mining codes for fixing and miners' privileges, see pp. 106–7 and 159 above.

[31] Editors' note in Agricola (1950), 281–2; Ludwig and Gruber (1987), 214; Nef (1952), 453.

resources. There they not merely transferred existing technology, but occasionally also developed their own innovations, as was the case with lead smelting in Derbyshire. It is a consequence of their influence that large numbers of technical terms used in mining in England and Sweden, and even in France and other Romance-speaking countries, are of German origin, though the term *Berghmaster* appeared in a Derbyshire lead-mining case as early as 1288. The German miners were also in demand as military engineers. One admirer wrote to Queen Elizabeth in 1567:

> Those places in Jockendall [Joachimsthal] that were woods, wastes and wilderness, are now strong, beautiful and populous cities. Not only nurseries to all European divers sciences and specially in knowledge of mineral affairs, dividing of metals, draining of waters, and such like, but also the same miners be worthy soldiers, most durable in all troubles and travails, and specially in winter and in hot and cold places.

Curiously enough, in 1444–5 the Elector of Saxony invited an 'English' mining expert, Adrian (?) Spierinc, to improve the productivity of his mines.[32] A 'large group of emigrant miners from Joachimsthal and Schwaz' set off for Central America in 1527–30 to develop the Welsers' mining property there. While many of the migrations of experts and skilled miners were motivated by the pull of other parts of the world in this manner, some were also driven by the 'push factor', because their own mines were in decline.[33]

The leading mining and smelting complexes described here disposed of enormous capital sums: they represented some of the largest concentrations of capital of the age. As noted above, their rise is to be explained in part by the demand factor of an increasing population in Europe enjoying rising prosperity, which in turn these companies helped to sustain, and which then became the basis of a larger economic surplus over bare subsistence than had existed in previous ages. Some of this surplus was to be found in the new mining towns; much more of it was transferred to increasingly absolutist princes who then proceeded to waste it in costly wars. The absolutism of these princes was also furthered by the fact that the same metallurgical revolution which had helped to put at their disposal the additional resources to fight these wars had also created the heavy artillery and other armament which had become too costly for even their richest subjects, and thus confirmed their own ascendancy. There was yet another link between mining and war: for the newly rich merchants who financed the mining companies also had control over much of the disposable surplus created by the European economy, some of which they used in turn to finance both the rulers and their wars. They also managed to absorb some

[32] Quotation from Donald (1955), 119, also (1961), 13 ff.; Gille (1980*a*), 558 and (1966), 42, 57 ff.; Bromehead (1956), 11; Raistrick (1975), i. 25–6; Hammersley (1991), 158; Henschke (1974), 172; Rowse (1978), 55; Ford and Rieuwerts (1968), 19; Stolz (1955), 268; Egg *et al.* (1986), 136; Kuhn (1955), 196; Unger (1983), 68; also p. 183 above. For a contrary view, see Burt (1991); Crossley and Kiernan (1992), 6–8; Rees (1968), 23; Raistrick and Jennings (1965), 73, 78–9; Spooner (1972), 24; Laube (1976), 14–15; Lander (1970), 325; Hardy (?1988), 15; Cirković (1987), 160–1.

[33] Schreiber (1965), 195; Riedmann (1988), 127; Spooner (1972), 24; Wilsdorf and Quellmalz (1971), 92.

of the more traditional surpluses: thus the Fuggers made their early killings by handling the financial transactions of wealthy churchmen and church institutions. Taking it all in all, without the Fuggers, the Welsers, and the rest, neither the mineral industries nor the Renaissance princes could have achieved as much as they did.

As far as mining was concerned, the need for large lumps of capital had come upon these districts gradually. In the beginning, when workings were small, groups of miners and other local people would club together to meet the original expenditure until the metal could be raised and sold. Furnaces and other equipment were also relatively limited in cost. In due course, as deeper workings and more advanced methods required larger investments, the mining communities evolved a form of shares known in Germany as *Kuxen*. Each of these entitled its holder to his share of the surplus, or obliged him to meet his share of the deficit, at the end of every reckoning period, without having any final capital investment sum laid down in advance. As investment grew, the periodic calls for fresh capital began to exceed the resources of the actual miners and other original holders. At this point, outside merchants from Augsburg, Nuremberg, Cracow, and elsewhere entered, and by acquiring the shares, assumed both the liabilities of the workings, and the control and profits which were to follow. The biggest of them, the Fugger partnership, was able to boost its income not merely by gaining monopoly powers over several markets, and co-ordinating the technically complementary works, like silver, copper, and lead mining and smelting, but also, and above all, by gaining mint, taxation, and other privileges in return for their loans to the Habsburgs.[34] Ultimately, this was to be their undoing, for in the end some of the princes repudiated their debts; but for the time being the merchants' riches grew at the same pace as their power.

The form of organization prevailing in the mining districts was thus purely capitalistic: the men engaged in them, capitalists and wage workers alike, were, not least, also pioneers of European capitalism. They represented 'a pocket of economic innovation in the surrounding feudal economy', and were bound to exert some pressure to undermine the status (*ständisch*) society out of which they had grown, although territorial rulers were at times among the leading shareholders. In one view, the whole drive had 'a modern aspect of a capital investment in underdeveloped areas'.[35] It seems natural that the larger firms, permeated as they were by a capitalist spirit, developed innovations in accounting; still less will the emergence of an early form of class struggle, the phenomenon of strikes and the recognition of labour management as a necessary skill, cause surprise.[36]

The new type of society which thus came to be established in some of the marginal lands of Europe was also largely an urban society. Typically for German conditions,

[34] Nef (1941*a*), 204; Probszt (1966), 74; Strieder (1929); Ritschel (1983), 41; Kellenbenz (1988), 32; Vlachovic (1971), 603–4; Lewis (1907), 177–81; Molenda (1976*b*), 162.

[35] Quotations from Wyrobisz (1976), 761 and Schreiber (1965), 200; also cf. Ludwig and Gruber (1987), 1; Hatcher (1973), 43; Paulinyi (1971), 564; Laube (1968), 577, 583; Braunstein (1983), 582; Molenda (1976*a*), 167–9.

[36] Agricola, book 1; Egg *et al.* (1986), 130; Pölnitz (1960), 363; Henschke (1974), 82 ff., 119 ff.

towns were granted charters from an early stage of their mining activity which provided for the kinds of freedom which would then attract miners and other skilled men from outside. Thus Schneeberg, originally planned as a colony of Zwickau, received its town and mining charter in 1479 and 1481, about eight years after silver ores were discovered, and it was granted a mint in 1483: by 1500, its estimated population had reached 10,000. Annaberg got its charter in 1497, some five years after the discovery of silver ores, and a mint in 1498. By 1540 its population was estimated at 12,000. Joachimsthal, the most successful at the time, had its charter granted in 1518, and in 1519 the minting of thalers began: by 1533 its population had reached 18,000. These figures meant that these towns were a good deal larger than the capitals of the surrounding German states. Many other mining towns were founded at this time, though none reached a similar size. By the later sixteenth century the three boroughs named above contained 40,000 inhabitants among them, while the mining district as a whole counted a population of some 130,000. Some of these mining settlements were so nearly contiguous as almost to form a single conurbation, though the smelting plants had to be located away from them because of their need for wood and water-power. Together with the other mining areas of Bohemia and Slovakia, they formed the most densely settled areas of their respective countries.[37]

In the Hungarian/central Slovakian mining area, of the eight mining towns, Schemnitz contained 4,000 miners in 1535, Neusohl around 1,000, and Kremnitz 400. Schemnitz received its charter in 1244. These towns also had a planned layout on the German model. From 1388, they had formed an association to defend their common interests, including the regulation of prices, contracts, religious freedom, law codes, and a *Bruderkasse*, or insurance fund.[38] Schwaz in Tyrol, which had had only 40 households in 1312, had grown to 20,000 inhabitants in its heyday in the sixteenth century. As such, it was the second largest city in the Austrian lands, ranking immediately behind Vienna: Innsbruck, the capital of Tyrol, had a mere 5,000–6,000 inhabitants, the whole county of Tyrol little more than 110,000. Hall, the other mining town there, had 2,500–3,000 inhabitants, Rattenberg another 750.[39] Mining and smelting in Styria and Carinthia and in the Harz region had also led to the creation of new towns.[40]

These towns, it should be stressed once more, were founded in what was largely a wilderness, in 'the extreme marginal edge of settlement', in 'districts hostile to colonization', in Mitterauer's words.[41] The whole process has been referred to, not unfairly, as a set of 'Klondike phenomena',[42] and indeed the towns' populations were made up almost exclusively of miners and metal-workers and their families. Thus in Zellerfeld in 1571, of 370 people in employment, 286 were miners and

[37] Kuhn (1955), 188–97; Unger (1983), 1–6; Schreiber (1965), 194; Ritschel (1983), 18; Sieber (1954), 25; Petran (1965), 220.

[38] Paulinyi (1971), 538; Vozár (1971), 568–80; Molenda (1976*a*), 166.

[39] Egg (1964), 7, 52; Riedmann (1988), 124; Klein (1980), 93.

[40] e.g. Henschke (1974), 161; Mitterauer (1974*b*), 255.

[41] Mitterauer (1974*b*), 234.

[42] Stromer (1986), 86.

another 38 were smelters and other associated workers, making 324, or 87.6 per cent of those at work. In Wildemann in 1571 the proportion was 86.5 per cent. For the Erzgebirge mining region as a whole, 29 of its 40 towns were pure mining towns, and the remainder, housing craftsmen, transport workers and others, were connected at least indirectly with the mines.[43] In the larger towns there would necessarily be a larger element for service and outside supplies; there was, among other things, an administrative and professional layer to be accommodated. However, even there, the mainly one-dimensional population structure, with an exceptionally large number of young men, was likely to have imposed its own character on the urban milieu.

It would nevertheless be quite wrong to assume that these centres were, like the goldrush townships of California, Alaska, or Australia in the nineteenth century, shanty towns bereft of culture and scarcely within the law. Quite the contrary: in addition to forming one of the leading edges of Europe's economy, they were also culturally and artistically among the most active centres of their day.

Georg Bauer, otherwise known as 'Agricola', author of the famous book on metals, may serve as an example. In the very first 'book' of his *magnum opus*, he claims that the successful mine manager must be not merely an expert geologist and mineralogist, a mining engineer and chemist and assayer, but also knowledgeable about 'philosophy', in order 'that he may discern the origin, cause, and nature of subterranean things'; medicine, to care for illnesses and accidents caused by working underground; astronomy; surveying; arithmetic; architecture; mechanical drawing; and finally law, 'that he may not take another man's property and so make trouble for himself, and that he may fulfil his obligations to others according to the law'.[44] The book itself does indeed contain sections on these, as well as on related subjects like labour management.

Nor is this the full extent of Agricola's contribution. He also published substantial works on physical geology; on subterranean water and gases; on mineralogy; on the history and topography of metals; on weights and measures; and on animals which live underground, all in the same general field of knowledge. But, additionally, he also found time to publish on entirely different subjects. Among the more important of these were books on the plague; a political tract on the war against the Turks; a family tree of the House of Saxony; a Latin grammar; some theological tracts; and there are hints of other works, including one on medical history, though no details have survived.

Agricola was a true Renaissance man, occupying 'a considerable place in the great awakening of learning', a correspondent of Erasmus, though he resisted the Reformation. Born in 1494 in Glauchau, Saxony, he studied at the University of Leipzig and after some years as schoolmaster in Zwickau, became a lecturer at the University in 1522. He thereafter studied medicine at Bologna and Padua and possibly also Ferrara, and stayed for three years in Bologna and Venice, helping to edit

[43] Kuhn (1955), 199; Unger (1983), 3. [44] Agricola (1950), 1–4.

the Aldine edition of Galen and Hippocrates, before returning to Zwickau in 1526. In the following year he became medical officer for the town of Joachimsthal, then the centre of the regional mining activity. He took up a share in the famous *Gottesgabe* (God's Gift) mine which was discovered in 1530, and about the same time he left Joachimsthal for travel and study. In 1533 he was appointed medical officer for the town of Chemnitz, where he remained until his death in 1555: his *magnum opus*, the *re metallica*, was thus published posthumously. The publication of his learned books on mining and metallurgy began in 1544, he was elected a Burgher of Chemnitz in 1546, and in the same year the Duke/Elector of Saxony made him Burgomaster, an office which he held for four terms. The Dukes Maurice (1521–53) and Augustus (1526–86) also showered other favours on him, which was all the more remarkable since he was a 'staunch Catholic under a Protestant Sovereign in a State seething with Protestantism'.[45]

Given the range and quality of his work, we can be sure that had he resided in Italy, France, the Rhineland, or wherever else conspicuous consumption has aroused the interest of historians of art and 'culture', he would generally have been acknowledged as one of the great men of his age. But, as is often the case with original minds working in marginal areas, his work was largely forgotten, until rescued from neglect in 1912 by Herbert Hoover and Lou Henry Hoover, the former of whom, then a young engineer, was later to make his mark on history in an altogether different field.[46]

Agricola, though the outstanding local contributor to the development of science and the scientific spirit in conjunction with practical industry and technology, was by no means the only one. Another was Dr Ulrich Rühlein von Kalbe or Calw ('Calbus'), physician, mathematician, founder of a school of liberal arts, surveyor of mines, and town planner of Annaberg (1497) and Marienberg (1521), town physician and Councillor of Freiberg (1509) and Burgomaster of that town (1514), to whom, in fact, some have attributed the *re metallica*. A third was Lazarus Ercker (*c*.1530–94)—born in Annaberg, mine and mint technician, studied at the University of Wittenberg, assayer of Dresden, mint assayer at Goslar, counter-assayer at Kuttenberg, and author of several practical and learned books. Others to be noted are Wenceslas Payer, who brought out the first book on mining medicine in 1523; Petrus Plateanus, co-founder of a mining dictionary in 1525; and Magnus Hunt, who produced the second mining medicine book, in 1529, all from Joachimsthal.[47] These engineers and others 'were at once humanists and technical experts', developing an 'intermediate culture between science and practice, a sort of general know-how'.[48]

[45] Introd. to Agricola (1950), pp. viii, xiv. This and the preceding paragaphs are largely based on the excellent work of the editors of that edition, Herbert Clark Hoover and Lou Henry Hoover. Also cf. Gille (1980*b*), 30; Long (1991), 334–5.

[46] Mokyr (1990), 64; also Gille (1966), 35.

[47] Introd. and appendix to Agricola (1950), book XVII and 610–11; Long (1991), 328, 346–9; Wilsdorf and Quellmalz (1971), 159.

[48] Braunstein (1983), 576, 577, also 591.

By contrast—and significantly—most of the contemporary authors on technical works who originated in Italy or France and who had some practical experience—such as Vanuccio Biringuccio (1480–1539)—were military engineers, or they had studied and were disciples of German practice.

In addition to the engineers, other contributors to the active intellectual life of the mining districts included Adam Riese of Annaberg (1492–1559), author of perhaps the most famous mathematical textbook in German history, and Friedrich Myconius (1490–1546), as well as the poet and hymn composer Nicolaus Hermann (1480–1561), and the poets Dr Johannes Salianus and Paulus Niavis who made the miners key figures in their writings. These were immigrants. Of those native to the area who became important in the following generation, Andreas Mensel (Schneeberg) and Johan Richter (Joachimsthal) deserve mention. Nor should the scientific-technological interest of regional rulers, among whom Duke Julius of Brunswick must occupy a leading place, be forgotten.[49]

Several of the mining towns were noted for their fine patrician houses, financed out of mining profits. Others erected splendid churches, like Schneeberg's St Wolfgang's (built 1516–36) or Annaberg's St Anne's (1499–1525), or town halls, like the Renaissance building at Marienberg (1533), together with a tithe hall and the *Knappschaftshaus* (miners' centre). Latin schools were founded in Annaberg (1500–5), Marienberg (1532–6), Schneeberg (1483–5), and Schlaggenwald (1553). Some of them also boasted a library, even a monastery. Marienberg had been laid out by Rühlein von Kalbe on a 'humanist plan, the most regular of all mining towns'. At a humbler level, craftsmen came to decorate the churches with paintings and sculptures, mystery plays emerged, and German schools and hospitals were founded.[50]

The miners themselves, as proto-proletarians, as men of freedom who had emancipated themselves from the surrounding feudal order, were possibly outsiders as far as the mainstream of the dominant culture was concerned. However, their towns became a 'breeding place of the Reformation and the first centre of Enlightenment to arise among an industrial proletariat'. Thus 'the beginning of the mining town settlement showed not only in the economic sphere, but also in cultural matters a seething unrest, an openness and receptivity towards the new and a certain lack of stability'.[51] This was perhaps nowhere more clearly marked than in their attitude to the Church.

The Erzgebirge mining communities, then at the zenith of their influence, were among the very first to embrace the new doctrines of Martin Luther. Luther's father, in fact, was one of them—a copper miner in the Mansfeld district near the Harz, who worked himself up from hewer to a modest fortune as a share proprietor, chosen at one time to be miners' spokesman in negotiations with the town council. How far the great Reformer was influenced directly by him is not clear. The elder

49 Kuhn (1955), 204–5; Moran (1981), 261–2.

50 Vozár (1971), 574; Molenda (1976*a*), 187; Niederer (1979), 243; Laube (1976), 27–40; Kellenbenz (1976), 115; Wilsdorf and Quellmalz (1971), *passim*.

51 Quotations from Schreiber (1965), 200 and Kuhn (1955), 202.

Luther appears to have been subject to the miner's typical fear of evil spirits, from which even Agricola was not entirely free, and 'told of one of his companions who had died in agony after Satan's minions had torn the skin off his back'.[52] There is something, too, in Luther of the dark brooding danger and the fear of hell which not unnaturally forced itself onto the mentality of men who spent much of their life in perilous work underground. Yet he himself seemed curiously loath to acknowledge this link, always emphasizing his peasant background, which was rather that of his grandparents.

Be that as it may, it seemed that, given their experience, 'it was a foregone conclusion that [the miners] would swiftly and unhesitatingly adopt [Luther's] creed. In the new and progressive border community of Joachimsthal, the first Bohemian town to hear Protestant preachers who arrived in 1521, the spiritual emancipation thus engendered inspired a number of outstanding men to develop their capacities to the full.'[53] Among them was Johannes Mathesius (1504–65), the parish priest of the town and first biographer of Luther.

Elsewhere also the miners were among the staunchest supporters of reform. In fact, the destruction of a Protestant church in the southern Bohemian mining town of Klostergrab in 1618 was one of the triggers that set off the Thirty Years War. More immediately, Neusohl in Hungary had a Protestant parish priest in 1527, as did Schemnitz in 1528, and Silberberg in Silesia became Protestant in 1532.[54]

The cultural liveliness of that region was mirrored by the mining town of Schwaz in Tyrol. It was in the van of progress in many fields. As early as 1477 the town established an isolation hospital for those suffering from syphilis and leprosy. The miners' main hospital provided some of the best medical attention then available, employing two doctors trained in Italy. They were visited in 1516 by no less than Paracelsus who came to the town, not to teach, but to learn from a leading 'alchemist', possibly a chemist, resident there. Another prominent person was the mine's silver refiner, Sigmund Fueger, who enjoyed a wide reputation as a metallurgist. In 1520 a local entrepreneur, Jörg Stöckl, set up a printworks and publishing house which brought out humanistic works among others. Fine buildings and portraits painted of the well-to-do proprietors were evidence of a certain educated taste among the inhabitants. The mining company had provided for a school as well as for a Latin school which educated the choir boys. There was also a well-known choir in the town, the miners had their mystery play and passion play, and there were almshouses and churches. Even a Franciscan monastery was built in 1507–14, followed in 1516 by an Augustinian convent.

By one of the quirks of religious territorial division, Schwaz lacked a parish priest in the sixteenth century. The official incumbent was based on Vomp and he did not know how to handle the unruly Schwazers who had, however, themselves provided for five chaplaincies. Luther's doctrines became known in 1520, and were immediately and enthusiastically welcomed by burghers, miners, and labourers alike. By

[52] Friedenthal (1970), 10. [53] Schreiber (1965), 196. [54] Kuhn (1955), 203.

1525 almost all the nuns had left the convent, having become Lutherans, though later some of them returned penitently to their original faith. However, the enthusiasm did not endure. By about 1530 the great wave of Lutheranism was over, and the people of the Tyrolean mining towns, especially the lower orders, turned to the Anabaptists, who were preaching an even more radical departure from the past, including the communalization of property. Their influence was strongest between 1530 and 1550, when some converts emigrated to Moravia and elsewhere. Eventually they were dissuaded from their heresies by the somewhat drastic method of execution by sword, fire, or drowning. All told, seventy-one were done to death in Rattenberg, while Schwaz mourned only two victims. In the Counter-Reformation which followed, no fewer than five Jesuit missions were established in the town.[55]

In the Gastein-Rauris district of Tyrol also, the Lutheran reformation made a deep impression, because the population there, too, 'stood in an intellectual-communicative interrelation which also fostered political consciousness'.[56] Other mining valleys in the eastern Alps were similarly affected by the Lutheran agitation, but all of them were ultimately returned to their original faith as a result of the brutal repressive measures taken against them by the authorities.

While these mining areas on the margin could not compare with Florence, Venice, or Paris in significance for the European Renaissance, and had no direct hand in the redrawing of the political map of Europe, or even in halting the Ottoman advance, yet they were more than temporary mining camps owing their prominence simply to the fortunate location of mineral ores. The ores, of course, were vital, but if the miners, the engineers, and the entrepreneurs—and the society they built up—became technical and economic pioneers, driving Europe a substantial step forward and laying the foundations for the advances of the next age, it was not merely because of the regional favourable conjunction of resources, but also because of the influence of these resources upon the society which emerged, and which they helped to shape. Among its characteristics were active entrepreneurship, including technical innovation and risk-taking, as well as an interest in the arts, in learning, and in what is generally considered to be 'culture'. But their culture had a balance of its own. Far more than that of the more renowned centres of the Renaissance, it was directed towards science and a scientific attitude, including necessarily the questioning of received wisdom, the testing by experiment rather than by reference to authority, and the intensive interest in the actual environment shown by advances in such sciences as geology, mineralogy, and medicine. It was in those significant scientific aspects of Renaissance culture that they were in the forefront, perhaps even in advance of their age. It thus appears that, in so far as they were up among the leaders, it was not in spite of their marginal location, but because of it. The minerals and fuel and water-power; the freedoms and privileges and the social openness; the practical ingenuity, the energy and initiative needed to

[55] Much of this paragraph is based on Egg *et al.* (1986), 134 ff.; also Kuhn (1955), 203; Cole and Wolf (1974), 41–4.

[56] Ludwig and Gruber (1987), 214.

survive: all typical attributes of marginal Europe, combined to push economy and society an important step forward.

But, as is always the case whenever marginal areas take the lead, the lead was to be temporary only. By the mid-sixteenth century the mining districts of central Europe suffered two blows to their prosperity almost simultaneously. On the one hand, the ore supplies began to give out, at least as far as existing technologies could reach them at acceptable cost; on the other, a stream of more cheaply acquired gold and silver from the Americas began to flood the European markets. In the second half of the sixteenth century, the signs of incipient decline were unmistakable. By the early seventeenth century, the mining towns which were most vulnerable, like Schwaz, had declined into insignificance.[57] Some others lingered on longer, and some survived even the disasters of the Thirty Years War to preserve some sort of mining and metallurgical activity into the modern age. But their pioneer role within Europe and the world was over.

Not all these settlements became wholly deserted when the ore gave out: there was enough there of the kind of enterprising spirit typical for many marginal areas, as well as the basic infrastructure that survived from the days of glory, to seek, and find, alternative productive occupations. Several former mining towns turned to a variety of domestic industries, for which they had at least some of the raw materials and which were based on skill and application, which they possessed in plenty, rather than on large-scale capital structures. The making of wooden toys and wood carvings, musical instruments including violins, glassware, metal pipe fittings, basket weaving, straw plaiting, lace making, embroidery and, in the Bohemian mountains, the beginnings of a flourishing linen industry, were among the activities taken up in the areas once famous for mines, furnaces, and forges.[58] Some of these regional industries, with appropriate modifications, continue to the present day. Others were at least to foreshadow, or become part of, the next phase of development in which marginal areas were to make their mark: the age of what has come to be known as proto-industry. It was a form of industrial organization in which workers engaged in production in their homes, villages, and towns, but supplied a world market; it will be discussed in more detail in Chapters 9 and 10 below.

[57] Egg *et al.* (1986), 156; Schwarz (1959), 220.

[58] e.g. Kuhn (1957), 264–8; Kaufhold (1986); Müller (1938); Kötschke and Kretzschmar (1965), 293–4; Wessely (1853), i. 266; Schremmer (1970), 341; Sandberger (1979), 763; Fried (1975), 186; Smith (1978), 577 (map); Bilz (1975), 5; Sieber (1967), 12, 15–17, 35–6, 76. Also pp. 201–2 below.

9

Some Later Case Studies

Chapters 6–8 have attempted to sketch the way in which, respectively, a broad belt of an extensive moving frontier, a type of organization—the Cistercian monastery—and a compact region came to provide a framework for technical and organizational progress and pioneering leadership. The present chapter takes the story up to a more recent period and sets out to provide examples of a different kind. It will deal with more specific, more limited concentrations of advanced industrial, mining, or similar activities in marginal areas. These, also, help to illustrate the peculiar role played by those areas in European economic history.

There were essentially two types of industry to be found in important concentrations in marshes, forests, and mountains between the seventeenth and nineteenth centuries. One of these depended for its location in marginal areas on the availability of the minerals themselves, of wood fuel and water-power as well as, in the later stages, of coal. It consisted of metal mining and smelting, salt mining, glass-making, and the early stages of metal manufacture.[1]

The second group is made up of the manufacture of textiles, of toys and other wooden goods, and of composite articles like musical instruments, clocks, and watches. For these, also, timber and possibly water-power might be of importance; but a main explanation for the location of these occupations in marginal areas was the availability of a certain type of labour. Often the men and women who lived there possessed a tradition of hard work and of manual skills; their industrial occupation would frequently fill a gap in the annual work cycle, normally in their winter when fields were snowed up or deep-sea fishing had to be suspended; and they would be willing to accept low wages, either because they were inured to hardship, or because they had small plots of land out of which they could make up their incomes.[2] In the period which we are now considering, many of these areas were engaged in the kind of domestic industry which is nowadays referred to as proto-industrial, working for merchant *Verleger* who supplied distant markets. Some of them went on to develop into centres of fully-fledged modern large-scale industry; others were to preserve some form of outwork; and others still were to lose their industries and their leading role altogether and become deindustrialized in the era of mechanical mass production.

Germany offers some of the most interesting examples of this kind of advanced activity in marginal lands. One of the best known of these was the Black Forest. It

[1] Fremdling (1985), 139. [2] Sieber (1967), 82.

was settled late, both because of its thick woodland and its mountainous nature: it was thus marginal in a double sense. By the early seventeenth century, however, it had become an important textile outworking area. It supplied the famous Calw Cloth company, which had something like monopsony rights over buying up the local product, but also worked for Swiss merchants in St Gallen and Appenzell (for embroidery) and in Basle, providing cotton and silk yarns in addition to woollen yarns and woven fabrics. In the deepest forest, where no one else would settle, glass-makers plied their trade, a select, privileged, endogamous group. Most famous, without doubt, was the clockmaking industry. Probably arising out of an older tradition of wood carving and box making, it developed rapidly from about 1720 after a false start in 1665. By 1815 there were said to be 688 masters, 127 suppliers, and an annual output of 187,000 clocks. In 1895, 34 factories as well as several hundred workshops were counted. The first musical clock was made in 1768, and musical boxes, mathematical puzzles, and complex automatons as playthings for the rich were other products. The competitive edge enjoyed by the region, as well as the technical advances registered, were said to be due to the high skill and excellent training of the local workforce.[3]

The Swabian Alb, another mountainous, though rather more accessible region, lying to the east of the Black Forest, also produced textiles, in part for Swiss *Verleger*: by 1798 there were estimated to be 30,000 linen weavers active there. One local firm which rose to world fame by 1914 on the basis of over 40 outworking branches scattered on the plateau and the hillsides was the Hohner company, makers of mouth-organs.[4]

Further east still, on the border with Bohemia, were the Bavarian Forest, the Upper Palatinate, and the Fichtelgebirge. All three were wooded and mountainous, as well as stretching along a political border area, and they were thus perhaps marginal in a threefold sense. They all contained important mining and manufacturing activities in our period.

In the Upper Palatinate, 20–25 per cent of the population depended on mining and metallurgy until the early seventeenth century; thereafter that share declined, and the region was largely deindustrialized, changing 'from a rich mining country to a considerably poorer arable and stockbreeding land'.[5] There was some revival of the iron industry in the late eighteenth century, and glass-works, sawmills—some of them taking over disused ironworks buildings—and textiles offered some industrial employment, but the heights of the Middle Ages were not regained. In the Fichtelgebirge, iron mining and smelting continued until the nineteenth century, and there, as indeed in the Upper Palatinate, in the Bavarian Forest, and in several of the other forested uplands of Germany, including the Spessart, the Thüringer Wald and, as noted above, the Black Forest, glass-making based on wood fuel survived until the age of coal.[6]

[3] Mayer (1938); Gothein (1970); Magnus (1897), 13; Discherl (1938), 103–4; Müller (1938), 87–90.
[4] Müller (1938), 78; Megerle (1982), 122; Schremmer (1979*a*), 1102; Berghoff (1994).
[5] Schremmer (1979*b*), 1372 and (1970), 340. [6] Discherl (1938); Schmidtill (1963).

In Silesia it was the south-western mountainous borderland, the *Grenzstreifen*, which had become much the most densely settled by the eighteenth century, even though it did not contain the capital, Breslau. The Prussian Census of 1748 'lists 5,672 domestic weavers in the Hirschberg-Schönau region, 2,657 in the County of Glatz and 12,000 in the mountains, this last figure being four times as many as were active in all the rest of Silesia'.[7] By the end of the century, Upper Silesia, rich in various minerals as well as in coal, had become one of the leading metallurgical centres in Europe, the first in Germany to turn to the coke smelting of iron, though it was situated 'far away from cultured men, at the limits of the Empire', according to Goethe, who had come to view the first steam engine at Tarnowitz in 1790. Despite its mineral riches, its 'marginal location' and difficult transport conditions were to remain a handicap throughout the nineteenth century.[8]

In the Saxon Erzgebirge, scene of the mining revolution in the fifteenth–seventeenth centuries, industrial work and even mining by no means died out completely thereafter, as noted in Chapter 8 above. In addition to the traditional copper and silver ore, nickel and wolfram were mined in the nineteenth century, and uranium, first proved in 1780, was traded from 1830. The Saxon uplands became, in fact, the most industrialized region of Germany, to the mid-century at least. In 1831, 30,335 people, or 2 per cent of the population, lived by mining and smelting. Mechanized cotton spinning developed first there in Germany: in the Erzgebirge district alone there were 210,000 mule spindles in 1817, and in due course the water-power, which had been one of the causes of the early industrial development of the region, gave way locally to the steam engine. It was to be in engineering that the Saxon lead was to become most marked within Germany by the first half of the nineteenth century, though much of this was centred in the cities of the foothills rather than in the high mountains, where, nevertheless, rolling mills and forges were to be found. The clocks, the toys, the embroidery and lace making have been noted above.[9]

The musical instrument manufacture of the Saxon Vogtland does perhaps deserve special mention. Allegedly first started by Protestant Bohemian refugees, it was boosted by further Bohemian immigration after the Thirty Years War, when its best period began. In addition to violins (there was a guild of violin-makers in Neukirchen in 1716), the region produced double basses and cellos, guitars, mandolins, lutes, harps, zithers, and timpani. Other instruments were added later: brass wind instruments, woodwinds, even accordions and barrel organs for a time. The local population was encouraged not merely to acquire the great skill needed to make the instruments, but also to develop their own musical talents: a musical Sunday School was started in Neukirchen in 1834, and musical schools were founded in Klingenthal in 1844 and in Adorf

[7] Ziekursch (1978), 133–4; Schreiber (1965), 203.

[8] Cf. Goethe's views cited in p. 67 above; also Magnus (1987), 13; Fremdling (1986), 354 and (1985), 148–9; Fuchs (1970).

[9] Sieber (1954), 47–8 and 1967; Kiesewetter (1988); Bilz (1975), 6–7; p. 198 above.

in 1860. To complete the picture, it should be added that the region also had a flourishing textile industry.[10]

On the other side of the mountain range, in Bohemia, similar centres of textiles and glass-making developed. Meanwhile, the Slovak-Hungarian mining districts further east, with Schemnitz in the lead, continued to install, and partly pioneer, advanced mining techniques. There were remarkably advanced units also in salt mining, including Wielicka, near Cracow, reported in 1670 to work at a depth of up to 350 metres and employing 1,000 men, a more reliable report of 1752 putting it at 700; as well as Ronaszek and Maros Ujvar in Transylvania.[11]

In the west of Germany, it was the mountainous areas of the county of Mark, of the duchy of Berg, of the Siegerland, and of the Eifel which contained much of the metallurgical and other industries at the time. The interdependence of Mark and Berg has been noted above. The Siegerland, further south, was forced to develop the 'hauberg system' of timber regeneration to preserve its diminishing forests. Described as a 'marginal land', even as 'extreme marginal land', it yet carried a large, highly industrialized population. The Eifel, rich in wood fuel and water-power, specialized in smelting iron and in a secondary iron industry.[12]

Though somewhat old-fashioned and limited in many ways, when compared with the leading British industrial regions of the day, it should be borne in mind that in the German and Austrian context, these remote mountain districts were among the leading, and technically most advanced centres of their countries. Even the latest technological innovations imported from Britain, such as Newcomen engines or mule spindles, were commonly introduced first in these marginal areas.

There were industrial centres also in the German (Bavarian) Alps. The wood carvings of Oberammergau and Berchtesgaden are well known, as are the violins made in Mittenwald. The making of the thick fabric known as *Loden* was widely spread, and there was glass-making and even, between the seventeenth and nineteenth centuries, an iron industry, with blast furnaces in Aschau and Bergen, using the ore found on the Kressenberg.[13]

In the Austrian Alps it was the iron industry of Styria and Carinthia which formed the main upland industrial concentration. It was largely owing to the richness and accessibility of the ore and the plentiful timber and water-power that the local industry survived into the modern age. It also proved to be capable of adopting new techniques: iron puddling was introduced in the 1830s, and the industry was well able to hold its own against outside competition in the nineteenth century. Because of its dependence on charcoal, the industry employed not only the actual smeltworkers and hammermen, but a large proportion of the farming peasantry—

[10] Bein (1884).

[11] Svoboda (1991), 122; Teich (1973); Raistrick and Jennings (1965), 219; Kunnert (1974); Multhauf (1978), 29–30.

[12] Plaum and Witthöft (1993), 318, 322; Müller (1938), 131–3; Gleitsmann (1982); Lange (1976); Eversmann (1804); Fremdling (1986), 357; and pp. 135–6 above.

[13] Schremmer (1970), 315–17; Zorn (1971), 197; Sandberger (1979), 763.

some one-third according to one calculation—engaged in cutting wood or burning charcoal. About $11\frac{1}{2}$ farmsteads, it was said, were necessary to keep one scythe forge supplied. Of the main product, about one million scythes, sickles, and straw knives a year were exported around 1700; by 1890, this had risen to 9 million scythes produced, and 8 million exported.[14] A small iron industry also survived in Tyrol into the nineteenth century, and there was wood carving, textile spinning and weaving, and lace making and embroidery in many other Austrian Alpine areas.[15]

Among Alpine developments it is the early appearance of an industrial revolution in Switzerland, located as it mostly was in the mountains, which has attracted most attention. One major contribution to this was the precocious development of the textile industry, including cotton manufacture and its finishing process of calico printing; later on, embroidery and lace making became highly successful. St Gallen, Appenzell and the Zurich uplands were among the leading regions. Local raw material supplies—wool in the Fribourg region of the Jura mountains, flax in Appenzell and the Zurich Oberland—no doubt helped in the beginning. Expansion was fostered by the existence of a class of small traders and middlemen who were required to export the dairy produce and bring in the bread grains and other lowland products needed by the mountain dwellers. Growth was furthered also by the availability of water-power and of cheap land, and was driven into the higher uplands by the restrictive policies of the lowland towns and villages which inhibited or prevented altogether the building of new houses and the setting up of new industries. In the end, upland textile work was not merely a spare-time activity between agricultural pursuits as in other areas, but a full-time occupation by workers who migrated in increasing numbers to the mountain mills and workshops.

In 1787 the canton of Zurich had 34,000 spinners at work, as well as 6,500 looms for cottons alone. When cheap yarn from Britain became available, the Swiss switched to importing it, until such time as their own mechanized spinning mills were got going, while expanding the later processes such as weaving and concentrating on high quality goods. By 1827 there were 12,000 cotton looms working in the canton of Zurich, two-thirds of them in the Oberland, and 6,000 silk looms; by 1842, this had risen to 17,000 and 11,000 respectively.[16]

There were considerable concentrations of textile manufacture also in other Swiss mountain regions. Woollens were to be found in the Engadine, silks and cottons in Schwyz and in the 'most distant valleys' of Uri, and cottons in Glarus. There was also an important woollen industry in the mountains above Fribourg.[17]

Of greater international significance still was watchmaking. Trading for this was centred in Geneva, as was the production of the most expensive models, though

[14] Pickl (1986*a*), 31–6; Sandgruber (1974); Paulinyi (1974); Haushofer (1986), 72.

[15] Löhr (1971), 17; Wessely (1853), i. 266; Egg (1977).

[16] Braun (1965), 31–2 and (1984), 48, 89, 97 ff.; Pfister (1991), 152 and (1992*a*), esp. 113, 250 ff.; Blache (1933), 84; Niederer (1993), 213; Göttmann (1991); Jäger *et al.* (1986).

[17] Mathieu (1987), 86–9 and (1992), 227–9; Kistler (1962), 69, 103; Arnold (thesis, 1989), 51–2; Mathieu and Stauffacher (1986), 337 ff.; Peyer (1975).

most of the actual ordinary work was carried out in the villages of the Jura mountains. 'As late as the seventeenth century, this was a frontier wilderness', into which the watch industry, started by French refugees, began to move in the eighteenth century. Its establishment there was helped by the freedom from guild restrictions, and by the fact that the high valleys were cut off by snow over many winter months, providing time for domestic industrial work. It was sustained by the skill of the mountain people, and by an increasingly sophisticated system of specialization and division of labour. Together all these factors helped the Swiss watchmakers to capture from the British the main world markets outside the United States by the early nineteenth century. In 1752, 464 watchmakers were counted in the Neuchâtel region. By 1792 it was 3,458, or one-quarter of the entire population, and in 1809 their number was estimated to have been around 6,000.[18]

Finally, the Alpine salt works had turned into important concentrations of industrial activity; some, indeed, had become technical pioneers. In terms of size, Reichenhall in Bavaria, by no means the largest, had 2,550 people directly dependent on the mine in 1780, plus 700 woodmen; Traunstein, linked to it, had 550 and 600, respectively. Other leading locations were Hallein, Ischl, Hallstatt, and Aussee in Salzburg, Hall in Tyrol, and Berchtesgaden in Bavaria. Their normal method, going back in its essentials to the tenth century, was not to hack the rock salt from the bowels of the earth, but to lead sweet water to it to dissolve it and separate out other material, and then pump out the brine to pans on the surface, where the water was boiled out of it. Only in Reichenhall was the salt found naturally in the form of brine. In order to link up with adequate fuel supplies, Hall had a pipeline of 9 km. in length between the mine and the pans as early as the thirteenth century. The most spectacular such construction was a pipeline of 33 km. in length built in 1616–17 to convey the brine from the salt mines at Reichenhall to the forest-rich region of Traunstein. It required seven pumps driven by water-power, with a lift of 238 metres over the intervening heights, considered to be technical marvels of their day. A pipeline of 29 km. in length was laid from Berchtesgaden in 1819. Other innovations were adits, water-pressure pumps, and boiling and drying apparatus.[19]

Pockets of industrial and mining activity were found also in the marginal areas of the British Isles. As on the Continent, their location in areas which at the current state of technology were difficult of access was explained not only by the fact that the necessary resources such as mineral ores, timber, and water-power were to be found there, but also by historical causes, including freedom from guild restrictions and from royal inspections, and land available for settlement. Once established there, the poor agricultural yields and/or the seasonal nature of agrarian employments would further encourage the population to take up industrial work.[20]

18 Landes (1983), 257–8, 271; Pfleghart (1908); Braun (1984), 120–1.

19 Bergier (1982), 188; Koller (1987); Schremmer (1970), 39–45 and (1980); Otruba (1974); Emons and Walter (1988); Multhauf (1978), 69; Hägermann and Ludwig (1984); and pp. 120, 186, and 202 above.

20 Clarkson (1971), 96; Smail (thesis, 1988) 18.

Among the most important upland mineral concentrations were the lead-mining areas of the Pennine chain. The Peak District of Derbyshire, at its southern extremity, was—and is—a bleak, inhospitable landscape, providing grazing for sheep, at most, on the lower slopes, with moors higher up, so that much of the food had to be imported. Though it has, like the Lake District, turned into a favourite tourist and recreation area in the twentieth century, its isolation in earlier ages and Defoe's description of it as a 'waste and houling Wilderness' are not difficult to picture today. Yet, distant from the main centres of population as it was, its populous villages and small townships derived their livelihood, apart from animal husbandry and some limestone quarrying, largely from lead mining and smelting. Celia Fiennes found 'only low dry stone walls round some ground, else its only hills and dales as thick as you can imagine, but tho' the surface looks barren yet those hills are impregnated with rich Marbles Stones Metals Iron and Copper and Coal mines in their bowels'.[21]

Lead mining developed from a long-established traditional base to a peak of activity between the seventeenth and nineteenth centuries. Its expansion and the stream of innovations which began to flow in the seventeenth century were driven by two parallel influences: a rising population and its more varied technical needs increased demand; while technical improvements and an enhanced flow of capital, itself made available by increased national wealth, enabled the local miners to increase their supply. Maximum employment was probably reached in the mid-eighteenth century, when 10,000 miners were said to have been employed[22]—a figure which is almost certainly greatly exaggerated, but represents the conviction that much growth had taken place. Active mining on a considerable scale continued until the end of the nineteenth century.

As miners were forced to go beyond easily accessible veins into ever deeper shafts, the hilly nature of the country allowed much of the necessary drainage to be performed for a time by underground channels, or 'soughs', which conveyed the water to exits on lower-lying ground. The first important such channel, planned by Cornelius Vermuyden for the Dovegang mine, was cut in 1632–51. The Cromford sough was probably started in 1672 and later extended to drain several other mines. By 1706 Ashover had a drainage level of almost one mile in length and other, longer ones were soon to follow. Hannage sough, near Wirksworth, finished in about 1740, had a length of 1¼ miles. One near Youlgrave, known as Hillcar sough, which was started in 1766, was navigable for two out of its ultimately 4½ miles. It took 21 years to build and cost £50,000, yet was still highly profitable. At Speedwell a complete underground canal system was driven in 1774–81. Yatestoop sough in the Winster area, 2¼ miles in length, was started in 1752, cost £30,000, and took 21 years to build; Meerbrook (1½ miles) allegedly cost £45,000 and Stoke (2 miles) some £35,000. Altogether, some 150 soughs, not counting branches, are known to have

[21] Defoe (1927), ii. 583; Fiennes (1988), 104; Thirsk (1961), 73.
[22] Parker and Willies (1979); Willies (1973), 55–6.

been cut in the Derbyshire mining area. These were generally built by separate companies, charging annual fees, calculated as a proportion of the sales or profits to the mines they helped to drain.

Where the ground or the depth of working did not allow this kind of drainage, the alternative was to install mechanical pumps. Much of the revival of drowned mines by this method was the result of the intervention of the highly capitalized London (Quaker) Lead Company, which entered the district in 1720, but there was some local enterprise also. Yatestoop was first in the field, erecting a Newcomen engine in 1715, only three years after its prototype had proved itself; by 1730 there were three more installed in the Winster area. Yatestoop was also the first in 1782 to install a Newcomen engine underground to reduce the weight of the pump rods; an underground waterwheel had been installed at Chapeldale in the 1720s, and another in nearby Crimbo. In 1811 Farey counted five engines at Yatestoop and another six in nearby Winster. The Gregory mine, which took over one of Yatestoop's Newcomen engines in 1768, added a Boulton and Watt engine in 1779. A more unusual water-pressure engine was installed by Richard Trevithick in 1805 at Alport; by 1848 six engines were at work for the Alport Mining Co., but the mine was nevertheless overwhelmed by water and had to close in 1852. Steam-power was also used for winding. The earliest local example was put up by the Gregory mine near Ashover in 1796, and others followed soon after. The deepest local mine shaft, at Eyam Edge mine, where mining began in 1711, reached 1,093 ft. (333 m.). The Ecton copper mine shaft, in the Manifold valley, however, went down even deeper to 1,300 ft. (396 m.).[23]

There were significant technical innovations also in the smelting of the lead ores, replacing the earlier primitive bole fires. The forerunner of the more advanced reverberatory furnace is generally held to have been built at Beauchief, in the Derbyshire foothills on the edge of Sheffield, by William Humphry in 1565, though there was a counter-claim for a similar invention by Burchard Kranich in respect of his furnace at Duffield built in 1552–3. The more advanced reverberatory cupola furnace was first installed in 1735 and spread rapidly thereafter. From the eighteenth century onwards, when smelting with pit coal began, the area was favoured by its nearby coal-mines.[24] It should be added that the Peak District was also not without its domestic textile industry.[25]

In its heyday, the raising of the lead ore turned the villagers of these remote valleys into an industrial and mining population. In the mid-nineteenth century, two-fifths of the active male population in Youlgrave and one-third of that of Bakewell

[23] Raistrick and Jennings (1965), 72, 128, 178, 187, 221; Ford and Rieuwerts (1968); Kirkham (1968), 85, 91; Spence (1992), 167 ff.; Farey (1811–17), i. 328–31; Fisher (1952); Heaney (thesis, 1982), 115, 120, 140–2; Pilkington (1789), 127–8; Hopkinson (thesis, 1958), 169.

[24] Ford and Rieuwerts (1968), 19; Raistrick and Jennings (1965), 78–80, 116; Rees (1968), 493–500; Raistrick (1975), 126 and (1982), 45; Aikin (1795), 81; Heaney (thesis, 1982), 121; Crossley and Kiernan (1992); Hopkinson (thesis, 1958), 152–5; Hall (1978), 77.

[25] Cf. p. 230 below.

were employed in lead mining and related activities. Some of these were immigrants. The decline of mining thereafter then led to a rapid loss of population. Between 1851 and 1881, 19 out of the 24 villages in a radius of 10 miles around Bakewell experienced an actual decline.[26]

Similar developments took place in the northern Pennine lead-mining districts. Here the London (Quaker) Lead Company had its main base, having moved its major investments from Wales to the Alston district, where Nent Head was first leased in 1750. Its Teesdale developments date from 1753, and Stanhope (Weardale) from 1800. Its organization as a joint-stock company employing wage labour, in place of the traditional miner-partnership, reflected the need for much larger capital, and as in Derbyshire, the Company was in the forefront of technical change. It had bought up the earlier patent for smelting lead with pit coal, then improved the reverberatory furnace and smelting by cupellation, erected stamp mills in all its plants by 1738 and a crusher roller in 1804, and was among the first to install Newcomen engines in its mines. Its Nent Force level was 5 miles long: it was started by John Smeaton in 1776 and took fifty years to complete at a cost of £80,000.[27]

Nent Head village, developed from 1753, became the centre of the Company's social activity. Set in rough moorland at a height of 1,460–1,600 ft. (445–488 m.), 'barren and mountainous', where 'the scene on every hand is dark and deplorable', the mines being at 1,500–2, 500 ft. (457–762 m.), its mining community was wholly dependent on the initiative of the Company and its managers. A workers' insurance Benefit Fund dates from 1755. A day school for all the 200 children of the village, well ahead of its time, was built in 1818, and enlarged in 1864. There was a library, a cricket club, medical staff, gardens and allotments, reasonable housing with a water supply from 1850, and baths and washhouses. A school was also built for Middleton in Teesdale, and among other provisions were churches and chapels, roads, and liming and drainage for the ground used for pastures. The Alston area communities alone contained over 1,000 families in 1811; altogether, in 1815–65, the Company employed an average of 850 miners underground.[28]

There was mining and smelting activity also in Swaledale, Arkengarthdale, and Wensleydale in the same period. Two smelting mills dating from the sixteenth century have been found there, and no fewer than 16 that were built in the course of the seventeenth century. The large capitalistic enterprise which became dominant here was the Arkengarthdale and Derwent Mining Co. formed in 1819. In Swaledale there was such a honeycomb of pits dug, that one could enter one mine and emerge 6 miles away without having emerged into the open.[29] In its heyday it attracted large numbers of immigrants, and in the period 1770–1815 the labour force of the area

26 Knowles (thesis, 1990), 16–17, 31–3; Hopkinson (thesis, 1958), 141; Heaney (thesis, 1982), 140, 146; Fuller (1965), 391.

27 Raistrick (1977) and (1975), ii. 40–4; Raistrick and Jennings (1965), 116–19, 193–4.

28 Raistrick (1977), 14–40, 74.

29 Hastings (1981), 26–7; Bogg (1908), 221, 351; Hardy (?1988), 17, 59; Raistrick (1982) and (1975*a*), 13–14.

grew to 2,000 miners. The Parish Register of Arkengarthdale shows a rise of annual baptisms from 25 in 1728–58 and 33 in 1759–83, to 50 in 1801–22 and 63 in 1823–37. The annual excess of baptism over burials, a reflection in part of the large number of young people, rose from 7 to 9, to 18.5, and to 33 for the same periods. By the final years, a large proportion of the grooms were entered in the marriage register as 'miners'.[30]

There were other significant or advanced upland mining and metallurgical works in the northern uplands which deserve at least brief mention. Copper mining in Middleton Tyas flourished in 1730–1880 and was early in the field with a reverberatory furnace, and a Newcomen engine dating from 1753. There were slate quarries in Coverdale and alum works on the North Yorkshire Moors. Furness and the Lake District possessed charcoal iron furnaces and slate quarries. The Wanlockhead lead mines in Scotland were also known for their paternal management in the eight-eenth century.[31]

In its early days as a producer of iron and steel goods, the Sheffield industrial region was also clearly 'marginal in position', situated as it was among bleak moorland hills on the edge of the Peak District, 'partly in Highland and partly in Lowland Britain'. It lay, according to Macaulay, 'on the verge of a wild moorland tract'. Ecclesfield church was even known in 1620 as the 'minster of the moors'. Cobbett, in 1830, noticed 'the ragged hills all round this town . . . bespangled with groups of houses inhabited by the working cutlers'. 'Sheffield', according to Mayhew in mid-century, 'stands about the point where the wild hill country—in part wooded, in part moorland—begins to fine away into the smooth expanse of the south-easterly plains of Yorkshire.' 'There is scarcely a street', according to the local directory of 1858, 'from which you cannot see the hills crowned by woods which environ the town.'

'In the Middle Ages the Sheffield Region was something of a backwater . . . it was comparatively barren, sparsely populated, and inaccessible except for the eastern parts which were within easy reach of the main route of north and south communication.' Right up until the railway age, 'Sheffield was among the most land-locked towns in the country and one of the most difficult to reach along the national highways . . . Sixty miles from the coast and twenty miles from a navigable river, surrounded by steep hills and deep valleys and approached from the west across formidable moors.' It was 'a small and remote town to which, astonishingly, fine ores from Sweden were imported through Hull, shipped up the Trent and its tributary to Bawtry, and then carried overland'. It had no borough government, no Member of Parliament, no resident magistrate until the end of the eighteenth century and, situated in a distant corner of the county, it was largely ignored also by the judicial system: it did not even host a meeting of the West Riding Quarter Session

30 Arkengarthdale Parish Register.

31 Marshall (1989), 142 and (1958), 17 ff., 110; Marshall and Davies-Shiel (1969), 29 ff., 154 ff.; Hornshaw (1975); Ord (1972), 326; Tuke (1800), 17–20; Smout (1962), 149–50; Chapman and Knoop (1908), 363.

until 1699. Even by the mid-eighteenth century, an annual income of £100 was considered handsome in Sheffield, and one of £500 'a fortune that required retiring from business'.[32]

Yet, on the basis of local iron ore (replaced later by imports from Sweden and elsewhere), water-power, wood fuel, coal, ganister for furnace lining, and stone suitable for grindstones, there were by 1679, alongside traditional crafts, 1,562 knifesmiths' (cutlers') marks awarded to independent suppliers by the local guild, together with 136 shearsmiths' and 284 scissorsmiths' marks. In addition to these, filesmiths, scythesmiths, nailers, and others were also active in the region. Of grooms recorded in marriages in 1653–60, two-thirds were in the cutlery and allied trades; in 1698–1703, it was one-half, as also in the baptisms and burials in 1728–33. The Hallamshire economy at the time was 'one of the most specialised in the land'.[33]

By the mid-eighteenth century, the region was in the forefront of fashionable design for tableware, silver and silver-plated goods, as well as leading in technical advance. Among its most significant innovations were Thomas Boulsover's invention of silver plating known as 'Old Sheffield Plate' (1742) and Benjamin Huntsman's crucible method of making cast steel, developed about the same time, which was destined to hold the field for over a century. By the 1840s, Sheffield made about one-half of the world's steel. Later local innovations included Robert Hadfield's development of steel alloys, the electric furnace (1910), and stainless steel (1912).[34] It was only the city's own development into a major conurbation in the last century and a half, based largely on mass-produced steel and the possibilities opened up by modern means of transport, which removed it, at least partially, from the geographical margin.

Lake District water-power drove numerous mills. Some turned to cotton spinning in the early days of the Industrial Revolution, but what emerged ultimately was the manufacture of bobbins for the mills and other wooden articles.[35] The region around Kendal was famous for its coarse woollen cloth—a product which survived into the nineteenth century. The upland cloths, woven from the coarse wool of mountain sheep by 'part-time farmers and other relatively unskilled operatives . . . of little financial or technical ability', were generally reckoned to be of poor quality. When new products came in, according to Kerridge,

> old products (and some of their producers) took refuge in remote parts, where no innovation was afoot, and costs were lower: the centrifugal diffusion of cast-off technology had commenced. The old coloured cloth industries of the woodland [sc. Essex and Suffolk], the Wealden Vales and the Chalk Country [sc. Wiltshire] took flight to backward countries, to central and eastern Europe and the Peak-Forest Country [sc. the Pennines].[36]

[32] Maxwell (1956), 121; Lewis (1956), 138; Macaulay (1913), 330; Hey (1979), 28 and (1991), 9, 145, 211; Lloyd (1992), 112; quotations from Cobbett, Mayhew, and White in Pybus (1994), 91, 119, 133; Leader (1905), 6.

[33] Walton (1952), 95; Jones (1956); Hey (1991), 94–101, 143; Hopkinson (thesis, 1958), 225–6.

[34] Tweedale (1993).

[35] Marshall and Davies-Shiel (1969), 20, 60–2; Marshall and Walton (1981), 27.

[36] Kerridge (1985), 8, 176, 177, 239; also Young (1770), iii. 172; Hughes (1965), 355.

This typical deprecation of upland production has not, however, been shared by everyone. The part-time farmers of the Halifax region, remote though it was, yet, according to at least one observer of 1588, 'excel the rest in policy and industrie for the use of their trade and groundes . . . [there is] begoon and mayntayned among the people a natural ardency of newe inventions annexid to an unyealdinge industry'.[37] This would offer one explanation why the region later became one of the world's leading textile areas. There was some linen made in northern Pennine areas, while in the eighteenth century, the Macclesfield silk trade, producing a fabric to cover buttons also led to its own form of upland enterprise in the 1790s: 'In the wild country between Buxton, Leek and Macclesfield called the Flash lived a set of pedestrian chapmen who hawked their buttons and other smallware' who had a bad reputation for dishonesty ('flash-men').[38]

Possibly most interesting in this context was the stocking knitting industry centred on Kendal. There was hand knitting also in East Anglia, in Dorset, in the East Midland forests, in Scotland and the Scottish Isles, among other areas, but pride of place must go to the area between Richmond and Kendal east to west, and between Kirkby Stephen and Dentdale north to south, including Swaledale and Wensleydale. In 1595 there were said to be 1,000 knitters within a radius of 20 miles around Kendal; by 1770 Arthur Young estimated their number at about 3,000, including 120 wool combers who each provided work for 5 spinners each of whom supplied 4–5 knitters, making 550 dozen per week. In 1801 Ravenstonedale, with a population of 1,138, made 1,000 pairs of stockings per week, or practically one pair per head. During the Seven Years War (1756–63), government agents came to Kirkby Lonsdale, Kirkby Stephen, and Kendal, to buy up for the army all that was made there.[39] Yet knitting never became a full-time concentrated industry, but remained an additional activity that people engaged in during slack seasons, in the evenings, while socializing in 'spinning galleries' and, according to some observers, even as they walked to market. It was never in the van of progress, and in fact finally succumbed to machine knitting; yet it bore witness to the skill and industriousness of large numbers of upland folk.

Altogether, across the country, there was scarcely a mountain or fen area without mining or industrial employment, engaged in supplying distant markets. The Weald, it is true, once the leading iron making and working region, was in decline: from 52 furnaces and 58 forges in 1574 it had shrunk to 3 furnaces in 1787.[40] But the Wiltshire and Cotswolds woollen industry was still flourishing; and one of the greatest industrial concentrations of the age was beginning to grow in the barren heathland of the Midlands around Birmingham, which was as late as 'the seventeenth

[37] Quoted in Heaton (1965), 77; also François (1966), 260; Holroyde (1988), 20–1; Jennings (1992) 45–7 and p. 90 above.

[38] Aikin (1795), 437.

[39] Hartley and Ingilby (1988); Thirsk (1984*a*), 244–5 and (1967), 96; Young (1770), iii. 170; Sellers (1912), 413; Searle (thesis, 1983), 252; Defoe (1927), ii. 629–30; Hallas (1990), 205.

[40] Cleere and Crossley (1985); Short (1989).

century . . . not easily accessible by any of the existing means of communication'. Much of its main raw material—pig and forge iron—came, in the years of expansion which followed, from the marginal regions of Shropshire. Even Coalbrookdale, the site of one of the most significant innovations that ushered in the Industrial Revolution, namely the coke-smelting process for iron, was situated in a gorge difficult of access except by the Severn itself. Arthur Young described it in 1785 as 'a romantic spot, in a winding glen set between two immense hills'.[41] Nor did industrial advance halt at the Scottish Highlands: next to the traditional whisky stills and the temporary boom of the kelp industry, domestic spinning was taking root.[42] Among many other examples, two areas deserve special mention: Cornwall and the Welsh mountains.

In the Middle Ages, the Cornish tin mines, which were mostly to be found on upland locations, formed one of Europe's major concentrations of mining activity. The miners provided much of the wealth of the region, and were suitably rewarded with legal rights and privileges. As everywhere else, problems arose when first the alluvial deposits, and then the easiest underground veins began to be worked out and miners had to dig deeper for the ore. By the end of the sixteenth century, some mines had reached a depth of 50 fathoms; soon after, the raising of water by pumps driven by water-power commenced and, as an alternative, the 'great county adit' began to be dug in 1748 which, after 50 years, reached a total length of 30 miles and drained 46 mines. Nevertheless, by the 1770s, large waterwheels had to be installed to move the necessary pumps, while elsewhere, in one extreme case, rag and chain pumps, moved by human muscle, required 60–80 men to clear the workings for 10–12 miners. Meanwhile, reverberatory furnaces had been developed from the early eighteenth century, permitting the use of coal in smelting, and there were innovations also in stamping and other processes.[43]

However, by the later eighteenth century, by which time copper mining was temporarily overtaking tin mining in importance (both had huge capital sums invested), the drainage problem was threatening the survival of Cornish mining altogether. At that point a new technology came to the rescue which was destined to move the region from marginal importance right into the centre of the Industrial Revolution: that was the steam engine. The earliest 'steam' pump had been designed by Thomas Savery, a Cornishman, in 1698. A much more effective type, that of Thomas Newcomen, a Devonian, was developed some ten years later, and between 1745 and 1775 over 40 Newcomen engines had been erected in Cornwall to help drain the mines. However, the Newcomen engine was greedy of coal and coal was expensive in Cornwall. Consequently, James Watt's steam engine, one of whose main advantages was the saving of fuel, found there one of its earliest customers. The first Watt engine was put up in Cornwall in 1777–8, and by the end of 1778 there

41 Arthur Young in *Annals of Agriculture*, iv (1785), 165; Court (1953), 3–4; Ponting (1971); Wanklyn (1982); Goodman (thesis, 1978); Johnson (1952); Trinder (1973), 9; Davies (1939–40), 31–2.

42 Ramsay (1965); Thirsk (1961), 74–5; Rowlands (1989); Collins (1978), 20, 24; Durie (1979), 88–91.

43 Jenkin (1972), 85–98; Barton (1967); Lewis (1907); Hatcher (1973), 46–50; Rowe (1953), 5–6.

were five; the welcome Cornish orders may well have tided the Boulton & Watt steam-engine partnership over its most critical early period. By 1800, a total of 173 steam engines are known to have been erected in the county, a figure exceeded only by Lancashire and the West Riding. A race of brilliant engineers, among them Richard Trevithick, the Hornblower brothers, John Nancarrow, Samuel Grose, and Arthur Woolf, made numerous improvements, including the pioneering of high-pressure steam and of the compound engine, which led to the development of the 'Cornish' pumping engine, together with early steam locomotive experiments. 'By 1840 Cornish engines and Cornish engineers had attained a pre-eminent position', it has been said truthfully. In 1838 there were over 200 mines at work in Cornwall, using 170 steam-pumping engines, 120 steam stamps and winding engines, and employing some 30,000 people. Hayle Foundry was one of the largest engine works in the kingdom, and there were several others. However, as the metal became more difficult to mine, and cheap supplies became available from overseas, Cornish mining declined precipitately in the second half of the century, forcing a large proportion of the skilled labour force to emigrate.[44]

In the Welsh hills, mining and manufacture were more widely dispersed before the Industrial Revolution than they were to become later. A woollen (flannel) industry flourished in Montgomeryshire, Merioneth, Anglesey, Denbigh, and Caernarfon, much of it carried on by domestic work in upland farmsteads, for sale in Welshpool, Oswestry, and Shrewsbury. Its decline in the late nineteenth century is thought to have been caused by the delay in introducing mechanization. There was scattered lead and silver, iron and coal mining, and iron working in such forges as Dolobran and Mathraval. The beginnings of the concentration of coal and iron in south Wales may be dated from 1686, when Sir Humphrey Mackworth occupied his works at Neath, but its development into one of Britain's leading industrial and mining regions had to wait another hundred years.[45]

North Wales reached its peak earlier. It was an area of progressive agriculture with marshes being drained in the eighteenth and nineteenth centuries and cultivation creeping further up the mountainsides when it was encouraged by high wartime prices. At the same time, it was also the location of some of the key developments of the early stages of the British Industrial Revolution. There was John Wilkinson's pioneer ironworks at Bersham and Brymbo; coal was mined at Wrexham and Holywell; the Anglesey copper mines dominated British markets for a time from the 1790s; there were slate quarries; and, in addition to the traditional woollens, transferred to factories in 1797–1837, some of the earliest British cotton mills were erected in north Wales, drawing their power from local streams.[46] Here

[44] Quotation from Rowe (1953), 127, also *passim*; Kanefsky and Robey (1994), 182; Jenkin (1972), 171–6; Lemon (1969); Carne (1969); Barton (1967), 84–6, 279; von Tunzelmann (1978), ch. 9 and (1970).

[45] Rees (1968), i. 212–17, 281 ff., ii. 71 ff.; John (1950), 6–8; Kerridge (1985), 177; Collins (1978), 24; Rowley (1986), 180; Powell (1967–8*b*), 117–23; Lewis (1963–4): Evans (1951–2), 22; Pearson (1913–15); Lloyd (1967–8), 104–5.

[46] Dodd (1951); Morris (1959–60).

was yet another marginal region which had a pioneer role in the Industrial Revolution, though in this case, the lead did not last long: most of the region's mining and manufacturing activities had ceased by the 1840s.

It is probably unnecessary to describe other countries in the same detail: similar developments occurred in all parts of Europe. In France, for example, there was weaving, lace making, and metalwork in the Massif Central, silk throwing, spinning and weaving in Ardèche, rural metallugy in the Pyrenees, glove making above Grenoble, textiles in the more remote regions of Languedoc and textiles, woodwork, and metal work in Dauphiné, the Vosges, and even in the Pyrenees. The interesting suggestion has also been made that in view of the slow population increase under the Third Republic, industry settled along the French border regions in order to attract surplus labour from abroad.[47] There was industrial activity, including some advanced work, in the Carpathians and mining in the Ural mountains and in areas farther east. Even in the Balkan mountains, charcoal and lime burning, and some proto-industry could be found in this period.[48]

A major point of attraction of upland sites, as appears from the literature again and again, was their wealth of timber resources. However, not all forests were located on mountains, and there were industrial concentrations also in many woodlands of the plains at a time when wood and charcoal were the main fuels for domestic as well as industrial use. Moreover, some forests of the plains also contained the kind of mineral resources which could become the basis of advanced industry.

Typical of these was the Forest of Dean. Its iron had been worked by the Romans and there are records of its renewed working in the Middle Ages. At least three of the new type of blast furnace were erected there in the sixteenth century, one in 1575, and two in the 1590s. In 1634, there were 11 furnaces and 11 forges in the Forest; there were also glass-works, and the fear was expressed that the timber resources were being used up at an alarming rate. The region was preserved as an industrial centre into the modern age by the development of the reverberatory furnace and the coke smelting of iron, both of which enabled the region to bring its rich coal resources into play.[49]

Elsewhere, possibly the most widespread forest industry of this period was glassmaking. The existence of medieval glass-works in the forests has been noted above; they were to be found in similar locations into the modern era wherever there were no cheap coal supplies available. This applied particularly to France, to Germany, and to other parts of central Europe.[50]

[47] Hanagan (1989), 79; Ogden (1989), 124–7; Lequin (1977), i. 73; Derruau-Boniol and Fel (1970), 71; Poitrineau (1986), 111; Le Bras (1986), 143; for the Catalonian side of the Pyrenees, see Thomson (1992), 46, 61; Weber (1976), 212–13.

[48] Podraza (1986), 286–8; Teich (1973); Blanchard (1989); Curtis (1956), 723; Palairet (1983), 180.

[49] Hart (1971), esp. 8, 10, 107–8.

[50] e.g. Henning (1983), 71; Slawinger (1966), 227–8; Piuz (1967), 72–3; Pischel (1928); Gleitsmann (1981), 54; Kellenbenz (1965), 391, 404 and (1963), 860; Discherl (1938); Schremmer (1970), 99; Deffontaines (1933), 87 ff.; Kuhn (1955), 229–38; Kreiner (1919), 118–19; Müller (1938), 12–15; Rose-Villequey (1971); Grossmann (1967), 159 ff.

Given the technical difficulties and the skill required, the wide dispersal of the industry among a large number of units may be surprising, but is largely explained by the fact that the other ingredients and materials needed, such as quartz or clay, were available almost everywhere, while the real bottleneck was caused by the vast quantities of timber which were required not merely to generate heat, but even more for the production of potash before other sources for it were developed in the nineteenth century. It was in search of trees that the glass-workers ventured ever deeper into the forests.[51] Their voracity for timber, together with the relatively limited fixed capital involved, also serves to explain the nomadic nature of many glass-works which had to move to new sites whenever they had used up all the local forest reserves.[52] Some forest glass-works were quite extensive: a typical eighteenth-century firm might employ over 60 people directly, with additional large numbers in the forests cutting wood, making barrels, carting, etc.[53] Next to glass-making, it was ironworks which were held responsible for the destruction of the forests. However, together with other potash users, such as soap works and gunpowder makers, they tended to be found outside marginal areas.[54]

The timber crisis was ultimately solved by the use of coal fuel. Here Britain was far in advance of the Continent. For glass-making, a coal-fired reverberatory furnace was developed in the early years of the seventeenth century; iron was first successfully smelted in a coke furnace in 1709 in Coalbrookdale, but the method was not adopted on any scale before the 1760s; the puddling process for making bar or forge iron was perfected in 1783–4. At the same time, coal or coke fuel began to be used in a wide range of other industries in Britain,[55] the rest of Europe following some fifty years or more behind.

An alternative to the replacement of wood fuel by coal was to import timber from the vast and under-used forests of northern and eastern Europe, thus using the still undeveloped riches of the European margin.[56] In the areas of intensive iron working in Russia and Sweden, local timber resources might themselves be endangered, but considerable export surpluses could be made available from the rest of these countries, as well as from Norway and Finland. By the second half of the nineteenth century, the steam sawmills introduced into the forests to prepare the timber for export became important centres of industrial activity in their own right, the forests thus seeing the first germs of the successful industrialization of parts of Scandinavia.[57]

51 Schwarz (1959), 223 and pp. 119–20 above.

52 e.g. Stromer (1986), 99; Rubner (1975), 99 ff.; Nef (1941*a*), 189 and (1936–7), 181–2; Scoville (1968), 164; Rose-Villequey (1971), 134; Deffontaines (1933), 89. On the problem of the denudation of forests, see p. 14 above.

53 Gothein (1970), 815; Wohlauf (1981), 270; Pischel (1928), 37.

54 Cleere and Crossley (1985), 168; Skipp (1978), 56–7, 93–7; Terrett (1962*b*), 362–4; Knoppers and Nicholls (1981), 67–8; Musson (1978), 41.

55 Musson (1978), 33–43; Kenyon (1967), 49; Godfrey (1975), 38; Pischel (1928), 45; Wrigley (1988).

56 Jones (1981), 4; Clow (1956), 87.

57 Lindqvist (1983); Åttman (1981); Haraldsson (1989), 193–5; Wohlert (1988), 17; Söderberg (1982), 393; Åström (1975), (1978), (1981), (1983); Hoffman (1982), 37–40; Hovland *et al.* (1982), 46–8.

As for the marshes and fens in this period, they did contain some domestic textile work and other small-scale businesses,[58] but more important than these for the future were the immense sums sunk in drainage schemes. Those that cleared the area around the English Wash from the seventeenth century onwards, for example, ultimately drained 307,000 acres. There were great works also undertaken, many of them by Dutch experts, in other parts of Britain, in Germany, and in France, among other areas.[59] All of these, together with their complex embankment and sluice constructions, represented a substantial infrastructural investment.

However, the changes wrought in these areas of Europe pale into insignificance when measured against the transformation of the waterlogged coastal plains of the northern Netherlands. Flanders and Brabant in the southern Netherlands, it has been noted above, managed to raise themselves to leading economic regions in Europe in the eleventh–fourteenth centuries in spite of their locational disadvantages. Much poldering and dyking had taken place also in the northern provinces to conquer 'a wilderness terrain either empty or given to livestock breeding'; yet the area was still left, by the end of the Middle Ages, 'remote and ill-drained, as uninhabitable and unfertilized lowlands, [where] inundation was in many ways a more immediate threat than ever before'.[60] Flooding disasters continued to punctuate the history of these districts at frequent intervals, causing immense destruction and loss of life well into the early modern period.

Even in the seventeenth century, the 'Golden Age', it could be said that 'geography . . . had isolated the Netherlands from the rest of Europe. On one side was the sea, on the other sandy moors and marshland; the country seemed to be surrounded by "deserts".' The Groningen peat mosses were still uninhabited, Gelderland had 'heaths and vast forests', and Drenthe had 'desert-like . . . infertile lands'.[61] But clearly the most difficult area, and most subject to the mockery of the country's enemies, was still the marshy landscape of the Holland and Zealand coastal strip, the heartland of the United Provinces. 'Holland, at the creation of the world, was no dwelling place for men', it was said as early as 1622; but it was above all at the time of the first and second Anglo-Dutch wars that English commentators were moved to express their contempt for the boggy enemy country. The Dutch Deputies, it was said, 'sprung out of mire and slime, and like a mushroom ripen'd in small time'. The Republic was 'a Canaan, but seated in a Bog and overflowing with milk and water instead of honey'; it was 'the buttock of the world, full of veins and blood but no bones in it'; 'the meanness of nature and calling [i.e. the merchants' trade] was said to incapacitate them (contrary to a great deal of historical evidence) to the honourable arts of war'; and, not least, 'insomuch that by drawing their

58 Thirsk (1987), 54; de Vries (1983), 167; Neeson (1993), 4–5.

59 Smith (1978), 506 ff., 518–19; Harris (1957), 303–12, 317; Abel (1966), 191–2; Slicher van Bath (1963), 200; Clay (1984), 111; Darby (1968), 29 ff. and (1973*c*), 333 ff.; Lindley (1982); Lucassen (1987), 139, 295; Marshall (1958), 64; Williams (1970), 55–67; Baines and Fairbairn (1869), i. 38–9, 46. Also see pp. 30, 34, 100, 132, and 157 above.

60 De Vries (1974), 25, 32.

61 De Vries (1974), 106; Zumthor (1994), 24, 25.

breath they must of necessity suck in the water which with long continuance forced all their inward parts coming out at the nose, ears and eyes, so stifling and choking them that it took away their breath'.[62]

No doubt all mendacious propaganda is fair in war, yet there is ample evidence that Dutch cities, surrounded as they were by much stagnant water, were extremely unhealthy: 'Dutch cities were, here as elsewhere, killers' and their extraordinarily fast growth in the sixteenth and seventeenth centuries was maintained only by immigration. There was some immigration from abroad, particularly of people persecuted because of their religion, but the doubling of the population of the whole country in the course of the sixteenth century, and the continuing growth rate that was faster than that of its neighbours in the seventeenth, were the result largely of natural increase.[63]

This population growth reflected the immense economic progress of the country. 'The Low Countries', it has not unreasonably been said, 'presented the greatest contrast between limited natural resources and abundant entrepreneurial achievement.' Their success puzzled many observers. 'How could a peripheral, swampy delta area—where nothing would grow—develop into the dynamic centre of the world economy in the seventeenth century?' How could Holland have 'developed from a peripheral and dominantly agricultural region to a very diversified and urbanised economy'? How was it that the area 'came to the fore', that 'it was in the northern Netherlands provinces, formerly poor relations of their more affluent southern neighbours, that a new and genuine form of growth was to be found in the . . . century [after 1590]'? After all, as an English commission reported in 1622, the Dutch were merely 'occupying a small country with no natural resources, not fully so big as two of our best shires'.[64] How was it done? It is a question repeatedly asked and answered in different ways by Dutch historiography. The arguments presented in this volume allow us to express the view that the achievements of the Dutch in the golden age, great though they were, were less miraculous than is often assumed.

It has to be noted, to begin with, that as a marginal marshland, the country that was to become the United Provinces enjoyed some natural, as well as social and historical advantages. Though it lacked adequate timber resources—or rather, the rapidly expanding demand outran the local supply—the country had extensive peat deposits, at the time when the potentialities of coal were by no means clear. Moreover, the flat, open landscape was ideal for using the energy of the wind in windmills. The soil, once it was drained, carried rich grass for the rearing of cattle, and there were fish and fowl. The waterways provided the possibility of cheap inland transport.

Of greater importance, as it turned out, was the long coastline to encourage shipping, and the accessibility of fishing grounds on the high seas. The Dutch were fortunate in the movement of the herring shoals, and the herring is widely believed to

[62] Quotation in Schama (1988), 262, 263, 265, 266.

[63] Wilson (1977), 23; Helleiner (1967), 37–8, 46–7.

[64] Supple (1977), 452; Zumthor (1994), 19, 30; Wolf (1990), 115; Wilson (1977), 22 and (1967), 518.

have been one of the bases of Dutch prosperity. Other main varieties of fish caught included Dogger Bank cod and Spitzbergen whales.[65] The expanses of water around and inside the Netherlands also did excellent duty for defensive purposes: at no time was this shown to greater effect than in the struggle for independence against the Spaniards. To use the dykes and the fleet against an enemy did, however, require more than the bounties of nature: it also required the skill and ingenuity of the population. We turn here to the field of social-historical, rather than purely natural resource explanations.

As noted above,[66] it was the co-operative skill required in winning land from the marshes, as well as the defensive possibilities of the terrain, which gave the Dutch the power to achieve their early freedom from feudal governance and exploitation. With that freedom they could develop their own form of self-rule, as well as their famous independent, enterprising spirit. At the same time, the unsuitableness of their soil for grain production forced them to import grain to feed their rising numbers. Thus it has been held that 'to bring in the enormous quantities of grain needed', enough to feed over half a million people in Holland, Utrecht, Friesland, and Groningen,[67] the Dutch had to build and manage shipping to the Baltic, which also carried cargoes of timber and naval stores, as well as to find export commodities to pay for them. In this way, the poverty of their own agrarian resources became a major cause of the rise of their shipping fleet, their search for colonial goods, and their industrial prowess.

There is a broad consensus that it is in the excellence of their shipping that a large part of the explanation of Dutch dominance over the European economy in their golden years between *c.*1590 and 1670 is to be sought. Their ships, above all the fishing *bus*, which allowed catches to be cleaned and salted at sea while still fresh, and the *fluyt*, were better designed and fitted their purpose better than other European long-distance vessels; they were more cheaply produced by an early form of mass production, and they were manned by sailors showing superb seamanship. As a result, 'in 1670 the volume of Dutch-owned shipping—some 568,000 tons—considerably exceeded that of Spanish, Portuguese, French, English, Scottish and German combined'.[68]

On the basis of that shipping, the Dutch acquired colonies and trading posts in many parts of the world—driving the Portuguese out of some of them in doing so—thus laying the foundation not merely of a lucrative entrepôt trade, but also of processing industries, such as sugar boiling, in the homeland. Other highly successful and competitive industries, beside the shipbuilding already noted, were those of book printing and map making, pottery and tiles, brewing, metal goods, precision instruments and diamond cutting. Despite their high labour costs, the Dutch also maintained a flourishing textile industry: Leiden was widely believed to have been

[65] De Vries (1974), 68; Michell (1977), 148–53; Parry (1967), 171–2; Wilson (1967), 520.

[66] See p. 100 above.

[67] Morineau (1978), 144; de Vries (1974), 170–2; van Houtte (1977), 191–2.

[68] Parry (1967), 210; Wilson (1977), 24; Sella (1974), 414; Tracy (1990), 12, 90, 95.

the largest single centre of the woollen industry in Europe, and Haarlem was supreme in linen.[69] According to a more recent view, it was the advances and innovations in agriculture which were the main base of Dutch economic success: by specialization, by innovative technology and much capital investment, and on the basis of the freedom over their methods and rotation systems, Dutch farmers made it possible for cities and industries to grow and enrich themselves without provoking a Malthusian crisis.[70] In the England of the 'agricultural revolution', it was the Netherlands which were looked upon as the main source of agrarian innovation.

All these were astonishing achievements for a nation of barely one and a half million people. Their enterprise in economic matters was impressive enough: it extended to banking and finance; to making Amsterdam the main grain storehouse, as well as stock exchange of Europe; to establishing trading posts and industries in Scandinavia, Germany, and elsewhere and, by the eighteenth century, financing much of the deficit of European rulers. They were no doubt helped by the fact that taxes, though high overall, lay lightly on merchants, and merchants enjoyed not only high status, but also much of the control over political decisions, including the relative free-trade policies of the United Provinces. It was a commonplace among British observers from Gregory King to Adam Smith that the Netherlands was the richest country in Europe.[71] Their cultural achievements in literature, science, and the arts—above all, their painting, religion, and philosophy—among other fields were surely as great as their success in the economic sphere.

It is not possible to do full justice in a few pages to the Dutch rise to dominance in the European economy in the later sixteenth century. Yet enough has been said to make clear how much that success owed to the marginal position and conditions in the country. The peripheral location, the difficulty of colonization and of making the land habitable, which led to freedom from feudalism—providing the opportunity for an early capitalistically inclined peasantry and a free land and labour market—have meant, in one view, that 'Holland's earlier backwardness would almost of its own be transferred into an advantage'.[72] Freedom of trading and fishing, a marginal location making conquest by outsiders difficult, a tough environment calling for initiative and ingenuity, poor agrarian endowment requiring grain and timber imports and consequently exportable goods in return, and the hidden merits of a marshland, including internal transport, were among other advantages. All these combined to allow the barren marshy lowlands of the Dutch coast to play, in their time, a more prominent part in the progress of the European economy than any other marginal region, until the time when a number of marginal uplands of Britain became the location of the key stages in the Industrial Revolution. At the height of their glory, of course, the Netherlands had ceased to be marginal, and had become the very heart of the European economy.

69 Sella (1974), 415; de Vries (1974), 119–20; Tracy (1990), 21.
70 It is the argument of de Vries as well as van Zanden; also Maddalena (1974), 316.
71 Wilson (1967), 518, 533; de Vries (1974), 234, 242–3; Glamann (1977), 287; Morris (1995), 216.
72 Van Zanden (1993), 19.

But, as elsewhere and at other times, marginal regions tend not to keep their leading position for long. The Dutch Republic lost out politically because it was small in relation to its rivals, necessitating a high level of taxation to maintain its defence, yet still left vulnerable; it lacked natural resources required in the next stage of development, especially coal and iron; initiative remained concentrated on commerce in a period when industry offered greater opportunities for profitable innovation; wages and social costs were kept above the level of those of neighbouring countries, although industrial efficiency was no longer superior; too much capital was lent abroad instead of being invested in home production; and there was a high cost involved in keeping drainage and dykes in repair.[73]

We are now in a position to draw some conclusions. The picture which has emerged from the cursory survey of this chapter differs in important detail from the conventional view of Europe's economic progress in the seventeenth–nineteenth centuries. That view recognizes, for the western half of the Continent at least, an undoubted sense of lively agricultural, commercial, and industrial growth, technical innovation and more sophisticated organization. Practical tinkerers come up with solutions to age-old problems; large joint-stock companies are formed, capable of providing the capital which many of the new industrial and commercial enterprises now demand; scientists of the leisured and professional classes take an active interest in this kind of progress and in turn help it along by new scientific insights.

Possibly nowhere is this trend better illustrated than in the publication of Diderot's *Encyclopédie* in ultimately 35 volumes between 1751 and 1780—itself inspired by a French translation of Ephraim Chambers's *Universal Dictionary* of 1728. Written mainly by bourgeois and other professionals, and intended for a similar readership, it attracted no fewer than 4,000 subscriptions. It was meant not only to register progress to date, but to inspire hope in further advance and indicate the direction which it might take. There is little doubt as to what was in the minds of the leading spirits in that respect. Apart from agriculture, which forms, in line with Physiocratic doctrine, the major thrust of the economic articles in the *Encyclopédie*, the interest is focused on urban workshops, on grand luxurious manufactories, on foundries and forges comfortably situated along well-banked streams, possibly surrounded by workers' settlements. The commerce which sustains this expansion and advance is the overseas trade conducted by ships from the major ports. The existence of mountains is scarcely acknowledged outside the fields of fauna, flora, and geology, and internal trade with marginal areas rates hardly a mention.

This was, no doubt, a reasonable representation of the most advanced contemporary thought generated in the cities and the country estates of the leaders of the French Enlightenment. They formed the 'polite' society which had emerged out of an earlier barbarism, an example and inspiration to all at home and abroad. Yet their treatment missed out one of the most significant aspects of

[73] Wilson (1977), 25–8; Mokyr (1976); de Vries (1974), 114.

the European economy at the time, for it missed out much of the work of the men living on the margin.

There, on mountains, in forests, in border regions, on marshlands, life was stirring in ways of its own. The people of the margins, unhampered as they were by restrictive regulations or strict traditions, were pioneering new methods, capturing markets, learning new skills, delving deeper into the bowels of the earth. Here much of the new engineering of pumping and haulage machinery was to be found; furnaces and stamping machines were experimented with and improved; new textiles were designed, or traditional ones made more cheaply and marketed in new ways; watches, musical instruments, and metal goods were produced more efficiently so that they could be afforded by larger numbers of consumers. It is also where specialization provided growing markets for the foodstuffs produced by plains people which encouraged them to find methods to increase yields and improve quality.

Much of this, we know, took place in areas largely unobserved from the favoured centres, often treated with contempt, viewed as romantic playthings or ignored altogether. Yet those marginal regions were contributing much of the growing stream of goods and flow of new ideas that marked the stirrings of the age. Marginal in geographical location, they were by no means marginal in history. To neglect them is to neglect one of the mainsprings of European progress.

To be sure, these were not the only regions from which initiatives sprung; many cities and plains were also among the pioneers, and they have been celebrated often enough in the literature. Innovations occurring in the margins have indeed been noted in their time also, but without the necessary observation that here was a distinct source, possessing its own social structure and economic logic, and that it was precisely these properties which were responsible for originating a considerable number of the key innovations which were to change the face of Europe. Among them were some of the earliest steps in what came to be known as the Industrial Revolution, as well as some of the most impressive examples of the 'proto-industrial' system. To these we turn in the following chapter.

10

The Industrial Revolution and the Location of Proto-Industry

The well-known term, the Industrial Revolution, is traditionally applied to the transformation of the British economy between *c.*1760 and 1850. There is some debate as to whether equivalent changes which followed in other countries should be described by the same term, or whether their experience was sufficiently different to merit a different appellation. As far as Britain is concerned, however, despite some recent criticism, an immense and still growing literature bears witness to its continuing usefulness.[1] Behind its popularity lies the need not only to find an apt expression for the economic upheavals which occurred in Britain in those years, but also to indicate that it was an indigenous growth without much help from the rest of Europe, but which yet heralded a new era not merely for one country, but for the whole world. An expanding and seemingly irreversible process, covering one country after another, was set in train by it. It is not unreasonable to hold that the Industrial Revolution was 'by any reckoning . . . probably the most important event in world history, at any rate since the invention of agriculture and cities. And it was initiated by Britain.'[2]

There is now a wide consensus that, in spite of its world-shaking significance, the Industrial Revolution did not in its earlier phases cover the whole country but, on the contrary, was an intensely regional phenomenon. [3] Among the most important regions which carried and were transformed by it were Lancashire, the West Riding of Yorkshire, Birmingham and the West Midlands, Clydeside, north-east England, and south Wales, with lesser concentrations in south Yorkshire, the East Midlands, Cornwall, and north Wales. By contrast, as has often been noted, the major long-established cities stood aloof: 'A surprising fact', according to Paul Bairoch, 'in that early phase of the Industrial Revolution was that there were no traditional cities, especially large traditional cities, among those in which the [Industrial] Revolution developed'. 'As is well known', confirmed de Vries, 'the early stages of the Industrial Revolution tended to be played out in relatively small cities and in rural locations.'[4]

In England, three regions among those listed stand out in terms of the technical and organizational innovations introduced, and the exceptional rate of growth of the leading local industries: Birmingham and its hinterland together with Shropshire;

[1] Pollard (1992*a*). [2] Hobsbawm (1962), 29. [3] Hudson (1989*b*); Pollard (1992*b*).
[4] Bairoch (1988), 503; de Vries (1981), 103; Hohenberg and Lees (1985), 241.

Lancashire; and the West Riding of Yorkshire. As noted in Chapter 9 above, the West Midlands was an area which was somewhat isolated before the mid-eighteenth century, a region containing several forests and relatively little fertile agricultural land; nevertheless, it is doubtful if it should be termed marginal in our sense. The position regarding the other two named regions, lying on the western and eastern slopes of the Pennine chain respectively, is quite different. Before the transformations brought about by the Industrial Revolution, these were classical marginal regions in the British economy.

To Lancashire, the future centre of the world's cotton industry, belongs pride of place for, as has often been repeated, 'whoever says Industrial Revolution says cotton'.[5] Yet there was little in the preceding history to lead one to expect the prominence which that county was to achieve. Until the sixteenth century, Lancashire was one of the poorest and most backward shires of England. At the time of Domesday it was hardly yet within the orbit of English civilization, and was not even credited with a name or existence of its own, but appeared partly as an appendage to Cheshire, and partly within the accounts for Yorkshire.[6] Nor did its relative position change much in the following five centuries, at least as far as taxation and assessments for royal contributions are concerned. Thus, in terms of tax assessments per acre, Lancashire was 34th out of 34 counties in 1275, and came bottom also in 1296, 1306, and 1332, when it was still 37th out of 37. Only thereafter did it register a very slight improvement: in 1503 it ranked 35th out of 37, and by 1693 it had advanced to 35th out of 39 counties.[7]

Apart from that last seventeenth century date, this ranking was in line with the similarly poor showing of the other counties which might be considered marginal. Thus for the lay subsidy of 1334 (which excluded church property by definition), the lowest poundage rates per acre were levied in Northumberland, Lancashire, Westmorland, West Riding, North Riding, Cornwall, Cumberland, Devon, Derbyshire, and Shropshire, in that order—a roll-call of the marginal regions. Again, the Poll Tax of 1377 appeared to show Cumberland, Westmorland, and Northumberland to be the thinnest settled, at under 10 people per square mile, followed by Lancashire and the North and West Ridings which carried 10–20 people per square mile. Lancashire did not then have a single town with over 1,000 inhabitants. In 1515 Lancashire had still the lowest assessment in terms of land, at £3.8 per 1,000 acres, the North Riding of Yorkshire coming next with £8.1, followed by the West Riding with £11.3, against an average of £66.6 for the whole country. Even as late as 1636, the ship money assessment for Lancashire was £1 per 1,219 acres, much the lowest except for Cumberland at 1,251 acres, against, at the other end of the scale, Devon at 184 acres and Wiltshire at 123 acres. In various other assessments between 1641 and 1693 Lancashire still ranked among the lowest, being surpassed only by Northumberland, Westmorland, Cumberland, and Durham.[8]

[5] Hobsbawm (1977), 56; also Farnie (1979), ch. 1. [6] Darby (1977), 2.

[7] Buckatzsch (1950–1), 186–7. By 1843, it had moved up to second place among 39: ibid.

[8] Glasscock (1973), 138; Jewell (1991), 17–18; Jordan (1962), 1; Schofield (1965), 504; Curtler (1908),

By the seventeenth century, however, considerable growth had taken place in terms of population, at least, and this accelerated in the eighteenth century.[9] The Land Tax of 1692, to be sure, which became fixed in its allocative distribution from 1697, still showed Lancashire and the other northern counties to be among the most lightly taxed, but by then this distribution no longer represented a fair share-out of the burden. It is not entirely clear why the northern counties were favoured in this way, unless it were simply because it continued a well-established tradition, but as industrialization progressed, their low assessment, which remained unaltered, became less and less justifiable: 'The original assessment was heavily biased in favour of the northern and western counties, a feature of the tax which became permanent.' Moreover, 'as the relative riches of the different counties and towns specifically charged altered, the unfairness increased.'[10] It did, in fact, prove to be of considerable benefit to the industrial counties at a time when they were pulling away from the rest by their industrialization, though it is not to be assumed that that was its intended objective.

There were two sets of factors responsible for the tradition of low taxation assessments in the marginal northern counties from the Middle Ages to the early modern period. One was the notion that they were poor and backward because they were distant from the centre; the other, that their actual climate, configuration, and soil would yield but poor agricultural returns in any circumstances.[11]

Distance from the centre was a complex issue, as noted in earlier chapters.[12] It implied a lack of political power and social influence for the leading regional personalities, ignorance of political events and delay in receiving important information, and, not least, long, tedious, and costly journeys for those who were forced to have business in London. Distance from the centre also meant that there were fewer trading links, less chance of reaching the richer markets of the core counties of England, and therefore less developed commercial and financial institutions in the north. In the case of Lancashire, there were also periodic and destructive raids by the Scots, and these were explicitly cited from time to time as grounds for reducing royal levies on the north or remitting them altogether. But at the same time, being out of reach of the court also implied less control from the political centre, and a greater measure of freedom and independence. If the north was sometimes ignorant of what went on in London, London was not always well informed on what went on in the distant periphery. The placing of lesser burdens on the taxpayers of the north was not unconnected with the fear that they were more likely to refuse and rebel, and that their rebellions would be more difficult to put down: 'in this respect as in others, remoteness from central government had its advantages'.[13]

421; also Miller (1991*b*), 42; Winchester (1987), 2; Williams (1982), 92 (map); Baker (1973*a*), 191–6; Swain (1986), 1–2; Law (1908), 271. But see Stanley (1980) for a critical review of the evidence.

[9] Emery (1973), 252; Darby (1973*c*), 307; Jordan (1962), 3 ff. and p. 222 above.

[10] Mingay (1964), 382; Dowell (1965), 50–1; also Wilson (1982), 423; Habakkuk (1940), 9; Musgrove (1990), 244.

[11] Winchester (1987), 2.

[12] See pp. 68 and 96–7 above.

[13] Walton (1987), 28.

Beyond these political and marketing considerations there was also the solid fact that, at the given agrarian technology, Lancashire, together with some other northern regions, could provide only a poor living to its people. Over much of the north of England, even in the lowlands, wheat could not be grown because of the climate, and oats, together with barley, became the main crop. One theory even suggests that it was the absence of a wheat crop from which the conquerors might have drawn their feudal dues that kept the leading Norman nobles out of the region in the first decades after the Conquest, and delayed the building of castles and the siting of monasteries there until the time of Henry I (1100–35).[14]

Ultimately, as population increased in all parts of England in the following two centuries, Lancashire, too, began to be more densely settled. Nevertheless, 'Lancashire presents, throughout the thirteenth century, a spectacle of unreclaimed wilderness of woodland, moss and fell.'[15]

Much of the country was high ground, where at most sheep and cattle could provide a living, while the lowlands were mostly wet, covered in large part by mosses and marshes, with only circumscribed areas suitable for cropping. There are some indications that it was the poverty of the land which forced its people to occupy themselves with textiles even in the Middle Ages. With the decline of population in the later fourteenth century, the cultivation line on the hillsides receded as it did everywhere else, and the textiles were given up again.[16]

In due course population rose once more, and by the early Tudor period was beginning to press again on the limits of the land. Conditions were not propitious. Around 1480, Lancashire could still be described as 'poor, isolated and backward', 'a remote and backward county . . . poor in natural resources, sparsely settled, and without strong leadership or mature institutions'. Its backwardness was due to its 'scant economic resources and its political vicissitudes during the Middle Ages . . . The region was on exposed frontiers which for generations bore very heavy military burdens and which suffered from repeated and damaging Scottish forays.' Its soil was thin and in many regions was 'of marginal agricultural value, with great stretches of land that were intractable waste'. It suffered from its 'barren' and 'rugged' hills, the 'harshness of the climate and the unproductiveness of the land'. The Honour of Clitheroe, for example, it was alleged in 1608, consisted of 'great and mountainous commons entirely barren and unprofitable'. As late as 1631, Gervase Markham 'considered the region as one of the most backward in England in its productivity and agricultural methods'.[17]

The county's backwardness was thought to be reflected also in its religious history: 'In Lancashire, retarded social development meant that the old institutions and forms of thought retained their vigour'; 'Lancashire could hope to attract only the dregs of the clerical population', for, as a backward and underdeveloped

14 Kapelle (1979), 221–9. 15 Hallam (1972), 217. 16 Swain (1986), 9.

17 Quotations from Jordan (1962), pp. vi, 1–2; Swain (1994), 71; also Baines and Fairbairn (1869), iv, p. ii.

county, it could provide only meagre incomes for its priests. In Tudor times, 16 of the richest 20 benefices were in the hands of absentees.[18]

Yet Lancashire was not without its assets. Its extensive forests and moorlands could be developed by clearing to provide land for settlers; the marshy low grounds could be turned into fertile agricultural land by drainage, as later generations discovered; and the moist atmosphere created lush meadows for animal husbandry. 'In spite of an inclement climate and a niggardly soil the population grew rapidly' in an area like Rossendale. Moreover, the marginality of the land and the social backwardness for which it was responsible could themselves be turned to favourable account when conditions were ripe. In some of the poorest areas, where 'land became increasingly scarce as population rose', holdings were 'fragmented to a point where supplementary income was essential for many, with and without land'.[19] There was pressure, therefore, to take up occupations that would supplement incomes: it was aided by the fact that there were few corporate towns in the county, 'so that Lancashire largely escaped the great struggle between urban gild interests and country interests which characterized the older clothing counties'. 'There can be no doubt that one explanation of the rapid rise in importance of Manchester cottons, and Lancashire rugs, friezes, linens and kerseys, lies in the absence of corporate towns with their guild restrictions.' To this freedom has to be added the essential failure of the government's attempts to control by the Acts of 1514, 1535, and later, the country trade through alnagers and by other means.[20]

We have here a theme which has occupied us before, and which will occur again: the advantages of marginality and backwardness at specific crucial times. In the case of Lancashire, the rise of a domestic textile industry in the early modern period was favoured in part by the poor soil and unfavourable agricultural conditions generally, and in part by the backward social structure of the region which meant that potential restraints from existing vested interests, in this case from the town guilds, could effectively be ignored. Furthermore, the mainly pastoral character of the agrarian economy, which in one sense reflected the poverty of the soil and the difficulty of its cultivation, had the advantage of freeing family members for non-farm work in certain seasons. Other assets possessed by Lancashire were the wool grown locally, and the relatively low incomes leading to low wage expectations. By the later sixteenth century, older centres like Preston and Wigan had lost much of their textile industry; this was now increasingly settling in upland farmsteads and hamlets, but towns like Manchester, Bolton, Bury, Rochdale, Blackburn, and Colne also benefited.

In the course of the sixteenth century, linens and fustian mixtures were added to the pre-existing woollen fabrics, while among these, kerseys were expanded and worsteds added. The following two centuries saw not merely expansion but also specialization. In place of the traditional part-time employment in the textile

[18] Haigh (1969), 27, 1, 2. [19] Tupling (1927), 161, 167 ff.; Swain (1986), 70; Porter (1977).

[20] Lowe (1972), 82, 83, 86; Daniels (1920), 3–4. 'Cottons' at the time were mainly woollen fabrics, not cotton materials as understood later.

industry, increasingly there were full-time weavers, while simultaneously agriculture experienced its own transformation. The improvement of the land was generally associated with enclosures which 'consisted of bringing into use of common pasture and large tracts of moorland, moss, marsh and sandhills'. What was once wasteland now began to be turned to profitable use. In the sixteenth and seventeenth centuries, enclosures affected mostly the manufacturing upland areas of east Lancashire; in 1710–70 they covered the lower-lying western linen and coal-mining areas; and from the 1770s onward, moors and marshes were reclaimed and 'great tracts of moorland were taken in' in north-east Lancashire, as in other parts of Britain. Given the growing urban population and its food demands in wartime, 'oats and potatoes were cultivated even on what now appear to be impossibly barren hilltops'.[21]

While there was merchanting in towns and some specialized production such as the significantly named 'Manchester goods', industry was still essentially rural up to at least 1750. Against that background, the seventeenth-century Justices refused to enforce the privileges of such urban guild monopolies as survived, for the significant reason that it would create poverty in the countryside. Typically, country weavers were part-time smallholders, and their womenfolk were engaged in spinning. Typically also, they were settled on the infertile hills and uplands. Full-time weavers even in non-privileged towns now began to complain of being undercut by the part-time farmer-weavers of the villages.[22]

If we were to stop and review the scene as it presented itself around the middle of the eighteenth century, we would find, together with significant change, also a great deal of continuity. The environmental framework was still largely unfavourable.

> Until the eighteenth century the society between Ribble and Mersey had maintained a largely self-contained existence upon the fringe of civilization; cut off from the rest of England by barriers of mountain and marshland, it lay far distant from the great centres of economic activity and from the main channels of commerce. The poverty of a barren frontier region was manifest in the small population . . . it also provided the great spur to the development of manufactures.[23]

In the north of the county, north of the Ribble, Defoe found no trade in the 1720s, no ships visible at sea, few people and, surrounding them, high hills which 'had a kind of unhospitable terror in them'.[24] As for the eastern uplands, 'the clay soil of east Lancashire . . . was unsuitable for arable cultivation and unrewarding to the farmer, being heavy, cold and damp'; 'soil and climate were decidedly unhospitable'. Even as late as 1838, in the east Lancashire weaving district,

> everywhere extend wild, naked hills, in many places totally unreclaimed, in others enclosed, but exhibiting all the signs of a neglected spiritless husbandry; with stunted fences or stone

[21] Wadsworth and Mann (1965), 321–2; also Sylvester (1969), 486–9; Davies (1960), 11; Lazenby (thesis, 1949), 2–4; Scola (1992); Kenworthy (thesis, 1949), 59, 96–7. For the national position, see p. 45 above.

[22] Wadsworth and Mann (1965), 25, 28, 59, 317; Davies (1960), 127; Phillips and Smith (1994), 43–4.

[23] Farnie (1979), 46, also 36–8.

[24] Defoe (1927), ii. 679.

> walls, and fields sodden with wet from want of drainage, and consequently overgrown with rushes. Over these naked and desolate hills are scattered to their very tops, in all directions, the habitations of a swarming population of weavers.

> The soil and climate of the hill country between Bolton and Blackburn . . . were poor for farming and the holdings were small. Thus the switch to textile manufactures was more rapid than in other areas, and leaseholders like the Ashworths and the neighbouring country gentry became manufacturers, while the labourers and cottagers became domestic spinners and weavers.

> With few exceptions, the strongest concentration of weavers occurred in the upland districts of the county [of Lancashire], where the soil was too cold, damp, and acidic for arable cultivation. Accordingly, as the textile industry prospered during the sixteenth and seventeenth centuries, surplus labour was readily available to work in spinning and weaving.

Indeed, so bleak was the landscape that people walking out from their upland factory villages found themselves in 'danger in windswept moors'.[25]

By contrast, the western lowlands turned out to be reasonably fertile once they had been drained and improved—a process that was both costly and long-drawn-out. The enormous growth of industry, of trade, and of population which followed in the nineteenth century was accompanied by the emergence of substantial urban concentrations there, above all in Liverpool and the coal-mining towns, while Manchester itself with its suburbs, though lying on the edge of the bleak hill landscape, became a great metropolis. It might thus be said that the marginality which covered the whole county until the Industrial Revolution was being pushed back to its eastern upland half: it is a classic example of the common experience that a marginal area, once it undergoes successful development, ceases thereby to be marginal for the time being. The western lowlands will therefore no longer be classified in those terms after the mid-eighteenth century in this study. What is truly significant is that in spite of the remarkable growth and developments in the west of the county, the dynamic of the Industrial Revolution, particularly in its early, critical stages, originated and continued to be located in the eastern, undoubtedly marginal districts of Lancashire, extending to the equally unhospitable territories of neighbouring counties.

It was not only in the agricultural scene that traditional elements survived: the industrial structure also contained many elements of apparent continuity. The textile manufacture, as it appeared around 1750, seems to have evolved smoothly from its earlier, more primitive beginnings into a classic domestic putting-out system of a kind which has recently come to be known as 'proto-industry' or 'industry before the industrial revolution'. Among the main characteristics of such a system are production for distant markets outside the region; the actual productive work being largely performed in the countryside by an agrarian population which might begin as part-timers, but could become a full-time industrial workforce in their own

[25] Quotations from Farnie (1979), 46; Walton (1989), 50; Aspin (1969), 52; Boyson (1970), 1–2; Coupe (1977), 109; also cf. Curtler (1908), 428; Daniels (1920), 139–40; Walton (1987), 74; Lazenby (thesis, 1949), 9–10; Geoff Timmins and Rex Pope in Pope (1989), 31; Fletcher (1962), 94–5.

homes, linked to towns where finishing processes and perhaps the more skilled tasks would be undertaken, possibly also in large workshops; and access to the food surpluses of agrarian regions to feed an increasingly dependent manufacturing population. What has come to be stressed, moreover, is the inherent growth potential of such a structure, as the putting-out merchants acquired capital and knowledge of world markets, as workers and others were provided with incentives to contrive technical innovations, and as means of transport in the region were improved and thereby encouraged further expansion.[26]

These features of a typical proto-industrial landscape apply to mid-eighteenth-century Lancashire with remarkable accuracy. While its towns, above all Manchester, concentrated on finishing processes—such as calico printing or the making of smallware—agents of the resident merchants swarmed out to the villages and hamlets, including those in the inhospitable upland valleys, to take work to the weavers, who in turn found work for the female village population in spinning and carding; alternatively, they supplied yarn to the weavers directly. The larger merchants might work through intermediate 'fustian masters'; the merchants resident in the smaller urban centres had direct contact with the weavers, who would walk into town once a week to deliver the finished cloth and collect fresh materials. There were still weavers buying their own cotton or yarn; others worked up what was provided for them, being little removed from piece-rate workers; while others still preserved a quasi-independence, but at the price of depending on credit from the merchants.[27]

All this, or something like it, could be found in any of the numerous proto-industrial regions of Europe. As was the case elsewhere, too, there was an increasing regional concentration of manufacturing activity. Cotton and mixed fabric production was now concentrated in Lancashire and the adjoining areas, together with the Clyde valley and Northern Ireland, while declining elsewhere: if the 1801 Census is to be trusted, an astonishing 36 per cent of the total population of the county worked in textiles; in the same period there were localities in which 50 per cent and up to 80 per cent of bridegrooms were weavers.[28]

In this development it was the weaving of fustian cloth, a material which normally consisted of linen warp and cotton weft, which had by the mid-eighteenth century taken the leading role. Well established by 1621 in Lancashire, its expansion was helped to some extent by the legislation of 1700 and 1721, which was intended to protect the woollen industry but incidentally encouraged both the finishing of calicoes in Britain and the production of a substitute for the Indian calicoes which British workers were as yet unable to imitate directly. This was fustian cloth; and by 1736 its importance had grown to the extent that the 'Manchester Act' of that year

26 For a good summary of an enormous literature see Mendels (1982), 77–80.

27 e.g. Mantoux (1961), 36–8; Chapman and Knoop (1908), 382; Walton (1987), 21 and (1989), 69; Lee (1972), 1–2; Daniels (1920), 36–9; Tupling (1927), 170, 178; Phillips and Smith (1994), 91; also, despite her misgivings, Rose (1992), 150–2.

28 Farnie (1979), 24; Rose (1992), 155; Walton (1987), 110; Chapman (1972), 13, 19; Lee (1972), 5–7.

specifically exempted it from the prohibitions of the earlier legislation.[29] Much of the linen yarn used by fustian weavers was imported from Ireland or the Continent, while cotton yarn was increasingly spun at home, of imported raw cotton.[30]

Other textile branches were also growing well, including the making of checks and the production of smallware, such as inkle, lace, and tapes: the tapes, it is worth noting, were produced on the 'Dutch' or 'engine' loom, a piece of equipment introduced at the beginning of the century,[31] which had the incidental effect of acclimatizing the local population to the idea of technological innovation. Another textile trade which expanded significantly on the fringes of the Lancashire industrial region was silk throwing and spinning, later complemented by weaving. After the Lombes' silk-throwing patent ran out in 1734 the silk industry settled in the marginal landscape in and around Congleton and Macclesfield as well as in Stockport, being attracted mainly by the availability of water-power.[32] The complicated, water-driven machinery of the silk mills can also be seen as offering a model of the potentialities of technology to local entrepreneurs. In the event, a considerable number of cotton mills were erected in due course in the three silk industry towns named above.

This, then, was the state of the regional textile industries around the middle of the eighteenth century. The sequence of technical innovations which were about to overwhelm the cotton industry at this point is too well known to need anything but the briefest mention. The first significant improvement was Kay's flying shuttle, invented in 1733, which after some delay spread rapidly in the 1760s. By itself it was hardly revolutionary, being capable of doing little more than doubling the output of a weaver. Yet in a situation where it needed 4–5 spinners to keep a weaver going, while the potential spinners, the women and children of the villages, were already fully engaged, 'and despite imports there was normally an almost critical shortage of thread',[33] it ushered in a spinning crisis. The spinners simply could not keep up with the needs of the weavers. An active search for means to break the bottleneck was set in train: it even reached London, where in 1760 the Society of Arts offered a prize for the best method of accelerating the spinning process. The situation was transformed by three major inventions which mechanized cotton spinning: Hargreave's jenny (1764–7, patented in 1770), Arkwright's frame (patented in 1769), and Crompton's mule (*c.*1779). The scope of each invention was soon extended by ancillary innovations, such as carding and roving machines, and each spinning machine was itself rapidly improved to take ever more spindles and to increase its speed, thus multiplying the output of a single worker ever more dramatically. Moreover, the quality and regularity of the machine-spun yarn were so much superior to the hand-spun variety that pure cotton cloth of every degree of fineness could be woven from it, thus making Britain completely independent of Indian supplies.

29 O'Brien *et al.* (1991); Daniels (1920), 10–23.

30 Daniels (1920), 57–60; Lee (1972), 3.

31 Daniels (1920), 25, 72; Walton (1987), 64.

32 Unwin *et al.* (1924), 27–8; Iredale (1970), 139; Kenworthy (thesis, 1949), 60–1; Malmgreen (thesis, 1981), 14 ff.; Ashmore (1982), 3, 29–30.

33 Mantoux (1961), 208; also Lee (1972), 4; Daniels (1920), 38. For Scotland, see Mitchell (1925), 102.

Jennies and mules could, in their early days, be installed in cottages, thus leaving the location of the spinning activity unchanged; but Arkwright's frame, significantly known almost from the start as the 'water frame', needed a waterwheel to power it, and so, before long, did the other two machines. Spinning had therefore to be transferred from homes or small workshops to 'mills' or factories. This is the origin of the factory system and, if a single point of entry for the new age is to be named, it is surely to be found at this exact spot.

There is no dispute as to what happened next. Large numbers of the new would-be entrepreneurs and spinning masters left the towns and the plains for the hills in search of suitable locations. Mills for the Arkwright frames which produced the strong, but coarse thread for warps, and mills for the mules producing finer, if weaker threads for the weft sprang up like mushrooms in all the uplands surrounding the Lancashire cotton district, as indeed they did along the rivers surrounding the other main cotton centre in Glasgow.

As Mantoux observed:

> The beginnings of the modern factory system are to be found in small hamlets, far removed from those great industrial centres round which the mass of working people has since gathered. These small places were scattered along the foot of the Pennine range, on all three sides of it; on the west towards Manchester and the Irish sea, on the south towards the Trent valley, and on the east towards the Yorkshire plain and the North Sea.

They were to be found even in the Derbyshire High Peak, difficult of access now and still more so in the eighteenth century. Names of Peak villages and towns otherwise known only then and now to the tourist—Edale, Tideswell, Bakewell, Calver, Castleton, Matlock, Bamford, Hartington, Youlgrave, Wirksworth, Ashford, Winster, Cressbrook, and Litton—came to denote places in which Arkwright and other pioneers built cotton mills or converted existing mills to cotton spinning.[34]

It is widely assumed that this undeniable centrifugal tendency of industry to move to the less accessible uplands in its most vulnerable yet most decisive phase of change was motivated mainly by the quest for water-power. 'The competition amongst industrial capitalists with considerable resources to secure water power in the most favourable situations and to develop it by ambitious feats of engineering is one of the most remarkable features of the last decades of the 18th century.' Not only cotton-mill owners, but also silk- and paper-mill proprietors began 'to join battle to control streams and rivers by the building of weirs or to buy rights to collect water and impound it for their own use'. A widespread trade in water rights made fortunes for those landlords who happened to own them, though they could also be a source of costly and long-drawn-out litigation. In this resource, the uplands of east Lancashire were well endowed: 'the most important natural resource of east Lancashire lay in its water supply'; indeed, 'the rivers of east Lancashire had excited a magnetic

[34] Mantoux (1961), 247; Chapman (1967), 54–68, 167; Pilkington (1789), 51, 393 ff.; also Rose (1992), 144; Dodd (1951), 284–90; Aikin (1795), 475 ff.; Wood and Wilmore (1927), 166–8; Hastings (1981), 32; Watts (1967*b*); Speight (1982), 94; Mackenzie (1959); Fletcher (1971), 12–13; Farey (1811–17), iii. 484–5; Knowles (thesis, 1990), 38.

attraction upon industry, drawing mills to their banks in such numbers as to become the hardest-working water courses in the world.' In 1835 the river Irwell together with its tributaries drove no fewer than 300 mills of all kinds.[35]

No doubt the quest for water-power was important, but a monocausal explanation of this kind leaves a number of questions unanswered. There was also water-power, after all, in existing towns, where some mills were, indeed, converted to cotton spinning. A water supply could be augmented or regularized to some extent by contemporary engineering techniques. The likelihood is that it was not so much, or not exclusively, the availability of upland water which made it attractive, but also, and perhaps mainly, its lower price, especially the cheaper land on the banks of streams.

Furthermore, weaving also tended to expand to the uplands, though there was no obvious technical need for water-power in the case of the weavers. Behind this increase in the number of weavers lay the fact that the cheapening of cotton fabrics and of others which were partly made of cotton yarn, brought about by machine spinning, had led to an astonishing increase in sales. Raw cotton net imports, the best measure available, rose from 3.3 million lb. in 1770 to 51.6 million lb. in 1800, and were to rise to 248 million lb. in 1830 and reach over 1,000 million lb. in 1860. Thus, from the 1780s onwards, the tables were completely turned on the weavers. It was now they who could not keep up with the demand. Consequently, men, women, and children rushed into the weavers' trade, from other occupations and from other parts of the country, to fill the gap. William Radcliffe's well-known comment sums up matters.

> There was not a village within thirty miles of Manchester, on the Cheshire and Derbyshire side in which some of us were not putting out cotton warps, and taking in goods . . . in short, we employed every person in cotton weaving who could be induced to learn the trade . . . every lumber room, even old barns, cart-houses, and outbuildings of every description were repaired, windows broken through the old blank walls, and all fitted up for loom-shops.[36]

A 'golden age' for handloom weavers set on in the 1790s, to last for something like two decades.

A mechanical loom was invented in 1785, but was of little practical use. It required a number of improvements before the power-loom began seriously to replace handloom weaving in the 1820s. Even then, however, the advantages of mechanization were not nearly as striking as in spinning, and skilled weavers, capable of producing complex fabrics, could hold their own until well into the 1850s. At its peak, therefore, in the first three decades of the century, some 200,000–250,000 workers, many of them full-time, were engaged in cotton weaving in the extended Lancashire region. They, like the spinners, were to be found in large numbers not in the towns, but in the 'straggling manufacturing villages or market towns which had sprung from obscurity earlier in the [nineteenth] century

[35] Quotations from Unwin *et al.* (1924), 119; Phillips and Smith (1994), 89; Farnie (1979), 51, 52; also Tupling (1927), 195; Walton (1987), 103; Aikin (1795), 262–3; Baines (1966), 85; Slaven (1975), 93; Bairoch (1988), 254–5; Chapman (1971); and p. 121 above.

[36] Radcliffe (1828), 121, 65.

with the rapid expansion of hand weaving'. The areas of Whalley, Darwen, Haslingden, Oswaldtwistle, Colne, Clitheroe, and Marsden were mentioned. In the Colne chapelry it was claimed at the time that the whole population of 17,000 souls lived by the loom. In the Peak District, too, 'handloom weaving was the more usual form of domestic industry in those remote parts of the Region up to the second decade of the nineteenth century'. On the Derbyshire and Cheshire side of Manchester 'every village had weavers'.[37]

Clearly, there must have been causes additional to the water resources, which were of no particular significance to weavers, to induce cotton masters and workers to move to the thinly populated and remote uplands. One potent factor was the long tradition of textile work culminating in the proto-industrial phase; however, this could not explain the specific move to the Peak District and the uplands of north Wales. Other favourable factors were cheap land and low rents; but also, as ever, there were the low wages and the industriousness associated with part-time farmer-weavers working within their family economy. These were people inured to hardship and exacting toil. Originally, the widespread occupation of weaving had arisen because of the inability to eke out a living from farming alone in those infertile regions: now the supply of weavers was met by the desperate need of mill owners to find ever larger numbers of people able to turn their yarn output into saleable cloth. From the point of view of the cotton masters, this may simply have appeared as spare capacity at a time when demand for several factors of production seemed to outrun supply.

Yet the distant upland village locations were not without problems, some of which led to increased costs in their turn. For one thing, the right sort of labour might be difficult to find: even Arkwright, setting up the very first spinning factory in Cromford in 1771—a location he may or may not have chosen for its constant water supply—appeared to have problems recruiting labour of sufficient skill and docility in that remote village. It has indeed been argued that the choice of Cromford was not a sensible one from the economic point of view in the light of all the circumstances, which makes the choice, followed as it was by the installation of several other mills in the same marginal region, all the more remarkable. Wages might well be lower in those marginal districts, but to attract and keep his labour force, the mill owner might have to erect whole townships in the wilderness at his own expense: this was the case for the largest mills in Scotland, at New Lanark, Catrine, Blantyre, and Deanston, and for the mills in remote locations in England, such as at Tottington and Low Moor.[38] It was the absence of an adequate local labour supply which was largely responsible, in this phase, for the notorious employment of pauper apprentices in cotton mills in the more isolated settlements. Additionally, there were high costs of transport and delays because of distance: even today some of these locations can be reached only with difficulty. Contacts with the markets, with

[37] Bythell (1969), 92; Phillips and Smith (1994), 173; Chapman (1967), 53; also Chapman (1972), 59–61; Daniels (1920), 136–7; Rose (1992), 156.

[38] Chapman (1972), 53–5, 64–7; Coupe (1977); Ashmore (1963–4); Campbell (1980), 17.

buyers and sellers, were also more difficult or, if a middleman was used, more expensive compared with the opportunities enjoyed by mill owners located in or near Manchester.

In opting for distant upland locations, therefore, cotton masters had to take on board a whole bundle of consequences, favourable and unfavourable, which followed from their decision. Essentially, it was the complete set of net advantages derived from a marginal location which determined their choice, and which made marginal lands a key location in what turned out to be the decisive breakthrough into modernity.

Two technological innovations were to pull much of the cotton industry back into the large towns. One was the Watt steam engine which replaced the waterwheel. Installed for the first time in a cotton spinning mill in 1785 in Nottinghamshire, followed by another in 1789 in Manchester, it became widespread after 1800. By 1830 steam had overtaken water as a source of power in cotton spinning and thereafter pulled ahead rapidly. By the time cotton mills returned to the towns they found labour more freely available while external economies in a highly competitive industry became increasingly significant. In addition, there was the availability of coal: in 1838, 96 per cent of steam-powered cotton mills were located where coal was cheapest.[39] The second innovation was the power-loom mentioned above. As its name implies, it required a factory rather than a home workshop, and thus led to the relocation of weaving into the larger towns. In some cases, weaving sheds were attached to spinning factories, but there was also an increasing regional specialization between weaving and spinning towns.

Some water-powered mills were still being built into the 1830s and, because of the low wages, some jenny spinning survived for up to a century 'in the hands of [the] marginal producers—the phrase is used in both the geographic and the economic sense—while elsewhere overtaken by better machines'. In general, however, the package of advantages beckoning from the active centres persuaded cotton masters to move into the towns, and led to closures in the marginal areas. In consequence, 'many of the valleys where the mills had flourished in the late eighteenth and early nineteenth centuries ran down into dereliction in the late nineteenth century'.[40]

On the basis of this enormously enlarged cotton textile manufacture, Lancashire in due course became the home of a huge agglomeration of other industries, linked more or less directly to basic cotton spinning and weaving. Rapid urban development followed, and Liverpool and Manchester grew into cities that were counted among the largest in the country. The proportion of the British population living in the 'North-West' region, of which Lancashire was the main component, rose from 4.9 per cent in 1701 to 8.3 per cent in 1801 and 12.0 per cent in 1851: this was much the fastest relative gain of any region.[41]

[39] Tunzelmann (1978), 66.

[40] Phillips and Smith (1994), 170; Chapman (1967), 51; also Chapman (1967), 211–13; Walton (1987), 107; Farnie (1979), 3.

[41] Lee (1986), 127.

There has been much debate on the causes of this extraordinary regional concentration of dynamic growth, both before and after the great inventions which were to transform the industry, the county, and, in the view of some, the whole world. It is worth once more going over the locational advantages of a county but recently among the poorest and least developed, which first favoured the domestic textile industry, and then took on the pioneering role of developing the modern factory system. Experience elsewhere was to show that it by no means followed that a region containing a well-established domestic manufacture would inevitably succeed in converting it into a successful factory industry, and still less that it would lead the world in doing so. We are therefore faced here by two separate issues. One is the emergence of a successful proto-industry mainly in the uplands of Lancashire before 1750–60; the other is the location of the first factory industry in the world in its critical early stages in the same unpromising landscape, before, in yet a third stage, the mills returned to the lowlands, and in the process turned the former marginal lowlands into a 'core' area.

In determining the original location of the domestic textile industry, the poverty of the soil and the unsuitability of the climate for agricultural productivity had, as we have seen, played a considerable and probably decisive part. A further advantage of the Pennine slopes for textile work was the ready availability of pure and plentiful water, necessary for washing, scouring, and bleaching—water which was also required in the towns, for dyeing and printing as these developed in the early eighteenth century. The beneficial effect of the moist atmosphere on the handling of the cotton fibre is also frequently mentioned, but is subject to some controversy. The freedom from guild restrictions and later from the Weavers' Acts and the Calico Acts were other local advantages, as was the low level of wages before the industrial boom. Beyond these, the character of the local population, especially as it was formed by poverty and adversity, may be considered a point in favour. Even as early as 1650, at least one visitor was struck by the fact that 'the people in and about the town [of Manchester] are said to be in general the most industrious in their callings of any in the northern part of this Kingdom'; it is a view which, even if not to be taken too literally, denotes a certain general impression. As industry grew, 'folkways [were] inherited from the rural past even in the largest towns, which were simply overgrown villages'. Among them were a preference for investment in real property, an irreverent attitude to established authority, family loyalty, 'respect for money', and 'a quasi-peasant cunning, shrewdness and tenacity which proved an effective substitute in daily life for book-learning'.[42] These, at a time of untried innovations, and an environment of cut-throat competition, played out against a background of rising demand for those who knew how to attempt to meet it, were considerable assets. Easy access to the raw material is omitted from this list, for by the early eighteenth century, most of it, apart from some rough wool, was imported,

[42] Quotations from Aikin (1795), 154 and Farnie (1979), 71; also Walton (1989), 65–6; Rose (1992), 150; Baines (1966), 85–7; Hunt (1986), 950.

but we may convert that factor to the existence of good ports and reasonable communications, including canals, for much of the county.

Up to this point, there was nothing to show, at least to a casual observer, that the classical proto-industry as it existed in Lancashire would have a future greatly different from other similar European regions. 'Many regional economies elsewhere in Europe', Walton argues persuasively, 'reached a similar position, without crossing the threshold to a new era of factory industry and large-scale urbanisation . . . At this stage, Lancashire's condition was remarkable, but not unique.'[43] How did it come about that when the next stage of industrialization, of the water-powered mills which are generally taken to have played a leading part in ushering in the nation-wide Industrial Revolution, became technically feasible, these were located in the Lancashire uplands, rather than elsewhere?

Part of the answer has to be sought outside Lancashire, in the British economy at large. The explanation for the leading role of Britain in industrializing the world has been the subject of an extensive debate. Among the factors generally listed are internal peace, the rule of law, an industrial tradition, including widely available mechanical skills, a reasonable surplus over and above subsistence which could be saved, and an abundance of appropriate raw materials. These and similar explanations have, of course, to bear the weight not only of the breakthrough in the cotton industry, but also of the British pioneer role in developing a wide range of coal technologies, of engineering, of chemical manufacturing, of the railways and numerous other innovations associated with the Industrial Revolution, in addition to the revolution in the textile industry. At the same time, the success of Lancashire had a large share in propelling forward the British economy as a whole. But even if we accept that there were good reasons why the decisive breakthrough into modernity should occur in Britain, we are still left to explain how Lancashire came to occupy the role of advance guard in this movement.

In trying to explain the pioneer position of that county, it is worth remembering that the material on which it built its prosperity, cotton fibre, was a relatively recent arrival: it was 'not bound in the customs of centuries', as was the woollen industry.[44] It also seems that, in the given state of technology, it happened to be easier to design machines that would spin cotton fibres than those of wool, let alone flax. If we accept that any technical progress depends, among other factors, on the material possibilities of what workmen and technologists can perform at the time, given their background and the manufacturing capacities of the age, there was a powerful advantage for Lancashire, arising from its specialization in fustians, in having lit upon a fibre in which the technical leap forward of spinning by machine proved to be feasible. Cotton had the further advantage of a potentially highly elastic supply of raw material from abroad, while the demand for the finished material proved to be equally elastic, not least because, among other factors, its cheapness allowed it to

[43] Walton (1987), 66.

[44] Heaton (1965), 323; Uwin, Introd. to Daniels (1920), p. xxv; Tupling (1927), 192.

replace the older linen and woollen fabrics.[45] At the same time, it might plausibly be argued that it was Lancastrian enterprise which explains the pioneering role of cotton, rather than the other way round.

Within that regional advantage, one reason why in the first phase of mechanized spinning the mills were drawn into the bleak uplands of Lancashire, Derbyshire, Cheshire, and north Wales, was because that is where they found the necessary plentiful water supply for power, scouring, and other purposes. Secondly, land was cheap: as was said of the Calder valley, 'the poor quality of a rough, hilly and humid land reduced its price well below the levels reached in South-East Lancashire'.[46] Thirdly, there was the pre-existence of a highly successful proto-industrial regional economy. There were, in the towns and villages of south-east Lancashire and the adjoining regions, men and women skilled in handling textiles; merchants with capital and a knowledge of markets; and a modern social and technical infrastructure, including improved means of transport. There were also the external economies associated with marketing and the pressure to absorb innovations.[47]

A possible fourth explanation lies in the social entrepreneurial factor. No one familiar with the Lancashire scene in the latter part of the eighteenth century and the beginnings of the nineteenth can fail to be struck by the vigorous, competitive, ruthless, and innovative nature of its industrial population, including those merchants fortunate enough to be able to draw on old wealth, and men rising from the bottom, eager to amass new riches. It may well be that the local strength of Nonconformity had some influence on this quality, also. That these characteristics contributed to the relative success of the following stages is not in doubt; it may, however, be argued that they have to be seen as a consequence of the economic expansion of the preceding phase, rather than as the cause of the following one. Be that as it may, an active class of potential entrepreneurs was one element which the incipient factory system in Lancashire owed to the preceding proto-industry in the same region.

No doubt other favourable factors could be cited to help explain the pioneer role of the Lancashire cotton industry in Europe's progress into industrialization. Enough has been said, however, to make clear that this was a complex matter in which explanation cannot be limited to a single cause, but must be grounded on a conjunction of several co-operating elements, among which the particular characteristics of the marginal uplands play a critical part.

When we now turn to the next stage, when water gave way to steam as the source of energy for factories, the Lancashire textile region was again fortunate: above all, it was found that it straddled a rich coalfield, there were iron supplies not too far away, and it had a long tradition of clockmaking on which early machine makers could draw. Regional salt- and coal-based technology became the basis of the flourishing chemical industry in south-west Lancashire, which helped to transform the

[45] Walton (1987), 111 and (1992), 366; Tupling (1927), 192. [46] Farnie (1979), 305–6.

[47] Walton (1987), 66–71, 111–12; Rose (1992), 160; Chapman (1972), 115 and (1967), 213.

dyeing and bleaching processes, among others.[48] The transport infrastructure—roads, canals, and ports at first, followed by railways later—was of a kind to allow industrial expansion to continue at breakneck speed. As water- and steam-power overlapped for many decades before steam ultimately gained the upper hand, it is evident that the concentration and traditions of the earlier form of power were major factors in the location of the later, despite the significant locational shifts which had occurred *within* the region on the change-over to steam. However, much of that took place in a region which, taken as a whole, was no longer marginal.

Thus the foundation of the pioneer industrial region in Lancashire may be said to have been laid in the early modern period, but its later transformation was made possible by the existence of a whole series of favourable factors which could be brought successively into play in two distinct phases as and when they were needed.

If we now turn to the other leading industrial region which we propose to treat in some detail, the West Riding of Yorkshire, we find a number of striking similarities with developments in Lancashire, along with some significant differences. Some of the similarities were geographic. Like the Lancashire cotton region, the West Riding woollen area was located in the poor north of England, along the slopes of the Pennine chain. Being on the eastern side, however, it had a lower rainfall, and the slopes were gentler, making for more extensive dales. The distance to the sea was much greater, a broad belt of mainly agricultural land lying between the industrial towns and the ocean, and the shore faced the North Sea and the Continent rather than the Irish Sea and the Atlantic.

In the Middle Ages the record of poverty and backwardness was a similar one. At Domesday, the annual value calculated per square mile was the second lowest in the country, at 3*s*. to 4*s*., only the North Riding being lower at 2*s*., against a national average of 32*s*.; measured as annual value per man, the West Riding was still at the bottom with 3*s*., though much closer to the average of 6*s*. In both calculations parts of Lancashire were included in the West Riding data.[49] Until the end of the seventeenth century, Yorkshire had, along with the other northern counties, extremely low tax assessments per acre, being 27th out of 34 counties in 1275, 32nd out of 37 in 1503, and 34th out of 39 in 1693. But this referred to the whole of the county, including its plains and cities. Within these totals for Yorkshire, the West Riding alone had the second lowest assessment of all in 1334 and the third lowest in 1515, only Lancashire being reckoned even less able to bear taxation. Judging from the Poll Tax returns of 1379, 'the future woollen district was then about the least populous and least wealthy area in the West Riding'. Other indications confirm that through the centuries contemporaries considered these Pennine slopes to have been among the poorest regions of the country.[50]

[48] Walton (1987), 66, 112–16. [49] Darby (1977), 228; also p. 222 above.

[50] Crump and Ghorbal (1935), 27; Buckatzsch (1950–1), 186–7; Schofield (1965), 504; also Jewell (1991), 18; Miller (1991*b*), 42; Glasscock (1973), 138; Donkin (1973), 78–9; Heaton (1965), 117; and p. 222 above.

Unlike cotton, the exotic and relatively new fibre on which the prosperity of Lancashire was built, the material which became the basis for the growth of the West Riding in the Industrial Revolution, namely wool, was old-established in England. Derived from the clip of English sheep, it was the basis of much the most important industry, and of the leading export commodity, from the Middle Ages onward until the end of the eighteenth century. There were then few areas in which there was no woollen manufacture of some kind, though the fulling mills were necessarily confined to rivers yielding water-power. By the end of the Middle Ages, however, a notable regional increased density had occurred in mainly three regions: the West Country, East Anglia, and the West Riding of Yorkshire.[51]

The woollen industry was among the first to pull out from urban guild control and settle in the open country or in unincorporated towns. In Yorkshire this had proceeded a long way by the mid-sixteenth century, possibly aided by the earlier pioneering by the monasteries of a sheep and wool economy in the remoter parts of the county, and it had led to the decay of such towns as Beverley, Ripon, and Pontetfract. York complained in 1561 that the industry had left for the uplands where it was not only closer to the water mills, 'but also the poor folk as spinners, carders, and other necessary workfolk for the weaving, may there beside their hand-labour have rye, fire, and other relief cheap, which in this city is very dear and wanting'.[52] This is a not unreasonable list of advantages of the margin. Looked at from the opposite perspective of the Pennine slopes, however, 'it was . . . the natural disadvantages of the region, the rigorous and rainy climate, the barren shallow soil, the great moors and wastes, that first compelled a scanty population to turn to the raising of cattle and sheep and to the wearing of the home-grown wool . . . Huddersfield, Halifax, Bradford, Leeds . . . have all risen . . . in spite of the palpable disadvantages of some of their sites. Set among the hills they have had to struggle for centuries.' They were helped in this quite considerably by freedom from guild control, on the one side, and from manorial control in those inhospitable regions, on the other.[53] However, the woollens produced locally at this time were of poor quality, made from coarse wool mainly for home consumption.

At the end of the following century, Yorkshire's Land-Tax assessment of the 1690s was still among the lowest, together with Lancashire's, in spite of the growing wealth engendered by industrial expansion. Yorkshire, with 10 per cent of the country's territory, paid only 4.7 per cent of the tax. Even in the assessment of 1707 the West Riding, at £15 per square mile, was grouped with the other five northern counties and the Welsh counties as among the least burdened.[54] However, while the county's population growth in the course of the seventeenth century, being at the rate of 14 per cent, was still only half the national average, some of the nascent industrial centres registered notable increases in population as well as in manufacturing

[51] Lipson (1965), 1–6, 222. [52] Quoted in Lipson (1965), 225, also 223, 226, 238.

[53] Quotation from Crump and Ghorbal (1935), 11, 12; also Hudson (1981), 44; Jennings (1992), 47; François (1966), 220; Heaton (1965), 205; Smail (thesis, 1988), 18.

[54] Musgrove (1990), 246; Darby (1973*c*), 308; and p. 223 above.

output. Above all, Halifax—a parish including a large, thinly settled upland area as well as the town itself—recorded a population increase from perhaps 10,000 in 1548 to 18,000–19,000 at the time of the Restoration in 1660, which then accelerated to 40,000 in 1764. This involved widespread encroachment and enclosure of the wastes: 'Much of this increased population moved into marginal agricultural holdings: either on waste, or in cottages on existing farms.' All of it occurred on the basis of an expanding woollen trade, especially the making of kerseys, a coarse, narrow cloth, in the parish.[55]

The preamble to the Halifax Act of 1555, cited many times since, had implied that the inhabitants had been driven into the textile trade because they lived on 'great waste and moors, where the fertility of the ground is not apt to bring forth any corn nor good grass, but in rare places, and by exceeding and great industry of the inhabitants'. A century later, when the water supply, the comparative freedom, and the local wool were noted as other factors favouring the location of the woollen industry there, the poverty caused by the harsh climate, the 'poor soil and the marked seasonality of agricultural activity' of the dominant animal husbandry, were still named as being among the most powerful causes of its concentration in those bleak parts of the Pennine uplands.[56]

Any earlier growth was put in the shade by the expansion of the West Riding woollen and worsted industries between *c.*1700 and 1770. This growth may be looked upon as being composed of two parts: a strong expansion of the output in Britain as a whole, and a substantial increase in the share of the West Riding in it. The first was one aspect of the general increase in incomes which helped to prepare the ground for the Industrial Revolution. The second emphasizes the significance of the marginal regions in it. According to Deane, British output rose by 8 per cent per decade to 1741 and by 13–14 per cent per decade in 1741–71; over the century as a whole, it rose about 2½ times, from £5 million to £14 million. Yorkshire's output rose from £1 million in 1700 to £3.3 million in 1772, and was then to jump to £8.4 million in 1800: its share thus rose from one-fifth to three-fifths in the course of the century. The success of the West Riding earlier in the century was particularly marked in its share of exports. 'By the end of the eighteenth century . . . the locus of domestic woollen production had shifted decisively northwards'.[57]

The rise of the worsted manufacture, formerly dominated by Norfolk, was particularly impressive. Halifax took the lead here in the early eighteenth century, turning above all to shalloons, though, interestingly enough, it was later overtaken by Bradford because it was alleged to have become smug and conservative—a fate which befell Bradford itself, in relation to French competition, later in the nineteenth century. The attempt to produce worsteds in the Calder and upper Dearne

[55] Smail (thesis, 1988), 16, also 80; Darby (1973*c*), 306; François (1966), 225; Raistrick (1970), 79; Ellis (1962), 423; Watson (1973), 146–7; Crump and Ghorbal (1935), 32.

[56] Hudson (1981), 35, also (1991), 265; Holroyde (1979), 60; Smail (thesis, 1988), 15–16. A rendering of the preamble will be found in Hudson (1986), 63.

[57] Gregory (1982), 47, also 27, 35, 6; Deane (1957); Ponting (1971), 35; Wilson (1973), 228–30, 242.

valleys in the 1770s–1790s is also said to have failed because the traditional industrial structure there, geared to the manufacture of woollens, was unable to keep up with the rapid changes in fashion required by the market for worsteds.[58] However, a large north-western portion of the West Riding industry had by then successfully turned to worsteds as its specialization.

There has been a great deal of debate on the causes of the success of the West Riding industry as against its two main rival regions, the West Country and East Anglia, even in the period before the mechanical inventions which introduced the factory system—after which Yorkshire pulled away from the rest even faster. In some respects, a parallel with Lancashire suggests itself. Both counties managed to assume the leadership in their respective industries well before the factory age, the one gaining control of an industry which, because it built on an imported raw material, might have settled almost anywhere, the other by beating off competition from other established active areas. Several commentators, beginning with Clapham, denied the significance of water-power and coal in the shift to the West Riding, since its pre-eminence occurred before the period of the power-driven mills, though contemporaries, such as Defoe, were apt to stress the advantages of a cheap fuel, especially in the dyeing process: 'the country has but little wood', the historian of Halifax observed in 1775, and 'without [coal] the manufactures would languish, if not be totally destroyed'.[59] Similarly, the role of pure water was not insignificant, even before 1770. Against this, access to the raw wool could not have made much difference to Yorkshire's success, since all districts by that time imported much of theirs from other areas, though it may have been a weakness of Norfolk that it tended to import, not raw wool, but yarn from elsewhere. Skill, experience, and reputation lay with the other districts, rather than Yorkshire, and Yorkshire was certainly not favoured by ease of transport.

The general tendency has therefore been to look to the 'human' factor or the organizational structure as the grounds for the emergent superiority of the West Riding. It could be pointed out that while both the other districts were dominated, in different ways, by large capitalists who had in practice reduced the craftsmen to wage workers, the West Riding industry was still in the hands of the weavers as independent masters, buying in their raw material, seeing to its spinning and weaving, and then selling the woven fabrics to the merchants to be finished and marketed. The system was therefore more flexible; it allowed energetic young men to rise to the top; and it suffered less from labour troubles. In Clapham's terse phrase, 'it is the ordinary case of a pushy, hard-working locality, with certain slight advantages, attacking the lower grades of an expanding industry'.[60] That last point was important: Yorkshire first began to encroach on the markets of the other districts

58 Hudson (1981), 45; Heaton (1965), 264, 286–7; Jenkins (1975), 35; Sigsworth (1958), 19; Lipson (1965), 240–1; Clapham (1906), 517.

59 Watson (1973), 2; Defoe (1927), ii. 601; Richards (1993), 211; Sigsworth (1958), 14; Crump and Ghorbal (1935), 19; Singleton (1970), 25; Aikin (1795), 576.

60 Clapham (1910), 201.

by offering cheaper imitations, and raising their quality gradually thereafter. Cheapness was achieved initially by low wages, though by the end of the eighteenth century, northern wages had climbed well above those paid in the south. 'It is likely', according to Gregory, 'that the West Riding of Yorkshire was in fact a labour surplus economy in the first half of the [eighteenth] century', and that, in turn, derived from its location on the margin. The marginal location was also considered to have been significant by Heaton: 'The supply of wool, the possibilities of water power, the possession of a population which could not produce by tillage on the bleak slopes all that was necessary for sustenance, and which, by the inherited skill of generations, was especially suited for industrial work', were among the chief causes of its progress before the great inventions. Inherited qualities were also given high prominence by Maud Sellers: Yorkshire's gains, she held, were due to the 'inherited thrifty tendencies of generations of forebears who had wrung a scanty living from a sterile soil, and the efficiency of the skilled weavers and spinners, with their inherited dexterity of fingers, in combination with the physical characteristics of the district'.[61]

As in Lancashire, the growth of the textile industry in the eighteenth century was associated with a change-over from a part-time to a full-time occupation for increasing numbers, and an increasing dependence of the local communities on textile work. Thus at Hebden Bridge, 84 out of 120 banns of marriage between 1754 and 1776 were for weavers or woolcombers, and 55 out of 119 burials in 1767–80 were of textile workers. In Sowerby, in the mid-eighteenth century, 70 per cent of the male population depended on textiles and in the early nineteenth century it was 68 per cent, not counting others associated with the trade. In Calverley, 70 per cent were classified as 'clothiers' and a further 1 per cent worked in other textiles.[62]

There were, however, considerable structural differences between the organization of the two main branches of the trade, the woollen and the worsted sections. At the same time, there was also a strongly marked locational segregation between them, the woollen district being itself sub-divided into locations making white cloth, coloured cloth, heavy cloth, narrow or broad cloth, etc.[63] One recent study has derived both the locational and industrial differences from the traditional manorial land-holding structure, which in turn was not unconnected with the lie of the land. According to that analysis, feudal lords had little interest in the bleaker uplands, manorial control was weak there, a free market in land developed early, and as a result, great inequalities of holdings emerged in the course of the centuries. The richer villagers were enabled to use their capital for merchanting and the financing of mills, while members of the poorer families were forced to take jobs as dependent outworkers, drifting later into the factories: 'the precarious position of the cottager

[61] Gregory (1982), 49; Heaton (1965), 281; Sellers (1912), 417; also Lipson (1965), 249–52; James (1968), 587; Wilson (1973), 235–8; Chapman (1973), 118–19; Hudson (1991), 264 and (1981), 44; Newell (1925), 256.

[62] Hebden Bridge (1981); Hudson (1991), 269–71.

[63] There was also a linen area immediately to the north: Thirsk (1978), 144; Jennings (1983), 171–81.

in the highland zone made him more receptive to the idea of working for an employer on a piece rate basis'. These were the areas of the worsted trade. In the agriculturally more favoured, lower reaches of the Pennines, however, the manorial framework survived longer, land holdings had less time to be distorted by the entrepreneurship or luck of individuals, and were thus more evenly distributed, and it was out of this more democratic society that an industrial structure, consisting of thousands of independent 'manufacturers', the hallmark of the West Riding, could emerge.[64] It follows that making the democratic structure of the West Riding industry responsible for its success before 1770 runs up against the difficulty that the much vaunted competitive organization of the market with its numerous small entrepreneurs applied to woollens only and precisely not to the more dynamic and faster growing section, the worsted trade.

It is these numerous woollen manufacturers, often referred to as 'yeomen clothiers', who have given rise to the established, and often romanticized picture of the West Riding industry before industrialization and well beyond. Working alone or with members of their family or perhaps a journeyman or two, these weavers were independent contractors. Each of them dwelt in his own home which also contained the workshop, surrounded by 'his enclosures, in which he keeps milch cows for the support of his family, and horses for the conveyance of his goods', which involved taking the weekly woven piece or two to the market hall in town, which might be as much as 5–6 miles distant. The description by Defoe as he first descried the weavers' houses dotted all over the hillsides on his way from Lancashire to Halifax in 1725, making him think that 'this is one of the most populous parts of Britain', has often been reprinted, but other travellers came away with the same impression. Even in the mid-nineteenth century one of them approaching Saddleworth from the west found that his 'eye wanders over clumps of rock and through straggling woods of sombre fir—from cottage to cottage, and hamlet to hamlet, and mill to mill—the former often perched high upon the hills, where the green of the pasture begins to give place to the brown sterility of moss and moor, and the latter invariably nestled in the very bottom of the glen'. Despite its poor soil, an enthusiastic contemporary, referring to the industrial employment, yet felt that 'I know not any country where, upon the whole [the poor] live better'.[65] While they kept to the tradition of a proper apprenticeship, and mostly still observed the rhythms of the agrarian calendar, these handloom weavers imposed something like a democratic form of government on their parishes. Yet they turned out to be flexible enough: as innovations poured in on them, many showed 'something like a poor man's frontier spirit', and survived into the middle of the nineteenth century.[66]

[64] Hudson (1981), 45 and *passim*, and (1991), 265–6.

[65] Quotations from Aikin (1795), 93; Defoe (1927), ii. 603; Aspin (1972), 111; Watson (1973), 8. Also Heaton (1965), 291–4; Smail (thesis, 1988), 52; Gregory (1982), 92–3, 111 ff.; and for the diary of a typical weaver-farmer, see Ashworth (1782–1816).

[66] Lipson (1965), 74–7; Smail (thesis, 1988), 193–4; Gregory (1982), 82; Glover (1961), 3.

In the worsted trade, by contrast, control had fallen early on into the hands mainly of large putting-out entrepreneurs, while the actual weavers had become wage workers, a 'virtual rural proletariat'.[67] It represented quite a different form of proto-industry. Numerous disputes between workers and employers were common, and the alleged widespread embezzlement of material by the outworkers led to the Worsted Acts of 1762 and 1777 and the formation of 'worsted committees' to organize and finance the prosecution of offenders. Some of the larger employers had spinners and weavers working for them as far distant as Wensleydale, Swaledale, Ormskirk, Preston, Craven, Westmorland, Cheshire and Derbyshire.[68] After the new technology of machine spinning and weaving became available from Lancashire, it was, with one important exception, the worsted section which applied it first in the West Riding.

Taking our stand about the year 1770 to view the West Riding, we would see a flourishing, expanding woollen and worsted domestic industry. Apart from the fulling mills strung out along the streams, using a technology which in its essence was then over 400 years old, and the fly shuttle, which had begun to spread in the 1760s, there was little sign of any technical breakthrough to explain the expansion up to that time. Growth had occurred by applying conventional methods to a growing number of units. Most of the industry was rural, with weavers living in scattered hillside cottages which allowed them to engage in a little farming, while spinners were found in most village households. There was little urbanization, the main towns of Leeds and Wakefield being on the border between the woollen district and the plain, to reap the advantage of easier transport facilities. The leading towns inside the industrial district, Halifax and Huddersfield, had cloth halls to which the weavers would bring their cloths for sale, and they also housed some of the finishing work, such as the dyeing, shearing, and pressing, which was done on the merchants' premises. Though the industry had been subject to innumerable legal restrictions (as well as much protection), the West Riding had either ignored them or been freed from them, and the region was known for its vigorous competitive spirit. Rather like Lancashire in the same period, it appeared to be a typical proto-industrial landscape on typical marginal land.

At this point, this traditional, yet alert industry was faced with a series of technological innovations, above all efficient spinning machines, many of them pioneered in neighbouring Lancashire, which were bound to change drastically both its structure and its social relationships. To contemporaries, who were by no means conscious of facing a new era, these presented themselves as a series of challenges and opportunities in the course of a continuing evolution. Nevertheless, they were obliged to deal with numerous changes in their economic and social life. How did the West Riding cope?

[67] Hudson (1981), 38–9.

[68] James (1968), 324–6; Heaton (1965), 294; Hudson (1991), 263, 286–7; Sigsworth (1958), 13.

Curiously enough, the first new type of mill was to be found, not in the worsted, but in the woollen section: this was the scribbling mill, introduced rapidly from the late 1770s. It replaced the carding process by a set of water-driven machines. Often situated next to existing fulling mills (which were needed in the woollen, but not the worsted trade), they were commonly put up by co-operative or joint-stock companies made up of the small 'clothier' firms that were to become their customers. In this way the traditional local independence was not compromised, and the structure of the industry not overturned. There had been something like 100 fulling mills in the area; by 1786 they were alleged to have been joined by 170 scribbling mills, though most of those were very small units.[69]

Thereafter it was the worsted section which mechanized its spinning first, leading the woollen trade by some 20–30 years while lagging itself behind cotton by about the same time span. Following an earlier prototype actually set to work in Lancashire, the first worsted mechanical spinning mill in Yorkshire was established in Addingham, on the river Wharfe, in 1787. The first steam mill, at Baildon, Bradford, dated from 1795, and by the 1820s the hand spinning of worsted yarn was 'almost extinct'. Among the reasons for the earlier mechanization of the worsted before the woollen section were its more capitalistic organization, the technical possibilities and, not least, the example of the cotton mills, some of which were situated adjacent to the worsted spinners in the Pennine valleys and were in some cases actually converted to worsted yarn.[70] Hand spinning of woollen yarns lingered on until the mid-century. In remote regions, such as Wensleydale and Swaledale, primitive water-driven mills, combined with cheap labour, lasted out until the end of the century.[71]

As in cotton, weaving was mechanized a good deal later than spinning. In the 1830s there were still 12,000 handloom weavers said to be active in the Huddersfield region, and 10,000 around Leeds. Once again woollens were lagging a generation or so behind worsteds. Power-looms weaving worsted cloths began to spread rapidly in the 1830s, while power-loom weaving among woollens did not win through fully until the 1880s. As a consequence of this time-lag between spinning and weaving, there was for more than half a century, over the whole period usually considered to cover the Industrial Revolution, a curious marriage between old and new, as each modern spinning mill would have large numbers of traditional handloom weavers associated with it. This organizational division was accompanied by a striking horizontal locational division. The spinning mill would be sited along the stream in the valley bottom, possibly next to the scribbling mill, with the cottages of its workers clustering around it, 'whilst the hill-top "town" of which it was the offshoot continued to carry on the hand [weaving] processes'. Even when weaving was

[69] Crump and Ghorbal (1935), 11, 17, 68; Jenkins (1975), 19; Bentley (1970), 44; Hudson (1986), 32–3 and (1981), 47; Gregory (1982), 88; Aikin (1795), 577; Bischoff (1842), ii. 391–2.

[70] Clapham (1906), 518; also Sigsworth (1958), 3, 16; Lipson (1965), 156; Heaton (1965), 283; Chapman (1965), 97, 112–13; Hudson (1981), 50–5; Wright (1986), 88–90.

[71] Hallas (1990), 204.

finally mechanized, many power-looms would be set up in sheds on the high ground where the settlement had always been, rather than along the narrow valley bottom alongside the spinning mills.[72]

The first half of the nineteenth century saw a remarkable growth in the overall size of the wool textile industry. The estimated domestic clip increased from 80 million lb. in 1775 to 100 million lb. in 1800–19 and 135 million lb. in 1850–4, while at the same time net imports rose from 8 million lb. in 1800 to 38 million lb. in 1850. The industry also became increasingly concentrated along the Pennine slopes. Employment in the Yorkshire woollen industry rose from 23,600 in 1835 to 40,600 in 1850, its share of the British total rising from 50 per cent to 65 per cent between those years. The share of Yorkshire and Humberside in the national population rose from 5.1 per cent in 1751 to 7.7 per cent in 1851.[73] This was a good deal less dramatic than the growth of the north-west (Lancashire), but within the overall figure, the expansion of the West Riding was diluted by the slower growing agrarian districts. A huge complex of iron and engineering works, chemical works, a transport network and one huge conurbation were built up in the region.

In 1816 the historian of Leeds was still of the opinion that 'unequal surface, rapid streams and plentiful fuel are the soul of manufactures',[74] but as water-power gave way to steam, as heavy industry was added and the concentration of population became ever denser, industry moved away from the hilly, outlying areas into the valleys and lowland towns as it did in Lancashire. By 1838 only 31 per cent of those employed in woollen mills were to be found in the western upland areas centred on Huddersfield, Halifax, and Almondbury,[75] while the larger cities themselves, by the very fact of their growth, had removed themselves from marginal status. The true margin, here too, had shrunk back.

When searching for the causes of the industrial concentration on the Pennine slopes of the West Riding, it is helpful, as in the case of Lancashire, to distinguish between the pre-industrial or proto-industrial stage, and the period of the Industrial Revolution. In the early, manual phase, the poor agricultural conditions, the freedom from guild and government control, the low taxation level, and the ease of settlement on unwanted marginal land, together with the hardihood and industriousness of the inhabitants—derived from their harsh environment and their willingness to accept low wages—must occupy a major share of the explanation. To these must be added the natural resources, including water-power, peat and coal fuel, and land suitable for pasture on which sheep and cattle could graze.

For the second stage, the breakthrough into industrialization, the pre-existing structure clearly played a critical role: the 'characteristic features of the Yorkshire woollen industry are in part an inheritance from the pre-factory organisation of the

72 Crump and Ghorbal (1935), 16, also 82–5; Hudson (1981), 46 and (1986), 37, 44–5; Gregory (1982), 66, 246; Lipson (1965), 176, 188; Heaton (1965), 357; Clapham (1906), 517–18.

73 Jenkins (1975), 17; Gregory (1982), 61; Lipson (1965), 216–18; Lee (1986), 127.

74 Quoted as an epigraph at the front of Sigsworth (1958).

75 Gregory (1982), 255; Jenkins (1975), 46–7; Singleton (1970), 37.

trade'.[76] But, as we know, not all proto-industrial concentrations turn into pioneer industrializers. Among the factors which favoured the West Riding at that point were local coal deposits, locally available iron ore, and plentiful building stone. A tradition of thrift helped to provide the needed capital. A flourishing home market and good connections to some potential overseas markets stood ready to offer rich rewards to those who could lower costs or improve efficiency in other ways. There was no lack of such individuals. The active entrepreneurial spirit—found both among manufacturers who adopted new technologies and anticipated changing fashions, and among the merchants who travelled at home and abroad to buy in the wool and sell the finished fabrics—was clearly another significant ingredient.

Looking at both these leading areas of the British Industrial Revolution together, we have to begin by taking it for granted, as we did above in the case of Lancashire,[77] that if a technical and organizational breakthrough were to occur, the pre-existing conditions would locate it in Britain, and that textiles, as the major industrial employer at the time, would be at the centre of it. Given the remarkable dynamic growth of both the textile industries in both these marginal regions in the phase immediately preceding, it is not entirely surprising that so many of the key innovations occurred and spread there first. It has been argued that in an unstable economy ripe for change it needs but a slight lead, achieved possibly accidentally, in any one location, to allow that location to pull away from the rest by cumulative advantages: 'making a decisive innovation first may vastly raise the probability of subsequent innovations being made.'[78] No doubt, but this view omits to note that the Industrial Revolution consisted not of a single lucky stroke, but of a sustained stream of innovations, and that other regions, even after having a single innovation implanted in them from outside or by a local genius, yet failed to 'take off'. Conversely, it was not merely that the British breakthrough allowed Lancashire and the West Riding to develop: these regions and their industrial bases were a most important ingredient of the success of the national economic revolution itself.

Were there any specific 'marginal' qualities which propelled these two regions into the lead? In line with the more general arguments in Part I of this book, the peculiar aptness, and the specific contribution of these marginal regions, may be classified into positive and negative characteristics. Among the leading positive resources were the availability of water-power, coal, and iron ore. To these could be added good pastureland which provided a tradable surplus and wool for local industry, as well as the kind of agriculture which left seasonal free time and a valuable labour supply for a manufacturing occupation. The remoteness itself, though generally considered an obstacle to economic progress, hid some advantages: among these were freedom from government, manorial, or guild control, and from vested or prying interests. It is worth noting in this context that it may not be a coincidence that some of the greatest individual innovators of the age, such as Abraham

[76] Clapham (1906), 520. [77] See p. 236 above.
[78] Davis (1973), 311–13; Crafts (1977), 432.

Darby, Arkwright, Wilkinson, Boulton and Watt, and Josiah Wedgwood, tended to settle outside the main centres of their respective trades.[79]

What might be called the chief negative factor which yet furthered progress was the combination of inferior soil, harsh climate, and elevation which provided a poor agricultural living for the population, especially in periods of population increase, and thus forced it to look for other sources of income. To recall Aikin's view, referring to Bolton in 1795: 'the barrenness of its situation has probably aided its progress in wealth and population by operating as a stimulus to the industry and ingenuity of its people.' The innovations in agricultural techniques of the eighteenth century widened the gap further in favour of the southern and eastern lowlands and made upland agriculture even less competitive. To this we may add the shortage of local timber which encouraged the search for iron and coal.[80] Meanwhile the disadvantages of distance from markets and centres of power and from the source of capital remained. It was their very poverty within these harsh conditions which spurred the inhabitants to seek alternative employments, which encouraged and rewarded those among them who were energetic, frugal, enterprising and quick to seize their chance, and indeed pushed the whole population into developing these qualities. The people both of Lancashire and of Yorkshire were again and again credited by visitors and observers with showing precisely these character features. The spurs of adversity were richly provided on the bleak, inhospitable slopes of the Pennines, east and west.

The character of the Industrial Revolution as a whole, as it developed in Great Britain, carried the clear imprint of having its roots in marginal lands. This was not merely a matter of building a technology on local resources, on coal rather than oil or timber which might have been available in other parts of the world. It was rather discernible in such matters as developing the kind of practical, down-to-earth engineering used on provincial streams rather than the splendid and pompous constructions more familiar in capital cities abroad; above all, it was recognizable in the concentration on the mass production of the most significant traded industrial commodity—textiles—followed by others such as coal, tools, nails, or pottery, rather than on expensive luxury goods on which so much continental ingenuity was expended. It is also worth stressing that the typical innovation of the Industrial Revolution was aggressive, rather than defensive, that is to say, it was designed to increase output to meet a beckoning expanding market, rather than being designed to cut costs to hold on to a threatened one.

All this is by no means equivalent to saying that it was only marginal areas which had a pioneering role in the Industrial Revolution. In fact, of the leading industrial regions, in addition to Lancashire and Yorkshire, only south Wales, south Yorkshire, and Cornwall were clearly marginal on the accepted definitions; the West Midlands and western Scotland had, at best, some marginal features; and the north-east of England, its pioneer role derived from its unmatched riches in coal

79 Hoskins (1955), 165–6.

80 Jones (1977), 497; Tunzelmann (1981), 162; Wrigley (1988).

supplies, was hardly marginal at all by the eighteenth century. Nevertheless, it is striking that with the inevitable exception of some particular corners of London, the whole of the south-eastern half of England, and the prosperous part of Scotland south and east of Edinburgh, made remarkably few contributions to the process, except to supply, as the holders of the country's wealth, some capital and merchanting to the activists in the north and west.

Thus, if we were to imagine, *per impossibile,* that the north-western half of the country had not existed, it is inconceivable that anything remotely resembling the Industrial Revolution could have been brought into being by the south-eastern half of Great Britain. Even if we make the somewhat less strained counterfactual assumption of a state frontier running between the Bristol Channel and the Wash, it would be difficult to resist the conclusion that the imaginary Southland, far from figuring in the textbooks as leading the transformation of the world into modernity, would have been the subject of the kind of critical assessment now extended to France: it would be described as possessing wealth and an advanced society, no doubt, but failing, by its structure and its very attitude to industry, to create any real basis for a pioneer role in the process of industrialization.[81] Nor was the whole of the north-west of England, Wales, and Scotland equipped to revolutionize the world. Rather it may be viewed as presenting three concentric rings in ascending order of effectiveness: the whole of that part of the British Isles containing a number of quite different structures; the key regions, like Lancashire and Yorkshire; and within them, the true marginal lands which carried so much of the innovational drive.

Not all marginal areas were to gain by the Industrial Revolution. Some, including the Highlands of Scotland, much of Wales, and the English border country, found that it destroyed much of what little they had. Industrialization meant the 'euthanasia of cottage industry' and 'the problems of the outlying regions were exacerbated, their disadvantages multiplied . . . For the distant and marginal zones of the system, the economic consequences were sometimes even more revolutionary and disruptive than those experienced at the industrial 'core'.[82]

Marginal areas are, after all, as a rule disadvantaged and handicapped, and their hours of glory, where they occur at all, tend to be bound to certain conjunctions and to be short-lived. The Industrial Revolution is one of the very few historical periods of 'particular northern distinction, importance, and power'. It was an 'extraordinary phase, as a development which could take place only in the most unusual combination of circumstances',[83] among which the creation and development of deeply penetrating, real 'revolutionary' innovations on a broad front were most significant. Even if we include the whole of their industrial zone, and not only the bleak uplands, the good years for Lancashire and Yorkshire lasted, at best, just over a century. In the end, 'the shift of resources into the exploitation of the northern

[81] For an excellent recent summary, see Landes (1994), 648–51.

[82] Richards (1993), quotations from pp. 212, 205, 203. Also, for a different age, cf. Husbands (1987), 352–5.

[83] Musgrove (1990), 1; Barrow (1969), 1.

provinces . . . in the eighteenth and nineteenth centuries might be represented as an interlude . . . in a much larger historical trend [towards London]'. Indeed, 'the tension between the metropolitan core-periphery structure and the resource-based structure' never ceased, and 'by 1900 the metropolitan economy was beginning to reassert itself against the earlier relative losses to the resource-based regions'. The drift had started even earlier. While the share of the national population living in London and Middlesex had fallen from 8.5 per cent in 1701 to 7.9 per cent in 1801, it had more than recovered even by 1851 to 12.1 per cent.[84] By the 1920s the core of the south-east was once again gaining strongly over the periphery,[85] the economy was reverting to type, and the marginal regions in the north and west were once more relatively poor and less well provided with all measurable social amenities. The English south-east was once again the centre of wealth and, as always, the centre of power.

Yet, looking at the process as a whole, the Industrial Revolution was a unique event, and therefore, by definition, could occur once only. Its leading regions had a one-off role in this unique process of world history and thus, by definition, could hardly be made to furnish an adequate basis for statements of probability. Could it be that it was not only an accident that England was 'first'[86], but even more of an accident that within that country, it was the marginal regions on the Pennine slopes which became the leading regions?

It will surely be generally conceded that it was to be expected that if the breakthrough into the Industrial Revolution were to occur, it would have strong bases in expansionary and successful proto-industrial regions. Given the advantages held by Great Britain over other countries, and given the resources which Lancashire and the West Riding had developed, it would be difficult to think of any other region beating them to a leading position in the next phase of development. The location of proto-industry thus becomes significant, and the question 'why these two marginal regions?' may therefore be pushed back one stage: was there any connection between the rising proto-industrial regions and the European marginal lands in the later eighteenth century? To answer that question, a brief glance may be cast at other European regions, to provide a firmer basis for understanding the locational concentration of the British Industrial Revolution.

There is now a widespread consensus that the conditions to be found on marginal lands were particularly well suited for the development of proto-industry in Europe by the eighteenth century. This does not mean that the kind of domestic industry working for a distant market which is covered by the term of 'proto-industry' would never be found in towns or on rich agricultural plains: things are never as clear-cut in economic history, and it is not difficult to list some examples of a combination of productive agriculture and active industrial work operating within one region.[87]

84 Dyos (1971), 91; Langton and Morris (1986), p. xxviii; Lee (1986), 127.
85 Keeble (1976), 46.
86 Crafts (1977); and discussion in Landes (1994) and Crafts (1995) with reply by Landes.
87 Gullickson (1983); Walton (1989), 42; Hudson (1989*b*), 25; Whyte (1989), 237.

However, to jump to the opposite conclusion, that 'agricultural systems had little or no influence on the distribution of manufactures' (Kerridge) does seem to be going a good deal too far.[88]

There may, in individual cases, be good reasons why a rich agricultural region also turned to domestic manufacture. Formally, it can be shown that the propensity to develop a cottage industry, or in other words the share of household labour devoted to agriculture and manufacturing, respectively, depended not merely on the conditions ruling in agriculture, but on the relative marginal returns on both these occupations, taking into account prices, capital needs, and other similar factors.[89] Of particular importance here was the density of population. Given relatively favourable conditions for work in domestic manufacture by some members of rural families, it was rational for them to opt for it even in agricultural surplus areas.

Nevertheless, there was overwhelming evidence of the tendency of proto-industry, particularly the expanding, more up-to-date sections of it, to settle on marginal areas all over Europe. The European countryside, it has been said, was gradually separating out into 'two sorts of ecosystem and economy, one agricultural, the other protoindustrial, linked by trade': 'topography, soil, and precipitation . . . could give rise to one set of regions with comparative advantage in growing food crops and another where comparative advantage lay somewhere among the following options: pastoral husbandry, mining, lumbering, the export of labour as harvesters, domestic servants, construction workers, or mercenary troops, and cottage industry.' While, to quote another observer, 'agricultural production increased in the fertile valleys, domestic industrial production grew in the poorer districts'. As a consequence, much of western, central, and northern Europe appeared to be 'bifurcated' into 'good arable plains, and smaller regions of pastoralism, where peasants increasingly added rural domestic manufacturing for the market to their economic activities'. Looked at the other way, 'handicraft industry is not altogether haphazard, but is associated with certain types of farming community and certain kinds of social organization'. Evidence from many parts of continental Europe as well as Britain confirms the common assumption of a link between animal husbandry and rural domestic industry.[90]

In many regions, the factor favourable to the rise of domestic industry was indeed seen simply to consist in the poverty of the soil, or the difficulty of working it. In addition to the examples of Lancashire and Yorkshire noted above, such was said to have been the case in the Netherlands, where industry had shifted to the poorer agrarian outlying districts, in Sweden, Denmark, on virtually all German and French uplands, in Switzerland, Austria, eastern Europe, and the Balkans, among

[88] Kerridge (1985), 241; more generally, Coleman (1983), 441.

[89] Pfister (1992*a*); also Jones (1975), 340.

[90] Quotations from Jones (1977), 494; Schön (1982), 61; Emery (1973), 280; Thirsk (1961), 88; also Wrightson (1982), 127; Klima (1989), 511; Frost (1981), 30; Kussmaul (1990), 139–42; Collins (1978), 20; Husbands (1987), 345.

others.[91] An additional factor was often an exploitative landowning class which used its power to raise rents on poor land above the agricultural yield, for the purpose of forcing the peasantry to seek industrial employment.

The reverse could also be observed. It was because 'the Dutch were too rich'—on the basis of their flourishing agriculture in their central areas—to find domestic industrial employment attractive that such work was forced to settle among the poor, pastoral outlying lands. Similarly in Württemberg it was said that the peasants were doing so well as agriculturists in the nineteenth century that they saw no attraction in working in industry. There was practically no proto-industry to be found in the eastern Prussian provinces, either: everyone was fully employed in agriculture which afforded expanding employment with its expanding export market. Poor as they were, the people of the Norwegian coastlands were fully engaged in forestry and fishing, so that there, too, employment in textiles could not take a hold.[92]

In some marginal regions, it was not so much the poverty of the soil as such, but rather the specialization in animal husbandry which provided the drive for additional sources of income. Stockbreeding and dairying generally allowed more free time than arable cultivation, either seasonally or within the working day, for some or all family members to engage in proto-industrial employment. The seasonally available free labour is sometimes seen as 'underemployment'. In one considered view, 'rural industry's expansion depended generally upon the well-known phenomenon of agricultural underemployment, that expansion occurred especially where three conditions converged: access to an urban market, farming with considerable emphasis on herding rather than tillage, growing population.'[93] These elements were often connected. It was frequently the poverty of the soil, the upland steep slopes, or the harsh climate to be found in mountainous regions which prevented the cultivation of grain and forced the population to specialize in animal husbandry.

Access to the market and population growth will be discussed below; here we may note that the gaps in the working year might easily have been filled with other work, but domestic industry offered better returns. Where upland villages became snowed up for long periods in the winter, as in the Swiss Jura mountains where watchmaking flourished, in the French Alps or the Black Forest, making it impossible for the villagers to leave their settlements[94], natural conditions provided a particularly strong incentive to fill the enforced idle day with paid industrial work. In

[91] De Vries (1985), 669; Heckscher (1963), 172–3; Ahlberger (1988), 70–2; Kriedte *et al.* (1977), 40; Assenmacher (1990), 689; Ziekursch (1978), 137–8; Bein (1884), ii. 127; Bickel (1947), 52; Braun (1960), map on p. 57; Kellenbenz (1965), 423–4; Viazzo (1989), 188, 274; Millward (1984); Palairet (1983), 180; Houston and Snell (1984); Müller (1938), 205; Schremmer (1972), 21; Klima (1989), 510; Stromer (1986), 51 ff.; Köllmann (1974), 6; Bücher (1901), 172–3; Magnus (1897), 13; Ogden (1989), 124–7; Poitrineau (1986), 111; Kiesewetter (1980), 317–18.

[92] De Vries (1983), 167; Dipper (1989), 69; Megerle (1982), 215–21; Schremmer (1978); Bruland (1989), 29; Schissler (1978), 60.

[93] Tilly and Tilly (1971), 189.

[94] Pfleghart (1908), 20; Blache (1933), 81.

the prevailing stockbreeding system, the animals would have been driven into byres or other protected places, where the peasants could feed them and look after them in the snowy season without leaving the shelter of their farmsteads.

Much of this, as we have seen, applied to earlier centuries also. What distinguished the eighteenth century was the relentless increase of population in all parts of Europe, an increase for which the impetus was to be found in part in the technical, organizational, and structural changes of the age themselves. The pressure of a growing population would tend to accentuate the tendency for poor or pastoral areas to turn to proto-industry.[95]

It has sometimes been held that in a phase of growth of population, a particularly close link between partible inheritance and the spread of domestic industry existed in certain areas. The presumption is that the splitting of holdings into ever smaller units with the passing of the generations produces plots that are inadequate to feed a family and forces some members of it to make up the family income by industrial employment, unless they escape by emigration. This notion seems plausible by itself, but it does not follow that people living in areas in which primogeniture (or any other system of a single heir) prevails are under any less pressure to seek industrial incomes or emigration, given the same underlying population pressure, such that each generational cohort is larger than the one preceding it. In those conditions, under primogeniture, there will be people who have no land at all. They will have to hire themselves out as labourers, but since, by definition, there is not enough land to feed them all, some will be forced to turn to industry. They might well then become full-timers, ahead of the men and women of the partible inheritance regions. Inheritance systems by themselves are thus not as important a factor for the rise of cottage industry as the population increase itself.[96]

Other factors were also involved in the dynamic changes affecting the European economy, in which both the population increase and the improvements in technology played a part. One key element of this was the rising productivity on the land, which at times not only kept pace with the regional rising population, but actually ran ahead of it, to allow a country like Britain to produce a food surplus for export. These advantages were not, however, available everywhere to the same extent. In Britain, they favoured mostly the lowlands, and cheapened arable field products to the point at which formerly viable upland agriculture could no longer compete. Here was a specific reason for the dwellers in some marginal regions to have to turn to manufacturing.[97]

One particular difference between marginal areas and rich agricultural regions in these conditions deserves special attention. In the latter, there would generally be no free land available within the overcrowded villages on which the additional

[95] Hey (1972), 31; Bucher (1974), 108.

[96] Thirsk (1967), 10 ff.; Swain (1986), 205; Viazzo (1989), 188; Jones (1960–3), 118; Schremmer (1970), 358 ff. and (1972), 21 and (1979*c*), 7–9; Hudson (1986), 63–4; Appleby (1978), 53, 63. For a similar argument regarding emigration, see p. 84–5 above.

[97] Jones (1968) and (1977); also Mastboom (1994), 95.

families might settle. If there was any spare land, it would most likely be in the margins, on uplands, moors, marshes, or in forests. For those unwilling to leave the country, their only chance then was to settle on the waste there. In numerous instances, therefore, it was these marginal areas which attracted immigrants, some of whom even came out of rich arable cultivation areas. There they might find freedom to settle and possibly also other freedoms, but they would also find, almost by definition, that the land on which they were forced to settle would not feed them adequately. There existed thus a particular incentive for recent immigrants to marginal areas to seek industrial work. Conversely, a domestic industry, once successfully established on marginal land, might attract other immigrants to it.[98]

Needless to say, a proto-industrial region of this type could not flourish if it were too remote, and in particular, too distant from its markets, both for selling its products and for buying in the foodstuffs and necessary raw materials. Textile regions might have to maintain weekly contacts with the putting-out merchants, by means of urban agents riding round the villages, or alternatively by weavers, knitters, and spinners carrying their materials to and from the warehouse. Other products—such as watches, toys, or musical instruments—needed less frequent sales, yet even they, in the end, had to be within reach at some time in the year. Thus it was 'the more accessible uplands [which] proved especially hospitable to protoindustrial developments' in France, but also elsewhere.[99] One has only to read the graphic description of the difficulties which the West Riding weavers faced as late as the 1830s—setting out from their hillside homes with a wagon loaded with textiles to the town market in the snow in winter, having to start off in the dark, and easing the wagon down step by step until it reached the road in the valley bottom—[100] to appreciate the limitations imposed by geography on industrialists living on the margins.

While our main emphasis so far has been on the mountainous margins, there is much evidence, from all parts of Europe, that some forested areas too were highly successful in attracting proto-industrial activities.[101] An interesting example is furnished by the linen weavers of Silesia. Their needs for the bleaching process included grounds facing the sun, water, and fuel and potash from the forest. As they used up the local fuel supplies, they were gradually forced to follow the receding forests upward, while the deserted former wooded areas were ploughed up to become agricultural. It was a process which delighted the landlords owning what had previously been upland forest territory of little value, who were now able to charge the weavers 'protection money' (*Schutzgeld*) as well as 'handicraft rent' or 'weaver' or 'bleaching' rent, in place of the earlier feudal impositions.[102] Heaths and

[98] Kussmaul (1990), 147; Schremmer (1970), 370 ff.; Frost (1981), 32; Schläpfer (1984), 8; Ogden (1989), 135; Ziekursch (1978), 118, 135; Müller (1938), 70; Löhr (1971), 17; Niederer (1993), 212–13.

[99] Hohenberg and Lees (1985), 94, also 196; Dewerpe (1984), 899; Braun (1984), 123–4; Moch (1983), 202.

[100] Gaskell (1987), 66.

[101] Baltzarek (1979), 339; Götschmann (1985), 8–9; Kellenbenz (1965), 420.

[102] Ziekursch (1978), 110–11; Kisch (1959), 546–7; also Klima (1989), 520.

the sandy wastes known as 'landes' were other likely areas favourable to proto-industrial activity. Kellenbenz grouped all of them together: 'this type of industry', he noted, 'prospered in forested and mountainous areas and in the landes, where the yield from the land was insufficient to provide a living for the inhabitants. There, where animal husbandry predominated, people had more time to devote to a handicraft occupation.'[103]

In due course, many of these domestic industries which were vital for the survival of considerable concentrations of population in marginal areas found themselves in competition with factory-made goods. Some managed to adopt or even take a leading part in that novel form of industry, as had the textile industries of Lancashire and Yorkshire before them. Others survived by switching to more complex, artistic, or high-quality goods production which the machine could not as yet imitate. Many, however, succumbed to the superior competitive power of the lowland or urban factory. These regions became deindustrialized and a large proportion of their population was frequently forced to emigrate.[104] Once again, the good times for marginal areas proved to have been but temporary.

Despite some conspicuous exceptions, therefore, the major share of the more advanced type of industrial and commercial activity of the eighteenth century described as 'proto-industry' was concentrated in the marginal areas of Europe. It follows that if, as is generally believed, the Industrial Revolution for which the European economy was becoming ripe was to find it easiest to take root in regions with a flourishing proto-industry, it was likely to emerge first in marginal areas.

If Britain, for a variety of reasons, was destined to play a pioneer role in that process, it would be a British marginal region in which novel machinery and organization would first take root. Among the leading industries were cotton and woollen textiles: it was not at all surprising, but rather to be expected, that Lancashire and the West Riding of Yorkshire were among the first to take to the new system. The argument of the whole of this study may be summarized by saying that, having been placed in that position, the marginal regions were exceptionally well equipped to push it forward vigorously, to lead the rest of Europe to a significant extent and for a considerable period of time.

[103] Kellenbenz (1963), 875 (S. P. translation); also Hoskins (1955), 162.

[104] e.g. Baltzarek (1979), 339; Kriedte *et al.* (1977), 302; Marshall (1958), 56; Schremmer (1979*c*), 9; Kiesewetter (1988), 274; Müller (1938), 162.

PART III

Conclusion

11

Conclusion

In all historical writing a decision has to be made not merely on what to include, but also on what to leave out. The present volume is not a general economic history. Much of the substantial and fruitful debate on what constitutes, as well as what helps to promote economic progress has been taken for granted. Developments in science and technology, capital provision and company organization, class struggles and the emergence of new classes and social strata and much else besides are noted only if they impinge directly on our theme. That theme is located on the borderline between geography and economic history.

This study has set out to investigate two separate, though interrelated topics. One is a survey of the way in which contemporaries and historians have viewed European marginal areas lying north and east of the Alps, from the Middle Ages onward, and the peculiar structures and experiences of the societies living in them which marked them out from those living in areas surrounding them. The other is the leading or pioneer role played by areas of this kind in some of the most significant developments within the European economy within this period, and in the British Industrial Revolution in particular. This then raised the question whether the remarkable contributions of the marginal regions to economic progress made at certain crucial times were to be considered as purely accidental, or whether, on the contrary, they may be derived directly from their special attributes.

To have covered satisfactorily the larger part of Europe over many centuries would have required many volumes. There has had to be some selection, and in order to do this, the topic has been narrowed down in two ways. As far as its geographical dimension is concerned, the treatment in any depth has been limited to two areas: the Pennines together with the Anglo-Scottish borderlands, and the Swiss and Bavarian Alps; but data derived from all parts of central and northern Europe have been drawn on additionally as and when required. Secondly, rather than covering the whole period, a number of important episodes have been picked out to illustrate the general theme: these include the German colonization of eastern Europe in the Middle Ages, the role of the Cistercian monasteries in opening up wasteland, sixteenth-century mining and metallurgy, a number of other marginal areas in the seventeenth, eighteenth, and nineteenth centuries (rather more briefly), and the British Industrial Revolution with its focus on Lancashire and the West Riding of Yorkshire, together with a general survey of European proto-industrial regions over the same period.

There is an evident danger that anyone basing himself on a small selection of hand-picked and unrepresentative examples is likely to jump to unjustified conclusions. For one thing, the two upland areas selected for special attention, though enjoying the advantage of a large literature, were in their different ways unique, and it may well be that the resulting bias will not have been fully removed by the briefer references to other areas. Secondly, and more seriously, the historical episodes chosen as illustrations were those in which marginal areas emerged from obscurity because of the innovatory activity to be found in them, and they were therefore anything but typical for the long run of European history. They were, however, picked deliberately to illuminate the second of our themes: how, and under what conditions, marginal areas came to play a leading role in the rise of the European economy. The object, put differently, is not to show that marginal regions were always in the lead, still less to allege that the dynamic of European society never came from the central or 'core' areas, but rather to enquire whether it was a matter of surprise if major breakthroughs originated in the marginal zones, or whether, on the contrary, the factors which were found to have marked out their constitution were of a kind to make them likely to become fertile grounds for progressive initiatives.

Beyond these specific doubts regarding the choice of regions and episodes to receive detailed attention, there may be more general doubts regarding the approach of this study. They are listed in its early pages, and it behoves us to return to them at this stage in the light of the intervening chapters. To begin with the most obvious: is a regional approach justified for an economic and historical study of this kind? To this question a positive answer can be given without hesitation. The region, as such, as a subject for study in economic history, by now surely needs no defence: it has long since become a commonplace and exceedingly fruitful basis for investigating questions relating to our economic past.[1] As far as our particular topic—the marginal regions—is concerned, the case for a regional framework is, if possible, even stronger, not least because the whole of the vast literature ranging over all parts of Europe, relating to life on the margin, simply takes its relevance for granted. The concept of marginality, indeed, would clearly lose its validity if we were to deny the general proposition that there are regions which have significant properties in common and which distinguish them from neighbouring regions. The alternative scheme of dividing up the world into countries is no doubt useful for many purposes; but it would make no sense in the categories required here, particularly in view of the shifting frontiers, and the great changes in the character of the political structures subsumed under the term of 'countries' in the course of the centuries which this study seeks to cover.

Secondly: is the limitation to an area of Europe north and east of the Alps (with occasional excursions to the Balkans and the southern slopes of the Alps and the Pyrenees) justified in a study which attempts to investigate the historical develop-

[1] For good summaries, see Hudson (1989*b*), or the whole issue of the *Jahrbuch für Wirtschaftsgeschichte*, 1992/I.

ment and the role of marginal areas in general? There are studies in existence which cover the whole of the globe, and it would no doubt have been most interesting to compare Andean villages, Himalayan settlements, or societies existing in semi-desert conditions with our European experience. Yet, quite apart from the general problem that the wider the extensive coverage, the weaker its intensive treatment, there is the evident danger that differences of culture and history will greatly complicate the task of isolating out the characteristics of a society to be derived specifically from its life on the margin. While a study which took the whole world for its purview would thus be highly desirable from some points of view, though it would be beyond the personal limitations of this author, it does not follow that the present, more limited study, which enjoys the advantage of starting out with a population which was fairly homogeneous quite apart from its shared marginal characteristics, is without value of its own. It is for reasons of relative homogeneity that the Mediterranean regions have been excluded, though from some points of view it might no doubt have been wiser to incorporate them with the rest of Europe: our understanding of the origins and features of transhumance, for example, would have been much enriched by including the experience of the Iberian and the Italian peninsulas. Yet, taking it all in all, it seemed best, in order to ensure a degree of comparability, to limit geographical coverage to what in effect were the outer reaches of the Roman Empire and the territories beyond.

This brings us to the third, and most important area of doubt: is the 'marginal' existence of a region a reasonable category for isolating out its historical problems? Do marginal areas have enough in common, and are they sufficiently differentiated from 'core' regions, to impart recognizable qualities to them which derive specifically from their marginality, rather than from any other source? Further, even if we were to grant some specific properties to societies living, say, in uplands, do they have enough in common with those living in forests, and on marshes, to justify us in lumping them all together as 'marginal'? Differences between their environments are only too obvious. Are they possibly greater than their similarities?

There is the further problem that over much of Europe, and over much of the Continent's history in the past millennium, the margin has been a moving one. This has been particularly so in the case of forests, which still covered much of the land surface in AD 1000, but were systematically encroached on and pushed back thereafter. As any territory which changed from forest to ploughed fields ceased to be marginal, its population similarly took on a different character, and its social structure, and the form of its exploitation by members of the ruling classes, changed accordingly. Marshes, also, were drained in time, and often become fertile, core country. Mountains, on the other hand, are immovable: yet on mountains, too, the line of occupation could be moved, their forests cleared for settlement or pasture, or roads or railways built to make formerly inaccessible districts quite easy to reach, and possibly even become gainers from through traffic or as holiday resorts. There is, moreover, likely to be a significant difference between people living in areas which are, as it were, permanently marginal, and those living in territories in the

process of being transformed into part of the settled core. Beyond this is the general problem, neatly illustrated by the case of Manchester and its surroundings in their heyday in the nineteenth century, that a marginal area, if it succeeds in lifting itself to a leading position, by that very fact ceases to be marginal. Marginal areas, like treason in a famous couplet, are, it appears, never able to achieve success. The concept of marginality thus has a tendency to disappear as we approach it.

Moreover, the enormous technical and social changes of a thousand years of history naturally also affected the concepts and realities of marginality. So in the Middle Ages a marginal existence would designate almost complete isolation, while by the later nineteenth century the media and modern means of transport made communication with a marginal area or within it at most only slightly more complex or costly than elsewhere, but certainly removed much of the effect of distance. Again, the abundance or shortage of a particular natural resource might be decisive in earlier ages, but a substitution could usually be found without much difficulty in modern times. This may be generalized by stating that the regional differentiation of marginal areas was much greater in the past, and has steadily shrunk with the changes of the centuries. It still exists today, but is of a different nature, and much less dominant in determining the character of life on the margins than it used to be.

The issue which we have chosen thus opens out a series of major problems.[2] It has been part of the object of this book not to tackle these purely by abstract thoughts, but to work towards their solution by an alternative, inductive approach. There exists, after all, an enormous literature which takes the peculiarity of societies living in marginal areas for granted: can we possibly be justified in treating all of it as merely chasing a will-o'-the-wisp? It seemed to be a more useful undertaking to summarize, and try to make sense of, the extensive, mainly descriptive writing on the subject. More: the subject demands attention not merely because of the interest which it has aroused in the past, but because of its practical utility. Has a case been made out by the historical study presented here, that life on the margin is different, and that it is the very marginality of a region which helps to explain its distinctiveness? More accurately, has a case been made out that these areas, impoverished and handicapped though they usually are, do at times rise to play a significant, possibly even a key part in the economic progress of Europe and the world, not by accident, but precisely because of their special characteristics? The reader must judge for himself or herself on the basis of the historical evidence presented: it has been the object of this study to allow such a judgement to be made. Our own conclusions, which have emerged from the material presented in the preceding chapters, will be summarized in the remaining pages.

It cannot be denied that the populations inhabiting the marginal areas of Europe, as defined here, were as a rule poorer, less privileged, and less well endowed with the material goods which form the basis of economic well-being than the rest of their countrymen at any given point in time. On mountain areas in particular, climate,

[2] It is discussed further in Pollard (1995).

soil, and slope often combined to render agricultural conditions difficult and yields poor. On marshes, any form of cultivation might be impossible, and the same applied to forests. All would have difficulty and face high costs in reaching the main markets of their time.

Further, it would also be true to say that these societies were often technically less advanced, less well informed, and more backward both in their economic and in their social organization than core areas. They were widely believed to have been 'marginal, weak, alienated, provincial and backward. [Their] Innovations come late.'[3] It is not difficult to make out a case that innovations were more likely to be introduced, and their diffusion to be pushed forward more rapidly and more effectively in urban environments[4] than in the more isolated marginal regions of a country.

Faced, on mountains and in forests in particular, by inexplicable and often disastrous natural phenomena, and confronting them frequently alone and far from the comforting circle of a settled population, marginal people tended to be more superstitious and to retain their belief in magic longer than the more sophisticated dwellers of the plains. Whether they were also to be classified as less knowledgeable in general, or more ignorant, is rather more doubtful, since it depends on the definition of 'knowledge'. In terms of the formal education made available for the bulk of the population, marginal societies were, as we have seen, not necessarily less well instructed.

As for political and social influence, the periphery was, almost by definition, and almost universally, underprivileged and discriminated against. It usually lacked access to the centres of power, and those who made decisions or passed legislation would tend to give priority to interests closer at hand. If it did try to exert some influence, this generally proved more difficult and more costly to carry through than for those fortunate enough to live in the centre of things, and was likely to be less effective. Similarly, marginal areas were, because of their remoteness, as a rule less able to influence their markets. Where a marginal area coincided with a frontier territory, as it often did, it might be subject to periodic harassment by the enemy while having to bear more than its share of the cost of the country's defence.

These initial disadvantages would tend to reinforce each other in a cumulative manner: 'the problems of the outlying areas were exacerbated, their disadvantages multiplied'[5] precisely by the factors which helped the more favourably placed areas to prosper. Those who wanted to escape the hampering conditions of their existence on the margins had no option but to emigrate. Emigration was a common feature of marginal areas, and may be taken as a proof of their less desirable environment.

Based on these real or perceived weaknesses imposed by their marginality, negative judgements on the dwellers in marginal areas were, as we have seen, common

[3] Strassoldo (1980), 52. [4] e.g. Lepetit and Hoock (1987).

[5] Richards (1993), 205; also (1988), 194 and (1982), 411.

among contemporaries. Some of these were informed by sympathy for the difficult environment in which the men and women on the margins had to spend their lives. Most of them, however, were rooted in prejudice and it was prejudice of a kind that arises from ignorance and fear of the strange and the different, rather than from knowledge and understanding. Commonly the inhabitants of forests, marshes, and mountains were classified as uncouth, dangerous, and barbarous. Where they were not viewed with contempt as being inferior, they were feared as being violent, lawless, and devoid of the finer feelings distinguishing the best of humanity. It was little help to their reputation that in fact they were not given the chance fully to benefit from the ministrations of religion, or the efforts of the schoolmaster, or by the application of the law, while their own framework of mores and regulation of social behaviour were either ignored or misunderstood and derided. In consequence, when they ventured into the world of the plains, the people from the margins were treated with disdain, prejudice, and unfairness, and they were liable to be exploited if they proved useful, and expelled if they did not.

Yet we are faced by the fact that they had their moments of glory in history. In some ways, at some times, they ceased to be outsiders and, at least for a brief period, were at the heart, or, as it has been termed, at the 'cutting edge'[6] of economic progress, becoming, at critical times, 'poles of development' and 'autonomous centres of decision-making'.[7] We are therefore driven to wonder whether their environment, or their social behaviour, was necessarily as inferior as it was believed to have been.

Among their advantages was commonly the possession of valuable natural resources: minerals were most frequently found in mountainous regions, often because the lie of the land made them more accessible, or at least drew attention to them earlier. Once discovered, mines were more easily worked, in part because they could be drained by gravity through soughs or adits without costly machinery, and partly because the surface land was of little value and access to it was granted eagerly by landlords in the hope of deriving a substantial revenue from the activity of miners. Mountains also usually had water-power, and land on the banks of streams was cheaper and was rented out more freely in marginal areas. Upland moors and rough grazing nearby might add large areas to the village lands to carry larger herds or flocks, producing meat, dairy products, or wool where arable lands were limited. There were also frequently substantial forests on mountain slopes, since the drive to cut down trees to make room for agriculture was commonly halted before rising ground. Timber also constituted the wealth of forest regions, to be used as fuel and as building material, for supplying potash, or bark for tanning, and for numerous other purposes. Fens and marshes had reeds, fish, wildfowl and well-watered meadows, among other resources.

The value of all these varied with current technology and the structure and capabilities of the communities living on the margins. The resources had always been

[6] Cole and Wolf (1974), 48. [7] Bergier (1988), 28.

there: their exploitation, tentative and sporadic before the tenth century, expanded steadily and systematically thereafter, as population pressure increased and technical innovation opened up new opportunities. But it is not merely social change which acted on the resources: it is important to bear in mind that in the process of the expansion of the European economy, resources also acted on society. Their availability called forth efforts to exploit them, and the technical gain of each stage made possible the advance to the next one. Solutions are most commonly found where desirable ends are almost, but not quite, attainable. This was eminently so in mining where, typically, ores might be suspected, or even seen, if only difficulties of pumping or hauling could be overcome, and they acted as a powerful spur to find methods of overcoming them; but it was true also of finding methods to preserve the freshness of products in upland dairying, of clearing woodland, and of many other activities. The important thing was that it was frequently in marginal areas, where conditions might be less favourable and needed conscious adaptation to reach the kind of results which were achieved more easily in the open plains, that this stimulus to innovation existed.

Almost by definition, the dwellers in marginal areas were unable to grow sufficient bread grain, their main food, to feed themselves from their own soil: unlike the happier communities in territories of mixed agriculture, they therefore had to trade to survive. It was, in some ways, their very disadvantages which forced them to be dependent on outside links in what has been termed, somewhat confusingly, 'parochial cosmopolitanism'.[8] Their enforced specialization on such tradable commodities as animal products, minerals, timber products or textiles, among others, having to be exchanged for foodstuffs, tended to create a class of trading entrepreneurs who could provide the initiative and commercial know-how for advancing to higher stages of development, besides channelling capital from the centre to the periphery. These contacts spread knowledge of conditions outside their own territories among entrepreneurs. Among other classes, wider horizons were fostered by the widespread need to seek temporary jobs outside their villages at certain seasons, including driving their cattle into the cities, or hiring themselves out as domestic servants or mercenaries. In the same way the colonists who at different times followed the call to greater freedom and wider opportunities, such as the settlers on the moving eastern frontier of Germany in the Middle Ages, developed less cramped views, and were more willing to experiment, than their kindred who stayed behind. Few can doubt that individuals who have travelled are more likely to embrace innovations than those who have never left their own hearths.

There were, to be sure, some generic differences between the three types of marginal lands discussed in this volume—mountains, forests, and marshes. In broad general terms it may be said that marshes scored on grounds of abundant food resources except for grain, they disposed of good transport after canalization, and

[8] Hohenberg and Lees (1985), 241. Kussmaul stresses the opposite, namely, that villagers in marginal areas were distinguished by their household self-sufficiency, Kussmaul (1990), 116–17.

they taught the people dwelling in them the skills of collaboration and the techniques of controlling their environment; forests offered a rich supply of raw materials and some protection, but tended to suffer from poor transport facilities and limited food supplies; while mountains had minerals, water, and (sometimes) timber, good grazing grounds and certain strategic advantages, and they bred a hardy race of self-sufficient people, but also possessed a harsh climate and poor soil, and they contained many obstacles to transport.

There were also some chronological differences of impact. With some simplification, we may note that in the Middle Ages it was forests which offered the greatest opportunities to enterprising men, their advantages declining with time. In the early modern period it was marshy territories, above all in the north-west of Europe, which seemed to succeed, not least because their water-borne economy formed the best springboard for societies who wished to take advantage of maritime trade and commercial capitalism, which were at the forefront of progress at the time. In the modern age it was the resources and characteristics of upland societies which tended to make most of the running, though in no phase were these advantages and drawbacks exclusive to one or other type of marginal territory.

No doubt circumstances affect individuals and their reaction to their environment. But can the kind of territory which they inhabit also be said to affect the qualities of societies, as if they were individuals?

We are on dangerous ground here. Do societies have characters, or dominant characteristics? Racism or ethnic prejudice have often enough been proved wrong. The English, for example, had the no doubt deserved reputation in the first Elizabethan age of being colourful, pleasure seeking, open to artistic stimuli. This was reversed under the rule of the Puritans, revived under the Restoration and (jumping the intervening period), converted to its very opposite in Victorian Britain which was generally described as dour, buttoned-up, taking both its work and its pleasures seriously, moralistic, but commercially pushful and industrially innovative. Post-war Britain, and the 'swinging London' of the recent period, in particular, have completely reversed all these once again. Similarly, the Germans of the early nineteenth century were still viewed as an ineffectual society of 'poets and thinkers', of pedantic professors and conservative bureaucrats; half a century later they were known to be ruthless militarists, efficient industrialists, and determined imperialists. National societies, it seems, have no inborn characteristics. Yet this does not mean that, at any given time, in given circumstances, there may not be a set of induced attitudes which amount to a distinct societal personality or character. May the peculiar environment of marginal regions have affected, and shaped the character, not merely of some individuals, but of whole societies in a discernible way?

There is certainly no lack of positive opinion in the literature on the 'influence of landscape on the character of men. We may wonder why, for example, the warriors and visionaries of the ages are invariably of the mountains, the merchants and scholars of the plain, why the Scots dance and the Welsh sing, why [somewhat

startlingly] so many mountain people, in Savoy and Lombardy, as in Scotland, have red hair.'[9] From Aristotle to Montesquieu, thinkers have taken for granted the influence of environment on politics and society. Thus, to take an example at random, few would object to the kind of thinking which derived the relatively advanced technology applied to the English Fens in the Middle Ages from 'the habits, customs, laws, traditions and sentiments . . . of this peculiar race, the Fenmen'.[10]

We may well believe that 'by itself geography explains nothing. Historical events, including specific technological innovations, are needed to put site or location to given uses. Yet geography may not be altogether dismissed.'[11] The question is always how to combine the two. Where the effect of environment on the character of marginal societies is concerned, there frequently occurs a subtle shift in the argument from the assured to the dubious. To state that people learn from their environment is probably uncontroversial: thus the mountain dweller will have an eye where the richest pastures on the alp may be found. From there it is a short step to the notion that individuals adapt to their environment: people living on the margins are more self-reliant, and they may have become so, either because they have learnt by experience, or because there is a process of the survival of the fittest at work. The next step would be to argue that based on the adaptation of individuals, societies also have to adapt: marginal settlements develop stronger family loyalties, are more martial, are more likely to embrace extreme or superstitious forms of religion. Finally, the necessities of the terrain may be said to affect social structure and influence a society's psychological characteristics: 'custom turns into nature', 'habits become natural'. Another observed sequence might be that geography will determine social forms, these influence social values and these, in turn, affect individual behaviour.[12] The conclusion does not necessarily follow from the premisses, yet the notion of the final stage of the argument—that some types of society such as marginal societies have a nature, a personality, or a character of their own—has been repeatedly taken for granted and accepted as valid in practical affairs.

People living on marginal lands have frequently been described as hardy, tough, resilient, undeterred by adversity. They tend to be adventurous, full of initiative, alert as well as inventive. So are their societies: 'there can be great energy and creative tension in perimeters, margins and intersections',[13] and that is so precisely because they are marginal, because of the environment which marginal lands provide for them.

Their environment has taught them to be modest in their demands, to live frugally and to spurn luxury and excess. Moralists frequently extolled those virtues, comparing favourably the qualities of dwellers on mountains or in remote forests and marshes with the hedonism and self-indulgence of city dwellers and of the people of

[9] Armstrong (1960), 27.
[10] Hallam (1965), 201; also e.g. Barber (1974), 79; Kennedy (1987), 21.
[11] Jones (1987), p. xxvii. [12] Bartlett (1982), 192, also 196; Womack (1989), 35.
[13] Musgrove (1990), 51.

the plains. People living on the margins, though materially poorer, were morally superior: 'virtues . . . [are] nourished by hard times.'[14] Their frugality also meant that wages were low, and costs could be kept down. Temporary migrants from the margins who hired themselves out as harvesters in the agricultural regions, or as building and service workers in the towns, accepted conditions which others would have spurned.

Yet these people were not unskilled. Their formal education—because of their religion, of smaller village classes, of enforced winter idleness or the greater emphasis which outsiders always place on education for their children—was not infrequently superior to that of the population living in 'core' areas. The handicraft skills of those engaged in specific trades, it is true, were normally lacking, but survival on the margins needed a range of other skills which were not always fully valued by townsfolk. Those who lived in marginal areas were frequently dependent on their own resources, and had to be able to turn a hand to many things. It was, in fact, the absence of narrow specialization which tended to make marginal society comparatively flexible and enterprising.

In addition to these advantages based on an assembly of individual characteristics, there were also social advantages enjoyed on the margins. For example, marginal lands benefited by the freedom from guild control: time and again, but especially in the early modern period, it turned out to be a sizeable advantage for the advancement of manufacturing in the margins to have escaped the dead hand of the guild system, so that 'it was . . . always more likely that radical changes of direction or adaptation would occur at the margin'.[15] This may be viewed as a particular example of the common rule that institutions which represent progress at their birth, as did the medieval guild, sooner or later turn into obstacles to progress, not least because they become ossified: similarly, regions badly placed to prosper in one age may, with changed circumstances, be propelled into the lead in another.

Being outside the traditional guild structure was, however, only one of the advantages which allowed marginal areas to be, from time to time, in the forefront of progress. Possibly more important still was the fact that the population of the margins was less likely to suffer tight political control from outside. Exploitation by feudal lord or church dignitary was kept to a minimum or shaken off completely early on; the people on margins, in forests and marshes, but above all in the uplands, gained personal freedom and rights of self-determination well ahead of the rest of Europe. The explanation for that freedom hinges, appropriately enough, on the collaborative effect of environment and personal or social qualities: these areas were difficult to conquer both because of the nature of the terrain and because of the martial skills and the resolution of their fighting men, and the two are not unconnected with each other.

Given this range of advantages, there were various ways in which the dwellers in the margins might take the lead or point the way forward in the history of Europe

[14] Womack (1989), 168. [15] Dodgshon (1987), 261, 262.

since the Middle Ages. The German colonization of the East attracted enterprising spirits and gave them wider freedoms and privileges, as well as more land than was available elsewhere. The Cistercian monasteries happened to combine, for a critical fertile period, a social organization of educated, self-assured men and their desire to settle on empty lands. The mines of central Europe in the fifteenth and sixteenth centuries had their hour of glory when European developments cried out for precious metals and other minerals, and technology had reached a level, and was encouraged to develop from it, to make the ore finds accessible, given sufficient energy and capital resources. In the following two centuries, other marginal areas came to enjoy temporary relative advantages, well into the phase of advanced 'proto-industry'. It was out of such areas that the most decisive economic break-through, the Industrial Revolution, was to emerge to take its triumphal course across the Continent.

Thus it was in no way paradoxical that occasions were seen to arise when the periphery led the centre, and the last turned out to be first: underdeveloped regions took the lead, in a kind of 'polarization reversal'.[16] The Flanders of the eleventh century, for example, was 'very much a frontier territory', 'a poor and dangerous no-man's land, unable to feed its burghers and unruly farmers except by massive imports'.[17] Yet, before long, it became the hub of north-western Europe and arguably a focal centre of economic progress of the age. Some centuries later, the northern Netherlands, water-logged, isolated, far from the political power centre though they were, became in their turn the pacemakers of the modernization of the European economy. Revolutionizing practices in agriculture and industry, in drainage and canalization, in commerce and shipping, for over a century they dominated European trade, finance, and colonization to a most striking extent for so small a country. Similarly, 'England began as a marginal and colonial country, lying off a continent populated by more powerful neighbours, wealthier and equipped with more elaborate institutions than its own.' 'From the fifteenth century to 1688, England and Wales, like Scotland, had been peripheral kingdoms in the European power game'; 'Britain was not only geographically peripheral, but also marginal in economic, technological and cultural developments.'[18] Yet she was on the threshold of a rise that would lead her to an economic pioneering role and a dominance that lasted a century and a half. These were major regions or whole countries, respectively, which took an economic lead on emerging from what appeared to be obscurity and poor natural endowments. *Mutatis mutandis*, similar role reversals could be found in more circumscribed marginal regions also.

We stated at the beginning that, instead of engaging in theoretical discussion, we would let the evidence speak for itself. The evidence collected in this volume is surely overwhelming that the margin, generally pitied or despised, could be, at

[16] Rauch (1984), 211; Verlinden (1983). [17] Nicholas (1991), 29, 33.
[18] Wolf (1990), 123; Colley (1984), 53; Glennie (1990), 199; and p. 10 above.

times, ahead of the rest, at the cutting edge of economic and social advance; and that there were good reasons, in the internal resources and social make-up of those regions, why this should have been so.

Yet margins, in the end, remained margins. Society gave them little thanks for their contribution, no matter how vital it had been. Their historic task performed, they tended to subside again into relative poverty and unaltered powerlessness. The centre might be eclipsed temporarily, but it would always reassert itself in the long run.

BIBLIOGRAPHY

ABBREVIATIONS

AgHist.	*Agricultural History*
AgHR	*Agricultural History Review*
Annales ESC	*Annales: Économies, Sociétés, Civilisations*
Antiq.	*Antiquarian*
Bull.Inst.HR	*Bulletin of the Institute of Historical Research*
BusH	*Business History*
CEHE	*Cambridge Economic History of Europe*
Comp.St.S&H	*Comparative Studies in Society and History*
DAJ	*Derbyshire Archaeological Journal*
DAS	*Derbyshire Archaeological Society*
EcHR	*Economic History Review*
EHR	*English Historical Review*
Expl. EcH	*Explorations in Economic History*
Hist.	*History*
J.	*Journal*
Jb.	*Jahrbuch*
JDA&NHS	*Journal of the Derbyshire Archaeological and Natural History Society*
JEcH	*Journal of Economic History*
JEEcH	*Journal of European Economic History*
J.Hist.G	*Journal of Historical Geography*
JPE	*Journal of Political Economy*
P&P	*Past and Present*
Rev.	*Review*
Soc.	*Society*
ScEHR	*Scandinavian Economic History Review*
SZG	*Schweizerische Zeitschrift für Geschichte*
Trans.	*Transactions*
TC&WAAS	*Transactions of the Cumberland and Westmorland Archaeological and Antiquarian Society*
T.Hist.SL&C	*Transactions of the Historic Society of Lancashire and Cheshire*
TL&CAS	*Transactions of the Lancashire and Cheshire Antiquarian Society*
TRHS	*Transactions of the Royal Historical Society*
VCH	*Victoria County History*
VSWG	*Vierteljahrschrift für Sozial- und Wirtschaftsgeschichte*
YAJ	*Yorkshire Archaeological Journal*

UNPUBLISHED MATERIAL

(a) Archives

Bavarian State Archive
Ministerium des Handels,

MH119, 126, 135, 137, 141, 176, 190, 216, 225, 251
Calderdale Archives
Ashworth Diaries 1782–1816, HAS 300–303
Cumberland Record Office
Lonsdale MSS, Surveys D/LONS/L8
Northumberland Record Office
Census of Population, Reels 24 and 25
Northumberland Parish Records
North Yorkshire Record Office
Parish Register: Arkengarthdale

(b) Theses

Arnold, Philip, 'Verarmung und Rückständigkeit in der Urner Markgenossenschaft (1. Hälfte des 19. Jahrhunderts)', Liz. thesis (Zurich, 1989).

Beckett, J. V., 'Landownership in Cumbria *c.*1680–*c.*1750', Ph.D. thesis (Lancaster, 1975).

Burgess, John, 'Methodism in Cumbria', M.Litt. thesis (Durham, 1979).

Burgess, John, 'A Religious History of Cumbria 1780–1920', Ph.D. thesis (Sheffield, 1984).

Clark, M. A., 'The Reformation in the Lake Counties', Ph.D. thesis (CNAA-Trinity College, Bristol, 1990).

Dilley, R. S., 'Agricultural Change and Common Land in Cumberland 1700–1850', Ph.D. thesis (McMaster, 1991).

Dixon, P. J., 'The Deserted Medieval Villages of North Northumberland', Ph.D. thesis (Wales, 1984).

Eyre, S. P., 'A Consideration of the Factors Limiting Land Improvement on the Upland East of the River Derwent', Ph.D. thesis (Sheffield, 1954).

Giger-Eschke, P., 'Kommunalpolitik Zürichs im 18. Jahrhundert', Liz. thesis (Zurich, 1985).

Goodman, K. W. G., 'The Land, People and Industry of the Titterstone Clee Hill Area of Shropshire from the Sixteenth to the Eighteenth Centuries', Ph.D. thesis (Keele, 1978).

Harrison, S. M., 'The Pilgrimage of Grace in the Lake Counties, 1536–7', M.Litt. thesis (Lancaster, 1975).

Heaney, C. P., 'The Development of the Peak District Village and the Influence of Lead Mining', B.Arch. dissertation (Nottingham, 1982).

Hopkinson, G. G., 'The Development of Lead Mining and of the Coal and Iron Industries in Northern Derbyshire and South Yorkshire 1700–1800', Ph.D. thesis (Sheffield, 1958).

Humphries, A. B., 'Agrarian Change in East Cumberland 1750–1900', M.Phil. thesis (Lancaster, 1993).

Kälin, Urs, 'Aspekte von Macht und Herrschaft in der Landsgemeindedemokratie: Zum Regierungs- und Lebensstil der Urner Magistratsfamilien 1803–1847', Liz. thesis (Zurich, 1985).

Kenworthy, P. F., 'Rural Settlement: East Cheshire', MA thesis (Manchester, 1949).

Knowles, Paul, 'Change and Development in Victorian Britain: The Case of Two Derbyshire Peakland Settlements, Youlgrave and Bakewell', BA dissertation (Newcastle upon Tyne, 1990).

Lazenby, Walter, 'The Social and Economic History of Styal 1750–1850', MA thesis (Manchester, 1949).

McCall, M. R., 'Welldressing in Tideswell: The Derbyshire Tradition', MA thesis (Leeds, 1976).

Malmgreen, Gail, 'Economy and Culture in an Industrialising Town: Macclesfield, Cheshire, 1750–1835', Ph.D. thesis (Indiana, 1981).

Rowley, R. T., 'The History of the South Shropshire Landscape 1086–1800', B.Litt. thesis (Oxford, 1967).

Ruckstuhl, Viktor, 'Aufbruch wider die Türken: Ein ungewöhnlicher Solddienst am Ende des 17. Jahrhunderts', Liz. thesis (Zurich, 1990).
Searle, C. E., '"The Odd Corner of England": A Study of a Rural Social Formation in Transition, Cumbria *c.*1700–*c.*1914', Ph.D. thesis (Essex, 1983).
Smail, John, 'From the Middling to the Middle: Class Formation in the Century Before the Industrial Revolution', Ph.D. thesis (Stanford, 1988).
Trocmé, Claire, 'Well Dressing: An Example of Water-Folklore in the Peak District', MA thesis (Strasburg, 1977).
Winchester, Angus, 'Agrarian Organisation in Copeland 1200–1600', Ph.D. thesis (Durham, 1978).
Wrathmell, Stuart, 'Deserted or Shrunken Villages in Southern Northumberland from the Twelfth to the Twentieth Centuries', Ph.D. thesis (Wales, 1975).

PRINTED BOOKS AND ARTICLES

(Place of publication is London unless otherwise specified)

Aarebrot (1982), F. A., 'Norway: Center and Periphery in a Peripheral State', in Rokkan and Urwin (1982*a*), 75–111.
Abel (1943[1], 1955[2]), W., *Die Wüstungen des ausgehenden Mittelalters* (Stuttgart).
Abel (1966[2]), W., *Agrarkrisen und Agrarkonjunktur* (Hamburg/Berlin).
Adamson (1970), D. A., 'The Hearth Tax', *Trans. Dumfries and Galloway Natural Hist. and Antiq. Soc.* 47 (1970), 147–77.
Advusin (1989), D. A., 'Rivers, Forests and Settlement Patterns of the Eastern Slavs between the 6th and the 9th Centuries', in Bergier (1989*a*), 135–46.
Agricola (1950), G., *De re metallica*, ed. H. C. and L. H. Hoover (New York).
Ahlberger (1988), C., 'Pauperization or Proletarization?', in M. Mörner, and T. Svenson (eds.), *Classes, Strata and Elites* (Göteborg), 69–82.
Aikin (1795), J., *Description of the Country from thirty to forty Miles round Manchester* (London).
Aitchison (1960), L., *A History of Metals*, ii.
Alapuro (1982), R., 'Finland: An Interface Periphery?', in Rokkan and Urwin (1982*a*), 113–64.
Albion (1926), R. G., *Forests and Seapower* (Cambridge, Mass.).
Ambrosiani (1985), B., 'Specialization and Urbanization in the Mälar Valley—a Question of Maturity', in Lindquist, 103–12.
Amman (1959), H., 'Die Bedeutung der südtiroler Notare für die Wirtschaftsgeschichte', in Troger and Zwanowetz, 1–19.
Amstadt (1969), J., *Die k.k. Militärgrenze 1522–1881* (Würzburg).
Anderson, G. M., Ekelund, R. B., Jr., Hebert, R. F., and Tollison, R. D. (1992), 'An Economic Interpretation of the Medieval Crusades', *JEEcH* 21, 339–63.
Anderson (1968[2]), J., *Observations on the Means of Exciting a Spirit of National Industry … of Scotland* (New York).
Andreae (1952), S. J. F., 'Embanking and Drainage Authorities in the Netherlands during the Middle Ages', *Speculum* 27, 158–67.
Anonymous (1874), 'Notes on the State of Religion in the Border Country', *TC&WAAS* 1, 81–5.
Appleby (1978), A. B., *Famine in Tudor and Stuart England* (Stanford).
Arbman (1961[2]), H., *The Vikings.*
Armstrong (1883), R. B., *The History of Liddesdale*, i (Edinburgh).
Armstrong (1911), R., *The Peel Towers of the Scottish Border* (Galashiels).
Armstrong (1960), W. A., *The Armstrong Borderland* (Galashiels).

Ashcroft (1984), M. Y. (ed.), *Documents Relating to the Swaledale Estate of Lord Wharton in the Sixteenth and Seventeenth Centuries* (Northallerton).

Asheim (1988), B. T., 'Peripheral Industrialisation and Capitalist Development', in Linge (1988*a*), 53–71.

Ashmore (1963–4), O., 'Low Moor, Clitheroe', *TL&CAS* 73/4, 124–52.

Ashmore (1977), O., *Historic Industries of Marple and Mellor* (Stockport).

Ashmore (1982), O., *The Industrial Archaeology of North-West England* (Manchester).

Ashtor (1989), E., 'The Factors of Technological and Industrial Progress in the Later Middle Ages', *JEEcH* 18, 7–36.

Aspin (1969), C., *Lancashire: The First Industrial Society* (Helmshore).

Aspin (1972), C. (ed.), *Manchester and the Textile Districts in 1849* (Helmshore).

Assenmacher (1990), M., 'Family Division of Labour and the Economic Status of Women in the Process of Industrialization', *JEEcH* 19, 687–96.

Åström (1975), S.-E. 'Technology and Timber Exports from the Gulf of Finland, 1661–1740', *ScEHR* 23, 1–23.

Åström (1978), S.-E., 'Foreign Trade and Forest Use in Northeastern Europe 1660–1860', in Maczak and Parker, 43–64.

Åström (1981), S.-E., 'North European Timber Exports to Great Britain', in P. L. Cottrell, and D. H. Aldcroft (eds.), *Shipping, Trade and Commerce* (Leicester), 81–97.

Åström (1983), S.-E., 'Commercial and Industrial Development in the Baltic Region in Relation to the Other Areas of Europe', in Guarducci, 435–53.

Athill (1976*a*), R. (ed.), *Mendip: A New Study* (Newton Abbot).

Athill (1976*b*), R., 'Industry', in Athill (1976*a*), 145–79.

Atkin (1954), C. W., 'Herefordshire', in Darby and Terrett, 57–64.

Atkinson (1987²), J. C., *Forty Years in a Moorland Parish* (Otley).

Åttman (1981), A., 'The Russian Market in World Trade, 1500–1860', *ScEHR* 29, 177–202.

Aubin (1939), H., *Zur Erforschung der deutschen Ostsiedlung* (Leipzig).

Aubin (1971²), H., 'The Land East of the Elbe and Colonization Eastwards', *CEHE* i. 449–86.

Aubin (1928¹, 1973²), H., 'Wirtschaftsgeschichtliche Bemerkungen zur ostdeutschen Kolonisation', in *Sozial- und Wirtschaftsgeschiche: Gedächtnisschrift für Georg von Below* (Aalen), 169–96.

Austin (1990), D., 'Medieval Settlement in the North-East of England', in Vyner, 141–50.

Austin (1973), M. R., 'Religion and Society in Derbyshire during the Industrial Revolution', *DAS* 93, 75–89.

Awty (1977), B. G., 'Force Forge in the Seventeenth Century', *TC&WAAS* 77, 97–112.

Awty (1981), B. G., 'The Continental Origins of Wealden Ironworks 1451–1544', *EcHR* 34, 524–39.

Bagwell (1988²), P. S., *The Transport Revolution 1770–1985.*

Bailey, J., and Culley, G. (1813), *General View of the Agriculture of the County of Cumberland.*

Bailey (1989*a*), M., *A Marginal Economy? East Anglian Breckland in the Middle Ages* (Cambridge).

Bailey (1989*b*), M., 'The Concept of Margin in the Medieval English Economy', *EcHR* 42, 1–17.

Bailey (1991), M., 'Per impetuum maris: Natural Disaster and Economic Decline in Eastern England, 1275–1350', in Campbell (1991*a*), 184–208.

Bain (1894), J., *The Border Papers*, i, *1560–1594* (Edinburgh); (1896), ii, *1595–1603.*

Bainbridge (1947), T. H., 'Eighteenth-century Agriculture in Cumbria', *TC&WAAS* 48, 56–66.

Baines (1991), D., *Emigration from Europe 1815–1930.*

Baines (1966²), E., Jr., *History of the Cotton Manufacture in Great Britain.*

Baines, T., and Fairbairn, W. (1869), *Lancashire and Cheshire, Past and Present* (4 vols.).

Bairoch (1981), P., 'Urbanisation and Economic Development in the Western World', in Schmal, 61–75.

Bairoch (1988), P., *Cities and Economic Development, from the Dawn of History to the Present* (Chicago).

Bairoch (1989), P., 'Urbanization and the Economy in Preindustrial Societies', *JEEcH* 18, 239–90.

Baker (1966), A. R. H., 'Evidence in the "Nonarum Inquisitiones" of Contracting Arable Lands in England during the Early Fourteenth Century', *EcHR* 19, 518–32.

Baker (1973*a*), A. R. H., 'Changes in the Later Middle Ages', in Darby (1973*a*), 186–247.

Baker (1973*b*), A. R. H., 'Field Systems in South-East England', in Baker and Butlin, 377–429.

Baker, A. R. H., and Butlin, R. A. (eds.) (1973), *Studies of Field Systems in the British Isles* (Cambridge).

Baldwin, J., and Whyte, I. D. (1973), *The Scandinavians in Cumbria.*

Baltzarek (1979), F., 'Zu den regionalen Ansätzen der frühen Industrialisierung in Europa', in H. Knittler (ed.), *Wirtschafts- und Sozialhistorische Beiträge* (Vienna), 334–55.

Barahona (1983), R., 'Basque Regionalism and Centre–Periphery Relations', *European Studies Review* 13, 271–95.

Barber (1974), B. R., *The Death of Communal Liberty: A History of Freedom in a Swiss Mountain Canton* (Princeton).

Barbour (1930), V., 'Dutch and English Merchant Shipping in the 17th Century', *EcHR* 2, 261–90.

Baring (1901), F., 'The Making of the New Forest', *EHR* 16, 427–38.

Barrière (1983), B., 'L'économie cistercienne du sud-ouest de la France', in Flaran, 75–99.

Barrière (1990), B., 'Les problèmes économiques d'une communauté cistercienne double: le cas d'Obazine-Coyroux XIIe-XVIIIe siècles', *Annales du Midi* 102, 149–59.

Barrow (1969), G. W. S., 'Northern English Society in the Twelfth and Thirteenth Centuries', *Northern History* 4, 1–28.

Barrow (1973), G. W. S., *The Kingdom of the Scots.*

Barta, G., and Dingsdale, A. (1988), 'Impacts of Change in Industrial Company Organisations in Peripheral Regions', in Linge (1988*a*), 165–83.

Bartels (1992), C., *Vom frühzeitlichen Montangewerbe Zur Bergbauindustrie* (Bochum).

Bartlett (1982), R., *Gerald of Wales 1146–1223* (Oxford).

Barton (1967), D. B., *Tin Mining and Smelting in Cornwall* (Truro).

Bätzing (1991), W., *Die Alpen* (Munich).

Baxter (1913), W., 'The Granges of Holme Cultram', *TC&WAAS* 14, 274–80.

Bazeley (1901), M. L., 'The Extent of the English Forest in the Thirteenth Century', *TRHS* 4th ser. 4, 140–72.

Bean (1958), J. M. W., *The Estates of the Percy Family 1416–1537.*

Bean (1963), J. M. W., 'Plague, Population and Economic Decline in England in the later Middle Ages', *EcHR* 15, 423–37.

Beaver, P. D., and Purrington, B. L. (eds.) (1982), *Cultural Adaptation to Mountain Environment* (Atlanta).

Beckett (1982), J. V., 'The Decline of the Small Landowner in Eighteenth- and Nineteenth-Century England: Some Regional Considerations', *AgHR* 30, 97–111.

Beckett (1990), J. V., *The Agricultural Revolution* (Oxford).

Bein (1884), L., *Die Industrie des sächsischen Voigtlandes* (2 vols., Leipzig).

Beinart, W., and Coates, P. (1995), *Environment and History: The Taming of Nature in the USA and South Africa* (London and New York).

Bekker-Nielsen (1989), T., 'Rivers and Urban Development in Roman Gaul', in Bergier (1989*a*), 111–22.

Bentley (1970[2]), P., *The Pennine Weaver from the Earliest Times to the Present Day* (Bath).

Beresford (1954[1], 1965[2]), M., *The Lost Villages of England.*

Beresford (1967), M., *New Towns of the Middle Ages.*

Beresford (1971), M., 'A Record of Historical Research', in M. Beresford and J. G. Hurst, (eds.), *Deserted Medieval Villages* (New York), 3–75.

Berg (1985), M., *The Age of Manufactures.*

Berg (1991*a*), M. (ed.), *Markets and Manufacture in Early Industrial Europe.*

Berg (1991*b*), M., 'Markets, Trade and European Manufacture', in Berg (1991*a*), 3–26.

Berg (1991*c*), M., 'Commerce and Creativity in Eighteenth-Century Birmingham', in Berg (1991*a*), 173–201.

Berghoff (1994), H., 'Industrialisierung im ländlichen Raum', in Tuttlinger Geschichtsverein, *Industrie und Industriebauten im Landkreis Tuttlingen* (Tuttlingen).

Bergier (1979), J.-F., 'Clio sur les Alpes', *SZG* 29, Special Issue, with Introduction 3–10.

Bergier (1980), J.-F., 'Le cycle médieval: des sociétés feodales aux États Territoriaux', in Guichonnet (1980*a*), i. 163–265.

Bergier (1982), J.-F., *Une histoire du sel* (Fribourg).

Bergier (1983), J.-F., *Die Wirtschaftsgeschichte der Schweiz* (Zurich and Cologne).

Bergier (1987), J.-F., 'Die Auswirkungen des Verkehrs auf die Bergbevölkerung im Mittelalter', in Lindgren, 119–22.

Bergier (1988), J.-F., 'La montagne: économies et sociétés', in M. Körner (ed.), *Wozu Geschichte und Wirtschaftsgeschichte?* (Berne), 27–34.

Bergier (1989*a*), J.-F. (ed.), *Montagnes, fleuves, forêts dans l'histoire* (St Katharinen).

Bergier (1989*b*), J.-F., 'Obstacles ou lignes de convergence?', in Bergier (1989*a*), 1–5.

Berthe (1990), M., 'Les territoires des Bastides', *Annales du Midi* 102, 97–108.

Berthet (1951), B., 'De la forêt inutile et la forêt précieuse', *Annales ESC* 6/2, 145–53.

Berthold (1964), R., 'Wachstumsprobleme der landwirtschaftlichen Nutzfläche im Spätfeudalismus', *Jb. für Wirtschaftsgeschichte* II/III, 5–23.

Bickel (1947), W., *Bevölkerungsgeschichte und Bevölkerungspolitik der Schweiz seit dem Ausgang des Mittelalters* (Zurich).

Biddick (1991), K., 'Agrarian Productivity on the Estates of the Bishopric of Winchester', in Campbell and Overton, 95–123.

Bielmann (1972), J., *Die Lebensverhältnisse im Urnerland während des 18. und zu Beginn des 19. Jahrhunderts* (Basle and Stuttgart).

Bigmore (1982), P., 'Villages and Towns', in Cantor (1982*a*), 154–92.

Bilz (1975), H., *Die gesellschaftliche Stellung und soziale Lage der hausindustriellen Seiffener Spielzeugmacher im 19. und Anfang des 20. Jahrhunderts* (Seiffen).

Bintliff (1977), J. L., 'New Approaches to Historical Geography', in Carter (1977*a*), 59–114.

Bircher (1938), R., *Wirtschaft und Lebenshaltung im schweizerischen 'Hirtenland' am Ende des 18. Jahrhunderts* (Lachen).

Birley (1981[2]), A., *Life in Roman Britain.*

Birnbaum (1987), H., 'Kiev, Novgorod, Moscow: Three Varieties of Urban Society in East Slav Territory', in Krekic, 1–62.

Birrell (1962), J., 'The Forest Economy of the Honour of Tutbury in the Fourteenth and Fifteenth Centuries', *University of Birmingham Historical J.* 8, 114–34.

Birrell (1969), J., 'Peasant Craftsmen in the Medieval Forest', *AgHR* 17, 91–107.

Bischoff (1842), J., *A Comprehensive History of the Woollen and Worsted Manufacture* (2 vols.).

Bishop (1935), T. A. M., 'Assarting and the Growth of the Open Fields', *EcHR* 6, 13–29.

Bishop (1936), T. A. M., 'Monastic Granges in Yorkshire', *EHR* 51, 193–214.

Bishop (1948), T. A. M., 'The Norman Settlement in Yorkshire', in R. W. Hunt, W. A. Pantin, and R. W. Southern, (eds.), *Studies in Medieval History* (Oxford), 1–14.

Bjorkvik (1965), H., 'Villages désertés: bilan de la recherche en Norvège et Suède', in *École des Hauts Études*, 581–605.

Blache (1933[6]), J., *L'homme et la montagne* (Paris).

Blaich (1981), F. (ed.), *Entwicklungsprobleme einer Region: Das Bergische Rheinland und Westfalen im 19. Jahrhundert* (Berlin).
Blanchard (1971), I. S. W., 'Derbyshire Lead Production', *DAJ* 91, 119–40.
Blanchard (1973), I. S. W., 'Seigneurial Entrepreneurship: The Bishops of Durham and the Weardale Lead Industry', *BusH* 15, 97–111.
Blanchard (1978), I. S. W., 'Resource Depletion and the European Mining and Metallurgial Industries, 1400–1800', in Maczak and Parker, 85–113.
Blanchard (1986), I., 'Continental European Cattle Trade 1400–1600', *EcHR* 39, 427–60.
Blanchard (1989), I., *Russia's Age of Silver.*
Blendinger (1977), F., 'Zur Geschichte der Messinghütte am Stainenberg bei Pflach bzw. Ruette', in Huter and Zwanowetz, 53–66.
Blickle (1973), P., *Landschaften im alten Reich* (Munich).
Bloch (1966), M., *French Rural History.*
Blum (1957), J., 'The Rise of Serfdom in Eastern Europe', *American Historical Rev.* 62, 801–36.
Boehm (1982), C., 'Mountain Refuge Area Adaptations', in Beaver and Purrington, 24–37.
Bog (1971), I. (ed.), *Der Aussenhandel Ostmitteleuropas 1450–1650* (Cologne and Vienna).
Bogg (1908), E., *Richmondshire* (Leeds and London).
Bogucka (1982), M., 'Polish Towns between the Sixteenth and Eighteenth Centuries', in Fedorowicz, 135–52.
Bohstedt (1983), J., *Riots and Community Politics in England and Wales 1790–1810* (Cambridge, Mass.).
Bolin (1971), S., 'Medieval Agrarian Society in its Prime: Scandinavia', *CEHE* i. 633–59.
Bonser (1970), K. J., *The Drovers: who they were and how they went.*
Borland (1898), R., *Border Raids and Reivers* (Dalbeattie).
Born (1957), M., *Siedlungsentwicklung am Osthang des Westerwaldes* (Marburg).
Boserup (1965), *The Conditions of Agricultural Growth* (New York).
Bosl (1979), K., 'Die ersten siebenhundert Jahre deutsch-bayerischer Geschichte Südtirols', *Jb. für bayerische Landesgeschichte* 42, 15–30.
Boswell (1932), A. B., 'The Teutonic Order', *Cambridge Medieval History*, vii (Cambridge) 248–69.
Bouch (1948), C. M. L., *Prelates and People of the Lake Counties* (Kendal).
Bouch, C. M. L., and Jones, G. P. (1961), *A Short Economic and Social History of the Lake Counties 1500–1830* (Manchester).
Bowes (1990), P., *Weardale: Clearing the Forest* (Bishop Auckland).
Bowie (1990), G. G. S., 'Northern Wolds and Wessex Downland: Contrasts in Sheep Husbandry and Farming Practice, 1770–1850', *AgHR* 38, 117–26.
Boyson (1970), R., *The Ashworth Cotton Enterprise* (Oxford).
Bradshaw (1916), F., 'The Lay Subsidy Roll of 1296: Northumberland at the End of the Thirteenth Century', *Archaeologia Aeliana* 3rd ser. 13, 186–302.
Bramke (1993), W., 'Die Industrieregion Sachsen', in Schulze, 211–317.
Brandon (1972), P. F., 'Cereal Yields on the Sussex Estates of Battle Abbey during the Later Middle Ages', *EcHR* 25, 403–20.
Brandon (1988*a*), P. F., 'South-Eastern England', in Thirsk, 174–89.
Brandon (1988*b*), P. F., 'South-Eastern England', in Thirsk, 341–68.
Brassley (1984), P., 'Northumberland and Durham', in Thirsk (1984*a*), 30–58.
Braudel (1976), F., *The Mediterranean and the Mediterranean World in the Age of Philip II* (2 vols., New York).
Braudel (1986), F., *L'identité de la France: Espace et histoire* (Paris).
Braudel, F., and Spooner, F. (1967), 'Prices in Europe from 1450 to 1750', *CEHE* iv. 378–486.
Braun (1960), R., *Industrialisierung und Volksleben* (Zurich and Stuttgart).

Braun (1965), R., *Sozialer und kultureller Wandel in einem ländlichen Industriegebiet im 19. und 20. Jahrhundert* (Zurich and Stuttgart).
Braun (1984), R., *Das ausgehende Ancien Régime in der Schweiz* (Göttingen).
Braunstein (1983), P., 'Innovations in Mining and Metal Production in Europe in the late Middle Ages', *JEEcH* 12, 573–91.
Bridbury (1973), A. R., 'The Black Death', *EcHR* 26, 577–92.
Britnell (1990), R. H., 'Feudal Reaction after the Black Death in the Palatinate of Durham', *P&P* 128, 28–47.
Brockstedt (1989), J., 'Wandel der Landwirtschaft durch Industrialisierung im Herzogtum Oldenburg und seinen drei Teilgebieten 1870–1914', in J. Bergmann (ed.), *Regionen im historischen Vergleich* (Opladen).
Broers (1990), M., 'Marx and the Four-hundred Metres Contour Line: Regional Response to the French Revolution in Rural Piedmont', *J.Hist.G* 16, 76–89.
Bromehead (1956), C. N., 'Mining and Quarrying to the Seventeenth Century', in Singer *et al.*, ii. 1–40.
Brooks (1954), F. W., *York and the Council of the North.*
Brown (1971), R. L., 'An Introduction to the Study of Witches and Witchcraft Superstition in the Eastern Borders', *Hist. of the Berwickshire Naturalists' Club* 39, 34–42.
Brugger, E. A., Furrer, G., Messerli, B., and Messerli, P. (eds.) (1984*a*), *The Transformation of Swiss Mountain Regions* (Berne and Stuttgart).
Brugger *et al.* (1984*b*), 'Introduction', in Brugger *et al.* (1984*a*), 11–16.
Brugger (?1979), H., *Die Schweizerische Landwirtschaft* (Frauenfeld).
Bruland (1989), K., *British Technology and European Industrialization* (Cambridge).
Brunner (1968), O., *Neue Wege der Verfassungs- und Sozialgeschichte* (Göttingen).
Brush (1982), S., 'The Anthropology of Highland Peoples', in Beaver and Purrington, 159–67.
Brustein (1991), W., 'An Endogenous Explanation of French Internal Peripheries', in Nolte, 91–117.
Bryden, J., and Scott, I. (1990), 'The Celtic Fringe: State Sponsored versus Indigenous Local Development Initiatives in Scotland and Ireland', in W. B. Stöhr (ed.), *Global Challenge and Local Response* (London and Tokyo), 90–132.
Buchanan (1973), R. H., 'Field Systems in Ireland', in Baker and Butlin, 580–618.
Buchanan, R. H., Butlin, R. A., and McCourt, D. (eds.) (1976), *Fields, Farms and Settlement in Europe* (Holywood, Co. Down).
Bucher (1974), S., *Bevölkerung und Wirtschaft des Amtes Entlebuch im 18. Jahrhundert* (Lucerne).
Buckatzsch (1950–1), E. J., 'The Geographical Distribution of Wealth in England, 1086–1843', *EcHR* 3, 180–202.
Bücher (1901), C., *Industrial Evolution.*
Bührer (1977), W., *Der Zürcher Solddienst des 18. Jahrhunderts* (Berne).
Burgess (1980), J., 'The Quakers, the Brethren and the Religious Census in Cumbria', *TC&WAAS* 80, 103–11.
Burgess (1988), J., *The Monasteries of Southern Scotland* (Carlisle).
Burt (1969), R. (ed.), *Cornish Mining* (Newton Abbot).
Burt (1991), R., 'The International Diffusion of Technology in the Early Modern Period: The Case of the British Non-ferrous Mining Industry', *EcHR* 44, 249–71.
Butler (1988), L. A. S., 'Building in England and Wales', in Thirsk, 931–65.
Butlin (1964), R. A., 'Northumberland Field Systems', *AgHR* 12, 99–120.
Butlin (1967), R. A., 'Enclosure and Improvement in Northumberland in the Sixteenth Century', *Archaeologia Aeliana* 4th ser. 45, 149–60.
Butlin (1973), R. A., 'Field Systems in Northumberland and Durham', in Baker and Butlin, 93–144.

Butlin (1976), R. A., 'Land and People, *c.*1600', in T. W. Moody, F. X. Martin, and F. J. Byrne (eds.), *A New History of Ireland*, iii, *Early Modern Ireland 1534–1691* (Oxford).

Byers (1952), J. *Liddesdale, Historical and Descriptive* (Galashiels).

Bythell (1969), D., *The Handloom Weavers* (Cambridge).

Camden (1971), W., *Britannia* (Hildesheim and New York).

Cameron (1954), A. D., 'Border Abbeys and Agriculture in the Middle Ages', *Hawick Archaeological Soc. Trans.* 35–46.

Cameron (1984), E., *The Reformation of Heretics: the Waldenses of the Alps 1480–1580* (Oxford).

Campbell (1990), B. M. S., 'People and Land in the Middle Ages, 1066–1500', in Dodgshon and Butlin, 69–121.

Campbell (1991*a*), B. M. S. (ed.), *Before the Black Death* (Manchester).

Campbell (1991*b*), B. M. S., 'Land, Labour, Livestock and Productivity Trends in English Seignorial Agriculture, 1208–1450', in Campbell and Overton, 144–82.

Campbell, B. M. S., and Overton, M. (eds.) (1991), *Land, Labour and Livestock: Historical Studies in European Agricultural Productivity* (Manchester).

Campbell, B. M. S., and Overton, M. (1993), 'A New Perspective on Medieval and Early Modern Agriculture: Six Centuries of Norfolk Farming *c.*1250–1850', *P&P* 141, 38–105.

Campbell (1960²), M., *The English Yeomen under Elizabeth and the Stuarts.*

Campbell (1980), R. H., *The Rise and Fall of Scottish Industry 1707–1939* (Edinburgh).

Canny (1994), N. (ed.), *Europeans on the Move: Studies on European Migration 1500–1800* (Oxford).

Cantor (1982*a*), L. (ed.), *The English Medieval Landscape.*

Cantor (1982*b*), L., 'Introduction', in Cantor (1982*a*), 17–23.

Cantor (1982*c*), L., 'Forests, Chases, Parks and Warrens', in Cantor (1982*a*), 56–85.

Cantor (1982*d*), L., 'Castles, Fortified Houses, Moated Homesteads and Monastic Settlements', in Cantor (1982*a*), 126–52.

Caputa (1984), J., 'Potential Agricultural Production in Highlands', in Brugger *et al.* (1984*a*), 149–56.

Carey (1967²), H. C., *The Past, the Present and the Future* (New York).

Carne (1969), J., 'Statistics of Tin Mining in Cornwall' [original edn. 1839], in Burt, 83–93.

Caron (1978), F., 'Les "pays suiveurs": France et Belgique', in L. Bergeron (ed.), *Histoire économique et sociale du monde*, iii, *Inerties et révolutions* (Paris), 453–503.

Caroni (1979), P., 'Die Bedeutung des Warentransportes für die Bevölkerung der Passgebiete', in Bergier (1979), 84–100.

Carr (1992), A. D., 'A Debatable Land: Arwystli in the Middle Ages', *Montgomeryshire Collections* 80, 39–54.

Carsten (1941), 'Slavs in North-Eastern Germany', *EcHR* 11, 61–76.

Carter (1971), F. W., 'The Commerce of the Dubrovnik Republic, 1500–1700', *EcHR* 24, 370–94.

Carter (1977*a*), F. W. (ed.), *An Historic Geography of the Balkans.*

Carter (1977*b*), F. W., 'Urban Development in the Western Balkans 1200–1800', in Carter (1977*a*), 147–95.

Carter (1980), I., 'The Highlands of Scotland as an Underdeveloped Region', in F. H. Buttel and H. Newby (eds.), *The Rural Sociology of the Advanced Societies* (Montclair, NJ), 353–85.

Carus-Wilson (1954), E. M., 'An Industrial Revolution in the Thirteenth Century', in ead. (ed.), *Essays in Economic History*, 41–60.

Carus-Wilson, E. M. (1962), 'Evidence of Industrial Growth on some Fifteenth-century Manors', in ead. (ed.), *Essays in Economic History*, ii. 151–67.

Cépède, M., and Abensour, E. S. (1961), *Rural Problems in the Alpine Region* (Rome).

Chalklin, C. W., and Havinden, M. A. (eds.) (1974), *Rural Change and Urban Growth 1500–1800.*

Chambers (1972), J. D., *Population, Economy and Society in Pre-Industrial England.*

Chambers, J. D., and Mingay, G. E. (1966), *The Agricultural Revolution.*

Chambers (1864), W., *A History of Peeblesshire* (Edinburgh).

Chandler (1991), L., *Dallowgill through the Ages* (Otley).

Chapman (1965), S. D., 'The Pioneers of Worsted Spinning by Power', *BusH* 7, 97–118.

Chapman (1967), S. D., *The Early Factory Masters* (Newton Abbot).

Chapman (1971), S. D., 'The Cost of Power in the Industrial Revolution in Britain: The Case of the Textile Industry', *Midland Hist.* 1/2, 1–23.

Chapman (1972), S. D., *The Cotton Industry in the Industrial Revolution.*

Chapman (1973), S. D., 'Industrial Capital before the Industrial Revolution', in Harte and Ponting, 113–37.

Chapman, S. J., and Knoop, D. (1908), 'Industries', in Farrer and Brownbill, 351–409.

Charlton (1859), E., 'Notes on North Tynedale in 1279', *Archaeologia Aeliana* 2nd ser. 3, 147–57.

Châtelain (1976), A., *Les migrants temporaires en France de 1800 à 1914* (2 vols., Lille).

Chauvin (1983), B., 'Réalités et evolution de l'économie cistercienne dans le duché et comté de Bourgogne au moyen âge', in Flaran, 13–52.

Chevalier (1973²), L., *Labouring Classes and Dangerous Classes in Paris in the First Half of the Nineteenth Century* (New York).

Chisholm (1979), M., *Rural Settlement and Land Use.*

Cipolla (1949–50), C. M., 'The Trends in Italian Economic History in the late Middle Ages', *EcHR* 2, 181–4.

Cipolla (1974), C. M. (ed.), *Fontana Economic History of Europe*, ii, *The Sixteenth and Seventeenth Centuries.*

Cirković (1987), S., 'Unfulfilled Autonomy: Urban Society in Serbia and Bosnia', in Krekic, 158–84.

Clapham (1906), J. H., 'Industrial Organisation in the Woollen and Worsted Industries of Yorkshire', *Economic J.* 16, 515–22.

Clapham (1910), J. H., 'The Transference of the Worsted Industry from Norfolk to the West Riding', *Economic J.* 20, 195–210.

Clark (1977²), C., *Population Growth and Land Use.*

Clark (1945), G., 'Farmers and Forests in Neolithic Europe', *Antiquity* 19, 57–71.

Clark (1947), G., 'Forest Clearance and Prehistoric Farming', *EcHR* 17, 45–51.

Clark (1992), G., 'The Economics of Exhaustion, the Postan Thesis, and the Agricultural Revolution', *JEcH* 52, 61–84.

Clark (1981), G. L., 'Regional Economic Systems, Spatial Interdependence and the Role of Money', in Rees *et al.*, 91–105.

Clark (1952), J. G. D., *Prehistoric Europe: The Economic Basis.*

Clarke (1985), H., 'English and Baltic Trade in the Middle Ages—an Evaluation of the Evidence', in Lindquist, 113–20.

Clarke (1988), P. D., 'The Sectarian "Theatre" and its Impact on Restoration Cumbria', *TC&WAAS* 88, 161–75.

Clarkson (1971), L. A., *The Pre-Industrial Economy in England 1500–1750.*

Clarkson (1989), L. A., 'The Environment and Dynamic Pre-Factory Industry in Northern Ireland', in Hudson (1989*a*), 252–70.

Clavadetscher (1976), O. P., 'Freiheit und Freiheiten im Mittelalter', *SZG* 26, 4–8.

Claval (1990), P., 'A Critical Review of the Centre-Periphery Model as Applied in a Global Context', in Shachar and Öberg, 13–27.

Clay (1984), C. G. A., *Economic Expansion and Social Change: England 1500–1700*, i, *People, Land and Towns* (Cambridge).

Cleary (1988), M., 'Transhumance in the Mediterranean World: The Case of Languedoc', *J.Hist.G* 14, 37–49.

Cleere, H., and Crossley, D. (1985), *The Iron Industry of the Weald* (Leicester).

Clout (1983), H. D., *The Land of France 1815–1914.*

Clow (1956), A. and N. L., 'The Timber Famine and the Development of Technology', *Annals of Science* 12, 85–102.

Cockcroft (1975), B., *The Dale that Died.*

Cohn (1975), N., *Europe's Inner Demons: An Enquiry Inspired by the Great Witch-Hunt* (Brighton).

Cole, J. W., and Wolf, E. R. (1974), *The Hidden Frontier: Ecology and Ethnicity in an Alpine Valley* (New York and London).

Coleman (1956), D. C., 'Labour in the English Economy of the Seventeenth Century', *EcHR* 8, 280–95.

Coleman (1973), D. C., 'Textile Growth', in Harte and Ponting, 1–21.

Coleman (1977), D. C., *The Economy of England 1450–1750.*

Coleman (1983), D. C., 'Proto-Industrialization: A Concept Too Many', *EcHR* 36, 435–48.

Coles (1989), B. and J., *People of the Wetlands.*

Colley (1984²), L., *Britons: Forging the Nation 1707–1837.*

Collingwood (1928²), W. G., *Lake District History* (Kendal).

Collins (1978), E. J. T., *The Economy of Upland Britain 1750–1950* (Reading).

Constantinescu (1982), N. N., *The Special Features of the Industrial Revolution in Romania* (Budapest).

Conti (1988), S., 'The Italian Model and the Problems of the Industrial Periphery', in Linge (1988*a*), 37–52.

Coombes (1958), L. C., 'Lead Mining in East and West Allendale', *Archaeologia Aeliana* 4th ser. 36, 245–70.

Cornholme (1986), W. E. P., *Shore in Stansfield: A Pennine Weaving Community* (Todmorden).

Coulton (1925), G. G., *The Medieval Village* (Cambridge).

Coulton (1933), G. G., *Scottish Abbeys and Social Life* (Cambridge).

Coupe (1977), G., 'Tottington: The Growth and Development of a Lancashire Village', *TL&CAS* 79, 95–122.

Court (1953²), W. H. B., *The Rise of the Midland Industries 1600–1838.*

Cowan, I. B., and Easson, D. E. (1976²), *Medieval Religious Houses in Scotland.*

Cowell (1984), A. H., 'An Approach to the Agrarian History of Upland Country: Ecology and Habitat', *AgHR* 32, 63–74.

Cox, J. C., and Forbes, A. C. (1907), 'Forestry', *VCH Durham.*

Crafts (1977), N. F. R., 'Industrial Revolution in Britain and France: Some Thoughts on the Question "why was England first"', *EcHR* 30, 429–41.

Crafts (1995), N. F. R., 'Macroinventions, Economic Growth and "Industrial Revolution" in Britain and France', *EcHR* 48, 591–8.

Cregeen (1979), E., 'Tradition and Change in the West Highlands of Scotland: A Case Study', in Dyrvik *et al.*, 99–119.

Crossley, D., and Kiernan, D. (1992), 'The Lead-Smelting Mills of Derbyshire', *DAJ* 112, 6–48.

Crouzet (1993), F., *La grande inflation: la monnaie en France de Louis XVI à Napoleon* (Paris).

Cruden (1960), S., *Scottish Abbeys* (Edinburgh).

Crump (1931), W. B. (ed.), *The Leeds Woollen Industry 1780–1820* (Leeds).

Crump (1941), W. B., 'Border Traffic: Illustrated from the Shuttleworth Accounts', *Trans. Halifax Antiq. Soc.* 21–8.

Crump, W. B., and Ghorbal, G. (1935), *History of the Huddersfield Woollen Industry* (Huddersfield).

Cullen (1972), L. M., *An Economic History of Ireland since 1660.*

Cullen (1981), L. M., 'Population Growth and Diet', in J. M. Goldstrom and L. A. Clarkson (eds.), *Irish Population, Economy and Society* (Oxford).

Cunningham (1892), W., *The Growth of English Industry and Commerce*, ii (Cambridge).

Curtis (1956), J. T., 'The Modification of Mid-Latitude Grasslands and Forests by Man', in Thomas, 721–36.

Curtler (1908), W. H. R., 'Agriculture', in Farrer and Brownbill, 419–36.

Daisenberger (1859–61), J. A., 'Geschichte des Dorfes Oberammergau', *Oberbayerisches Archiv für vaterländische Geschichte* 20, 53–312.

Dale (1980), B., 'Subjective and Objective Social Indicators in Studies of Regional Social Wellbeing', *Regional Studies* 14, 503–15.

Daniels (1920), G. W., *The Early English Cotton Industry* (Manchester).

Darby (1940), H. C., *The Medieval Fenland* (Cambridge).

Darby (1950–1), H. C., 'Domesday Woodland', *EcHR* 3, 21–43.

Darby (1951), H. C., 'The Clearing of English Woodlands', *Geography* 36, 71–83.

Darby (1954*a*), H. C., 'Gloucestershire', in Darby and Terrett, 1–31.

Darby (1954*b*), 'The Midland Counties', in Darby and Terrett, 417–47.

Darby (1956), H. C., 'The Clearing of the Woodlands in Europe', in Thomas, 183–216.

Darby (1962), H. C., 'The Northern Counties', in Darby and Maxwell, 419–54.

Darby (1967*a*), H. C., 'Dorset', in Darby and Finn, 67–131.

Darby (1967*b*), H. C., 'The South-Western Counties', in Darby and Finn, 348–95.

Darby (1968[2]), H. C., *The Draining of the Fens* (Cambridge).

Darby (1971), H. C., *The Domesday Geography of Eastern England* (Cambridge).

Darby (1973*a*), H. C. (ed.), *A New Historical Geography of England* (Cambridge).

Darby (1973*b*), H. C., 'The Anglo-Scandinavian Foundations', in Darby (1973*a*), 1–38.

Darby (1973*c*), H. C., 'The Age of the Improver, 1600–1800', in Darby (1973*a*), 302–88.

Darby (1977), H. C., *Domesday England* (Cambridge).

Darby, H. C., and Finn, R. W. (eds.) (1967), *The Domesday Geography of South-West England* (Cambridge).

Darby, H. C., Glasscock, R. E., Sheail, J., and Versey, G. R. (1979), 'The Changing Geographical Distribution of Wealth in England: 1086–1334–1525', *J.Hist.G* 5, 247–62.

Darby, H. C., and Maxwell, I. S. (eds.) (1962), *The Domesday Geography of Northern England* (Cambridge).

Darby, H. C., and Terrett, I. B. (eds.) (1954), *The Domesday Geography of Midland England* (Cambridge).

Davico (1972), R., 'Populations marginales et développement industriel: L'économie du Piémont à la fin du XVIIIe et au début du XIXe siècle', *Revue d'histoire moderne et contemporaine* 19, 469–97.

David (1987), R., 'The Slate Quarrying Industry in Westmorland', *TC&WAAS* 87, 215–25.

Davie, G., and Hearl, D. (1991), 'Religion and Politics in Cornwall and Devon', in Havinden *et al.* (1991*a*) 214–23.

Davies (1939–40), A. S., 'The Charcoal Iron Industry of Powysland', *Montgomeryshire Collections* 46, 31–66.

Davies (1960), C. S., *The Agricultural History of Cheshire 1750–1850* (Manchester).

Davies (1991), E. H. C., 'Property and Landownership in Llangadfan', *Montgomeryshire Collections* 79, 29–112.

Davies (1981), N., *God's Playground: A History of Poland*, i, *The Origins to 1795* (Oxford).

Davies-Shiel (1972), M., 'A Little-Known Late Medieval Industry. Part I. The Making of Potash for Soap in Lakeland', *TC&WAAS* 72, 85–111.

Davies-Shiel (1974), M., 'A Little-Known Late Medieval Industry. Part II. The Ash Burners', *TC&WAAS* 74, 33–64.

Davis (1962), R., 'English Foreign Trade, 1700–1774', *EcHR* 15, 285–303.

Davis (1973), R., *Rise of the Atlantic Economies* (Ithaca).

Davis (1979), R., *The Industrial Revolution and British Overseas Trade* (Leicester).

Deane (1957), P., 'The Output of the British Woollen Industry in the Eighteenth Century', *EcHR* 17, 207–23.
Décarreaux (1964), J., *Monks and Civilization.*
Deffontaines (1933^5), P., *L'homme et la forêt* (Paris).
Defoe (1927), D., *A Tour Thro' the whole Island of Great Britain* (2 vols.).
Defoe (1992), D., *A Tour Through the whole Island of Great Britain.*
Denecke (1992), D., 'Ideology in the Planned Order upon the Land: The Example of Germany', in A. R. H. Baker and G. Biger (eds.), *Ideology and Landscape in Historical Perspective* (Cambridge).
Denholm-Young (1934), N., 'The Yorkshire Estates of Isabella de Fortibus', *YAJ* 31, 389–420.
Denholm-Young (1964^2), N., *Seignorial Administration in England* (New York).
Denis, M., Pihan, J., and Stanyer, J. (1991), 'The Peripheries Today', in Havinden *et al.* (1991*a*), 37–48.
De Rosa (1988), L., 'Urbanization and Industrialization in Italy (1861–1921)', *JEEcH* 17, 467–90.
Derruau-Boniol (1979^3), S., *Le Massif Central* (Paris).
Derruau-Boniol, S., and Fel, A. (1970^3), *Le Massif Central* (Paris).
Derry (1957), T. K., *A Short History of Norway.*
Devèze (1961), M., *La vie de la forêt française au XVIe siècle* (2 vols., Paris).
Devine (1983), T. M., 'Highland Migration to Lowland Scotland, 1760–1860', *Scottish Historical Rev.* 62, 137–49.
Devine (1988), T. M., *The Great Highland Famine. Hunger, Emigration and the Scottish Highlands in the Nineteenth Century* (Edinburgh).
De Vries (1973), J., 'On the Modernity of the Dutch Republic', *JEcH* 33, 191–202.
De Vries (1974), J., *The Dutch Rural Economy in the Golden Age 1500–1700* (New Haven).
De Vries (1980^2), J., *The Economy of Europe in an Age of Crisis 1600–1750* (Cambridge).
De Vries (1981), J., 'Patterns of Urbanization in pre-industrial Europe 1500–1800', in Schmal, 77–109.
De Vries (1983), J., 'The strengths and limitations of Dutch capitalism', in Guarducci, 153–73.
De Vries (1984), J., *European Urbanization 1500–1800.*
De Vries (1985), J., 'The Population and Economy of the Pre-Industrial Netherlands', *J. of Interdisciplinary Hist.* 15, 661–82.
Dewerpe (1984), A., 'Genèse protoindustrielle d'une région développé: L'Italie septentrionale (1800–1880)', *Annales ESC* 39, 896–914.
Dickens (1966), A. G., *Lollards and Protestants in the Diocese of York* (Oxford).
Diener (1974^2), H. O., *Geschichte der Besiedlung und Kultivierung des Erdinger Mooses* (Aalen).
Dilley (1967), R. S., 'The Cumberland Court Leet and the Use of Common Lands', *TC&WAAS* 67, 125–51.
Dilley (1991), R. S., 'Livestock in Cumberland 1660–1870', in B. A. Holderness and M. Turner (eds.), *Land, Labour and Agriculture, 1700–1920*, 133–147.
Dipper (1989), C., 'Bauernbefreiung, landwirtschaftliche Entwicklung und Industrialisierung in Deutschland: Die nichtpreussischen Staaten', in Pierenkemper, 63–75.
Discherl (1938), J. F., *Das ostbayerische Grenzgebirge als Standraum der Glasindustrie* (Würzburg).
Ditt, K., and Pollard, S. (eds.) (1992), *Von der Haimarbeit in die Fabrik* (Paderborn).
Dixon (1972), P., 'Shielings and Bastles', *Archaeologia Aeliana* 4th ser. 50, 249–58.
Dlugoborski (1992), W., 'Die schlesischen Magnate in der frühen Phase der Industrialisierung Oberschlesiens', in Pierenkemper (1992*a*), 107–28.
Dodd (1932^1, 1951^2), A. H., *The Industrial Revolution in North Wales* (Cardiff).
Dodd (1954–6), J. P., 'The State of Agriculture in Shropshire, 1775–1825', *Trans. Shropshire Archaeological Soc.*, 55, 1–31.

Dodgshon (1975), R. A., 'Infield-outfield and the territorial expansion of the English township', *J.Hist.G* 1/4, 327–45.

Dodgshon (1981), R. A., *Land and Society in Early Scotland* (Oxford).

Dodgshon (1987), R. A., *The European Past: Social Evolution and Spatial Order.*

Dodgshon (1988), R. A., 'West Highland Chiefdoms, 1500–1745: A Study in Redistributive Exchange', in Mitchison and Roebuck, 27–37.

Dodgshon (1993), R. A., 'Strategies of Farming in the Western Highlands and Islands of Scotland', *EcHR* 46, 679–701.

Dodgshon, R. A., and Butlin, R. A. (eds.) (1990²), *An Historical Geography of England and Wales.*

Donald (1955), M. B., *Elizabethan Copper.*

Donald (1961), M. B., *Elizabethan Monopolies* (Edinburgh).

Donkin (1960), R. A., 'Settlement and Depopulation on Cistercian Estates during the Twelfth and Thirteenth Centuries', *Bull.Inst.HR* 23, 141–65.

Donkin (1962), R. A., 'Cattle on the Estates of Medieval Cistercian Monasteries in England and Wales', *EcHR* 15, 31–53.

Donkin (1963), R. A., 'The Cistercian Order in Medieval England: Some Conclusions', *Institute of British Geographers, Trans. and Papers* 33, 181–98.

Donkin (1973), R. A., 'Changes in the Early Middle Ages', in Darby (1973*a*), 71–135.

Donkin (1978), R. A., *The Cistercian Studies in the Geography of Medieval England and Wales* (Toronto).

Donnelly (1954), J. S., 'Changes in the Grange Economy of English and Welsh Cistercian Abbeys, 1300–1450', *Traditio*, 10, 399–458.

Douglas (1899), G., *A History of the Border Counties* (*Roxburgh, Selkirk, Peebles*) (Edinburgh and London).

Douglas (1798), R., *General View of the Agriculture in the Counties of Roxburgh and Selkirk* (Edinburgh).

Douie (1932), D. L., *The Nature and the Effect of the Heresy of the Fraticelli* (Manchester).

Dovring (1966), F., 'The Transformation of European Agriculture', *CEHE* vi. 604–72.

Dowd (1961), D. F., 'The Economic Expansion of Lombardy, 1300–1500: A Study in Political Stimuli to Economic Change', *JEcH* 21, 139–160.

Dowell (1965²), S., *A History of Taxation and Taxes in England*, ii, *Taxation from the Civil War to the Present Day.*

Drew (1947), J. S., 'Manorial Accounts of St. Swithin's Priory, Winchester', *EHR* 62.

Druzhinina (1991), E. I., 'Southern Ukraine in the 18th and 19th Centuries', in Nolte, 219–29.

Dubuis (1979), P., 'Demographie et peuplement dans le diocèse de Sion au moyen âge', in Bergier, 144–158.

Dubuis (1986), P., 'Les hommes et le milieu montagnard dans l'histoire européenne', in Economic History Congress, 3–19.

Duby (1968), G., *Rural Economy and Country Life in the Medieval West.*

Duby (1974), G., *The Early Growth of the European Economy* (Ithaca, NY).

Dudley, D. R., and Webster, G. (1962), *The Rebellion of Boudicca.*

Dujcev, I., Velkov, V., Mitev, I., and Panayatov, L. (1977), *Histoire de la Bulgarie des origines à nos jours* (Roanne).

Durie (1979), A. J., *The Scottish Linen Industry in the Eighteenth Century* (Edinburgh).

Duval (1953), M., 'En Bretagne: Forêts Seignorales et Droits d'usage', *Annales ESC* 8, 482–92.

Duxbury (1985), A., 'Wealth and the Standard of Living in Ravenstonedale 1691–1840', *TC&WAAS* 85, 219–227.

Dyer (1980), C., *Lords and Peasants in a Changing Society* (Cambridge).

Dyer (1988*a*), C., 'West Midlands', in Thirsk, 224–34.

Dyer (1988*b*), C., 'West Midlands', in Thirsk, 369–83.

Dyer (1989), C., 'The Retreat from Marginal Land', in M. Aston, D. Austin, and C. Dyer (eds.), *The Rural Settlements of Medieval England* (Oxford), 45–57.

Dyos (1971), H. J., 'Greater and Greater London: Notes on Metropolis and Provinces in the Nineteenth and Twentieth Centuries', in J. S. Bromley and E. H. Kossman (eds.), *Britain and the Netherlands*, iv, *Dominion and Province*.

Dyrvik, S., Mykland, K., and Oldervoll J. (eds.) (1979), *The Satellite State in the 17th and 18th Centuries* (Bergen, Oslo, and Tromso).

East (1938^1, 1965^2), W. G., *The Geography Behind History*.

École des Hautes Études, VIe Section (1965), *Les hommes et la terre. XI. Villages désertés et histoire économique, XIe–XVIII siècles* (Paris).

Economic History Congress (1986), *Debates and Controversies* (Zürich).

Edlin (1962), H. L., 'The Land and the People', in J. Walton (ed.), *Border Guide*.

Egg (1964), E., 'Schwaz ist aller Bergwerke Mutter', *Der Anschnitt* 16/3, 3–63.

Egg (1977), E., 'Manufakturen in Tirol im Vormärz', in Huter and Zwanowetz, 125–45.

Egg, E., Gstrcin, P., and Sternad, H. (1986), *Stadtbuch Schwaz: Natur-Bergbau-Geschichte* (Schwaz).

Egli (1984), E., 'Science—the Burden of Responsibility', in Brugger *et al.* (1984*a*), 31–42.

Eisenstadt, S. N., and Rokkan, S. (eds.) (1973), *Building States and Nations*, i (Beverley Hills and London).

Eliot (1970), J., 'Armstrong—a Famous Border Clan', *Hawick Archaeological Soc. Trans.* 16–28.

Elliott (1959), G., 'The System of Cultivation and Evidence of Enclosure in Cumberland Open Fields in the 16th Century', *TC&WAAS* 59, 85–104.

Elliott (1973), G., 'Field Systems in Northwest England', in Baker and Butlin (1973*a*), 41–92.

Ellis (1962), M. J., 'A Study of the Manorial History of Halifax Parish in the Sixteenth and Early Seventeenth Centuries', *YAJ* 90, 250–64 and 420–442.

Elm (1992), K. (ed.), *Erwerbspolitik und Wirtschaftweise mittelalterlicher Orden und Klöster* (Berlin).

Emery (1973), F. V., 'England circa 1600', in Darby (1973*a*), 248–301.

Emons, H. H., and Walter, H.-H. (1988), *Alte Salinen in Mitteleuropa* (Leipzig).

Engerman (1986), S. L., 'Slavery and Emancipation in Comparative Perspective', *JEcH* 46, 312–39.

Epperlein (1967), S., 'Gründungsmythos deutscher Zisterzienserklöster westlich und östlich der Elbe im hohen Mittelalter', *Jb. für Wirtschaftsgeschichte*, iii. 303–35.

Erickson (1976), C., *Emigration from Europe 1815–1914: Select Documents*.

Erickson (1981), R. A., 'Corporations, Branch Plants and Employment Stability in Non-metropolitan Areas', in Rees *et al.*, 135–53.

Evans (1951–2), D. J., 'The Drapers of Shrewsbury and the Welshpool Flannel Market in the Seventeenth Century', *Montgomeryshire Collections* 52, 22–8.

Evans (1949–50), E., 'Arwystli and Cyfeiliog in the Sixteenth Century: An Elizabethan Inquisition', *Montgomeryshire Collections* 51, 23–37.

Evans, E., and Beckett, J. V. (1984), 'Cumberland and Westmorland', in Thirsk (1984*a*), 3–29.

Evans (1940), E. E., 'Transhumance in Europe', *Geography* 25, 172–80.

Evans (1956), E. E., 'The Ecology of Peasant Life in Western Europe', in Thomas, 217–39.

Evans (1982), F. T., 'Wood since the Industrial Revolution: A Strategic Retreat?', *History of Technology* 7, 37–55.

Evans (1985), N., *The East Anglian Linen Industry*.

Evans (1989), N., 'Two Paths to Economic Development: Wales and the North-East of England', in Hudson (1989*a*), 201–27.

Evans (1987), R. P., 'Thomas Pennant (1726–1798), the Father of Cambrian Tourists', *Welsh Hist. Rev.* 13, 395–467.

Everitt (1967), A., 'The Marketing of Agricultural Produce', in J. Thirsk (ed.), *The Agrarian History of England and Wales*, iv, *1500–1640* (Cambridge), 466–92.

Everitt (1970), A., 'Nonconformity in Country Parishes', *AgHR* 18, 178–99.

Everitt (1977), A., 'River and Wold: Reflexions on the Historical Origin of Region and Pays', *J.Hist.G* 3, 1–19.

Everitt (1979), A., 'Country, Community and Town: Patterns of Regional Evolution in England', *TRHS* 5th ser. 29, 79–108.

Eversmann (1804), F. A. A., *Übersicht der Eisen- und Stahlerzeugung auf Wasserwerken in den Ländern zwischen Lahn und Lippe* (Dortmund, repr. Werdohl, n.d.).

Faber (1979), K.-G., 'Geschichtslandschaft—Région historique—Section in History', *Saeculum* 30, 4–21.

Farey (1811–17), J., Sr., *General View of the Agriculture and Minerals of Derbyshire* (3 vols.).

Farmer (1977), D. L., 'Grain Yields on the Winchester Manors in the Late Middle Ages', *EcHR* 30, 555–66.

Farnie (1979), D. A., *The English Cotton Industry and the World Market 1815–1896* (Oxford).

Farrer (1911), W., 'North Lonsdale after the Restoration', *TC&WAAS* 12, 202–15.

Farrer, W., and Brownbill, J. (eds.) (1908), *VCH, County of Lancaster*, ii.

Febvre (1973), L., 'Frontière: The Word and the Concept', in P. Burke (ed.), *A New Kind of History from the Writings of Febvre.*

Fedorowicz (1982), J. K. (ed.), *A Republic of Nobles: Studies in Polish History* (Cambridge).

Fehn (1979), H., 'Das Land Bayern und seine Bevölkerung', in Spindler, 647–707.

Fehn (1968), K., 'Almen und Almwirtschaft im Berchtesgadener Land vom Mittelalter bis zur Gegenwart', *Zeitschrift für Agrargeschichte und Agrarsoziologie* 16, 36–55.

Fel (1962), A., *Les hautes terres du Massif Central: Tradition paysanne et économie agricole* (Paris).

Feldenkirchen (1981), W., 'Zum Einfluss der Standortfaktoren auf die Eisen- und Stahlindustrie des Ruhrgebiets (bis 1914)', in Blaich, 47–87.

Fiennes (1982), C., *The Illustrated Journey of Celia Fiennes c.1682–1712.*

Fiennes (1988), C., *Through England on a Side Saddle.*

Finn (1967*a*), R. W., 'Wiltshire', in Darby and Finn, 1–66.

Finn (1967*b*), R. W., 'Somerset', ibid. 132–222.

Finn (1967*c*), R. W., 'Devonshire', ibid. 223–95.

Firbas (1949), F., *Spät- und nacheiszeitliche Waldgeschichte Mitteleuropas nördlich der Alpen*, i, *Allgemeine Waldgeschichte* (Jena).

Fisher (1957), F. J., 'The Sixteenth and Seventeenth Centuries: The Dark Ages of English Economic History', *Economica* 24, 2–18.

Fisher (1952), F. N., 'Sir Cornelius Vermuyden and the Dovegang Lead Mine', *JDA&NHS* 72, 74–118.

Fisher, S., and Havinden, M. (1991), 'The Long-Term Evolution of the Economy of South-West England, from Autonomy to Dependence', in Havinden *et al.* (1991*a*), 76–85.

Flaran (1983), Abbaye de, *L'économie cistercienne: Geographie—mutations du Moyen Âge aux Temps Modernes* (Auch).

Fleming (1882), D., *Description of the County of Westmoreland* [*sic*] *AD 1671.*

Fleming (1889), D., *Description of the County of Cumberland AD 1671* (Kendal).

Fletcher (1971), A. J. *et al.*, *The Hope Valley in 1851* (Sheffield).

Fletcher (1962), T. W., 'The Agrarian Revolution in Arable Lancashire', *TL&CAS* 72, 93–122.

Flinn (1958–9), M. W., 'The Growth of the English Iron Industry 1660–1760', *EcHR* 11, 144–53.

Flinn (1959), M. W., 'Timber and the Advance of Technology: A Reconsideration', *Annals of Science* 15, 109–20.

Foerster (1968²), R. F., *The Italian Emigration of Our Times* (New York).

Fohlen (1967), C. (ed.), *Actes du Colloque sur la Forêt* (Paris).

Folz (1980²), R., *The Concept of Empire in Western Europe, from the Fifth to the Fourteenth Century* (Westport, Conn.).

Forberger (1958), R., *Die Manufaktur in Sachsen* (Berlin).

Forbes (1956), A. K., 'Metallurgy', in Singer *et al.*, 41–80.

Ford (1908), J. R., 'The Customary Tenant-Right of the Manors of Yealand', *TC&WAAS* 9, 147–60.

Ford, T. D., and Rieuwerts, J. H. (eds.) (1968^1, 1983^3), *Lead Mining in the Peak District* (Bakewell).

Ford (1976), W. J., 'Settlement Patterns in the Central Region of the Warwickshire Avon', in Sawyer (1976*a*), 274–94.

Forster (1957), R., 'The Noble Landlord in the Region of Toulouse at the End of the Old Regime', *JEcH* 17, 224–44.

Fossier (1983), R., 'L'économie cistercienne dans les plains de Nord-Ouest de l'Europe', in Flaran, 53–74.

Fowler (1976), P. J., 'Early Mendip', in Athill (1976*a*), 50–75.

Fox (1932), C., *The Personality of Britain* (Cardiff).

Fox (1989), E. W., 'The Argument: Some Reinforcements and Projections', in Genovese and Hochberg, 331–42.

Fox (1991*a*), H. S. A., 'Devon and Cornwall', in Miller (1991*a*), 152–74.

Fox (1991*b*), H. S. A., 'Devon and Cornwall', ibid. 303–23.

Fox (1991*c*), H. S. A., 'Devon and Cornwall', ibid. 722–43.

François (1966), M. E., *The Social and Economic Development of Halifax 1558–1640* (no loc.).

Franklin (1952), T. B., *A History of Scottish Farming.*

Franz (1939), G., *Deutsches Bauerntum*, ii, *Neuzeit* (Weimar).

Fraser (1968), C. M. (ed.), *The Northumberland Lay Subsidy Roll of 1296* (Newcastle upon Tyne).

Fraser (1972), M., *Welsh Border Country.*

Fremdling (1985), R., *Technologischer Wandel* (Berlin).

Fremdling (1986), R., 'Eisen, Stahl und Kohle', in Pohl (1986*a*), 347–70.

Fried (1975), P., 'Reagrarisierung Südbayerns seit dem 19. Jahrhundert', in Kellenbenz, 177–93.

Friedenthal (1970), R., *Luther.*

Friedl (1982), J., 'Education and Social Mobility: Some Parallels between Appalachia and the Alps', in Beaver and Purrington, 38–49.

Friedmann (1966), J., *Regional Development Policy* (Cambridge, Mass.).

Friedmann. J., and Alonso, W. (eds.) (1975), *Regional Policy: Readings in Theory and Application* (Cambridge, Mass.).

Frödin (1940), J., *Zentraleuropas Alpenwirtschaft*, i (Oslo).

Frognier, A. P., Quevit, M., and Stenbock, M. (1982), 'Regional Imbalances and Centre-Periphery Relationships in Belgium', in Rokkan and Urwin (1982*a*), 251–78.

Frost (1981), P., 'Yeomen and Metalsmiths: Livestock and Dual Economy in South Staffordshire 1560–1720', *AgHR* 29, 29–41.

Fuchs (1970), K., *Vom Dirigismus zum Liberalismus: Die Entstehung Oberschlesiens als preussisches Berg- und Hüttenrevier* (Wiesbaden).

Fuchs (1992), K., 'Städtewachstum und Wohnungsversorgung in Oberschlesien im 19. Jahrhundert', in Pierenkemper (1992*a*), 145–64.

Fügedi (1975), E., 'Das mittelalterliche Königreich Ungarn als Gastland', in Schlesinger (1975*a*), 471–507.

Fuller (1965), G. J., 'Lead Mining in Derbyshire in the mid-Nineteenth Century', *East Midlands Geographer* iii/7, 373–93.

Fussell (1951–3), G. E., 'Four Centuries of Farming Systems in Shropshire, 1500–1900', *Trans, Shropshire Archaeological Soc.* 54, 1–29.

Gadrin, D., and MacMillen, M. (1991), 'The Way Ahead: Economic Integration or Marginalisation', in Havinden *et al.*, (1991*a*), 63–75.

Gaffney (1959), V., 'Summer Shielings', *Scottish Hist. Rev.* 38, 20–35.

Gailey (1962), R. A., 'The Evolution of Highland Rural Settlement', *Scottish Studies* 6, 155–77.

Gallagher (1976), P. F., 'Conditions of land tenure and their religious implications', in J. R. Sommerfeldt (ed.), *Studies in Medieval Cistercian History*, ii (Kalamazoo).

Galtung (1971), J., 'A Structural Theory of Imperialism', *J. of Peace Research* 8, 81–110.

Garnett (1945), A., 'The Loess Regions of Central Europe in Prehistoric Times', *Geographical J.* 106, 132–43.

Garnsey (1986), P., 'Mountain Economies in Southern Europe', in Mattmüller, 7–29.

Gaskell (1987), E., *The Life of Charlotte Brontë* (Harmondsworth).

Genovese, E. D., and Hochberg, L. (eds.) (1989), *Geographical Perspectives in History* (Oxford).

Gerhard (1959), D., 'The Frontier in Comparative View', *Comp.St.S&H* 1, 205–29.

Gilbert (1993[2]), M., *Altas of British History*.

Gilchrist (1907), D. A., 'Agriculture', *VCH Durham*, 357–72.

Gille (1956), B., 'Machines', in Singer *et al.*, 629–62.

Gille (1966), B., *The Renaissance Engineers*.

Gille (1980*a*), B., 'The Medieval Age of the West', in M. Daumas (ed.), *A History of Technology and Invention* (3 vols.), i. 422–576.

Gille (1980*b*), B., 'The Fifteenth and Sixteenth Centuries', ibid. ii. 16–148.

Gilliard (1929), C., 'L'ouverture du Gothard', *Annales d'histoire économique et sociale* 1, 177–82.

Gilly (1841/1842), W. S., *The Peasantry of the Border* (Berwick upon Tweed).

Gilomen (1991), H. J., 'Sozial- und Wirtschaftsgeschichte der Schweiz im Mittelalter' *SZG* 41, 467–92.

Gilpin (1792[2]), W., *Observations on the Mountains, and Lakes, of Cumberland and Westmorland* (2 vols.).

Ginter (1992), D. C., *A Measure of Wealth: The English Land Tax in Historical Analysis* (Hambledon).

Giraldus Cambrensis (1908, 1919), *The Itinerary through Wales and the Description of Wales*.

Gissel, S., Juttikala, E., Österberg, E., Sandnes, J., and Teittson, B. (1981), *Desertion and Land Colonization in the Northern Countries c.1300–1600* (Stockholm).

Glacken (1956), C. J., 'Changing Ideas of the Habitable World', in Thomas, 70–92.

Glamann (1977), K., 'The Changing Pattern of Trade', *CEHE* v. 185–289.

Glasscock (1973), R. E., 'England circa 1334', in Darby (1973*a*), 136–85.

Glauser (1971), F., 'Handel mit Entlebucher Käse und Butter vom 16. bis 19. Jahrhundert', *SZG* 21, 1–63.

Glauser (1979), F., 'Der Gotthardtransit von 1500 bis 1650', in Bergier, 3–10.

Gleitsmann (1981), R.-J., 'Aspekte der Ressourcenproblematik in historischer Sicht', *Scripta Mercaturiae* 15/2, 33–89.

Gleitsmann (1982), R.-J., 'Die Haubergwirtschaft des Siegerlandes als Beispiel für ressourcenschonende Kreislaufwirtschaft', *Scripta Mercaturiae* 16, 23–55.

Gleitsmann (1984), R.-J., 'Der Einfluss der Marktwirtschaft auf die Waldentwicklung Mitteleuropas' in Kroker and Westermann, 24–39.

Glennie (1990), P. D., 'Industry and Towns 1500–1730', in Dodgshon and Butlin, 199–222.

Glover (1961), F. J., 'The Rise of the Heavy Woollen Trade of the West Riding of Yorkshire in the Nineteenth Century', *BusH* 4, 1–21.

Glyn-Jones (1991), A., 'The Repopulation of the Countryside in Cornwall and Devon', in Havinden *et al.*, 132–42.

Godfrey (1975), E. S., *The Development of English Glassmaking* (Oxford).

Goehrke (1980), C., 'Die russischen Kosaken im Wandel des Geschichtsbildes', *SZG* 30, 181–207.

Gore (1984), C., *Regions in Question: Space, Development Theory and Regional Policy*.

Gothein (1970[2]), E., *Wirtschaftsgeschichte des Schwarzwaldes und der angrenzenden Landschaften* (New York).

Götschmann (1985), D., *Oberpfälzer Eisen* (Theuern).
Götschmann (1986), D., 'Der Sulzbacher Bergbau im Mittelalter und in der frühen Neuzeit', *SZG* 49, 41–123.
Göttmann (1991), F., 'Der Raum Zwischen oberer Donau und Schweizer Alpen im 18. Jahrhundert', *Scripta Mercaturiae* 1/2, 1–40.
Gottmann, J. (ed.) (1980*a*), *Centre and Periphery: Spatial Variations in Politics* (Beverley Hills).
Gottmann, J. (1980*b*), 'Confronting Centre and Periphery', in Gottmann (1980*a*), 11–25.
Gottschalk (1966), J., 'Die Bedeutung der Zisterzienser für die Ostsiedlung, besonders in Schlesien', *Zeitschrift für Ostforschung* 15, 67–106.
Goudie (1986[2]), A., *The Human Impact on the Natural Environment* (Oxford).
Gradmann (1901), R., 'Das mitteleuropäische Landschaftsbild nach seiner geschichtlichen Entwicklung', *Geographische Zeitschrift* 7, 361–77 and 435–47.
Graham (1976), B., 'The Evolution of the Settlement Pattern of Anglo-Norman Eastmeath', in Buchanan *et al.*, 38–47.
Graham (1905), J., *Condition of the Border at the Union.*
Graham (1907), T. H. B., 'The Parish of Hayton', *TC&WAAS* 8, 55–71.
Graham (1911), T. H. B., 'The Debatable Land, Part I', *TC&WAAS* 12, 33–58.
Graham (1913), T. H. B., 'The Debatable Land, Part II', *TC&WAAS* 14, 132–57.
Graham (1925), T. H. B., 'Border Tenure', *TC&WAAS* 25, 86–95.
Grainger (1908), F., 'Agriculture in Cumberland in Ancient Times', *TC&WAAS* 9, 120–46.
Grainger (1913), F., 'The Cumberland Yeoman in Past Times', *TC&WAAS* 14, 281–91.
Gramulla (1977), S., 'Fedi di Sanitá als Zeugnisse des Kölner transalpinen Verkehrs um 1720', in Huter and Zwanowetz, 147–55.
Grant (1930), I. F., *The Social and Economic Development of Scotland before 1603* (Edinburgh).
Graus (1975), F., 'Die Problematik der deutschen Ostsiedlung aus tschechischer Sicht', in Schlesinger (1975*a*), 31–75.
Gravier (1964), J. F., *L'amènagement du territoire et l'avenir des régions françaises* (Paris).
Gray (1951–2), M., 'The Kelp Industry in the Highlands and Islands', *EcHR* 4, 197–210.
Gray (1957), M., *The Highland Economy 1750–1850* (Edinburgh).
Gregory (1982), D., *Regional Transformation and Industrial Revolution: A Geography of the Yorkshire Woollen Industry.*
Gregson (1989), 'Tawney Revisited: Custom and the Emergence of Capitalist Class Relations in North-East Cumbria 1660–1830', *EcHR* 42, 18–42.
Grenier (1930), A., 'Aux origines de l'économie rurale: la conquête du sol français', *Annales d'Histoire Économique et Sociale* 2, 26–47.
Griffiths (1988), M., 'Country and Town: Agrarian Change and Urban Fortunes', in T. Herbert and G. E. Jones, *Tudor Wales*, 67–106.
Grigg (1980), D., *Population Growth and Agrarian Change: An Historical Perspective* (Cambridge).
Grill (1987), B., 'Deutschland—ein Waldesmärchen', *Die Zeit* 53, 25 Dec. 1987.
Gripaios, P., Bishop, P., Gripaios, R., and Herbert, C. (1989), 'High Technology Industry in a Peripheral Area: The Case of Plymouth', *Regional Studies* 23/2, 151–7.
Grossmann (1934), H., 'Der Einfluss der alten Glashütten auf den schweizerischen Wald', in E. Rühl, *Bericht über das Geobotanische Forschungsinstitut ... 1933* (Zurich).
Grossmann (1967), H., 'Influence des métiers et des activités industrielles sur la forêt Suisse de 1600 à 1860', in Fohlen, 159–64.
Guarducci (1983), A. (ed.), *Sviluppo e Sottosviluppo in Europa e Fuori d'Europa dal Seculo XIII alla Revoluzione Industriale* (Florence).
Guichonnet (1972), P., 'Vers de nouvelles formes d'industrialisation: le type Alpin, l'expérience italienne', in Léon *et al.*, 547–55.
Guichonnet (1980*a*), P., *Histoire et Civilisations des Alpes* (2 vols., Toulouse and Lausanne).
Guichonnet (1980*b*), P., 'Le milieu natural alpin', in Guichonnet (1980*a*), i. 11–54.

Guichonnet (1980*c*), P., 'Les Alpes occidentales franco-italiennes', in Guichonnet (1980*a*), i. 266–310.

Guichonnet (1980*d*), P., 'L'homme devant les Alpes', in Guichonnet (1980*a*), ii. 169–248.

Guichonnet (1980*e*), P., De l'autarcie à la dépendance', in Guichonnet (1980*a*), ii. 249–80.

Gülich (1844), G. von, *Über die Urbarmachung wüster Ländereien als Mittel, viele Erwerbslose zu beschäftigen* (Cassel).

Gullickson (1983), G. L., 'Agriculture and Cottage Industry: Redefining the Causes of Proto-Industrialization', *JEcH* 43, 831–50.

Günther (1930), A., *Die alpenländische Gesellschaft* (Jena).

Guth (1989), K., 'Wanderungsbewegungen in und aus Franken im 19. Jahrhundert', *Jb. für fränkische Geschichtsforschung* 49, 109–33.

Guttmann (1986), M. P., 'The Dynamics of Urban Decline in the Late Middle Ages and Early Modern Times', in Economic History Congress 23–56.

Habakkuk (1940), H. J., 'English Landownership, 1680–1740', *EcHR* 10, 2–17.

Habakkuk (1953), H. J., 'English Population in the Eighteenth Century', *EcHR* 6, 117–33.

Habakkuk (1971), H. J., *Population Growth and Economic Development since 1750* (Leicester).

Haddon (1958), A., 'The Border Laws', *Hawick Archaeological Soc. Trans.* 14–19.

Hafner, H., and Günter, T. (1984), 'Land-Use Changes and Ecological Effects in the Swiss Alps', in Brugger *et al.* (1984*a*), 101–24.

Hägermann, D., and Ludwig, K.-H. (1984), 'Mittelalterliche Salinenbetriebe', *Technikgeschichte* 51, 155–89.

Hagmann, H.-M., and Menthonnex, J. (1979), 'Éléments de démographie Alpine', in Bergier, 216–31.

Haigh (1969), C., *The Last Days of the Lancashire Monasteries and the Pilgrimage of Grace* (Manchester).

Haldane (1953^2), A. R. B., *The Drove Roads of Scotland* (Edinburgh).

Halecki (1952), O., *Borderlands of Western Civilization: A History of East Central Europe* (New York).

Hall (1978), 'Economy and Society in the Derbyshire Peak District', *DAJ* 98, 72–82.

Hallam (1954), H. E., *The New Lands of Elloe* (Leicester).

Hallam (1958), H. E., 'Some Thirteenth-Century Censuses', *EcHR* 10, 340–61.

Hallam (1965), H. E., *Settlement and Society: A Study of the Early Agrarian History of South Lincolnshire* (Cambridge).

Hallam (1972), H. E., 'The Postan Thesis', *Historical Studies* 15/58, 203–22.

Hallam (1988*a*), H. E., 'New Settlements: Eastern England', in Thirsk, 139–74.

Hallam (1988*b*), H. E., 'Southern England', ibid. 203–24.

Hallam (1988*c*), H. E., 'Foreign Techniques: Eastern England', ibid. 272–311.

Hallam (1988*d*), H. E., 'Southern England', ibid. 341–68.

Hallam (1988*e*), H. E., 'Drainage Techniques', ibid. 497–507.

Hallas (1990), C., 'Cottage and Mill: The Textile Industry in Wensleydale and Swaledale', *Textile History* 21, 203–21.

Hallas (1991), C., 'Migration in Nineteenth-Century Wensleydale and Swaledale', *Northern History* 27, 139–61.

Hamilton (1937–8), E. J., 'The Decline of Spain' *EcHR* 8, 168–79.

Hamilton (1963), H., *An Economic History of Scotland in the Eighteenth Century* (Oxford).

Hammersley (1957), G., 'The Crown Woods and their Exploitation in the Sixteenth and Seventeenth Centuries', *Bull.Inst.HR* 30, 136–61.

Hammersley (1973*a*), G., 'The Charcoal Iron Industry and its Fuel, 1540–1750', *EcHR* 26, 593–613.

Hammersley (1973*b*), G., 'Technique or Economy? The Rise and Decline of the English Copper Industry, ca. 1550–1660', *BusH* 15, 1–31.

Hammersley (1988), G., *Daniel Hochstetter the Younger* (Stuttgart).

Hammersley (1991), G., 'The Effect of Technical Change in the British Copper Industry between the Sixteenth and the Eighteenth Centuries', *JEEcH* 20, 155–73.

Hanagan (1989), M., 'Nascent proletarians: migration patterns and class formation in the Stéphanois region, 1840–1880', in Ogden and White, 74–96.

Handley (1953), J. E., *Scottish Farming in the Eighteenth Century.*

Hansen (1978), N. M., 'Border Regions: A Critique of Spatial Theory and a European Case Study', in N. M. Hansen (ed.), *Human Settlement Systems* (Cambridge, Mass.), 247–62.

Hansen (1976), V., 'The Medieval Dispersal of Rural Settlement in Denmark as a Function of Distance from Primary Nucleations', in Buchanan *et al.*, 53–9.

Haraldsson (1989), K., *Tradition, regional specialisiering och industriell utveckling* (Uppsala).

Harbottle, B., and Newman, T. G. (1973), 'Excavation and Survey on the Starsley Burn, North Tynedale, 1972', *Archaeologia Aeliana* 5th ser. 1, 137–75.

Hardy (?1988), J., *The Hidden Side of Swaledale* (Kendal).

Harley (1958), J. B., 'Population Trends and Agricultural Developments from the Warwickshire Hundred Rolls', *EcHR* 11, 8–18.

Harnisch (1984), H., *Kapitalistische Agrarreform und industrielle Revolution* (Weimar).

Harris (1973), A., 'Changes in the Early Railway Age, 1800–1850', in Darby (1973*a*), 465–526.

Harris (1957), L. E., 'Land Drainage and Reclamation', in Singer *et al.*, 300–23.

Harrison (1990), B., 'New Settlements in the North Yorkshire Moors, 1086–1340', in Vyner, 19–31.

Harrison, R., and Hart, M., (1990), 'The Nature and Extent of Innovative Activity in a Peripheral Economy', *Regional Studies* 24/5, 383–93.

Hart (1971), C., *The Industrial History of Dean* (Newton Abbot).

t'Hart (1993), M. C., *The Making of a Bourgeois State* (Manchester).

Harte, N. B., and Ponting, K. G. (eds.) (1973), *Textile History and Economic History* (Manchester).

Hartley, M., and Ingilby, J. (1968), *Life and Tradition in the Yorkshire Dales.*

Hartley, M., and Ingilby, J. (1979[2]), *Yorkshire Village.*

Hartley, M., and Ingilby, J. (1988[2]), *The Old Hand-Knitters of the Dales* (Clapham).

Hartley, M., and Ingilby, J. (1990[2]), *Life and Tradition in the Moorlands of North-East Yorkshire* (Otley).

Hartwell (1973), R. M., 'A Revolution in the Character and Destiny of British Wool', in Harte and Ponting, 320–38.

Harvey (1966), B., 'The Population Trend in England between 1300 and 1348', *TRHS* 5th ser. 16, 23–42.

Harvey (1991), B. F., 'Introduction: the crisis of the early fourteenth century', in Campbell (1991*a*), 1–24.

Harvey (1994), P. D. A., 'Manorial Accounts', in R. H. Parker and B. S. Yamey (eds.) *Accounting History* (Oxford), 91–115.

Harvey (1976), S. P. J., 'Evidence for Settlement Study: Domesday Book', in Sawyer (1976*a*), 195–99.

Hassinger (1969), H., 'Der Verkehr über Brenner und Resche vom Ende des 13. bis in die zweite Hälfte des 18. Jahrhunderts', in Troger and Zwanowetz, 137–94.

Hastings (1981), R. P., *Essays in North Riding History* (Northallerton).

Hatcher (1970), J., *Rural Economy and Society in the Duchy of Cornwall 1300–1500* (Cambridge).

Hatcher (1973), J., *English Tin Production and Trade before 1550* (Oxford).

Hatcher (1977), J., *Plague, Population and the English Economy 1348–1530.*

Hatcher (1988*a*), J., 'South-Western England', in Thirsk, 234–45.

Hatcher (1988*b*), J., 'South-Western England', ibid. 383–98.

Hatcher (1993), J., *The History of the British Coal Industry*, i, *Before 1700: Towards the Age of Coal* (Oxford).

Hauser (1964), A., 'Wald und Forst in der Gründerzeit der Eidgenossenschaft', *Schweizerische Zeitschrift für Forstwesen* 11, 637–58.

Hauser (1972), A., *Wald und Feld in der alten Schweiz* (Zurich and Munich).

Haushofer (1986), H., *Aus der Bayerischen Agrargeschichte 1525–1978* (Munich/Vienna/Zurich).

Hausmann (1975), F., *Die Agrarpolitik der Regierung Montgelas* (Berne and Frankfurt).

Havinden, M. A., Quéniart, J., and Stanyer, J. (eds.) (1991*a*), *Centre and Periphery* (Exeter).

Havinden (1991*b*), M. A. *et al.*, 'How the Regions became peripheral', in Havinden *et al.* (1991*a*), 13–23.

Havinden M., and Stanes, R. (1991), 'Agriculture in South West England. The Legacy of History', in Havinden *et al.* (1991*a*), 143–53.

Hay (1966), D., *Europe in the Fourteenth and Fifteenth Centuries.*

Head (1979), A-L., 'Quelques remarques sur l'emigration des régions préalpines—le cas Glaronnais', in Bergier, 181–93.

Heaton (1931), H., 'Benjamin Gott and the Industrial Revolution in Yorkshire', *EcHR* 3, 45–66.

Heaton (1965²), H., *The Yorkshire Woollen and Worsted Trades* (Oxford).

Hebden Bridge WEA Branch (1981), *Heptonstall Township in the Eighteenth Century* (Halifax).

Hechter (1975), M., *Internal Colonisation: The Celtic Fringe in British National Development.*

Hechter, M., and Brustein, W. (1980), 'Regional Modes of Production and State Formation in Western Europe', *American J. of Sociology* 85/5, 1061–94.

Heckscher (1963²), E. F., *An Economic History of Sweden* (Cambridge, Mass.).

Hedley (1950), W. P., 'The Medieval Forests of Northumberland', *Archaeologia Aeliana* 4th ser. 28, 96–104.

Hefner (1839), J. von, 'Leistungen des Benediktstiftes Tegernsee in Kunst und Wissenschaft', *Oberbayerisches Archiv für vaterländische Geschichte* 1, 15–35.

Heichelheim (1956), F., 'Effects of Classical Antiquity on the Land', in Thomas, 165–82.

Helbig (1975), H., 'Die Ungarische Gesetzgebung des 13. Jahrhunderts und die Deutschen', in Schlesinger (1975*a*), 511–26.

Helleiner (1967), K. F., 'The Population of Europe from the Black Death to the Eve of the Vital Revolution', *CEHE* iv. 1–95.

Hellen (1972), J. A., 'Agricultural Innovation and Detectable Landscape Margins', *AgHR* 20, 140–54.

Heller (1993), W., 'Politische Grenzen und Grenzräume', in Weisbrod, 173–94.

Helmolt (1896), H. F., 'Die Entwicklung der Grenzlinie aus dem Grenzsaume im alten Deutschland', *Historisches Jb.* 17, 235–64.

Henderson (1879), W., *Notes on the Folk-Lore of the Northern Counties of England and the Borders.*

Henning (1983), F. W., 'Vorindustrielles Gewerbe und wirtschaftlicher Wandel im Paderborner Land im 19. Jahrhundert', *Vortragsreihe der Gesellschaft für Westfälische Wirtschaftsgeschichte* 25, 5–41.

Henschke (1974), E., *Landesherrschaft und Bergbauwirtschaft* (Berlin).

Herrmann (1989), J., 'Zum Wechselverhältnis von naturräumlicher Siedlung, sozialökonomischer Entwicklung und Staatsbildung in Mitteleuropa vom 7. bis 11. Jahrhundert', in Bergier (1989*a*), 227–35.

Hey (1972), D., *The Rural Metalworkers of the Sheffield Region* (Leicester).

Hey (1979), D., *The Making of South Yorkshire* (Ashbourne).

Hey (1984*a*), D., 'Yorkshire and Lancashire', in Thirsk (1984*a*), 59–88.

Hey (1984*b*), D., 'North-East Midlands: Derbyshire. Staffordshire, Cheshire and Shropshire', ibid. 129–58.

Hey (1991), D., *The Fiery Blades of Hallamshire* (Leicester).

Higham (1973), M. C., 'The Pre-Conquest Settlement in the Forest of Bowland', in Baldwin and Whyte, 119–34.

Higham (1986), N., *The Northern Counties to AD 1000.*
Higounet (1950), C., 'Cisterciens et bastides', *Le Moyen Âge* 56, 69–84.
Higounet (1965), C., 'Villeneuves et bastides désertés', in École des Hautes Études, 253–65.
Higounet (1975), C., 'Zur Siedlungsgeschichte Südwestfrankreichs vom 11. bis zum 14. Jahrhundert', in Schlesinger (1975*a*), 657–94.
Higounet (1983), C., 'Essay sur les granges cisterciennes', in Flaran, 157–80.
Higounet (1986), C., *Die deutsche Ostsiedlung im Mittelalter* (Berlin).
Hildebrand (1992), K-G., *Swedish Iron in the Seventeenth and Eighteenth Centuries* (Jernkontorets Berghistoriska Skriftserie 29).
Hill (1968), B. D., *English Cistercian Monasteries and their Patrons in the Twelfth Century* (Chicago).
Hills (1970), R. L., *Power in the Industrial Revolution* (Manchester).
Hilton (1980), J. A., 'The Cumbrian Catholics', *Northern History* 16, 40–58.
Hilton (1950^1, 1972^2), R. H., *Social Structure of Rural Warwickshire in the Middle Ages* (Oxford).
Hinde (1857), J. H., 'Cornage of Northumberland', *Archaeologia Aeliana* 2nd ser. 1, 44–7.
Hinds (1896–1922), *A History of Northumberland* (10 vols., Newcastle upon Tyne and London).
Hobsbawm (1962), E. J., *The Age of Revolution: Europe 1789–1848.*
Hobsbawm (1969), E. J., *Bandits.*
Hobsbawm (1977^2), E. J., *Industry and Empire* (Harmondsworth).
Hocevar (1987), T., 'The Albanian Economy 1912–1944: A Survey', *JEcH* 16, 561–18.
Hodgen (1939), M. T., 'Domesday Water Mills', *Antiquity* 13, 261–79.
Hodges (1982), R., *Dark Age Economics.*
Hodgkins (1987), D. J., 'The Peak Forest Canal—Lime and Limestone', *DAJ* 107, 73–91.
Hodgson (1827–58), J., *History of Northumberland in Three Parts* (6 vols., Newcastle upon Tyne).
Hodgson (1901), T. H., 'The Military Road in Cumberland', *TC&WAAS* 2, 274–81.
Hoffman (1977), G. W., 'The Evolution of the Ethnographic Map of Yugoslavia', in Carter (1977*a*), 437–499.
Hoffman (1980), G. W., 'Variations in Centre–Periphery Relations in South-East Europe', in Gottmann (1980*a*), 111–33.
Hoffman (1982), K., 'Sawmills—Finland's Proto-Industry', *ScEHR* 30, 35–43.
Hoffmann (1975), A., 'Zur Problematik der agrarischen Nebengewerbe und der Reagrarisierung', in Kellenbenz, 29–37.
Hoffmann (1910), E., 'Die Entwicklung der Wirtschaftsprinzipien im Zisterzienserorden während des 12. und 13. Jahrhunderts', *Historisches Jb.* 31, 699–727.
Hogg (1972), R., 'Factors which Affected the Spread of Early Settlement in the Lake Counties', *TC&WAAS* 72, 1–35.
Hohenberg, P. M., and Lees, L. H. (1985), *The Making of Urban Europe 1000–1950* (Cambridge, Mass.).
Holderness (1976), B. A., *Pre-Industrial England: Economy and Society from 1500 to 1750.*
Hollander (1960–1), A. N. J. den, 'The Great Hungarian Plain: A European Frontier Area', *Comp. St. S&H* 3, 74–88 and 155–69.
Hollander (1979), S., *The Economics of David Ricardo* (Toronto).
Holly (1954), D., 'Leicestershire', in Darby and Terrett, 309–25.
Holly (1962), D., 'Derbyshire', in Darby and Maxwell, 278–329.
Holroyde (1979), H., 'Textile Mills, Masters and Men in the Halifax District 1770–1851', *Trans. Halifax Antiq. Soc.*, 57–73.
Holroyde (1988), H., 'Protestantism and Dissent in the Parishes of Halifax 1509–1640', *Trans. Halifax Antiq. Soc.*, 17–40.
Hooke (1978), D., 'Early Cotswold Woodland', *J. Hist. G* 4, 333–41.
Hooke (1982), D., 'Pre-Conquest Estates in the West Midlands: Preliminary Thoughts', *J. Hist. G* 8, 227–44.
Hooke (1989), D., 'Pre-Conquest Woodland: its Distribution and Usage', *AgHR* 37, 113–29.

Hope (1899), W. H. St. J., 'Fountains Abbey', *YAJ* 15, 269–402.

Hornshaw (1975), T. R., *Copper Mining in Middleton Tyas* (Northallerton).

Hornstein (1951), F. von, *Wald und Mensch* (Ravensburg).

Hösch (1972), E., *The Balkans: A Short History from Greek Times to the Present Day*.

Hoskins (1943), W. G., 'The Reclamation of the Waste in Devon, 1550–1800', *EcHR* 13, 80–92.

Hoskins (1955, 1971^2), W. G., *The Making of the English Landscape*.

Houseman (1800), J., *Topographical Description of Cumberland, Westmorland, Lancashire and a Part of the West Riding of Yorkshire* (Carlisle).

Houston, R. and Snell, K. D. M. (1984), 'Proto-Industrialization? Cottage Industry, Social Change and Industrial Revolution', *Historical J.* 27, 473–92.

Hovland, E., Nordvik, H. W., and Tveite, S. (1982), 'Proto-Industrialisation in Norway, 1750–1850: Fact or Fiction?', *ScEHR* 30, 45–56.

Howell (1963), R., 'Puritanism in Newcastle Before the Summoning of the Long Parliament', *Archaeologia Aeliana* 4th ser. 41, 135–55.

Hudson (1981), P., 'Proto-Industrialisation: The Case of the West Riding Wool Textile Industry in the 18th and 19th Centuries', *History Workshop* 12, 34–61.

Hudson (1986), P., *The Genesis of Industrial Capital* (Cambridge).

Hudson (1989*a*), P. (ed.), *Regions and Industries* (Cambridge).

Hudson (1989*b*), P., 'The Regional Perspective', in Hudson (1989*a*), 5–38.

Hudson (1989*c*), P., 'Capital and Credit in the West Riding Wool Textile Industry *c.*1750–1850', in Hudson (1989*a*), 69–99.

Hudson (1991), P., 'Landholding and the Organisation of Textile Manufacture in Yorkshire Rural Townships, *c.*1660–1810', in Berg (1991*a*), 261–91.

Hufton (1972), O., 'Begging, Vagrancy, Vagabondage and the Law', *European Studies Rev.* 2, 97–123.

Hufton (1974), O., *The Poor of Eighteenth-Century France 1750–1789* (Oxford).

Hufton (1983), O., 'Social Conflict and the Grain Supply of Eighteenth-Century France'. *J. Interdisciplinary Hist.* 14, 303–31.

Hughes (1965), E., *North Country Life in the Eighteenth Century*, ii, *Cumberland and Westmorland 1700–1830*.

Hügi (1984), 'Mineral Wealth', in Brugger *et al.* (1984*a*), 197–212.

Hunt (1986), H. E., 'Industrialization and Regional Inequalities: Wages in Britain, 1760–1914', *JEcH* 46, 935–66.

Hurst (1988), J. G., 'Rural Building in England and Wales: England', in Thirsk, 854–930.

Husa (1965), V., 'L'importance de la production du charbon au moyen âge en Europe Centrale', in *Second International Conference of Economic History, Aix-en-Provence 1962* (The Hague), 472–81.

Husbands (1987), C., 'Regional Change in a Pre-Industrial Economy', *J. Hist. G* 13, 345–59.

Hutchinson (1794), W., *The History and Antiquities of Cumberland*, i (Carlisle).

Huter, F., and Zwanowetz, G. (eds.) (1977), *Erzeugung, Verkehr und Handel in der Geschichte der Alpenländer* (Innsbruck).

Hutton (1995), R., 'The English Reformation and the Evidence of Folklore', *P&P* 148, 89–116.

Inkster (1975), I., *Marginal Men: Aspects of the Social Role of the Medical Community in Sheffield 1790–1850* (Cyclost., New South Wales University).

Iredale (1970), D., 'Industry, Trade and People since 1700', in W. B. Stephens (ed.), *History of Congleton* (Manchester), 121–200.

Jack (1988*a*), R. I., 'Wales and the Marches', in Thirsk (1988), 260–71.

Jack (1988*b*), R. I., 'Wales and the Marches', ibid. 412–96.

Jäger (1875), A., 'Beitrag zur tirolerisch-salzburgischen Bergwerksgeschichte', *Archiv für österreichische Geschichte* 53, 335–456.

Jäger (1954), H., 'Zur Entstehung der heutigen grossen Forsten in Deutschland', *Berichte zur deutschen Landeskunde*, 156–71.

Jäger (1958), H., *Entwicklungsperioden agrarer Siedlungsgebiete im mittleren Westdeutschland seit dem frühen 13. Jahrhundert* (Würzburg).

Jäger, R., Lemmenmeier, M., Rohr, A., and Wiher, P. (1986), *Baumwollgarn als Schicksalsfaden* (Zurich).

Jakob (1984), H., 'Königsfeld—ein Zentrum frühmittelalterlicher Eisenverhüttungen', *Archiv für Geschichte von Oberfranken* 64, 79–94.

James (1968²), J., *History of the Worsted Manufacture in England.*

James (1966), M. E., 'The First Earl of Cumberland (1493–1542) and the Decline of Northern Feudalism', *Northern History* 1, 43–69.

James (1981), N. D. G., *A History of English Forestry* (Oxford).

Jameson (1989), M. H., 'Mountains and the Greek City States', in Bergier (1989*a*), 7–17.

Janeczek (1994), A., 'Settlement of the Polish-Ruthenian Borderland', in Subacci, 19–27.

Jeannin (1974), P., 'Conjuncture et production du cuivre dans les Vosges méridionales à la fin du XVIe et au début du XVIIe siècle', in F. Braudel (ed.), *Conjuncture économique, structures sociales* (Paris), 121–38.

Jeffrey (1857–64), A., *The History and Antiquities of Roxburghshire* (4 vols., Edinburgh).

Jegorov (1930), D. N., *Die Kolonisation Mecklenburgs im 13. Jahrhundert* (2 vols., Breslau).

Jelavich (1984), B., *History of the Balkans*, i, *Eighteenth and Nineteenth Centuries* (Cambridge).

Jelecek, L., and Bohac, Z. (1989), 'Mountains, Forests, Rivers: Medieval Bohemia in the Context of Central Europe', in Bergier (1989*a*), 147–66.

Jenkin (1972²), A. K. H., *The Cornish Miner* (Newton Abbot)

Jenkins (1990), D., 'The Demography of late Stuart Montgomeryshire, *c.*1660–1720', *Montgomeryshire Collections* 78, 73–113.

Jenkins (1973), D. T., 'Early Factory Development in the West Riding of Yorkshire, 1770–1800', in Harte and Ponting, 247–80.

Jenkins (1975), D. T., *The West Riding Wool Textile Industry 1770–1835* (Edington).

Jenks (1885), J. W., *Henry Carey als Nationalökonom* (Jena).

Jennett (1964), S., *Deserts of England.*

Jennings, B. (and Pately Bridge Tutorial Class) (1983²), *A History of Nidderdale* (Huddersfield).

Jennings (1992), B. (ed.), *Pennine Valley* (Otley).

Jewell (1991), H. M., 'North and South: the Antiquity of the Great Divide', *Northern History* 27, 1–25.

Jewell (1994), H. M., *The North–South Divide: The Origins of Northern Consciousness in England* (Manchester).

John (1950), A. H., *The Industrial Development of South Wales, 1750–1850* (Cardiff).

Johnson (1952), B. L. C., 'The Foley Partnerships: The Iron Industry at the End of the Charcoal Era', *EcHR* 4, 322–40.

Johnson (1984), S., *A Journey Through the Western Islands of Scotland* (*1775*) in D., Greene (ed.), *The Oxford Authors: Samuel Johnson*, 593–641.

Joliffe (1926), J. E. A., 'Northumberland Institutions', *EHR* 41, 1–42.

Jollie (1974²), F., *Manners and Customs of Cumberland* (Moon, Cumberland).

Jones (1967), E. L., 'Agriculture and Economic Growth in England 1660–1750: Agricultural Change', in id., *Agriculture and Economic Growth in England 1650–1815*, 152–71.

Jones (1968), E. L., 'The Agricultural Origins of Industry', *P&P* 40, 58–71.

Jones (1975), E. L., 'Afterword', in W. N. Parker and E. L. Jones (eds.), *European Peasants and their Markets* (Princeton), 327–60.

Jones (1977), E. L., 'Environment, Agriculture, and Industrialization in Europe', *AgHist* 51, 491–502.

Jones (1981¹, 1987²), E. L., *European Miracle.*

Jones (1973*a*), G., *A History of the Vikings*.

Jones (1955), G. P., 'The Poverty of Cumberland and Westmorland', *TC&WAAS* 55, 198–208.

Jones (1956), G. P., 'Early Industrial Development', in Linton, 146–154.

Jones (1958), G. P., 'Some Population Problems relating to Cumberland and Westmorland in the 18th Century', *TC&WAAS* 58, 123–39.

Jones (1962), G. P., 'The Decline of the Yeomanry in the Lake Counties', *TC&WAAS* 62, 198–223.

Jones (1969), G. P., 'King James I and the Western Border', *TC&WAAS* 69, 129–51.

Jones (1960), G. R. J., 'The Pattern of Settlement on the Welsh Border', *AgHR* 8, 66–81.

Jones (1960–3), G. R. J., 'The Tribal System in Wales', *Welsh Hist. Rev.* 1, 111–32.

Jones (1973*b*), G. R. J., 'Field Systems in North Wales', in Baker and Butlin, 430–79.

Jones (1976), G. R. J., 'Multiple Estates and Early Settlement', in Sawyer (1976*a*), 15–40.

Jones, H. *et al.* (1986), 'Peripheral Counter-Urbanization', *Regional Studies* 20, 15–26.

Jones (1980), M., 'Notes from the Margin: Class and Society in Nineteenth-Century Gwynedd', in Smith, 199–214.

Jones (1971), P., 'Medieval Agrarian Society in its Prime: Italy', *CEHE* i. 340–431.

Jones (1993), R. M., 'The Historical Consequences of Early Industrialisation in a Welsh District: The Case of North Wales, 1780–1980', in Schulze, 227–43.

Joos (1946), L., 'Die Walserwanderungen vom 13. bis 16. Jahrhundert', *SZG* 26, 289–344.

Jope (1956), E. M., 'Agricultural Implements', in Singer *et al.*, ii. 81–102.

Jordan (1962), W. K., *The Social Institutions of Lancashire* (Manchester).

Juillard (1976), É., *Histoire de la France rurale*, iii, *Apogée et crise de la civilisation paysanne 1789–1914* (Paris).

Juillard, É. and Nonn, H. (eds.) (1976), *Espaces et régions en Europe Occidentale* (Paris).

Kahk (1989), J. J., 'About the Historical Meaning of the Zone of Natural Barriers in the Way of German Eastern Expansion in XIth–XIVth Centuries', in Bergier (1989*a*), 167–80.

Kallbrunner (1934), J., 'Hans Steinberger: Ein Beitrag zur Geschichte der Montanwirtschaft im Zeitalter Rudolfs II', *VSWG* 27, 1–27.

Kampus (1981), I., 'Das System der öffentlichen Finanzen und Abgaben in Kroation … im 16. Jahrhundert', in Pferschy, 515–20.

Kanefsky, J., and Robey, J. (1994), 'Steam Engines in 18th-Century Britain: A Quantitative Assessment', in S. Pollard (ed.), *The Metal Fabrication and Engineering Industries* (Oxford), 167–92.

Kapelle (1979), W. E., *The Norman Conquest of the North: The Region and its Transformation 1000–1135*.

Kasiske (1941), K., 'Das Wesen der ostdeutschen Kolonisation', *Historische Zeitschrift* 164, 285–315.

Kaufhold (1986), K. H., 'Gewerbelandschaften in der frühen Neuzeit', in Pohl (1986*a*), 112–202.

Keeble (1976), D., *Industrial Location and Planning in the United Kingdom*.

Keeble, D., Owens, P. L., and Thompson, C., (1982), *Centrality, Peripherality and EEC Regional Development* (Cambridge).

Kellenbenz (1963), H., 'Industries rurales en occident: De la fin du moyen âge au XVIIIe siècle', *Annales ESC* 18, 833–82.

Kellenbenz (1965), H., 'Ländliches Gewerbe und bäuerliches Unternehmertum in Westeuropa vom Spätmittelalter bis ins 18. Jahrhundert', *Second International Conference of Economic History, Aix-en-Provence 1962* (The Hague), 377–472.

Kellenbenz H. (ed.) (1975), *Agrarisches Nebengewerbe und Formen der Reagrarisierung im Spätmittelalter und 19./20. Jahrhundert* (Stuttgart).

Kellenbenz (1976), H., *The Rise of the European Economy*.

Kellenbenz (1981), H., 'Technologie und Produktivität im Metallsektor (Ende 15. bis Anfang 18. Jahrhundert)', in Mariotti, 363–89.

Kellenbenz (1988), H., 'Kapitalverflechtung im Mittleren Alpenraum', *Zeitschrift für bayerische Landesgeschichte* 51, 13–50.

Kendrick (1968[2]), T. D., *A History of the Vikings*.

Kennedy (1987), P., *The Rise and Fall of the Great Powers*.

Kent (1955–6), H. S. K., 'The Anglo-Norwegian Timber Trade in the Eighteenth Century', *EcHR* 8, 62–74.

Kenyon (1967), G. H., *The Glass Industry of the Weald* (Leicester).

Kermack (1967), W. R., *The Scottish Borders (with Galloway) to 1603* (Edinburgh and London).

Kerr (1986), A. J. C., *The Common Market and how it works* (Oxford).

Kerridge (1985), E., *Textile Manufacture in Early Modern England* (Manchester).

Kershaw (1973*a*), I., *Bolton Priory: The Economy of a Northern Monastery 1286–1325*.

Kershaw (1973*b*), I., 'The Great Famine and Agrarian Crisis in England, 1315–1322', *P&P* 59, 3–50.

Kiefner (1983), T., 'In der Herberge der Barmherzigkeit (die letzte grosse Vertreibung der Waldenser im Jahr 1730)', *SZG* 33, 5–46.

Kienholz (1984), H., 'Natural Hazards: A Growing Menace?', in Brugger *et al.* (1984*a*), 385–405.

Kiernan (1988), V. G., 'The Covenanters: A Problem of Creed and Class', in Krantz, 53–81.

Kiesewetter (1980), H., 'Erklärungshypothesen zur regionalen Industrialisierung in Deutschland im 19. Jahrhundert', *VSWG* 67, 305–33.

Kiesewetter (1981), H., 'Agrarreform, landwirtschaftliche Produktion und Industrialisierung im Königreich Sachsen 1832–1861', in Blaich, 89–137.

Kiesewetter (1988), H., *Industrialisierung und Landwirtschaft: Sachsens Stellung im regionalen Industrialisierungsprozess Deutschlands im 19. Jahrhundert* (Cologne and Vienna).

King (1973), E., *Peterborough Abbey 1086–1310* (Cambridge).

Kinvig (1954), R. H., 'Warwickshire', in Darby and Terrett, 270–92.

Kirkham (1968), N., *Derbyshire Lead Mining through the Centuries* (Truro).

Kisch (1959), H., 'The Textile Industries in Silesia and the Rhineland: A Comparative Study in Industrialization', *JEcH* 19, 541–64.

Kisch (1964), H., 'Growth Deterrent of a Medieval Heritage: The Aachen-area Woollen Trades', *JEcH* 24, 517–37.

Kistler (1962), R., *Die Wirtschaftliche Entwicklung des Kantons Schwyz* (Stans).

Klein (1965), H., 'Salzburg, ein unvollendeter Passstaat', in Mayer, 275–91.

Klein (1920), J., *The Mesta: A Study in Spanish Economic History* (Cambridge, Mass.).

Klein (1980), K., *Daten zur Siedlungsgeschichte der österreichischen Länder bis zum 16. Jahrhundert* (Munich).

Klima (1989), A., 'Domestic Industry, Manufactory and Early Industrialization in Bohemia', *JEEcH* 18, 509–27.

Kluge (1969), R-D., 'Darstellung und Bewertung des deutschen Ordens in der deutschen und polnischen Literatur', *Zeitschrift für Ostforschung* 18, 15–53.

Knoppers, J. V. T., and Nicholls, R. V. V. (1981), 'Der Ostseeraum und der Welthandel mit Pottasche … 1650–1825', in K. Friedland and F. Irsigler (eds.), *Seehandel und Wirtschaftswege Nordeuropas im 17. und 18. Jahrhundert* (Ostfildern), 59–83.

Knowles (1940), D., *The Monastic Order in England … 943–1216* (Cambridge).

Knowles (1944), D., 'Some Developments in English Monastic Life, 1216–1336', *TRHS* 4th ser. 26, 37–52.

Knowles (1948), D., *The Religious Orders in England*, i, *The Old Orders 1216–1340* (Cambridge).

Knowles (1955), D., *The Religious Orders in England*, ii, *The End of the Middle Ages* (Cambridge).

Knowles, D., and Hadcock, R. N. (1953), *Medieval Religious Houses in England and Wales*.

Knox (1985), S. A., *The Making of the Shetland Landscape* (Edinburgh).
Kocka (1990), J., *Arbeitsverhältnisse und Arbeiterexistenzen* (Bonn).
Koebner (1932), R., 'Deutsche Kolonisation und deutsches Recht in den Piastenländern', *VSWG* 25, 313–52.
Koebner (1971), R., 'The Settlement and Colonization of Europe', *CEHE* i. 1–91.
Koller (1987), F., 'Bayern-Salzburg-Bechtesgaden: der Streit um den Salzhandel 1587–1611', *Zeitschrift für bayerische Landesgeschichte* 50, 767–821.
Köllmann (1974), W., *Wirtschaftsentwicklung des bergisch-märkischen Raumes im Industriezeitalter* (Remscheid).
Kötzschke, R., and Ebert, W. (1937), *Geschichte der ostdeutschen Kolonisation* (Leipzig).
Kötzschke, R., and Kretzschmar, H. (1965), *Sächsische Geschichte* (Frankfurt am Main).
Kovacevic (1960), D., 'Dans la Serbie et la Bosnie médiévales: les mines d'or et d'argent', *Annales ESC* 15/1, 246–58.
Kramer (1977), H., 'Zur Geschichte der Agrarwirtschaft, des Agrarhandels und des späteren Fremdenverkehrs in Steinach (Tirol)', in Huter and Zwanowetz, 235–45.
Krantz (1988), F. (ed.), *History from Below* (Oxford).
Kraschewski (1984), H-J., 'Der Bergbau des Harzes im 16. und zu Beginn des 17. Jahrhunderts', in Kroker and Westermann, 134–43.
Kreiner (1919), K., *Wirtschaftsleben im Bayerisch-Böhmischen Waldgebiet* (Erlangen).
Krekic (1987), B. (ed.), *The Urban Society in Eastern Europe in Premodern Times* (Chicago).
Krenzlin (1952), A., *Dorf, Feld und Wirtschaft im Gebiet der grossen Täler und Platten östlich der Elbe* (Remagen).
Krenzlin (1959), A., 'Das Wüstungsproblem im Lichte ostdeutscher Siedlungsforschung', *Zeitschrift für Agrargeschichte und Agrarsoziologie* 7, 153–69.
Kriedte, P., Medick, H., and Schlumbohm, J. (1977), *Industrialisierung vor der Industrialisierung* (Göttingen).
Kroker, W., and Westermann, E. (eds.) (1984), *Montanwirtschaft Mitteleuropas vom 12. bis 17. Jahrhundert* (Bochum).
Krollmann (1928), C., 'Die Besiedlung Ostpreussens durch den deutschen Orden', *VSWG* 21, 280–98.
Krüger (1958), H., *Zur Geschichte der Manufakturen und Manufakturarbeiter in Preussen* (Berlin).
Kruker (1979), R., 'Inneralpine Transportprobleme und kulturelle Lösungsmittel', in Bergier, 101–23.
Kubinyi (1975), A., 'Zur Frage der deutschen Siedlungen im mittleren Teil des Königreichs Ungarn (1200–1541)', in Schlesinger (1975*a*), 537–66.
Kuhn (1955, 1957), W., *Geschichte der deutschen Ostsiedlung in der Neuzeit*, i, *Das 15. bis 17. Jahrhundert (Allgemeiner Teil)*; ii, *Das 15. bis 17. Jahrhundert (Landschaftlicher Teil)* (Cologne and Graz).
Kuhn (1971), W., *Beiträge zur schlesischen Siedlungsgeschichte* (Munich).
Kuhn (1973), W., *Vergleichende Untersuchungen zur mittelalterlichen Ostsiedlung* (Cologne and Vienna).
Kuhn (1975*a*), W., 'Westslawische Landesherren als Organisatoren der mittelalterlichen Ostsiedlung', in Schlesinger (1975*a*), 225–61.
Kuhn (1975*b*), W., 'Die deutschrechtliche Siedlung in Kleinpolen', ibid. 369–415.
Kula (1976), W., *An Economic Theory of the Feudal System.*
Kunnert (1974), 'Bergbauwissenschaft und technische Neuerungen im 18. Jahrhundert', in Mitterauer (1974*a*), 181–98.
Kussmaul (1981), A., *Servants in Husbandry in Early Modern England* (Cambridge).
Kussmaul (1990), A., *A General View of the Rural Economy of England 1538–1840* (Cambridge).
Ladurie (1974), E. L., *The Peasants of Languedoc* (Chicago).
Ladurie (1977), E. L., *The French Peasantry 1450–1660* (Aldershot).

Ladurie (1981), E. L., *Montaillou, Cathars and Catholics in a French Village 1294–1324* (Harmondsworth).

Lambert (1971), A. M., *The Making of the Dutch Landscape* (London and New York).

Lampe (1983), J. R., 'Debating the Balkan Potential for Pre-1914 Development', *JEEcH* 12/1, 187–96.

Lampe, J. R., and Jackson, M. R. (1982), *Balkan Economic History, 1550–1950: From Imperial Borderland to Developing Nations* (Bloomington, Ind.).

Lander (1970^2), J. H., 'Lead Mining' and 'Textile Trades', in *VCH Derbyshire*, ii.

Landes (1983), D. S., *Revolution in Time* (Cambridge, Mass.).

Landes (1994), D. S., 'What Room for Accident in History? Explaining Big Changes by Small Events', *EcHR* 47, 637–56.

Langdon (1986), J., *Horses, Oxen and Technological Innovation … 1066–1500* (Cambridge).

Lange (1976), G., *Das ländliche Gewerbe in der Grafschaft Mark am Vorabend der Industrialisierung* (Cologne).

Langton, J., and Morris, R. J. (eds.) (1986), *Atlas of Industrializing Britain 1780–1914*.

Latouche (1937), R., 'Un aspect de la vie rurale dans la Maine au XIe et au XIIe siècle', *Le Moyen Âge* 47, 44–64.

Latouche (1948), R., 'Défrichement et peuplement rural dans la Maine du XIe au XIIIe siècle', *Le Moyen Âge* 54, 77–87.

Latouche (1967^2), R., *The Birth of Western Economy*.

Lattimore (1980), O., 'The Periphery as Locus of Innovation', in Gottmann (1980*a*), 205–15.

Laube (1968), A., 'Bergbau, Bergstädte und Landesherrschaft in Sachsen im 15./16. Jahrhundert', *Zeitschrift für Geschichtswissenschaft* 16, 1577–91.

Laube (1976), A., *Studien über den erzgebirgischen Silberbergbau von 1470 bis 1546* (Berlin).

Law (1908), A., 'Social and Economic History', in Farrer and Brownbill, 261–326.

Lawson (1973), W., 'The Construction of the Military Road in Northumberland 1751–1757', *Archeologia Aeliana* 5th ser. 1, 177–93.

Layer (1979), A., 'Die innere Entwicklung', in Spindler, iii/2, 854–9.

Leader (1905^2), R. E., *Sheffield in the Eighteenth Century* (Sheffield).

Lebon (1935), J. H. G., 'The Jezera, a Mountain Community in South-West Yugoslavia', *Geography* 20, 271–82.

Le Bras (1986), H., *Les trois France* (Paris).

Lee (1972), C. H., *A Cotton Enterprise 1795–1840: A History of M'Connell & Kennedy, Fine Cotton Spinners* (Manchester).

Lee (1986), C. H., *The British Economy since 1700: A Macroeconomic Perspective* (Cambridge).

Lefebvre (1973), G., *The Great Fear of 1789* (New York).

Le Goff (1972), J., 'The Town as an Agent of Civilization *c.*1200–*c.*1500', in C. Cipolla (ed.), *Fontana Economic History of Europe*, i. 71–106.

Leibundgut (1986), H., *Unsere Gebirgswälder: Natur, Zustand, Bewirtschaftung* (Berne and Stuttgart).

Leiser (1983), P., *Annette von Droste-Hülshoff: Die Judenbuche. Interpretationen und Hinweise* (Hollfeld).

Lekai (1977), L. J., *The Cistercians: Ideals and Reality* (Kent, Ohio).

Lemon (1969), C., 'The Statistics of the Copper Mines of Cornwall [1838]', in Burt, 49–82.

Leneman, L., and Mitchison, R. (1987), 'Scottish Illegitimacy Ratios in the Early Modern Period', *EcHR* 40, 41–63.

Lennard (1959), R., *Rural England 1086–1135* (Oxford).

Léon, P., Crouzet, F., and Gascon, R. (eds.) (1972), *L'industrialisation en Europe au XIXe siècle* (Paris).

Léon, P. *et al.* (eds.) (1976), *Histoire Économique et Sociale de la France*, iii, *L'avènement de l'ere industrielle* (Paris).

Lepetit, B., and Hoock, J. (eds.) (1987), *La ville et l'innovation* (Paris).

Lequin (1977), Y., *Les ouvriers de la région Lyonnaise* (2 vols., Paris).

Lewis (1958), A. R., 'The Closing of the Medieval Frontier 1250–1350', *Speculum* 33, 475–83.

Lewis (1907), G. R., *The Stannaries* (Cambridge, Mass.).

Lewis (1982), H. M., 'Industrialization, Class and Regional Consciousness in two Highland Societies: Wales and Appalachia', in Beaver and Purrington, 50–70.

Lewis, J., and Williams, A. M. (1988), 'Factories in Fields: Small Manufacturing Firms in Rural Southern Europe', in Linge (1988*a*), 113–30.

Lewis (1970), M. J. T., *Early Wooden Railways.*

Lewis (1956), N. B., 'The Middle Ages', in Linton, 138–41.

Lewis (1963–4), W. J., 'Lead Mining in Eastern Montgomeryshire in 1751', *Montgomeryshire Collections* 58, 114–24 .

Lichtenberger (1978), E., 'The Crisis in Rural Settlement and Farming in the High Mountain Region of Continental Europe', *Geographia Polonica* 38, 181–17.

Liddell (1966), W. H., 'The Private Forests of Southwest Cumberland', *TC&WAAS* 66, 106–30.

Ligou (1967), D., 'Forêts, garrigues et maquis dans la guerre des Camisards', in Fohlen, 129–40.

Lindgren (1987*a*), U. (ed.), *Alpenübergänge vor 1850* (Stuttgart).

Lindgren (1987*b*), U. 'Vorwort', in Lindgren (1987*a*), 7–8.

Lindley (1982), K., *Fenland Riots and the English Revolution.*

Lindquist (1985), S.-O. (ed.), *Society and Trade in the Baltic during the Viking Age* (Visby).

Lindqvist (1983), S., 'Natural Resources and Technology', *Scandinavian J. of Hist.* 8, 83–107.

Lindsay (1977), J. M., 'The Iron Industry in the Highlands: Charcoal Blast Furnaces', *Scottish Historical Review* 56, 49–63.

Linge (1988*a*), G. J. R. (ed.), *Peripheralisation and Industrial Change.*

Linge (1988*b*), G. J. R., 'Peripheralisation and Industrial Change', in Linge (1988*a*), 1–21.

Linton (1956), D. L. (ed.), *Sheffield and Its Region* (Sheffield).

Lipson (1965[2]), E., *The History of the Woollen and Worsted Industries.*

Lloyd (1992[2]), D. W., *The Making of English Towns: 2000 Years of Evolution.*

Lloyd (1967–8), H., 'The Iron Forges of the Vyrnwy Valley', *Montgomeryshire Collections* 60, 104–10.

Lloyd (1977), J. H., *The English Wool Trade in the Middle Ages* (Cambridge).

Logan (1983), F. D., *The Vikings in History.*

Löhr (1971), L., *Bergbauernwirtschaft im Alpenraum* (Graz and Stuttgart).

Lohrmann (1979), D., 'Energieprobleme im Mittelalter', *VSWG* 66/3, 297–316.

Lohrmann (1989), D., 'Die Bedeutung der Wasserscheide zwischen Schelda und Somme bis ins 18. Jahrhundert', in Bergier (1989*a*), 218–26.

Lombard (1959), M., 'Un problème cartographié: le bois dans la Mediterranée Musulmane', *Annales ESC* 14, 234–54.

Long (1991), P. O., 'The Openness of Knowledge: An Ideal and its Context in 16th-Century Writings on Mining and Metallurgy', *Technology and Culture* 32, 318–55.

Longworth (1970), P., *The Cossacks* (New York, Chicago, and San Francisco).

Lönnroth (1971), E., 'The Baltic Countries', *CEHE* iii. 361–96.

Lösch (1954[1], 1971[2]), A., *The Economics of Location* (New Haven and London).

Lopez (1976[1], 1984[2]), R. S., *The Commercial Revolution of the Middle Ages 950–1350* (Cambridge).

Louis (1907), H., 'Mining', *VCH Durham*, 319–56.

Low (1819), D., *Report Relating to the Lordship and Estate of Marchmont.*

Lowe (1972), N., *The Lancashire Textile Industry in the Sixteenth Century* (Manchester).

Lowndes (1963), R. A. C., 'Celtic Fields, Farmsteads and Burial Mounds in the Lune Valley', *TC&WAAS* 63, 77–94.

Loyn (1962[1], 1970[2]), H. R., *Anglo-Saxon England and the Norman Conquest.*

Lucas (*c.*1880), J., *Studies in Nidderdale.*

Lucassen (1987), J., *Migrant Labour in Europe 1600–1900.*

Lucassen (1994), J., 'The Netherlands, the Dutch and long-distance migration in the late sixteenth to the early nineteenth centuries', in Canny, 153–91.

Lucassen (1993), L., 'A Blind Spot. Migratory and Travelling Groups in Western European Historiography', *International Rev. of Social Hist.* 38, 209–35.

Ludwig, K.-H., and Gruber, F. (1987), *Gold- und Silberbergbau im Übergang vom Mittelalter zur Neuzeit* (Cologne and Vienna).

Lund (1974), N. W., 'Land Clearance and New Settlements on the Wastelands of Europe in the 18th Century', *6th International Congress of Economic History, Copenhagen, Section C.*

Lyon (1957–8), B., 'Medieval Real Estate Developments and Freedom', *American Historical Rev.* 63, 47–61.

Lyons (1989), J. S., 'Family Response to Economic Decline: Handloom Weavers in early nineteenth-century Lancashire', *Research in Economic History* 12, 45–91.

Lythe, S. G. E., and Butt, J. (1975), *An Economic History of Scotland 1100–1939* (Glasgow/London).

Macaulay (1913), Lord, *A History of England from the Accession of James the Second*, i.

McCracken (1958–9), E., 'The Woodlands of Ireland circa 1600', *Irish Historical Studies* 11, 271–96.

McDonnell (1963), J. (ed.), *A History of Helmsley, Rivaulx and District* (York).

McDonnell (1988), J., 'The Role of Transhumance in Northern England', *Northern History* 24, 1–17.

McDonnell (1990), J., 'Upland Pennine Hamlets', *Northern History* 26, 20–39.

McDonnell (1992), J., 'Pressures on Yorkshire Woodland in the late Middle Ages', *Northern History* 28, 110–125.

McDonnell (1994), J., 'Antecedents of Border Tenant Rights', *Northern History* 30, 22–30.

McDowall, R. W., and Mercer, E. (1970), 'Bastles of Cumberland and Northumberland', in Ramm *et al.*, 61–95.

McGowan (1981), B., *Economic Life in Ottoman Europe: Taxation, Trade and the Struggle for Land, 1600–1800* (Cambridge and Paris).

MacInnes (1988), A. I., 'The Impact of the Civil Wars and Interregnum: Political Disruption and Social Change within Scottish Gaeldom', in Mitchison and Roebuck, 58–69.

McIntire (1942), W. T., 'The Salt Pans of the Solway', *TC&WAAS* 42, 1–12.

Mackenzie (1959), H. M., 'The Bakewell Cotton Mill and the Arkwrights', *DAJ* 79, 61–87.

MacMillen (1991), M. J., 'The Core-Periphery Concept in Economic Terms with Special Reference to Brittany and Cornwall-Devon', in Havinden *et al.*, 95–103.

McNeill (1992), J. R., *The Mountains of the Mediterranean World* (Cambridge).

McNeill (1964), W. H., *Europe's Steppe Frontier* (Chicago).

MacSween (1959), M. D., 'Transhumance in North Skye', *Scottish Geographical Magazine* 75, 75–88.

Maczak, A., and Parker, W. N. (eds.) (1978), *Natural Resources in European History* (Washington).

Maddalena (1974), A., 'Rural Europe 1500–1750', in Cipolla, 273–358.

Madurowicz-Urbanska (1986), H., 'Die Raumstrukturen und Dorfansiedlungen in den Westkarpaten', in Mattmüller, 300–19.

Maeder, H., and Kruker, R. (1983), *Hirten und Herden: Alpenkultur in der Schweiz* (Olten).

Magnus (1897), Sir P., *Report on a Visit to Germany* (British Parl. Papers, C.8301, 403 ff.

Magnusson (1994), L., *The Contest for Control* (Oxford and Providence).

Maitland (1960[2]), F. W., *Domesday Book and Beyond.*

Malowist (1959), M., 'The Economic and Social Development of the Baltic Countries from the Fifteenth to the Seventeenth Centuries', *EcHR* 12, 177–89.

Maltézov (1989), C., 'Frontières sociales at frontières géographiques en Romanie venitienne: le cas des révolts crétoises', in Bergier (1989*a*), 60–4.

Mann (1986), M., *The Sources of Social Power*, i, *A History of Power from the Beginning to AD 1760* (Cambridge).

Manning (1975), B., 'The Peasantry and the English Revolution', *J. of Peasant Studies* 2, 133–58.

Mantoux (1961^2), P., *The Industrial Revolution of the Eighteenth Century*.

Manuel (1922), D. G., *Dryburgh Abbey in the Light of its Historical and Ecclesiastical Setting* (Edinburgh).

Mariotti (1981), S. (ed.), *Produttività e Technologie nei Secoli XII–XVII* (Florence).

Marsh (1974), G. P., *Man and Nation* (Cambridge, Mass.).

Marshall (1958), J. D., *Furness and the Industrial Revolution* (Barrow-in-Furness).

Marshall (1969), J. D., 'Some Aspects of the Social History of 19th-Century Cumbria, i, Migration and Literacy', *TC&WAAS* 69, 280–307.

Marshall (1970), J. D., 'Some Aspects of the Social History of 19th-Century Cumbria, ii, Crime, Police, Morals and the Countryman', *TC&WAAS* 70, 221–45.

Marshall (1972), J. D., '"Statesmen" in Cumbria: The Vicissitudes of an Expression', *TC&WAAS* 72, 248–73.

Marshall (1973), J. D., 'The Domestic Economy of the Lakeland Yeoman, 1660–1749', *TC&WAAS* 73, 190–219.

Marshall (1989), J. D., 'Stages of Industrialisation in Cumbria', in Hudson, (1989*a*), 132–55.

Marshall, J. D., and Davies-Shiel, M. (1969), *The Industrial Archaeology of the Lake Counties* (Newton Abbot).

Marshall, J. D., and Walton, J. (1981), *The Lake Counties from 1830 to the mid-twentieth century* (Manchester).

Marshall (1788), W., *The Rural Economy of Yorkshire* (2 vols.).

Marshall (1794), W., *General View of the Agriculture of the Central Highlands of Scotland.*

Marty (1951), A., *Die Viehwirtschaft der Urschweiz und Luzerns, insbesondere der Welschlandhandel 1500–1798* (Lachen).

Marwick (1924), W. H., 'The Cotton Industry and the Industrial Revolution in Scotland', *Scottish Historical Rev.* 21, 207–18.

Massey (1984), D., *Spatial Divisions of Labour.*

Mastboom (1994), J. M., 'The Role of Eastern Gelderland in Dutch Economic Development 1650–1850', in Subacci, 93–100.

Mate (1985), M., 'Medieval Agrarian Practices: The Determining Factors?', *AgHR* 33, 22–31.

Mate (1991), M., 'The Agrarian Economy of South-West England before the Black Death: Depressed or Buoyant?', in Campbell (1991*b*), 78–109.

Mathieu (1987), J., *Bauern und Bären: Eine Geschichte Unterengadins von 1650 bis 1800* (Chur).

Mathieu (1992), J., *Eine Agrargeschichte der inneren Alpen: Graubünden, Tessin, Wallis 1500–1800* (Zurich).

Mathieu, J., and Stauffacher, H. (1986), 'Alpine Gemeindedemokratie oder aristokratische Herrschaft', in Mattmüller, 320–60.

Mattmüller (1986), M. (ed.), *Wirtschaft und Gesellschaft in Berggebieten, Itinera*, 5/6.

Mauersberg (1960), H., *Wirtschafts- und Sozialgeschichte zentraleuropäischer Städte in neuerer Zeit* (Göttingen).

Maxwell (1956), I. S., 'The Age of Settlement', in Linton, 121–37.

Maxwell (1962*a*), I. S., 'Yorkshire, the West Riding', in Darby and Maxwell, 1–84.

Maxwell (1962*b*), I. S., 'Yorkshire, the North Riding', ibid. 85–163.

Maxwell (1962*c*), I. S., 'Yorkshire, the East Riding', ibid. 164–232.

Mayer (1952), K. B., *The Population of Switzerland* (New York).

Mayer (1937), T., 'Die Entstehung des "modernen" Staates im Mittelalter und die freien Bauern', *Zeitschrift der Savigny-Stiftung für Rechtsgeschichte (Germanistische Abteilung)* 57, 210–88.

Mayer (1938), T., 'Die Besiedlung und politische Erfassung des Schwarzwaldes im Hochmittelalter', *Zeitschrift für die Geschichte des Oberrheins* 52–91, 500–22.

Mayer (1959), T., 'Über die Freiheit des Bauern in Tirol und in der schweizer Eidgenossenschaft', in Troger und Zwanowetz, 231–40.

Mayer (1965*a*), T., *Die Alpen in der europäischen Geschichte des Mittelalters* (Konstanz and Stuttgart).

Mayer (1965*b*), T., 'Die Alpen als Staatsgrenze und Völkerbrücke im europäischen Mittelalter', in Mayer (1965*a*), 7–14.

Mazoyer (1932), L., 'Exploitation forestière et conflicts sociaux', *Annales d'histoire économique et sociale* 4, 339–58.

Medick (1993), H., 'Grenzziehung und die Herstellung des politisch-sozialen Raumes', in Weisbrod, 195–211.

Megerle (1982), K., *Württemberg im Industrialisierungsprozess Deutschlands* (Stuttgart).

Meiggs (1982), R., *Trees and Timber in the Ancient Mediterranean World* (Oxford).

Mellor (1989), R. E. H., *Nation, State and Territory*.

Mendels (1982), F., 'Proto-Industrialization: Theory and Reality', *Eighth International Economic History Congress, 'A' Themes*, 69–107.

Menzel (1975), J. J., 'Der Beitrag der Urkundenwissenschaft zur Erforschung der deutschen Ostsiedlung am Beispiel Schlesiens', in Schlesinger (1975*a*), 131–59.

Mercer (1991), R. J., 'The Highland Zone: Reaction and Reality 5000 BC–2000 AD', *Proceedings of the British Academy* 76, 120–150.

Merl (1989), S., 'Agrarreformen und nichtmarktwirtschaftliche Bedingungen—Agrarsektor und Industrialisierung in Russland und in der Sowjetunion', in Pierenkemper, 175–209.

Merlin (1971), P., *L'exode rural, suivi de deux études sur les migrations par Robert Hérin et Robert Nadot* (Paris).

Merritt (1974), R. L., 'Locational Aspects of Political Integration', in K. R. Cox, D. R. Reynolds, and S. Rokkan (eds.), *Locational Approaches to Power and Conflict* (New York), 187–211.

Messerli (1989), P., *Mensch und Natur im alpinen Lebensraum* (Berne/Stuttgart).

Messerli, P., and Brugger, E. A. (1984*a*), 'Theoretical Guidelines for the Analysis of Problems in Mountain Areas', in Brugger *et al.* (1984*a*), 43–66.

Messerli, P., and Brugger, E. A. (1984*b*), 'Mountain Areas between Self-Reliance and Dependency', ibid. 603–18.

Meyer (1979), W., 'Wüstungen als Zeugen des mittelalterlichen Alpwesens', in Bergier, 256–64.

Meyer-Marthaler (1944), E., 'Der heutige Stand der Walserfrage', *SZG* 24, 1–27.

Miani (1964), G., 'L'économie lombarde aux XIVe et XVe siècles: Une exception à la règle', *Annales ESC* 19.

Michaud (1959), G. (ed.), *Les routes de France depuis les origins jusqu'à nos jours* (Paris).

Michell (1977), A. R., 'The European Fisheries in Early Modern History', *CEHE* v. 134–84.

Micklethwaite (1899), J. T., 'The Cistercian Order', *YAJ* 15, 245–68.

Middleton (1973), T., *Annals of Hyde and District* (Longden).

Miller (1964), E., 'The English Economy in the Thirteenth Century: Implications of Recent Research', *P&P* 28, 21–40.

Miller (1988), E., 'Northern England', in Thirsk, 245–59.

Miller (1991*a*), E. (ed.), *The Agrarian History of England and Wales*, iii, *1348–1500* (Cambridge).

Miller (1991*b*), E., 'Yorkshire and Lancashire', in Miller (1991*a*), 42–52.

Miller (1991*c*), E., 'Yorkshire and Lancashire', ibid. 182–94.

Miller, E., and Hatcher, J. (1978), *Medieval England—Rural Society and Economic Change 1086–1348*.

Millward (1974), R., 'The Cumbrian Towns between 1600 and 1800', in Chalklin and Havinden, 202–28.

Millward (1984), R., 'The Early Stages of European Industrialization: Organization and Serfdom', *Expl. EcH* 21, 406–28.

Millward, R., and Robinson, A. (1970), *The Lake District.*

Mingay (1964), G. E., 'The Land Tax Assessment and the Small Landowner', *EcHR* 17, 381–8.

Mingay (1990), G. E., *A Social History of the English Countryside.*

Mironov (1992), B. N., 'Consequences of the Price Revolution in Eighteenth-Century Russia', *EcHR* 45, 457–78.

Mitchell (1925), G. M., 'The English and Scottish Cotton Industries: A Study in Interrelations', *Scottish Historical Rev.* 22, 101–14.

Mitchell (1968), H., *The Hard Way Up.*

Mitchison, R., and Roebuck, P. (eds.) (1988), *Economy and Society in Scotland and Ireland 1500–1939* (Edinburgh).

Mitterauer (1974*a*), M. (ed.), *Österreichisches Montanwesen. Produktion, Verteilung, Sozialformen* (Munich).

Mitterauer (1974*b*), M., 'Produktionsweise, Siedlungsstruktur und Sozialformen im österreichischen Montanwesen des Mittelalters und der frühen Neuzeit', in Mitterauer (1974*a*), 234–315.

Moch (1983), L. P., *Paths to the City* (Beverley Hills and London).

Moch (1989), L. P., 'The Importance of Mundane Movements . . . in the History of Migration', in Ogden and White, 97–117.

Mokyr (1976), J., *Industrialization in the Low Countries 1795–1850* (New Haven).

Mokyr (1990), J., *The Lever of Riches: Technological Creativity and Economic Progress* (New York).

Mol (1992), J. A., 'Besitzerwerbungen der friesischen Zisterzienserklöster Klarkamp, Bloemkamp und Gerkeskloster', in Elm, 67–96.

Molenda (1976*a*), D., 'Mining Towns in Central-Eastern Europe in Feudal Times', *Acta Poloniae Historica* 34, 165–88.

Molenda (1976*b*), D., 'Investments in Ore Mining in Poland from the 13th to the 17th Centuries,' *JEEcH* 5/1, 151–69.

Molenda (1981), D., 'Le progrès technique et l'organisation économique de l'extraction des metaux non ferreux en Pologne du XIVe au XVIIIe siècle', in Mariotti, 399–410.

Monkhouse (1954), F. J., 'Worcestershire', in Darby and Terrett, 215–26.

Monter (1976), E. W., *Witchcraft in France and Switzerland* (Ithaca).

Moore (1965), J. S., *Langton: A Study in the Evolution of the Wealden Landscape* (Leicester).

Moran (1981), 'German Prince-Practitioners: Aspects in the Development of Courtly Science, Technology, and Procedures in the Renaissance', *Technology and Culture* 22, 253–75.

Morard (1971), N., 'Les premières enclosures dans le Canton de Fribourg à la fin du moyen âge et les progrès de l'individualisme agraire', *SZG* 21, 249–81.

Morawitzky (1856–7), M. T., 'Übersicht der von dem Kloster Benediktbeuern für das allgemeine Landes-Defensivwesen im spanischen Erbfolgekrieg aufgebotenen Unterntanen', *Oberbayerisches Archiv für vaterländische Geschichte* 16, 306–29.

Morineau (1978), M., 'Les Mancelliniers de l'Europe', in P. Léon *et al.* (eds.), *Histoire* économique et sociale du monde, ii (Paris).

Morris (1995), C. T., 'How Fast and Why Did Early Capitalism Benefit the Majority?', *JEcH* 55, 211–26.

Morris (1959–60), E. R., 'The Dolobran Family in Religion and Industry in Montgomeryshire', *Montgomeryshire Collections* 56, 124–47.

Morris (1901), J. E., *The Welsh Wars of Edward I.*

Morsel (1972), H., 'Les industries électrotechniques dans les Alpes Français du Nord de 1869 à 1921', in Léon *et al.*, 557–92.

Mortensen (1951), H., 'Neue Beobachtungen über Wüstungs-Brandfluren und ihre Bedeutung für die mittelalterliche deutsche Kulturlandschaft', *Berichte zur deutschen Landeskunde* 10, 341–61.

Morton (1832), J., *The Monastic Annals of Teviotdale* (Edinburgh).

Müller (1905), J., 'Das Rodwesen Bayerns und Tirols im Spätmittelalter und zu Beginn der Neuzeit', *VSWG* 3, 362–420.

Müller (1938), J., *Die Industrialisierung der deutschen Mittelgebirge* (Jena).

Multhauf (1978), R. P., *Neptune's Gift: A History of Common Salt* (Baltimore and London).

Murra (1989), J. V., 'High Altitude Andean Societies and their Economies', in Genovese and Hochberg, 205–14.

Murray (1875), R., 'Border Superstitions', *Hawick Archaeological Soc. Trans.*, 165–7.

Musgrove (1990), F., *The North of England* (Oxford).

Musson (1976), A. E., 'Industrial Motive Power in the United Kingdom, 1800–70', *EcHR* 29, 415–39.

Musson (1978), A. E., *The Growth of British Industry*.

Mutschlechner (1969), G., 'Die Bergwerksordnung für Gossensass und Sterzing vom Jahre 1510', in Troger and Zwanowetz, 293–314.

Myrdal (1957), G., *Economic Theory and Underdeveloped Regions*.

Myres (1989), J. N. L., *The English Settlements* (Oxford).

Nabholz (1924), H., 'Aus der Geschichte der Zürcher Landwirtschaft', in Zürcher landwirtschaftlicher Kantonalverein, *Die Landwirtschaft im Kanton Zürich* (Zurich).

Nabholz (1931), H., 'Die Eidgenossenschaft in der Dauphiné', *Archiv des Historischen Vereins des Kanton Bern* 31, 17–31.

Nabholz (1938), H., 'Der Kampf der Schweizer Bauern um Autonomie und Befreiung von den Grundlasten', *Wirtschaft und Kultur, Festschrift Alfons Dopsch* (Baden-bei-Wien), 484–502.

Nadal, J., and Giralt, E. (1960), *La population Catalane de 1553 à 1717: L'immigration française* (Paris).

Narr (1956), C. J., 'Early Food-Producing Populations', in Thomas, 134–51.

Naujoks (1982), E., 'Stadt und Industrialisierung im Bereich der Schwäbischen Alb', *Zeitschrift für Württembergische Landesgeschichte* 41, 165–93.

Neale (1976), F., 'Saxon and Medieval Landscapes', in Athill (1976*a*), 75–101.

Neeson (1993), J. M., *Commoners: Common Right, Enclosure and Social Change in England, 1700–1820* (Cambridge).

Nef (1934), J. U., 'The Progress of Technology and the Growth of Large-Scale Industry in Great Britain, 1540–1640', *EcHR* 5, 3–24.

Nef (1936–7), J. U., 'Prices and Industrial Capitalism in France and England, 1540–1640', *EcHR* 7, 155–85.

Nef (1941*a*), J. U., 'Industrial Europe at the Time of the Reformation (ca. 1515–ca. 1540)', *JPE* 49, 183–224.

Nef (1941*b*), J. U., 'Silver Production in Central Europe, 1450–1618', *JPE* 49, 375–591.

Nef (1950), J. U., *War and Human Progress* (Cambridge, Mass.).

Nef (1952[1] and 1987[2]), J. U., 'Mining and Metallurgy in Medieval Civilization', *CEHE* ii. 429–92, 691–761 resp.

Nef (1966[2]), J. U., *The Rise of the British Coal Industry* (2 vols.).

Netting (1981), R. M., *Balancing on an Alp* (Cambridge).

Neville (1994), C. J., 'Keeping the Peace in the Northern Marches in the later Middle Ages', *EHR* 109, 1–25.

Newell (1925), A., *A Hillside View of Industrial History* (Todmorden).

Newton (1912), J., 'Agriculture', in Page, 455–480.

Newton (1974), R., 'The Decay of the Border: Tudor Northumberland in Transition', in Chalklin and Havinden, 2–31.

Nicholas (1991), D., 'Of Poverty and Primacy: Demand, Liquidity and the Flemish Economic Miracle, 1050–1200', *American Historical Rev.* 96, 17–41.

Nicholas, S., and Steckel, R. H. (1992), *Tall but Poor: Nutrition, Health and Living Standards in Pre-Famine Ireland* (NBER Working Paper Series no. 39, Cambridge, Mass.).

Nicholls (1961), W. H., 'Industrialization, Factor Markets and Agricultural Development', *JPE* 69, 319–340.

Nicolson, J., and Burn, R. (1976²), *The History and Antiquities of the Counties of Westmorland and Cumberland* (2 vols., Carlisle).

Niederer (1979), A., 'Die alpine Alltagskultur', in Bergier (1989*a*), 233–55.

Niederer (1980*a*), A., 'Économie et forme de vie traditionelle dans les Alpes', in Guichonnet (1980*a*), ii. 5–90.

Niederer (1980*b*), A., 'Mentalités et sensibilités', ibid. ii. 91–168.

Niederer (1993), A., *Alpine Alltagskultur zwischen Beharrung und Wandel* (Berne, Stuttgart, and Vienna).

Nietsch (1939), H., *Wald und Siedlung im vorgeschichtlichen Mitteleuropa* (Leipzig).

Nitz (1983), H.-J., 'The Church as Colonist: The Benedictine Abbey of Lorsch and Planned Waldhufen Colonization in the Odenwald', *J.Hist.G* 9, 105–26.

Nolte (1991), H.-H. (ed.), *Internal Peripheries in European History* (Göttingen and Zurich).

North, D. C., and Thomas, R. P. (1973), *The Rise of the Western World* (Cambridge).

Novosel'tsev (1986), A. P., 'Economy and Social System of Highlands in the Middle Ages', *Contributions to 9th International Economic History Conference, Moscow*—(Cyclost.).

Nutley (1980), S. D., 'The Concept of Isolation—A Method of Evaluation and West Highland Example', *Regional Studies* 14, 111–23.

Oakey, R. P., and Cooper, S. Y. (1989), 'High Technology Industry, Agglomeration and the Potential for Peripherally Sited Small Firms', *Regional Studies* 23, 347–60.

Öberg (1990), S., 'An Historical Background to the Geography of Creativity', in Shachar and Öberg, 128–48.

O'Brien (1919), G., *The Economic History of Ireland in the Seventeenth Century* (Dublin and London).

O'Brien, P., Griffiths, T., and Hunt, P. (1991), 'Politial Components of the Industrial Revolution: Parliament and the English Cotton Textile Industry, 1660–1774', *EcHR* 44, 395–423.

O'Dell, A. C., and Walton, K. (1962), *The Highlands* and *Islands of Scotland* (London and Edinburgh).

Odermatt (1981), L., *Die Alpenlandschaft in Nidwalden: Geschichtliche Entwicklung und Anpassung an die Agrarstrukturen der Neuzeit* (Stans).

Offer (1985), A., 'Ricardo's Paradox and the Movement of Rents in England, *c.*1870–1910', in Wood, iv. 156–73.

Ogden (1989), P. E., 'Industry, Mobility and the Evolution of Rural Society in the Ardèche in the Late Nineteenth and Early Twentieth Centuries', in Ogden and White, 118–41.

Ogden, P. E., and White, P. E. (eds.) (1989), *Migrants in Modern France.*

O'Grada (1994), C., *Ireland, a New Economic History 1780–1939* (Oxford).

Ord (1972²), J. W., *The History and Antiquities of Cleveland* (Stockton on Tees).

Ormrod (1991), W. M., 'The Crown and the English Economy, 1290–1348', in Campbell (1991*a*), 149–83.

Osborne (1978), B. S., 'Common Lands, Mineral Rights and Industry: Changing Evaluations in an Industrializing Society', *J.Hist.G* 4, 231–49.

Oschinsky (1971), D., *Walter of Henley and other Treatises on Estate Management and Accounting* (Oxford).

Otruba (1974), G., 'Quantitative Aspekte der Salzproduktion im 19. Jahrhundert', in Mitterauer (1974*a*), 29–71.

Outhwaite (1986), R. B., 'Progress and Backwardness in English Agriculture, 1500–1650', *EcHR* 39, 1–18.

Overton, M., and Campbell, B. M. S. (1991), 'Productivity Change in European Agricultural Development', in Campbell and Overton, 1–50.

Owen (1976), D., 'Chapelries and Rural Settlement: An Examination of some of the Kesteven Evidence', in Sawyer (1976*a*), 66–71.

Owen (1991*a*), D. H., 'Wales and the Marshes', in Miller (1991*a*), 92–106.

Owen (1991*b*), D. H., 'Wales and the Marshes', ibid. 238–54.

Owen (1991*c*), D. H., 'Wales and the Marshes', ibid. 648–61.

Page, W. (ed.) (1912), *VCH of the County of York*, ii.

Page (1914), W. (ed.), *VCH, Yorkshire North Riding*, i.

Palairet (1979), M., 'The New Immigration and the Newest: Slavic Migrations from the Balkans to America and Industrial Europe since the Late Nineteenth Century', in T. C. Smout (ed.), *The Search for Wealth and Stability*, 43–65.

Palairet (1983), M., 'Land, Labour and Industrial Progress in Bulgaria and Serbia Before 1914', *JEEcH* 12, 163–85.

Palairet (1986), M., 'The Culture of Economic Stagnation in Montenegro', in Mattmüller, 392–438.

Palairet (1995), M., 'Rural Serbia in the light of the Census of 1863', *JEEcH* 24, 41–107.

Palliser (1993), D. M., 'Domesday Book and the Harrying of the North', *Northern History* 29, 1–23.

Palme (1983), R., *Rechts-, Wirtschafts- und Sozialgeschichte der inneralpinen Salzwerke bis zu deren Monopolisierung* (Frankfurt am Main/Berne).

Palme (1984*a*), R., 'Rechtliche und soziale Probleme im Tiroler Erzbergbau vom 12. bis zum 16. Jahrhundert', in Kroker and Westermann, 111–17.

Palme (1984*b*), R., 'Die Entstehung des Tiroler Bergrechts 1185–1214', *Mitteilungen des Instituts für österreichische Geschichtsforschung* 92, 317–40.

Pappas (1981), N. C., 'Balkan Foreign Legions in Eighteenth-Century Italy. The "Reggimento Real Macedone" and its Successors', in I. Banac, J. G. Ackerman, and R. Szporluk (eds.), *Nation and Ideology* (New York), 33–59.

Parker (1908), F. H. M., 'Inglewood Forest, Part IV', *TC&WAAS* 9, 24–37.

Parker (1909), F. H. M., 'Inglewood Forest, Parts V and VI', *TC&WAAS* 10, 1–28.

Parker, H. M., and Willies, L. (1979), *Peakland Lead Mining and Mines* (Ashbourne).

Parry (1967), J. H., 'Transport and Trade Routes', *CEHE* iv. 155–219.

Parry (1978), M. L., *Climatic Change, Agriculture and Settlement* (Folkestone).

Paulinyi (1974), A., 'Der technische Fortschritt im Eisenhüttenwesen der Alpenländer ... 1600–1860', in Mitterauer (1974*a*), 144–80.

Paulinyi (1971), O., 'Eigentum und Gesellschaft in den niederungarischen Bergstädten', in Bog, 525–68.

Pearsall, W. K., and Pennington, W. (eds.) (1973), *The Lake District: A Landscape History.*

Pearson (1913–15), J. M., 'The Decayed and Decaying Industries of Powysland', *Montgomeryshire Collections* 37, 15–30.

Pease (1913), E., *The Lord Wardens of the Marches of England and Scotland.*

Pedreira (1990), J. M., 'Social Structure and the Persistence of Rural Domestic Industry', *JEEcH* 19, 521–47.

Perloff, H., and Wingo, L. (1975), 'National Resource Endowment and Regional Economic Growth', in Friedmann and Alonso, 307–31.

Perrot (1983), J.-C., 'Développement et sous-développement régionales', in Guarducci, 91–102.

Pesez, J.-M., and Ladurie, E. L. (1965), 'Le cas français: vue d'ensemble', in École des Hautes Études, 127–252.

Petmezas (1990), S. D., 'Patterns of Proto-Industrialization in the Ottoman Empire. The Case of Eastern Thessaly, *c.*1750–1860', *JEEcH* 19, 575–603.

Petran (1965), J., 'A propos de la formation des régions de la production specialisée en Europe centrale', Second International Conference of Economic History, Aix-en-Provence, 1962, 217–22.

Petri (1975), F., 'Entstehung und Verbreitung der niederländischen Marschenkolonisation in Europa', in Schlesinger (1975*a*), 695–754.

Pettit (1968), P. A. J., *The Royal Forests of Northamptonshire* (Northamptonshire Record Society).

Peyer (1975), C., 'Wollgewerbe, Viehzucht, Solddienst und Bevölkerungsentwicklung in Stadt und Landschaft Freiburg i. Ue. vom 14. bis 16. Jahrhundert', in Kellenbenz, 79–95.

Peyer (1979), H. C., *Gewässer, Grenzen und Märkte in der Schweizergeschichte* (Zurich).

Pferschy (1981), G. (ed.), *Siedlung, Macht und Wirtschaft* (Graz).

Pfister (1986), C., 'Bevölkerung, Wirtschaft und Ernährung in den Berg- und Talgebieten des Kantons Bern 1760–1869', in Mattmüller, 361–91.

Pfister (1985), U., *Die Anfänge der Geburtenbeschränkung* (Berne, Frankfurt am Main, and New York).

Pfister (1989), U., 'Proto-industrialization and Demographic Change: The Canton of Zürich', *JEEcH* 18, 629–62.

Pfister (1991), U., 'Protoindustrialisierung: die Herausbildung einer Gewerberegion, 15.–18. Jahrhundert', *SZG* 41, 149–61.

Pfister (1992*a*), U., *Die Zürcher Fabriques* (Zurich).

Pfister (1992*b*), U., 'The Proto-Industrial Household Economy: Toward a Formal Analysis', *J. of Family History* 17, 201–22.

Pfister (1994), U., 'Regionale Spezialisierung und Handelsinfrastruktur im Alpenraum, 15.–19. Jahrhundert', in 11th International Economic History Congress, Milan, *Section C 28* (Milan).

Pfleghart (1908), A., *Die schweizerische Uhrenindustrie* (Leipzig).

Philipson, J., and Child, F. A. (1960), 'Remains of Illicit Distilleries in Upper Coquetdale', *Archaeologia Aeliana* 4th ser. 38, 99–112.

Phillips (1980), A. D. M., 'Mossland Reclamation in Nineteenth-Century Cheshire', *T.Hist.SL&C* 129, 93–107.

Phillips, C. B., and Smith, J. H. (1994), *Lancashire and Cheshire from AD 1540.*

Phillips (1977), P., *A View of Old Montgomeryshire* (Swansea).

Pickl (1974), O., 'Die Salzproduktion im Ostalpenraum am Beginn der Neuzeit', in Mitterauer (1974*a*), 11–28.

Pickl (1981), O., 'Technischer Fortschritt im Tiroler Bergbau des 16. Jahrhunderts', in Mariotti, 411–15.

Pickl (1986*a*), O., 'Die Steiermark als Gewerbe- und Industrielandschaft', in Pohl (1986*a*), 16–38.

Pickl (1986*b*), O., 'Wirtschaft und Gesellschaft in den Ostalpenländern Kärnten und Steiermark', in Mattmüller, 38–101.

Pickles (1981), M. F., 'Agrarian Society and Wealth in Mid-Wharfedale 1664–1743', *YAJ* 53, 63–78.

Pierce (1972), T. J., *Medieval Welsh Society* (Cardiff).

Pierenkemper (1989), T. (ed.), *Landwirtschaft und industrielle Entwicklung* (Stuttgart).

Pierenkemper (1992*a*), T. (ed.), *Industriegeschichte Schlesiens im 19. Jahrhundert* (Wiesbaden).

Pierenkemper (1992*b*), T., 'Gestaltende Kräfte: Staat, Unternehmer und Arbeiter', in Pierenkemper (1992*a*), 77–106.

Pilkington (1789), J., *A View of the Present State of Derbyshire* (2 vols., Derby).

Pinkney (1953), D. H., 'Migrations to Paris during the Second Empire', *J. of Modern Hist.* 25, 1–12.

Pirenne (1908–9), H., 'The Formation and Constitution of the Burgundian State (Fifteenth and Sixteenth Centuries)', *American Historical Rev.* 14, 477–502.

Pischel (1928), F., *Thüringische Glashüttengeschichte* (Weimar).

Piskorski (1991), J., 'Die deutsche Ostsiedlung des Mittelalters in der Entwicklung des östlichen Mitteleuropa', *Jb. für die Geschichte Mittel- und Ostdeutschlands* 40, 27–84.

Piuz (1967), A.-M., 'La forêt dans l'histoire', *SZG* 17, 72–9.

Platt (1969), C., *The Monastic Granges in Medieval England.*

Plaum, B. D., and Witthöft, H. (1993), 'Das Siegerland: Ein historisches Profil', in Schulze, 318–63.

Plymley (1813), J., *General View of the Agriculture of Shropshire.*

Podraza (1986), A., 'Die Naturbedingungen und die Entwicklungsrichtungen der Produktion am Beispiel der Westkarpaten', in Mattmüller, 283–99.

Pohl (1986*a*), H. (cd.), *Gewerbe- und Industrielandschaften vom späten Mittelalter bis ins 20. Jahrhundert* (Stuttgart).

Pohl (1986*b*), H., 'Einführung', in Pohl (1986*a*), 3–15.

Pohlendt (1950), H., *Die Verbreitung der mittelalterlichen Wüstungen* (Marburg).

Poitrineau (1986), A., 'Quelques aspects specifiques de l'économie montagnarde française à l'époque moderne', in Mattmüller, 102–22.

Pollard (1992*a*), S., 'The Concept of the Industrial Revolution', in G. Dosi, R. Giannetti, and P. A. Tominelli (eds.), *Technology and Enterprise in an Historical Perspective* (Oxford), 29–62.

Pollard (1992*b*), S., 'The Concept of Regional Industrialization: The British Experience', *Jb. für Wirtschaftsgeschichte* 1992/I, 4–35.

Pollard (1995), S., 'Marginal Areas: Do They Have a Common History?', in B. Etemad, J. Batou, and T. David (eds.), *Towards an International Economic and Social History* (Geneva), 121–36.

Pollard, S., and Crossley, D. W., (1968), *The Wealth of Britain.*

Poller (1970), H., 'Erzgebirgige Einflüsse im Bergbau der Markgrafschaft Bayreuth vom 16. bis 19. Jahrhundert', *Archiv für Geschichte von Oberfranken* 50, 319–38.

Pölnitz (1960²), G. Frh. von, *Die Fugger* (Frankfurt am Main).

Ponting (1971), K. G., *The Woollen Industry of South-West England* (Bath).

Pope (1989), R. (ed.), *Atlas of British Social and Economic History since c.1700.*

Porter (1974), J., 'A Forest in Transition: Bowland 1500–1650', *T.Hist.SL&C* 125, 40–60.

Porter (1977), J., 'Waste Land Reclamation in the Sixteenth and Seventeenth Centuries: The Case of South-Eastern Bowland, 1550–1630', *T.Hist.SL&C* 127, 1–23.

Posch (1966), F. (ed.), *Der steirische Bauer* (Graz).

Postan (1938–9), M. M., 'The Fifteenth Century', *EcHR* 9, 160–7.

Postan (1950), M. M., 'Some Evidence of Declining Population in the Late Middle Ages', *EcHR* 2, 221–46.

Postan (1967), M. M., 'Investment in Medieval Agriculture', *JEcH* 27, 576–87.

Postan (1971), M. M., 'Medieval Agrarian Society in its Prime: England', *CEHE* i. 548–632.

Postan (1972), M. M., *The Medieval Economy and Society.*

Postan (1973), M. M., *Essays on Medieval Agriculture and General Problems of the Medieval Economy* (Cambridge).

Potter (1996), D., 'The International Mercenary Market in the Sixteenth Century', *EHR* 111, 24–58.

Pounds (1973), N. J. G., *An Historical Geography of Europe 450 BC–AD 1330* (Cambridge).

Poussou (1970), J.-P., 'Les mouvements migratoires en France et à partir de la France du XVe siècle au début du XIXe siècle', *Annales de Démographie Historique* 11–78.

Powell (1967–8*a*), J. M., 'Agriculture in Montgomeryshire in the early nineteenth century', *Montgomeryshire Collections* 60, 67–84.

Powell (1967–8*b*), J. M., 'The Industrial Structure of Montgomeryshire in the early nineteenth century', ibid. 111–24.

Prebble (1963), J., *The Highland Clearances.*

Prestwich (1979), M., 'Italian Merchants in the Late 13th and Early 14th Centuries', in Centre for Medieval and Renaissance Studies, UCLA, *The Dawn of Modern Banking* (Newhaven/London), 77–104.

Price (1969), L. L., 'West Barbary; or Notes on the System of Work and Wages in the Cornish Mines [1891]', in Burt, 111–206.

Price (1981), R., *An Economic History of Modern France 1730–1914.*

Price (1983), R., *The Modernization of Rural France.*

Prince (1973), H. C., 'England circa 1800', in Darby (1973*a*), 389–464.

Pringle (1813), A., 'General View of the Agriculture of the County of Westmorland', in Bailey and Culley.

Probszt (1966), G. Frh. von, *Die niederungarischen Bergstädte* (Munich).

Purrington (1982), B. L., 'The Context of Cultural Ecology in Highland Environments', in Beaver and Purrington, 3–11.

Pybus (1994), S., *'Damned Bad Place, Sheffield': An Anthology of Writing about Sheffield through the Ages* (Sheffield).

Quirin (1954), K., *Die deutsche Ostsiedlung im Mittelalter* (Göttingen, Frankfurt am Main, and Berlin).

Rackham (1976), O., *Trees and Woodland in the British Landscape.*

Rackham (1980), O., *Ancient Woodland, its history, vegetation and uses in England.*

Rackham (1990), O., *The History of the Countryside.*

Radcliffe (1828), W., *The Origin of the New System of Manufacture called Powerloom Weaving* (Stockport).

Radkau (1983), J., 'Holzverknappung and Krisenbewusstsein im 18. Jahrhundert', *Geschichte und Gesellschaft* 9, 513–43.

Rae (1958), T. I., 'Some Aspects of Border Administration in the 16th Century', *Hawick Archaeological Soc. Trans.*, 5–13.

Rae (1966), T. I., *The Administration of the Scottish Frontier 1513–1603* (Edinburgh).

Raftis (1960–1), J. A., 'Western Monasticism and Economic Organization', *Comp.St.S&H* 3, 452–69.

Raftis (1974), J. A., *Assart Data and Land Values* (Toronto).

Raftis (1988), J. A., 'East Midlands', in Thirsk, 189–202.

Rainer (1977), J., 'Die Messingfabrik Möllbrücke in Kärnten', in Huter and Zwanowetz, 331–49.

Raistrick (1970), A., *West Riding of Yorkshire.*

Raistrick (1975), A., *The Lead Industry of Wensleydale and Swaledale* (2 vols., Hartington).

Raistrick (1977[2]), A., *Two Centuries of Industrial Welfare: the London (Quaker) Lead Company 1692–1905* (Hartington).

Raistrick (1982), A., *The Wharton Mines in Swaledale in the Seventeenth Century* (Northallerton).

Raistrick, A., and Jennings, B. (1965), *A History of Lead Mining in the Pennines.*

Ramana (1985), D. V., 'Ricardo's Environment', in Wood, i. 196–208.

Ramm, H. G., McDowall, R. W., and Mercer, E. (1970), *Shielings and Bastles.*

Ramsay (1965[2]), G. D., *The Wiltshire Woollen Industry in the Sixteenth and Seventeenth Centuries.*

Randall (1989), A. J., 'Work, Culture and Resistance to Machinery in the West of England Woollen Industry', in Hudson (1989*a*), 175–98.

Randsborg (1992), K., 'Barbarians, Classical Antiquity and the Rise of Western Europe: an Archaeological Essay', *P&P* 137, 8–24.

Ratkos (1971), P., 'Das Kupferwesen in der Slowakei vor der Entstehung der Thurzo-Fuggerschen Handelsgesellschaft', in Bog, 584–99.

Rauch (1984), T., 'The Accumulation Theory Approach to the Explanation of Peripheral Disparities of Underdeveloped Countries', *Geoforum* 15, 209–29.

Rauch (1988), T., 'The Accumulation Theory Approach to Peripheralisation in Underdeveloped Countries: The Examples of Nigeria and Zambia', in Linge (1988*a*), 22–36.

Raumolin (1982*a*), J., *The Relationship of Forest Sector to Rural Development* (Cyclost., University of Oulu, Finland).

Raumolin (1982*b*), J., *Center-periphery Theories before Center-periphery Theories and the Problem of the Organisation of Space* (Cyclost., Rovaniemi, Finland).

Ravenhill (1967), W. L. D., 'Cornwall', in Darby and Finn, 296–347.

Rees (1951), A., *Life in a Welsh Countryside* (Cardiff).

Rees, J., Hewings, G. J. D., and Stafford, H. A. (1981), *Industrial Location and Regional Systems.*

Rees (1968), W., *Industry before the Industrial Revolution* (2 vols., Cardiff).

Reid (1920), R. R., 'Barony and Thanage', *EHR* 35, 161–99.

Renouard (1958), Y., '1212–1216: Comment les traits durables de l'Europe occidentale moderne se sont définis au début du XIIIe siècle', *Annales de l'Université de Paris* 28, 5–21.

Ress (1954), F. M., 'Unternehmungen, Unternehmer und Arbeiter im Eisenerzbergbau und in der Eisenverhüttung der Oberpfalz von 1300 bis um 1630', *Schmollers Jahrbuch* 74, 49–106.

Reulecke (1980), J., 'Nachzügler und Pionier zugleich: das Bergische Land und der Beginn der Industrialisierung in Deutschland', in S. Pollard (ed.), *Region und Industrialisierung* (Göttingen), 52–68.

Rey (1967), M., 'La forêt de Chaux au Moyen Âge', in Fohlen, 67–85.

Ricardo (n.d.), D., *The Principles of Political Economy and Taxation* (Everyman's, London).

Ricardo (1951*a*), D., 'An Essay on the Influence of the Price of Corn on the Profit of Stock', *Works and Correspondence*, iv (Cambridge).

Ricardo (1951*b*), D., 'On Protection to Agriculture', ibid. 201–70.

Richards (1982–5), E., *A History of the Highland Clearances* (2 vols.).

Richards (1988), E., 'Regional Imbalance and Poverty in Early Nineteenth-Century Britain', in Mitchison and Roebuck, 193–207.

Richards (1993), E., 'Margins of the Industrial Revolution', in P. O'Brien and R. Quinault, (eds.), *The Industrial Revolution and British Society* (Cambridge).

Richter (1976), M., *Giraldus Cambrensis: The Growth of the Welsh Nation* (Aberystwyth).

Riden (1978), P., 'The Population of Derbyshire in 1561', *DAJ* 98, 61–71.

Riden (1991), P., 'The Charcoal Iron Industry in the East Midlands 1580–1780', *DAJ* 111, 64–8.

Riedenauer (1983), E., 'Die Geschichte des Alpenraums als Feld überregionaler Forschung', *Zeitschrift für bayerische Landesgeschichte* 46, 593–606.

Riedmann (1988[2]), J., *Geschichte Tirols* (Vienna).

Rieuwerts (1973), J. H., *Lathkill Dale: Its Mines and Miners* (Hartington).

Ritschel (1983), B., 'Zur Bergwerksgeschichte Goldkronachs', *Archiv für Geschichte von Oberfranken* 63, 15–51.

Roberts (1968), B. K., 'A Study of Medieval Colonization in the Forest of Arden, Warwickshire', *AgHR* 16, 101–13.

Roberts (1973), B. K., 'Field Systems in the West Midlands', in Baker and Butlin, 188–231.

Robson (1989), R., *The Rise and Fall of the English Highland Clans* (Edinburgh).

Rocquebert (1982), M., 'Le paysage et les hommes', in R. Lafont (ed.), *Les Cathars en Occitanie* (Paris), 263–338.

Roehl (1972), R., 'Plan and Reality in a Medieval Monastic Economy: The Cistercians', *Studies in Medieval and Renaissance Hist.* 9, 83–113.

Roglić (1970), J., 'Die Gebirge als die Wiege des geschichtlichen Geschehens in Südosteuropa', *Colloquium Geographicum, Argumenta Geographica* 12, 225–39.

Rokkan (1973*a*), S., 'Centre Formation, Nation Building and Cultural Diversity', in Eisenstadt and Rokkan, 13–38.

Rokkan (1973*b*), S., 'Cities, States and Nations', ibid. 73–97.

Rokkan (1975), S., 'Dimensions of State Formation and Nation Building', in Tilly (1975*a*), 562–600.

Rokkan (1980), S., 'Territories, Centers and Peripheries ... within Western Europe', in Gottmann (1980*a*), 163–204.

Rokkan, S., and Urwin, D. W. (eds.) (1982*a*), *The Politics of Territorial Identity* (London, Beverley Hills, and New Delhi).

Rokkan, S., and Urwin, D. W. (1982*b*), 'Introduction', to Rokkan and Urwin (1982*a*), 1–17.

Rollinson (1963), W., 'The Lost Villages and Hamlets of Low Furness', *TC&WAAS* 63, 160–9.

Rollinson (1978), W., *A History of Cumberland and Westmorland* (London and Chichester).

Rose (1992), M., 'Lancashire, die Baumwollindustrie und die industrielle Revolution: Der Übergang zum Fabriksystem', in Ditt and Pollard, 138–61.

Rosenberg (1988), H. G., *A Negotiated World: Three Centuries of Change in a French Alpine Community* (Toronto).

Rösener (1992), W., *Peasants in the Middle Ages.*

Rose-Villequey (1971), G., *Verre et verriers de Lorraine au début des temps modernes* (Paris).

Rosset (1984), P., 'Culture et élevage dans la viguerie de Cerdagne à la fin de l'ancien régime', *Revue d'histoire moderne et contemporaine* 31, 131–42.

Rothenburg (1960), G. E., *The Austrian Military Border in Croatia, 1522–1747* (Urbana).

Rowe (1953), J., *Cornwall in the Age of the Industrial Revolution* (Liverpool).

Rowlands (1989), M., 'Continuity and Change in an Industrialising Society: The Case of the West Midlands Industries', in Hudson (1989*a*), 103–31.

Rowley (1972), T., *The Shropshire Landscape.*

Rowley (1986), T., *The Landscape of the Welsh Marches.*

Rowling (1976), M., *The Folklore of the Lake District.*

Rowse (1941[1], 1969[2]), A. L., *Tudor Cornwall: Portrait of a Society.*

Rowse (1978[2]), A. L., *The England of Elizabeth*, i (Madison).

Rubner (1967), H., *Forstgeschichte im Zeitalter der industriellen Revolution* (Berlin).

Rubner (1975), H., 'Waldgewerbe und Agrarlandschaft im Spätmittelalter und im 19. und 20. Jahrhundert', in Kellenbenz, 97–108.

Rubner (1984), H., 'Technisch-industrielle Entwicklung, Waldzerstörung und Waldwirtschaft von der Aufklärung bis zur Gründung des Deutschen Reiches', *Technikgeschichte* 51, 94–103.

Ruesch (1979), H., 'Die Demographie der Alpen zwischen 1650 und 1850', in Bergier, 159–80.

Ruffieux (1980), R., 'Singularité de la Suisse', in Guichonnet (1980*a*), i. 311–68.

Rule (1970), J. G., 'Some Social Aspects of the Cornish Industrial Revolution', in R. Burt (ed.), *Industry and Society in the South-West* (Exeter).

Russell (1972*a*), J. C., *Medieval Regions and their Cities* (Newton Abbot).

Russell (1972*b*), J. C., 'Population in Europe', in C. Cipolla (ed.), *Fontana Economic History of Europe*, i.

Russell (1967), W. M. S., *Man, Nature and History.*

Rutkowski (1971), J., 'Medieval Agriculture in its Prime: Poland, Lithuania and Hungary', *CEHE* i. 487–506.

Sahlins (1989), P., *Boundaries: The Making of France and Spain in the Pyrenees* (Berkeley, Los Angeles, and Oxford).

Sainclivier (1991), J., 'Structure et évolution économique de la Bretagne dépuis le XVIIIe siècle', in Havinden *et al.* 86–94.

Saint-Blanquat (1949), O. de, 'Comment sont créés les bastides du sud-ouest', *Annales ESC* 4, 278–89.

Salaman (1957), R. A., 'Tradesmen's Tools, *c.*1500–1850', in Singer *et al.*, 110–23.

Salaman (1987[2]), R. N., *The History and Social Influence of the Potato* (Cambridge).

Saltmarsh (1941), J., 'Plague and Economic Decline in England in the later Middle Ages', *Cambridge Historical J.* 7, 23–41.

Salzman (1950), L. F., 'Mines and Stannaries', in J. F. Willard, W. A. Morris, and W. H. Dunham (eds.), *The English Government at Work, 1327–1336*, iii (Cambridge, Mass.), 67–104.

Sandberg (1982), L. G., 'Ignorance, Poverty and Economic Backwardness in the Early Stages of European Industrialization', *JEEcH* 11, 675–97.

Sandberger (1979), A., 'Die Landwirtschaft', in Spindler, iv/2, 732–48.

Sandgruber (1974), R., 'Die Innerberger Eisenproduktion in der frühen Neuzeit', in Mitterauer (1974*a*), 72–105.

Sandgruber (1989), R., 'Die Landwirtschaft als Nachfragefaktor in den Anfängen der Industrialisierung: das Beispiel Österreich', in Pierenkemper, 79–93.

Sandvik (1979), G., 'The Norwegian Economy in the 18th Century—a Satellite of Denmark?', in Dyrvik *et al.*, 36–48.

Sassoon (1960), J., 'Leadmining at Woodhead, Carsphairn', *Trans. Dumfries and Galloway Natural Hist. and Antiq. Soc.* 46, 170–7.

Satchell (1983), J. E., 'A History of Meathop Woods, i', *TC&WAAS* 83, 25–32.

Satchell (1984), J. E., 'A History of Meathop Woods, ii, The Middle Ages to the Present', *TC&WAAS* 84, 85–98.

Saunders (1954), V. A., 'Shropshire', in Darby and Terrett, 113–19.

Sawyer (1976*a*), P. H. (ed.), *Medieval Settlement: Continuity and Change.*

Sawyer (1976*b*), P. H., 'Introduction', in Sawyer (1976*a*), 1–7.

Sawyer (1979), P. H., 'Medieval English Settlement: New Interpretations', in id. (ed.), *English Medieval Settlement*, 1–8.

Sayce (1955–6, 1957–8), R. U., 'The Old Summer Pastures. A Comparative Study', *Montgomeryshire Collections*, 54, 117–45 and 55, 37–86.

Schama (1988), S., *The Embarrassment of Riches: An Interpretation of Dutch Culture in the Golden Age* (Berkeley and Los Angeles).

Schelbert (1976), L., *Einführung in die schweizerische Auswanderungsgeschichte der Neuzeit* (Zurich).

Schich (1979), W., 'Zur Rolle des Handels in der Wirtschaft der Zisterzienserklöster während der zweiten Hälfte des 12. und der ersten Hälfte des 13. Jahrhunderts', *Zisterzienserstudien* 4 (Berlin).

Schissler (1978), H., *Preussische Agrargesellschaft im Wandel* (Göttingen).

Schläpfer (1984), W., *Wirtschaftsgeschichte des Kantons Appenzell Ausserrhoden* (Gais).

Schlender (1987), T., *Der Wald in Mythen, Märchen und Erzählungen* (Munich).

Schlenger (1965), H., 'Historische Geographie der Sowjetunion', in O. Brunner *et al.* (eds.), *Festschrift Hermann Aubin zum 80. Geburtstag* (2 vols., Wiesbaden), i. 54–86.

Schlesinger (1975*a*), W. (ed.), *Die deutsche Ostsiedlung des Mittelalters als Problem der europäischen Geschichte* (Sigmaringen).

Schlesinger (1975*b*), W., 'Zur Problematik der Erforschung der deutschen Ostsiedlung', in Schlesinger (1975*a*), 11–30.

Schlesinger (1975*c*), W., 'Flemmingen und Kühren: zur Siedlungsform niederländischer Siedlungen des 12. Jahrhunderts im mitteldeutschen Osten', in Schlesinger (1975*a*), 263–309.

Schlüter (1952–3), O., *Die Siedlungsräume Mitteleuropas in frühgeschichtlicher Zeit* (2 vols., Remagen).

Schmal (1981), H. (ed.), *Patterns of European Urbanisation since 1500.*

Schmidthenner (1923), H., 'Die Reetbergwirtschaft in Deutschland', *Geographische Zeitschrift* 29, 115–27.

Schmidtill (1963), E., *Zur Geschichte des Eisenerzbergbaus im südlichen Fichtelgebirge* (Kulmbach).

Schnath (1963), G., 'Vom Wesen und Wirken der Zisterzienser in Niedersachsen im 12. Jahrhundert', *Niedersächsiches Jb. für Landesgeschichte* 35, 78–97.

Schnyder (1973), W., *Handel und Verkehr über die Bündner Pässe im Mittelalter* (2 vols., Zurich).

Schofield (1965), R. S., 'The Geographical Distribution of Wealth in England, 1334–1649', *EcHR* 18, 483–510.

Schön (1982), L., 'Proto-Industrialisation and Factories: Textiles in Sweden in the Mid-Nineteenth Century', *ScEHR* 30, 57–71.

Schrank (1992), G., 'Crossroads of the North: Proto-Industrialization in the Orkney Islands, 1730–1840', *JEcH* 21, 365–88.

Schreiber (1965), H., *Teuton and Slav: The Struggle for Central Europe.*

Schremmer (1970), E., *Die Wirtschaft Bayerns* (Munich).

Schremmer, E. (1972), 'Standortausweitung der Warenproduktion im langfristigen Wirtschaftswachstum', *VSWG* 59, 1–40.

Schremmer (1978), E., 'Industrielle Rückständigkeit und strukturstabilisierender Fortschritt', in H. Kellenbenz (ed.), *Wirtschaftswachstum, Energie und Verkehr* (Stuttgart and New York), 205–33.

Schremmer (1979*a*), E., 'Wirtschaft', in Spindler, iii/2, 1067–118.

Schremmer (1979*b*), E., 'Wirtschaft', in Spindler, iii/2, 1371–86.

Schremmer (1979*c*), E., 'Der Süddeutsche Odenwald. Ein Beispiel für ein wirtschaftliches Randgebiet während der Zeit der Industrialisierung 1871–1913', *Zeitschrift für Agrargeschichte und Agrarsoziologie* 27, 1–18.

Schremmer (1980), E., *Technischer Fortschritt an der Schwelle zur Industrialisierung* (Munich).

Schubert (1957), H. R., *History of the British Iron and Steel Industry from c.450 BC to AD 1775.*

Schuler (1984), M., 'Migration Patterns in the Swiss Mountain Areas', in Brugger *et al.* (1984*a*), 244–53.

Schulte (1959), F., *Die Entwicklung der gewerblichen Wirtschaft in Rheinland-Westfalen im 18. Jahrhundert* (Cologne).

Schulz (1931), H., *Die wirtschaftliche Struktur des Oberharzes und seines nördlichen Vorlandes, vom Ende des 10. bis zum Beginn des 15. Jahrhunderts* (Chemnitz-Schönau).

Schulze (1993), R. (ed.), *Industrieregionen im Umbruch* (Essen).

Schumacher (1967), E., *Die kurkölnischen Westfalen im Zeitalter der Aufklärung* (Olpe).

Schumer (1984), B., *The Evolution of Wychwood to 1400: Pioneers, Frontiers and Forests* (Leicester).

Schumpeter (1972[8]), J. A., *History of Economic Analysis.*

Schwabe (1984), E., 'Development of Settlement Structures in Swiss Mountain Areas', in Brugger *et al.* (1984*a*), 125–43.

Schwarz (1959), G., *Allgemeine Siedlungsgeographie* (Berlin).

Schwarzenbach (1931), A., 'Beiträge zur Geschichte des Oberengadin im Mittelalter und in der Neuzeit', *Schweizer Studien zur Geschichtswissenschaft* 16/3, 303–485.

Scola (1992), R., *Feeding the Victorian City: The Food Supply of Manchester 1770–1870* (Manchester).

Scoville (1968[2]), W. C., *Capitalism and French Glassmaking, 1640–1789* (Berkeley and Los Angeles).

Scurfield (1986), G., 'Seventeenth-Century Sheffield and its Environs', *YAJ* 58, 147–71.

Searle (1986), C. E., 'Custom, Class Conflict and Agrarian Capitalism: the Cumbrian Customary Economy in the Eighteenth Century', *P&P* 110, 106–33.

Searle (1993), C. E., 'Customary Tenants and the Enclosure of the Cumbrian Commons', *Northern History* 29, 126–53.

Seebass (1928), F., *Bergslagen. Versuch einer kulturgeographischen Beschreibung und Umgrenzung* (Brunswick).

Seidenfus (1981), H. S., 'Was erwartet die Nationalökonomie von einer regionalen Wirtschaftsgeschichte?', in Blaich, 139–66.

Sella (1974), D., 'European Industries, 1500–1700', in Cipolla, 354–426.

Sella (1979), D., *Crisis and Continuity: The Economy of Spanish Lombardy in the Seventeenth Century* (Cambridge, Mass.).

Sellers (1912), M., 'Industries', in Page, 329–37 and 381–448.

Semmingsen (1960), I., 'Norwegian Emigration in the Nineteenth Century', *ScEHR* 8, 150–60.

Semple (1911), E. C., *Influence of Geographic Environment on the Basis of Ratzel's System of Anthropo-Geography* (New York).

Semple (1932), E. C., *The Geography of the Mediterranean Region: Its Relation to Ancient History.*

Seward (1972), D., *The Monks at War: The Military Religious Orders.*

Shachar, A., and Öberg, S. (eds.) (1990), *The World Economy and the Spatial Organization of Power* (Aldershot).

Shaw (1980), F., *The Northern and Western Islands of Scotland: Their Economy and Society in the Seventeenth Century* (Edinburgh).

Sheppard (1973), J. A., 'Field Systems in Yorkshire', in Baker and Butlin, 145–87.

Shils (1975), E., *Center and Periphery* (Chicago).

Short (1989), B., 'The De-Industrialisation Process: A Case Study of the Weald, 1600–1850', in Hudson (1989*a*), 156–74.

Sieber (1954), S., *Zur Geschichte des Erzgebirgischen Bergbaues* (Halle on Saale).

Sieber (1967), S., *Studien zur Industriegeschichte des Erzgebirges* (Cologne and Graz).

Siebter Bericht (1992), *Über die Lage der schweizerischen Landwirtschaft und die Agrarpolitik des Bundes* (Berne).

Sieferle (1982), R. P., *Der Unterirdische Wald. Energiekrise und Industrielle Revolution* (Munich).

Sigg (1974), O., 'Bevölkerungs- Agrar- und Sozialgeschichtliche Probleme des 16. Jahrhunderts am Beispiel der Zürcher Landschaft, *SZG* 24, 1–25.

Sigsworth (1958), E. M., *Black Dyke Mills* (Liverpool).

Simms (1976), A., 'Deserted Medieval Villages and Fields in Germany', *J.Hist.G* 2/3, 223–8.

Sinclair (1979²), John, *The Statistical Account of Scotland*, iii, *The Eastern Borders* (East Ardsley).

Singer, C., Holmyard, E. J., Hall, A. R., and Williams, T. I. (eds.) (1956–7), *A History of Technology*, ii and iii (Oxford).

Singer (1971), F. W., 'Die Wüstung "Forchheim" im Kohlwald bei Arzberg', *Archiv für Geschichte von Oberfranken* 51, 5–38.

Singleton (1970), F., *Industrial Revolution in Yorkshire* (Clapham).

Sitwell (1986), N. H. H., *Outside the Empire: The World the Romans Knew.*

Skipp (1970), V. H. T., 'Economic and Social Change in the Forest of Arden, 1530–1649', in J. Thirsk (ed.), *Land, Church and People* (Reading), 84–111.

Skipp (1978), V., *Crisis and Development: An Ecological Case Study of the Forest of Arden 1570–1674* (Cambridge).

Slaski (1979), K., 'North-Western Slavs in Baltic Sea Trade from the VIIIth to the XIIIth Century', *JEEcH* 8, 83–107.

Slaven (1975), A., *The Development of the West of Scotland 1750–1960.*

Slawinger (1966), G., *Die Manufaktur in Kurbayern ... 1740–1833* (Stuttgart).

Slicher van Bath (1946), B. H., 'Manor, Mark and Village in the Eastern Netherlands', *Speculum* 21, 115–28.

Slicher van Bath (1963¹, 1966²), B. H., *The Agrarian History of Western Europe, AD 500–1850.*

Slicher van Bath (1977), B. H., 'Agriculture in the Vital Revolution', *CEHE* v. 42–133.

Slicher van Bath (1982), B. H., 'The Economic Situation in the Dutch Republic During the Seventeenth Century', in M. Aymard (ed.), *Dutch Capitalism and World Capitalism* (Cambridge and Paris).

Smailes (1960), A. E., *North England.*

Smith (1863 edn.), A., *Wealth of Nations* (Edinburgh).

Smith, C. S., and Forbes, R. J. (1957), 'Metallurgy and Assaying', in Singer *et al.*, 27–71.

Smith (1980), D. (ed.), *A People and a Proletariat: Essays in the History of Wales 1780–1980.*

Smith (1981²), D. M., *Industrial Location* (New York).

Smith (1798), J., *General View of the Agriculture of the County of Argyll* (Edinburgh).

Smith (1991), R., 'Demographic Developments in Rural England, 1300–48: A Survey', in Campbell (1991*a*), 25–77.

Smith (1943), R. A. L., *Canterbury Cathedral Priory* (Cambridge).

Smith (1947), R. A. L., 'The Benedictine Contribution to Medieval English Agriculture', in id., *Collected Papers*, 103–16.

Smith (1970), R. B., *Land and Politics in the England of Henry VIII* (Oxford).

Smith (1971*b*), R. E. F., 'Medieval Agrarian Society in its Prime: Russia', *CEHE* i. 507–47.

Smith (1990), R. M., 'Geographical Aspects of Population Change in England 1500–1730', in Dodgshon and Butlin, 151–79.

Smith (1971*a*), R. S., 'Medieval Agrarian Society in its Prime: Spain', *CEHE* i. 432–48.

Smith (1978²), T. C., *An Historical Geography of Western Europe before 1800* (London and New York).

Smout (1962), T. C., 'The Lead Mines at Wanlockhead', *Trans. Dumfries and Galloway Natural Hist. and Antiq. Soc.* 39, 144–58.

Smout (1969), T. C., *A History of the Scottish People, 1560–1830.*

Smout (1979), T. C., 'Scotland in the 17th and 18th centuries—a Satellite Economy?' in Dyrvik *et al.*, 9–35.

Smout (1983), T. C., 'Scotland and England, 16th–18th centuries: is dependency a symptom or a cause of underdevelopment?', in Guarducci, 319–42.

Smout (1991), T. C., 'The Highlands and the Roots of Green Consciousness', *Proceedings of the British Academy* (for 1990), 237–63.

Smout, T. C., Landsman, N. C., and Devine, T. M. (1994), 'Scottish Emigration in the Seventeenth and Eighteenth Centuries', in Canny, 76–112.

Søderberg (1984), J., 'A long-term perspective on regional economic development in Sweden, ca. 1550–1914', *ScEHR* 32, 1–16.

Søderberg (1982), J., 'Causes of Poverty in Sweden in the Nineteenth Century', *JEEcH* 11, 369–402.

Sombart (1922, 1987), W., *Der Moderne Kapitalismus* (3 vols., Munich).

Somerville (1977), R., 'Commons and Wastes in North-West Derbyshire', *DAJ* 97, 16–22.

Speight (1892), H., *The Craven and North-West Yorkshire Highlands.*

Speight (1900), H., *Upper Wharfedale.*

Speight (1902), H., *Lower Wharfedale.*

Spence (1980), R. T., 'The Graham Clans and Lands on the Eve of the Jacobean Pacification', *TC&WAAS 80, 79–102.*

Spence (1992), R. T., 'Mining and Smelting in Yorkshire by the Cliffords ... in the Tudor and Early Stuart Period', *YAJ* 64, 157–83.

Spencer (1991), C., *The History of Hebden Bridge* (Hebden Bridge).

Spindler (1979²), M. (ed.), *Handbuch der bayerischen Geschichte*, iii/1–2, iv/2 (Munich).

Spooner (1972), F. C., *The International Economy and Monetary Movements in France 1493–1725* (Cambridge, Mass.).

Spufford (1965), M., *A Cambridgeshire Community. Chippenham from Settlement to Enclosure* (Leicester).

Spufford (1974), M., *Contrasting Communities* (Cambridge).

Srbik (1947), H. R. von, 'Rodordnungen des Ausferngebietes in neueren Jahrhunderten', in Wopfner, 247–69.

Standing (1981), G., 'Migration and Modes of Exploitation', *J. of Peasant Studies* 8/2, 173–211.

Stanley (1980), M., 'The Geographical Distribution of Wealth in Medieval England', *J.Hist.G* 6/3, 315–20.

Steensberg (1976), A., 'Store Valby and Borup: Two Case Studies in the History of Danish Settlement', in Sawyer (1976*a*), 94–113.

Stefanescu (1989), S., 'Les Carpates dans l'histoire du peuple romain', in Bergier (1989*a*), 84–99.

Steinacker (1947), 'Staatswerdung und politische Willensbildung im Alpenraum', in Wopfner, 271–316.

Steiner (1987), M., 'Contrasts in Regional Potential', *Papers of the Regional Science Association* 61, 79–92.

Stevenson (1905), R. L., *Essays on Travel.*

Stevenson (1911), R. L., 'Travels with a Donkey in the Cevennes', in *The Works of R. L. Stevenson*, i.

Stevenson (1981), W. B., 'The Monastic Presence in Scottish Burghs in the Twelfth and Thirteenth Centuries', *Scottish Historical Rev.* 60, 97–118.

Stewart (1956), O. C., 'Fire as the First Great Force Employed by Man', in Thomas, 115–33.

Stoianovich (1989), T., 'The Segmentary State and la grande nation', in Genovese and Hochberg, 256–80.

Stökl (1953), G., *Die Entstehung des Kosakentums* (Munich).

Stökl (1975), G., 'Siedlung und Siedlungsbewegungen im alten Russland (13.–16. Jahrhundert)', in Schlesinger (1975*a*), 755–79.

Stolz (1955), O., *Die Geschichte des Landes Tirol*, i (Innsbruck).

Storper (1981), M., 'Towards a Structural Theory of Industrial Location', in Rees *et al.*, 17–40.

Strassoldo (1980), R., 'Centre-Periphery and System-Boundary: Culturological [*sic*] Perspectives', in Gottmann (1980*a*), 27–61.

Strätz (1976), H.-W., 'Bergmännisches Arbeitsrecht im 15. und 16. Jahrhundert', *Der Anschnitt* 28, 86–94, 114–22.

Strieder (1929), J., 'Die Entstehung eines deutschen frühkapitalistischen Montanunternehmertums im Zeitalter Jacob Fugger des Reichen (1459–1525)', *Beiträge zur Geschichte der Technik und Industrie* 19, 1–12.

Stromer (1984), W. von, 'Wassernot und Wasserkünste im Bergbau des Mittelalters und der frühen Neuzeit', in Kroker and Westermann, 50–72.

Stromer (1986), W. von, 'Gewerbereviere und Protoindustrien im Spätmittelalter und Frühneuzeit', in Pohl (1986*a*), 39–111.

Subacci (1994), P. (ed.), *Recent Doctoral Research in Economic History* (Milan).

Sugar (1977), P. F., *Southeastern Europe under Ottoman Rule, 1354–1804* (Seattle).

Summerson (1982), H., 'Crime and Society in Medieval Cumberland', *TC&WAAS* 82, 111–24.

Supple (1977), B., 'The Nature of Enterprise', in *CEHE* v. 394–461.

Suter (1971), H., 'Innerschweizerisches Militärunternehmertum im 18. Jahrhundert', *Mitteilungen der Antiquarischen Gesellschaft, Zürich* 45/3.

Svoboda (1991), G. J., 'The Foreign Trade of Eighteenth Century Bohemia', *JEEcH* 20/1, 93–123.

Swain (1986), J. T., *Industry Before the Industrial Revolution: North-East Lancashire c.1500–1640* (Manchester).

Swain (1994), J. T., 'The Lancashire Witch Trials of 1612 and 1634 and the Economics of Witchcraft', *Northern Hist.* 30, 64–85.

Sweeney (1987), G. P., *Innovation, Entrepreneurs and Regional Development.*

Swiss Economy (1991), *A Trilogy 1291–1991* (St Sulpice).

Sylvester (1969), D., *The Rural Landscape of the Welsh Borderland.*

Symon (1959), J. A., *Scottish Farming, Past and Present* (Edinburgh and London).

Tann (1973), J., 'The Employment of Power in the West-of-England Wool Textile Industry, 1790–1840', in Harte and Ponting, 196–224.

Taylor (1965), G. R. (ed.), *The Turner Thesis* (Boston).
Taylor (1969*a*), J., 'On the Economy of Mines in Cornwall and Devon [1814]', in Burt, 15–29.
Taylor (1969*b*), J., 'On the Economy of Mining [1837]', ibid. 31–48.
TeBrake (1985), W. H., *Medieval Frontier. Culture and Ecology in Rijnland* (Austin, Texas).
Teich (1973), M., 'Diffusion of steam-, water- and air-power to and from Slovakia during the 18th century', in Centre National de la Recherche Scientifique, *L'acquisition des techniques par les pays non-initiateurs* (Paris), 349–76.
Terrett (1954*a*), I. B., 'Rutland', in Darby and Terrett, 355–65.
Terrett (1954*b*), I. B., 'Northamptonshire', ibid. 379–89.
Terrett (1962*a*), I. B., 'Nottinghamshire', in Darby and Maxwell, 233–77.
Terrett (1962*b*), I. B., 'Cheshire', ibid. 330–91.
Terrett (1962*c*), I. B., 'Lancashire', ibid. 392–418.
Thirsk (1953), J., *Fenland Farming in the Sixteenth Century* (Leicester).
Thirsk (1961), J., 'Industries in the Countryside', in F. J. Fisher (ed.), *Essays in the Economic and Social History of Tudor and Stuart England* (Cambridge), 70–88.
Thirsk (1964), J., 'The Common Fields', *P&P* 29, 3–25.
Thirsk (1967), J., 'The Farming Regions of England', in J. Thirsk (ed.), *The Agrarian History of England and Wales*, iv, *1500–1640* (Cambridge).
Thirsk (1978), J., *Economic Policy and Projects* (Oxford).
Thirsk (1984*a*), J. (ed.), *The Agrarian History of England and Wales*, v/1, *1640–1750: Regional Farming Systems* (Cambridge).
Thirsk (1984*b*), J., *The Rural Economy of England*.
Thirsk (1985), J., 'Escaping from Constraints: The Industrial Revolution in a Malthusian Context', *J. of Interdisciplinary Hist.* 15/4, 729–53.
Thirsk (1987), J., *England's Agricultural Regions and Agrarian History, 1500–1750*.
Thirsk (1988), J. (ed.), *The Agrarian History of England and Wales*, ii, *1042–1350* (Cambridge).
Thomas (1986), B., 'Was there an Energy Crisis in Britain in the 17th Century', *Expl.EcH* 23, 124–52.
Thomas (1976), C., 'Towards a Definition of the term "Field" in the Light of Prehistory', in Sawyer (1976*a*), 145–51.
Thomas (1956), W. L., Jr. (ed.), *Man's Role in Changing the Face of the Earth* (Chicago).
Thompson (1918–19), J. W., 'Dutch and Flemish Colonization in Medieval Germany', *American J. of Sociology* 24, 159–86.
Thomson (1983), J. K. J., 'Variations in Industrial Structure in Pre-industrial Languedoc', in M. Berg *et al.* (eds.), *Manufacture in Town and Country Before the Factory* (Cambridge), 61–91.
Thomson (1992), J. K. J., *A Distinctive Industrialization: Cotton in Barcelona, 1728–1832* (Cambridge).
Thornton (1991), C., 'The Determinants of Land Productivity on the Bishop of Winchester's Demesne of Rimpton, 1208–1403', in Campbell and Overton, 183–210.
Thrupp (1972), S., 'Medieval Industry 1000–1500', in C. Cipolla (ed.), *The Fontana Economic History of Europe*, i. 221–73.
Thünen (1966), J. H. von, *The Isolated State* (Oxford).
Tilly, C. (ed.) (1975*a*), *The Formation of Nation States in Western Europe* (Princeton).
Tilly (1975*b*), C., 'Reflections on the History of European State-Making', in Tilly (1975*a*), 3–83.
Tilly, C., Tilly, L., and Tilly, R. (1975), *The Rebellious Century* (Cambridge, Mass.).
Tilly, R., and Tilly, C. (1971), 'Agenda for European Economic History in the 1970s', *JEcH* 31, 184–98.
Timm (1960), A., *Die Waldnutzung in Nordwestdeutschland im Spiegel der Weistümer* (Cologne and Graz).

Timmermann (?1959), O. F., 'Zur Frage der Landnahme in den deutschen Alpen', *Berichte zur deutschen Landeskunde* 18, 194–223.

Titow (1969), J. Z., *English Rural Society 1200–1350*.

Titow (1972), J. Z., *Winchester Yields: A Study in Medieval Agricultural Productivity* (Cambridge).

Toch (1986), M., 'Voralpine Grundherrschaft und alpine Bauern im Spätmittelalter', in Mattmüller, 30–7.

Toch (1989), M., 'Peasants of the Mountains, Peasants of the Valleys and Medieval State Building: The Case of the Alps', in Bergier (1989*a*), 65–70.

Todd (1987), M., *The South West to AD 1000* (London and New York).

Todorov (1983), N., *The Balkan City 1400–1900* (Seattle).

Tödtling (1984), F., 'Organizational Characteristics of Plants in Core and Peripheral Regions of Austria', *Regional Studies* 18/5, 397–412.

Topolski (1982), J., 'Seventeenth-Century Poland and the Turning Point in European Economic Development', in Fedorowicz, 70–91.

Topolski (1991), J., 'The Problem of Internal Economic Peripheries in Poland in Early Modern Times', in Nolte, 205–17.

Tough (1928), D. L. W., *The Last Years of a Frontier* (Oxford).

Toynbee (1959–64), A. J., *A Study of History*, i (1962), ii (1962), xi (1959), xii (1964) (Oxford).

Tracy (1990), J. D., *Holland under Habsburg Rule, 1506–1566* (Berkeley and Los Angeles).

Trawkowski (1975), S., 'Die Rolle der deutschen Dorfkolonisation und des deutschen Rechtes in Polen im 13. Jahrhundert', in Schlesinger (1975*a*), 349–68.

Tremel (1981), 'Die ostalpine Landwirtschaft vom 13. bis zum 17. Jahrhundert', in Mariotti, 89–98.

Trevor-Roper (1969), H. R., *The European Witch-Craze of the Sixteenth and Seventeenth Centuries and other Essays* (New York).

Trinder (1973), B., *The Industrial Revolution in Shropshire* (London and Chichester).

Troger, E., and Zwanowetz, G. (eds.) (1959), *Beiträge zur Geschichtlichen Landeskunde Tirols* (Innsbruck).

Troger, E., and Zwanowetz, G. (eds.) (1969), *Neue Beiträge zur Geschichte der Landeskunde Tirols* (Innsbruck and Munich).

Tubbs (1986), C. R., *The New Forest*.

Tuck (1991*a*), J. A., 'The Northern Borders', in Miller (1991*a*), 34–42.

Tuck (1991*b*), J. A., 'The Northern Borders', ibid. 175–82.

Tuck (1991*c*), J. A., 'The Northern Borders', ibid. 587–98.

Tuke (1800), J., *General View of the Agriculture of the North Riding of Yorkshire*.

Tunzelmann (1970), G. N. von, 'Technological Diffusion during the Industrial Revolution', in R. M. Hartwell (ed.), *The Industrial Revolution* (Oxford).

Tunzelmann (1978), G. N. von, *Steam Power and British Industrialization to 1860* (Oxford).

Tunzelmann (1981), G. N. von, 'Technical Progress during the Industrial Revolution', in R. Floud and D. McCloskey (eds.), *The Economic History of Britain since 1700*, i, *1700–1850* (Cambridge).

Tupling (1927), G. H., *The Economic History of Rossendale* (Manchester).

Turner (1985), J. R., 'Henry C. Carey's Attitude towards the Ricardian Theory of Rent', in Wood, iii. 51–66.

Turnock (1970), D., *Patterns of Highland Development*.

Turnock (1982), D., *The Historical Geography of Scotland since 1707* (Cambridge).

Turnock (1983), D., 'The Highlands: Changing Approaches to Regional Development', in G. Whittington and I. D. Whyte (eds.), *An Historical Geography of Scotland*.

Tweedale (1993), G., 'The Business and Technology of Sheffield Steelmaking', in C. Binfield *et al.* (eds.), *The History of the City of Sheffield* (3 vols., Sheffield), ii. 142–93.

Ubersfeld (1967), A., 'Fontainebleau et le recueil Denecourt', in Fohlen, 45–55.

Ullmann (1956), E. L., 'The Role of Transportation and the Bases for Interaction', in Thomas, 862–80.

Ulmer (1935), F., *Höhenflucht. Eine statistische Untersuchung der Gebirgsentsiedlung Deutschtirols* (Innsbruck).

Unger (1983), M., *Stadtgemeinde und Bergwesen Freibergs im Mittelalter* (Weimar).

Unwin, G., Hulme, A., and Taylor, G. (1924), *Samuel Oldknow and the Arkwrights* (Manchester).

Unwin (1990), T., 'Towns and Trade 1066–1500', in Dodgshon and Butlin, 123–49.

Urban (1973), W., 'The Organization of Defense of the Livonian Frontier in the Thirteenth Century', Speculum 48, 525–32.

Urban (1975), W., *The Baltic Crusade* (DeKalb, Ill.).

Urwin (1982), D. W., 'Territorial Structures and Political Developments in the United Kingdom', in Rokkan and Urwin (1982*a*), 19–73.

Usher (1957), A. P., 'Machines and Mechanisms', in Singer *et al.*, 324–46.

Valentinitsch (1981), H., 'Die windische Grenze und das steirische Proviantwesen', in Pferschy, 521–32.

Van Berchem (1980), D., 'Les Alpes sous domination romain', in Guichonnet (1980*a*), i. 95–161.

Van Houtte, (1977), J. A., *An Economic History of the Low Countries 800–1800.*

Van Zanden (1993), J. L., *The Rise and Decline of Holland's Economy: Merchant Capitalism and the Labour Market* (Manchester).

Vellacott (1912), C. H., 'Mining and Smelting (Medieval)', in Page, 338–54.

Venturi (1991), F., *The End of the Old Regime in Europe 1776–1789* (2 vols., Princeton).

Vergil (1950), P., *Anglica Historia* (Camden Series 3, vol. 74).

Verlinden (1983), C., 'Ou sont les peripheries?', in Guarducci, 235–60.

Veyret (1978[2]), P., *Les Alpes* (Paris).

Viazzo (1989), P. P., *Upland Communities: Environment, Population and Social Structure in the Alps since the Sixteenth Century* (Cambridge).

Viazzo, P. P., and Albera, S. (1986), 'Population, Resources and Homeostatic Regulation in the Alps, the Role of Nuptuality' in Mattmüller, 182–231.

Vilar (1976), P., *A History of Gold and Money, 1450–1920.*

Vilar (1988), P., 'Peasant Worker and National Rebellion: The Case of Nineteenth-Century Catalonia', in Krantz, 319–42.

Vilfan (1975), S., 'Die deutsche Kolonisation nordöstlich der oberen Adria und ihre sozialgeschichtlichen Grundlagen', in Schlesinger (1975*a*), 567–604.

Vincent (1973), P., 'Pre-Viking Changes in the Cumbrian Landscape', in Baldwin and Whyte, 7–16.

Vinogradoff (1905), P., *The Growth of the Manor.*

Vinogradoff (1908), P., *English Society in the Eleventh Century* (Oxford).

Virtue (1976), A., *Memoirs of a Derbyshire Hill Farmer.*

Vivelo (1978), F. R., *Cultural Anthropology Handbook* (New York).

Vlachovic (1971), J., 'Produktion und Handel mit ungarischem Kupfer im 16. und im ersten Viertel des 17. Jahrhunderts', in Bog, 600–27.

Volk (1984), O., *Salzproduktion und Salzhandel mittelalterlicher Zisterzienserklöster* (Sigmaringen).

Vozár (1971), J., 'Die sozialen Folgen des Bergbaues für die Bevölkerung des mittelslovakischen Bergreviers im XVI. Jahrhundert', in Bog, 569–83.

Vyner (1990), B. E. (ed.), *Medieval Rural settlement in North-East England* (Durham).

Wace, A. J. B., and Thompson, M. S. (1972), *The Nomads of the Balkans.*

Wadsworth, A. P., and Mann, J. deL. (1965[2]), *The Cotton Trade and Industrial Lancashire 1600–1780.*

Wagner (1931), E., *Die Holzversorgung der Lüneburger Saline* (Düsseldorf).

Waites (1959–62*a*), B., 'The Monastic Settlement of North-East Yorkshire', *YAJ* 40, 478–95.

Waites (1959–62*b*), B., 'The Monastic Grange as a Factor in the Settlement of North-East Yorkshire', ibid. 627–56.

Waites (1967), B., *Moorland and Vale-Land Farming in North-East Yorkshire: The Monastic Contribution in the Thirteenth and Fourteenth Centuries* (York).

Wakefield (1974), W. L., *Heresy, Crusade and Inquisition in Southern France 1100–1250*.

Walker (1964), M., *Germany and the Emigration 1816–1885* (Cambridge, Mass.).

Wallace (1990), I., *The Global Economic System*.

Wallerstein (1974–89), I., *The Modern World System* (3 vols., San Diego and New York).

Walton (1986), J. K., 'The Strange Decline of the Lakeland Yeoman: Some Thoughts on Sources, Methods and Definitions', *TC&WAAS* 86, 221–33.

Walton (1987), J. K., *Lancashire: A Social History* (Manchester).

Walton (1989), J. K., 'Proto-Industrialisation and the First Industrial Revolution: The Case of Lancashire', in Hudson (1989*a*), 41–68.

Walton (1992), J. K., 'Die Baumwollindustrie und die Arbeiterklasse von Lancashire', in Ditt and Pollard, 364–87.

Walton (1952[2]), M., *Sheffield, its Story and its Achievements* (Sheffield).

Wanderwitz (1987), H., 'Salz auf den Pässen der Alpen', in Lindgren (1987*a*), 173–8.

Wandruszka (1980), A., 'Les Alpes orientales', in Guichonnet (1980*a*), 369–91.

Wanklyn (1982), M. D. G., 'Industrial Development in the Ironbridge Gorge before Abraham Darby', *West Midlands Studies* 15, 3–7.

Watson (1877), D., 'Moss-Troopers and the March-Laws', *Hawick Archaeological S. Trans.* 8–14.

Watson (1973[2]), J., *The History and Antiquities of the Parish of Halifax in Yorkshire* (Didsbury).

Watts (1967*a*), D. G., 'A Model for the Early Fourteenth Century', *EcHR* 20, 543–7.

Watts (1967*b*), D. G., 'Water-power and the Industrial Revolution', *TC&WAAS* 67, 199–205.

Watts (1971), S. J., 'Tenant-Right in Early Seventeenth-Century Northumberland', *Northern History* 6, 64–87.

Watts, S. J., and Watts, S. J. (1975), *From Border to Middle Shire: Northumberland 1586–1625* (Leicester).

Weber (1969[6]), A., *Theory of the Location of Industry* (Chicago).

Weber (1976), E., *Peasants into Frenchmen: The Modernization of Rural France, 1870–1914* (Stanford).

Weisbrod (1993), B. (ed.), *Grenzland. Beiträge zur Geschichte der deutsch-deutschen Grenze* (Hanover).

Weishaupt (1992*a*), M., *Bauern, Hirten und 'frume edle puren'* (Basel and Frankfurt am Main).

Weishaupt (1992*b*), M., 'Hirten, "Bauern und Bürger" und Bauensoldaten', in A. Tanner and A.-L. Head-König (eds.), *Die Bauern in der Geschichte der Schweiz* (Zurich), 23–39.

Weiss (1979), H., 'Das Agrarwesen vom Spätmittelalter bis zum Ende des 18. Jahrhunderts', in Spindler, iii/1, 456–78.

Weiss (1941), R., *Das Alpwesen Graubündens* (Erlenbach and Zurich).

Wellhofer (1989), E. S., 'Core and Periphery: Territorial Dimensions in Politics', *Urban Studies* 26, 340–55.

Wells (1988), R., *Wretched Faces* (Gloucester).

Wenskus (1975), R., 'Der deutsche Orden und die nichtdeutsche Bevölkerung des Preussenlandes mit besonderer Berücksichtigung der Siedlung', in Schlesinger (1975*a*), 417–38.

Wessely (1853), J., *Die österreichischen Alpenländer und ihre Forsten* (2 vols., Vienna).

Westermann (1971), E., *Das Eislebener Garkupfer und seine Bedeutung für den europäischen Kupfermarkt 1460–1560* (Cologne and Vienna).

Whealey (1954), P., 'Staffordshire', in Darby and Terrett, 160–9.

White (1973), J. T., *The Scottish Border and Northumberland*.

White (1963), L., 'What Accelerated Technical Progress in the Western Middle Ages?', in A. C. Crombie (ed.), *Scientific Change*, 272–91.

White (1972), L., 'The Expansion of Technology 500–1500', in C. Cipolla (ed.), *Fontana Economic History of Europe*, i. 143–74.

White (1989), P., 'Internal Migration in the nineteenth and twentieth centuries', in Ogden and White, 13–33.

Whittington (1973), G. H., 'Field Systems in Scotland', in Baker and Butlin, 530–79.

Whittlesey (1939), D., *The Earth and the State* (New York).

Whitwell (1904), R. J., 'English Monasteries and the Wool Trade in the 13th Century', *VSWG* 2, 1–33.

Whyte (1973), I. D., 'Shielings and the Upland Pastoral Economy of the Lake District', in Baldwin and Whyte, 103–18.

Whyte (1989), I. D., 'Proto-Industrialization in Scotland', in Hudson (1989*a*), 228–51.

Wiessner (1950), H., *Geschichte des Kärntner Edelmetallbergbaues* (Klagenfurt).

Wightman (1975), W. E., 'The Significance of "Waste" in the Yorkshire Domesday', *Northern History* 10, 55–71.

Wijkman (1990), P. M., 'Patterns of Production and Trade', in W. Wallace (ed.), *The Dynamics of European Integration*, 89–105.

Wilkinson (1904), T., 'Local Folklore', *Trans. Halifax Antiq. Soc.*, 2–9.

Williams (1991), A. M., 'Endogenous and Exogenous Sources of Growth in the Economy of Cornwall and Devon', in Havinden *et al.* 108–19.

Williams (1969), D. H., *The Welsh Cistercians* (Pontypool).

Williams (1980), G. A., 'Locating a Welsh Working Class: The Frontier Years', in Smith, 16–46.

Williams (1970), M., 'The Enclosure and Reclamation of Waste Land in England and Wales in the Eighteenth and Nineteenth Centuries', *Trans. of the Institute of British Geographers* 51, 55–70.

Williams (1971), M., 'The Enclosure and Reclamation of the Mendip Hills, 1770–1870', *AgHR* 19, 65–81.

Williams (1976), M., 'Mendip Farming', in Athill (1976*a*), 102–25.

Williams (1982), M., 'Marshland and Waste', in Cantor (1982*a*), 86–125.

Williams (1960–3), P., 'The Welsh Borderland under Queen Elizabeth', *Welsh Hist. Rev.* 1, 19–36.

Williams (1964), P., 'The Northern Borderlands under the Early Stuarts', in H. E. Bell and R. L. Ollard (eds.), *Historical Essays 1600–1750*, 1–17.

Williamson (1996), A. H., 'Scots, Indians and Empire: The Scottish Politics of Civilization 1519–1609', *P&P* 150, 46–83.

Williamson (1975), J. G., 'Regional Inequality and National Development', in Friedmann and Alonso, 158–200.

Willies (1973), L., 'The Barker Family and the Eighteenth Century Lead Business', *DAJ* 93, 55–74.

Wilsdorf, H., and Quellmalz, W. (1971), *Bergwerke und Hüttenlagen der Agricola-Zeit* (Berlin).

Wilson (1966^2), C., *Anglo-Dutch Commerce and Finance in the Eighteenth Century* (Cambridge).

Wilson (1967), C. H., 'Trade, Society and the State', *CEHE* iv. 487–575.

Wilson (1977), C. H., 'The Historical Study of Economic Growth and Decline in Early Modern History', *CEHE* v. 1–41.

Wilson (1970), D. M., *The Vikings and their Origins*.

Wilson (1982), G. J., 'The Land Tax Problem', *EcHR* 35, 422–6.

Wilson (1901), J., 'Domesday Book, Pipe Rolls and Testa de Nevill', in J. Wilson (ed.), *VCH Cumberland*, i. 295–335.

Wilson (1973), R. G., 'The Supremacy of the Yorkshire Cloth Industry in the Eighteenth Century', in Harte and Ponting, 225–46.

Winchester (1973), A. J. L., 'The Multiple Estate', in Baldwin and Whyte, 89–102.

Winchester (1987), A. J. L., *Landscape and Society in Medieval Cumbria* (Edinburgh).

Wiswe (1953), H., 'Grangien niedersächsischer Zisterzienserklöster', *Braunschweigisches Jb.* 34, 5–134.

Witney (1990), K. P., 'The Woodland Economy of Kent, 1066–1348', *AgHR* 38, 20–39.

Wohlauf (1981), G., *Die Spiegelmanufaktur Grüneplan im 18. Jahrhundert* (Hamburg).

Wohlert (1988), K., 'Concentration Tendencies in Swedish Industry Before World War I', in H. Pohl (ed.), *The Concentration Process in the Entrepreneurial Economy since the late 19th Century* (Stuttgart).

Wolf (1990[2]), E. R., *Europe and the People without a History* (Berkeley, Los Angeles, and London).

Wolfstrigl-Wolfskron (1903), M.Rr.von, *Die Tiroler Erzbergbaue 1301–1665* (Innsbruck).

Wollenberg (1992), K., 'Die Erwerbspolitik und Wirtschaftsweise des oberbayerischen Zisterzienserklosters Fürstenfeld', in Elm, 51–66.

Womack (1989), P., *Improvement and Romance: Constructing the Myth of the Highlands.*

Wood (1985), J. C. (ed.), *David Ricardo: Critical Assessments* (4 vols.).

Wood, L. S., and Wilmore, A. (1927), *The Romance of the Cotton Industry* (Oxford).

Woolf (1986), S., *The Poor in Western Europe in the Eighteenth and Nineteenth Centuries.*

Woolf (1991), S., *Napoleon's Integration of Europe.*

Wopfner (1903), H., *Beiträge zur Geschichte der freien bäuerlichen Erbleihen Deutschtirols im Mittelalter* (Breslau).

Wopfner (1931), H., 'Beiträge zur Geschichte der alpinen Schwaighöfe', *VSWG* 24, 36–70.

Wopfner (1947, 1948), H. (Festschrift for), *Beiträge zur Geschichte und Heimatkunde Tirols* (2 vols., Innsbruck).

Wopfner (n.d.), H., *Tiroler Bauer und Tiroler Landesfreiheit* (Innsbruck).

Wordsworth (1974[5]), W., *A Guide through the District of the Lakes,* in *The Prose Works of William Wordsworth,* ed. W. J. B. Owen and J. Worthington ii (Oxford).

Wright (1986), G. N., *The Yorkshire Dales* (Newton Abbot).

Wrightson (1982), K., *English Society 1580–1680.*

Wrigley (1969), E. A., *Population and History.*

Wrigley (1988), E. A., *Continuity, Chance and Change* (Cambridge).

Wroot (1930), 'The Yorkshire Abbeys and the Wool Trade', *Thorsby Soc. Publications—Miscellanea* 33, 1–21.

Wuthnow (1989), R., 'Towns, Regions and Religious Movements in the Reformation', in Genovese and Hochberg, 34–56.

Wyrobisz (1976), A., 'Mining in Medieval and Modern Poland', *JEEcH* 5, 757–62.

Wyrobisz (1978), A., 'Resources and Construction Materials in Pre-Industrial Europe', in Maczak and Parker, 65–84.

Yatsunsky (1974), V. K., 'Geography of the Iron Market in Prereform Russia', in W. L. Blackwell (ed.), *Russian Economic Development from Peter the Great to Stalin* (New York), 71–107.

Young (1770), A., *A Six Months Tour through the North of England* (4 vols.).

Youngson (1973), A. J., *After the Forty-Five* (Edinburgh).

Youngson (1974), A. J., *Beyond the Highland Line.*

Zahnbrecher (1907), F. X., *Die Kolonisationstätigkeit des Hochstifts Freising in den Ostalpenländern* (Munich).

Zahnd (1990), U. M., 'Zur Wirtschaftsordnung hochmittelalterlicher Zisterzienserklöster im Oberdeutschen und Schweizerischen Raum', *SZG* 40, 55–66.

Zajchowska (1976), S., 'Changes in Land Use in the North-East Part of Great Poland during the Nineteenth and Twentieth Centuries', in Buchanan *et al.*, 118–30.

Zeeuw (1978), J. W. de, 'Peat and the Dutch Golden Age', *Afdeling Agrarische Geschiedenis, Bijdragen* 21, 3–31.

Zernack (1975), K., 'Zusammenfassung: die hochmittelalterliche Kolonisation in Ostmitteleuropa und ihre Stellung in der europäischen Geschichte', in Schlesinger (1975*a*), 783–804.

Ziegler (1982[2]), P., *The Black Death.*

Ziekursch (1978[3]), J., *Hundert Jahre Schlesische Agrargeschichte* (Aalen).

Zientara (1975), B., 'Die deutschen Einwanderer in Polen vom 12. bis zum 14. Jahrhundert', in Schlesinger (1975*a*), 333–48.

Zimmermann (1989), C., 'Entwicklungshemmnisse im bürgerlichen Milieu: die Individualisierung der Allmenden und Gemeinheiten um 1780', in Pierenkemper (1992*a*), 99–112.

Zon (1920), R., 'Forests and Human Progress', *Geographical Rev.* 10, 139–66.

Zorn (1971), W., 'Die wirtschaftliche Struktur Altbayerns im Vormärz (1815–1848)', *Oberbayerisches Archiv* 93, 190–206.

Zumthor (1994), P., *Daily Life in Rembrandt's Holland* (Stanford).

Zurfluh (1982), A., 'Urseren 1640–1830, les populations des hautes vallées alpines', *SZG* 32, 293–323.

Zurfluh (1986), A., 'Gibt es den homo alpinus?', in Mattmüller, 232–82.

Zwanowetz (1977), G., 'Zur Wirtschaftslage Tirols und Vorarlbergs gegen Ende der Regierungszeit Kaiser Josephs II', in Huter and Zwanowetz, 417–44.

Zytkowicz (1983), L., 'Développement et sous-développement dans le monde slave', in Guarducci, 261–90.

INDEX